CASES IN MARKETING

CASES IN MARKETING

ORIENTATION, ANALYSIS, AND PROBLEMS

FOURTH EDITION

THOMAS V. GREER
University of Maryland

MACMILLAN PUBLISHING COMPANY
New York

COLLIER MACMILLAN PUBLISHERS
London

Macmillan Publishing Company
866 Third Avenue, New York, New York 10022

Collier Macmillan Canada, Inc.

Library of Congress Cataloging-in-Publication Data

Greer, Thomas V.
    Cases in marketing.

    Includes bibliographical references.
    1. Marketing—Case studies.   I. Title.
HF5415.G665   1987   658.8   86-12653
ISBN 0-02-347080-1

Printing   2 3 4 5 6 7   Years: 7 8 9 0 1 2 3
ISBN 0-02-347080-1

PREFACE
TO THE FOURTH EDITION

The fourth edition of this book, like its predecessors, is intended as an educational tool for the training of students of business administration. It is my hope that students and their instructors will find this edition both appealing and useful.

Twelve of the forty-nine cases in this edition are new, and thirteen retained from the third edition have been updated. In selecting the cases, I have tried to meet the need of professors of business administration for a comprehensive and well-organized teaching aid. This edition continues to maintain a balance between large and small organizations. Because services are of growing importance in the American economy and because the discipline of marketing is showing an increased interest in services, I have increased the attention given to this area in this edition. Eighteen cases focus on services, six of them on nonprofit organizations, whereas twenty-four cases deal with consumer goods and seven with industrial goods. Newer avenues for the application of marketing skills, such as professional sports, the arts, health care, philanthropy, and social marketing, are given prominent places in this new edition. In response to the social concern of many students, this edition includes several cases that can be used as springboards for discussions of the legal, societal, and ethical environment of marketing. Two cases deal with organizations owned by blacks.

The cases are of varying levels of difficulty, and most of them can be used at more than one academic level. They vary in length from three to twenty-five pages, and the average length is between seven and eight pages. This intermediate length provides ample content for student thought and analysis without the time demands of extremely long cases. Besides stimulating student analysis, these cases have been found to arouse vigorous discussion. All have been tested in the classroom. A sufficient number of cases is included to allow a professor to use the book for several semesters without assigning a case more than once—if that is his or her policy.

Some cases lend themselves to chapters other than those in which they appear in this book. For example, "Huffy Bicycles" is placed in "Nature and Scope of Marketing"; "Le Drugstore," in "Consumer

Behavior"; and "Tonka Toys," in "Advertising and Public Relations"; but all three can also be used effectively in "International Marketing." "Thompson Funeral Home" is placed in "Pricing" but can also be used in "Consumer Behavior" or "Social Responsibility." "McIlhenny–Tabasco Products" is categorized under "Products and Product Strategy" but can also be used in "Pricing." Although associated with "Consumer Behavior," "Lily Crest Modes" is also pertinent to "Planning and Forecasting." "St. Teresa's School" is included in "Products and Product Strategy" but can be adapted for "Social Responsibility." By giving some limited direction, the professor could also use the four overview "Marketing Programs" cases at the end of the book for specialized purposes with specific chapters. It is important to note that the cases were prepared as a basis for class analysis and discussion rather than to illustrate either effective or ineffective handling of administrative situations.

Considerable attention has been given to preparing the student for tackling cases effectively. The expository material at the beginning of the book should aid both the beginning case analyst and the student who has had previous case experience. This material includes a general discussion of the rationale of teaching and learning by cases and explanation of a five-step methodology for analyzing cases. A sample case is then presented, followed by an analysis by one of my *real* students and by my responses to that beginner's work. The student who reads these sections thoroughly before attempting the remainder of the cases will avoid many pitfalls. Some instructors may ask their students to study the cases differently or use a variety of approaches, depending on the type of case. Suggested discussion questions are provided separately in the *Instructor's Manual* for the instructor's convenience.

An effort has been made to provide factual role models in the case content for the increasing number of women majoring in business. In addition, five professional women have contributed cases to this edition.

The case materials reflect the true diversity of both marketers and customers in society by including persons of differing socio-economic status of both sexes and of several racial, cultural, and ethnic groups.

I happily acknowledge the cooperation of people in many organizations who made this compilation of cases possible. Also, I thank the adopters on the many campuses who have used the first, second, and third editions. A gratifying number of them have offered helpful advice.

For the preparation of cases, I extend special thanks to Richard Rosecky, "Power Tools, Inc." (A) and (B); Helena Poist, "Romano

Olive Oil, Inc."; Patricia Stocker, "Denver Art Museum"; Robert Krapfel, "Universal Motors Parts Division"; Dee Wewer, "Head Sports Wear"; Sheryl Ferrucci, "Unilever"; and Joanne G. Greer, "Volunteers in Health Care, Inc.," "Women's Exercise and Fitness Centers," and "Maple Hill Clinic." Dr. Rosecky is a marketing executive with his company; Ms. Poist is director of marketing in her organization; Professor Stocker is on the faculty at the University of Maryland and was formerly with the Denver Art Museum; Dr. Krapfel is on the marketing staff of his organization; Ms. Wewer is vice president of Head Sports Wear, Inc.; Ms. Ferrucci is on the marketing staff of Leo Burnett & Company in Milan, Italy; and Dr. Joanne G. Greer is on the Inspector General's staff, U.S. Department of Health and Human Services, Washington, D.C.

Comments of users of the book are welcome.

College Park, Maryland   *T.V.G.*

CONTENTS

4
CONSUMER BEHAVIOR   51

5
MARKETING RESEARCH   103

6
PRODUCTS AND PRODUCT STRATEGY   121

7
CHANNELS OF DISTRIBUTION   167

16
MARKETING PROGRAMS
(OVERVIEW) 411

CASES IN MARKETING

1

RATIONALE AND METHODOLOGY OF THE CASE METHOD

AN INTRODUCTION TO THE CASE METHOD

You are about to use the case method in a marketing course. If you have not encountered this approach to learning before, you are probably wondering what it is and what it can do for you as a student.

The case method is a teaching device aimed at bridging the gap between classroom training and work organizations. The case presents to the student, in narrative and tabular form, a set of facts about a specific business situation. The student must sort out the relevant from the irrelevant, organize the facts into a clear exposition of the problem at hand, formulate possible solutions, choose and defend a particular solution, and design implementation for that solution.

Case development may take several forms, such as group discussion, recitation, written work at home, a timed written analysis in class, an individual or group oral report, a debate between teams, or role playing of a major incident in a case. Combinations of these forms are also used.

Many professors in colleges, officials in government, and executives in industry want to see students involved in the realistic problems faced by organizations. Some of these problems are in day-to-day operations, whereas others involve less frequent but highly important occurrences. In using the case technique, instructors are not attacking the place of theories and facts in the student's training.

Rather they are combining these with practical business problems or issues and developing a task integrating theory and practice, called a "case." Their purpose is to provide a more fruitful learning situation for you.

A well-organized lecture on several concepts concerned with, for example, product-line policy may seem clear and succinct, and the student may conclude that he sees the ramifications and could apply these concepts as needed. Perhaps that is true. However, if the student has to put himself into the position of a manager, carefully determine his problems, and think his way through them (all in relation to the composition of a product line), he may (1) take the material on product-line policy more seriously, (2) see that the presented material does not stand majestically alone but is interrelated with other factors, and, most importantly, (3) learn something about the process of making a decision on behalf of an organization. That decision-making ability is highly useful to the person in his own personal life as a consumer, but it is indispensable if he is to become—and remain—a manager. The essence of the manager's work is making decisions.

Instruction by the case method is *participative*, and the main responsibility is on the student. In a sense, the case is raw material on which the student is asked to practice. The student's benefit from the case method will be approximately proportional to the effort he puts into his analysis of the case. Superficial treatment of the case will result in a superficial learning experience.

The use of the case method is not primarily to help the student to accumulate a store of knowledge or to acquaint him with current business practices. These may come as side benefits. The primary purpose is to develop and sharpen the student's skills in working through a complex problem. The first stage of that invaluable process is learning to identify the problem or problems. Sometimes this is surprisingly elusive. If one lacks considerable experience with the work, one may discover to one's chagrin (and cost) that one is dealing with symptoms and side issues only. Other stages in the process may include screening and interpreting the facts, setting up alternative courses of action and calculating their relative costs and payoffs, making a specific recommendation and showing why it is the best alternative, and finally, designing implementation.

Many students have remarked to the author that they are familiar with the case method because they have received instruction in business law through their study of court cases. Business cases are like law cases only in rare instances. In fact, they are different both in nature and purpose. A law case represents a decision that has already been made; it is history. It is important, even though the legal decision may seem illogical, because precedent is infinitely more important to law than to management. The law case is an official judgment and becomes an addition to the body of law. It is to be studied and heeded. Moreover, it was decided by an outsider, in fact, a third party outsider. A judge is imposing his judgment on the situation. In a business case, a manager can disregard precedent unless that precedent has been blessed as organization policy. Even in the latter instance he normally has ample opportunity to overturn the policy by objectively showing that it does not suffice. Business managers seldom, if ever, use precedent to keep an issue from arising or to compel a certain solution to a problem. Even if they so desired, they could not do so, for the manifold factors of the business world change so rapidly that old solutions to uncertainties may furnish useful analogies but rarely definitive answers. In a sense, business cases are more like medical school cases, that is, patients to be studied by advanced trainees. The student makes his examination, collects and interprets data to produce a diagnosis, chooses among alternative treatments available, prescribes the specific treatment, and gives treatment.

Cases do not come in one standardized length or form. Some collections emphasize fairly lengthy cases of, for example, fifteen to thirty pages or more. Other collections emphasize short cases averaging one to three pages. This group averages seven pages. The intent of the cases presented in this collection is to provide the student with a challenging amount of problem material without getting into the depth that he will probably encounter in some later courses. However, the more sophisticated student should bear in mind that some lengthy cases are not any more challenging intellectually than some cases of medium length. Whatever the length of a case or the average length in a collection, there is challenge to be found. Students with differing amounts of course background and business experience will see differing depths of material in the same case. Having a stronger background does not necessarily imply solving the case more quickly. A group of students in their second marketing course would probably carry the analysis of a given case far beyond what they did with the same case in their first course. Instructors in various settings may expect and demand different levels of quality from the student in his analytical work. All instructors will expect the students to grow as they gain experience with the case method and to perform a better quality of analysis as they handle more cases.

The author has assembled a wide variety of cases, all of which are new, in order to expose the student to many kinds of problems These cases are a shortcut in your development as a manager. It would take many years of varied work experience to meet the equivalent of the problems illustrated in the whole collection of cases. They are of varying degrees of intricacy, scope, and challenge. The cases are set in many different industries, but the abilities they will develop in the conscientious student are almost totally transferable from the given settings to any number of other settings. It is the skill of analytical problem solving that the cases seek to develop, rather than bits of knowledge about specific types of enterprises.

Practice in analyzing the cases will help the student prepare for a career of making decisions. Most persons will start out their careers with little authority to make decisions. Within that limited authority the student must try to reach the best decisions and be able to explain why he or she has reached those decisions. With experience the student will develop ability to make better decisions. When you are promoted to a position with more authority you will have more problems about which to reach decisions. A large proportion of the student's time will be spent on this function. This collection of cases should assist in preparing the student to do something constructive with that first job. But more important, the experience of analyzing these cases should assist the student in handling later more responsible positions in the business world. The person with the analytical mind is going to move forward in the organization.

TO THE STUDENT: A SUGGESTED METHODOLOGY FOR YOUR WORK ON CASES

No single methodology for handling cases is ideal or holds a monopoly on logic. Various persons experienced in cases can offer alternative approaches. If your instructor does not assign you a methodology that he prefers, it is suggested that you use the one presented as follows.

You may find the case method somewhat perplexing when you work on your first case assignment. This happens because you may not have built up a background of knowledge about marketing and you may not have developed a logical framework of analysis for problem solving.

Your first effort should be to read the case assigned carefully enough to remember many of the details presented in it. Most students find that they need to read the materials several times. After reading the case with great care it is important to identify the major problem(s) or questions(s) involved.

Step 1: The Problem(s) or Question(s)

Every cases analysis requires the identification of the principal question or problem that requires an answer. Unfortunately, business problems do not arrive labeled "problem." Therefore, the student must learn to identify the problem(s) raised. It is often appropriate to state the question in the form of agreement or disagreement with the decision or recommendation made by one of the persons in the case. Such a question might be, "Do you agree with Belmont's proposed price change?" Or you might state your question in the following form: "What should the price be?" On occasion the main question needs to be broken down into subquestions, such as the following: "What should the price be? Should someone have the authority to adjust that price in dealing with customers and, if so, in what range? Should the price have a specified period of time in which it is in effect?"

It is imperative that you locate the basic problem(s) or question(s). For example, it is not meaningful to assert that low sales volume is the problem, since low sales volume is only symptomatic of an underlying problem such as poor supervision and control by sales managers, inadequate coordination of the several kinds of promotion, a poor compensation plan, or something else.

Step 2: The Facts

Some persons find it very helpful to visualize the system under consideration and to identify who is managing the various systems or subsystems. See if you find this to be of assistance. You may want to prepare a diagram depicting these relationships. Some students like to use a systems framework around the system under consideration, so that they can perceive the inputs and outputs of the system, the goals, the organization structure, the resources available, the set of products and/or services offered the market, the routine operations, the accomplishments, and the past and probable actions and responses of competitive and complementary systems.

It is vital that you sift and sort the facts of the case, even if there are a very large number of them. A time-consuming technique but one that many persons find productive is to rank order the facts. List the most important fact first and the least important fact last. Between them fill in the various facts in descending order of importance for answering the question. Use your best judgment in building this list, but always ask yourself, "Just what do I need to know in order to answer the question?" Note that some facts may be irrelevant, but care should be taken in discarding any fact. Let your imagination play with the fact and see if it fits together with another seemingly irrelevant fact to make one highly relevant fact. When the facts have been completely arranged in order, you should review and revise your list once again on the basis of logic and your intuition.

A necessary categorization is to separate objective facts from particulars that are the opinions, assumptions, or premises of persons in the case. The latter are by no means unimportant, but they should be correctly labeled for future use and suitable weighting. Moreover, try to identify your own speculation and opinions that you may have formed, for they are not the facts of the case.

Remember the human factor in all of this. You must be alert to personal characteristics and personal relationships among the principals of the case. Given their life-style, sex, age, rank in the organization, job background, socioeconomic background, personality, and other factors, what would you expect them to do or say? What would surprise you or appear atypical? Not only must you look for these aspects but you must use them substantively and use them to help you judge the degree of objectivity in supposedly objective facts.

Enough facts have been presented in each case for you to develop intelligent solutions. However, if you feel it is imperative that you make an assumption in the absence of some extremely important fact, go ahead and make a reasonable assumption. Be sure to state that assumption clearly in your write-up. Exercise restraint in deciding whether to make an assumption. Because some instructors may not want you to make any assumption, clarify the policy in your class.

Additional information on some problems can be obtained from marketing textbooks and other reference materials in libraries. Some cases in this book include footnotes referring you to helpful readings. Carefully selected interviews are also a possibility. All of these may be worthwhile pursuits. However, you should be watchful for both conscious and unconscious biases. In interviews, you should remember that some of the information supplied you is probably indicative of the unique set of circumstances and experiences of the interviewee. It may be helpful background and provocative, but try to put it in perspective. Moreover, one must not postpone a decision until every conceivable information resource has been exhausted. Such behavior is both uneconomic and unreasonable. No manager has in front of him every piece of data that may have a bearing on his problem. Time, cost, cost/benefit relationships, and lack of access to some data preclude such an extreme view.

Step 3: The Alternative Courses of Action

What can be done to take care of the problem? Stated in a more formal manner, what are the action alternatives or alternative courses of action?

Often you will think of five or six alternative courses of action. However, you may need to dismiss some of these alternatives as unfeasible. For example, some courses may clearly violate the long-term objectives of the organization or some short-term goals of the operating period (such as a year or a quarter). These objectives and goals are sometimes stated but more often must be inferred. Capital constraints might rule out some alternatives and behavioral factors may also rule some out. If practicable, you should reduce the list of alternative courses of action to those three or four that need to receive the most careful, detailed consideration.

These remaining alternatives must be formally evaluated. You should list the advantages and disadvantages of each. Think in terms of the utility that each action alternative can deliver and the risk that it entails. This procedure requires great care but if it is done well it puts you in good condition for step number four.

Step 4: Your Decision and Reasoning

You should now select the action alternative that provides the best answer to the problem. In so doing, compare and contrast the sets of advantages and disadvantages developed in Step 3. Make your selection. Be sure that you articulate the main reasons that you select one alternative over the others. For each rejected alternative, state why your chosen alternative is better. This not only clarifies your own thinking but also enables you to coherently ask other students during class discussion why they chose an alternative that you rejected and equips you to defend your choice. Your process of reaching a decision is a crucially important analytical ability—and you must do everything you can to make it a smoothly working ability. Articulating the process by trying to communicate it orally and in writing to other persons is excellent practice for developing and sharpening this vital managerial ability.

Step 5: Implementation of Your Decision

Your decision is not complete until you prepare at least gross operational plans for its implementation. Draw up a statement of (a) what must be done to carry out your decision; (b) what personnel must be assigned to do it; (c) when this act(s) should be carried out; and (d) about how much it will cost to do it. You are dealing with acts, existing or new personnel, a timetable, and a rough budget. Usually you cannot give highly detailed or precise answers to the questions of Step 5. However, gross estimates are infinitely better than no estimates at all, for they force you to bring to a logical conclusion a logical process of thinking.

2

A SAMPLE CASE ANALYSIS AND CRITIQUE

This chapter contains a typical case, "Cherry Tree Learning Materials Company," followed by an analysis that was written by a student for regular classroom work. This analysis is then critiqued by the author for your instruction.

It is suggested that you attempt to analyze the Cherry Tree Learning Materials Company case. Compare your work with the student work given and with the author's critique. This will give you a good preparation for your first case assignment.

CHERRY TREE LEARNING MATERIALS COMPANY—A SAMPLE CASE

Cherry Tree Learning Materials Company, founded in the middle 1950s, was a successful manufacturer of sixty different "special education" toys and games. *Special education* is the term generally used for the education of children with various physical, mental, or emotional disabilities. Sales had been growing by 7 to 8 per cent annually for the past four years and in the latest year were about $4,800,000. Net profits after taxes the past year were about $179,000 and slightly less the year before that. Dividends totaling about $70,000 were paid out in each of those years.

The organization manufactured a line of toys and games designed to assist in the development of children with five types of problems, specifically dealing with motor skills, visual-motor skills, auditory skills, phonology skills, and structural and verbal syntax skills. For example, a product that had sold well and received much favorable comment from teachers and parents was the balance disc. About twenty-five inches in diameter, it was a rigid, round platform made of wood that could be locked in any preselected direction or left free for circular movement. The degree of tilt was scientifically determined and set at the factory. Safety treads on the surface discouraged slipping down or falling off. The child could stand, sit, or kneel on the surface. An edging protected the child's hand and fingers. This toy assisted in several ways, the most obvious of which was teaching equilibrium. It also helped the child learn body alignment, and coordinated mental and muscular activity, as well as developing the child's body image concept. The device also helped relate visual skills to body alignment and stato-kinetic functioning. This product was sold at $26.

Another example was sewing cards. These were cardboard rectangles with simple outline designs, such as a tree, a pear, or a house. The child was to use the thick, semisharp needles and colored yarn enclosed in the package. Several colors of yarn and eighteen designs were provided in the box of thirty-six cards. The objective was to develop eye-hand coordination, assist in learning colors, and furnish a vehicle for creative expression. This product was sold for $5.65 a box.

The executives of the company were interested in whether they could successfully offer their line of toys and games to children who had no difficulties. In other words, could they expand outside the "special education" market? This subject had been under extended discussion among all the executives.

One executive, Lawrence Teilman, stated that he opposed such a change of basic strategy because he thought Cherry Tree had done little to serve the special education market through *parents* of children who needed the products. He reasoned that, although schools might buy one or two units of an item for the classroom, promoting this item to parents for home use might result in the sale of eight or ten additional units per classroom of special education children. No one in the company perceived a problem of persuading teachers of the great usefulness of the products, and the executives believed that sales were limited primarily by school board budgets. Nevertheless, tax appropriations for special education were growing all over the United States. Their rate of growth was much faster than educational appropriations in total. Teilman believed that many teachers, if approached by a parent, would encourage the parent to buy additional materials for home use. The problem, in Teilman's opinion, was one of obtaining suitable mailing lists and sending catalogs with carefully worded cover letters directly into the homes of disabled children. However, he wondered if most educators would cooperate in compiling such lists. He also wondered if the U.S. Department of Education would release its extensive national mailing list for "Closer Look," a newsletter edited for the parents of disabled children. It was noted by several persons in Cherry Tree Company that most parents of disabled children ordinarily have rather small discretionary income because they incur extra costs with such children, especially medical costs.

The president of Cherry Tree, Terence Halsey, asked the sales department for a report on where orders had been coming from. About a week later the information came back that in the past year 86 per cent of sales had been to schools and 14 per cent to individuals. It was almost exactly the same the year before. A small percentage of the individuals might have been teachers in special education departments of schools or private tutors, but there was no way of finding out without inquiring.

Another executive, John Dearborn, noted approvingly that Teilman's proposal would not require any changes in the product line or any changes in promotion. Marketing to parents of normal children would, in Dearborn's opinion, require careful playing down of the fact that the products were originally designed for disabled children. However effective Cherry Tree's materials might be in facilitating learning, Dearborn believed that the typical parent of a normal child would feel some stigma in using them. Also, many of the skills taught by Cherry Tree materials were not difficult for a normal child to master without assistance, and the parent might conclude that the more expensive items in the product line were not worth the investment.

Clarence Stett agreed with Dearborn's objections. Nevertheless, he believed that a certain subset of the Cherry Tree product line had great potential for the market of normal children. Stett reasoned that some of these products were built around skills essential for pre-reading, reading, and writing, namely the visual-motor and visual-perceptual toys and games. The company's consulting psychologist, Elizabeth Freeman, reported that it appeared to her that there was near panic among conscientious middle-class parents lest their children not learn to read. Several executives said that their reading and observations supported Dr. Freeman completely. Stett believed that it would be necessary only to call these products to the attention of such parents. He believed that a mere knowledge of their existence would induce a sense of obligation to purchase them. If a new campaign were confined to these materials, a much smaller catalog could be used and advertising could focus on parents of four-to seven-year-olds who could be reached through women's magazines.

George Higgins, another executive, thought that Stett's idea had potential but that advertising should focus on more specialized magazines such as *Parents* or the magazines of the Parent-Teacher Association. He said that subscribers to these periodicals probably were more committed to their role as parents than were nonsubscribers.

Roy Pasek, another executive, pointed out that, although expenditures for general education could be projected to stabilize or possibly decrease in the future because of the declining birthrate, expenditures for special education were increasing. He conjectured that parents of disabled children had now been politicized to the extent that they would demand public services for their children. Recent court decisions indicated that appropriate public special education programs would in time be the legal right of every child. Some estimates of involved children ran as high as 15 per cent of the school population. Equipping of these new special education classrooms would be an attractive proposition for companies in the field. Pasek also said that thus far Cherry Tree had provided sturdy, good quality, conveniently assembled, but noninnovative teaching materials, many of which were available from other companies in a slightly different form or could even be built by the teacher herself. Pasek stated that perhaps Cherry Tree should cultivate its image as a specialist in educational toys and games for the disabled child and try to expand the product line with new items, as many as possible of which should be patentable.

Advise the executives of Cherry Tree Learning Materials Company.

A STUDENT ANALYSIS OF THE CHERRY TREE COMPANY CASE

Step 1: The Problem or Question

As I see it, the problem in this case is to find the best way to improve the market share of Cherry Tree Learning Materials Company, with particular emphasis on the possibility of expanding from a restricted market (handicapped children) to a much broader market (normal children). Probably the most pertinent question in this problem is, What market segment should Cherry Tree strive to obtain? Should the company keep the same market segment and try to achieve more sales there? (The present market is primarily schools.) Or should it attempt to make more sales to parents of these children? Should Cherry Tree bring out a new product line? Should it attempt to become a specialist in classroom equipment? And finally, should it attempt to market some or all of its products to normal children?

EXHIBIT 1 Best-Selling Items in Cherry Tree's Product Line[*]

Item	Price	Skill Taught
Body puzzles	$ 3.00	body concept
Bead-sequencing kit	6.50	visual perceptual
Parquetry blocks	5.75	visual perceptual
Pegboards	10.50	fine motor; visual perceptual
Sponge balls	1.50	gross motor; body concept; visual perceptual
Storytelling posters (series of 10)	.75 each	prereading; concept development; language development
Balance disc	26.00	gross motor; body concept; etc.
Sorting box	11.00	fine motor; visual perceptual
Shape dominoes	1.75	fine motor; visual perceptual; procedural organization
Balance beam walking board	28.00	dynamic body balance; coordination; orthopedic correction
Stencil boards	5.75	visual motor; figure-ground discrimination
Sequential memory exercise cards	2.75	memory; visual-motor sequencing
Halves-and-wholes matching cards	1.75	visual discrimination
Dimensional puzzles, models 1 through 5	2.25 each	small muscle control; visual perception; spatial relations
Prewriting design cards	3.00	visual perception
Same-or-different cards, 4 sets	1.00 each	visual perception and discrimination
Color discovery cards	1.00	matching; memory
Comparison weighing scale	15.00	fine motor; visual perceptual; concept development
Coin rubber stamps	4.50	money value
Time teacher	4.25	clock reading
Sequencing picture cards, 4 sets	3.50 each	memory; concept development; prereading
Rhyming pictures	1.50	prereading; auditory discrimination
Talking letters	4.50	prereading; auditory discrimination
Sewing cards	5.65	visual perception; visual-motor coordination

[*]The items in the exhibit accounted for about 82 per cent of sales.

Step 2: The Facts

Cherry Tree Learning Materials Company is a successful manufacturer of sixty different special education toys and games. For the past four years, sales had been growing by 7 to 8 per cent annually, with sales last year approximately $4,800,000. Following are some facts and opinions, which I believe are important to this case, ranked in order of their importance.

Facts
1. In the past year, 86 per cent of sales had been to schools, whereas only 14 per cent had been to individuals.
2. Tax money given to schools for special education purposes has been increasing.
3. Keeping within the special education market would require very little change in products or promotion.
4. Expanding the market to normal children would require extensive changes, particularly in promotion.
5. Teachers were already convinced of the usefulness of Cherry Tree's products.
6. Many of the lower-priced toys were too simple for normal children to provide them any benefit.

Opinions
1. Teachers could convince parents of handicapped children of the usefulness of the toys.
2. Parents of handicapped children have small discretionary incomes because of high medical bills.
3. Parents will demand more money from government for their handicapped children.
4. Educators may not cooperate with Cherry Tree by releasing mailing lists of parents with handicapped children.
5. Normal children, and their parents, may feel uneasy using a product that they know was originally designed for a handicapped child.
6. Some executives believe that there would be a high demand for reading skills games and toys.
7. Expanded health services will soon become the right of every child.
8. Parents of normal children may feel that an expensive toy is not worth the investment.

Using these facts and opinions, together with the material presented in the case, I see six alternatives open to Cherry Tree. After listing these alternatives, I briefly explain them and then state the advantages and disadvantages of each.

Step 3: The Alternative Courses of Action

1. Keep the same market segment; i.e., sales primarily to schools and some sales to individuals. (Some of these individuals are perhaps teachers and private tutors.)

2. Attempt to market the entire current product line to parents of normal children.
3. Establish an additional product line, composed mainly of lower-priced items aimed at normal children, while retaining the present product line.
4. Place increased emphasis on marketing to *parents* of handicapped children.
5. Attempt to market only reading and prereading skills toys and games to parents of normal children. (These items are part of the company's current product line.)
6. Attempt to become a leading specialist in equipping special education classrooms while retaining the current market.

Alternatives 1 and 2 will be abandoned at this point, because neither would achieve Cherry Tree Learning Materials Company's objectives. The former should be abandoned because, although the company had been increasing its sales in this market, it has expressed a desire to expand, and the latter because all the executives seem to agree that an attempt to market the entire line to parents of normal children would result in failure. These collective judgments must be given great weight. This leaves us to consider alternatives 3, 4, 5, and 6.

Alternative 3

This choice would require a new product line, particularly of lower-priced items, which many parents could afford to buy.

Advantages of Alternative 3
1. There would be a better opportunity to sell to a large number of individuals, including parents of both normal and handicapped children.
2. There would be increased awareness of Cherry Tree's products because more consumers would own them.
3. With an expanded line of products, Cherry Tree could establish itself as a leader in the field of educational toys and games.

Disadvantages of Alternative 3
1. There are ever-present new product failures.
2. A very costly promotional program would be necessary to change the image of Cherry Tree so that parents of normal children would not be hesitant to buy products supposedly for "abnormal" children.
3. Loss of old customers because of this new image may occur.

Alternative 4

This action alternative, proposed by Lawrence Teilman, suggested emphasis on marketing products to parents of handicapped children, to be used in addition to those provided at school.

Advantages of Alternative 4
1. It would require no changes in the products or promotion.
2. Teachers would convince parents of the usefulness of the products.
3. Cherry Tree's current product line included some low-priced toys that parents could almost certainly afford.

Disadvantages of Alternative 4
1. Without the cooperation of educators and government, it would be extremely difficult to contact these parents.
2. Even if contacted by the company, many of these parents may have such high medical and other expenses that they would not be interested in buying the products.

Alternative 5

This action alternative was suggested by Dr. Elizabeth Freeman, a consulting psychologist, and an executive, Clarence Stett. They believe that a large number of parents would seize the chance to help their children learn to read, especially middle-class parents. In fact, they believed that many parents would feel obligated to purchase reading skills toys and games.

Advantages of Alternative 5
1. There is an opportunity for a much larger market.
2. If the assumptions were correct, there would be an everpresent demand for these products.
3. About sixteen of the existing products in Exhibit 1 are applicable.

Disadvantages of Alternative 5
1. Parents of normal children may feel uneasy about having their children use a product associated with disabled children.
2. Cost of promotion to overcome this uneasiness must be incurred.
3. Some inexpensive toys and games would be too simple for normal children.
4. Parents may believe that the more expensive toys and games are not worth the money, because in time their normal children would master the skills involved anyway.

Alternative 6

This last action alternative, proposed by another executive, Roy Pasek, involved Cherry Tree's becoming a leading specialist in what Pasek saw as a booming field in the years to come. He believed that with increased special education budgets, the schools would be looking for companies to install specially equipped classrooms to handle the needs of these special students. He also believed that Cherry Tree, which already had a fine reputation in this field, would be a logical choice to take on this added responsibility. He believed that Cherry Tree should take the leadership of the industry, develop the needed products, patent as many of the new products as possible, and cultivate the image of a specialist and leader.

Advantages of Alternative 6

1. It is a fact that schools are receiving more funds for special education.
2. Cherry Tree could establish itself as a leader in the industry.
3. There should be a need for these special classrooms as teaching methods become more advanced.

Disadvantages of Alternative 6

1. There is the possibility of new product failures.
2. The factor of competition exists in a new branch of the industry with which Cherry Tree is not familiar.
3. Cost of promotional programs to cultivate this new image may be excessive.

Step 4: My Decision and Reasoning

I believe that alternative 6, Pasek's specialty and leadership concept, is the best action alternative in this case. I think it is superior to the new product line idea (alternative 3) for three reasons. First, it involves less risk to develop products for which there will almost certainly be a demand than to develop products in the hope of creating a demand. Second, it would be an easier project to promote an expansion of the company's image, one with even more responsibility, than to try to *change* the image from a producer of toys and games for disabled children only to a producer of such goods for *all* children. Finally, the opportunity to make a profit is greater because the company would be marketing a specialty good to organizations that have the necessary funds rather than a shopping or possibly even a convenience good to individuals who may not have the necessary purchasing power to afford it.

Pasek's action alternative is superior to alternative 4 (marketing to the parents of disabled children) for three reasons. First, obtaining adequate mailing lists is a prerequisite for this alternative course of action. Company executives have already expressed concern about the possibility of educators and government officials not releasing this information, or at least being reluctant to do so. Pasek's idea, on the other hand, would have the strong approval, if not all-out cooperation, of school officials, who I am sure would do everything in their power to obtain the latest, most modern equipment for their schools. A school's program is a reflection of the administrators in charge, and they are spending state and federal and local funds, not their own. The second reason again deals with monetary reasons. On the one hand, Cherry Tree would be trying to market to individuals with very limited incomes, and, on the other hand, Cherry Tree would be competing for contracts with state and local governments who, as we all know, never run out of money. Finally, whereas parents may not recognize the need for Cherry Tree's products, objective evidence seems to indicate that there are increased benefits and opportunities being offered to disabled children in public school systems and officials do recognize the need for special toys, games, and other equipment with which to teach "special children."

Alternative 5, proposed by Dr. Freeman and Clarence Stett, is a good idea and one that probably would succeed given the necessary effort. However, I feel that it is inferior to Pasek's idea for a number of reasons. First, I believe the fear that parents of normal children would feel uneasy about buying products that they associate with "abnormal" children is a very real one, a fear that promotional programs may not be able to overcome. The handling of motivational themes would be intricate. This would not be a problem with alternative 6, although the promotional programs would have to stress the idea of increased responsibility of the firm. Second, profit margins would be lower on the inexpensive home toys and games than on the institutional classroom equipment. Third, we come to a basic question again—who can better afford the products? As stated before, educational institutions using governments funds have more purchasing power than individuals unless one is talking about very large numbers of individuals.

Step 5: Implementation of My Decision

Now that I have made my decision, I will attempt to implement it. To enable this plan to succeed, I believe Cherry Tree Learning Materials Company should do the following:

a. Expand its research and development department.

b. Slowly increase its promotional efforts.
c. Establish solid lines of communication with members of local and state school boards.
d. Continue its present successful operations.

I believe that the company should expand its research and development program immediately, possibly hiring one or two professionals if needed. I also believe that the company should hire as a consultant a school administrator with a good background in methods of teaching special education students, one who really knows what it is like to work directly with these children. This person would be invaluable in helping to determine the future needs of the teaching field.

The company should start slowly to increase its promotional programs, advertising in various education magazines, engaging in public-relations type activities, and perhaps sponsoring a project similar to Washington, D.C.'s, own Special Olympics for handicapped children. Slowly but surely the company should make itself known. Also, I would suggest sending a lobbyist to Washington, D.C., to try to encourage increased government support of special education in the school systems. I would set one year as this image-building goal.

During the implementation of this plan, I would expect Cherry Tree to carry on with its already successful operations. Therefore, it may be necessary to hire additional employees to handle tasks that might be overlooked in the effort to make the new plan successful. In other words, the company should not sacrifice those tasks that have been working in the past. With all efforts running smoothly, I would expect Cherry Tree to be able to take on its additional responsibility as specialist in equipping special educational classrooms in approximately one year.

I make no claims of being able to predict accurately the total cost of this program, but the following provides a breakdown of the types of costs and some "ball-park" estimates of such costs:

Costs of Program

Two new R & D people at $21,000 per year	$ 42,000	
One new consultant—part-time	10,000	
One lobbyist	27,000	
Other additional labor cost	25,000	
Total employee cost		$104,000
R & D program	50,000	
Advertising and public-relations costs	100,000	
Total initial investment		150,000
Total (ball-park estimate)		$254,000

A COMMENTARY ON THE FOREGOING
STUDENT'S ANALYSIS

The foregoing analysis of the Cherry Tree Learning Materials Company case was prepared by one of the author's students as part of regular course work and was the first case analysis this student had ever prepared. It is not at all bad. However, in the following paragraphs a number of observations are made that would strengthen the analysis and add perspective. The comments are not offered in order of importance and certainly are not all that could be said about the case and the student's analysis. One should note that the action alternatives in the Cherry Tree Company case are more readily visualized than in some of the later cases.

Among the several executives of the company only Terence Halsey, the president, is identified by position in the organization structure. If one knew the positions of the other men, it would be helpful in judging their views and proposals for resolving the problem. Such views and proposals sometimes reflect the defense of a job, the seeking of influence or power, or other in-house political strategy. Regardless of internal company politics, one's outlook may be narrow and lack company perspective because one is well acquainted with only one specialty. The president of this organization is apparently remaining silent and listening to the ideas and arguments of his subordinates. In doing so he gains some freewheeling discussion and criticism of one manager's reasoning by another. However, after a decision has been made it will be somewhat harder in human-relations terms to bury the disagreements than if strong positions on the problem or issue had never been taken. It is a gamble taken by many top executives who believe the open forum does more good than harm. Some others believe in consensus or in limited discussion.

One does not know the rate of inflation or other change in prices and costs, but one should recognize that part of a sales growth curve may be the result of that inflation. Competitors probably experienced similar cost and price trends, but a company must not mislead itself about its real growth.

Cherry Tree Company did not know what fraction of its sales was going to schools and what fraction to individuals, an indication that there was little, if any, ongoing analysis in the marketing area of the firm. Such breakdowns of data are commonly known several times a year. Moreover, the company does not know how much of the 14 per cent of sales that goes to individuals is really to parents. It is noted in the case that some of this segment may be educators (teachers or private tutors) ordering as individuals rather than through the schools. If 14 per cent of sales is coming truly from parents when there has been no effort to cultivate such a market segment, it is quite encouraging to one contemplating the development of that segment. With small-scale sampling of the individual accounts, one could determine the real situation. The case does not make it clear whether these individuals who order are put on the mailing list for future company catalogs and, if so, for how long. The length of time that the account-holder's child needed the company's products would vary enormously, of course, according to type of disability, severity, and age of the child. Because such information is usually unavailable on the account, one might want to send the catalog until there had been no sales to that account for a designated number of periods.

One may be convinced that the status quo is not the best action alternative, but one should examine it and see what is encouraging and what is discouraging about it. One could infer that, given the status quo, Cherry Tree Company could live a rather comfortable life for a period of time and enjoy a rising demand fueled by tax appropriations and social awareness trends in government. Yet there are discouraging factors, such as the potential for market disruption by innovative competitors, potential entry of new competitors into an expanding market, and the apparent desire among the executives for the company to expand in a more directed and planned manner and more rapidly. One does not really know how long full development of the judicial and legislative trend toward social education will require. In addition, one should note the declining birthrate. This factor may be fully or partially offset for a period of years by the trend toward special education but eventually will be of importance to firms in the educational materials industry.

Although parents of mildly disabled children may be hesitant to admit that anything is wrong, it is a known fact that the parents who have above average education, income, and occupations will seek professional "special education" for their children before other parents will do so. In instances of mild disability, parental seeking of service may long precede the referral by the nursery school, kindergarten, or first grade teacher to these special services. Therefore, for mild disabilities among children about ages four to seven, the income argument in the case does not hold well. Parents of such special education children are likely to have as much if not more discretionary income than parents of normal children. After about age seven or eight, most children needing special education, regardless of the income of the homes they come from, have been referred by their teachers or parents. However, some of these children are not receiving the special services to which they have been referred. Of course, the definition of need for special attention and the measurement criteria by which children are classified vary from state to state and sometimes from school district to school district within a state. The trend is for the criteria to become more generous so that more children, even with marginal problems, are beginning to receive some professional assistance. In the United States, the trend is national in scope. States that are slow to change policies on such matters are prodded by federal grants that, as a prerequisite, may require adoption of better criteria.

The figure of 15 per cent for the proportion of children ultimately involved in special education is not the average or a conservative estimate. Rather it is the highest estimate and so must be used with caution. A prudent manager would not normally use the top end of a range of estimates.

One must note that some teachers and parents regard extra teaching at home by the parents as more harmful than helpful. It may overtire the child, cut into his play time, raise his anxiety level, offset the novelty of the school and its teaching equipment, or pose the parent as a competitor of the teacher. In addition, some parents have no teaching skills, and some others have inadequate patience in a teaching situation. On the other hand, the Cherry Tree materials could be made available to the child in the home without formal teaching by a parent being involved.

If a national health insurance plan is adopted in the United States, parents of all disabled children or at least low-income parents of such children would find themselves with increased discretionary income. This result would depend, of course, on the specific benefit characteristics and income deduction features of such a national health insurance plan. Even if no such plan were instituted, rising public expenditures on special education might free some parents' income by absorbing all or part of the costs of testing, evaluation, periodic trained observation, and therapy that are now borne by the parents.

Most of the twenty-four items in Exhibit 1, which collectively comprise 82 per cent of company sales, are low-priced relative to average family income in the United States. Fifteen of the twenty-four items are priced under $5. Only three are priced $15 or more. Also, if these items are specifically recommended by a pediatrician, other medical practitioner, psychologist, or physical therapist, one may be able to count them as medical expenses for purposes of income tax reporting.

The prices of the items in Exhibit 1 are low enough that one could logically consider whether rising demand would permit a general increase, thus increasing profits. This is unlikely, because the case states that the generic products of the company can be obtained from competitors. Apparently Cherry Tree has achieved only a limited degree of brand preference within generic categories. Increased prices do seem within the realm of possibility but only if all significant competitors also raise prices by similar accounts. Such behavior would have to avoid any conscious concerted action or consultation. If there were instances of company bidding for potentially large unit purchases by large school districts, the competitive bidding process might undo the general price rise.

One may wish to consider that, if Cherry Tree made even a small fraction of its sales to normal children, the parents of disabled children might gain more emotional utility from the brand name. It would serve to normalize and legitimize the consumption of Cherry Tree brand products in those parents' perceptions. This might result even if only three or four products for normal children were involved. For the market of normal children the manufacturer could emphasize such factors as sturdiness, safety, and general quality. However, the necessary advertising and creation of a new distribution channel for these few items might result in a net loss on them. In order to have a set of products for normal children that is large enough to interest retailers, Cherry Tree might have to spend a disproportionate share of its product development time and money in preparing more games and toys for normal children. The manufacturer might utilize direct-mail advertising to parents of normal children, but again a small number of products would be involved over which to spread the costs. Reaching people through direct mail can be costly per unit unless there is pre-existing motivation in the market. However, losses might be offset by gains made by sales to parents of disabled children. On the other hand, it is probable that special education teachers and supervisors would prefer to buy educational devices from a manufacturer known for excellence in educational matters rather than a manufacturer known for turning out toys and games per se. A point supporting the offering of products to normal children is that the company's salemen might find it expeditious to call on supervisors of kindergartens and early elementary grades in conjunction with their calls on supervisors of special education, because such people frequently maintain their offices in the same school district headquarters building. Some existing products, such as pegboards and sorting boxes, might be suitable for normal children through this channel.

One interesting strategy would be to label the goods marketed for normal children as, for example, "Made by Kingston, a Division of Cherry Tree Learning Materials Company." The average price would be fairly low and attractive, because the most expensive items in the current line seem to be the ones that normal children are least likely to need. Parents of normal children might not recognize the brand name "Cherry Tree" anyway, and the alleged stigma probably would not be operative if the Cherry Tree label were not recognized. If the products offered to normal children were not redesigned and then failed to gain acceptance, there might be little cost in reclaiming them for the traditional market of the company. It might mean shipping, handling, and repackaging costs.

An interesting facet of the alleged stigma is that among some parents it would apply more to the disability of mental retardation than to other rather common disabilities, such as partial sight, difficulties of hearing and speech, muscular malfunctions, or hyperactivity. However, some parents of normal children do not distinguish among the disabilities. For some others the term *special education* connotes only mental retardation.

In contemplating the combination of the market composed of parents of the disabled, the company would want to consider the potential of the motivational theme "Used in N thousand special education classrooms." It would be accurate and would contain much emotional implication. If the company attempted to develop this market, it might consider offering "learning systems," sets or series of products aimed at specific disability patterns. A carefully written manual for parents' use of the products would be advisable. For example, a series shipped in three or four stages and aimed at assisting in visual-motor and visual-perception skills might include the following: sponge ball, bead-sequencing kit, pegboards, shape dominoes, parquetry blocks, storytelling posters, sorting box, stencil boards, sequential memory exercise cards, halves-and-wholes matching cards, dimensional puzzles, prewriting design cards, same-or-different cards, and sewing cards. These items total $78.65. Sold together with a manual, the price might be slightly cut, such as $73.50. The shipments might start with the simplest and work upward. Determining such a sequence might be difficult for many parents and impossible for others. Without such package deals, the unit purchase by individuals would almost always be smaller than unit purchases by schools. Order filling and handling lend themselves to economies of scale. The more stages a package deal has in it, the smaller are the economies of scale in order filling and handling.

Professional issues are involved in whether Cherry Tree can secure mailing lists of parents of handicapped children. It is unlikely that it will get much cooperation from any level of government or from schools, and it will get only limited amounts of cooperation from special education teachers. However, some parents would probably provide their names and addresses voluntarily if company salesmen could get blanks made available to them by their children's teachers. Some teachers would cooperate and some would not. Also salesmen could pass out literature and address blanks at meetings of organizations of parents of the disabled, if this action was not in violation of the regulations of the place in which the meetings were held. Many clubs issue rosters of the membership free of charge. The officers of many voluntary organizations sell or rent the membership lists to list brokers in order to raise some funds or because they think the membership would like selected direct mail.

Because the company makes sixty products and only twenty-four are listed in Exhibit 1, the remaining thirty-six products must account for 18 per cent of sales. This is an average of 0.5 per cent of sales for each of these products. This situation may be justified, perhaps in light of having a complete teaching line, a desire to meet the needs of the rare case, and getting a school to order all or most of its needs from Cherry Tree instead of having to go to several competitors' catalogs. However, a firm should let the burden of proof rest with the low-volume products.

The possibility of copyrights and patents on future products gets one into areas of legal sophistication. Brand names and trademarks would be relatively easy for the company to protect, but patents for devices would be difficult to secure, would involve significant legal fees, would usually require several years to obtain, and probably could be designed around by competitors. Very few new toys and games even qualify for a patent. Manuals for products could be copyrighted, of course, without much problem. However, a competitor could paraphrase the manual and discuss the same learning principles and create a competitive manual without any copyright infringement. The copyright idea lends itself fairly well to the expansion of the company into children's books and magazines. Cherry Tree might find such items to have commercial potential especially for the partially sighted or for those with visual perceptual problems.

The case does not reveal if Cherry Tree has a new products department or other structure for developing products in an orderly and controlled manner. If the company remains a specialist in special education devices, it might wish to consider seeking research and development contracts from the federal government. Such contracts are sometimes the springboard for a product breakthrough or even product leadership in an industry.

Pasek's proposal in the case did not necessarily imply the student's interpretation of designing and offering complete classroom packages. It is not unreasonable to make that interpretation, but an equally plausible interpretation is that Cherry Tree should be a strong and innovative leader in the industry and seek a larger share of the market in the expanding and increasingly sophisticated field of special education materials.

The idea of classroom packages proposed by the student does not take cognizance of several difficulties. One is that the group of disabilities to be dealt with might vary enormously from classroom to classroom, with some children having multiple disabilities. The stages of development of the children in a classroom may be diverse. And some teachers would take offense at being handed a preplanned package instead of carefully selecting their materials piece by piece with specific reference to each current pupil. This prepackaged concept has worked well in marketing whole curriculums, such as elementary science for normal children, but the logistics seems formidable for any type of instruction as individualized as special education. The student did not sufficiently grasp this characteristic of the market. Even if the schools gave the teachers considerable discretion in working with the Cherry Tree Learning Materials Company representatives to put together the appropriate combination of products, the combination of pupils assigned to each teacher (and thus the combination of needs) would change from year to year. An interesting variant would be an attempt to market rather complete pools of educational equipment with varying numbers of units of some of the components. A pool would go to a certain school or subdistrict of a large school system and teachers would draw from it to meet their needs. Potential quantity price discounts might make it more attractive to school boards.

The student's implementation section, like many other attempts at showing implementation, is difficult to comment on. Some companies lobby in Washington, D.C., and in some of the state capitals. Much of the tax money spent on special education comes from the federal government. In addition, state monies usually subsidize school districts. Cherry Tree may be too small to attempt a lobbying effort. Moreover, it would be supporting mainly a generic cause rather than its brand and would benefit from only a fraction of the total effect, if any. Some trade associations representing many companies of similar interests also lobby.

The indicated $50,000 expenditure on R & D programs may well be not just a one-time effort but one running for many years or indefinitely. The figure itself may be understated heavily. New salesmen may be necessary. Moreover, if output is to increase, a not unreasonable assumption, there may have to be additional investment in plant and equipment. The one-year estimate for the time required for advertising, public relations, and general image change is probably too short.

The amount of net profit after taxes in recent years can be related to the potential implementation costs. One may even consider the wisdom of reducing dividends in order to raise more cash for purposes of expansion without incurring further indebtedness or selling stock.

3

NATURE
AND SCOPE
OF
MARKETING

HUFFY BICYCLES

Huffy Corporation, the largest manufacturer of bicycles in the United States, was established in 1928 as The Huffman Manufacturing Company. The name was changed in 1977, in part to reflect what many people had called it for years and also to make it agree with the brand name on the bicycles. The name change was received by the relevant publics without problem. Operating data are presented in Exhibit 1.

This company also had three other investments. There was a sporting goods division, which made basketball backboards, rims, nets, and other basketball accessories. This was a natural outgrowth of the company's long involvement in bicycle riding for recreation and better health. This division was the former Frabill Company of Milwaukee, Wisconsin, which was acquired in 1977. The fishing and marine equipment portion of the Frabill product line was sold off in the early 1980s. An exercise equipment line was bought from a small California company, Pyramid Sports, Inc., in the early 1980s and added to the sporting goods division. However, after heavy losses, exercise equipment was eliminated in 1985. Gerico, Inc., was purchased in February 1983. This wholly owned subsidiary in Denver made infant carriers, strollers, swings, bathtubs, and several other juvenile products. YLC Enterprises, Inc., provided in-store assembly,

EXHIBIT 1 Huffy Corporation Financial and Operating Review

	(Dollar Amounts in Thousands, Except Per Share Data) Years Ended December 31	1985	1984	1983
	NET SALES	$263,935	$269,482	$255,752
Summary of Operations	Operating Profit	6,722	16,240	14,073
	Interest Expense	(2,901)	(3,016)	(3,674)
	Other Income/(Deductions) Net	(4,222)	1,465	(4,271)
	Earnings (Loss) before Income Taxes (Benefit)	(401)	14,689	6,128
	Federal and State Income Taxes (Benefit)	(646)	6,433	2,115
	NET EARNINGS (LOSS)	245	8,256	4,013
	EARNINGS (LOSS) PER COMMON SHARE:			
	Primary	.05	1.48	.73
	Fully Diluted	.05	1.43	.73
Other Financial Data	Common Dividends Paid	2,137	2,140	1,647
	Common Dividends per Share	.40	.40	.33
	Capital Expenditures for Plant and Equipment, Net	5,356	5,605	2,824
	Average Common and Common Equivalent Shares Outstanding (in Thousands):			
	Primary	5,375	5,374	5,373
	Fully Diluted	5,375	5,837	5,834
Financial Position at Year End	Total Assets	129,264	136,603	138,812
	Working Capital	50,034	58,110	55,741
	Current Ratio	2.2	2.6	2.3
	Net Investment in Plant and Equipment	26,679	26,869	26,545
	Long-Term Obligations	19,529	28,253	29,284
	Redeemable Preferred Stock	—	—	5,000
	Shareholders' Equity	64,678	66,573	60,615
	Equity per Common Share	12.10	12.47	11.41
Additional Data*	Number of Common Shareholders	3,019	3,467	2,821
	Number of Employees	3,073	2,749	2,928

*1976 thru 1984 data at June 30; 1985 data at December 31

1982	1981	1980	1979	1978
$195,288	$246,206	$221,644	$232,131	$178,307
(3,902)	16,914	15,740	17,620	10,725
(5,884)	(5,456)	(4,708)	(3,163)	3,339)
73	2,619	590	212	421
(9,713)	14,077	11,622	14,669	7,807
(5,938)	6,659	4,937	6,365	3,773
(3,775)	7,418	6,685	8,304	4,034
(.99)	1.66	1.53	2.02	1.00
(.99)	1.56	1.53	2.02	1.00
2,311	2,282	1,933	1,715	1,550
.53	.56	.48	.43	.39
6,012	7,378	11,831	13,336	3,466
4,269	4,255	4,137	4,030	4,031
4,734	4,719	4,445	4,030	4,031
108,618	132,606	112,241	105,232	78,913
42,683	49,419	47,656	38,084	30,624
2.7	2.2	2.8	2.1	2.1
36,983	38,409	35,903	29,051	29,099
30,703	31,941	34,974	23,771	18,484
5,000	5,000	5,000	5,000	—
44,020	50,970	43,714	39,354	32,782
10.37	12.07	10.79	9.73	8.21
3,221	2,930	2,848	2,356	2,187
1,924	3,137	2,457	2,987	2,815

warranty service, and general repair services for several types of products, including bicycles, physical fitness equipment, gas grills, and shopping carts, for 4,100 retail stores across the United States, most of them units of national and regional chains. This subsidiary relieved many retailers of service work they did not like and for which they did not want to be responsible. Most consumers were put off by the idea of assembling something themselves when the retailer was unable or unwilling to do it. Consumers also typically did not do the work right and often wound up with unsafe products. Operating in 196 of the 200 largest geographical markets of the United States, YLC was the only national organization of its type. The sales growth of YLC had been remarkably high, but saturation of its market would come in time. YLC was founded in 1978 with Huffy as a 50 per cent owner, but Huffy bought the other half in 1982. An automative products division in Delphos, Ohio, that made gasoline cans, tire pumps, and several other automotive service products was sold in April 1982. In the early 1970s there was a lawn-mower operation, but it did not succeed. Huffy Corporation had never made a decision on whether to diversify seriously and, if so, how.

Bicycles accounted for the vast majority of the company's sales, in most years over 85 per cent. Sales were mainly to large national and regional chains of department stores and sporting goods stores, some other mass retailers, and a few wholesalers. The heart of the distribution network was over 200 department store companies, some with many branches. In the latest year, one customer, K-Mart, accounted for 13 per cent of all corporate sales. In the previous year, the corresponding figure was 18 per cent, and, in the year before that, the corresponding figure was 14 per cent. Some other highly significant customers were J. C. Penney Co., Inc., Montgomery Ward & Co., and F. W. Woolworth Co. Some large merchants offered Huffy-made bicycles with the Huffy name on them whereas others preferred that their house brand be shown. In the late 1970s and in 1980, about 40 per cent of the company's bicycles were sold under the private labels of major customers. This figure became 35 per cent in 1981. In 1982 it became 24 per cent and began to stabilize thereafter. The chains provided about 90 per cent of all corporate sales until the beginning of the 1980s. The most recent figure was about 65 per cent. Huffy was anxious to get this figure down to 50 per cent and preferably a little below. In the 1982–1984 period, several large U.S. retail chains switched much of their bicycle buying to foreign sources, the majority of which were Taiwanese. However, disappointed with quality, some of these chains switched a fraction of their purchases back to U.S. suppliers, including Huffy, as of 1985. It was a perplexing topic area for Huffy to consider for long-run policy. Archrival Murray Ohio Manufacturing Company, now based in Tennessee after a relocation, made the house brand carried by Sears Roebuck, its number one customer. A little over 50 per cent of Murray Ohio's sales were as house brands.

The other principal domestic suppliers to the mass market were Murray Ohio and AMF. Murray Ohio was the second largest bicycle maker in the United States and growing considerably faster than Huffy whereas AMF was number four. Schwinn, the third largest company, carefully avoided the mass merchants. Columbia (MTD) sold mainly to mass merchants but sold some units to specialty shops. Ross (Chain Bike Corporation) sold mainly to specialty shops but a few units to mass merchants.

There were slightly over 100 million bicycles in the United States in usable condition. A well-made, reasonably maintained bicycle had a life of 10 to 20 years, but children's bicycles were not maintained as well as adults' bicycles. At least half of the bicycles that were abandoned were not worn out. Instead, the reasons were that the owner became bored with riding, wanted a different type or model of bicycle, or had outgrown the size of the product.

Nearly 100 million Americans rode a bicycle at least once in a while. Swimming was the number one type of recreational exercise, but bicycle riding was one of the three or four other important types of recreation vying for second rank. Of the bicycles sold in the United States in a typical year, about 25 to 30 per cent were sold to adults for their own use.

Unit sales of bicycles in the United States increased at an average annual rate of 7.7 per cent from 1960 through 1978. The industry referred to the years 1972 through 1974 as the Bicycle Boom. About 13.9 million units were sold in 1972; 15.2 million, in 1973; and 14.1 million, in 1974. The peak year occurred 13 years after the peak in the birthrate, but it was also influenced by widening interest in outdoor recreation and physical fitness. Throughout the 1970s, bicycles sales were helped a little by rapidly rising gasoline prices and frequent strikes by public transit workers, but the press drastically exaggerated the contribution of these two factors. Industry sales slowed in the late 1970s and early 1980s but still remained rather good. However, the year 1982, with only 6.7 million units sold, was the worst since 1965. Most of the industry had been unreasonably optimistic for some years. In 1983, 8.9 million units were sold, in 1984, 9.7 million units; and in 1985, 11.0 million units. Further industry growth was expected to settle down to an annual rate of approximately 2 or 3 per cent for several years.

Huffy Corporation was quite expansionist and optimistic in the late 1970s. The organization enlarged its main bicycle factory in

Celina, Ohio, in 1978. Construction of a large bicycle plant in Ponca City, Oklahoma, which cost $16 million, was started in 1979; and its first bicycle came off the assembly line in 1980. The company believed it was the most modern bicycle production facility in the world and enlarged it in 1982. Huffy closed its Azusa, California, bicycle plant in October 1982 and shifted that production to its facility in Ponca City, Oklahoma. When the Oklahoma plant was planned, there was no intention to close the California plant. Demand did not justify keeping the Azusa factory open, however. Then in April 1983 the company closed its Ponca City plant and centralized all bicycle production in the Celina, Ohio, facility. Estimation of demand had been incorrect to an alarming degree.

Huffy's share of the combined imports and domestic production of bicycles (in units) was about 25 per cent in the latest year, compared to about 23 per cent for Murray Ohio. Huffy Corporation's share of domestically produced units was about 39 per cent and had been that for several years. The corresponding Huffy figures for 1974 and 1980 were 23 per cent and 35 per cent respectively. Because, on the average, the bicycles sold in specialty shops commanded a much higher price and Huffy did not have much distribution through such shops, Huffy's share of the market in terms of dollars was around 18 per cent, much lower than its share calculated on units of product. Huffy's top-of-the-line Huffy brand bicycle sold for about $195 whereas the prestigious brands started about that price.

Bicycle specialty shops sold about 25 per cent of all bicycles in the United States as of the mid-1980s, down from 46 per cent in 1968. However, this one-fourth share in units amounted to a 40 per cent share in dollars because, on average, a bicycle in a specialty shop sold for about 60 per cent more than a bicycle sold in a large national or regional chain store. Some of the many prestige brands usually found in specialty shops were Schwinn, Puch, Gitane, Fuji, and Motobecane.

Adult consumers were more important to specialty shops than to mass retailers. There were several reasons: (1) higher prices, (2) greater brand prestige, (3) greater retailer prestige in the local community, (4) claimed and perceived higher quality of products, (5) claimed and perceived higher quality of information before the sale, and (6) claimed and perceived higher quality of service after the sale. People were hesitant to pay specialty shop prices for a child's bicycle, especially because the child would outgrow it rather quickly.

Huffy had had a significant problem with the image of its bicycles. The company's products were perceived by the great majority of people as toys. Most adults who did not see them as toys, nevertheless, saw them as too inexpensive and aimed at unknowledgeable or klutzy consumers or both. It was embarrassing to most adults to be seen on a Huffy. Schwinn spokespersons were openly, publicly contemptuous of Huffy. Even among children there was a problem. On the sissiness scale, Huffy ranked rather high. The older the consumer, the more at a disadvantage Huffy was. Bicycle specialty shops did not want to stock Huffy brand products mainly because of the reasons sketched out earlier. A secondary reason was that such shops were fearful, with very good reason, that some regional or national chain stores or both would undercut the prices of Huffies that the locally owned specialty shops would try to charge.

To combat these problems, Huffy did quite a number of things. It worked on product design so as to offer a greater assortment of bicycles, including several types of bicycles that might satisfy the swings of fashion. The company saw the potential for the BMX (bicycle motocross) style of product rather early and began to make it successfully. This product was a motorcycle-styled bicycle with wide, knobby tires. The main appeal was to teenagers. Huffy also brought out sidewalk bicycles for children and Huffy Scat tricycles for young children. Contests were held in conjunction with Cap'n Crunch's Peanut Butter Cereal, a Quaker Oats Company product, the prizes being Huffy brand bicycles. The company also formed a professional racing team, and it heavily publicized all racing team victories. Advertising became more dynamic and interesting.

However, two other actions loomed larger in the company's overall strategy to alter its image. First, Huffy acquired an exclusive, long-term license to manufacture and distribute Raleigh brand bicycles in the United States from T I Raleigh Industries, Ltd., of England, a prestigious maker of bicycles for over a century. Also included was the right to use the Raleigh name on exercise equipment. This brand, which had about 3 per cent of the American market, had been made in Taiwan and Japan for Raleigh under contract for several years. Huffy planned to continue using this source for some of its Raleigh supply, but it also leased manufacturing buildings in Kent, Washington for production. These facilities were leased until 1988, subject to six consecutive options to renew for additional terms of three years each at a rent to be determined. Raleigh sold at retail for about $245 to $1,400. Raleigh was the second-largest brand, after Schwinn, sold in the specialty shop segment of the U.S. market. Despite the Oriental sourcing in recent years, the Raleigh name still carried a very special mystique, that of a high-quality European bicycle ridden by a knowledgeable, sophisticated person through the leafy English countryside. The visual image was remarkably strong. Huffy Corporation established its Raleigh effort as a wholly owned subsidiary, Raleigh Cycle Company of

America, to try to separate this line as much as possible psychologically from the Huffy line. Some Raleigh dealers refused to handle Raleigh after Huffy began to have responsibility for its production and marketing. As one such dealer put it to a customer, "The quality of Raleigh is now just as good as the Huffy you see in the big chain toy store down the street. It's just a painted-over Huffy." Credibility was a problem for Huffy Corporation. Clearly, things were not going to be easy for Huffy's Raleigh subsidiary.

The second major part of the corporate strategy was to gain some presence in the 1984 Olympics, emphasize the results indefinitely, and then aim for later Olympic Games also. The U.S. Cycling Federation selected Huffy Corporation and its Raleigh subsidiary to produce bicycles at Huffy's Technical Development Center in Dayton, Ohio, to be used by the U.S. National Cycling Team in worldwide competition, including the Olympics. These bicycles were designed by people with expensive scientific and engineering talent and were hand-built. Every bicycle was tailored to the individual characteristics of the rider as well. These products were put to the competitive test rather early on in their development at the 1984 Summer Olympics. Americans had not won an Olympic bicycling medal since 1912, but this time they won nine of them, five of the nine on Huffy-made Raleigh bicycles. Included were the gold medal earned by Connie Carpenter for the women's road race and a gold earned by Stephen Hegg for the individual pursuit race. Hegg's bicycle received considerable news media coverage because of its unusual appearance. Called the "High Tech Bike" and the "Funny Bike," it had a 24-inch front wheel, a 27-inch solid disc rear wheel, and aerodynamic style handlebars. Silver medals were won by Norman Vail in the sprint race and the U.S. team in the 4,000-meter pursuit race. A bronze medal was taken by the 100-kilometer road race team. Of the 23 Americans participating in the Olympics, 13 rode bicycles made by Huffy technical development personnel.

Dumping

Most of the U.S. bicycle industry believed that there was some "dumping" of bicycles in the U.S. market in violation of U.S. laws and a loose set of understandings more or less agreed on in an international treaty. Much of the industry and certainly Huffy believed that Taiwan was the chief culprit. The Bicycle Manufacturers Association, a trade group and often the spokesperson for the U.S. industry, filed antidumping charges with the International Trade Commission against Taiwan and several other countries. There was very little chance of winning the legal dispute, however.

The U.S. tariff on foreign-made bicycles ranged from 5½ to 11 per cent and had been stable for many years. The sizes usually bought for children paid a tariff of 11 per cent; and those usually bought by adults and older teenagers, 5½ per cent. The tariff on bicycle parts was from 6 to 10 per cent depending on type of part. The Bicycle Manufacturers Association had long claimed that the average bicycle tariff in the world was 24 per cent and that no country had lower bicycle tariffs than the United States. In 1985 the association reduced the claimed figure of 24 per cent to 20 per cent but reiterated that U.S. producers had to pay their workers extraordinarily high wages and fringe benefits and needed the protection of a higher tariff. The U.S. bicycle manufacturers, including Huffy, imported selected components. For example, a large fraction of the multispeed hubs came from Great Britain, West Germany, and Japan. Many of the tires came from India, South Korea, and Taiwan; and many of the coaster brakes, from Mexico, Japan, and West Germany; and derailleur systems, from France.

The word "dumping" had to do with the sale of foreign-made goods at questionably low prices. There had never been a really clear meeting of the minds on what constituted dumping. Moreover, even when a definition could be temporarily adopted for the sake of argument, the relevant economic data were difficult to gather and extraordinarily difficult to verify. Dumping was usually thought of as the pricing policy whereby a company sold a product abroad for a figure either below its cost or for less than it charged in its home country. There was no general meeting of the minds on how to handle fixed versus variable costs or what a reasonable profit was. There was also no general agreement on what role was played in "cost" by subsidies that the government of a country might make to a producer in that country.

The uncertainty was given some structure by a major international treaty, the General Agreement on Tariffs and Trade, signed in 1947 by many countries, including the United States. Many other countries signed later, and the number of signatories was now 90. This treaty was administered by a permanent secretariat in Geneva, Switzerland. In prohibiting the dumping, Article Six of the treaty contained the following language:

> For purposes of this article, a product is to be considered as being introduced into the commerce of an importing country at less than its normal value, if the price of the product exported from one country to another (a) is less than the comparable price, in the ordinary course of trade, for the like product destined for consumption in the exporting country or, (b) in the absence of such domestic price, it is less than either (i) the highest comparable price for the like product for export to any third country in the ordinary course of trade,

or (ii) the cost of production of the product in the country of origin plus a reasonable addition for selling cost and profit.

However, the preceding failed to take into account the level of the effects of imports on the companies in the importing country. Less developed countries were able to write into the treaty agreement a clause that limited the right to prohibit importation of low-priced goods implied in the preceding definitional language. This resulted in the following further language of the treaty:

If as a result of unforseen developments and of the effect of the obligations incurred by either party to this agreement, any product is imported into the territory of one of the parties in such increased quantities and under such conditions as to (a) cause or threaten serious injury to domestic producers or to the establishment of domestic production in that territory of like or directly competitive products, or (b) cause serious disruption of traditional patterns of trade in that product or directly competitive products, the injured party shall have the right, in respect of such products, and to the extent and for such time as may be necessary to prevent or remedy such injury, to suspend the obligation in whole or in part.

The treaty and a subsequent code of interpretation of Article Six authorized any member nation to adopt antidumping taxes, often called countervailing duties, against an offending nation. For example, if the illicit price in nation X was determined to be $10 per unit of product too low, then a tariff or additional tariff could be imposed by nation X for $10 per unit of relevant product against the imports from the offending nation. The number of allegations and formal complaints was rising in some countries, including the United States. Most did not result in any action. These complaints were handled by the International Trade Administration, part of the Commerce Department, and the International Trade Commission. In the United States, a complainant had to prove both price discrimination and significant injury to the domestic industry. Minor injury or injury to the complainant only was not sufficient.

Imported bicycles became quite important in the United States in the 1950s and temporarily peaked in 1972 at 37 percent of the U.S. market. U.S. tariffs on bicycles were reduced in 1968. The import percentage fell for several years and bottomed out at 17 per cent in 1979. See Exhibit 2. It turned up in 1980 with a 23 per cent share. Huffy believed that the upturn in 1980 came about because many U.S. mass merchants expected a domestic shortage of bicycles in 1980 that did not materialize. In 1981 and 1982 imports took 23 per cent; and in 1983, 30 per cent. In 1984 and 1985 the share surged to 42 per cent and 49 per cent, respectively.

Industry analysts had developed some data about the imports. See Exhibit 3. This exhibit showed, for example, that about 17 per cent of the bicycles entering the United States from Japan were sold through large merchants, the remainder going through shops that specialized in bicycles. The corresponding figure for the largest supplier, Taiwan, had been declining for several years. It was 60 per cent in 1980. This was explained by both rising quality of Taiwanese bicycles and carefully planned marketing attempts by Taiwan to place the goods in bicycle specialty shops in the United States.

Advise Huffy Corporation.

EXHIBIT 2 Share of the U.S. Market Held by Imported Bicycles in Selected Years

	Percentage of Units
1960	31
1965	18
1968	21
1969	28
1970	28
1971	26
1972	37
1973	34
1974	28
1975	23
1976	21
1977	20
1978	20
1979	17
1980	23
1981	23
1982	23
1983	30
1984	42
1985	49

EXHIBIT 3 Bicycles Sold Through Mass Merchants as a Percentage of All Bicycles Imported from the Source Nation

Source Nation (in order of number of bicycles sold in U.S.)	Percentage of Units
Taiwan	23
Japan	17
South Korea	100
Poland	100
France	0
Britain	0

LONDON FOG

London Fog was an extraordinarily well-known brand name. In fact, the brand name was far better known than the company, whose official name was Londontown Corporation. Located in a suburb of Baltimore, this organization was founded in 1922 and was the oldest as well as the largest rainwear maker in the United States. Its sales exceeded $165 million per year and were growing.

The United States rainwear industry lost about seventy-five manufacturers between the late 1960s and the middle 1980s through merger and bankruptcy. About twenty firms remained, several of which were in some difficulty.

The extent to which the London Fog brand name was familiar to American male consumers was quite impressive. In standard, unaided tests among properly constituted samples of men, more than 90 per cent said, "London Fog" after the interviewer said, "Raincoat." The corresponding figure for women was less but still impressively high. Thus, the brand awareness, recognition, and recall were among the highest ever achieved by an American manufacturer.

Londontown Corporation made men's and women's raincoats and rainproof outerwear. It had about 60 per cent of the men's raincoat market and about one-third of the women's raincoat market in the United States. The company added men's and women's other outerwear to its product line only in the late 1970s. Among the types of outerwear were quilted jackets in several lengths and weights and light-weight windbreakers and golf jackets. These were marketed as a collection under the trade name "Outdoors Unlimited by London Fog." It was hoped that use of the word "unlimited" would call to the consumer's attention that the garments were for warmth as well as protection from the rain. Company advertising headlined the collection as "rugged and ready jackets and coats for women and men." In 1983 and 1984, Londontown introduced the London Towne label. According to company executives, this was done so as to add some new and different channels of distribution. In 1985 the organization added another collection of men's and women's outerwear and gave it the brand name "Winning Edge by London Fog."

Moreover, Londontown Corporation licensed several other companies to manufacture rain hats, umbrellas, shoes, and other products using the name London Fog. Some of the firms paying to use this famous brand name were Gold Star Hat Corporation, Bowen Shoe Company, Fashion Rite, Miller Brothers Industries, and Schertz Umbrellas, Inc.

The advertising of London Fog typically utilized a line drawing modeled on the Big Ben tower of the Houses of Parliament in London. Often the advertisements also used a statement that had become strongly associated with the brand: "London Fog lets you laugh at the weather." Both print and electronic media were used heavily. Among the minor types of advertising were multicolor leaflets for retailers to stuff inside regular monthly bills to their customers. Some consumers thought of London Fog as a British organization. Britain enjoyed a reputation as a source of fine clothing for men.

A much larger organization, Interco, Inc., acquired a majority interest in Londontown Corporation on February 25, 1976. Interco was a conglomerate that manufactured apparel, footwear, and furniture and owned several retailing firms. The headquarters office was in St. Louis. Realizing "the importance of the entrepreneurial spirit in its executives," one of Interco's stated corporate policies was to acquire a company only if the management wished to continue on an active basis.

The Apparel Manufacturing Group in Interco consisted of 11 apparel companies operating 51 manufacturing plants and 12 major distribution centers across the United States. In March 1984, Interco acquired Abe Schrader Corporation, which made women's dresses, suits, coats, sportswear, and ensembles in the medium- to medium-high price ranges. The sales of the Apparel manufacturing Group in fiscal 1985 were $943,077,000. See Exhibit 1 for other years. London Fog was by far the best-known brand name in the entire Apparel Manufacturing Group.

Among the clothing brands Interco owned were Don Robbie, Devon, Clipper Mist, College-Town, Queen Casuals, John Alexander, Stuffed Shirt, Stuffed Jeans, Pant-her, Smith & Jones, LeTigre, Petite Concept, Rejoice, Cowden, It's Pure Gould, T. A. Whitney, Tour de France, Big Yank, Donegal, Cherokee, and Campus. Interco also manufactured large amounts of clothing for the house brands

EXHIBIT 1 Sales of Interco and Its Apparel Group
by Year, 1977–1985 (in thousands)

	Interco	Apparel Group
1985	$2,625,746	$943,077
1984	2,678,886	880,122
1983	2,566,606	877,341
1982	2,673,769	899,161
1981	2,368,456	850,970
1980	2,024,307	818,380
1979	1,851,458	731,259
1978	1,666,657	640,487
1977	1,566,432	576,019

of several retail chains. Among Interco's footwear brands were Florsheim, Winthrop, Rand, Worthmore, Hy-Test, Grizzlies, Thayer McNeil, Miller Taylor, Avenue, Crawdads, Personality, Miss Wonderful, J. G. Hook, diVina, Phillips, and Thompson, Boland & Lee. The major furniture brands owned by Interco were Ethan Allen, Broyhill, Kling, Knob Creek, and Restocrat. The conglomorate entered the furniture business in the calendar year 1980. Ethan Allen, Inc., was purchased February 1, 1980; and Broyhill Furniture Industries, Inc., December 1, 1980. The products of these two large furniture makers were almost all upper-middle-priced and were very well known. Through these two acquisitions just ten months apart, Interco became the largest furniture manufacturer in the world.

The Interco retailers included, among others, Golde's, a department store with ten branches in and near St. Louis, and Idaho Department Stores, a chain of 77 junior department stores in Texas and the Northwest. Other operations included 30 large home improvement centers in the Midwest called Central Hardware, 88 men's specialty shops in the Midwest and South called Fine's or Fine's United, 72 discount department stores in the Southeast under the name Sky City Discount, and a national chain of Florsheim shoe shops. The company opened 39 new Florsheim shops in 1985 alone. Interco also operated stores under the names of Benchley, Carithers, Jeans Galore, Keith O'Brien, Standard Sportswear, United Shirt, and Thornton's. In addition, Interco owned Senack, Inc., which operated a large national chain of leased shoe departments in many independent department stores and large apparel stores. The heavy emphasis in the Retail Group was on clothing and shoes. In 1984, Interco sold most of P. N. Hirsch & Company, a chain of 385 junior department stores in the Northwest and Southwest, and consolidated the retained units into the Idaho Department Stores operation. Interco also sold Albert's, a chain of 63 women's specialty shops, in late 1984 and Eagle Family Discount Stores, a chain of 210 self-service stores, in early 1985. All three components were sold because of their poor earnings. There was concern in Interco and within the Retail Group about performance, priorities, and emphasis just as there was concern in the four divisions or groups of the conglomerate about the importance of each to Interco.

The Apparel Manufacturing Group provided 35.9 per cent of Interco's sales. Londontown Corporation provided over one-sixth of the apparel sales and between 6 and 7 per cent of Interco's total sales. The conglomerate had annual sales of $2,625,000,000 and about 48,000 employees. The corresponding figures four years earlier were $2,368,000,000 and about 56,000 employees. See Exhibits 2 and 3.

EXHIBIT 2 Sales by Group as a Percentage of Interco's Total Sales,
by Fiscal Year, 1977-1985

	1985	1984	1983	1982	1981	1980	1979	1978	1977
Apparel	35.9	32.9	34.2	33.6	35.9	40.4	39.5	38.4	36.8
Footwear	22.1	21.1	21.3	22.0	23.6	27.4	29.0	30.3	31.4
Furniture	21.2	20.1	17.8	19.3	13.2	1.0	0	0	0
General Retailing	20.8	25.9	26.7	25.1	27.3	31.2	31.5	31.3	31.8

EXHIBIT 3 Operating Earnings to Sales as a Percentage, by Interco Group,
by Fiscal Year, 1977-1985

	1985	1984	1983	1982	1981	1980	1979	1978	1977
Apparel	8.8	11.4	10.8	11.7	12.9	12.9	13.1	13.5	13.5
Footwear	9.4	10.3	10.5	13.4	15.0	11.8	11.4	8.8	9.9
Furniture	9.7	11.0	6.3	10.7	12.8	15.0	—	—	—
General Retailing	3.2	4.2	3.3	3.4	4.2	6.5	7.0	7.3	6.5

Londontown was no longer independent. As with any subsidiary of a conglomerate, fundamental changes in the company and its product line and capital investments were subject to review by the management at the Interco headquarters. However, Londontown was rewarded with much more quasi-independence than a typical subsidiary of a typical conglomerate.

The president of Londontown at the time of the acquisition, Jonathan P. Myers, was appointed to be one of the six vice-presidents of Interco. Four of them, including Myers, were appointed to the Interco Board of Directors. Myers, his father, his wife, his sister, and his brother-in-law together had owned about 42 per cent of the Londontown corporate stock and thus became sizable stockholders of the conglomerate. The market value of their shares on the stock exchange more than doubled when the acquisition was concluded. Jonathan's elderly father, Israel Myers, had begun working for London Fog in 1923 at the age of sixteen. He was largely responsible for the later growth of the company until he chose to go into retirement as his son and son-in-law gradually assumed active management roles.

Londontown Corporation had a history of considerable innovation. Israel Myers detected a rising consumer interest in lightweight rainwear in the early 1940s. His first such sale was to the U.S. Army, which awarded him a contract for 10,000 raincoats. Because rubber was scarce, the company made coats of synthetic rubber on a sheet of cotton. Soon after World War II, as supplies became plentiful again. Londontown began making private label rainwear for J. C. Penney and Sears, Roebuck and Co. In 1951, London Fog experimented with a new synthetic fabric, Dacron polyester, made by a process developed by Du Pont. London Fog was one of the first manufacturers to buy the revolutionary new cloth, which repelled water, did not wrinkle, and had good visual appeal. The source was Wamsutta Mills, which had been licensed by Du Pont to manufacture the new fabric. However, the first Dacron melted during the sewing process. Du Pont, Wamsutta, and London Fog worked together to develop a lubricant that solved the problem, and by 1953 satisfactory London Fog Dacron rainwear was in production. In early 1954, Saks Fifth Avenue stores, in a major promotion paid for by Londontown, were the first to introduce the revolutionary new raincoats. This retailer had thirty days of exclusive rights to sell the product. This introduction gave the new product a high-fashion and status stamp. The sales growth thereafter was quite rapid. The status of the new product was ironic. Israel Myers was very fond of recalling that in earlier years the manufacturing of raincoats was the lowest-status portion of the entire apparel industry.

There was a noteworthy difference in the risks involved in manufacturing raincoats for women as opposed to those for men. Men demanded the same raincoats not just year after year but decade after decade. Although women's rainwear did not exhibit the extremes of design or rapid change of the women's dress industry, it did change appreciably. London Fog did not give adequate attention to those changes prior to 1970. In 1969 the company suffered high losses by not responding to the women's fashion cycle. London Fog became acutely conscious of the need to forecast women's fashion, to observe the slow changes in men's fashion, and to remain alert to the possibility that men's fashion might begin to change more rapidly than in the past. Major rainwear manufacturers might have the ability to influence the men's fashion cycle to change more quickly. Most business observers considered London Fog to be a trendsetter for women's raincoats.

The company had many competitors, but all of them were much smaller. For women, two of the largest were Forecaster of Boston and Misty Harbor. Two well-established imports from Britain, Burberry's and Aquascutum of London, England, were peripheral competitors in that their price lines were from 40 to 90 per cent higher than London Fog's, whose price lines were considered in the medium- to upper-medium range and topped out at about $200. Some other important imports were Induyco and Cortefiel from

Spain, and Diane Von Furstenberg and Calvin Klein from Hong Kong. For men's rainwear a major competitor was Gleneagles, Inc., also located in Baltimore. It was a division of Hart, Schaffner & Marx but was only a fraction the size of London Fog.

The number and sizes of competitors in the future were in doubt even though the number of domestic producers had declined markedly. The fundamental facts were that the production of raincoats was extremely simple and low-skilled, such production required relatively low capital investment and unsophisticated equipment (that is, it was labor-intensive), and the United States was moving toward fewer restrictions on international trade.

London Fog used a selective distribution policy in selling goods to retailers. The company had traditionally placed a suggested retail price on each garment and had carefully avoided selling to discounters. Virtually all stores charged the full list price on London Fog products. In 1977 and 1978 the Federal Trade Commission accused the manufacturer of price-fixing, that is, dictating to the retail accounts the prices to charge ultimate consumers. This ability of manufacturers to practice resale price maintenance had been legally rescinded by Congress as of early 1976. London Fog signed a consent order, not admitting any wrongdoing but promising not to dictate the prices that retailers could charge in the future.

At the time of the case, Mark H. Lieberman, previously the marketing vice president, had succeeded to the office of president of Londontown Corporation. Jonathan Myers, now age 47, became chairperson of Londontown's board of directors but was no longer an Interco vice president or a member of the Interco Board of Directors. Lieberman was appointed to the Operating Board of Interco but not its Board of Directors. The conglomerate's Operating Board had 24 members, 20 of whom were what Interco called "the principal officers of Interco's major operating companies." The other four persons were Interco's chairperson of the Board of Directors, president, executive vice president, and senior vice president. The executives of the conglomerate referred to this body, which met monthly, as "the heart of our business." Londontown Corporation also had an Operating Board, consisting of its management team plus four Interco senior corporate officers, which met quarterly.

Advise the London Fog organization.

H. G. PARKS SAUSAGE

Founded in 1951, H. G. Parks, Inc., was a well-known manufacturer of pork sausage. It was established by Henry G. Parks, Sr., when he was thirty-five years old, and it grew to become the seventh largest minority-owned firm and the second largest publicly held minority-owned firm in the United States. This second fact means, of course, that the Parks stock was publicly traded on the open market. From the beginning there was another large investor besides Parks. However, that man, William L. Adams, was a silent partner. Adams was a prominent black business executive in Baltimore and a member of the city council. H. G. Parks, Sr., also served on the city council from 1963 to 1969.

The Parks enterprise was sold in 1977 for $5 million to Norin Corporation of Miami, Florida, a conglomerate with annual sales of about $650 million. Besides the principal owners, Parks and Adams, there were about 900 other stockholders. The price received by each stockholder was more than twice the price of the stock on the open market. H. G. Parks, Sr., stayed on as a consultant, but not as an employee of Norin, under a seven-year contract. According to some people in the corporation and in the community, a great sense of loss was felt by the Parks employees and many members of the community. The company had been successful and respected and carried symbolic value.

Although H. G. Parks, Inc., had sales of $15 million and a net profit of almost $1 million in the year before the sale, it did not prosper under Norin's ownership. Although there were allegations of poor management decisions and insufficient management involvement and interest, the underlying causes were not clear. However, it was clear that H. G. Parks, Inc., was severely affected by the high inflation rates of the late 1970s. For example, the prices of the raw materials went up 100 percent, and annual insurance premiums went up by $70,000. Sales began to decrease. A severe cash flow problem developed.

In August 1980, Norin sold the Parks organization to Canadian Pacific Enterprises, a manufacturing subsidiary of Canadian Pacific Railroad. Shortly thereafter, H. G. Parks, Inc., was transferred to the jurisdiction of another Canadian Pacific Railroad subsidiary, Canellus, Inc., based in Syracuse, New York. After a short delay, Canellus put Parks up for sale and gave H. G. Parks, Sr., and the company employees a forty-five-day first right of refusal to buy the business. The founder of the firm, then aged sixty-four, declined to buy it back or to become a major investor in it. He said, "My day is past."

During the next few weeks nine persons pooled savings and borrowed money in order to purchase the Parks corporation. A short extension of the forty-five-day period was necessary. Leading the investment group was sixty-year-old Raymond V. Haysbert, president of H. G. Parks, Inc., since 1975. A former college professor of business administration, Haysbert joined Parks, Inc., in 1952, when the organization employed only six people. Haysbert put in his personal savings of $100,000, took out a second mortgage on his house, and borrowed $22,000 on his Visa, MasterCard, and American Express credit cards.

Although the investors together had a large amount of funds, they did not have enough to meet the asking price of $4.6 million. At that point they approached the Baltimore City Council and its subsidiary board of finance and requested assistance.

Specifically, the nine investors asked that $2.5 million of low-interest, industrial development bonds be issued to help them finance the purchase. Such bonds were a popular but controversial device for local or state government or both to subsidize the building of such projects as stadiums, industrial parks, docks, and factories. A state, county, or city issued bonds either for itself or on behalf of selected private projects. These securities were for the purpose of economic development of local areas and the creation of the accompanying jobs.

Issuance of such bonds specifically to benefit private enterprises was authorized in the 1960s. Their usefulness depended on the fundamental point that the federal income tax does not apply to securities issued by state and local governments as part of the traditional division of powers between the national government and the state governments. These bonds were attractive to individual buyers because the interest the bonds paid was exempt from federal income tax. The bonds were economical to the issuer because they carried an interest rate that was below prevailing market rates for other loans. Most tax experts and many business executives, politicians, and consumer activists contended that this device was undesirable and had been abused and that all private enterprise should utilize the usual money markets for funds.

After a lengthy debate on the desirability and propriety of issuing such bonds for the benefit of the nine investors at Parks, Inc., the City Council voted thirteen to two to do so. A major issue was the criticism that H. G. Parks, Sr., would be back in a position of considerable economic power at Parks, Inc., using local government financial aid after he had sold that same company at a substantial gain and kept that gain. All this was, of course, legal. Victorine Q. Adams, wife of William L. Adams, was a member of the City Council but abstained on this vote. Such bonds had already been voted earlier for several other companies by the City Council.

The city issued $2 million in bonds for Parks, Inc., at low interest rates and sold $600,000 worth to Commercial Credit Corporation and $1.4 million to Equitable Trust Company, at which time the $2 million was paid to Canellus on behalf of the nine investors. Now the company was theirs, but, of course, they were responsible for repayment of the bonds and the accompanying interest over a long time period.

Haysbert, the largest investor, was named president and chief executive officer of H. G. Parks, Inc., and his son was appointed the personnel manager. The manufacturing vice president, G. T. Day, and the vice president-comptroller, A. S. Choksi, were also major investors. Choksi was a naturalized American citizen originally from India. H. G. Parks, Sr., made a token investment in the company and was appointed chairperson of the Board of Directors and given a lifetime contract as a consultant to the company. Haysbert was a well-known community leader, articulate and witty, and president of HUB (Help United Baltimore), an organization of about 600 black business and professional people. He served on the board of directors of several corporations and numerous nonprofit organizations.

The Parks firm was well known in its trade territory, partially because of its advertising. Just before the purchase by Norin, Parks, Inc., was spending $1 million per year on advertising, but Norin required this figure to be cut substantially. Parks, Inc., did not spend a greater share of its sales on advertising than was common in the industry, but its advertising tended to be noticed. The company popularized a statement, "More Parks sausage, Mom, please!" This statement was widely used in the company's advertisements, both print and electronic. This expression was usually accompanied by a photograph of a young child, usually a boy. Many different children of all races were used. The child was always cute and appealing and spoke the sentence enthusiastically. The sentence sought to integrate auditorily or visually or both the words "Parks" and "pork." On the front of the company's plant, a bold sign in red proclaimed, "The House of More Parks Sausages, Mom, Please!" Interestingly, for several years the company used the expression "More Parks sausage, Mom!" without the word "please." Parks, Inc., received thousands of letters from consumers saying the children in the advertisements were brats for not saying "please." When this word was added, the company received thousands of letters of approval from consumers. Moreover, the company made intensive use of the two following expressions: "Famous flavor found only in Parks. Famous flavor!"; and "Nothing pleases people like Parks." Both were sometimes sung to a simple tune in advertisements appearing in the electronic media. Both of these statements relied on a principle in communication design: emphasis on the sound of one letter, F or P in these instances, stated fairly rapidly and with an interesting meter. Most familiar English language sounds, if deliberately repeated several times with a small planned sequence of variations, are noticeable and memorable. The statements were more effective in electronic media than in print media. Often two of the three statements were used in the same advertising, separated by some space on the page or by a few seconds of time.

In addition, the Parks organization had recently begun to advertise its sausages as an excellent ingredient to add to the stuffing served with roast turkey. Such messages were directed toward the Thanksgiving and Christmas holiday periods. The use of sausage to give stuffing a different flavor was the resumption of an old American and British tradition but presented as a new idea in cooking.

The sausage industry was highly competitive. Competitors included all the large national meat-packing companies, such as Oscar Meyer, Hormel, Armour, Wilson, Swift, Jimmy Dean, and Bob Evans plus many regional operations, most notably Mash's, Briggs, Fischer's, Green Hill, Hillshire, Esskay, Gwaltney, and Smithfield. Formerly owned by LTV, Inc., a large Dallas-based conglomerate, Briggs had recently been sold to Mash's but was to operate with its own production and marketing. Mash's management planned for Briggs to provide in-house competition for Mash's existing products. Formerly a subsidiary of ITT (International Telephone and Telegraph), another conglomerate, Gwaltney had recently been sold to Smithfield Foods, Inc. Also, Esskay, a Baltimore independent that had been experiencing difficulties with labor and production costs and was losing money, was sold to Smithfield Foods. Like Briggs, Gwaltney was to operate with its own production and marketing, and Smithfield's management was planning to encourage competition between Gwaltney and the existing Smithfield business. On the other hand, Smithfield had planned to operate the Esskay facility in Baltimore as a physical distribution center with no production there. Under enormous pressure from militant labor unions and many community leaders, the company agreed to have some production in Baltimore. Processing of some cured pork products, including sliced bacon and ham, was thus moved to the Esskay facility. Smithfield's corporate headquarters was in the suburbs of Washington, D.C., but the plant bearing its name and the Gwaltney plant were about 185 miles south in Smithfield, Virginia. Founded in 1936, Smithfield was by far the largest meat company in the East with almost $900 million in annual sales. This aggressive organization also had recently bought Patrick Cudahy, Inc., a century-old firm in Wisconsin.

Another competitor entered the East Coast in 1986, but its products could not be offered for sale until 1987 because of lengthy curing of the meats. Fiorucci Foods, Inc. (U.S.A.), a wholly owned subsidiary of 100-year-old Salumificio Cesare Fiorucci, S.p.A. of Rome, built an ultramodern plant in the suburbs of Richmond, Virginia. One of the largest makers of cured meats in Europe, it was known for spicy and other strong-flavored products. If successful along the East Coast, Fiorucci Foods would seriously consider going national.

All these national companies and most of the regional companies had broader meat product lines than did H. G. Parks, Inc. However, Parks, Inc., had been adding some new meat products. Its line already included very spicy, spicy, and mild products. Pork sausage, available in both rolled form and links, dominated the line, but there was also a pork scrapple and an all-beef sausage. The all-beef sausage was developed specifically to meet a need expressed by two important institutional customers, the Department of Corrections in both New York City and the District of Columbia. Moslem inmates could not eat the pork sausage that Parks, Inc., was already supplying these two organizations. Bacon and brown-and-serve sausage were added in 1982 and 1983. The latter product was not only convenient to the consumer but also had the majority of the fat removed. Another health-related step was to reduce slightly the salt content of the entire product line. In recent years, U.S. per capita consumption of pork and beef had declined slightly, mainly because of serious concern about cholesterol content and high calories. The prices of most Parks products were slightly above those of most of its competitors.

Besides new products, Parks, Inc., was pursuing food service contracts. This type of agreement called for the supplying of large quantities of food to lodging places, restaurant chains, and institutional accounts. The corporation already had contracts with the Eastern region of Pizza Huts, the Philadelphia public school system, some military installations through the U.S. Defense Department, the Northeastern New England part of the Howard Johnson hotel and restaurant chain, and, as noted, the correctional operations of New York City and the District of Columbia. Expansion opportunities with Howard Johnson had looked promising. However, Howard Johnson had just been divided and sold. A relatively unknown but highly successful company, Prime Motor Inns, based in Fairfield, New Jersey, was the new owner of the hotel operation, which had 500 locations, and 199 of the freestanding restaurants. Marriott Corporation was the new owner of the remaining 350 freestanding restaurants. Several years earlier, Parks, Inc., had had a sizeable contract to supply Marriott Corporation but had given it up after finding it could not earn a profit and still meet the prices which that company was willing to pay.

Parks, Inc., was giving considerable attention to 8-A-type sales contracts. Such agreements derived from provisions in federal (and some state) laws that allocate a certain percentage of the government procurement budget or a certain sum of money to be used exclusively to buy goods and services from the minority-owned sector of the economy. This was often termed the "set aside" rule. A minority-owned business might, of course, face stiff competition for such contracts from other minority-owned firms. The federal government was planning to modify its policy so that larger minority-owned companies would enjoy such benefits for a limited time period only. The political process of making such a change, if at all, would require several years.

The output of the company was distributed through most of the Northeast from northern Virginia to Massachusetts. The plant and offices were in the Camden Industrial Park in Baltimore. The distribution area extended approximately 440 miles north, 175 miles west, and 80 miles south of Baltimore. Physical distribution centers were operated in West Haven, Connecticut; Somerset, New Jersey; New York City; and Philadelphia, as well as Baltimore. The company's brand sold at a satisfactory rate in the Baltimore metropolitan area, which had a population of about 2.5 million, but no better than many out-of-town competitors. This area provided about 4 per cent of company sales. On the other hand, metropolitan New York City, with about 12 million population, accounted for 55 per cent of company sales. Parks, Inc., entered Richmond, Virginia, in 1982 but did not succeed there.

There were about 240 employees, about 80 percent of whom were members of minorities. Of the total, 110 were production and maintenance workers. This category of employees was unionized and was paid relatively high wages and fringe benefits. The union had recently won a substantial increase in compensation, with the increments spread over a period of several years. For this reason, plus the fact that quite a few local manufacturing companies were slowly reducing their work forces, it appeared that there would be labor peace for several years.

Sales for 1980 were about $16 million, thus exceeding the 1977 level, but the company sustained a loss of $400,000. Sales for 1981 reached about $17 million, but the financial results were borderline, and the plant was operating at only 65 per cent of production capacity. In 1983 the company made a net profit of almost $1 million. In 1984 sales reached $21 million, and the company was again profitable. Sales rose to $25.5 million in 1985, and the company remained profitable. Yet there was some concern about future directions of the company.

Advise H. G. Parks, Inc.

4

CONSUMER BEHAVIOR

MAPLE HILL PSYCHIATRIC CLINIC

Jane Finley, M.D., was a psychiatrist at a large hospital in Washington, D.C. She now had five years' postresidency experience and was interested in establishing a private practice. Although she felt her work at the hospital was socially useful and academically interesting, it was also exhausting and one-sided. Because her hospital was a general, short-term facility, the psychiatric admissions were usually of an emergency nature. The patients tended to be in chaotic personal or family situations or both and were difficult to handle. They also tended to stay only a few weeks to a month, and the most rewarding to work with were usually taken over by a more experienced outside psychiatrist as soon as the family physician could see the patient and make a referral. This left for the hospital staff only the poorest and most socially isolated patients. Often these patients were quickly transferred to a public mental health facility, but, even if they remained, they were usually contentious, remote, or violent. This made the work very fatiguing.

Dr. Finley needed to plan strategies to acquire private practice patients to replace her hospital salary income and to cover the overhead associated with independent practice. For this reason, she needed to evaluate potential sources of referrals and the types of patients that might come from each source. She then could plan a series of contacts with the most promising sources.

Two options were possible to Dr. Finley as an independent entrepreneur. She could operate a "solo" practice—with or without a receptionist. Many solo practitioners, especially psychoanalysts, operated this way. Because their patients came three or four times a

This case was prepared by Joanne G. Greer, Ph.D.

week, often for several years, there was little need for a receptionist to receive the infrequent new patients. In fact, it was common for psychoanalysts to have offices in their own homes after the European tradition. Another approach would be to establish a group practice, sharing one receptionist and waiting room with several other mental health professionals. These could be other psychiatrists, in which case the relationship was usually limited to shared overhead and covering emergency calls from patients during each other's vacations. Some psychiatrists who were comfortable with a multidisciplinary group would take psychologists and social workers as employees or partners. As neither of these groups could prescribe medication, the psychiatrist added an essential skill to the group. Psychologists were especially skilled in diagnostic testing, and social workers historically were strong in working with practical problems such as family organization or workplace difficulties. This structure appealed to Dr. Finley, but she felt her older colleagues might consider her presumptuous to set out in private practice with her own multidisciplinary clinic. In addition, it would cause her some social difficulties with other psychiatrists to take a psychologist as a partner because of the keen market competition between the two groups.

She had culled the following facts and opinions from other junior psychiatrists of her acquaintance:

1. There had been a drastic cutback in insurance coverage of psychiatric outpatient services. Formerly most good insurance plans had given equal coverage to psychiatric and other types of medical care visits. Now it was common to impose a limit of 50 or even 20 visits a year in most local insurance plans. Only a few upscale employers such as major law firms were willing to fund coverage for psychoanalysis, which required four visits a week.

2. Psychologists in independent private practice were steadily eroding the market for psychiatrists' outpatient services. Many persons who needed help were less put off by visiting a psychologist. In addition, psychologists often promoted their services from an upbeat "wellness" point of view rather than the "mental illness" model that patients and their families disliked. For example, psychologists were more prone to refer to "clients" rather than "patients." They tended to be less formal in their behavior and to accept more input from clients on the treatment plan.

3. Whereas enrollment for the further postdoctoral study at the local Psychoanalytic Institute had formerly given a young psychiatrist a certain cachet and guaranteed extra referrals of interesting patients, this was no longer true. Institute faculty no longer had

excess cases for psychoanalysis that they were inclined to refer to Institute candidates (trainees). For the four psychoanalytic cases required for graduation papers, candidates now had to search for appropriate referrals whereas, in the past, the institute's faculty had carefully selected them for the candidates.

4. Membership in the local psychiatric society had also become a poor source of referrals. No one had excess work at present. One friend told of accepting a referral based on his supposed special expertise only to find that the patient was exceedingly contentious and refused to pay her bills. He suspected his older colleague of "dumping" the patient on him to get rid of her.

5. Joining the local branch of the American Medical Association was probably a good move. Activity in the organization could lead to referrals from general practitioners and pediatricians. However, a contradictory fact cited by one colleague was that more and more general practitioners were choosing to treat emotional problems of patients themselves with prescription drugs. This was legal in spite of the fact that these doctors' knowledge of such drugs was less detailed than that of a psychiatrist. It was encouraged by the manufacturers of psychoactive drugs, who sent sales representatives with samples and literature to general practitioners as well as to psychiatrists.

Mental health services, unlike medical services, could be legally provided by several different types of individuals. Any M.D. could legally provide prescriptions for psychoactive drugs. Psychiatrists were M.D.'s with at least four years' of post-M.D. "clinical" training in mental illness in hospital settings. Clinical training simply meant actually taking care of patients while being tutorially supervised by more experienced doctors. This supervision consisted of small-group seminars in which one psychiatric resident would read his or her treatment notes to the group, and the group would discuss and critique the trainee's strategy with the patient. In addition, the trainee's psychotherapy work with some patients would be supervised on a one-on-one basis. The trainee would meet the case supervisor to review notes after every two to four meetings with the patient.

Clinical psychologists and counseling psychologists held either the M.S. or the Ph.D. degree. Their training differed from that of industrial, social, experimental, or educational psychologists although they all received the same basic foundation in psychology. During the latter phases of training, clinical and counseling psychologists received supervised experience with clients, similar to that given psychiatric residents. In fact, Ph.D. candidates and psychiatric residents sometimes attended the same seminars at hospital training centers. Psychologists were licensed for independent (unsupervised) practice in almost all states but only if they held the Ph.D. Master's level psychologists had to work under the supervision of a Ph.D. or M.D.

Psychiatric social workers usually held only a master's degree, the M.S.W. They received the same generic training as other types of social workers, but during the latter part of their training they received some limited training in doing psychotherapy. Traditionally, they worked as assistants to psychiatrists, taking care of contacts with the patient's family and employer or other practical matters. More and more, they were going into independent private practice, but most insurance companies would pay for their services only when supervised by an M.D. Some insurance companies would not pay them at all, and in some states they were not legally permitted to have an unsupervised clinical practice.

In addition to the three main groups of (1) psychiatrists, (2) psychologists, and (3) social workers, in some states some other groups could legally practice psychotherapy. Psychiatric nurses usually worked in mental hospitals either in physical patient care or sometimes as group therapists. Group therapy was a common adjunct to hospital treatment, offering a forum for patients to discuss practical problems under professional leadership. Educational settings and rehabilitative settings often used master's level counselors. Although their work with clients was practical in nature, it overlapped with that of the major mental health providers. In most states, counselors were not reimbursed by insurance companies, and, in some, they could not legally practice independently.

Sex therapists and marriage therapists were multidisciplinary groups. They had their own professional organizations and issued certificates to members who completed three years' of supervised clinical work in these specialties under the supervision of senior members of the organizations. Few insurance companies reimbursed marriage counseling. Sex therapy was usually reimbursed only when provided in the context of more general problems of living and when provided by a licensed M.D. or Ph.D. Although it was generally conceded that these organizations were reputable, there was opposition to regarding their services as "medical." In the past, the reputation of sex therapists and marriage counselors had been somewhat tarnished because untrained persons had set themselves up to practice these specialties. Few consumers knew how to locate a reputable certified counselor in these areas.

A final group was the pastoral counselors. Usually clergymen, priests, nuns, deacons, or other career religious staff, they provided various types of counseling to members of their denominations. Services were usually only short term (one to ten visits), and usually charges were nominal. Typical clients might be feuding married couples, a family with a drug user, or a person who recently lost a parent or spouse. Some pastoral counselors were fully qualified as licensed social workers or psychologists. Their clients seemed to lie outside the usual market for mental health services in that they turned to their churches for assistance in preference to the medical community. If referrals were needed, pastoral counselors usually referred clients to other church members.

Dr. Finley was able to obtain some data on patient characteristics from a study funded by the federal mental health research agency, the National Institute of Mental Health. This data compared the patients of various mental health-care workers on age, income, and other useful variables. However, the data was national, and Dr. Finley was not sure how relevant it was to her city. See Exhibits 1 and 2.

In spite of the fact that drug treatment was one of her unique market advantages, Dr. Finley was really not interested in a large practice of managing patients who required long-term psychoactive drug treatment. Long-term drug treatment tended to be given to persons who were either severely impaired or who lacked the intelligence, motivation, or opportunity to undertake psychotherapy or psychoanalysis. She found such patients less interesting. The infrequent visits for the supervision of the medication and monitoring of side effects were not the sorts of professional relationships she enjoyed.

On completing her residency, she had taken a research fellowship at her current hospital. In actual fact, this mostly involved functioning as a junior faculty member, supervising the hospital work of medical students and residents. However, she did conduct a research study on the effect of nutrition on psychotic behavior. She also enrolled in the local training institute of the American Psychoanalytic Association to pursue an eight-year, part-time curriculum to qualify for a certificate in psychoanalysis. She attended classes with other institute candidates on Saturdays, was psychoanalyzed herself, and began seeing "analysands" (persons in psychoanalysis) under faculty supervision. These training cases tended to be university students and housewives, drawn by the low-fee arrangement. They were interesting to work with but were no real source of income. She often received less each week from an analysand than she, in turn, paid to her case supervisor for the obligatory weekly tutorial session for that case. Of her four cases for graduation, only one paid her the usual fee of $75 a session. This analysand was enthusiastic and well-to-do and would probably remain in treatment for several years.

EXHIBIT 1 Last Five Patients and Treatment Characteristics for the More Severe Mental and Emotional Conditions: Comparison of Ambulatory Care Settings

Characteristic	Current Patient				Terminated Patient			
	Psychiatrist Mdn or %	Psychologist Mdn or %	Social Worker Mdn or %	Primary Care Physician Mdn or %	Psychiatrist Mdn or %	Psychologist Mdn or %	Social Worker Mdn or %	Primary Care Physician Mdn or %
n	154–173	52–57	98–112	0	83–91	16–18	51–62	3
				Providers in community mental health centers and other community settings				
Age	35.0	35.0	33.0	—	32.0	35.0	33.0	—
% female	47.1	54.4	61.6	—	47.3	55.6	67.7	—
Income ($1,000s)	7.4	6.0	6.0	—	6.0	8.0	7.4	—
Total no. visits[a]	20.0	15.0	24.0	—	12.0	21.0	18.0	—
Total no. months[a]	13.0	10.0	10.0	—	12.0	10.0	8.0	—
Visit length (minutes)	30.0	50.0	50.0	—	25.0	50.0	50.0	—
Initial severity[b]	30.0	25.0	35.0	—	40.0	30.0	40.0	—
Final severity[a,b]	65.0	60.0	65.0	—	60.0	65.0	61.0	—
% drugs used[c]	97.7	69.2	79.6	—	96.7	41.2	65.5	—
% no inpatient care	78.6	71.9	76.7	—	69.3	83.3	82.0	—

Characteristic	Current Patient				Terminated Patient			
	Psychiatrist Mdn or %	Psychologist Mdn or %	Social Worker Mdn or %	Primary Care Physician Mdn or %	Psychiatrist Mdn or %	Psychologist Mdn or %	Social Worker Mdn or %	Primary Care Physician Mdn or %
	Providers in private office							
n	460–537	207–227	81–90	41–48	205–235	135–145	37–45	16–21
Age	38.0	35.0	37.0	48.0	38.0	35.0	35.0	40.0
% female	57.0	61.2	70.8	72.9	58.3	54.5	75.0	55.0
Income ($1,000s)	20.0	20.0	18.5	11.0	20.0	20.0	19.0	20.0
Total no. visits[a]	30.0	30.0	40.0	10.0	20.0	20.0	10.0	6.0
Total no. months[a]	13.0	9.0	10.0	10.0	6.0	5.0	3.0	7.0
Visit length (minutes)	45.0	50.0	50.0	20.0	45.0	50.0	55.0	20.0
Initial severity[b]	30.0	30.0	35.0	50.0	35.0	30.0	40.0	50.0
Final severity[a,b]	80.0	70.0	75.0	80.0	60.0	55.0	60.0	50.0
% drugs used[c]	92.1	48.8	44.3	NA	88.8	42.6	46.5	NA
% no inpatient care	63.1	82.1	90.9	76.6	59.5	80.6	84.1	66.7

Note. Conditions included are schizophrenia, schizophreniform disorder, major depression (excluding mild depressive neurosis), and mania. — = Insufficient data to report findings.

[a] For current patients, the respondent estimated the patient's total number of visits, months in treatment, and final severity.

[b] Severity was measured using a modified version of the Global Assessment Scale of Endicott, Spitzer, Fleiss, and Cohen (1976), which ranges from 1 (unable to function in many areas) to 100 (superior functioning).

[c] Not asked of primary care physicians.

EXHIBIT 2 Last Five Patients and Treatment Characteristics for the Less Severe Mental and Emotional Conditions: Comparison of Ambulatory Care Settings

Characteristic	Current Patient				Terminated Patient			
	Psychiatrist Mdn or %	Psychologist Mdn or %	Social Worker Mdn or %	Primary Care Physician Mdn or %	Psychiatrist Mdn or %	Psychologist Mdn or %	Social Worker Mdn or %	Primary Care Physician Mdn or %
	Providers in community mental health centers and other community settings							
n	76–86	167–179	310–348	0	55–60	71–91	185–213	5
Age	34.0	33.0	33.0	—	33.0	32.0	33.0	—
% female	64.0	64.8	73.6	—	61.8	63.7	69.0	—
Income ($1,000s)	12.0	15.0	12.0	—	12.0	13.0	12.0	—
Total no. visits[a]	10.0	12.0	15.0	—	8.0	6.0	8.0	—
Total no. months[a]	6.0	4.0	6.0	—	4.0	3.0	3.0	—
Visit length (minutes)	50.0	50.0	55.0	—	45.0	50.0	55.0	—
Initial severity[b]	50.0	50.0	55.0	—	50.0	60.0	60.0	—
Final severity[a,b]	80.0	80.0	80.0	—	75.0	70.0	72.0	—
% drugs used[c]	66.7	13.0	14.2	—	55.0	12.7	9.6	—
% no inpatient care	86.0	96.1	96.4	—	83.1	92.3	91.3	—

		Providers in private office						
n	981-1,114	1,746-1,882	622-670	93-110	519-601	1,244-1,354	353-410	34-43
Age	36.0	35.0	34.0	40.0	35.0	34.0	34.0	40.0
% female	61.8	64.6	72.8	69.1	61.4	63.3	68.1	76.7
Income ($1,000s)	25.0	25.0	21.0	12.3	25.0	24.0	25.0	15.0
Total no. visits[a]	40.0	24.0	26.0	5.0	15.0	13.0	15.0	6.0
Total no. months[a]	12.0	7.0	8.0	6.0	4.0	4.0	5.0	4.0
Visit length (minutes)	50.0	50.0	50.0	20.0	50.0	50.0	55.0	20.0
Initial severity[b]	50.0	55.0	55.0	60.0	55.0	55.0	58.0	50.0
Final severity[a,b]	85.0	85.0	84.0	80.0	80.0	75.0	75.0	80.0
% drugs used[c]	35.9	8.6	8.0	NA	27.6	6.4	7.7	NA
% no inpatient care	87.6	93.0	98.0	72.0	89.2	93.7	94.2	74.4

Note. Conditions included are anxiety disorders, neuroses, personality disorders, and relationship problems. — = insufficient data to report findings.
[a] For current patients, the respondent estimated the patient's total number of visits, months in treatment, and final severity.
[b] Severity was measured using a modified version of the Global Assessment Scale of Endicott, Spitzer, Fleiss, and Cohen (1976), which ranges from 1 (unable to function in many areas) to 100 (superior functioning).
[c] Not asked of primary care physicians.

Dr. Finley really liked doing psychoanalysis. She felt that the patient became a real person to her, and she was actively involved in a growth process. She felt the same enthusiasm for doing psychotherapy with children, who often seemed to change so rapidly and profit so much from treatment, compared with older adults. However, she had found it disappointing and upsetting whenever a child's parents terminated the child's treatment prematurely either because they became jealous of the child's affection for the psychiatrist or to save money. One of her supervisors at the Psychoanalytic Institute suggested that she could ward off this outcome by cultivating a relationship with her young patients' parents, perhaps scheduling a meeting with them once a month. She felt this would work with elementary school children but suspected that adolescent patients would no longer trust her.

Because of her interest in children, she wondered whether she should become active in the local public schools as a volunteer, lecturer to PTA groups, and so on. One of her teachers at the institute had a consultant position with a prestigious girls' prep school. She received referrals from the school in return for providing free advice to the faculty on problems that came up. Over the years, parents who had been pleased with her work became sources of other referrals. At this school, all the families could afford to pay full fee, but this would not be so at a public school.

At the other end of the spectrum, the county in which Dr. Finley lived was willing to pay $45 an hour for treatment of Medicaid-eligible children but only to an incorporated nonprofit clinic or hospital. The fee to a private doctor was only $7 an hour. Dr. Finley was willing to try seeing these children although their families had a reputation for little patience with psychological explanations of misbehavior. In order to get the $45 per hour fee, she had tentatively decided to incorporate as "Maple Hill Clinic," named after her section of the Washington, D.C., metropolitan area. However, she feared that better-off patients would not come to a clinic. Also, although her low-fee psychoanalytic cases would be willing to visit a clinic, it might put off any full-fee analysands. Her neighborhood was adjacent to the more affluent northwest quadrant of the city, only a few blocks over the state line in the Maryland suburbs, and it actually contained quite a mixture of incomes. Older residents tended to be retirees on fixed incomes who had bought their neat brick houses when the Maryland suburbs of Washington were considered remote, and so the neighborhood was less desirable. Newer residents were upwardly mobile young professionals who bought the old houses for their convenience to the D.C. subway system. There were also some middle-aged couples with young adult children in residence. The average educational attainment of the neighbor-hood was quite high compared to the D.C. area as a whole. Almost all adults held college degrees, and many had advanced degrees.

There were several other prospective "bundles" of patients. A group that might be interesting to work with were the "worried well." This was a term recently coined by mental health researchers to describe persons whose life worries caused them to have various psychosomatic complaints, such as headaches, dizziness, difficulty in swallowing, heart-pounding, shortness of breath, or nausea. For such persons, extensive diagnostic tests revealed no bodily disease to explain the patient's complaints. These persons caused great expense to insurance companies because their symptoms were often the same as those of serious illnesses such as heart disease or cancer. The attending physicians felt ethically obligated to carry out expensive diagnostic workups even when they knew from experience that a particular patient was inclined to "somatize" under stress. There was a problem in getting these patients to accept the services of a psychiatrist even when the insurance company provided coverage. They usually became angry at the suggestion that their very real bodily suffering was a product of their emotions.

Another interesting group of patients were "bulimics" and "anorexics." Mostly women, these persons were obsessed with having a very slender figure. Anorexics reduced their food intake to danger-ously low levels whereas bulimics controlled their weights by binge-eating followed by induced vomiting. These persons also resisted recognizing their psychological difficulties and usually entered treatment only when their low weight became a danger to life and only at family insistence. Their characteristically high level of energy helped them deny the risk of their behavior. As an undergraduate, Dr. Finley had worked for a summer at the National Institutes of Health, coding data for a research team studying anorexia. One of these doctors had given her a letter of reference for application to medical school, but she had since lost touch with him.

Phobias were a type of mental problem that had suddenly become stylish and received lots of media coverage. Typically, phobics avoided seeking treatment. Often phobics simply rearranged their lives to avoid the feared object or experience. Flying in airplanes and visiting crowded places were two common phobias that often inter-fered with normal life. A person whose work required travel might spend the weekend on a train to be at a meeting on Tuesday without flying on Monday. A person who feared crowds might shop by phone or mail and limit his or her social life. Phobics were both male and female, but more women sought treatment. In fact, women predom-inated in all types of mental health patients except the criminally insane, and for a long time it had been believed that women were more subject to neurosis and psychosis. A long-term study by the National Institute of Mental Health of three typical communities had pretty well disproved this assumption. Using diagnostic interviews administered in household visits to sampled households, the researchers found that both sexes had equal difficulties, but women were more likely than men to seek treatment.

Interestingly enough, nonphysicians had had some success in marketing specialized services such as "phobia clinics" or "eating disorder clinics." These nonmedical therapists seemed better able to get the patient to accept treatment in comparison to the family M.D.'s usually unsuccessful referrals of these patients to psychiatrists. The treatment at such clinics was typically only "supportive," as compared to "problem-solving" or "insight-oriented." For example, a phobia clinic might treat a person's fear of shopping centers simply by providing a supportive companion to hold hands with and talk with as they made trips into crowded places in a graduated fashion. They might start with only talking about the trip, work up to a two-minute visit, and then lengthen the visits gradually. At termination of treatment, the patient would visit a crowded place alone. These therapists were very practically oriented and were neither trained for nor interested in probing deep motives for the patient's behavior. Some of them had no formal training—or very little—in mental health work, and they operated under the supervision of a psychologist. Such persons had been found useful in keeping costs down, and the patients liked them. A nearby university offered a formal training program for them, giving a degree called "Master in Mental Health." It was not legal for them to work without supervision by a psychologist or psychiatrist. The training program was open only to persons over age 40 who had been highly recommended for community volunteer achievements.

Dr. Finley's favorite teachers during her psychiatric residency training had been the psychoanalytically oriented faculty. She was enthusiastic about their philosophy of treatment. Whereas supportive psychotherapy was aimed at getting the patient to *feel* better and to solve immediate practical problems, psychoanalytic psychotherapy and psychoanalysis were designed to be learning experiences for the patient. If successful, they aimed to weaken the less desirable aspects of personality and to strengthen the more desirable aspects. So, for example, a person who was inhibited from competing in his or her profession would be treated differently by a supportive therapist versus a psychoanalytic therapist. The supportive therapist would encourage the person with pep talks, examples, suggestions, and praise. The psychoanalytic therapist would explore with him or her the probable reasons for his or her behavior, especially from child-hood. The hoped-for result would be that such patients would decide they had outgrown the nonproductive behavior and feel free to give it up on their own.

The psychoanalyst aimed to improve the quality of life of the patient and not simply to help solve the most pressing problems quickly. However, this aspect of psychoanalysis was not emphasized in communications to the public. This was probably because most American psychoanalysts were M.D.'s and psychiatrists although in the rest of the world this was not so. The American medical psycho-analysts were sensitive to any suggestion that they did not cure diseases just like their other M.D. colleagues. They felt that such an idea would make them less like doctors and more like psychologists. Psychologists had been traditionally excluded from the training institutes of the American Psychoanalytic Association although a few hundred had been trained during the last thirty years under a special "waiver" of their lack of the medical training prerequisite. Currently, the American Psychological Association was supporting a lawsuit against the American Psychoanalytic Association by some of its members, claiming restraint of trade at their traditional exclusion from the prestigious postdoctoral clinical training available only at the psychoanalytic institutes. The American psychologists had already appealed to the International Psychoanalytic Association to recognize their claims to be treated equally with foreign psychologists, but this group had refused to get involved in a national-level dispute.

In psychoanalysis per se, the meetings were more frequent than in psychotherapy, and the treatment lasted several years. Psychoanalysis was distinguished from psychoanalytic psychotherapy by length and intensity of treatment but not by philosophy. Psychanalysis was usually recommended for persons who were rather intelligent but had such significant personal difficulties that the time involved would be worth it to them.

The one fact that most of the public knew about psychoanalysis was that the analysand lay on a couch and that the psychoanalyst sat out of sight. Freud, the founder of psychoanalysis, had stated simply that he did not care for being stared at all day, but the arrangement developed a mystique for his followers. Most of them followed the procedure faithfully, believing that it helped the analysand relax and allow a free flow of thoughts. The analysand was instructed simply to say whatever came to mind. This became progressively harder to do as the material became more troubling. The task of the psychoanalyst was to listen until the pattern of the communications made some sense and then attempt to pull them together into a coherent return communication. This communication, traditionally called an "interpretation," could be summarizing or confrontational or could extend the analysand's ideas a step further. If the interpretation were properly formulated and timed, the analysand often responded with confirmatory recollections from the past or information from the present.

Freud's greatest discovery, detailed in one of his first psychoanalytic writings, was "transference." This was the tendency of the analysand to "transfer" feelings about childhood's significant figures more and more to the present-day psychoanalyst. Freud maintained that transference was universal and that it caused many everyday problems. Workers tended to react to a male boss as if he were their childhood father, repeating both the pleasant and the painful aspects of the childhood relationship. Young adults tended to seek out mates that were either negative or positive images of their opposite-sex parent. Transference tended to "heat up" in the intimacy of the analyst-analysand relationship, particularly if the analysand tried to cooperate and actually say whatever came to mind without blocking thoughts. Such feelings were usually patently illogical, for, in fact, the analyst took no active role whatever in the analysand's life. As soon as the analyst identified a transference manifestation, the next task was to fit it into the analysand's childhood history tentatively and offer these ideas to the analysand for consideration. If the communication was well-timed, the analysand saw things about his or her behavior and unconscious feelings that had never been clear before and may have caused significant trouble in everyday relationships. This recognition was a first step toward change.

Psychoanalysts were convinced that no one who had not been psychoanalyzed could really understand how psychoanalysis worked. The older psychoanalysts who had established private practices were not particularly concerned about this. They were accustomed to receiving sufficient referrals to keep busy from long-established contacts in the medical community. They also received referrals through past patients. Because it took from eight to fifteen years to complete the training and one could not start it until completing the psychiatric residency, the senior members of the group were age fifty-five to seventy. At age seventy, they were required by their professional association to stop taking new patients for psychoanalysis although they could continue to teach and to do psychotherapy. It was considered undesirable for an analysand to have to contend with the death of the psychoanalyst in the middle of the treatment.

Dr. Finley and her classmates at the institute felt that their teachers were rather out of touch with the current generation. The candidates were convinced that their contemporaries were unlikely to spend $10,000 a year on a treatment without understanding how it worked. The prescription of a physician no longer had that kind of influence over educated people. They were aware that there were cheaper and less time-consuming options. At the same time, the candidates were also at a loss for any ideas on how to promote psychoanalysis. To get their four supervised cases for graduation, most of them had persuaded patients who originally came to them for psychotherapy to try psychoanalysis instead. Often this involved bargaining on the fee so that the cost for the analysand was no greater than twice a week psychotherapy. Even then, some people resisted doubling their weekly time commitment to the treatment.

The candidates at the institute enjoyed other aspects of their teachers' "old fashioned" point of view. The psychoanalytic training process had remained essentially unchanged since Freud's day, and the candidates enjoyed the idea of participating in an unbroken intellectual tradition of such stature. No distinction was made before the public between the candidates and the faculty in that candidates were permitted to hold themselves out to the public as psychoanalysts as soon as they began their first psychoanalysis. Although classes and seminars were required, the heart of the training was considered to be the candidate's own personal psychoanalysis, done by a faculty member, and the candidate's four required pieces of psychoanalytic work. Graduation was not guaranteed at any point; the training process was completely personalized. Each of the four "graduation" cases was supervised by a different faculty member to expose the candidate to various approaches to the work. If the candidate's work did not progress satisfactorily, a fifth or sixth case might be required, or the candidate might be advised that his or her talents lay in psychiatry rather than psychoanalysis. Following the tradition of Freud's training of his own students, when the candidate seemed ready, he or she was invited to present a clinical paper to the local psychoanalytic society as a gesture of welcome.

Several aspects of psychoanalysis had combined to give it a tarnished reputation in the popular press and among many ordinary persons in the last twenty years. Discovery of the major antipsychotic drugs had cut deeply into the general psychotherapy market back in the early 1960s. Psychoanalysts were seen as opposing drug treatment unnecessarily. The women's movement had been deeply offended by some of the writings of the founder of psychoanalysis, Sigmund Freud. The general consumer of services was unaware that present-day psychoanalysts also took Freud's ideas about women with a grain of salt. Finally, one of the basic tools of the psychoanalyst, transference, had been misinterpreted in movies and novels as "falling in love with the doctor." Each of these popularly held beliefs alienated different market segments. Dr. Finley wondered, in fact, whether it might be counterproductive to her success in private practice to identify herself to the general public as a psychoanalyst. A possibility was to label her work with the vaguer term "insight-oriented" rather than "psychoanalytic."

It was unfortunately true that any "insight-oriented" approach often involved much more time and, as a result, more cost to the patient or the insurance company. Furthermore, no scientifically designed research to compare the various approaches had yet been carried out. What comparative studies had been done were of limited scope and did not have proper statistical designs. Although she believed strongly that the methods she had been taught were effective, Dr. Finley had no scientific proof to offer to the more sophisticated consumer. She had to rely on the traditionally favorable attitude of the intelligentsia toward her type of therapy.

Advise Dr. Finley.

LE DRUGSTORE

The idea of the now well-known business Le Drugstore was unconventional at the time of its founding, 1958, and remains so today. The corporate, legally proper name was Publicis, S.A., and this name appeared on some objects in the store, such as the napkins and ashtrays. But the usual operating name and the one by which customers knew the firm was Le Drugstore. It was owned by a large French advertising agency.

On a business trip to New York in the mid-1950s, Paris advertising executive Marcel Bleustein-Blanchet caught a head cold during a spell of unpleasant weather. To complicate matters, he ran out of tissues at two in the morning. Bleustein-Blanchet knew that one could not buy tissues in Paris at that hour at any price and assumed that New York City would be the same. Nevertheless, he looked. To his delight he found that not just one but many New York City drug stores were open, and he bought the tissues he needed.

This little episode caused Bleustein-Blanchet a great deal of thought on his trip home and afterward. What would happen if someone were hungry and wanted a meal in Paris at that time of the night? French eating places and shops were notoriously rigid in their hours of operation and they stayed open relatively few hours. Yet, very probably most French consumers had never recognized this characteristic, for they had grown up with it and expected nothing different. Bleustein-Blanchet began to seriously consider setting up a business in Paris where one could buy a meal and tissues for one's cold and a great many other items, even late at night.

No equivalent of the American drugstore existed in the French economy and society, regardless of the question of operating hours. Bleustein-Blanchet's investment needed a name to describe this type of business, but nothing in the French language appeared to be suitable. Thus he selected the English-language word *drugstore* and Gallicized it to "le drugstore."

Location was judged to be a critical factor. Bleustein-Blanchet bought the old Astoria Hotel, an elegant building on the celebrated Avenue des Champs Elysées near the Arc de Triomphe, and placed Le Drugstore there. It was a choice that was bound to capture people's attention. If they did not see it, at least they would probably hear about it. Moreover, this location was on one of the most beautiful and famous streets in the world and was reasonably convenient for a large number of persons. This site was near many other shops, several specialized museums, embassies, office buildings, and some apartment houses, but it was well to the northwest of the real center of downtown. In fact, it was considered to be at the edge of downtown. However, it was fairly close to the Bois de Boulogne, a large beautiful park, and several high income, close-in residential neighborhoods composed mainly of townhouses and apartment houses. Le Drugstore was not the sort of place one would probably go downtown specifically to visit, unlike the major department stores or fashionable boutiques, and other specialty shops in the center of the city. Yet, perhaps in time it would come to attract passerby on the Champs Elysées and people who lived nearby. Le Drugstore opened its doors in 1958.

The store offered not only time convenience to those who lived or worked nearby but merchandise-mix convenience and innovation as well. Le Drugstore was set up to include several departments, which many persons connected with the firm preferred to call shops or boutiques. It included a soda fountain, which was both an American-style soda shop and American-style medium-priced restaurant; a pharmacy; a department for sundries; a tobacco shop; perfume boutique; record shop; toy shop; luggage shop; and a clothing shop. To top off the variety, the founder included two small movie theaters in Le Drugstore. Copper fixtures from an old luxury cruise ship were used to carry out a nautical decorative theme. Publicis spent more than U.S. $1 million in readying the old hotel structure for this highly unconventional package of goods and services.

Besides many French dishes, Le Drugstore served an American-style breakfast and, of course, American snack foods such as hamburgers. Eggs and toast were available for the tourist, visiting business person, or French consumer satiated with croissants. Even the unthinkable catsup was available for the hamburger. What is more, breakfast was available from 8:30 A.M. until 2 A.M., and dinner service began at 5 P.M. Both schedules were unique in France and perceived as barbarian by virtually all French people. The typical French breakfast was a hot beverage plus croissants or rolls with butter and sometimes jam or jelly. The French dinner time was normally no earlier than 7:30 P.M. and more commonly about 8:30 P.M.

Commercial success came quickly to Le Drugstore. It was considered chic for some time, but instead of dying as a fad usually does, it was accepted by enough people to make it a viable business.

Nevertheless, most Francophiles, especially of the American variety, were noisily critical of Le Drugstore, calling it a gross, ugly intrusion of the American culture into the French culture. Countless French also were angered by this new institution. The many French language purists were outraged. Concern about the name *Le Drugstore* was greater than concern about the breaks with tradition in products, product mix, and hours of operation. Some Parisian merchants and restaurateurs resented the competition and the unusual and aggressive style in which it was offered.

Most native English-speakers found it difficult to comprehend the anger of the French-language purists, especially when linguistic experts estimated that only about 40 per cent of contemporary English word stock came from Old English. In fact, most English language experts maintained that the migration of words from one living language to another was a natural process. Many added that it made a language more fun and more interesting.

After a short while it was realized that the underlying cause was apparently a large, long build-up of concern and resentment about word transplants from many other languages, most notably English, and about a century of decline in the international use of French as the world language of diplomacy and business. English had pushed ahead of French on a global basis, but French had a strong command of second place. Moreover, English was the most popular choice of foreign languages among students in French schools.

Most cultures of the world have no organization that attempts to govern the language, monitor its use in publications, rule on the appropriateness of words, or prepare the official dictionary, but both France and Spain do. In France it is called the French Academy. However, a much more militant group, called the Office of the French Vocabulary, had organized in 1957 with about 3,500 distinguished members. This new organization noted disdainfully that it had taken the French Academy twenty-four years to critically review the words beginning with the letters *A* through *C* in the latest round of work. The Office of the French Vocabulary launched a major crusade to purge the French language of expressions such as weekend, business-man, parking, hardware, software, and drugstore. Some broad-minded French noted that the language was derived from Latin and had a strong component of Greek and a noteworthy amount of German. General Charles de Gaulle was elected president of France in 1958 on the general theme of returning France to *gloire* (glory). He instituted many changes and actively led an increasing hostility to the United States and Britain and rejection of their cultures. Nevertheless, Publicis, S.A. persevered in its operations, weathered the public relations storm, and kept its trade name as well as its mode of operating.

In 1965 Le Drugstore was bold enough to add a branch two miles southeast of the original. Bleustein-Blanchet bought the Royal Café at the corner of Boulevard Saint Germain and Rue de Rennes, one of the busiest intersections on the Left Bank. This was at the heart of the literary district of the city, St. Germain des Pres, in the neighborhood so loved by many English language writers and at the edge of the university district. Le Drugstore number two was given approximately the same mix of departments as the parent location, except that a car rental service was installed and a large book department was placed in the basement. The cinema seated 300 and the soda fountain 200. This new branch became quite popular rather quickly. Also in that year, 1965, President Charles De Gaulle was re-elected, principally on a platform of hostility to almost everything Anglo-American and a revival of French glory.

The language debate never completely ceased, but it diminished somewhat through the late 1960s. However, in 1970 President Georges Pompidou appointed fifteen committees to identify popular foreign words and think of possible French-language replacements. In 1973 he denounced the influence of Anglo-Americanism. Pompidou appointed three large committees of prominent people to again investigate the problem and prescribe how to rid the language of foreign influences. The president and many French scholars and intellectuals took the position that their language was the foundation of their civilization and that their civilization was the highest ever achieved on earth. Some 350 foreign terms, mostly from the English language, were immediately and officially banned from use in the conduct of French government affairs, even without waiting for the predictable reports from the committees. The motivation was not just long years of anger and frustration but the increased threat of more English-language incursions because of the entry in 1973 of Britain and Ireland into the European Economic Community, which France, one of the EEC founders, had previously opposed.

Publicis, S.A. was ready for expansion again by 1970. The management selected a busy location slightly over one mile east of the first location and closer to the heart of downtown than the original location. This branch number three was on Avenue Matignon at Le Rond Point, a major circle formed by the Avenue des Champs Elysées, Avenue Franklin Roosevelt, Avenue Matignon, and other streets. It was one and six-tenths miles northwest of branch number two. This third branch also included a sidewalk cafe, a cinema with 350 seats, and a restaurant with 312 seats. The decor emphasized wood, marble, stainless steel, and leather. Within a short time this new branch was successful. Moreover, Publicis negotiated a part ownership in Pub Renault, a semi-British-style operation on the Champs Elysées about midway between Le Drugstore branches numbers one and three.

A disastrous fire destroyed the original Le Drugstore in 1972. Over 1100 customers and employees were evacuated successfully in just over six minutes. Many regular customers expressed great disappointment and emotional support for the company. The management rebuilt but this time stressed a modernistic design and used a decorating scheme of "railway car chic." The new store included all the old features. The restaurant was enlarged to seat 300 and the two cinemas enlarged to seat 500 and 280. A bar and a terrace facing the Champs Elysées were added to the sidewalk cafe. The re-opened Le Drugstore number one was an instant success.

In 1981 Le Drugstore finally reached the very busy heart of the downtown area. The company opened branch number four at 6 Boulevard des Capucines extremely close to the Paris opera house about one and a fourth miles east of the Avenue Matignon branch. Departmentation was similar to branches one and three.

Le Drugstore number one had a sales volume of about U.S. $16 million in the most recent fiscal year, and the three other locations had combined sales of about U.S. $23 million. Employment at the four totaled about 750. Approximately one million Parisians lived within one and a half miles of one of the four Le Drugstore locations.

As in several nations of the world, the capital city of France is the undisputed leader in more than government. Paris dominates France in the fine arts, performing arts, communications, finance, manufacturing, and distribution. It is the hub of transportation for the country. As of the latest government count in 1975, there were 2,317,227 persons within the city limits of Paris. The suburbs contained another 6,232,671 persons, for a metropolitan area total of 8,549,898. Population density in the city was very high, and population density in the suburban areas was higher than in the United States. The population of France was 52,599,430. Neither the Paris metropolitan area nor the nation was showing any significant population growth.

Advise Le Drugstore.

LILY CREST MODES

Lily Crest Modes' director of marketing, Perry Robbins, was reviewing the characteristics of demand for apparel[1] among elderly women, who, in his tentative estimation, were women sixty-five years of age or older. This company was already a sizable manufacturer of daytime dresses in the popular "misses" sizes, intended for the adult woman of average height. Currently the firm did not manufacture in "junior" sizes, which were popular with slightly shorter females in their teens and twenties, or in "half" sizes, meant for older women with shorter proportions. Lily Crest Modes was expansion-minded and well-financed. Its dresses retailed at $35 to $65. About 75 per cent of its dresses retailed at prices under $50.

Persons aged sixty or over had risen as an absolute number and as a percentage of the total United States population in recent years. See Exhibit 1. Moreover, there had been a growing public awareness of the problems of older persons. The average life expectancy in the United States was seventy-one, but this was a combined figure made up of a figure of sixty-seven for males and seventy-five for females. In 1920 the average life expectancy for males was fifty-three and for females it was fifty-four. About 53 per cent of women age sixty-five or over in 1979 were widows. Because men tended to marry women two years younger than they were, and because the life expectancy for women was rising more rapidly than for men, this proportion was expected to increase.

In studying the apparel needs of the elderly, researchers have severe problems in obtaining adequate frames for their sampling and in getting representative samples of such people. Using the institutionalized or those who have membership in senior citizens' clubs is not satisfactory, because such conditions are not randomly distributed throughout the population of the elderly. Moreover, for several reasons, mail questionnaries are not suitable. The elderly have more

---

[1] Helpful background on fashion apparel can be found in William H. Reynolds, "Cars and Clothing: Understanding Fashion Trends," *Journal of Marketing*, **32** (July 1968), pp. 44–49; Chester R. Wasson, "How Predictable Are Fashion and Other Product Life Cycles?" *Journal of Marketing*, **32** (July 1968), pp. 36–43; and Kent L. Granzin and John J. Painter, "Fashion Innovativeness and Price Proneness," in Henry Nash and Donald Robin, Eds., *Southern Marketing Association Proceedings 1975*, pp. 175–177.

EXHIBIT 1 Female Population of the United States, By Age Group, Selected Years (in thousands)

	1974	1979	1985	1990	1995	2000
Ages 60–64	4,906	5,095	5,629	5,459	5,093	5,364
	(4.52%)	(4.51%)	(4.71%)	(4.37%)	(3.92%)	(4.00%)
Ages 65–69	4,326	4,820	5,138	5,551	5,389	5,039
	(4.02%)	(4.27%)	(4.30%)	(4.44%)	(4.15%)	(3.77%)
Ages 70–74	3,291	3,803	4,227	4,501	4,861	4,723
	(3.03%)	(3.37%)	(3.54%)	(3.60%)	(3.74%)	(3.53%)
Ages 75–79	2,378	2,583	3,117	3,353	3,584	3,884
	(2.19%)	(2.29%)	(2.61%)	(2.68%)	(2.76%)	(2.90%)
Ages 80 or over	2,818	3,307	3,811	4,420	4,964	5,457
	(2.60%)	(2.93%)	(3.19%)	(3.54%)	(3.82%)	(4.08%)
Total age 60 or over	17,755	19,608	21,922	23,284	23,891	24,449
	(16.37%)	(17.36%)	(18.34%)	(18.62%)	(18.40%)	(18.27%)

Source: Derived from Bureau of the Census, *Projections of the Population of the U.S.*, Publications Series P-25, No. 704, Series II, issued July 1977. Series II of the population forecast is the "medium" forecast, which assumes continuation of recent birthrates and relies on survey data as to the number of children women want. Series I assumes a higher birthrate, whereas Series III assumes a lower birthrate.

time but less energy and they fatigue easily. Their eyesight may have declined and the print on the questionnaire may not be large enough. Most older persons do not respond well to new or unaccustomed tasks such as a mail questionnaire, and some totally shun new tasks of any kind. Responses to mail questionnaires among the elderly are likely to be from sharply separated groups, such as the more socially active, more healthy, or better educated. The personal interview ordinarily must be used. This may raise unit costs, but the superior results obtained may be worth the higher costs.

It was possible for Robbins to pin down certain physiological facts about the elderly female. These facts are not uniformly true for all older women, but tend to be what occurs. One tends to gain weight until the late sixties and then to lose weight slightly. Body fat tends to shift downward, with the bust and upper arms becoming smaller, the bust line sagging, and the abdomen and buttocks becoming larger. The indentation at the waist may become insignificant and the body may take on something of a pear shape. The fact that the shoulders become rounded adds to this effect. Moreover, a roll of fatty tissue develops at the base of the neck in back. This set of evolving conditions makes for severe problems of fitting. Standard measurements for clothing patterns are derived from younger women. So-called "half sizes" were introduced by industry to help the older or other women exhibiting these conditions, but have not been very successful. This was true not only of Lily Crest but of the women's apparel industry in general. See Exhibit 2.

There are related physiological facts. Some subcutaneous fat that in a younger person acts as insulation is dissipated. There is less muscular vigor and less physical movement and the movement is slower. Thus, the older person tends to feel colder in the winter and warmer in the summer than other persons.

One likely demand characteristic that seems to emerge from these findings and that is partially confirmed by observation is that elderly women need long sleeves or three-quarter length sleeves in their dresses. Sleeveless and short-sleeve dresses are not suitable most of the time for most such women. Stoles and sweaters are needed if the dress does not have appropriate sleeves. Two-piece dresses have been quite popular with the elderly for a long time.

There are other physical factors. Skin color and hair color tend to change. Some colors of clothing that looked good in earlier years do not compliment the elderly. On the other hand, the elderly can wear some colors that they could not wear in earlier years. The clearly proven favorites colors of elderly women are first blue and second green.[2] Moreover, more elderly women need dresses that are easy to put on and take off. This is explained by loss of energy and muscle tone and a high incidence of arthritis and related illnesses. This goal can be accomplished by modifications such as larger armholes and more and larger zippers, especially in the front.

Robbins' assistants had estimated that in the United States around 12 to 14 million dresses a year were manufactured with the elderly woman as the target market. In addition, many other dresses were turned out that the manufacturer hoped would appeal to either the elderly or those in the latter half of middle age, roughly fifty through sixty-four. There was no agreement on exactly which ages constituted the logical demand brackets in the industry.

In most households in which there is a woman age sixty-five or over, the breadwinner has retired. This usually means decreased income, but a portion (sometimes all) of that income is tax free. Public and private programs of social insurance have reduced the incidence of extreme poverty but provide very little discretionary purchasing power. Most money earned by the elderly goes to pay for the basics of life. The economic strains of the elderly are further complicated

---

[2] See Mary Shaw Ryan, *Clothing: A Study in Human Behavior* (New York: Holt, Rinehart and Winston, 1966), especially pp. 306–323, and the references cited therein.

74

EXHIBIT 2 Selected Data on Types of Figures and Sizes of Clothing

Type of Figure	Sizes of Clothing	Measurements of Figure (Inches)				Description of the Figure
			Height	Bust	Hip	
Juniors	Standardized: 7-19	Short	59½-61	32-36½	33½-39	More slender than Misses' with shorter waist and higher bust. Juniors' garments are styled for the young and active.
		Regular	62½-65½	30½-39½	32-43	
		Tall	67-69	32-38	34-41	
Misses'	Standardized: 8-22	Short	59½-62	31-39½	32½-42	More developed than Junior's; less developed than Women's. Misses' garments are styled for young women.
		Regular	63-66½	31-43	32½-46	
		Tall	67½-70	32½-40	34½-44	
Women's	Standardized: 28-42	Short (See Half-size Figure)				Normally developed and larger waisted than Misses. Women's garments are styled for mature women.
		Regular	63½-66½	33-45½	34-46	
		Tall	68-70	33-43	36-44	
Half-size (Women's)	Standardized: 8½-24½	Short	59½-63½	33-47½	34-48	A short Women's figure with a short waist. Bust, waist, and hips larger than average. Half-size styles are for mature women.
		Regular	See Women's Figure			
		Tall				

by the fact that fewer of them live with their children than did in past generations. But even among those who have no financial strain, there is a decline in the proportion of income spent for apparel. This is probably explained in that the elderly women goes out less socially and, because she is less active physically, her clothing does not wear out as quickly. The elderly woman receives some gifts of clothing, but these are seldom dresses.

In a 1958 study[3] based on data for 196 elderly women, one market researcher found that on the average they bought less than one better dress per year. For this garment they paid between $25 and $49. On the average, they bought one and one third housedresses, each costing under $6.

A 1963 study[4] sheds additional light on the elderly woman. The researcher studied sixty active, socially participating women over age sixty-five who were average in education, income, professional position, and social participation. Approximately half of these women enjoyed shopping for clothing and half did not. The researcher concluded that a remark by one interviewee accurately summarized the prevailing attitude toward apparel shopping: "I like it less each year." They gave several reasons (not in any order) for their decreasing enjoyment of shopping for apparel: a decline in energy; reduced income; an inability to locate clothing that fit and that they liked; lack of desire to spend their time in shopping; and the preference of many sales persons to assist younger customers. Despite these factors, only nine of the sixty women interviewed bought any clothing from mail-order firms, and the items they bought were not readily available in stores in Iowa City, Iowa, where the investigation was conducted.

A study in 1977 of 380 persons over sixty-five found that the average household of this age spent $520 per year on clothing. Within this age group the average female spent twice as much as the average male. About 73 per cent of these 380 persons had made a major purchase of apparel within the past six months.[5]

---

[3] Robert E. Dodge, "Selling the Older Consumer," *Journal of Retailing*, **34**, No. 2 (1958), pp. 73–81, 100. Also see references in footnote 1. Also see Sidney Goldstein, "The Aged Segment of the Market," *Journal of Marketing*, **32** (April 1968), pp. 62–68.

[4] Iva M. Bader, "An Exploratory Study of Clothing Problems and Attitudes of a Group of Older Women in Iowa City." *Adding Life to Years*. Institute of Gerontology, State University of Iowa, **10**, Supplement No. 10 (1963), pp. 3–6. Also see the nine articles on women in the July 1977 thematic issue of *Journal of Marketing*; and David Loudon, "Senior Citizens: An Underdeveloped Market Segment," in Henry Nash and Donald Robin, Eds., *Proceedings of the Southern Marketing Association, 1976*, pp. 124–126.

[5] Hale N. Tongren, "Major Item Purchases by Over-65 Consumers," in Henry Nash and Donald Robin, Eds., *Proceedings of the Southern Marketing Association, 1977*, pp. 188–190. Also see Tongren, "Imputed Income as a Factor in Purchasing Power of the Over-65 Age Group," in Nash and Robin, Eds., *Proceedings of the Southern Marketing Association, 1976*, pp. 127–129.

A 1977 analysis and thought paper on elderly women stated the following about women age sixty-five or over:

> These senior citizens are not the doddering, old, decrepit grandmothers so often envisaged. . . . Often, they are cosmopolitan in taste, well traveled, educated, knowledgeable, and very politically active. . . . They are interested in the "maintenance of self," both medically and in appearance."[6]

Advise Perry Robbins of Lily Crest Modes.

ROMANO OLIVE OIL, INC.

Founded in the early 1900s in Baltimore, Romano had been importing only the finest quality olive oil from the Mediterranean countries for more than seven decades. Much of the olive oil came directly from groves and processing plants of the parent organization, a growers' cooperative in Spain. Under the policies of the parent organization, the rest of the olive oil had to be purchased through the cooperative. The Spanish cooperative utilized Romano as its marketing organization in the United States. Although the parent wanted to sell as much gallonage as possible through Romano, the American subsidiary's management, almost all United States citizens, strongly preferred a healthier "bottom line" (net profit) than what they were achieving. These two goals were somewhat in conflict, apparently because of the price the parent company was charging the American subsidiary for the olive oil. This price was above that that could be obtained on the open, free market. Romano accounted for about 10 per cent of all olive oil imports into the United States. Since almost all olive oil consumed in the United States was imported, Romano also accounted for about 10 per cent of United States olive oil sales and was by far the largest marketer of the product.

Olive Oil

In its wild state the olive plant is a low, thorny bush, but in its domesticated form it is a tree that can reach thirty feet in height. Native to the Middle East, the olive plant prefers a semidry, mild climate. Because of the fruit and the rich oil obtained from the fruit, the olive became a staple of the diet in the Middle East and spread to all the countries of the Mediterranean Basin in the early years of civilization. Later the olive was brought to California and a few areas

---

[6]William Lazer and John E. Smallwood, "The Changing Demographics of Women," *Journal of Marketing*, **41** (July 1977), pp. 14–22 at p. 15.

The Romano case was prepared by Helena Poist.

of Latin America. Olives and, to a great extent, olive oil became very important exports of Italy, Greece, Spain, and Portugal. California olives were generally sold as canned fruit and were seldom made into oil.

Olive oil was versatile and had been used in various cultures and eras for a variety of purposes besides food preparation. For example, ancient Greeks used olive oil as a body liniment, muscle toner, and relaxant, and for medicinal purposes. The Egyptians mixed it with special herbs and spices to make a perfumed body ointment and cosmetic base. In biblical times olive oil was used in lamps and for religious rituals and blessings. In such times it was used even as a weapon, such as in pouring boiling oil over a fortress wall.

In modern times, however, the primary use of olive oil has been in food preparation. Olive oil has a unique flavor, and it was generally agreed that it surpassed the various vegetable oils in quality. Of particular value was virgin olive oil, which came from the first extraction of the olives. Such a product involved a "cold press" process, which meant that no hot water or chemical solvents were added to obtain the oil.

Romano's Operations

The oil arrived in drums and tanks in Baltimore harbor, where it was inspected for quality by United States Customs, the Food and Drug Administration, and company technicians. At the Romano plant, also in Baltimore, there was continuous quality control by the company laboratory until the product was shipped out to customers. The oil was stored in thirty-two large, 30,000-gallon, glass-lined, temperature-controlled tanks. The bottling and canning facilities of the plant could process all of the company's retail sizes, that is, two ounces, eight ounces, sixteen ounces, and thirty-two ounces (one quart), as well as the bulk-size institutional and industrial containers. Romano wanted retail distribution of the gallon-size containers but had not been able to convince retailers.

Romano produced a line of olive oil products to suit the various consumer needs. This line consisted of the following: Romano 100 per cent Virgin Olive Oil, Romanza 100 per cent Olive Oil, Laco Pure Olive Oil, and Avallo 10 and 20 per cent Blended Oil. Romanza combined the special flavors of select olive oils and was slightly lower in price than virgin olive oil. Laco had the taste of pure olive oil but was much inferior in quality to virgin and used primarily for the institutional trade. Avallo was a special blend of the less expensive soya cooking oil with a mild taste of pure oil in 10 per cent and 20 per cent quantities. The Romano brand was the primary line in retail sizes, whereas the other brands were sold primarily to food service establishments in the gallon and larger sizes only.

The Spanish parent company sold only the finest grades of olive oil, even though olive oil came in many different grades. At the same time, the average consumer was unable to distinguish among these different grades. Similarly, the prices of the higher grades of olive oil were far above those of the lower grades. Therefore, it was difficult for Romano, Inc., to market a superior product while its competitors marketed an inferior product.

Currently Romano had national distribution, but not in all major supermarket chains and not in all container sizes. The leading seller was the eight-ounce package followed by the sixteen-ounce and the quart container. Romano had no retail distribution of the gallon size. The main product competition consisted of other imported olive oils, oils that were blended (olive oil and soybean), and the domestic vegetable oils such as Wesson and Mazola. These competitors tended to sell oil in quart and gallon size containers.

Romano had a network of nineteen warehouses throughout the country from which the company served customers in all fifty states. One hundred food brokers represented Romano in their respective marketing areas. Four regional managers and a national sales manager worked closely with these people and the headquarters marketing team to provide the best quality and service possible for all retail and wholesale customers.

Major firms importing olive oil obtained their supplies in several different ways. These included the following:

1. Importing prepackaged oil bearing the exporter's name.
2. Importing prepackaged oil bearing the brand name designed and controlled by the importer.
3. Importing in 128-ounce (one gallon) cans and repacking into retail containers bearing the importer's brand.
4. Importing bulk oil and repacking into retail containers bearing the importer's brand.

Because of the ease of entering the industry, there were a great many regional competitors. They were entrenched in local markets and usually enjoyed lower retail prices than firms that sold nationally. These lower prices were mainly the result of higher freight costs incurred by national competitors to reship the goods. More than 100 different olive oil brands were marketed in the metropolitan New York City market. Romano chose to import in bulk in order to ensure quality and to control shipments to customers. Although this method of importing was the cheapest, freight differentials resulted in the local and regional competitors having lower prices regardless of the form in which they imported the olive oil.

Because it was both pure and imported, Romano brand olive oil had the disadvantage in the marketplace of selling at a premium price. As indicated previously, Romano competed with several vegetable oils, such as Wesson, which came from much larger companies who had large advertising budgets behind them. Besides being lower in price, such oils made claims of other advantages that might or might not be deterrents to Romano. The first consisted of health-related selling points, that is, polyunsaturated fats and low cholesterol. The second was taste appeal, that is, low flavor level.

As to health-related selling points, the consumer was presented with data on fat, cholesterol, and saturated and polyunsaturated fat. The corn oil companies heavily advertised and publicized these data in selling the benefits of corn oil. Whereas the cholesterol content of both corn oil and olive oil was zero, olive oil had a higher percentage of the nonsaturated and saturated fats than did corn oil. Corn oil had the advantage of being higher in the polyunsaturated fats. In restricted diets and diets designed to regulate cholesterol, physicians tended to recommend a restriction of the saturated and nonsaturated fats and an increase of the polyunsaturated fats. How much of a factor this had been in terms of influencing the sale of olive oil was not known, but it had to be faced as a possible deterrent to sales. Perhaps because of the heavy use and sales appeal of corn oil and other vegetable oils, many consumers had not acquired a taste for olive oil. In fact, the younger generation had grown up in an era of news, publicity, and advertising of corn oil. It might be possible, however, to counteract this negative factor.

Total olive oil industry sales in the United States had been declining for several years. Two of the reasons were the ethnic connotation of the product and the high and increasing prices of olive oil to the consumer. As Romano's management saw it, the real challenge, in terms of growth, was to expose the nonethnic consumer to the benefits of olive oil.

Romano's strategy of exposing the nonethnic consumer was in line with its current consumer profile. Although its consumers could not be precisely defined in terms of demographics, the majority of them were ethnic. The nonethnic users were primarily (1) women in their early twenties who were inexperienced cooks and followed recipes to the letter and (2) middle-aged women who were gourmet cooks. Most of Romano's sales were in the smaller containers, whereas many competitors sold primarily the gallon sizes. This led the company to believe that a good many of its consumers were nonethnic users, and that this would ensure Romano an edge in this market if the benefits of olive oil were known by the public.

Olive oil was primarily a commodity, as many people viewed it. Many ethnic consumers bought whatever olive oil was lowest in price, regardless of quality. Also, because of the high price of olive oil, some of these consumers were also moving toward the olive oil and soybean blends. On the other hand, nonethnic consumers tended to buy only the best olive oil and shop for a brand. A company objective was for consumers to buy Romano olive oil and to pay the premium price for it.

Olive oil was almost exclusively a consumer product. Specific data on the end use were currently unavailable. However, trade estimates suggested that upwards of 85 per cent of all olive oil was sold at retail for home consumption. Commercial and institutional users accounted for the remaining 15 per cent or less. Trade sources indicated that commercial users consisted only of high-priced hotels and restaurants specializing in European cuisine, which bought olive oil for the sake of authenticity. However, because the price of olive oil was higher than substitute oils, the current use of olive oil was minimal. Generally, olive oil was not used by other sectors of the hotel and restaurant trade. The manufacturing sector did not use olive oil to any appreciable extent because substitute oils were just as good and cost less. The exceptions were small manufacturers of European-style cuisine and gourmet foods. However, the quantity of olive oil used by such firms was insignificant.

Importers believed that the relatively high price of olive oil was the prime reason that consumption was not greater. In their view, this was an almost insoluble problem. The relative price of olive oil was slowly dropping, but the likelihood of the price of olive oil approaching the price of other oils was remote. The price of olive oil was expected to remain at least an order of magnitude greater than that of the vegetable oils. In 1971, the price of olive oil was twice the average price of similar oils, but by 1975 it was three times the price of other oils. The price of olive oil reached a peak of 3.35 times the average of other oils in 1976. After that time the relative price of olive oil declined to about 3.0 and leveled off.

Olive oil was not heavily or widely promoted. The limited promotional monies and activities were aimed at ethnic markets. This was especially true in areas with large numbers of Italians and Puerto Ricans, such as San Francisco, New York City, Miami, Houston, and several New England cities. Actual national expenditures for advertising and sales promotion of olive oil were not available. However, estimates indicated that these figures were insignificant compared to the promotional and advertising expenditures on cooking and salad oils in general.

All importers of olive oil sponsored trade promotions. Various forms were used, but the most common was the conventional "off-invoice." This meant that the retailer received the promotional money off the regular price. In return for $1 or possibly $2 per case (on a $40 per case value), the retailer provided some or all of the following: in-store displays; reduced retail price; and mention in the retailer's local flier (handbill).

Most of the olive oil industry trade promotions were staged with small retailers in ethnic areas. The major retail chains avoided these trade promotions because the per-case cost was prohibitive. Such a chain's initial outlay was high, but the anticipated sales volume was relatively modest compared to the high turnover items competing for the large retailer's attention. Olive oil trade deals seldom warranted even advertising space in the local newspapers because of the low volume and other items competing for the valuable space.

Research Studies

In order to better understand the consumer, Romano conducted a small but carefully done survey of 250 people in the Baltimore area. The majority of respondents had not used any olive oil within the past year. In rank order the main reasons given by the respondents were the following:

1. Cost too much.
2. Never thought of it.
3. Too greasy.
4. Dislike flavor.
5. No reason.
6. Not good for health.

Those who used olive oil offered two main reasons for doing so. The first was that recipes called for it and the second was the flavor. The differences between light and heavy users of olive oil appeared to be the following:

1. Light users used olive oil when recipes called for it. (They tended to buy two- and four-ounce packages.)
2. Medium users used olive oil because of flavor and preference as well as the fact that recipes called for it. (They tended to buy eight- and sixteen-ounce packages.)
3. Heavy users used olive oil because they preferred the taste. They also believed that it was more healthful than other oils. Recipes emerged as only a minor factor for heavy users. (They tended to buy quarts and gallon-size packages.)

Several interesting things had been fairly well established in previous studies in the industry and were rather widely known in the

EXHIBIT 1 Romano, Inc., Selling Expenses Most Recent Year

	Amount
Salaries and wages	$150,112
Fringe benefits	24,225
Supplies	3,842
Telephone	20,505
Advertising	45,404
Contract services	7,500
Travel and entertainment	90,001
Dues and subscriptions	1,230
Warehouse breakage	4,538
Brokerage commissions	301,446
Unsalable merchandise	6,154
External samples	18,125
Taxes, licenses, and permits	9,545
Insurance	13,494
Depreciation	8,209
Miscellaneous expenses	537
	$704,867

industry. Different ethnic groups bought varying types of olive oil. Preference for olive oil appeared to differ among ethnic groups in the following ways:

1. People of Italian descent preferred a lighter olive oil typical of that supplied by Spanish and Italian exporters.
2. People of Greek and Portuguese descent preferred a heavier oil. In addition, they bought oil to which they were most accustomed. The Greeks bought Greek oil and the Portuguese bought Portuguese oil.
3. First-generation Americans of Mediterranean descent had a latent preference for olive oil. They would prefer to use olive oil whenever they required oil because they preferred its distinct flavor and believed in its health-giving properties. But, because of high prices they restricted their use of olive oil to salads and other purposes where its taste was critical. Where taste was not important they used a cheaper vegetable oil. The implication was that lower prices could induce users to use more olive oil and for all cooking purposes.
4. Upon arrival in the United States most immigrants did not have much discretionary income. As a result, they used cheaper oils. Over time, they became more affluent and switched back to the more costly but preferred oils. The implication was that increasing incomes of new immigrants might result in increased demand for olive oil.

5. High prices and inflation had switched some ethnic users away from olive oil, either partially or completely. Over time, some came to like and prefer these substitute oils. The implication was that some users may have been irrevocably converted to other oils.

Two demographic variables also appeared to influence the use of olive oil. These were the following:

1. The greatest use of olive oil occurred among affluent families. Use declined sharply among families with an annual income of less than $20,000.
2. Most of the users of olive oil resided in large metropolitan areas.

In evaluating the nonethnic market, olive oil and salad oils were directly or nearly directly substitutable. That is, one might be substituted for another without significantly affecting the taste, texture, and smell of the oil or any product made from it. However, for some purposes only a specific oil could be used. The degree to which an oil had a uniquely desirable property determined, at least in part, the price that users were prepared to pay for it.

Advice Romano Olive Oil, Inc.

EXHIBIT 2 Romano, Inc., Profit and Loss Statement End of Most Recent Year

		Amount
Gallons sold		1,207,069
Gross sales		$11,022,150
Less freight	$443,413	
—Promotional allowances	381,447	
—Discounts allowed	159,130	
—Storage and handling	93,242	
Net sales		$ 9,944,918
Cost of sales		7,448,892
Gross contribution		$ 2,496,026
Manufacturing overhead		288,182
Net contribution		$ 2,207,844
Selling expenses	$704,867	
Administrative expenses	325,350	
Net operating income		$ 1,177,627
Other income		42,147
Other deductions		331,168
Net profit before taxes		$ 888,606
Estimated income taxes		455,158
Net profit		$ 433,448

BOY SCOUTS OF AMERICA

The Boy Scouts of America was one of the most well-known and respected social service organizations in the United States. Although it was successful by ordinary and prevailing standards, it had several problems that needed careful analysis and thought.

History and Background

This organization was the largest national group in the 102-nation Boy Scout World Conference. Around the world there were slightly over 10 million members. The movement started in 1907 in Britain with an experimental camp for twenty-two boys conducted by the then inspector general of cavalry in the British Army, Lieutenant General Sir Robert Stephenson Smyth Baden-Powell, First Baron Baden-Powell of Gilwell, who was better known in Britain as a hero of the South African (Boer) War of 1899–1902. A few months later he published his famous book *Scouting for Boys*. Although Baden-Powell merely wanted to furnish advice to existing youth organizations and did not intend to start a separate organization, it was soon obvious that a separate movement had begun. The Boy Scouts movement quickly spread, first to Chile; then to Canada, Australia, and New Zealand; and in 1910 to the United States, the result, in part, of some missionary work conducted by Canadians. In the same year, the movement spread to Sweden, Norway, France, Mexico, and Argentina. Baden-Powell, who was designated Chief Scout of the World, lived until 1941.

Baden-Powell's experimental camp, held on Brownsea Island in Poole Harbour, Dorsetshire, allowed him to try out some of the ideas he had accumulated in a long career of largely outdoor activities, much of it spent in India, Afghanistan, and Africa. It emphasized hiking, sailing, canoeing, camping, mapping and map reading, signaling, knotting, and first aid. Just as important to the founder, the participating boy had to promise that on his honor he would do his best to do his duty to God and country, to help other people at all times, and to obey the Scout law, which was a simple code of chivalrous behavior easily comprehended by the child. All this training was to complement, not substitute for, the boy's formal education. Baden-Powell thought that boys should organize themselves into small groups of about six or seven. Their training should progress in steps with periodic recognition of accomplishments. Designation of ranks and award of badges would constitute the recognition.

As Scouting spread internationally, the basic pattern was retained: an outdoors orientation, programmed learning rewarded by the granting of rank and badges, and doing a daily good turn. Minor adaptations were made for national traditions and cultures, and different uniforms were designed for different age groups. However, there was a universal theme in the Scouting literature: "To develop desirable qualities of character, citizenship, and personal fitness." Scouts were expected to be trustworthy, loyal, helpful, friendly, courteous, kind, obedient, cheerful, thrifty, brave, clean, and reverent.

A permanent secretariat, the Boy Scout World Bureau, was established in Ottawa, Canada, to gather and disseminate information, help members with problems, and unify the international movement. The U.S. Scouting movement annually donated about $500,000 to the World Bureau. A world meeting for professionals and adult volunteers was held periodically, two recent locations of which were Copenhagen, Denmark, and Dearborn, Michigan. Scouts held a world jamboree every four years, two recent locations of which were Lillehammer, Norway, and a park in the province of Alberta, Canada.

Baden-Powell intended Scouting for boys of ages eleven to fifteen, but it was soon apparent that there was a social need and viable demand for service to boys both younger and older. In 1916, Baden-Powell introduced the Wolf Cubs, based on ideas in Rudyard Kipling's famous novels. This organization was to serve boys of ages eight to ten and to prepare them to become Scouts at age eleven. The Wolf Cubs spread quickly across Europe but did not reach the United States until 1930, where the organization was termed the Cub Scouts. The United States version of the Wolf Cubs had much more parental participation than the European version.

Organization Structure and Policies

The basic unit of the Cub Scouts was called a den and was guided by a person called a den leader, who was sometimes assisted by a Boy Scout called the den chief. At the beginning of the 1980s the title "den mother" was abandoned, and the title "den leader" established as men were permitted to take on these duties for the first time. Ten-year-old boys, although members of Cub Scouts, held separate meetings if there were enough of them. They were termed Webelos, an acronym for "We'll be loyal Scouts." The Webelos unit had to be led by a man. A pack was made up of several dens. Each den normally met once a week except in the summer. Once a month the pack met under the direction of the cubmaster. Both men and women could be cubmasters, but men outnumbered women by a ratio of six to one. A member started at the Bobcat rank and could work upward to the Wolf rank and then the Bear rank. A Webelo could earn the Arrow of Light Award. The den leaders and Webelos leader were accountable to the Pack Committee, a group of adult volunteers responsible for the welfare of the pack. The activities of the Cub Scouts were centered in the immediate neighborhood, and most were conducted in the houses of the adult leaders. Nearly all boys lived within walking distance of the meetings. Occasionally, some community service was performed, such as gathering items for Goodwill Industries or collecting waste paper. Meetings often consisted of work on crafts and study of American Indian lore, religious symbols, and patriotic and historical themes. Each meeting, lasting about forty minutes to an hour, contained several minutes of recreation; and some trips were made to museums, historical locations, and other places of interest.

Cub Scouts had always worn uniforms of dark blue and gold. In response to vigorous criticism about rigidity, waste, and the fact that families do not have unlimited income, Scouting finally made one small concession in 1983. The pack henceforth could elect to have the boys in its Webelos den wear either the traditional blue and gold or the Boy Scout khaki uniform with insignia, neckerchief, and cap that would identify them as Webelos Scouts. The individual, however, had no choice.

A new program, or division, of Scouting was launched in 1982, specifically as a remedy for the disappointing and falling membership size of the Cub Scouts. This program was name Tiger Cubs and was designed for seven-year-old boys. According to national headquarters, "It introduces families to the values of Scouting one year earlier than had been possible previously. It provides a natural flow into Cub Scouting when these boys become eight years of age." In its first year it enrolled 84,050, and this figure climbed to 123,643 in 1983 and 145,310 in 1984.

The names of the total organization and of the intermediate age group of eleven to thirteen were the same—Boy Scouts. The exact range of years that was to be included in this intermediate group had always been subject to disagreement. The Boy Scouts included a good many fourteen-year-olds who were in the eighth grade in school, for the Explorer Scouts did not want boys until they were at least in the ninth grade. Boy Scouts were organized into patrols and troops, the former consisting of usually five to eight boys who elected a patrol leader from among their membership. Most patrols adopted names, often humorous, such as the Tweety Birds, and designed flags for themselves. Two or more patrols made up a troop, which was headed by an adult termed the scoutmaster. The various patrol leaders in the troop constituted the Patrol Leaders Council, which planned the activities for the entire troop. They elected a senior boy leader who presided at the planning meetings. The scoutmaster was accountable to the Troop Committee, a group of adults responsible for the troop's welfare. The scouts all wore khaki uniforms, but the neckerchief color and design were chosen locally.

The Boy Scout started as a Tenderfoot. After passing a specified number of tests, mostly concerned with his ability to take care of himself outdoors, he gained the rank of Second Class Scout. After mastering specified camping and hiking skills, he advanced to First Class Scout. Promotions were not related directly to age or passage of time but to passing tests, demonstrations, and completing tasks. Advancement to the rank of Star Scout and then Life Scout depended on service to Scouting and superior proficiency demonstrated through the earning of badges. The highest rank was Eagle Scout, which required the earning of 11 specified badges in outdoors, fitness, and service subjects plus 13 badges in fields of the boy's own choice. Examples of these were dog care, woodworking, oceanography, gardening, journalism, consumer buying, traffic safety, and hog production. Over 115 different modules leading to badges were available. The Eagle Scout rank was further divided in that one could earn an Eagle Palm in the ascending order of bronze, gold, or silver, for every 5 additional merit badges beyond the 24 required. Very few boys progressed as far as the Eagle Scout rank.

The Explorer Scouts were set up many years ago for boys who were in high school. The precise time varied from area to area, but in the early 1970s girls were permitted to join the Explorers. This change raised concern among the Girl Scouts, Campfire Girls, and some other girls' groups. The number of female members of the Explorers' division was a sensitive topic and usually not announced. Significant participation by girls in the Explorer Scouts seemed to depend on the principal activity of the post. It was noticed that, if the vocational focus was paramedical, there tended to be good participation by girls. For example, a post that was sponsored by a community rescue squad that let the girl and boy Explorers ride in the ambulances with them was quite popular and was considered successful.

Organizational units were usually called "posts," but a few specializing as Sea Scouts called their units "ships." Although an adult supervised activities, the unit was largely self-governing. There were no ranks within the group, but there were various merit badges to be won. Explorers wore green field uniforms or blazer dress uniforms, depending on the occasion, whereas Sea Explorers wore navy blue or white sailor suits.

Explorer activities included experiences in citizenship, community service, outdoor activities, social events, and learning about vocations. There were two types of posts, general interest and special interest. The general interest post spent its time primarily in outdoor activities, such as camping, hiking, and water sports. The special interest post spent its time on one particular subject area, usually a vocational area, so as to give Explorers an opportunity to investigate future careers. Examples were law, law enforcement, medicine and health services, veterinary medicine, aviation, and engineering. This program derived from a pilot test conducted in 1976 under a grant from the U.S. Department of Education. Programming for some occupations was subsidized by grants. The American Bar Association funded the programs in law, the Law Enforcement and Assistance Administration funded the program in law enforcement, the American Medical Association funded the programs in medicine and health services, and the Aircraft Owners and Pilots Association funded the program in aviation. The Air Force provided no funds but furnished time, talent, and general assistance for the aviation efforts. Area or regional conferences were sometimes held on specific vocations or issues, an example of which was an ecology conference for Explorers at Slippery Rock College. Each year several sports, normally sailing, surfing, and target skills, were played all the way to a national championship. There was also a competition in public speaking extending to the national level.

There was considerable dissatisfaction about the Explorers' segment of Scouting. In 1984 the Scouting movement reorganized and restructured the Explorer operation after running a pilot program in selected councils in 1983. A program called Varsity Scouts was set up strictly for boys of ages 14 to 18, which amounted to reestablishment of pre-1970s operations. The Explorers' division as constituted since the early 1970s was retained and recognized as a valuable program. Moreover, the scope of the Explorer program was expanded to age 20 and assigned the title Career Awareness Exploring. Scouting headquarters revealed in 1985 that 43 per cent of Explorers in 1984 were female. Although the age span for Explorers had been increased from 15–17 to 15–20, there was little realistic hope of attracting many members of age 18 through 20.

Cub Scout packs, Boy Scout troops, and Explorer Scout posts belonged to districts, which in turn, belonged to "local" councils. There were 413 councils in the United States and Puerto Rico, examples of which were Indianhead Council, St. Paul, Minnesota; Long's Peak Council, Greeley, Colorado; Theodore Roosevelt Council, Phoenix, Arizona; and West Michigan Shores Council, Grand Rapids, Michigan. For several years there had been a trend toward a consolidation of smaller local councils, and about 110 had been eliminated as separate entities. For example, Montclair Council Number 346, Orange Mountain Council Number 337, and Newark Council Number 349 became Essex Council Number 336 with offices in Newark, New Jersey. Several local councils made up an area, and several areas made up a region. There were six regions in the United States. For example, the East Central Region comprised Ohio, Indiana, Michigan, West Virginia, most of Wisconsin and Illinois, and parts of Kentucky; and it was divided into six areas and seventy-eight local councils.

All the local councils belonged to the national organization, and they elected the National Council, which governed the Boy Scout movement and appointed the chief scout executive. Management was in the hands of this executive and about 3,850 paid, full-time professional and professional-technical employees, about 580 of whom were in the national headquarters office in Irving, Texas, a suburb of Dallas. Formerly in North Brunswick, New Jersey, the headquarters was moved in 1979. The remaining professional and professional-technical employees were in regional, area, and local council offices. For example, sixty-six professional staff members were in the office of the New York metropolitan councils whereas the corresponding figures were fifty-six in Chicago, thirty-two in Pittsburgh, and thirty-four in Washington, D.C. There were also a good many other employees, such as office clerks and warehouse workers. The chief scout executive administered an annual national budget of more than $100 million, which did not include council, district, and unit budgets. The aggregate of the council annual budgets was over $200 million. Unit budgets varied greatly but would normally not be above a few thousand dollars or below $250. The new national headquarters building suffered damage of $1.5 million from a fire caused by arson in 1980, but it was all covered by insurance.

There was some low-key feeling on the part of many professionals at the local council level that the national office was perhaps oriented too much toward change. On the other hand, some observers and some of the people in the national headquarters thought that the local councils were somewhat resistant to change.

The full-time professional and professional-technical employees in national and regional offices prepared programs, program aids, and training materials; offered courses of instruction for adult volunteers; planned and controlled production and sales of uniforms and equipment; and generally assisted local councils in their work. National headquarters published *Boy's Life*, a magazine for boys; *Exploring*, a magazine for Explorer Scouts and their adult leaders; *Scouting*, a magazine of program aids for adult leaders; and *Cub Scout Handbook, Boy Scout Handbook, Explorer Scout Handbook*; and miscellaneous instruction books and pamphlets. All in all, there were about 2,000 separate publications. The Magazine Publications Division consistently earned a large net profit. See Exhibit 6.

Like many other nonprofit organizations, Boy Scouts of America did not practice full public disclosure of information on its finances and number of members. It was rather loathe to release data, especially in detail, in a timely manner and in a consistent way so as to permit objective, thorough analysis of comparable blocks, segments, and series of data. Statements of officials and publications were often vague. This manner of handling data was completely legal for nonprofit organizations but would have been inappropriate for business organizations with publicly traded shares of stock. It was not at all clear to what extent the historical problem with data was attributable to carelessness, inadequate management expertise, evasiveness, lack of time, or perhaps the nature of the organization. Of course, regular financial audits by outside accountants confirmed that there was no dishonesty with funds.

National headquarters also included the Supply Division, which specialized in equipment and uniforms. It maintained a network of five physical distribution centers around the nation. The product line included almost 6,000 items; for example, there were eight types of pocket knives and five types of wallets. The most widely needed products were stocked in approximately 3,000 department stores and sporting goods and apparel shops that had entered into distribution contracts with Boy Scouts of America. The more uncommon items could be ordered from the physical distribution centers. The supply division shipped more than 200,000 orders a year to these retailers, to the 600 Scout camps, and to the local councils.

In 1979 the Scouts had a world-famous designer, Oscar de la Renta, create a new uniform, and the supply division promoted it as "the sharp new look." The uniform cost a boy a minimum of $38 for one pair of long trousers, one long-sleeved shirt, a belt, a cap, a neckerchief, and a metal neckerchief slide for a Cub Scout and a minimum of $41 for a similar outfit for a Boy Scout or Explorer. A boy also needed a short-sleeved shirt, short pants, and high top socks for use in late spring or early fall. This outfit cost $24 for a Cub Scout and $29 for a Boy Scout or an Explorer. A sales tax was added in some jurisdictions. The national organization continuously emphasized to its subordinate organizations that boys had to wear uniforms, and adult volunteers had an ethical obligation to wear uniforms. The usual advertising theme for this was, "You owe it to your Scout team to set the proper uniform example." Leaders were strongly urged to conduct formal inspections of the boys for proper and complete uniforms. The wearing of medals and ribbons on the uniform was encouraged by the hierarchy. Many accessories were available, such as raincoats, warm jackets, vests, swim trunks, shoes, ties, and a variety of special headgear and shirts, all bearing Scouting insignia. The Supply Division consistently earned a large net profit. See Exhibit 6.

Financial support for Scouting came from the United Way (or its equivalent in some communities); direct donations; interest earnings on endowments; profits from sale of equipment, uniforms, and publications; membership fees; and, at the unit level, profits from unit sale of such fund-raising merchandise as candy, light bulbs, or seeds. The national organization's Local Council Finance Division published a manual entitled *Developing Prospects to Finance the Local Council* and furnished advice to local Scout workers on how to raise money and manage their finances. Typically, the United Way supplied 30 per cent to 35 per cent of council budgets. The annual national membership fee consisted of $2.00 for Cubs and Boy Scouts and $3.50 for Explorers and adult leaders. Each of these figures represented a $1.00 increase put into effect September 15, 1975. Packs, troops, and posts added varying amounts to the national fee for their local use, so that a member usually paid about four or five times the national fee. The national fee and usually the local fee were prorated for boys who joined after the beginning of the Scout year. The activities year in most units ran from early fall to early summer. Boarding camps were available for a charge in many locations, the most famous and prestigious of which was the Philmont Scout ranch in New Mexico.

Scout units regularly raised extra money by selling various kinds of merchandise. A common example was the arrangement with Hershey, which would charge the Scout unit $22.50 for a case of 48 bars of Hershey's milk chocolate with almonds, Krackel, or Reese's Peanut Butter Cups in the $.75 size. The sales revenue would be $36.00, and the gross profit was $13.50. Because there was no expense, the net profit was also $13.50. At the same time, either as individuals or a unit, the Scouts earned ten "gift points" per case sold, which were redeemable in merchandise. For example, 30 points were required for a football; 40, for an Everready flashlight; 270, for a Hot Foot sleeping bag; and 420, for a Coleman camp stove. Unsold candy could not be returned.

Some Issues and Problem Areas

During its history, the U.S. Scouting movement had been of enormous proportions. Cumulatively, approximately 61 million American males had been members of the Scouts at some time during the years when they were between ages eight and seventeen. Because the movement began only in 1910 and membership was relatively low in the formative period, about one half of American males of age eight or above living in the mid-1980s had been Scouts at some time.

Nevertheless, size of membership in the Cubs, Boy Scouts, and Explorers was a problem. The situation was even worse, however, for analysis of the data showed that the fraction of the youth market being reached at any given time was low. Exhibit 1 presents Scout membership for recent years broken down into Cubs, Boy Scouts, and Explorers; the United States male population in each age category for the nearest date; and the percentage share of the market. One experienced, knowledgeable Scouting official made this comment on the problem: "To many pack and troop leaders who already have all the boys they can handle, there is simply no personal satisfaction in an expanding membership for Scouting." He pointed out, however, that in the view of high-level volunteers and Scouting professionals, "a steady intake of new boys is what Scouting needs, above all else, to stay alive and healthy."[1]

It was also a source of great concern that so many boys dropped out of the organization. Some boys were active for a few weeks or months and then stopped participating or dropped their membership. Exhibit 2 shows the year-end membership as a percentage of all who were active at some point during the year for the sixteen-year period 1965–1980 and selected ealier years. Cub Scouts are separated out in this exhibit, but the data for Boy Scouts and Explorer Scouts were inextricably mixed.

Although they do not constitute a random sample, a few critical excerpts from people's comments on Scouting might be noted. Two boys whose sister had enjoyed Girl Scouts and whose parents, both of whom worked, were supportive and willing to have them join, said, "Scouting is irrelevant." A dependable but dissident scoutmaster stated, "It's sort of paramilitary." One parent said, "I don't like the gun ads in the magazine," whereas another said, "The higher-ups tell you too much about what you don't need to know but not enough about what you do need to know." One adult volunteer complained, "Parents don't really understand the problems of the leaders or even appreciate our hard work," whereas another adult volunteer, a Cub Scout leader, stated, "I think a good many parents send us their little boys just to be baby sat."

The ups and downs but long-term decline in membership of

---

[1] Robert W. Peterson, "Scouting's 'Middle Man': The Commissioner," *Scouting*, **65**: 6, (November–December 1977), pp. 8–10.

Explorer Scouts was especially troubling. Exhibit 3 presents the types of organizations that sponsored Explorer Scout units at the end of 1980 and in four earlier years dating back to 1965. The units sponsored by schools and PTAs as a percentage of all units declined by a very small amount, but the corresponding decline among religious institutions was sizable. The fraction sponsored by civic and community organizations rose sharply, however. Many different civic and community organizations cooperated; but the largest, in terms of number of Explorer units sponsored, were, in order, business firms, Lions Clubs, American Legion and Women's Auxiliary, fire departments, professional and scientific societies, police departments, Kiwanis Clubs, Rotary Clubs, settlement houses, Veterans of Foreign Wars and Women's Auxiliary, Knights of Columbus, Junior Chambers of Commerce, and Elks.

A severe drop in the number of Explorer posts sponsored by religious bodies occurred between December 31, 1965, and December 31, 1980. On the earlier date, such institutions sponsored 11,908 Explorer posts, which represented 51.8 per cent of such posts. On December 31, 1980, fifteen years later, religious bodies sponsored 6,854 Explorer posts, which represented 30.5 per cent of such posts. Moreover, these posts contained only 16.8 per cent of Explorer Scout membership, down from 23.8 per cent at the end of 1976. See Exhibit 3.

Within the category of religious sponsors, an interesting change occurred. At the end of 1965, the Church of Latter-Day Saints (Mormons) sponsored 2,788 Explorer Scout posts, or 23.4 per cent of all such posts. Mormons were the first in sponsorship among religious bodies, the Methodist Church was second with 2,370 posts (19.9 per cent of all posts), the Roman Catholic Church was third with 1,560 posts (13.1 per cent of all posts), the Presbyterian Church was fourth with 1,214 posts (10.2 per cent of all posts), and the Baptist Church (all branches) was fifth with 1,110 posts (9.3 per cent of all posts). At the end of 1980, however, the Mormon Church sponsored 4,257 Explorer posts with 34,977 members, which accounted for 62.1 per cent of all Explorer posts and 46.6 per cent of Explorer members in the religious sponsorship category. As of December 31, 1980, the Methodist Church sponsored only 557 posts numbering 9,078 members; the Roman Catholic Church, 559 posts numbering 9,964 members; the Presbyterian Church, 299 posts numbering 4,589 members; and the Baptist Church (all branches), 320 posts numbering 4,268 members. It should be noted that the Knights of Columbus, an organization that the Scouts records classified as civic and community, was a Roman Catholic laymen's organization but not related to any one Catholic parish.

The Knights of Columbus sponsored 47 Explorer posts with 652 members at December 31, 1980. Among churches in the United States, the largest in total membership was the Roman Catholic, followed by the Baptist (all branches), and then the Methodist.

Separate records of Scouting membership by race and ethnic background were not maintained. However, it was clear that blacks and Hispanics had never participated very heavily in the Scout movement, especially in the inner cities. Therefore, in 1965, the National Council subsidized several local councils in special projects to reach some blacks and Hispanics. Included were Chicago, Cleveland, Newark, Philadelphia, Los Angeles, Baltimore, Washington, St. Louis, Cincinnati, and Detroit. Practically all program materials became available in Spanish although some were previously available. There was an additional small outreach effort centered in Bluefield, West Virginia, and Springfield, Missouri, for disadvantaged rural youths. Responses in the inner cities were moderately encouraging. A second effort, launched in 1969, again produced moderately encouraging results. It had been extremely difficult to find adult volunteers in the inner cities to work with Scouts. Turnover of such workers was several times as high as in suburbs and small towns. One Scouting professional summarized it this way in a newspaper interview: "The trouble is, people don't stay around. If they're interested in helping kids, they're also interested in bettering themselves. And if they succeed, they move."[2] David Barrie, the head of the Cadet Corps, a friendly rival of the Boy Scouts in New York City, summarized the Scouts this way: "The virtues are impeccable, but the needs of children in the ghetto are different."[3] Participation by minorities in suburban areas was reasonably good and remained so. Data from the Bureau of the Census, summarized in Exhibit 4, showed that on July 1, 1976, 14.1 per cent of all boys in the United States in the age groups eight through seventeen were black and that this figure was forecast to rise to 15.1 per cent by mid-1982 because of a higher birthrate among blacks than in the population at large.

There were currently two important legal disputes, and a third dispute had been settled without litigation. A woman in Connecticut was suing because she wanted to be a scoutmaster, but females were not allowed. The rationale for the defense was that boys need men as role models. A man in California who was a self-avowed homosexual was suing to gain registration as a Scout leader. Scouting defended by arguing it was a private organization and as such had the right to set standards for its recognition of adult volunteer workers. The Scouting movement was particularly sensitive on the

[2] Barry Newman, "Boy Power," *The Wall Street Journal*, February 9, 1974, pp. 1, 19.
[3] Ibid.

homosexual issue because of a major scandal in Louisiana a short time before in which several male adult volunteers who were not self-avowed homosexuals had allegedly sexually abused a large number of young boys. Despite defending both legal actions vigorously, Scouting lost both disputes at the trial level but was appealing these decisions to the next judicial level.

In the third dispute, just settled without litigation, the membership of a fifteen-year-old boy in West Virginia, Paul Trout, was in process of cancellation because he was an atheist. He had been a Scout for seven years. This six-month-long dispute did not become a lawsuit, but it attracted extensive international attention. Letters to Scout headquarters ran in favor of permitting atheists to participate. The National Executive Board of the Scouts voted to change policy so that Trout could remain in the organization. The board reaffirmed the Scout oath, which requires duty to God. At the same time it decided to remove the definition of God as a Supreme Being from all Scouting materials. A formal resolution was adopted: "While not intending to define what constitutes belief in God, the Boy Scouts of America is proud to reaffirm the Scout Oath and its declaration of duty to God." Some observers considered the statement to be classic double-talk. The parents of Trout stated that they had not planned to sue and that they respected the right of the Boy Scouts to be a religious organization. However, they believed that the Scouts organization had not been aboveboard and open about such matters.

Charter renewal was a perennial problem, virtually every adult volunteer perceiving it as a terrible chore. The rate of noncooperation was rather high, as much as 15 per cent in a few large cities. In addition, a great many units were late in complying. According to professional Scout executives, most adult leaders at the grass-roots level were action-oriented people who disliked and often had a low regard for paper work of any type. Many volunteers saw paper work as an interference with getting the real job done. Charter renewal amounted to filling in extensive forms and collecting money once a year. These forms had to do with continuing the sponsorship agreement between the civic, religious, or educational organization and the area council of the Boy Scouts of America, listing all members and adult volunteers and their addresses and what position they would hold in the organization, reporting whether the adult leaders needed further training, and collecting and transmitting all required fees plus optional fees for magazine subscriptions. Recently, the whole process of rechartering had been renamed the "annual service plan" in an attempt to persuade adult volunteers that it had the purpose of helping units.

Advise the Boy Scouts of America.

EXHIBIT 1 Scouting's Share of the Market in Recent Years

	U.S. Population	Scouting Membership	Share of Market
	July 1, 1986	Dec. 31, 1985	
Age 7	1,729,000[1]	169,051	9.8%
Age 8-10	4,951,000[1]	1,499,259	30.3
Age 11-13	4,944,000[1]	1,014,456	20.5
Age 14-17	7,455,000[1]	48,430	.6
Age 15-20	22,206,000	1,023,812	4.6
Unduplicated potential	35,571,000	3,755,008	10.6%
	July 1, 1985	Dec. 31, 1984	
Age 7	1,658,000[1]	145,310	8.8%
Age 8-10	4,929,000[1]	1,492,890	30.3
Age 11-13	5,024,000[1]	1,040,828	20.7
Age 14-17	7,527,000[1]	36,949	.5
Age 15-20	22,442,000[2]	940,918	4.2
Unduplicated potential	35,973,000	3,656,895	10.2%
	July 1, 1981	Dec. 31, 1980	
Ages 8-10	5,176,000[1]	1,696,552	32.8%
Ages 11-13	5,347,000[1]	1,065,004	19.9
Ages 14-17	15,764,000[2]	447,469	2.8
	26,287,000	3,209,025	12.2%
	July 1, 1980	Dec. 31, 1979	
Ages 8-10	5,379,000[1]	1,711,237	31.8%
Ages 11-13	5,320,000[1] ⎫	1,446,057	7.0
Ages 14-17	15,219,000[2] ⎭		
	25,918,000	3,157,294	12.2%
	July 1, 1979	Dec. 31, 1978	
Ages 8-10	5,447,000[1]	1,787,791	32.8%
Ages 11-13	5,391,000[1] ⎫	1,515,478	7.0
Ages 14-17	16,276,000[2] ⎭		
	27,114,000	3,303,269	12.2%
	July 1, 1978	Dec. 31, 1977	
Ages 8-10	5,336,000[1]	1,843,033	34.5%
Ages 11-13	5,588,000[1] ⎫	1,622,854	7.3
Ages 14-17	16,651,000[2] ⎭		
	27,575,000	3,465,887	12.6%

EXHIBIT 1 (Continued)

	U.S. Population	Scout Membership	Share of Market
	July 1, 1977	Dec. 31, 1976	
Ages 8-10	5,311,000[1]	1,873,898	35.3%
Ages 11-13	5,833,000[1]	1,338,959	23.0
Ages 14-17	16,773,000[2]	386,914	2.3
	27,917,000	3,599,771	12.9%
	July 1, 1976	Dec. 31, 1975	
Ages 8-10	5,384,000[1]	1,966,570	37.1%
Ages 11-13	6,057,000[1]	1,502,495	24.8
Ages 14-17	16,879,000[2]	433,500	2.6
	28,320,000	3,932,565	13.9%
	July 1, 1975	Dec. 31, 1974	
Ages 8-10	5,583,000[1]	2,178,315	39.0%
Ages 11-13	6,208,000[1]	1,678,003	27.0
Ages 14-17	16,922,000[2]	471,336	2.8
	28,713,000	4,327,654	15.1%
	July 1, 1974	Dec. 31, 1973	
Ages 8-10	5,829,000[1]	2,447,607	42.0%
Ages 11-13	6,308,000[1]	1,907,180	30.2
Ages 14-17	16,881,000[2]	488,324[3]	2.9
	29,018,000	4,843,111	16.7%
	July 1, 1973	Dec. 31, 1972	
Ages 8-10	6,054,000[1]	2,486,706	41.1%
Ages 11-13	6,350,000[1]	1,954,697	30.8
Ages 14-17	16,747,000[2]	459,283	2.7
	29,151,000	4,900,686	16.8%
	July 1, 1972	Dec. 31, 1971	
Ages 8-10	6,204,000[1]	2,476,564	39.9%
Ages 11-13	6,365,000[1]	1,932,413	30.4
Ages 14-17	16,556,000[2]	396,542	2.4
	29,125,000	4,805,519	16.5%
	July 1, 1971	Dec. 31, 1970	
Ages 8-10	6,308,000[1]	2,438,009	38.6%
Ages 11-13	6,346,000[1]	1,915,457	30.2
Ages 14-17	16,281,000[2]	329,192	2.0
	28,935,000	4,682,658	16.2%

EXHIBIT 1 (Continued)

	U.S. Population	Scout Membership	Share of Market
	July 1, 1970	Dec. 31, 1969	
Ages 8–10	6,346,000[1]	2,380,336	37.5%
Ages 11–13	6,355,000[1]	1,909,299	30.0
Ages 14–17	8,101,000[1]	302,349	3.7
	20,802,000	4,591,984	22.1%

[1] Male only.
[2] Male and female.
[3] According to Scouts headquarters, this figure included "over 100,000 girls." This is the only time that data, even approximated, had been released on female members before 1985.

EXHIBIT 2 "End of Year" Membership Compared to "During Year" Membership of Scouts, 1965–1980, and Selected Earlier Years

December 31	Boy Scouts and Explorers	Cub Scouts	Combined
1980	72.8%	62.2%	66.7%
1979	71.2	62.9	66.4
1978	70.4	64.0	66.8
1977	73.6	67.3	70.1
1976	69.3%	64.9%	66.9%
1975	69.4	64.0	66.6
1974	68.4	62.0	65.1
1973	71.8	65.1	68.2
1972	73.8	66.1	69.6
1971	74.1	66.2	69.8
1970	72.6	66.5	69.3
1969	71.1	66.1	68.4
1968	72.8	67.8	70.2
1967	73.0	68.4	70.6
1966	72.5	68.2	70.3
1965	72.8	68.1	70.4
1960	72.2	67.5	69.8
1955	70.6	71.9	71.2
1950	70.1	65.6	68.2
1945	69.4	68.1	69.0
1940	71.2	68.2	70.6
1935	71.5	69.5	71.4

EXHIBIT 3 Sponsorship of Scout Units by Type of Organization, Five Selected Years

Sponsors of Units	Cub Scouts Per Cent of		Boy Scouts Per Cent of		Explorers Per Cent of		Total Per Cent of	
	Units	Members	Units	Members	Units	Members	Units	Members
Religious Bodies								
December 31, 1980	43.4	40.6	57.8	56.8	30.5	16.8	47.1	42.7
December 31, 1976	41.8	38.9	54.1	55.3	35.2	23.8	46.1	43.4
December 31, 1972	42.1	NA	53.1	NA	38.6	NA	46.4	NA
December 31, 1970	41.6	NA	53.9	NA	44.2	NA	47.6	NA
December 31, 1965	43.0	NA	55.7	NA	51.8	NA	50.3	NA
Civic and Community Organizations								
December 31, 1980	24.9	25.4	28.9	29.0	55.6	58.3	31.9	31.2
December 31, 1976	25.8	24.9	31.5	29.8	55.1	60.7	33.0	30.6
December 31, 1972	25.7	NA	31.1	NA	52.7	NA	32.6	NA
December 31, 1970	25.3	NA	30.6	NA	47.3	NA	31.0	NA
December 31, 1965	22.3	NA	28.8	NA	37.5	NA	27.7	NA
Schools and PTAs								
December 31, 1980	31.7	34.0	13.3	14.2	13.9	24.9	21.0	26.1
December 31, 1976	32.4	36.2	14.4	14.9	9.8	15.5	20.9	26.1
December 31, 1972	32.3	NA	15.8	NA	8.7	NA	21.0	NA
December 31, 1970	33.1	NA	15.5	NA	8.5	NA	21.4	NA
December 31, 1965	34.7	NA	15.5	NA	10.7	NA	22.0	NA

EXHIBIT 4 Black Boys as Percentage of All Boys, By Scout Age Group, United States, 1976 and 1982

July 1	Cub Scout Age		Boy Scout Age		Explorer Age		Total	
	Black Boys	All Boys	Black Boys	All Boys	Black Boys	All Boys	Black Boys	All Boys
1976	778,000	5,384,000	856,000	6,057,000	1,186,000	8,597,000	2,820,000	20,038,000
	14.5%		14.1%		13.8%		14.1%	
1982	761,000	4,906,000	813,000	5,460,000	1,110,000	7,467,000	2,684,000	17,833,000
	15.5%		14.9%		14.9%		15.1%	

EXHIBIT 5 Merit Badges, Most Frequently and Least Frequently Awarded, in Rank Order, Five Recent Years Combined and Sixty-Three Years Combined

Most Frequently Awarded, in Rank Order

Five Recent Years Combined	Sixty-three Years Combined
1. Swimming	1. Swimming
2. First aid	2. First aid
3. Cooking	3. Cooking
4. Camping	4. Firemanship
5. Lifesaving	5. Camping
6. Conservation of natural resources	6. Home repairs
7. Canoeing	7. Lifesaving
8. Nature	8. Safety
9. Home repairs	9. Public health
10. Safety	10. Pioneering
11. Citizenship in nation	11. Personal fitness
12. Citizenship in community	12. Nature
13. Fishing	13. Canoeing
14. Rowing	14. Citizenship in home
15. Hiking	15. Citizenship in community
16. Pioneering	16. Scholarship
17. Reading	17. Reptile study
18. Basketry	18. Citizenship in nation
19. Firemanship	19. Athletics
20. Personal fitness	20. Hiking
21. Music	21. Wood carving
22. Leather work	22. Rowing
23. Citizenship in home	23. Woodwork
24. Rifle and shotgun	24. Music
25. Archery	25. Fishing

Least Frequently Awarded, in Rank Order

Five Recent Years Combined	Sixty-three Years Combined
1. Small grains	1. Metallurgy
2. Cotton farming	2. Engineering
3. Fruit and nut growing	3. Radio
4. Forage crops	4. Landscape architecture
5. Sheep farming	5. Railroading
6. Farm records	6. Theater
7. Beekeeping	7. Fruit and nut growing
8. Pigeon raising	8. Small grains
9. Textiles	9. Cotton farming
10. Farm management	10. American business

EXHIBIT 6 Financial Results from Two Activities in Recent Years, Boy Scouts of America

Year	Magazine Publishing Revenue	Magazine Publishing Profit	Supply Operations Revenue	Supply Operations Profit
1978	$10,614,000	$ 742,050	$36,253,000	$3,959,000
1979	10,629,000	933,000	38,726,000	3,770,000
1980	10,768,000	930,000	41,489,000	2,774,000
1981	10,596,000	832,000	52,897,000	4,523,000
1982	11,413,000	647,000	51,417,000	6,215,000
1983	13,144,000	1,892,000	54,074,000	7,251,000
1984	Not available	934,000	51,813,000	5,921,000
1985	Not available	486,000	61,995,000	8,496,000

5

MARKETING RESEARCH

WATERSIDE SAVINGS AND LOAN ASSOCIATION

A large, out-of-state savings and loan (S & L) association acquired a smaller Florida savings and loan association. This long-established, federally chartered Florida company had not failed and, in fact, was now in average financial condition, but earlier it had been in marginal condition. The entire savings and loan industry in the United States, including Florida, had been somewhat depressed for several years, and many organizations had suffered severe losses. Some had gone out of business, and many had merged with stronger organizations. An organization about twice as large as Waterside and whose trade territory overlapped the northern half of Waterside's trade territory had failed a few months before and been taken over by the federal government for the protection of depositors and disposition of assets.

The savings and loan industry in the United States was composed of 3,400 institutions and many thousands of branches of those institutions. Aggregate assets of the industry were over $900 billion. Traditionally, savings and loan organizations were in only the home mortgage business; and they could not offer checking accounts, consumer loans, commercial loans, or trust services. Savings and loan organizations could legally pay a higher interest rate on savings than commercial banks and enjoyed some special income tax breaks. The rationale from a public policy viewpoint was that savings and loans provided a special and highly desirable service, the financing of housing, and thus deserved special treatment. However, such institutions were highly vulnerable to interest rate risk, something quite dangerous to their survival. They borrowed, that is, took in deposits, on the short term but lent for long periods of years. Thus, if interest rates rose significantly, the savings and loans institutions had to pay more while at the same time being saddled with assets that were bringing in interest income at the older, lower rates of interest. This fact of life, as interest rates rose through the years, was proving devastating to the industry. Through a series of change in U.S. law and regulations culminating in extensive deregulation and change in the form of the Garn-St. Germain bill of 1982, these institutions began to resemble commercial banks. It became lawful for savings and loans to offer checking accounts, consumer and commercial loans, and trust services. This statute also permitted savings and loans institutions and commercial banks to pay whatever rate was necessary to attract deposits. Savings and loans continued to enjoy the special privileges of lenient capital requirements and the ability to get cheap money from Federal Home Loan banks, which borrowed it by using the U.S. Treasury's credit rating. ARMs (adjustable rate mortgages) were also developed.

The acquired Florida company had no distinctive reputation. Rather, it was considered a dependable, middle-of-the-road "thrift." This term in financial circles had long been used to help distinguish S & Ls from the commercial banks. By industry standards, Waterside was considered just barely a medium-sized institution. The acquired organization operated five branches in several small cities adjacent to each other. In fact, these small cities were almost one continuous large city, and many real estate experts believed the towns would constitute a continuous developed strip within 15 years. Waterside's organizational headquarters, formerly in the original branch, number 1, had been moved to the newest and largest branch, number 5, two and a half years earlier when that branch opened. At the time of the case, there were no plans for new branches although it was widely assumed within the organization that eventually new branches would be needed. Branch number 1 was the northernmost in the network of locations, and the other four branches were scattered to the south over a range of about 18 miles. Branch number 5 was about halfway between the northernmost and southernmost branches.

All the branches observed the same days and hours of operations. All branch lobbies were closed on Saturdays and Sundays. However, drive-up windows were open in all branches on Saturday mornings to 12:00 noon. ATMs (automatic teller machines) could be used at all hours on all days of the week.

The new parent did not assign its own name to the Florida subsidiary but instead gave it the name Waterside Savings and Loan. The reasoning was primarily that the acquirer's name would not carry much, if any, meaning to most present and potential customers. The new parent did not judge the old name of the Florida organization to have great market worth and, in fact, considered it rather innocuous. Therefore, a new name was thought up and adopted.

In Waterside's trade territory there were several competitors. There were five commercial banks, each with three to eight branches, and four other savings and loan associations, each with three to six branches. There was a sizable credit union serving the employees of a major company and two very small credit unions.

Two years after the change of ownership, the director of marketing for Waterside, Ivan Lassiter, launched a research study. An experienced middle-aged banker, he had worked for Waterside for several years before the takeover. He was transferred to the marketing position at the time of the takeover. Lassiter handled advertising and public relations work for Waterside.

Lassiter designed the questionnaire reproduced as Exhibit 1. This survey form was neatly stacked at every teller's window in all branches for people to fill in. Lassiter instructed the tellers to keep the stack of forms in clear view of the customers, and his careful observations indicated that this instruction was carried out. Because of lack of time and considerable pressure of other duties, the tellers could not invite all customers to fill in the form. The marketing director understood this point, and in order to have consistent research procedures, he instructed *all* tellers not to invite customers specifically to participate in the project. If people took forms, they were asked politely but firmly to fill them in before they left the teller's window and then to hand them back to the teller. People were not permitted to take the forms away with them. The study got under way on July 8.

The number of customers who filled in the form as a percentage of customers who visited the bank intrigued Lassiter. He established the number of transactions conducted during one recent week at branch number two, a location that the bank officers considered to be average. Then, based on previous research conducted by the bank that showed the average customer's visit took care of 1.1 transactions, Lassiter estimated the number of customers. He compared the number of customers to the number who filled in the form. He was disappointed to find a participation figure of about 8 per cent.

Waterside had 27,510 accounts. About 3,400 people had multiple accounts. There were approximately 23,900 unduplicated names on the customer lists of the organization.

Lassiter began to wonder if perhaps there should be a set of weights used in interpreting the survey data collected. Should the views of a customer who maintained two accounts with the bank be accorded twice as much weight as those of a customer who maintained one account? Alternatively, if the average month-end balance in customer number one's account was three times as high as that of customer number two, should the views of customer one be assigned more weight? Lassiter's administrative assistant, Charles Rivera, noted that alternatively perhaps customers who came to the bank most often should be accorded more weight. Rivera had been with Waterside since finishing college about two years earlier.

EXHIBIT 1 Data Collection Instrument Used by Waterside Savings and Loan

Dear Customer,

As a customer, you are very important to us here at Waterside Savings. Please help us to serve you better by answering this short questionnaire concerning our hours and branch locations.

Thank you for banking at Waterside Savings!

1. How frequently do you come to the bank to do business?
   - _____ More often than once a week
   - _____ Once a week
   - _____ Once every two weeks
   - _____ Once a month
   - _____ Once a quarter

2. Would you prefer to:
   - _____ Come in the lobby to do business
   - _____ Use the walk-up
   - _____ Use the drive-up
   - _____ Use the ATM

3. Do you:
   - _____ Conduct business at one particular branch
   - _____ Use whichever branch is convenient

4. If you conduct business at one particular branch, which one is it?

   _____

5. Is the branch where you bank:
   - _____ Close to your home
   - _____ Close to your office
   - _____ Close to shopping
   - _____ Other

6. Do you bank:
   - _____ In the early morning (8:00 A.M. – 10:00 A.M.)
   - _____ At lunchtime (11:00 A.M. – 2:00 P.M.)
   - _____ In the late afternoon (3:00 P.M. – 5:00 P.M.)
   - _____ In the early evening (5:00 P.M. – 7:00 P.M.)

7. Do you most fequently bank on:
   - _____ Monday
   - _____ Tuesday
   - _____ Wednesday
   - _____ Thursday
   - _____ Friday
   - _____ Saturday

8. Would you like to be able to bank in the branch lobby:
   _____ On Saturday mornings from 9:00 A.M. - 12:00 P.M.
   _____ On Saturday afternoon from 12:00 P.M. - 3:00 P.M.

9. Are our hours and locations convenient for you?
   _____ YES   _____ NO

10. If "No," what would be most convenient for you?

   _____
   _____

Exhibit 2 displays the data collected for question 1 divided by branch. Exhibit 3 displays the data collected for question 9 cross-tabulated to the answers for question 1. Exhibit 4 displays the data collected for question 9 cross-tabulated to the answers to question 5.

Lassiter had instructed the tellers to urge the respondents to be thorough in filling in the questionnaire. Nevertheless, there were 30 incomplete forms, which he discarded. The marketing director noticed with great interest that two people had written on their questionnaires that they usually banked by mail and two others had written sentences whose essential message was that they appreciated the bank's showing enough concern about the consumer to make such an inquiry. One teller voluntarily reported to Lassiter that, although not certain, she thought she noticed the same elderly woman fill in the form near the beginning of the project and again about two weeks later. The teller did not question the customer about this possibility.

The marketing director stated that he was especially looking forward to the analysis of the data from this project in that he had a benchmark for question number 9. Two and a half years earlier, his predecessor, Miles Swenson, no longer with Waterside, had asked that single question in a skeletal study. Swenson conducted that study in the headquarters, branch number 5. In that simple project every customer had had a chance to fill in a card-size form containing that single question and hand it back to the teller. During that study, lasting exactly three weeks, 451 people had participated. Of these 451 people, 321 had said yes, and 130 had said no in answer to the question. Those who had participated constituted about 8 per cent of those who had visited the branch during that time period. Charles Rivera added that he thought it would be useful to establish a second benchmark. He explained that he meant a determination of what the customers of First Federal Savings and Loan, the leading competitor, thought of that competitor on the same set of questions Waterside was asking.

At the end of three full weeks, Lassiter was wondering if the collection of data should stop, for it seemed that they had in hand a great number of completed questionnaires, 2,032 to be exact. He was eager to analyze the information and interpret it in a report to Clarence Lazini, the president and chairperson of the board of Waterside Savings and Loan. Lazini had indicated earlier that he was not completely familiar with such research methods but was pleased to see the work being done and would try to be reasonably receptive to its results as he guided the organization.

Advise Waterside Savings and Loan Association.

EXHIBIT 2 Answers to Question 1 by Branch

	Branch					
	1	2	3	4	5	Total
More often than once a week	21	33	43	47	29	173
Once a week	40	61	82	86	62	331
Once every two weeks	49	72	100	103	74	398
Once a month	103	153	206	208	169	839
Once a quarter	41	61	81	41	67	291
	254	380	512	485	401	2032

EXHIBIT 4 Answers to Question 9
Cross-tabulated to Answers to Question 5

	Yes	No	Total
Close to your home	674	188	862
Close to your office	641	229	870
Close to shopping	145	58	203
Other	50	47	97
	1510	522	2032

EXHIBIT 3 Answers to Question 9 Cross-tabulated to Answers to Question 1

	Branch 1		Branch 2		Branch 3		Branch 4		Branch 5		Total	
	Yes	No	Yes	No	Yes	No	Yes	No	Yes	No	Yes	No
More often than once a week	18	3	29	4	40	3	26	3	42	5	155	18
Once a week	33	7	54	7	72	10	53	9	73	13	285	46
Once every two weeks	39	10	61	11	85	15	62	12	85	18	332	66
Once a month	69	34	106	47	143	63	118	51	145	63	581	258
Once a quarter	21	20	32	29	42	39	38	29	24	17	157	134
	180	74	282	98	382	130	297	104	369	116	1510	522

VOLUNTEERS IN HEALTH CARE, INC.

Volunteers in Health Care, Inc. (VHC) was a nonprofit corporation that was organized in 1968 to provide medical, psychological, and dental care for the medically indigent and other selected low-income populations in the northern suburbs of an Eastern city. The founders, a group of medical doctors who were predominantly psychiatrists, were still active in the group, although younger colleagues had assumed some of the management.

The original group of physicians augmented their ranks with their own former students, younger colleagues, and professional friends. There had never been a problem with recruitment of volunteer medical professionals, and the medical director had to decline additional volunteers in certain specialty areas. For example, there was consistently an excess of volunteers in pediatrics. A CPA, a former member of the board of directors, performed the annual financial audit free of charge. There had never been a volunteer lawyer, however, in spite of efforts to recruit one. In addition, no one with formal training in business management had ever been involved in VHC. The value of services donated in the most recent year, based on the county health department wage schedule, is displayed in Exhibit 1.

The founders had multiple interests in the organization, including the following:

1. Indignation about the plight of elderly persons and children who "fell through the cracks" of the health care system. Such persons either had too much income to qualify for welfare or did not apply for it. But because they or their parents were unemployed or marginally employed, they lacked private health insurance or were insured only intermittently. Preventive health care, such as checkups, shots, and monitoring of chronic illnesses such as high blood pressure, was particularly lacking. Hospital care was less of a problem because hospitals built with federal or state funds could not turn indigents away. A major regional children's hospital, although a private foundation, also accepted all indigent patients.
2. A research interest in psychosomatic disorders and a related need to stay active in general medical work, although they earned their living as psychiatrists.
3. A desire to demonstrate to their psychiatric colleagues the effectiveness of "talk" therapy with lower-class persons, who in the United States usually were given tranquilizers when stressed or

This case was prepared by Joanne G. Greer, Ph.D.

depressed. The founders were particularly influenced in this research interest by the writings of psychiatrists who had worked in the British national health service.

EXHIBIT 1 Estimated Value of Donated Services

Number of Volunteers	Staff	Hours	Rate	County Pay Rate
14	Physicians	1,306	$23.02	$30,064.12
22	Board members[1]	781	23.02	17,978.62
12	Psychologists	1,145	15.99	18,308.55
20	Nurses	779	9.69	7,548.51
5	Lab technicians	159	8.84	1,405.56
4	Medical students	24	8.84	212.16
2	Dieticians	61	10.63	648.43
12	Clinic assistants	411	6.05	2,486.55
2	Registrars	51	6.05	308.55
7	Office	209	7.72	1,613.48
1	Auditor	80	23.02	1,841.60
101		5,006		$82,416.13
		FICA		5,266.39
		State Unemployment		1,648.32
		Workmen's Compensation		346.14
		Total		$89,676.98

[1] Board member compensation is the same for all board members, physician, nonphysician, professional, or client, according to county policy.

VHC provided services at six sites, visiting a different site each evening from 7:30 to 10:30 P.M. The sites were located in county-subsidized housing units which were reserved for the elderly and a few totally disabled persons. Paid county employees furnished other services to these buildings, such as security guards, maintenance, and minimal recreational programs. Most residents lived on social security incomes from retirement or from total disability ratings, and had too much income to qualify for the state's Medicaid program but too little income to afford private doctors' fees. Transportation to physicians was a severe problem even to residents who had funds to pay the doctors' charges, because public transportation was poor and they were fearful of being injured while entering and leaving buses and crossing busy streets.

The space for the medical clinics at each site was donated by the county, although it was not exclusively dedicated to VHC. Examining rooms were often utilized by other personnel, such as county social workers, outside of clinic hours, and the only space reserved for VHC was a large closet at each site to hold basic equipment such as centrifuges and equipment for specimen collection. Patients made appointments by telephoning VHC's one-room office, located in a converted former county school building, which had been subdivided for use by various volunteer groups. Each evening a volunteer registrar picked up the files of patients expected at the clinic, set up the examining rooms, and arranged folding chairs at the waiting area. He or she greeted the patients, supervised their flow through the clinic, and recorded the services rendered. Payments were accepted on a voluntary system, and the usual total receipts for an evening were less than $10, with individual payments as low as fifty cents. Many paid nothing, although recently a sign had been posted stating, "VHC is staffed entirely by volunteers. Contributions gratefully accepted."

In reality, VHC had four paid staff: a nurse, a social worker, a secretary, and a lower-level manager who was promoted from secretarial work. The nurse took calls from patients, made appointments, and made decisions during the day about patient emergencies. For example, she might consult by telephone with a patient's doctor at his regular employment, or direct a patient to go to the hospital emergency room for a medical crisis. The social worker assisted new patients in contacting various sources of volunteer or tax-subsidized services in the county. Patients requiring medical services not available through VHC were assisted by the social worker to find local sources of help. For example, a patient requiring oral surgery for receding gums was put in touch with the clinic of a local dental school, and a nutritionist was found to assist several diabetic patients with menu planning on a fixed income.

Wives of the male physicians and their women friends sometimes volunteered for typing and filing for a few hours a day, and the supply of clerical help was more than adequate. It was particularly easy to get office volunteers ever since the county had recently moved VHC to an attractive suite in a new senior citizens day-care center. VHC had had only one daytime professional volunteer, a retired social worker, who made home visits and school visits to coordinate care for children receiving psychotherapy from VHC evening volunteers. She also took initial case histories of psychotherapy patients, which were presented to volunteer therapists at their weekly group meeting so they could each choose the type of patient they preferred working with. She had recently resigned, and psychotherapists now received only a name and telephone number for each referral.

Psychotherapists also had to "hustle" office space in the county buildings to see their patients, because there wasn't sufficient auditory privacy to conduct psychotherapy in the physician's examining rooms during evening clinics, even when the rooms were free. Never-

theless, there was no lack of psychotherapists because of an important career benefit they received by volunteering. Several distinguished
senior professors of psychiatry provided the volunteers with free case
supervision, a form of tutorial teaching, for each of their clinic cases.
Ordinarily, such supervision cost $60 to $80 an hour, and therapists
regarded supervision by a well-known educator as a prestige form of
continuing education.

VHC's sources of income and types of expenditures for the past
year are displayed in Exhibits 2 and 3. The main sources of income
were grants from United Way, the county health department, and
an "adolescent parent" grant program. The services to adolescent
mothers and their infants had been eliminated from the state and
federal plans for the coming fiscal year, so no further funds would
be available from that source. The previous week United Way had
notified the chairman of the VHC board of directors that no further
United Way funds would be available until VHC performed an evaluation and hired a professional manager. United Way also objected to
the research interest the physicians had in the patients, in spite of
the fact that any patient included in a research study signed an informed consent form. The fees received from Medicare, Medicaid,
and the county health department grant would not be sufficient to

**EXHIBIT 2 Volunteers in Health Care, Inc. Statement of Revenues and
Expenditures and Changes in Fund Balance**

Most Recent Fiscal Year Ended June 30	
Revenues	
United Way	$50,962.00
County Health Dept.	17,385.00
CETA	1,041.01
Medical Fees	15,409.00
Donations	550.00
Interest	211.49
Miscellaneous	144.34
Total Revenues	$82,148.26
Expenditures	
Program	
Clinic	62,558.51
CETA	5,914.77
Adolescent Parent Education	6,282.93
Total Program	$74,756.21
General & Administrative	14,932.28
Total Expenditures	$89,688.49
Excess of Revenues (deficiency) over Expenditures	(7,540.23)

EXHIBIT 3 Volunteers in Health Care, Inc. Analysis of Functional Expenditures Most Recent Fiscal Year Ended June 30

	Program			General &	
	Clinic	CETA	Total	Administrative	Total
Salaries & registrar fees	$51,062.97	$775.25	$51,838.22	$13,653.00	$65,491.22
Payroll taxes	4,257.86	51.55	4,309.41	1,169.92	5,479.33
Employee benefits	1,102.03	–	1,102.03	310.84	1,412.87
Total personnel costs	$56,422.86	$826.80	$57,249.66	$15,133.76	$72,383.42
Interest	–	–	–	5.59	5.59
Transportation	4,171.82	–	4,171.82	77.95	4,249.77
Contributions	–	–	–	–	400.00
Depreciation	424.50	–	424.50	92.32	516.82
Insurance	2,557.00	–	2,567.00	87.00	2,654.00
Laboratory fees	3,238.20	–	3,288.20	–	3,288.20
Office supplies & expenses	1,302.60	–	1,302.60	367.40	1,670.00
Repairs & maintenance	650.26	–	650.26	159.50	809.76
Medical supplies	1,471.40	–	1,471.40	–	1,471.40
Telephone	427.65	–	427.65	646.41	1,074.26
Miscellaneous	296.13	–	296.13	1,036.58	1,332.71
	$71,022.42	$826.80	$71,849.22	$17,606.71	$89,455.93

even maintain current operations, much less recruit a manager. Some of the patients had private health insurance, but the largest company refused to consider VHC for direct payment because VHC did not have a fixed fee schedule for services, but simply accepted whatever the patient was willing to pay. Consequently, the patients collected the insurance reimbursements and usually pocketed them, making a token donation to VHC. One patient was known to have collected $500 from an insurance company in reimbursement for psychotherapy visits, had donated $50 to VHC, and then used the remainder to take a vacation.

Two letters to the insurance company to negotiate a contract for direct payment to VHC had received short, stereotyped responses of refusal, signed by a correspondence clerk.

In a special meeting to discuss strategy, board members were offended by United Way's demand for an evaluation. Claire Washburn, the board president and wife of a former volunteer, commented, "Our program is sterling, and it breaks my heart to think they would question our integrity." Dr. Vincent Jones, one of the original founders, questioned whether the United Way's funds were worth the effort and wanted to pursue more vigorously obtaining direct reimbursement status with private insurors. VHC was currently receiving a grant from the county health department because VHC could care for the medically indigent more cheaply than county clinics, and Dr. Jones thought the county would give more business if pressed. He also thought there was a possibility of taking over the county operation completely, under a "capitation rate" payment arrangement. The county clinics had high costs, were poorly run, and had just received a large amount of negative coverage in the news media.

Because the county clinics primarily delivered care to medically indigent children, assuming responsibility for these patients would enable VHC to use the volunteer pediatricians it was currently turning away for lack of work.

Under the capitation rate mode of payment, the responsible payor, in this case the county, negotiates a per head annual payment with a health care provider, usually a clinic. The health care provider is responsible for service even if the provider incurs a loss. On the other hand, the provider receives the payment for all covered persons, even those who use no services that year. Medicaid experiments with capitation rate had been quite successful in that equal-quality care for patients with lower annual costs had resulted. Under capitation rate reimbursement, there is no financial incentive for the provider to provide unnecessary services, or to "ping-pong" the patient from doctor to doctor.

Washburn, the board president, was hesitant at the risks involved in giving up the United Way money, but Barry Water, a community activist board member, noted that if VHC dropped out of United Way, it would be completely free to hold its own annual fund-raising drive, an activity that United Way strongly discouraged in recipient agencies. He also noted that the children's hospital had successfully gone this route. Washburn pointed out that some response had to be made to United Way's request for an evaluation of the VHC program, but she, for one, had no idea how to go about it, particularly in light of United Way's expressed dislike for research in the clinics.

Advise Volunteers in Health Care, Inc.

STEPIK AND NEWCOMB MARKETING RESEARCH AGENCY

Stepik and Newcomb was a successful marketing research agency operating in several cities, including a large city in the Eastern United States. It enjoyed a reputation for integrity and quality service. As was true of most marketing research companies, most of this firm's experience with the consumer had been with the middle and upper middle classes. It appeared that proper servicing of a major new client, Harvest World Corporation, might require some changes in the firm's orientation. Harvest World was a regional retail chain with stores in New York, Connecticut, Massachusetts, Rhode Island, New Jersey, Pennsylvania, and Maryland. It characterized its stores as discount houses. They were all located in small cities and in middle-class suburbs of large cities. Harvest World operated two suburban stores in this metropolitan area.

This client was interested in setting up inner-city stores but not necessarily downtown stores. It was interested in string street locations that often occur from two to four miles from downtown shopping districts but not far enough out to compete with suburban planned shopping centers.

Stepik and Newcomb was quite aware of its lack of experience in analyzing low-income consumers.[1] It was also vaguely aware of a problem that one writer described in the following manner:

> The marketing executive who relies on information derived from his own life experiences is usually handicapped when faced with the problems of market-

---

[1] David A. Schwartz, "Coping with Field Problems of Large Surveys Among the Urban Poor," *Public Opinion Quarterly*, **34** (Summer 1970), pp. 267–272; and Herschel Shosteck, "Survey Research in the Inner City," in Fred C. Allvine, Ed., *Combined Proceedings of the 1971 Conferences* (Chicago: American Marketing Association, 1971), pp. 640–643.

ing to low-income groups, because their life-style is quite different from his middle-class one.[2]

One of Harvest World's research questions was to establish the current company image. Another was to determine an appropriate merchandise mix for the new stores. The company dealt in few soft goods but many hard lines. It stressed furniture, rugs, carpeting, major appliances, small appliances, lamps, phonographs, radios, television sets, records, clocks, watches, jewelry, typewriters, bibelots, table flatware, plastic dishes, and toys. It also had ready-made curtains, furniture slip-covers, tablecloths, and place mats. Another question dealt with appropriate pricing policies, and yet another was concerned with appropriate advertising themes and effective media to reach the prospective inner-city customers.

Stepik and Newcomb began by thoroughly studying the data for the city in question from the latest census of population and of housing. Second, the agency conducted traffic counts of pedestrians, cars, and buses at many different possible locations and analyzed the store affinity advantages, if any, for Harvest World at the various locations.

Next, in order to study the client's image, the agency designed a semantic differential instrument based on the work of Osgood and his colleagues.[3] The researchers used a seven-interval scale and bipolar adjectival pairs, as given in Exhibit 1. For the purpose of cross-classification, questions were asked on the following: occupation, place of employment, income, age, size of household, and places where credit had been established.

On the basis of a pilot study of thirty-seven addresses, in which there was an unusually high incidence of no one at home or no adult at home, the agency decided that it would need to start with a larger than average sample. This was decided despite the fact that the client was willing to pay for a call-back, or second visit, to the households in question. Being conservative, the agency feared that even on the second visit a sizable fraction of the sample still would not be at

[2]Kelvin A. Wall, "Marketing to Low-Income Neighborhoods. A Systems Approach," *University of Washington Business Review* (Autumn 1969), pp. 18–26. Reprinted in William Lazer and Eugene Kelley, *Social Marketing: Perspectives and Viewpoints* (Homewood, Ill.: Richard D. Irwin, Inc., 1973), pp. 453–461. Also see Bradley Greenberg and Brenda Dervin, "Mass Communication Among the Urban Poor," *Public Opinion Quarterly*, 34 (Spring 1970), pp. 232–234.

[3]See Charles E. Osgood, G. I. Suci, and P. H. Tannenbaum, *The Measurement of Meaning* (Urbana: University of Illinois Press, 1957). Also see William A. Mindak, "Fitting the Semantic Differential to the Marketing Problem," *Journal of Marketing*, 25 (April 1961), pp. 28–33; and Robert F. Kelly and Ronald Stephenson, "The Semantic Differential: An Information Source for Designing Retail Patronage Appeals," *Journal of Marketing*, 31 (October 1967), pp. 43–47.

EXHIBIT 1 The Semantic Differential Instrument Used By Stepik and Newcomb

Mean		7 Extremely	6 Very	5 Slightly	4 Both, Neither, or No Opinion	3 Slightly	2 Very	1 Extremely	
4.1	Happy	:	:	:	:	:	:	:	Sad
4.9	Inexpensive	:	:	:	:	:	:	:	Expensive
3.9	Neat	:	:	:	:	:	:	:	Unkempt
4.0	Dependable	:	:	:	:	:	:	:	Undependable
3.9	Fair	:	:	:	:	:	:	:	Unfair
4.0	Truthful	:	:	:	:	:	:	:	Deceptive
4.1	Spacious	:	:	:	:	:	:	:	Crowded
4.0	Public-minded	:	:	:	:	:	:	:	Self-serving
4.3	Modern company	:	:	:	:	:	:	:	Old-fashioned company
	Distinctive atmosphere	:	:	:	:	:	:	:	Ordinary atmosphere
	Relaxing	:	:	:	:	:	:	:	Not relaxing
	Strong	:	:	:	:	:	:	:	Weak
	Friendly	:	:	:	:	:	:	:	Stern

home. The pilot study also indicated that the length of the personal interview would have to be limited, for many became impatient or bored before it was over, and two terminated the interview before the interviewer was finished. For this reason, the final four pairs of adjectives were deleted from the semantic differential instrument, leaving nine pairs.

Stepik and Newcomb generated a proper geographical cluster sample and sent experienced field interviewers out to conduct the interviews. Some problems arose with the agency's local interviewer staff, which was composed of people who worked on an on-call basis. They held no full-time jobs. Stepik and Newcomb had on-call arrangements with seven undergraduate men and seven undergraduate women at local universities and seven housewives aged thirty-seven to fifty-six. All were white. The agency had given intensive interviewer training to all when they were first hired. For this project the agency chose to use the more mature women. To start with, one woman reported that she was sick and another refused to participate in this project. Later two other women dropped out. This put a heavy work load on the remaining three women, but they completed the interviews only four days behind schedule. One consolation in this turn of events was that the fewer the interviewers, the greater was the consistency among the interviews conducted.

The marketing research agency's usual experience had been that about 64 per cent of the intended household sample was obtained on the first visit and another 15 per cent was obtained on the second attempt. In the Harvest World project the agency found 50 per cent at home on the first visit and 13 per cent at home on the second attempt. No substitutions were allowed. The refusal rate was in line with the agency's general experience.

The mean ratings on the semantic differential instrument are given in the left-hand column of Exhibit 1.

Advise Stepik and Newcomb as to the remainder of the research project.

6

PRODUCTS
AND
PRODUCT STRATEGY

LA-Z-BOY CHAIR COMPANY

La-Z-Boy Chair Company perceived itself as the most widely recognized name in motion furniture. Although it made several other furniture products, it was best known for its upholstered reclining chairs. Exhibit 1 shows the firm's recent operating statements.

This organization was traceable back to the mid-1920s in southeastern Michigan, when Edward M. Knabusch and his younger cousin Edwin J. Shoemaker formed a partnership with the intention of manufacturing specialty furniture, including a reclining wooden chair that they had invented. They envisioned it for lawn and porch use. They took this chair to a furniture retailer in nearby Toledo, Ohio. "Clever idea," the store manager told them, "but folks will want something more comfortable. If you can make an upholstered chair that reclines, you'll have something you can sell."

A self-taught artisan, Knabusch took this as a challenge. He developed a chair and in 1928 opened a roadside business, a combination workshop and retail store, called Floral City Furniture Company, on the highway between Detroit and Toledo. A good showperson, Knabusch put the place of business on the map by staging tent shows, a miniature circus for children, and other colorful events.

EXHIBIT 1 La-Z-Boy Chair Company Statement of Operations

Year ended in April	1985	1984
Sales and other income		
Net sales	$282,741,371	$254,865,647
Other income	3,116,899	3,036,849
	285,858,270	257,902,496
Costs and expenses		
Cost of sales	191,312,763	167,387,155
Selling, general and administrative	54,712,479	45,962,187
Interest	1,146,079	962,868
Provision for income taxes	17,328,000	20,305,000
	264,499,321	234,617,210
Net income for the year	$ 21,358,949	$ 23,285,286
Weighted average shares outstanding	4,574,424	4,639,884
Per common share outstanding		
Net income	$ 4.67	$ 5.02
Cash dividends paid	$ 1.28	$ .95
Book value on shares outstanding at end of year	$28.34	$25.10
Return on opening shareholders' equity	18%	24%
Depreciation and amortization	$ 5,132,893	$ 4,156,978
Capital expenditures	$ 14,766,228	$ 7,798,920
Property, plant and equipment—Net	$ 44,748,748	$ 35,828,037
Working capital	$ 95,472,063	$ 94,913,666
Current ratio	3.10 to 1	3.48 to 1
Total assets	$193,429,929	$171,523,315
Long-term debt	$ 11,165,000	$ 13,221,754
Retained earnings	$122,335,619	$106,843,050
Shareholders	3,200	2,971
Employees	4,504	4,007

A modern manufacturing plant and headquarters offices were built in 1941 in nearby Monroe, Michigan, for the organization. It incorporated on May 1, 1941, and renamed itself La-Z-Boy Chair Company. The new plant was then converted to war goods production for almost four years. Afterward the company resumed making the reclining chair and gradually began to offer several models of the basic product.

1983	1982	1981	1980	1979
$196,973,340	$175,660,035	$155,616,665	$158,194,103	$146,168,368
2,062,320	2,070,075	2,394,079	1,805,111	1,416,421
199,035,660	177,730,110	158,010,744	159,999,214	147,584,789
136,952,128	125,271,646	107,333,728	110,453,246	103,875,833
38,595,170	36,680,054	31,988,181	30,170,113	28,991,704
1,031,140	1,370,951	1,256,431	977,088	368,385
9,686,000	6,446,000	7,800,000	8,592,000	6,665,000
186,264,438	169,768,651	148,378,340	150,192,447	139,900,922
$ 12,771,222	$ 7,961,459	$ 9,632,404	$ 9,806,767	$ 7,683,867
4,607,071	4,596,121	4,591,012	4,585,283	4,648,258
$ 2.77	$ 1.73	$ 2.10	$ 2.14	$ 1.65
$ .80	$ .76	$ .72	$ .72	$ .72
$21.03	$19.11	$18.17	$16.81	$15.38
15%	10%	13%	14%	11%
$ 3,542,901	$ 3,412,728	$ 3,259,692	$ 2,904,248	$ 2,495,377
$ 7,141,341	$ 2,437,146	$ 3,179,548	$ 7,022,123	$ 8,508,655
$ 32,296,591	$ 28,818,138	$ 29,946,661	$ 30,146,657	$ 26,312,012
$ 78,418,335	$ 67,307,350	$ 67,040,559	$ 61,029,411	$ 53,558,139
3.66 to 1	4.07 to 1	4.11 to 1	4.19 to 1	4.48 to 1
$140,724,447	$118,679,780	$119,139,673	$111,583,280	$ 96,842,445
$ 11,762,690	$ 7,672,290	$ 13,432,690	$ 15,055,097	$ 10,395,131
$ 87,964,629	$ 78,877,594	$ 74,409,394	$ 68,081,977	$ 61,578,222
2,942	3,161	3,324	3,130	3,260
3,568	3,074	3,449	3,628	3,713

Corporate growth in the 1960s and 1970s was centered around the launching in 1961 of the Reclina-Rocker chair, which was introduced to succeed the company's original upholstered reclining chair. According to company executives, "Our business has been built around a singularly successful product, the world-famous and widely imitated Reclina-Rocker." This product was a breakthrough in technology and comfort. It incorporated various features that previously

EXHIBIT 1 La-Z-Boy Chair Company Statement of Operations, cont'd.

1978	1977	1976
$132,722,901	$128,915,840	$105,182,395
1,448,070	1,282,216	971,153
134,170,971	130,198,056	106,153,548
92,802,139	87,098,178	71,596,625
24,401,989	21,264,512	16,962,794
363,061	304,697	338,741
8,019,000	10,403,000	8,533,000
125,586,189	119,070,387	97,431,160
$ 8,584,782	$ 11,127,669	$ 8,722,388
4,644,354	4,644,208	4,644,045
$ 1.85	$ 2.40	$ 1.88
$ .72	$ .52	$ .40
$14.44	$13.31	$11.44
14%	21%	19%
$ 2,128,907	$ 2,074,576	$ 1,997,644
$ 2,415,660	$ 3,778,591	$ 1,250,377
$ 20,356,781	$ 20,199,398	$ 18,542,804
$ 51,518,077	$ 46,161,260	$ 38,704,590
4.97 to 1	4.63 to 1	3.86 to 1
$ 85,096,849	$ 80,291,499	$ 71,300,464
$ 5,068,216	$ 5,746,383	$ 4,647,042
$ 57,243,118	$ 52,022,275	$ 43,289,587
3,544	3,034	3,093
3,440	3,628	3,423

had not been combined in one chair. It was built to rock and recline and had a movable footrest, which could be raised from its normal vertical position at the lower front of the chair to the desired horizontal position by use of a hand lever on the side of the chair. Much later, a swivel base was designed and offered as a customer option.

Subsequent to that introduction, the company vastly expanded its upholstered residential furniture line. After considerable research and development work, the organization in 1970 brought out the Sofette, a two-seat reclining unit in which each seat operated independently of the other. In 1973, La-Z-Boy introduced La-Z-Rocker, a line of swivel rockers that flexed their backs based on the weight of the individual. A line of sleep sofas called La-Z-Sleeper was brought out in 1977; and a line of ottomans to accompany the La-Z-Rockers, in 1978. In late 1979 the company introduced the Reclina-Way reclining chair to replace the former Wall-Recliner chair. Placed only a few inches from the wall, the smooth glide action of this product required only gentle shoulder motion to put it into operation. A helpful device was patented and put into use in 1981. This innovation, called the Swivel-Stop, locked La-Z-Rocker swivel rocker chairs in position when not in use. This device maintained a stable position when one sat down or got up. Also, according to company executives, "People had one objection to all swivel rocker chairs: they invariably faced the wrong direction. With Swivel-Stop the chair stays facing the direction you want when it is unoccupied." In late 1982 the company brought out a line of stationary sofas called La-Z-Sofa. A line of reclining chairs with high legs of exposed wood was introduced in 1983 and called the La-Z-Lounger. Also in that year the company brought out Reclina-Rest, a new line of reclining chairs. This stationary, multiposition recliner offered a footrest and reclining action that operated independently of each other, so that the number of combinations of positions expanded greatly. The La-Z-Sleeper was replaced in early 1984 by a new line of sleep sofas called Signature II, which offered a new exclusive mechanism and optional quilted innerspring mattress. In late 1984 the company introduced Eurostyled models in the Signature II sleep sofa line together with coordinated Reclina-Rocker chairs and La-Z-Sofa stationary sofas. Eurostyles reflected a movement in the fashion centers of Europe toward understatement and relaxed contours. La-Z-Boy's interpretation of this trend incorporated softly plumped saddlebag arms, double-pillowed seat backs that were adjustable for individual comfort, and shirred front rails. These changes not only produced attractive, interesting furniture, but they were also an overt attempt to appeal to trend-conscious consumers.

The company introduced a line of modular units in 1985 that featured the Reclina-Way mechanism and named them Motion-Modulars. This set of products was not only an expansion but also a rational response to the strong U.S. trend toward smaller houses and the mixed trend toward smaller living rooms or family rooms or both. Motion-Modulars could be arranged in many configurations, creating, for example, a straight or curved sofa, a love seat and a chair with an ottoman, a corner grouping, or even a sleep sofa in two sizes. Units could be bought individually or together, of course. Adding a unit later exposed the consumer to the risk of a tiny change in the color or texture of fabric. La-Z-Boy did not manufacture its own fabrics. Even if it had done so and concentrated on consistency, absolutely perfect uniformity in textures and especially in colors was impossible. What interior decorators and furniture salespersons often recommended in this case was for a consumer to add another piece of upholstered furniture in an obviously different but carefully coordinated color. In fact, most consumers did not want all the upholstered furniture in a room to match, thinking it looked rather dull.

An interesting piece of work was perfected in 1981, a new handle-footrest mechanism for Contract Division chairs. It was more simple and durable than the previous device. Because of the lower profile of this new mechanism, the company began experimenting with a high leg recliner for the residential market. This mechanism permitted the design of a chair that had a lighter look and higher style.

The La-Z-Boy residential products, on the whole, had always been casual-looking. For houses with both a living room and a family room, La-Z-Boy was more likely to be considered for purchase for the latter. The introduction of chairs with exposed wooden legs was an attempt to attract people with more formal tastes. In 1983 the company made an appeal to the person who preferred elegance and tradition by launching its Presidential Collection. This line combined reclining features with eighteenth-century styling. Skirted bottoms were replaced with exposed wooden legs in a choice of Queen Anne or Chippendale styles.

Earlier, the corporation had made an interesting diversification of the product line. In 1971 it entered the office seating market by designing and offering an item unique in its field, a high-backed executive recliner. Several other chairs for office use were designed and added to this initial offering. Thereafter the company operated as though it had two suborganizations, the Residential Division and the Contract Division. However, this arrangement was not formalized and each division assigned its own vice president until 1984. In 1982 the company expanded into desks and office furniture components, specifically, credenzas, bookshelves, and tables. They were offered in traditional, modern, and contemporary styling and in sizes and qualities suitable for what the company described as "executive, middle management, and secretarial requirements." However, La-Z-Boy was the distributor of these case goods, not the manufacturer. The company acquired and modernized a 153,500-square foot manufacturing plant in Leland, Mississippi, in 1985 and dedicated it to the making of contract market products. This was the smallest of the organization's nine manufacturing facilities. Pilot production of desks and other case goods began in 1985, and the company became self-sufficient in these goods by 1986. Compared to the case goods previously offered, La-Z-Boy now felt that it could offer better construction, styling, features, and finish. For example, the new in-house production of desks offered central locking systems, improved slide mechanisms for heavily loaded drawers, and hand-rubbed desktops for greater beauty and wear resistance.

In 1973 the company went into health-care seating for hospitals, clinics, and nursing homes. Although the potential demand of the health-care industry did not match that of office furniture, it was large and showed some signs of growing. La-Z-Boy reclining chairs were used in patient rooms, where they presented a comfortable alternative to the bed for people who were well enough to get up and down. They were also used in some specialized treatment situations such as hemodialysis and in many kinds of treatment for the very old and feeble. A new product about to be launched was a reclining chair on casters with an articulating arm tray table and a concealed footrest. Cheerful fabrics and vinyl coverings were available and emphasized.

The Contract Division acquired the rights in 1981 to make the BackJack floor rest from Concept Engineering, Inc., of Lincoln Nebraska, and introduced it at once. Shaped like the number 7 lying on its open side, this item was upholstered, lightweight, and portable leisure seating meant mainly for the beach, pool, or camping. Unlike the rest of the company's product line, it was distributed through sporting goods stores, home improvement centers, and mail-order catalogs and even in some redemption catalogs for trading stamps. La-Z-Boy abandoned this product at the end of 1983.

The lodging industry was selected by the Contract Division in 1984 as another area for sales development efforts. In gratifyingly short time, the division sold several large orders for chairs and sleep sofas to well-known hotel and motel chains and felt rather encouraged.

All sales growth in the company had been internally generated except for one acquisition. La Z-Boy acquired Deluxe Upholstering Ltd. of Waterloo, Ontario, in 1979, which had previously manufactured La-Z-Boy products for fifty years under a licensing agreement. Annual sales volume of this wholly owned subsidiary was about $9,530,000 in the most recent year, and the manufacturing facility was being approximately doubled in size.

The strong sales growth trend of early years stumbled in 1975 as an actual decrease occurred, but there was a rebound in 1976 and again in 1977. Growth in 1978, 1979, and 1980 was no greater than the rate of inflation in the economy. In 1981 there was a decline of

1.6 per cent, which of course represented an extremely large decline when adjusted for inflation. In 1981 and 1982 there was great self-examination in the corporation, and in 1982 there was the largest number of new style introductions in the organization's history. In 1982 the momentum resumed, and there was again noteworthy growth in 1983, 1984, and 1985. The year 1984 saw a surge of 29 per cent; and 1985, a rise of 8 per cent in sales.

The company was the eighth largest manufacturer of residential furniture in the United States and the largest of 15 makers of reclining chairs. It employed about 4,600 people. For its other residential furniture, La-Z-Boy faced 30 competitors. Its Reclina-Rocker as of 1986 enjoyed 33 per cent of the market for such a chair, and the competitor with the second-largest market share sold only half as much of this product type. The Reclina-Rocker still provided about 70 per cent of the company's sales.

Patents were highly important in the growth and development of the La-Z-Boy Chair Company, especially on its reclining-chair and rocking-chair mechanisms, and to its present competitive position. As of 1986 the corporation had 50 patents, all but six of which involved residential products. The original reclining mechanism patent, so crucial to the success of the company from 1961 forward, expired in 1978. According to R. G Micka, vice president of La-Z-Boy, "Patents are guarded carefully and are very important to the conduct of business in the nation's furniture trade." Competitors arose but did not copy the La-Z-Boy reclining chair mechanism, instead developing their own. According to Micka, "Tooling up for production on this mechanism is cost-prohibitive for most manufacturers if La-Z-Boy specifications and tolerances are to be met." The corporate executives believed that La-Z-Boy was now so well established in the industry that the loss of any single or small group of patents would not materially affect the business.

Most products were made on the receipt of an order from the retailer or business user. A few popular models were made for stock and held in warehouses for immediate shipment. Company sales were considerably lower in the summer than in the remainder of the year, but the scheduling of production, when possible, was planned to maintain a uniform level of manufacturing activity throughout the year. The company operated manufacturing plants in Redlands, California; Neosho, Missouri; Dayton, Tennessee; Siloam Springs, Arkansas; Leland, Mississippi; Newton, Mississippi; Tremonton, Utah; and Waterloo, Ontario. It had two facilities in Florence, South Carolina, a manufacturing plant and a fabric-processing center. The one dealing in fabrics was small and employed only 14 people, but it received and redistributed all fabrics to all the company's manufacturing plants. The headquarters people calculated fabric requirements of each plant based on furniture production schedules, and the fabric-processing center then shipped the appropriate amounts of the appropriate fabrics. Each plant made only a few items in the product line. The Monroe headquarters plus the facilities in Redlands, Dayton, Siloam Springs, and Waterloo were owned whereas the others were occupied under long-term leases. The company received small amounts of royalty income from the sale and licensing of its trademarks, trade names, and patents to foreign manufacturers in Norway, Italy, West Germany, South Africa, New Zealand, and Australia.

The principal raw materials used by La-Z-Boy in the manufacture of its furniture were hardwoods for frames; plywood and chipwood for internal parts; steel for the mechanisms; cotton, wool, synthetic; and vinyl fabrics, and leather and polyurethane foam for cushioning. The steel and wood products were purchased from several sources, usually located in the vicinity of the particular plant having the need whereas covering materials and polyurethane were purchased from a sizable number of sources on a centralized basis. La-Z-Boy fabricated the majority of the parts in its products, largely because parts of suitable quality made to its exact specifications were not obtainable at reasonable prices from outside suppliers.

Fabrics were highly important in the residential furniture business. There was extensive testing of fabric samples for strength, abrasion, fading, and general wear. The fabric-buying function was housed in the Monroe headquarters. Fabric buyers' recommendations, based on both functional and aesthetic considerations, were presented to the Fabric Review Committee and then to corporate management for final approval. Because of its large buying power, La-Z-Boy was able to obtain a few fabrics on an exclusive basis.

A new testing laboratory went into operation in 1985. It was twice as large as the facility it replaced and was equipped better. Not only were fabrics tested, but padding, springs, finishes, frames, glues, reinforcements, and mechanisms also were tested.

Research and development (R & D) typically amounted to about 0.7 per cent of sales. An activity carried out at corporate headquarters, R & D was a combination of pure engineering and the application of artistic design and comfort to engineering concepts. Increasingly, the R & D effort was converting to CAD (computer-aided design), which was adopted in 1983. This allowed almost instant recombinations of variables and minute alterations to proposals. The computer display screen was more versatile than the printed or hand-drawn diagram. Electronics also were being applied effectively to the cutting of fabric so as to minimize wastage.

The Residential Division maintained year-round showrooms in six cities for dealers and participated in several furniture shows/markets annually. It had 94 sales representatives, all paid on a commission basis. The company shipped its residential products to approximately 7,500 locations, but the number of retail stores carrying some or all of the line was an unknown but larger figure. This was because some shipping destinations served several branches of one retailer. The largest retailer account was Montgomery Ward, which had over 300 branches. The company also distributed through about 230 Showcase Shoppes. Such a business was a locally owned merchant who had agreed through contract to handle only La-Z-Boy products and use the name Showcase Shoppe. This permitted a consumer to see the full range of the La-Z-Boy furniture displayed to advantage in coordinated room settings. Nearly all these stores were in metropolitan areas. In rural areas and small cities, La-Z-Boy dominated the motion furniture business, but in metropolitan markets the company was only one of several strong and several marginal contenders. The Showcase Shoppes began in 1975, and by now only a small number were added each year. As this network grew; the number of shipping destinations for the Residential Division had declined by about 33 per cent. La-Z-Boy dropped a few accounts on its own initiative.

The Contract Division maintained its own sales force. About 65 per cent of contract furniture orders were placed by interior designers, architects, and Contract Division dealers. The contract line was handled through selected retail outlets, office supply stores, and mail-order catalog companies. This division also maintained permanent showrooms in Chicago, Atlanta, and Dallas and set up numerous temporary exhibits at shows that specialized by industry.

Advise La-Z-Boy Chair Company.

McDONALD'S

McDonald's Corporation was one of the best-known companies in the United States and Canada and constituted a success story seldom equaled. Systemwide sales were about $11 billion, and total assets and stockholders' equity were rising nicely. Net profits after taxes were very good and were rising rapidly. No dividends were paid until the twenty-second year of the organization's life, all the profits being plowed back into fast expansion of the system.

Restaurants operated by McDonald's itself furnished about 25 per cent of systemwide sales whereas franchised restaurants accounted for 69 per cent of sales. Most franchisors operated from 15 per cent to 20 per cent of their outlets, but McDonald's operated 26 per cent of its outlets. The 353 restaurants operated by several affiliates in foreign countries, chiefly Japan, were responsible for about 6 per cent of the sales. An affiliate was a company in which McDonald's share of equity was 50 per cent or less. The combined sales of foreign affiliates, foreign franchises, and company-owned units abroad amounted to about 20 per cent of company sales, but these sales were increasing faster than domestic sales. There were McDonald's restaurants in forty-one countries.

McDonald's held about a 21 per cent share of the U.S. market for fast foods in total but almost 45 per cent of the burger market, and it was much larger than its competitors. In terms of sales, it was twice as large as Kentucky Fried Chicken and Burger King; three times as large as Wendy's; and more than four times as large as Hardee's, Pizza Hut, and Church's Fried Chicken; and it completely dwarfed many companies such as Dairy Queen, Big Boy, and Roy Rogers.

McDonald's selected each location and constructed the facilities. A franchisee who operated an establishment paid McDonald's a large initial franchising fee, half in cash and half to be paid later, plus an annual franchise fee of 3 per cent of sales and an annual building rental of 8.5 per cent of sales. The franchise lasted for twenty years and included intensive training at the company's Hamburger University in Elk Grove Village, Illinois; management counseling; assistance with operations, advertising, and public relations; financial advice; materials for employee training; and the financial benefits of volume purchasing. However, McDonald's was not in the business of supplying the franchisees. Instead, it negotiated supply contracts with outside companies.

Growth, Development, and Policies

The company was founded in 1955 by Ray Kroc, who sold malted-milk machines. His curiosity was piqued in 1954, when he received an order for eight units from one hamburger restaurant, for that meant someone had found it necessary to make very large numbers of malts simultaneously. That establishment was McDonald's in San Bernardino, California, an eight-year-old firm owned and operated by Maurice "Mac" and Richard McDonald. The two brothers had developed the concept of the assembly-line hamburger and accompanying french fries. They had pioneered in the use of a standardized beef patty, with a standardized sauce, and an infrared lamp to keep the cooked potatoes crisp. In front of the restaurant was a large sign displaying two golden arches. The prices were quite low. Kroc was extremely impressed with what he saw: good value for the money, speedy service, elimination of wastefulness, cleanliness, the absence of anything to be stolen, and standardization. The McDonald brothers had franchised six other establishments in California to use their name and their complete set of procedures, but they were cautious and conservative about expanding further and wanted very much to avoid the traveling that inevitably would go with expanded operations. Kroc talked with them for three days while they assembled hamburgers. Finally, they worked out a contract whereby Kroc would have the exclusive right to sell the McDonald's name and complete package of procedures to franchisees and would get a percentage of sales made by franchisees. Six years later, in 1960, Kroc completely bought out the McDonald brothers' interests for $2.7 million.

Ray Kroc believed strongly in the concept of systems. He frequently instructed people, especially franchisees, that there was a science to making and serving a hamburger. He described his operating philosophy with two anagrams, QSC/TLC, which meant "Quality, Service, Cleanliness/Tender Loving Care." He emphasized that the company gave a person a chance to get into business for himself or herself without taking the entire risk alone. But that person had to agree to follow a proved way of conducting the business. Although Kroc saw the extreme importance of systems in creating and running an organization, he believed that systems should be no more complex than necessary. He frequently called attention to a favorite rule of thumb called K.I.S.S. for short, which translated "Keep it simple, stupid."

The system included physical standardization. Kroc believed that the public would react positively to a standardization that featured not only places that turned out the same food but that were extremely clean inside and outside and were staffed by courteous people. Most of the industry of which McDonald's was part had a reputation for slovenly conditions and unconcerned, often surly employees. Another point emphasized to franchisees, managers, and employees was the need to maintain scrupulously clean rest rooms.

McDonald's believed strongly in monitoring the work of franchisees and its own restaurant managers. Standardization and enforcement of policies could not really be accomplished without management audits. Accordingly, twice a year, internal consultants conducted a highly detailed inspection lasting about three days and rendered a written report with grades and comments on management practices. Among the categories critiqued were the food and beverages, cleanliness, speed of service, courtesy, and friendliness.

The company emphasized suburban locations, thus tapping the great population movements of the late 1950s and 1960s. Most existing fast-food firms chose to remain in the cities and ignored the suburbs. In the 1970s, McDonald's expanded into the cities and into some small towns.

The Product Line

Although it was realized that the "product" was far more than the food, the heart of McDonald's product was the food itself, The company was devoted to simple, bland foods that would have a rather broad, repetitive appeal and would be easy to make. The hamburger sandwich fitted these criteria, but as food traditions go, it was a relative newcomer. Hamburger meat originated in medieval Eastern Europe as raw beef shredded by a dull knife. Baltic region traders brought it to Hamburg, where it is still eaten both cooked and raw. German immigrants later brought it encased in bread to the United States. It is claimed that the hamburger was introduced by these immigrants in the Cincinnati area and also in St. Louis. There is good documentation that the first large-scale public offering of the hamburger was at the St. Louis World's Fair of 1904. New Haven, Connecticut, however, claims that a restaurant called Louis Lunch was the first to popularize this German dish.

There was always great concern for appropriate product characteristics and an appropriate product mix. Kroc determined that the company's first hamburger patty must measure 1.6 ounces and go in a bun that was 3.5 inches in diameter. He decreed that the bun must contain extra sugar so that it would brown faster and that the sandwich must contain exactly one-fourth of an ounce of onion. In 1963 the company introduced its double burger and double-cheeseburger. Although it believed passionately in standardization, McDonald's was always interested in new product development and in the improvement of the product line. Despite the fact that it had people engaged in research, McDonald's was quite receptive to product ideas arising from its franchisees. One of the great breakthroughs came from franchisee Lou Groen, who operated a restaurant in a Roman Catholic neighborhood in Cincinnati. On Fridays his sales dropped by about half. In 1961 he began experimenting with a breaded fish filet sandwich and his Friday sales increased. In 1963 this product became an official part of the McDonald's menu and soon thereafter was named the Filet-o'-Fish. This was the first expansion beyond burgers, french fries, and beverages. Franchisee Jim Delligatti of Pittsburgh saw that he was losing some trade to a nearby competitor who offered an oversized hamburger. Accordingly, he put two all-beef patties, special sauce, lettuce, cheese, pickles, and onions on a sesame seed bun. The company adopted it in 1968, called it the Big Mac, and it became the best-selling item in the product line.

Something more radical was developed in 1972 by franchisee Herbert Peterson in Santa Barbara, California, who saw that his restaurants might be more profitable if they opened at 7 A.M. rather than 10 A.M. Peterson had always enjoyed eggs Benedict and thought that the masses would like something similar if he could adapt it to the company's price structure and operating system. After six months of experimentation he introduced his Fast-Break Breakfast, a sandwich of Canadian bacon, cheese, and an egg on an English muffin. Along with earlier openings, this product was introduced in most McDonald's restaurants in the United States in 1976 under the name Egg McMuffin. This product added over 10 per cent to sales the first year. Soon thereafter the breakfast menu in the chain was expanded by adding fruit juices; Danish pastries; English muffins; a platter of sausage and hot cakes; and a platter of sausage, scrambled eggs, and hash brown potatoes. Most units of the chain adopted the 7 A.M. opening except on Sundays, when the opening was usually set at 8 A.M.

The company developed the Quarter Pounder in 1972 to replace the double hamburger. This new product caused McDonald's great public relations difficulties, for an official investigation by the U.S. Department of Agriculture showed that in no instance did the meat used exceed three ounces in weight. A belated advertising campaign by McDonald's emphasized the point that the patty used in the Quarter Pounder weighed a quarter of a pound *before* cooking.

In 1975 the company successfully added McDonaldland cookies, a bland, vanilla-flavored product made of flour, sugar, shortening, corn syrup, salt, leavening, lecithin, and artificial flavoring in the shape of fantasy characters from the company advertising and sales promotion. It was sold in two-ounce (fifty-six grams) portions packed in pasteboard boxes. Very much like the traditional "animal crackers," these were a hit, especially with children. The cookies were manufactured by the Keebler Company, already well known to children through its famous elves. Hot cherry and apple pies cooked in an individual serving size followed in all locations. Pumpkin and blueberry pies were offered seasonally starting in the mid-1980s. Ice cream sundaes were introduced in many locations as a test market. Hot tea was added in most locations in 1977, and biscuits were added in most locations in 1984 and 1985.

Exhaustive product development research on chicken began in 1971. The cooking of chicken, even merely frying it, offered many options to be evaluated carefully. For example, Kentucky Fried Chicken restaurants in the United States offered a choice of soft or extremely crispy chicken. In 1980 two major chicken products entered test markets. One was the McChicken sandwich, composed of a boneless chicken patty of combined dark and light meat, shredded lettuce, and a dressing that resembled mayonnaise—all on a bun. The other was Chicken McNuggets, bite-size lumps of boneless chicken served with a choice of sauces or dips. The basic idea for Chicken McNuggets resulted from an elevator conversation between Fred Turner, the company chairperson, and René Arend, the head chef in the organization's laboratory kitchens. At the time Arend was experimenting with recipes for the proposed Onion McNuggets, but Turner suggested experimentation with chicken as well. After a long, careful test-marketing effort, the decision went against the chicken sandwich, but the McNuggets were added to the product line.

On average, McDonald's kept about twenty proposed products in various stages of research and development. Most would not even reach the test-marketing phase. Besides risk of failure of a product, there was the grave concern that a new product that sold well might really accomplish nothing for the company but shift demand from an established product.

The company began testing the McFeast in 1978. This product was an extra large burger topped with tomato slices and lettuce. It finally evolved into the McDLT, a regular size cheeseburger with tomato slices and lettuce that was introduced in 1985. In that year, small-scale test marketing began on bacon, egg, and cheese biscuits.

Test marketing of salads was begun in late 1984, and by 1986 this testing had spread to numerous cities. Instead of a salad bar, the proposed products were individually made and wrapped salads in three varieties. McDonald's management emphasized the convenience of the products, whereas competitors pointed out the inflexibility and lack of freshness.

In markets abroad, McDonald's made a few additions to the standard menu. For example, it added soup in Japan, chicken croquettes and apple sauce in Holland, fried chicken in Australia, wine in France, and beer in West Germany. Market research conducted by various fast-food corporations indicated that foreign customers wanted the standard American menus with only a few additions. McDonald's had much more business abroad than any other American restaurant organization. Interestingly enough, when one McDonald's branch in the United States applied to authorities for a beer license in 1984, there was an avalanche of complaints, and the application was withdrawn.

McDonald's had been ultraconservative and cautious in accepting new product ideas. The company used a long lead time and finished off the development process with extensive test marketing. Nevertheless, it had had some failures: the roast beef sandwich, the pineapple burger, the Triple Ripple ice-cream cone, and the chopped beef sandwich. While still in test markets, the McRib sandwich was judged a failure. It was made of "restructured beef," which was less desirable cuts of beef re-formed into attractive shapes to look like steaks. Many people in the company were emotionally attached to the McRib and found its failure terribly depressing. About the same time, Burger King also failed with a steak sandwich. McDonald's widely test-marketed fried onion cubes in 1979 but decided against them. In the fast-food restaurant industry as a whole, a clear majority of the new products introduced had failed. McDonald's had always done much better than the average.

The company was anxious to ensure that the cooking process be systematic so as to keep its products consistent. Cybernetic deep fryers continuously adjusted to the moisture in potatoes so that all servings would have the same degree of brownness, and lights on the grills alerted the attendant to flip the patties. In 1984 ten seconds of cooking time was added to the cooking of a burger. Size of potatoes was controlled carefully in purchasing contracts. Because potatoes could not be controlled in advance, special scoops were designed to apportion the cooked potatoes correctly.

Besides preparing the foods according to company policy, McDonald's was vitally interested that the food also be in good condition when served. Therefore, the chain had a policy of throwing away unserved burger patties after ten minutes, french fries after seven minutes, and coffee after thirty minutes. Such losses were minimized through careful planning and control, of course. Norms for such losses were built into the budgeting process, and franchisees and managers were fully advised about these expectations. The paper and Styrofoam packages around the food and beverages had evoked many complaints from ecologists but served to insulate the products better than those of competitors.

Major competitors of McDonald's were giving increasing attention to their own product development and improvement of their own present product lines. Whereas McDonald's was an independent organization, two major competitors had been purchased by large conglomerates. Thus, each of these two restaurant chains, although much smaller than McDonald's, had access to its parent's considerable capital, product development laboratories and expertise, and a tradition of commitment to new product development. Heublein, a large distiller and importer, owned Kentucky Fried Chicken (and was itself owned by R. J. Reynolds Industries), and Pillsbury owned Burger King. Moreover, through aggressive advertising and on-premises sales promotion, Burger King was well on its way toward making the King character as well known as Ronald McDonald. Wendy's now employed forty-two people in its new product development operation.

Besides the matters already mentioned, there was concern about the image of employment at McDonald's, demographic trends, the protests about use of Canadian fish, the taste of the company's food, and criticism of the nutritional characteristics of the company's product line. The first was not as great a problem as the others but was significant. Company employee rolls were dominated by about 165,000 teenagers in the United States. Despite the facts that it was furnishing jobs to an age group that exhibited a relatively high rate of unemployment and that it got along well with nearly all its employees, McDonald's was attacked by social critics and officials of various labor unions for paying hourly wages that were below average for the nation, although legal. Employee turnover was high compared to business at large but not any higher than the rest of the fast-food industry. The company might have objectively answered these attacks, but could not, for public relations reasons, by pointing out that the employees were, in the words of Theodore Levitt, "totally unskilled machine tenders." This marketing professor and consultant added, "The only choice available to the attendant is to operate it exactly as the designers intended."[1]

Demographic trends were extremely unsettling. It was clear that the company's trade was primarily with children, teenagers, and adults under age thirty-five. Customers thirty-five years of age or over contributed only about 23 per cent of sales although they constituted about 42 per cent of the U. S. population. Children age fifteen or under accounted for 20 per cent of sales whereas persons age sixteen to thirty-four accounted for 57 per cent. This fact was acceptable as an application of the principle of aiming at a target market. However, the United States' birthrate had declined dramatically, and the population was aging. Wendy's, a competitive hamburger chain founded in Ohio in 1969 and not affiliated with any parent or conglomerate, was aiming at the over twenty-five market and was faring quite well. It featured a stylish decor, and its customers were not expected to clear off their tables.

After Ray Kroc went into semiretirement and ownership of McDonald's corporate stock became slightly more diffused, the new board chairperson, forty-six-year-old Fred L. Turner, who had started out as a McDonald's cook, encouraged some physical changes. There were several objectives, one of which was to attract more

---

[1] "The Burger That Conquered the Country," *Time*, September 17, 1973, p. 85.

middle-aged and older adults. McDonald's worked quickly to moderate the garish exterior look of the restaurants, which were often in multicolored candy stripes. Other factors to be dealt with were the feelings of upper middle-class people who found McDonald's visually jarring at best and unacceptably offensive at worst, occasional ethnic feelings, and occasional zoning regulations. A neat brown brick exterior of no particular architectural style was the usual result. Moreover, many golden arches signs were greatly reduced in size and some were merely attached to one wall of the building. In addition, the policy that the building had to be freestanding was dropped. Drive-through service bays were added in about 1,000 units in warmer regions of the United States, a throwback to the early years of some competitors. New uniforms for employees were designed and made available in a variety of colors to suit the decor. A few California and Maryland units of the chain experimented with having a hostess, attired at night in an attractive long gown, and substituting candlelight for the usual lighting. In a second cycle of architectural changes, McDonald's authorized fifteen new exterior and interior designs: English Tudor, Country French, New England, Western, Spanish, Old English, Dutch Colonial, Tahitian, Caribbean, French Quarter, Alpine, Midwesterner, Williamsburg, Cambridge and Gaslight.

In addition, the company began to broaden what was acceptable as a location. It started to seek sites in educational institutions, airports, zoos, military bases, and elsewhere. It even opened a branch in a children's hospital. In a unique arrangement, a McDonald's in College Park, Maryland, near the University of Maryland began to offer regular free McShuttle bus service to and from several places on the campus. The same branch was the first in the chain to offer home delivery, but this service failed. Burger King was test-marketing the use of mobile restaurants built on oversized vans. McDonald's had been successful with a number of mall restaurants, but it began an interesting experimental restaurant in a suburban Minneapolis mall in which there was no seating area and no burgers were on the menu.

A small but perplexing problem was a series of protests and restaurant picketings by some environmentalists and animal lovers against McDonald's use of fish from Canada. McDonald's was the world's largest purchaser of Canadian fish. Protestors hoped to pressure the Canadian authorities to eliminate or reduce the killing of baby seals.

Although many peole were virtually oblivious to the taste of the food they were eating and many were unable or unwilling to give the time it took to savor the taste, there was a modest trend toward increasing American interest in cooking. Gourmet authors and food commentators drew large audiences in person and through the media. Craig Claiborne and Julia Child both found McDonald's french fries good, and James Beard concluded, "The whole thing is aimed at the six-year-old palate." Gael Greene noted that the cheese tasted like glue and added, "I love the malts—thick, sweet and ice cold. They're better than if they were real."[2]

Social criticism of the nutritional characteristics of food served by McDonald's and other fast-food organizations had been growing for several years.[3] These products were termed "junk food." McDonald's was frequently the focus of criticism, not because it was the worst but because it was the largest. Among the most vocal were black critics who charged that McDonald's expansion into the inner city enticed the poor with low-nutrition food. As a matter of fact, McDonald's had a month-long advertising campaign in the early 1970s on the theme that each person should eat other foods in addition to what the company offered. A detailed research project done by Consumers Union and published in its *Consumer Reports* showed that Big Macs contained more salt per ounce than the burgers served by McDonald's major competitors but that McDonald's shakes and french fries contained less salt per ounce than the average for the fast-food industry.[4] In late 1984, McDonald's began a test market of unsalted burgers and pancakes in the Chicago metropolitan area. Nearly all the company's product line was unquestionably high in fats, sugar, salt, and calories. The real nutritional problem was not just McDonald's food but the severely unbalanced and overcaloric diet of a substantial fraction of the United States population, which included many millions of McDonald's regular customers.

Advise McDonald's Corporation.

---

[2] Ibid; and "Love in the Kitchen: The Outcome? Cuisine, Now Chow," *Time*, December 19, 1977, pp. 54–61.

[3] The social criticism of McDonald's early years and up to 1976 can be found in the highly opinionated book by Max Boas and Steve Chain, *Big Mac: The Unauthorized Story of McDonald's* (New York: E. P. Dutton & Co., Inc., 1976).

[4] "Fast Food Chains," *Consumer Reports* (September 1979), pp. 508–513.

POWER TOOLS, INC. (A)

Power Tools, Inc., was a large and diversified manufacturer of power tools and labor-saving devices for home and industry. Founded in the early 1900s, the firm's headquarters was in the Middle Atlantic states. It was included in the *Fortune 500* list of large U.S. corporations and produced and marketed its products on a worldwide basis.

During the early years of its existence, the company was primarily a manufacturer of a variety of machines and equipment. For example, at one time it manufactured industrial scales. As time passed, however, the firm expanded into the production of universal electric motors. This lead to the placement of a chuck onto the spindle of an electric motor; this was the earliest electric drill. It was large and cumbersome but offered the user the ability to drill holes without being tied to the traditional fixed-in-place drill press.

During the 1930s and extending into the 1940s the firm grew to specialize in the manufacture of electrically driven portable power tools. The firm grew and prospered. It developed a variety of electrically driven tools, such as various sizes of drills, percussion hammers, and a variety of grinders. During the late 1940s and early 1950s the firm entered the "do it yourself" market. It was able to develop the previously unexplored homeowner's market. This propelled the firm into a period of tremendous growth. In addition to the industrial markets, the firm increased in size by selling tools to the homeowner. This provided the firm with very large economies of scale. The price of the typical one-fourth-inch drill dropped from the $50 or $60 range to the $10 range. In the process, the firm doubled its sales about every ten years.

The Industrial/Construction Division

During its early years, the primary focus of Power Tools, Inc., was on the industrial user. As mentioned, the company provided grinders, drills, and a variety of other expensive engineered products. The company considered itself to be a pioneer in the growth of the industrial markets. It sold its products exclusively through the traditional "mill supply" houses. This emphasis on the industrial nature of the business was continued in the Industrial/Construction Division even as the phenomenal growth in the Consumer Products Division occurred.

During the 1950s, however, there was considerable growth in con-

This case was prepared by Richard Rosecky, Ph.D., who is on the staff of the company being considered.

struction products offered by the Industrial/Construction Division. Circular saws, finishing sanders, routers, and a variety of other new products were developed in parallel with the Consumer Products Division. Thus, the Industrial/Construction Division was able to take advantage of the economies of scale being produced in the factories of the Consumer Products Division. Specifically, the construction type of product continued to be sold through a distribution channel intermediary now called "Industrial Distributors" that also included a new variety of business that served construction contractors directly. These new distributors were unlike the traditional mill supply houses in that they were considerably smaller and catered to a construction contractor rather than to the traditional plant engineer or plant maintenance manager.

The growth of the construction products portion of the Industrial/ Construction Division propelled the division to impressive new heights. The company viewed its traditional industrial products as slow growth areas. The traditional products were now characterized by very cyclical and low growth rates. The construction products were viewed differently; their rate of sale growth was twice the rate of growth of similar industrial products.

The Development of New Products

The growth of the Consumer Products Division was visible to the public, which drove the price of the company's common stock to new highs. What was not as visible, although it was quite profitable, was the growth of new products in the Industrial/Construction Division. A variety of improvements upon existing products was made in addition to the introduction of completely new products. The division was well able to market these new products, often at a considerable profit. The circular saw was developed specifically for the Consumer Products Division, but it could be improved on and added to so as to make it a high-quality construction device.

In addition, the division prided itself on being a broad line manufacturer. It offered a variety of alternative tools in terms of size, quality, and performance. The division offered utility-duty products, heavy-duty products, and super-duty products. As an example, the division offered one-fourth inch, three-eighths inch, five-sixteenths inch, half-inch, one-inch, and larger sizes of drills. It offered end handle drills, pistol grip drills, right angle drills, all insulated drills, and others.

The concept of driving a screw with a drill evolved as part of the development of the drill line. This led to the development of the electrically driven power screwdriver, which was essentially a drill with a chuck that was designed to hold a screw and then drive it into the material. This product development was quickly found to be popular, and soon the other major manufacturers of power tools were eager to enter the market. The product exhibited all the attributes of the life-cycle curve. Only recently had the annual rate of growth begun to taper, and, in fact, the sales of this product by Power Tools, Inc., recently started a rapid decline.

Electric Screwdrivers Today

The total United States demand for electric screwdrivers was approaching $17 million per year. Because it viewed itself as the pioneer in the electric screwdriver business, Power Tools, Inc., was perplexed and annoyed by its present situation in that business. Several salient facts that had been gathered and are presented as Exhibit 1

EXHIBIT 1 Pertinent Data on Electric Screwdrivers

Total U.S. Market Size		
	$ Millions	Units (000)
1970/71	$ 6.1	87.5
1974	$10.4	146.7
Latest year	$16.6	188.0

U.S. Power Tool Market as a Per Cent of U.S. Total Tool Market ($)	
1970/71	13%
1974	17%
Latest year	20%

Company Share of Electric Screwdrivers Market ($)	
1970/71	32%
1974	24%
Latest year	13%

Makita Share of Electric Screwdrivers Market ($)	
1970/71	NA
1974	NA
Latest year	8%

seemed to portend danger to the company's valued and profitable line of electric screwdrivers. These products were manufactured in the company's oldest plant, which was located in the East.

The Influx of Domestic Competition

The concept of the electric screwdriver flowered in the late 1960s and was further developed throughout the 1970s. The fundamental economic strength of this product concept was the labor-saving aspect. Parallel to the labor-saving aspect were the many useful refinements and variations of the basic product. Depth-sensitive models, models with adjustable clutches, models with reversing features, and other variations were developed to serve specific market segments. However, no sooner had Power Tools, Inc., developed a new advance than a competitor would copy the idea and enter the market. This was possible because any manufacturer of a drill could convert it to a screwdriver by modifying the front end of the drill to accommodate the screwdriver attachments. Soon Power Tools, Inc., noticed that it had many competitors in the sale of electric screwdrivers.

This pattern of events led to a corresponding decline in the firm's market share. In the early years this organization had dominated the market, holding about a two-thirds share. As time had passed, its share had slipped gradually to 24 per cent in 1974 and an estimated 13 per cent currently. In a recent general sales slump, the electric screwdriver market declined as badly as, or worse than, other sectors of the power tool business. Sales of the product then increased but did not recover to quite the preslump level.

The Influx of Foreign Competition

During the late 1970s the firm was intensely bothered by the aggressive new efforts of Japanese manufacturers in the screwdriver market. The introduction of the Makita brand of power tools was especially noteworthy. This line of power tools was offered for sale in the United States at prices that were well below the general price level. Power Tools, Inc., viewed the quality of the Makita power tools as being commensurate with their price.

In recent years the Makita Company added insult to injury by announcing its intention to commence manufacturing at a West Coast facility that it proposed to finance in the United States. The total bond offering was made for $60 million and the plant was built. This new facility was soon to come on line. Power Tools, Inc., estimated that a majority of the new Makita plant's output would be electric screwdrivers that would compete directly with the company's own screwdrivers.

Advise Power Tools, Inc.

McILHENNY COMPANY—PRODUCERS OF TABASCO BRAND PRODUCTS

McIlhenny Company, located on Avery Island in the Louisiana coastal marshes about seven miles south of the town of New Iberia, manufactured two products. One was very old and extremely well known around the world and the other was a much later addition. The first was Tabasco Brand Pepper Sauce, introduced in 1868, and the other was Tabasco Brand Bloody Mary Mix, introduced more than 100 years later in 1972.

The key ingredient in the two products was the red pepper, known more technically as the *capsicum frutescens*. Ranging from three to four feet in height, this plant is a genus of the *Solanaceae* (nightshade) family. Its pungent flavored fruit is known as *tabasco pepper*, a varietal name. Cayenne pepper is a distinct variety not to be confused with *tabasco pepper*. Some species of this plant are bushy in appearance and are cultivated in tropical and subtropical regions. It is native only to the Western Hemisphere. Under its Central American and Mexican name, chili, the fruit was widely used in various sauces and to some extent as a flavoring in pickled foods.

The McIlhenny Company took great interest and pride in *capsicum*. The Indians of Central America and southern Mexico domesticated this plant around 2500 B.C. and used it widely as a seasoning for their diet of corn, squash, tomatoes, fish, and game. A friend of the founder of the present company brought back some of the seeds from Mexico following the Mexican-American War of 1848. By the late 1850s Edmund McIlhenny was growing *capsicum* plants in his vegetable garden on Avery Island. The company and the family worked for the next 130 years on improving the *capsicum* plant. Family members constantly involved themselves in selecting seed peppers for each new crop, and no outside pepper contaminated the strain in all those years. Botanists recognized the present plant as a distinct variety.

Until recently all the peppers used in the company's production had been grown on Avery Island, and 40 per cent of the peppers were still grown there. With the advent of federal and state unemployment compensation, food stamps, and many other welfare benefits, agricultural labor became increasingly difficult to obtain. Beginning in the early 1970s pepper crops brought to maturity could not be harvested because of a lack of agricultural labor.

The company started raising peppers in Mexico, Guatemala, Honduras, Colombia, and Venezuela. The seeds for all foreign-grown peppers were supplied by McIlhenny Company and no peppers were ever purchased on the open market. Some of the foreign peppers were propagated by contract under supervision of McIlhenny field people. In some instances the company leased land and raised the crop itself. The foreign-grown peppers were shipped to Avery Island for curing and aging as soon as their condition permitted transportation.

After the picked peppers were ground up they were steeped in their own juices in large white oak reusable casks that were similar to whiskey barrels. A wooden cover with tiny holes drilled through it was placed on top of each cask. Next, a thick layer of salt from the company's Avery Island salt mine was spread over the cover. This salt seal allowed the actual vapors of fermentation to escape and at the same time prevented fresh air from ever entering the barrel. This mash had to be aged for three warm seasons of fermentation and strengthening. These seasons might be three summers or two summers and a warm spring. The company president personally inspected every single barrel for both smell and taste before releasing it for mixing with 100 grain vinegar and salt. Approximately 30 per cent mash was combined with 60 per cent vinegar and 10 per cent salt and the resulting mixture was stirred constantly for about a month. Then the remaining pieces of pepper seeds and skins were screened out of the sauce. The seeds and skins, called "chaff" after drying, were sold to unaffiliated organizations that steamed them to obtain oil of capsaicin, the stinging material in Ben-Gay balm, "red hot" candies, and other products.

Tabasco brand pepper sauce was also made abroad. The first foreign production was in London, which was soon followed by production in Montreal. Mexico City, Caracas, and Madrid production operations were added later. However, the pepper mash used in these foreign operations was made on Avery Island and shipped abroad. All in all, approximately 55 million bottles were sold in 125 countries annually. Some foreign production was under licensing agreements and some was under partnership agreements. However, in every case it was required that samples of the finished sauce be submitted periodically to Avery Island for examination and approval. Foreign sales accounted for about 40 per cent of total sales and the percentage was rising.

McIlhenny Company distributed Tabasco Sauce and its newer product, Tabasco Brand Bloody Mary Mix, in the United States civilian market through food brokers. The personal selling effort was under the supervision of regional sales managers who were directed by a national sales manager. Military food brokers were used for the military segment of demand. The regular two-fluid-ounce container of Tabasco pepper sauce was supplemented by the development of a twelve-fluid-ounce size for restaurant chefs and a 128-fluid-ounce size for food manufacturers.

The company president, Walter Stauffer McIlhenny, thought that the company would aim toward further product diversification. He explained his thoughts in the following manner:

> We are constantly considering the addition of new products and have reviewed hundreds of suggestions. Obviously our prime purpose in adding a new product is to increase our profit. An important second consideration is that your account with your broker becomes more important with two or more items bringing greater revenues into his office. Accordingly the manufacturer is then in a position to command more effort from the brokers' retail force and their management team as well.

The advertising medium used for the pepper sauce was magazines, both consumer-type publications and those directed to restaurants and distributors. Among those selected in the latter category were *Food Service Marketing*, *Restaurant Business*, and *Institutions/ Volume Feeding Management*. For the Bloody Mary mix the choice was basically the same, although a small amount of newspaper advertising was also placed. For both products consumer magazines were emphasized. For sales purposes the planning unit was one dozen. The advertising allocation for pepper sauce was 40 cents per dozen, a figure that had not varied for the past twenty years. Of course, as physical sales volumes had grown so had the total advertising budget.

The name Tabasco and the familiar diamond-shaped label were protected by a U.S. Patent Office trademark registration at an early date. Nevertheless, much litigation was required to combat firms that attempted copies or near copies of the famous name and marks. McIlhenny Company succeeded in confirming its exclusive rights to the name, the diamond label, and the color pattern of the packaging.

The "Bloody Mary" was one of the two or three most popular alcoholic mixed drinks in the United States. Apparently an American creation and still strongly identified with the United States abroad, it surfaced in the mid-1930s. The Bloody Mary was popular in its own right but also acquired a reputation within a few years as an antidote to hangovers. In the United States well over half of all vodka, the top selling distilled spirit, went into this type of beverage. Recipes for Bloody Marys varied, of course, as to stirring or shaking, serving with ice cubes or strained, ratios of ingredients, and the use of additives such as a sprig of mint or a wedge of lime. What is more, product spin-offs had developed, including the Bloody Maria, made with tequila instead of vodka; the Danish Mary, made with aquavit instead of vodka; the Bull Shot, in which beef bouillon replaced tomato juice; and the Bloody Bull Shot, half tomato juice and half beef bouillon. However, virtually everyone included Tabasco Sauce and Worcestershire sauce with the spirits and juice or bouillon. Some people were purists and refused to use prepared mixes, but their numbers were apparently decreasing.

Over a period of years, Tabasco Brand Bloody Mary Mix achieved nationwide but somewhat spotty distribution. First a six-fluid-ounce can with an easy-open flip top was introduced, and later a twelve-fluid-ounce version in the same sort of can was brought out. Still later a thirty-fluid-ounce clear glass bottle with a screw-type lid was introduced. The most common price at retail for the first product was two for 69 cents, whereas for the second and third products the most common figures were 59 cents and $1.29, respectively. The ingredients were listed on the containers in the following order: concentrated tomato juice, water, fresh frozen concentrated lime juice, Worcestershire sauce, salt, and Tabasco pepper sauce.

McIlhenny Company had never experienced a product failure, but it had dropped two items many years before. In the early 1900s the firm operated a successful oyster canning plant. However, when the pressures of the Mississippi River at New Orleans began to pose a continuing threat to the city and the United States Army Corps of Engineers permanently diverted some of the water into the Atchafalaya Basin, the nearby oyster beds became muddy and could not survive. In addition, for a good many years McIlhenny packed green Tabasco peppers in vinegar under the label Island Pride peppers-in-vinegar. However, rising sales of the pepper sauce, which required ripened peppers, forced withdrawal of this item from the market.

Besides the pepper sauce and Bloody Mary mix, the McIlhenny family had other business interests. They owned but leased the island salt mine to International Salt Company of Clarks Summit, Pennsylvania, which produced Sterling brand salt. Exxon Company produced oil on, and adjacent to, the island. Moreover, the family of Edward A. McIlhenny operated Jungle Gardens, a 200-acre area that was devoted to natural vegetation, botanical exhibits, and Bird City, a noted refuge. McIlhenny Company, of course, continued to be owned by the descendants of Edmund McIlhenny and his wife Mary Eliza Avery McIlhenny, whose grandfather had first acquired the property.

Further Background on the McIlhenny Organization and Avery Island

McIlhenny Company was started in 1868 by Edmund McIlhenny, a former New Orleans banker and grandfather of the present head of the enterprise, Walter S. McIlhenny. However, Edmund's father-in-law, Judge Daniel Dudley Avery of Baton Rouge, had acquired the island on which the business was located many years earlier. And Avery's father-in-law, John Craig Marsh, had acquired partial ownership in 1818. At the time of the case younger men of the family had also entered the management, so six generations of the extended family had been involved in the island's economic activities. Known earlier by the names of E. McIlhenny and E. McIlhenny Sons, the organization was renamed McIlhenny Company in 1907.

Geologists do not consider Avery Island, once called Petite Anse (little handle), a real island. Yet it appears to be one, set as it is among a great expanse of marshes, swamps, and bayous about six miles from Vermillion Bay. Rising 152 feet above sea level, this island is really a column of solid salt about ten miles deep over which there is a cap of rich soil. Part of the island is covered with subtropical forest.

Indians produced salt on the island in early times. In the late 1700s John Hayes rediscovered the long-abandoned brine springs and began producing salt. Because of a rise in demand occasioned by the need for salt in making munitions for the War of 1812, the salt works were expanded. However, after that war foreign competitors nearly put the salt operation out of business and the island's economy turned to the growing of sugar cane. Demand for salt again surged at the opening of the Civil War in 1861. John Marsh Avery, son of Daniel Dudley Avery, then re-established the island's salt industry, which quickly became the principal salt supplier to the Confederacy. In expanding the salt works Avery made the first discovery of rock salt on the North American continent. Admiral David Farragut of the Union Navy shelled the facility in 1862 in an unsuccessful attempt to halt company operations. In April 1863 a Union land force under General Banks attacked and destroyed the company's facilities. The family had to flee to San Antonio, Texas, for safety and to live with relatives. They could not return for over three years, during which time their rich plantation land and crops suffered from neglect.

The hardy pepper plants survived the years of neglect. With the salt business in ruins and food supplies monotonous in the post-Civil War period, gourmet Edmund McIlhenny had both the time and the inclination to experiment with recipes. He began experimenting with various ways of making a piquant yet pleasing pepper sauce. He refined the basic methods for making the sauce, which was to crush the peppers, thus making a mash, then straining the mash, and adding salt and vinegar. The resulting aromatic mixture was then put into wooden barrels to age, so that the flavors and fragrances could steep and intermingle. McIlhenny let friends taste the concoction and found that they liked it. In 1868 he processed enough sauce for 350 bottles and sent the entire output as free samples to a selected group of wholesalers. In 1869 he received his first order for the sauce, which was assigned a wholesauce price of $1 per bottle. Always highly conscious of spices and condiments, Europeans also accepted the new product. Like many other companies of the coastal South, McIlhenny was international in its outlook and opened an office in London in 1872.

Edmund McIlhenny died in 1890 and was succeeded by his son John Avery McIlhenny. Some members of the family were interested in the island's salt deposit. A firm called Chouteau and Price sank a shaft 90 feet deep in 1867 but abandoned operations in 1870. The American Salt Company and the family agreed on a lease in 1880 and the lessee began producing large quantities of salt, using the early shaft.

Transportation of the salt had always been a severe problem and promised to be so for the new product. Three alternatives were tried and all failed: a causeway running north toward New Iberia; an embankment and tramway to Bayou Petite Anse; and a canal to Vermillion Bay. In 1883 railway service from New Orleans to the West was inaugurated and in 1886 a branch was opened from New Iberia south to the island, thus solving the problem. By this time the New Iberia Salt Company had taken over the salt operations. In 1898 the family organized its own Avery Rock Salt Mining Company, which sank a new shaft, still in use, to a depth of 518 feet. The mining operation was put in the hands of Sidney Bradford, an engineer married to Edmund's daughter Marigold.

During the 1890s Avery Island became established as an important wildlife refuge. Edmund's second son, Edward (Ned) Avery McIlhenny, became a naturalist who made several scientific expeditions to the Arctic. Edward McIlhenny became alarmed that the snowy egret, a beautiful white heron native to the Louisiana swamps, was rapidly declining in number and faced extinction. This bird had been slaughtered by hunters who wanted a few special plumes for use in women's hats. After a long search Ned found egret chicks, which he took back to Avery Island and successfully raised. Counting on a trait found in some birds he released them in the late fall for their natural migration south across the Gulf of Mexico. In the spring, six of the birds returned to him to form the nucleus of the island's large bird colony called Bird City. Thereafter the company continued to show extraordinary interest in ecology and conservation.

In 1906 John McIlhenny was appointed a U.S. Civil Service commissioner and turned the firm over to his brother Ned, who served as president of the company for the next forty years. Ned wrote several books and many magazine articles on the topics of egrets, alligators, wild turkeys, and folk music. He personally banded 189,289 birds in order to accumulate data to study their migratory routes. Despite Ned's other interests, sales of Tabasco Sauce continued to rise during his long administration. He worked well with his brother Rufus, who took on some of the management burden in the later years.

Rufus died in 1940, at which time the company called in Walter Stauffer McIlhenny, the son of John McIlhenny and nephew of Ned, to participate in the management. However, World War II intervened and Walter McIlhenny, a Marine Corps reserve officer, went on active duty. Ned suffered a stroke and Walter succeeded him in 1949. Walter's interest in the corps continued and he rose in the Reserve to the rank of Brigadier General. He modernized the Tabasco production line with up-to-date filling and labeling equipment but retained the picturesque, atmospheric buildings. He selected a new advertising agency, hired the company's first national sales manager, and expanded company interests abroad.

Humble Oil brought in an oil well at the edge of the island in 1942, and in a few years there was an extensive field. Although oil was a severe potential threat to the island's ecology, the problem was solved in a variety of ways, such as by burying the pipelines, bypassing certain trees, and filling and sodding over pits.

APPENDIX TO McILHENNY COMPANY

Principal Competitors of Tabasco Brand Bloody Mary Mix

There were several noteworthy competitors of McIlhenny's new Bloody Mary mix, All of them were nonalcoholic, as was the McIlhenny entry. Selected information about the competitive products follows:

1. Holland House Bloody Mary Cocktail Mix, made by Holland House Brands Company, Ridgefield, New Jersey, a division of National Distillers. This organization had a line of drink mixes, which included Manhattan, Screwdriver, Side Car, Tom Collins, Whiskey

Sour, Daiquiri, Pink Squirrel, and eighteen others, including a low-calorie version of the popular Whiskey Sour. A few of these products, including the Bloody Mary, were available in both liquid and instant dry mixes. However, the Screwdriver, Pink Squirrel, Love Bird, Grasshopper, Wallbanger, Tequila Sunrise, and Vodka (White) Sour were only availabe in an instant dry mix.

This brand of Bloody Mary mix was offered in three variations. The first was Regular, which was designed and promoted to be a traditional Bloody Mary, whereas the second was Extra Tangy, "the traditional Bloody Mary with extra zesty flavor." The third was Smooth Ń' Spicy, "a unique flavor system consistent with contemporary taste preferences; a welcome change of pace from the traditional." These three mixes were promoted on the label as "skillful blends of choice ingredients backed by experience that dates back to 1887." The traditional version from Holland House included tomato juice from tomato juice concentrate, lemon juice concentrate, natural flavors, salt, citric acid, monosodium glutamate, calcium carrageenan, hydrolyzed vegetable protein, iso-ascorbic acid, spice extractives, and less than 0.1 per cent each of sodium benzoate and sodium metabisulfite as preservatives. This brand was offered at a prevailing retail price of $1.09 in a twenty-four-fluid-ounce clear bottle with a screw-type lid. It was also offered in a six-fluid-ounce can at a prevailing price of 35 cents. Both the regular and extra tangy versions were available in such cans. At first the can had a solid top, but it was replaced by the easy-open flip top in 1978. Holland House Smooth N' Spicy was also available in a thirty-two-fluid-ounce (one quart) clear glass bottle with a screw-type lid at a prevailing price of $1.30.

2. Snap-E-Tom, made by Heublein, Inc., Hartford, Connecticut. Heublein made several other mixes, such as the Hereford's Cows series. Snap-E-Tom had the following ingredients: water, tomato paste, green chilies, salt, onion, and citric acid. It was available as a single pack and a three-pack. The can had a solid top and contained six fluid ounces. The prevailing retail prices were 27 cents and 79 cents, respectively. Because Heublein had just introduced a bottled whiskey sour that contained the alcohol, many industry observers were watching to see if later there would be a bottled Bloody Mary that contained the vodka.

3. Libby's Bloody Mary Mix, made by Libby, McNeill, & Libby, Chicago. This product had the following ingredients: water, tomato paste, cider and distilled vinegar, salt, spices, dextrose, hydrolyzed vegetable protein, citric acid, onion powder, jalapeno peppers, soy sauce solids and dextrans, flavorings, sugar, monosodium glutamate, garlic powder, caramel color, and hydrogenated vegetable oils. It was

offered only in a five-and-a-half-fluid-ounce can with an easy-open flip top, which was shipped and displayed as a six-pack. The prevailing price at retail was $1.25 per six-pack. Some retailers were willing to sell an individual can removed from the six-pack at a prevailing price of 21 cents.

4. Schweppes Bloody Mary Mixer, made by Schweppes U.S.A., Ltd., Stamford, Connecticut. This product had the following ingredients: concentrated tomato juice, water, Worcestershire sauce, lemon juice, vinegar, sucrose, citric acid, salt, red pepper, celery salt, black pepper, carrageenan. It was available in a twenty-five-fluid-ounce clear glass bottle with a screw-type lid at a prevailing price of 95 cents. This product was also offered in a four-fluid-ounce clear glass bottle in a three-pack at a prevailing retail price of $1.05. Some retailers were willing to break the three-pack and sell an individual bottle at 35 cents.

5. Mr and Mrs "T" Bloody Mary Mix, made by Mr. and Mrs. T. Products, a division of Taylor Food Products, Inc., El Segundo, California. This product had the following ingredients: water, tomato paste, concentrated tomato juice, vinegar, salt, sugar, invert sugar, dried onion, concentrated lemon juice, Worcestershire sauce, artificial flavor, spices, potassium sorbate and sodium benzoate as preservatives, and dry garlic. It was available as a single pack and consisted of a six-fluid-ounce can with an easy-open flip-type top. The prevailing price at retail was two for 65 cents. This brand was available also in a twenty-four-fluid-ounce size in a clear glass bottle with a screw-type lid at a prevailing price of 99 cents.

6. Heinz Bloody Mary Mix, made by H. J. Heinz Company, Pittsburgh, Pennsylvania. This product had the following ingredients: tomatoes, water, vinegar, corn sweetener, salt, concentrated lemon juice, hydrolyzed vegetable protein (with disodium inosinate, disodium guanylate), potassium sorbate as a preservative, molasses, spices, natural flavoring, anchovies, and onion powder. It was available in a thirty-two-fluid-ounce clear glass bottle with a screw-type lid. The prevailing price was $1.55.

7. Angostura Bloody Merry-Maker, made by A-W Brands, Inc., Carteret, New Jersey, a subsidiary of Iroquois Brands, Ltd., under license from Angostura, International, Ltd., Toronto, Canada. This product had the following ingredients: Worcestershire sauce, Angostura aromatic bitters, red pepper sauce, salt, celery flavoring, natural lemon flavor, and 0.1 per cent sodium benzoate as a preservative. It was available only in an eight-fluid-ounce clear glass bottle with a screw-type lid at a prevailing retail price of $1.59. This product was added in small amounts, usually three to five dashes, to vodka and plain tomato juice.

8. V-8 Spicy Hot Vegetable Juice Cocktail, made by Campbell's Soup Company, Camden, New Jersey. This product was being promoted both as an appetizer and as a mixer for alcoholic drinks. The ingredients were water, tomato concentrate, concentrated juices of carrots, celery, beets, parsley, lettuce, watercress, and spinach, with salt, ascorbic acid (vitamin C), natural flavoring, and citric acid. It was available only in a six-fluid-ounce can with an easy-open flip top, and these cans were in a six-pack. The prevailing retail price was $1.09 per six-pack. Some retailers were willing to sell an individual can at a prevailing price of 19 cents.

9. Steero Bloody Mary Cocktail Mix, made by American Kitchen Products Company, Jersey City, New Jersey. This product had the following ingredients: tomato juice, water, lemon juice, Worcestershire sauce, salt, sugar, and spices. It was offered in an eight-fluid-ounce can with a solid top at a prevailing retail of 39 cents. This company had just introduced a closely related product, Bullshot Cocktail Mix, which contained the following ingredients: water, tomato paste, monosodium glutamate, lemon juice, salt, citric acid, sugar, beef extract, caramel color, natural and artificial flavorings, spices, and Worcestershire sauce. This product was offered in an eight-fluid-ounce can with a solid top at a prevailing retail price of 43 cents.

In addition, three other brands should be acknowledged. Master's Mix Bloody Mary Mix, made by several companies under licenses from Professional Mixers, Inc., a Sacramento, California, firm, was available in a 25.6-fluid-ounce clear glass bottle with a screw-type lid. There was variation, but the prevailing retail price was about $1.39.

Schweppe's U.S.A., Ltd., was beginning to distribute Rose's Bloody Mary Mix under license from L. Rose and Company, Ltd. Both Schweppes and Rose were British organizations. Policies on package sizes and preferred prices were not completely settled yet. It appeared certain that Rose's would be in a twenty-four-fluid-ounce clear glass bottle with a screw-type lid and the retail price would be relatively high. Promotion as a prestige product was likely.

Sacramento Tomato Plus Vegetable Cocktail, made by Borden, Inc., New York City, had recently moved from western to national distribution. It was made of the following ingredients: water, tomato paste, salt, dried chili pepper, ground celery seed, dehydrated onion, powdered onion, ascorbic acid (vitamin C), natural flavorings, and spices. Although this product was now being promoted as a self-contained beverage, observers considered it probable that the product would later be promoted as a mixer for vodka, gin, and aquavit. It was offered in a five-and-a-half-fluid-ounce can, and these were in a six-pack. The prevailing retail price was 99 cents. Some retailers were willing to sell an individual can removed from the pack at a prevailing retail price of 17 cents. This product was also available in a forty-six-fluid-ounce can with a solid top at a prevailing retail price of 81 cents.

Advise the McIlhenny Company.

DURAFASHION KITCHEN UTENSILS

Durafashion Kitchen Utensils was one of the largest producers of kitchen utensils in the United States. From the founding of the firm until the middle 1960s, new products had come from a process that might be described as ad hoc. A person or persons had an idea for a product and suggested it. If the idea survived the criticism and was aggressively backed by its proponents, it was eventually accepted by top management and added to the product line. Such ideas had come from customers and potential customers and within the firm from salesmen, industrial engineers, the product repair department, and the purchasing department. One time there had been a valuable suggestion from a secretary and another time the suggestion had come from the advertising agency serving Durafashion. The company had tried to instill in all employees a sense of duty to constantly monitor the product line with the objective of suggesting logical additions.

In the middle 1960s a new products committee was established to consider new product development. At first the group met each time that enough suggestions had accumulated to warrant a meeting. Later it adopted a periodic meeting schedule of once every three months. Several years later it changed to a meeting every sixty days. The new products committee was composed of a person from production (usually an engineer), one from the finance and accounting office, one from purchasing, one from sales, and the marketing research director.

If this committee was impressed favorably with the idea, it might ask the marketing research director to conduct a commercial feasibility study. It might also ask the engineers to study physical feasibility, or both studies might be requested. Based on the outcome of these studies, the committee either recommended to the company president, Roy Bannerman, that the product be added to the line or it recommended that the work on the idea be abandoned. By this time, of course, the idea was termed a project. Most people in the company seemed to be pleased that this approach to new product development was more systematic, objective, open-minded, and thorough than the old ad hoc approach had been. Using this new approach to the development of products, Durafashion Kitchen Utensils Company had doubled the length of its product line, and annual sales had risen from $8,030,000 in the middle 1960s to a current figure of $13,100,000. Profits had risen by 59 percent in the same period of time.

About a year ago several new people were appointed to the new products committee but from the same organizational units that had always staffed the committee. The new marketing research director, Todd Lewis, was one of the new persons. Moreover, he was appointed

EXHIBIT 1 Number of Items in Product Line of Durafashion Kitchen Utensils Company

	1965	At Present
Canisters	4	11
Trivets	4	6
Colanders	1	2
Teakettles	2	6
Gelatin molds	3	7
Manual can openers	2	3
Cookie cutters	6	6
Fruit and vegetable presses	0	1
Timers	1	4
Manual juicer-grinders	0	1
Measuring spoons	2	2
Fondue pots	0	2
Spice racks	0	2
Cheese boards	0	3
Noodle rollers	0	1
Towel racks	2	2
Capper-corkers	0	1
Napkin holders	1	1
Butcher knives	2	3
Paring knives	4	5
Weighing scales	0	2
Spoons	3	5
Spatulas	2	6
Cookware		
Saucepans	3	6
Dutch ovens	1	2
Skillets	3	8
Double boilers	1	2
Egg poachers	1	1
Stock pots	1	2
Muffin pans	0	1
	49	104

chairman of the committee by the president of the corporation, whereas previously the committee had chosen its own chairman. Lewis immediately entered into negotiations with a commercial designer and stylist and after a few weeks entered into a twelve-month contract with him. These actions surprised most people in the company. Subsequently, it became common knowledge that Lewis had secured the permission of Bannerman before talking with the outside designer and again before signing the contract. This association with the outside designer had created some hostility for Lewis in the company, and even a little from the committee. It created even more skepticism and tension than hostility. However, before the year had passed, it became apparent that the outsider had supplied some valuable ideas and had modified some Durafashion employees' ideas to the point that commercial prospects were excellent for two new products and two redesigned old products. The total cost to Durafashion for the outside designer's services was $30,000.

The marketing research department continued to have ample amounts of work. As always, its work load was erratic. Hence, it utilized several outside consultants from time to time and the services of companies that supplied personal interviewers, clerks, and stenographers, and, of course, computer programming and computer time. The marketing research department consisted of Lewis, another professional, a clerk, and a secretary.

Lewis had introduced additional uncertainty by asserting that products have a life cycle and that the manufacturer benefits to a different extent and incurs different costs in the various parts of the product's life cycle. The prevailing sentiment in the company and among its competitors had always been that once in the line products remained indefinitely or until they showed a sustained period of unprofitable sale. Systematic reevaluation of the entire product line and every component in it had been adopted at a few firms in other industries.[1] Many people thought that this policy led to premature abandonment of products, premature redesign of products, and an emphasis on extremely minor modifications. They argued that in a resource-conscious society waste, whether on an assembly line or in the design of products, could be unpopular and even damaging to

---

[1] For example, see Conrad Berenson, "Pruning the Product Line," *Business Horizons*, 6 (Summer 1963), pp. 62-72; Philip Kotler, "Phasing Out Weak Products," *Harvard Business Review*, 43 (March–April 1965), p. 109; James T. Rothe, "The Product Elimination Decision," *MSU Business Topics*, 18 (Autumn 1970), pp. 45-51; Paul W. Hamelman and Edward M. Mazze, "Improving Product Abandonment Decisions," *Journal of Marketing*, 36 (April 1972), pp. 20-26; Gary M. Armstrong, "Comments on the Hamelman-Masse Model for Product Abandonment Decisions," *Journal of Marketing*, 37 (October 1973), pp. 75-77.

a corporate image. However, proponents of the idea argued vigorously that efficiency was served when an organization gave none of its products the benefit of the doubt. Where the societal environment for product innovation was evolving was unclear. It had long been thought that American society was receptive and sympathetic to change, and that perhaps change itself represented a form of utility to the American consumer.

Within Durafashion the production manager, Dale Redding, voiced some reservations about Lewis and his proposals. He noted the possibility of shorter production runs, new or more frequently modified tooling and dies, and the discomfort and fatigue of frequent change of duties on production workers. He also noted that published research has shown that one may find only one or two commercially feasible ideas out of every 500 ideas that were formally studied.

Todd Lewis also proposed a new products department consisting of a permanent staff including at least the following: a chemist, a metallurgist, a home economist, a cost accountant, and a marketing researcher. The proposed unit would have extensive laboratories. Lewis's estimate of the capital investment required for such laboratories was $120,000. He said that there should be a standing liaison committee made up of people from all over the company who would serve fixed terms to ensure accurate and timely communications with the new products department. According to his recommendation, product suggestions could still come from anywhere but would flow to the new products department for physical research, cost research,

EXHIBIT 2 Organization Structure of Durafashion

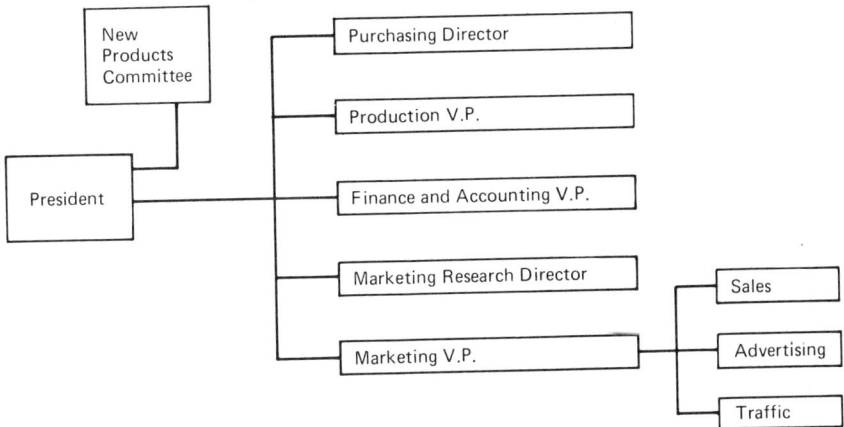

EXHIBIT 3 Current Balance Sheet, Durafashion Kitchen Utensils Company

Current Assets		
Cash		$ 27,240
U.S. government securities		19,000
Amounts due from customers	$351,200	
Less estimated uncollectables	1,756	349,444
Inventories		
Raw materials, operating supplies, and goods in process	$476,781	
Finished goods	441,858	918,639
Other current assets		4,300
		$1,318,623
Current Liabilities		
Notes payable to banks		15,000
Accounts payable		401,310
Taxes payable		46,401
Other		3,009
		$ 465,720
Property, Plant, and Equipment		
Total cost	$290,410	
Cost applied to past operations	145,305	145,105
Common stock		250,000
Reinvestment of profits		748,008

and preliminary market feasibility studies. If they survived these types of investigation, the suggestions would go to the marketing research department for final commercial evaluation and perhaps a test market. If they survived again, they would proceed to the company president for his approval.

Advise Durafashion Kitchen Utensils Company.

ST. TERESA'S SCHOOL FOR GIRLS

St. Teresa's School for Girls had been in continuous operation in a large city in the South since 1850. It had opened a branch, St. Elizabeth's School for Girls, about eighty miles away in a smaller city in 1880. The schools were owned by the Sisters of St. Emilie, who had sent a band of ten nuns from France in 1849 to open an American branch of the order. To support themselves the sisters opened a bilingual twelve-year boarding and day school for girls and on the same grounds ran a free school for poor boys ages five to eleven.

The order of St. Emilie was rather small but vigorous, having about

400 members in France, Italy, and Switzerland. The European branch was engaged in teaching the deaf and mute, managing two hospitals for the insane, operating four boarding schools for girls, and doing social work in many poor parishes. Over a period of 100 years the American branch grew to 350 members and was divided into three "Provinces," or jurisdictions, Northwest, Middle West, and Southern. Ultimate administrative control remained with the mother house in Marseilles, although each province had a head nun known as the mother provincial. The Southern United States group ultimately restricted itself completely to the teaching of middle- and upper-class children, in grades one through twelve in Catholic private and parochial schools. St. Teresa's elementary school division and the school for poor boys were closed in 1928. The Middle West branch went into both the teaching of girls and the operation of homes for working girls in large cities. The Northwest branch restricted itself to high schools for girls. The American establishments prospered to the extent that they subsidized the European endeavors financially and furnished the full support of a very small branch in West Africa, which opened in 1950.

The Catholic school system in the diocese[1] in which St. Teresa's School was located was extensive and diversified. Each parish maintained an elementary school. The tuition for church members was usually about $20 per month for the first child, whereas rates decreased for additional children from the same household simultaneously enrolled. The diocese as a whole maintained four high schools, two for boys and two for girls. The tuition for these institutions was usually about $40 per month for the first child and decreasing rates for additional children simultaneously enrolled. They were open to any student of the diocese, regardless of academic ability. The diocese also played host to a number of male and female religious orders who practiced a variety of good works, including the operation of hospitals, orphanages, a home for unwed mothers, a school for the deaf and mute, a four-year college, a university, and a number of private[2] schools somewhat more exclusive than those owned by the parishes and the diocese. These institutions sought to

---

[1] The Catholic Church in the United States is organized into parishes on the lowest level. A number of parishes makes up a diocese, which is presided over by a bishop. The bishop reports to a representative of the Pope. All Catholic persons conducting religious work within the boundaries of a diocese are required to have the approval of the presiding bishop.

[2] The schools were commonly classified by ownership. A school owned by a parish was called a parochial school and was open to all parish members. A school owned by the diocese (high schools and special education facilities) was called diocesan and open to all residents of the diocese. A school owned by a religious order was called private and was in fact run similarly to nonsectarian private schools except for the teaching of religion. The private Catholic schools were profit-making ventures on the part of their owners. Profits gained from these private schools were used to offset losses from other charitable works, making each religious order technically nonprofit in its consolidated financial statements.

earn a profit for their religious order-owners, who spent the profits for other endeavors that were not self-supporting. These schools were under the general supervision of the bishop of the diocese but were not financially accountable to him. Occasionally the bishop would give some aid to a financially distressed religious order in some endeavor. All the religious orders reported to their "generals" usually located elsewhere, for some as far away as Europe.

At this time there were six private high schools for girls in the city, each run by a different religious order of women. St. Mary's was the oldest of these schools and had from its earliest existence functioned as a boarding school for girls of high social status. St. Mary's was located in a well-preserved residential area close to the downtown business district. Most of the homes in this area were large and well over 125 years old. Holy Spirit Academy and St. Margaret's Academy were both located just a little farther out in a middle- and upper-middle-class area dating back more than 100 years. Mt. St. Agnes, a relatively new school only about thirty years old in the far northern portion of the city, operated a large middle- to upper-class development that sprang up as the city grew in that direction. In the oldest part of the city, where the first settlements were made, and in its immediately adjoining neighborhoods were located St. Teresa's and the Academy of the Holy Child. Because of the ethnic and socioeconomic characteristics of the immediate neighborhood in which it originally was set up, St. Teresa's had an enrollment that came from middle-class families engaged mostly in trade and lucrative blue-collar occupations. It never acquired the exclusive image of its competitors with the local people but was nevertheless highly successful. It was, however, extremely popular with upper-class girls from Central and South America. In some years 80 per cent of the boarding students were of this type. Oddly enough, the branch of St. Teresa's in the smaller city about eighty miles distant, because it was the first private school for girls in that city, became quite exclusive but remained smaller than the parent location. All of the schools mentioned previously catered to white students, the Catholic school system in nearly all of the South being racially segregated at that time.

In 1961, because of the deterioration of the neighborhood, St. Teresa's relocated from its historic and charming old buildings to a modern plant on the far north side in a neighborhood of upper-middle-class homes. The parcel of land was a gift from the bishop. The sisters did not provide for boarding students in the new facility. At the time that the plans were drawn for the new buildings, middle- and upper-class rural Catholic girls were no longer routinely boarded at city schools, as had been the tradition of the area in the past, but often attended Catholic or public schools in their hometowns. Consequently, the boarding enrollment of St. Teresa's had become predominantly upper-class students from Latin America. These students took a great deal of staff time, because they arrived knowing little English and were accustomed to being waited on by servants. The sisters had to show them how to perform many personal and household tasks and these girls often resented demands made on them. By consensus the older nuns concluded that the relocation would allow them to withdraw tactfully from the boarding school operation, which they had begun to find unprofitable and a thankless task. In addition, they noted that no recruits to the religious order ever came from this group of students. At the time of the relocation, boarding students made up about 5 per cent of the enrollment. Nearly all of the boarding students were from Latin America at this time.

For the first four years after relocation, enrollment at St. Teresa's flourished. The new facilities were actually quite crowded. For example, study halls were held on gymnasium bleachers because all classrooms were in constant use for instruction, and additional rest room facilities had to be built. In the new location St. Teresa's began to draw more upper-middle-class students than before. However, these were of only marginal academic ability, the brighter girls continuing to attend the more exclusive schools where they passed the entrance examinations with ease. Popularity of Catholic education in this city, which had a sizable Catholic population, both white and black, was such that the more exclusive nondiocesan Catholic schools were able to upgrade the academic caliber of their students substantially. Only St. Teresa's refused to establish an entrance examination requirement and accepted pupils on a first come, first served basis. Because of this fact its academic reputation with the local metropolitan area was adequate but not outstanding. During the four boom years, two new parishes on the extreme periphery of the suburbs, which lacked Catholic high schools, car-pooled their girls to St. Teresa's. Children from these two suburban parishes made up about 12 per cent of St. Teresa's enrollment.

After St. Teresa's had been in the new northside location for four years, the bishop of the diocese ordered the Catholic schools throughout the diocese to end racial segregation. The speed of desegregation varied greatly from one institution to another. Private Catholic schools having entrance examinations often enforced their minimum cutoff scores. The effect at first was to hold the blacks down to small numbers. St. Teresa's continued its policy of no entrance examination and became 10 per cent black the first year following the bishop's command. Exhibit 1 shows the racial composition of enrollment in St. Teresa's in the year prior to racial integration and the five years

EXHIBIT 1 Enrollment Data for St. Teresa's School for Girls

	Year Preceding Integration	Integrated Years				
		1	2	3	4	5
Freshmen	175	159	139	123	104	86
Sophomores	158	157	138	122	109	90
Juniors	122	145	132	121	103	87
Seniors	105	109	124	118	108	87
Total	560	570	523	484	424	350
Per cent black for four grades combined	0	10	21	34	41	45

thereafter. Like many other religious orders, the Sisters of St. Emilie were all white.

In the fourth year of integration a new diocesan high school was built on the outskirts of the city, serving the parishes that had been operating car pools to St. Teresa's. Most of these pupils, except those entering their senior year, transferred from St. Teresa's to the more conveniently located diocesan school.

In this same year an abrupt change took place in the disciplinary policies at St. Teresa's. Discipline in the preceding ten years had been quite military, contradicting a long former tradition of rather gentle firmness. The policy of regimentation had come in with a new principal, Sister Rose.

Although an efficient administrator, Sister Rose had little sympathy for girlish faults and believed her charges were likely to fall into evil ways unless they were constantly monitored. Her attitudes were enthusiastically seconded by many parents who regarded a convent school as primarily a guard for their daughters' morals. The students, however, were unhappy with many policies such as total silence between classes, censoring of student publications, strict dress codes, and a demerit system in which ten peccadilloes in nine weeks could deprive one of an elected office or a varsity team position. Anger over the situation by the younger nun teachers finally resulted in complaints going up through channels to the mother general in France and the abrupt removal and reassignment of Sister Rose. Her successor, Sister Catherine, brought in a relaxed and warm atmosphere that delighted the students. However, the change alienated a minority of parents, who thought Sister Catherine was less supportive of their authority and their principles. Sister Catherine held a master's degree in theology and was in the habit of introducing puzzling or con-

EXHIBIT 2 Per Cent Black for Year 5, by Grade,
St. Teresa's School for Girls

Freshmen	55
Sophomores	50
Juniors	45
Seniors	30

troversial issues into her discussions with students, encouraging them to discuss their own ideas on various religious and moral subjects. A larger minority of parents also found this facet of the new principal offensive.

In the fifth year of racial integration St. Teresa's encountered a financial crisis. Debts that had been growing slowly underwent a sudden spurt. Short-term liabilities totaled about $50,000. St. Teresa's was experiencing a drop in enrollment, whereas enrollment was at capacity at the other private girls' schools of the city. At the time of peak enrollment in the school, the religious order in all three American provinces had also begun to experience a decline in membership. Fewer high school seniors were considering seriously the idea of becoming nuns. Those seniors who were actually recruited more often left during training or during their first few years of teaching. Costs associated with a religious teacher were dormitory space, food, and a modest quantity of clothing. Medical care was donated by some of the physicians in the city. Costs associated with a lay teacher were an average salary of about $5,300 (in the year of integration) and Social Security taxes. St. Teresa's was also experiencing a rising ratio of bad debts to accounts receivable. About 80 per cent of the

EXHIBIT 3 Composition of Faculty of St. Teresa's School for Girls

	Year Preceding Integration	Integration Years				
		1	2	3	4	5
Religious						
Full-time	15	13	10	8	7	7
Half-time*	2	2	2	2	2	0
Lay						
Full-time	6	8	8	7	8	6
Half-time	2	2	4	4	2	1

*These half-time religious faculty members were full members of the religious order and caused the establishment the same per-capita expense for maintenance as full-time religious teachers. They were elderly.

EXHIBIT 4 Tuition Per Year

	Tuition Only	Tuition and Board
St. Mary's	$2,500	$5,200
St. Teresa's	455	—
Holy Spirit Academy	635	2,950
St. Margaret's	625	3,000
Mt. St. Agnes	685	3,075
Academy of the Holy Child	500	—
Diocesan Number 1	365	—
Diocesan Number 2	355	—
St. Elizabeth's	500	—

EXHIBIT 5 Enrollment Data for St. Elizabeth's School for Girls

	Year Preceding Integration	Integration Years				
		1	2	3	4	5
Kindergarten	22	20	21	23	22	24
Grades 1 through 6	180	175	170	172	168	174
Grade 7	25	28	23	27	29	30
Grade 8	23	25	28	23	26	28
Freshmen	80	85	87	90	89	92
Sophomores	75	79	82	85	87	86
Juniors	70	68	73	78	79	82
Seniors	67	68	67	71	76	78
Total						
Per cent black	0	0	0.5	1.5	1.8	2.0

EXHIBIT 6 Composition of Faculty of St. Elizabeth's School for Girls

	Year Preceding Integration	Integration Years				
		1	2	3	4	5
Religious						
Full-time	16	16	14	13	12	10
Half-time	2	2	1	0	0	0
Lay						
Full-time	1	1	3	5	7	9
Half-time	4	4	5	4	2	2

defaulters were white. No student in default had ever been asked to leave St. Teresa's. In addition to exclusion, there was the option of withholding the transcript when a defaulting alumna needed it for entrance into college or in getting a job. The bishop was adamant, however, in refusing to allow the withholding of academic transcripts from graduates who had not finished paying their tuition. In this same year there also occurred a storm that damaged the ground floor of one wing of the school building. Damage ran about $25,000. None of this amount was covered by the institution's insurance policy, which excluded flood damage.

Advise the mother provincial of the Southern branch of the Sisters of St. Emilie.

7

CHANNELS
OF
DISTRIBUTION

GIBSON GREETINGS, INC.

Gibson Greetings, Inc., was the oldest and third-largest producer of greeting cards in the United States. It was successful and had been growing rapidly in recent years but now faced some challenging problems and some opportunities to develop further certain of its successful strategies.

Composition of the Industry

The greeting card industry in the United States was comprised of three large companies and many small companies. The number of small firms varied from time to time but averaged around 500. Hallmark Cards, Inc., based in Kansas City, Missouri, held approximately a 40 per cent share of the card market whereas American Greetings Corporation, based in Cleveland, Ohio, held about 30 per cent, and Gibson Greetings, Inc., based in Cincinnati, held about 10 per cent. Norcross was once prominent and a challenger for third place but had gone bankrupt.

Established in 1910, Hallmark was clearly the leader, but its market share had slowly fallen from well over 50 per cent in the 1960s. Both American Greetings Corporation, established in 1906, and Gibson Greetings were highly aggressive and increasing their share of the annual national market for cards of about $3.5 billion. Gibson had doubled its share of the market during a six-year period.

All three organizations made wrapping supplies and paper party goods as well as cards. Hallmark's total sales were about five times as high as Gibson's; and American Greetings Corporation's sales, about three times as high as Gibson's. Hallmark had about 18,000 employees; and American Greetings, about 21,800. Exhibits 1 and 2 present Gibson's recent operating statements and balance sheets, respectively.

The whole card industry was characterized by intense competition, but it was a growth industry. Consumption of cards grew rapidly from the mid-1960s into the 1970s, then approximately stabilized over a short period, and then began to rise rapidly again. The no-growth period coincided with widespread sluggishness in the economy and some increases in the use of long-distance telephone calls. The long-distance people were seemingly influential in saying, "Reach out and touch someone." Over the period 1965–1986, industry sales rose an average of about eight and a half per cent per annum.

Although Gibson and American Greetings Corporation were rather specialized, Hallmark was already diversified and becoming more so. In 1984 the industry leader acquired Binney & Smith, Inc., makers of Crayola crayons, a product whose brand name was virtually synonymous with crayons. Hallmark also had ownership interests in real estate, textbook publishing, and broadcasting. Earlier, of course, it had added new products such as paper goods for parties, candles, mugs, and albums. Greeting cards provided about half of Hallmark's sales volume, down from nine-tenths in the 1960s. About 200 of Hallmark's employees worked in the company's new Technical and Innovation Center opened in 1983; and 700, in research and creativity. The select 200 were working on new ways to design and print cards. At any given time, Hallmark had an average of 32,000 different card designs in its entire line. Only about 10 per cent of designs lasted for more than a year, but the company's general-use card with purple pansies had been in production since 1941. Although the Hall family still held 70 per cent of the shares and employees held the rest, Hallmark was slowly transferring much of the significant authority to professional executives who were not emotionally attached to the greeting card industry. Both Hallmark and American Greetings had export sales, but they were not large in the total sales mix. Gibson had only trivial foreign sales.

The small card company portion of the industry was healthy and could not be taken lightly. Although the average life of a small

EXHIBIT 1 Statement of Income, Gibson Greetings, Inc., for Years Ended December 31, 1985, 1984, and 1983 (dollars in thousands except per share amounts)

	1985	1984	1983
Revenues:			
Net sales	$328,782	$300,385	$240,574
Royalty income	1,130	1,133	963
Total revenues	329,912	301,518	241,537
Costs and expenses:			
Cost of products sold	159,004	143,704	112,311
Selling, distribution and administrative expenses	111,848	98,894	79,360
Interest expense, net	7,493	6,426	7,950
Total costs and expenses	278,345	249,024	199,621
Income before income taxes and extraordinary items	51,567	52,494	41,916
Income taxes	22,900	24,147	19,524
Income before extraordinary items	28,667	28,347	22,392
Extraordinary items, net of income taxes of $2,947	2,797	—	—
Net income	$ 31,464	$ 28,347	$ 22,392
Income per share:			
Income before extraordinary items	$ 1.81	$ 1.79	$ 1.44
Extraordinary items	.18	—	—
Net income	$ 1.99	$ 1.79	$ 1.44

EXHIBIT 2 Balance Sheet, Gibson Greetings, Inc., for December 31, 1985 and 1984 (dollars in thousands except per share amounts)

	1985	1984
Assets		
Current assets:		
Cash and equivalents	$ 5,518	$ 3,064
Trade receivables, net	107,887	83,681
Inventories	79,356	71,853
Prepaid expenses	2,392	1,564
Deferred income taxes	16,164	13,655
Total current assets	211,317	173,817
Plant and equipment, net	50,054	38,492
Note receivable from related party	—	30,954
	$261,371	$243,263
Liabilities and Stockholders' Equity		
Current liabilities:		
Debt due within one year	$ 52,000	$ 29,500
Accounts payable	7,038	8,633
Income taxes payable	10,124	9,266
Other accrued liabilities	24,631	23,214
Total current liabilities	93,793	70,613
Deferred income taxes	7,327	3,628
Income taxes payable	—	1,892
Long-term debt	32,700	35,200
Subordinated note payable to related party	—	30,778
Total liabilities	133,820	142,111
Excess of fair value of companies acquired over cost, net	8,680	10,130
Stockholders' equity:		
Preferred stock, par value $1.00; authorized 5,000,000 shares, none issued	—	—
Common stock, par value $.01; authorized 25,000,000 shares, issued: 1985—15,684,899, 1984—15,660,555	157	157
Paid-in capital	32,642	32,503
Retained earnings	86,768	59,053
	119,567	91,713
Less cost of treasury stock, 49,108 shares in 1985 and 48,909 shares in 1984	696	691
Total stockholders' equity	118,871	91,022
Commitments and contingencies (Notes 9, 11 and 12)		
	$261,371	$243,263

company was short, any one of them might become another Gibson quickly. On the whole, this part of the industry was inventive and daring, especially in designing products and finding market niches. Among the most noteworthy small competitors were Papercraft Corporation, CPS Inc., California Dreamers, Paper Moon Graphics, Avanti, Inc., Current, Inc., Maine Line, Broom Designs, Inc., and Sun Cards. Paper Moon Graphics, a Chicago organization, was distinguished for quirky humor and striking drawings. Avanti, a Detroit company, was known for contemporary color photography. Founded in 1950 and based in Colorado Springs, Current sold its cards only by the box (including mixed use assortments) and only by mail and offered low prices and good value. Maine Line, of Rockport, Maine, emphasized cards that appealed principally to women. Broom, established in Detroit in 1971, and Sun, established in Washington, D.C., in 1982, made cards that showed only black people. Retailers in Detroit and Washington, D.C., in particular, were enthusiastic about these two firms. A few small firms—but also Gibson—had started offering Spanish language cards in the United States.

The best-known small company was Recycled Paper Products, Inc., of Chicago. Founded in 1971 by two men just finishing college and enthusiastic about conservation issues, this organization was intended only to influence large card makers to switch to recycled paper stock. The founders anticipated going out of business when that occurred, satisfied that they would have done their bit for conservation. Instead, the company had been quite successful and grown rather large, and the founders had added on cards made from regular paper so that printing could be clearer and colors true. It now ranked fourth in the industry with over $60 million annual sales and was still growing faster than the industry.

Gibson's Assets, Policies, and Practices

The Gibson organization was founded by Robert H. Gibson in 1850 as a small manufacturer of greeting cards. It was incorporated in 1885 in Ohio under the name Gibson Art Company. The name was changed to Gibson Greeting Cards, Inc., in 1960, and the common stock was listed on the New York Stock Exchange from 1962 to 1964 C.I.T. Financial Corporation purchased all of Gibson in 1964 and set it up as a wholly owned subsidiary with the name Gibson Greeting Cards, Inc. RCA Corporation acquired C.I.T. in 1980. In January 1982, RCA sold the Gibson organization to investors William E. Simon and Raymond G. Chambers and several members of the operating management of Gibson. Together Simon and Chambers bought about 65 per cent of the common stock; and the several managers, about 23 per cent. The remainder was bought by the general public.

Both Simon and Chambers were investment bankers, and the two were chairperson of the board and president, respectively, of Wesray Corporation, a private investment banking firm. Simon was formerly deputy secretary of the U.S. Treasury in 1973, the first administrator of the Federal Energy Office between 1973 and 1974, secretary of the Treasury from 1974 to 1977, chairperson of President Reagan's Productivity Committee, a member of President Reagan's Economic Policy Advisory Council, and a director of several major corporations, including Xerox, United Technologies, Dart and Kraft, Halliburton Company, Power Corporation of Canada, and Citicorp and Citibank. He was active in many national charities and was also president of the U.S. Olympic Committee. Chambers was a well-known investor and banker. Both Simon and Chambers were directors, but not officers, of Gibson.

The president was Thomas M. Cooney, who was previously the executive vice president of Fairmont Foods Company. The organization structure of Gibson below the presidency had been and still was uncommon. The executive vice president was Donald R. Taub, who was previously Gibson's vice president for distribution and manufacturing, a position that no longer existed. Before that job, he was president of Rust Craft Greeting Cards, Inc., a wholly owned subsidiary of American Greetings Corporation but formerly an independent manufacturer. There was now a vice president—marketing and creative, a position held since 1979 by Webster Schott, who was previously vice president and creative director of American Greetings Corporation and before that job was vice president, executive editor, and publisher of Hallmark Cards, Inc. There was also now a sales vice president, a position held by Harris W. Halvorson, who had been with Gibson Greetings for over forty years.

In 1984 and early 1985 there was considerable negotiation between Gibson and Walt Disney Productions. An agreement for Disney to acquire Gibson was reached, but this plan was canceled in February 1985 at a time when Disney itself was in a state of flux and new principal stockholders were taking over there.

Gibson employed about 2,500 people on a full-time basis and about 1,600 on a part-time basis. In addition, it hired full-time seasonal workers, typically about 700 to 800, because the work load of the organization was influenced by seasonality. Need grew in the summer and peaked in September. This variation in need was in both manufacturing and warehousing workers. The seasonality of sales is shown in Exhibit 3.

EXHIBIT 3 Gibson Greetings, Inc., Quarterly Sales as a Percentage
of Annual Sales

Year	Quarter 1 Jan. 1–Mar. 31	Quarter 2 Apr. 1–June 30	Quarter 3 July 1–Sept. 30	Quarter 4 Oct. 1–Dec. 31
Most recent	14.4	14.3	31.6	39.7
Two years ago	13.4	14.0	30.6	42.0
Three years ago	14.3	13.0	31.2	41.5
Four years ago	11.2	14.0	35.5	39.3

The company operated manufacturing facilities in Cincinnati, Ohio, and Memphis, Tennessee. Most cards were designed and printed in Cincinnati; and most gift-wrapping merchandise, in Memphis. Gibson had a physical distribution center near Berea, Kentucky, about seventy miles south of Cincinnati. The company opened a new physical distribution center in Kenton County, Kentucky, in the southern suburbs of Cincinnati in 1984. This new facility was built by using the proceeds from industrial revenue bonds. The company bought a few specialty items, such as tins and ceramic mugs, which it could not make. Besides the headquarters sales office in Cincinnati, Gibson maintained two sales offices in Texas, two in New York, and one each in California, Pennsylvania, Massachusetts, and Georgia.

The land and buildings in Cincinnati, Memphis, and Berea were all leased, not owned. The leases ran to 2002, with two options of five years each to renew. Rent was adjusted every five years to reflect changes in the Consumer Price Index. The company had a considerable investment in machinery and equipment, but store display fixtures accounted for well over half of the plant and equipment category of assets on the balance sheet.

Gibson designed and manufactured greeting cards, gift-wrapping paper, paper party goods, gift-wrapping accessories, and several specialty products such as calendars, stationery, plaques, candles, and related gift items. The paper party goods included tablecloths, cups, plates, and napkins in various sizes. The gift-wrapping accessories included tissue paper, kraft paper, tags, ribbons, bows, and assorted decorative trim items. Greeting cards provided about 50 per cent of the company's sales; gift wrap, about 45 per cent; and other items, about 5 per cent. At American Greetings Corporation, cards provided 64 per cent of sales, and that percentage was rather steady. Gibson enjoyed a larger share of the market for wrapping paper than for greeting cards, but company sales of cards were growing faster than those of wrapping paper. The company's share of the market was also rising faster for cards than for wrapping paper. Moreover, retail and wholesale prices were rising faster for cards than for paper. It was now common for the industry to offer many cards at retail for $1.75 or more, and cards under $.60 were becoming rare. Mean price in the industry was about $1.10.

There were several ways of segmenting the greeting card product line, but the most common, traditional way was to divide between "everyday" and seasonal cards. The everyday cards accounted for about 52 per cent of Gibson's card sales; and the seasonal cards, for about 48 per cent. The corresponding figures for American Greetings Corporation were 58 and 42 per cent. For the industry as a whole, everyday cards and seasonal cards were tied at 50 per cent each, but the share for everyday cards was slowly increasing. Everyday cards were divided into conventional and studio, that is, humorous cards. Studio cards were sometimes called "contemporary." The seasonal cards were devoted to holiday or festive periods, which included, in declining order of Gibson's sales, Christmas, Valentine's Day, Mother's Day, Easter, Father's Day, graduation, and Thanksgiving. In the industry at large, however, Easter was a little better than Mother's Day. Christmas cards, which once accounted for well over half of the industry's seasonal sales, now accounted for one-half, and the share was decreasing although extremely slowly. Halloween was considered by some people a good target for expansion. Some people in the industry distinguished between conventional and contemporary seasonal cards. Some new festive events were being identified through marketing research and cards created to honor them. One successful example, especially popular with teenagers, conveyed congratulations on getting a driver's license. Another honored the completion of a successful diet. Because of changing family relationships, demographics, and life-styles, some cards had been introduced recently that said, "To Mom and her husband" or "To Dad and his wife."

There was less artistic freedom in creating the Mother's Day products than in most of the other seasonals. Most Mother's Day cards used floral themes and decorations. Males bought the majority of cards for that occasion, and males associated flowers with femininity. There were very few contemporary cards for Mother's Day and virtually none with goofy drawings and wisecracking messages. The marketing research had established that the demand for such cards was tiny and that very few consumers felt comfortable joking about their mother although feelings about Father's Day were more varied. Hallmark alone made 1,000 different cards for Mother's Day.

Gibson maintained a full-time staff of artists, art directors, writers, and creative planners who designed the majority of the company's products. It also purchased the services of Helen Steiner Rice, called the "poet laureate of inspirational verse" by *The New York Times.* Writing exclusively for Gibson cards, she prepared warm, traditional verse that some people described as "syrupy."

Design of Gibson's everyday cards began approximately 18 months in advance. Finished designs of seasonal cards started into production about 15 months before the holiday. The majority of the designs for Gibson's everyday cards were replaced every 15 months, but birthday and get-well cards were replaced every 12 months; and sympathy, wedding, and baby congratulations, every 18 months. The life of a gift-wrap design was longer, occasionally exceeding two years.

All three leading companies introduced their first audio cards in late 1983, after several small manufacturers pioneered them principally through novelty and gift shops. The technology consisted of a chip and a miniaturized battery and speaker embedded in the card. Only a few designs were attempted. Gibson offered a card that played Christmas carols, and American Greetings offered a card with a printed message "Keep a song in your heart and me on your mind" and the music from the song "Let Me Call You Sweetheart." Hallmark offered a card showing two fat bears dancing, one with a rose clenched flamenco style in its teeth, to the lilting strains of "I'm in the Mood for Love." Initial retail price was about $7 for all three companies, but some designs that came out a little later sold for about $5. A small percentage of units produced did not work, and a few played even though the card was closed. Some people reported being startled by sudden bursts of spirited music. The price plus undependability and the tinny quality of the music produced less than encouraging results. There was the perpetual hope in the industry that expensive cards could replace inexpensive gifts, such as handkerchiefs or candy, in consumers' buying habits.

Many people in the U.S. greeting card industry referred to it as the "social expression" business, and many retailers spoke of their "personal expression" department. These were apt terms as applied to the U.S. culture. Americans bought more cards per capita than did Europeans. The latter preferred cards that were decorated but had no message, a product hard to sell to Americans. Europeans were more formal and under most circumstances expected to write in the appropriate message themselves. Most of them found cards made for the United States lacking in taste. Most Americans admired sentiment but were too inhibited to express it in their own words and handwriting whereas most Europeans were more restrained in what they wanted to say but had very little trouble writing it down. Most

Europeans perceived appropriate greeting cards as just another type of stationery, yet there was a small but detectable change going on among younger Europeans. Another point was that Americans thought of themselves as too busy to write a letter, even a short note on a small card, but actually were not any busier than most Europeans. Some U.S.-made cards or adaptations of U.S. cards made abroad by American firms or both had been doing rather well in Great Britain for quite a few years. In the United States, women sent the great majority of cards. The highest frequency of use occurred among middle-aged women of middle income.

Gibson's gift-wrapping paper was sold under several brand names, but Cleo brand accounted for most, and the great majority of that volume was for Christmas. In fact, it was the largest-selling brand of Christmas wrapping paper in the world. Cleo Wrap Division's annual production of wrapping paper could encircle the earth 16 times, and its printing plant capacity was enlarged by 25 per cent in 1984. Cleo brand also included several accessories such as ribbons, bows, and gift boxes. Cleo Wrap Division was the innovator of reversible wrapping paper, paper with a different pattern printed on each side. Some slow, uneven upgrading of Cleo brand products was occurring. There were several producers of gift wrap that did not produce greeting cards.

Cleo brand commanded retail prices well below Gibson's other gift-wrapping brands. It was sold primarily to mass merchandisers, variety store chains, discount department stores, supermarket chains, and drugstore chains, not to gift shops and conventional department stores. Gibson did not provide merchandising support services or advice for the retailers who handled Cleo brand. Such merchandise was shipped in corrugated paper cartons, which could be used as temporary freestanding displays. They were tall enough that they could be set on the floor but not so tall that they could not be set on a waist-high shelf. Such cartons carried the words "Cleo Wrap" in large clear print. These cartons were shipped directly to stores or to chain-operated central warehouses for subsequent redistribution to branch stores. Many of these retailers carried little or no gift-wrapping material except in the pre-Christmas season.

Traditionally, gift-wrapping paper suffered serious shelf wear. It soiled quickly, sometimes faded, and was occasionally torn. Recent progress in printing made the paper less likely to fade, and improved plastic film provided a stronger, more dependable cover. The three leading companies stayed about equal on this topic of development.

Gibson also marketed some cards under the Cleo brand. Cleo emphasized packaged juvenile valentine cards and was the leading producer of such cards in the nation but also produced a few boxed

Christmas cards. Some of the cards as well as some of the wraps featured the long popular Fuzzy Friends characters created by Gibson and the newer but successful Classroom Classics, which were actually created by children.

Gibson gave considerable emphasis to the use of the proprietary characters in card design. It had purchased licenses to use the following: Garfield; the Super Powers (Superman, Batman, and Wonder Woman); Sesame Street (Big Bird, Cookie Monster, Kermit, Miss Piggy, Bert, and Ernie); Loony Tunes (Bugs Bunny, Elmer Fudd, Porky Pig, Tweety Bird, Sylvester, Pepe LePew, Yosemite Sam, and Road Runner); the Hummel figurine characters; Cracker Jack; and Hershey's. Licenses were usually for one to four years, and some were nonexclusive. In 1984, Gibson bought the rights to use My Little Pony and Charmkins from Hasbro-Bradley, Inc., the largest toy maker in the United States.

Garfield the cat, a character developed by the cartoonist Jim Davis that drew about 70 million newspaper readers a day, was the single most popular character and was not licensed to any competitor of Gibson. Each Garfield card was designed and edited by Davis. Gibson sold an average of about 40 million greeting cards per year that used Garfield themes. In stores having large card departments, the Garfield products were assigned their own separate section.

In a major coup the exclusive right to the Disney characters (Donald Duck, Mickey Mouse, Pluto, Goofy, and others) was acquired in early 1985. Previously, Hallmark had enjoyed these rights. According to short-term plans, such properties were to be used only in the Gibson and Buzza brands. As a result of this licensing arrangement, Gibson received the exclusive right to operate card shops at both Walt Disney World in Florida and the Disneyland theme parks. Hallmark had the Peanuts characters, Heathcliff, and Jim Henson's Muppets, but American Greetings did not rely much on proprietary characters. Gibson had the strongest collection of proprietary characters in the industry.

Among appealing animal ideas, an underexploited theme was the koala, an Australian marsupial that most North Americans thought of as a cuddly little bear. QANTAS, an Australian airline, frequently showed this animal in its advertising. Gibson created Kirby Koala, and it immediately proved to be the most successful character the company had ever created. Some three million cards per year were being sold, and the koala theme extended to wrapping paper, party supplies, and gummed trim. Gibson began licensing other manufacturers to use Kirby Koala on infant wear, puzzles, stuffed toys, and ceramics. The company also started licensing the Gibson mouse created by Jean O'Brien exclusively for Gibson.

Archrival American Greetings, Inc., had scored a rousing success in recent years with its Strawberry Shortcake. Introduced in 1980, it was a little doll-like character with a pink bonnet and was surrounded by a sprinkling of polka dots and strawberries. Young girls liked it very much, and American Greetings licensed this character for use on countless items, earning tens of millions of dollars from it. In late 1982, Hallmark belatedly tried to match Strawberry Shortcake with its introduction of Shirt Tales. This was a group of tiny animals all living in a hollow tree wearing T-shirts with their shirttails hanging out and going about performing good deeds. Commercial results were not impressive.

Gibson showed considerable ability to innovate in matters besides products. In late 1982 the company introduced electronic reordering, the first in the industry, in a few major retail accounts. It spread to other major retail accounts by 1984. In this computerized reordering service, reorder tickets were converted at store level into electronic data, which were then transmitted to Gibson's central computer. This information was processed and relayed to a company distribution center, where the order was assembled and then shipped to the retailer. On average, three to four days of time in the mail one-way was eliminated. This cut turnaround time for an order by well over 40 percent and simultaneously permitted some reduction of inventory level in the store because less safety stock had to be kept on hand there. The service was not available to stores lacking computerization and very small stores.

The large manufacturers of greeting cards and gift-wrapping paper normally provided retailers in the United States with appropriate display fixtures. This custom was really necessary if such merchandise was to be handled well and look presentable. Moreover, retailers needed help in getting more productivity out of limited floor space.

Traditional fixtures for cards and gift-wrapping materials, although supplied by the concerned manufacturer, had had some problems. Drawers at the bottom were for reserve stock. Moving that stock up where it could be seen was seldom done in an orderly, timely manner; shoppers were alienated; countless sales were lost; and some seasonal merchandise did not see the light of day until too late. Moreover, the drawers were often a handy place to put reserves of unrelated goods from nearby departments and also to dump trash. In 1978, Gibson launched a concept that it called the "Everything-Up System." What this amounted to was that Gibson hired dozens of new merchandising personnel to call regularly on retailers handling company goods, and these personnel saw to it that no reserves were kept. As part of this concept, the manufacturer reduced the unit packing count that was virtually standard in the industry from twelve to six or sometimes less. Gibson increased frequency of merchandising visits to make sure that displays were kept well supplied and neat. Meanwhile, design work was going on for a new generation of fixtures. In 1980, Gibson brought out drawerless fixtures for everyday cards. Then in 1982, Gibson innovated with "Everything-Up Plus," which was the use of the now inactive, low spaces previously occupied by drawers for sloped displays of other Gibson products such as napkins, paper plates and cups, candles, and gift wrap. This 1982 innovation raised capacity by about 35 per cent.

In 1984, Gibson introduced an innovative store fixture that was superior to those provided by the principal competitors. Gibson termed its fixture concept "Everything Cubed." What this concept did was to reduce greatly wasted cubic air space occupied by the fixture. It accomplished this goal in three ways: first, by decreasing the depth of the fixture, moving from twenty-four inches in most cases to twelve inches in most cases; second, by sloping the display front at a steeper angle; and third, stocking merchandise all the way to the top of the fixture. There was virtually a doubling of the amount that could be shown in the same floor space. Retailer reaction was positive.

More than 50,000 stores in the United States sold Gibson products, compared to about 37,000 for Hallmark. The dominant practice for stores carrying one of the big three of the industry was not to carry the line of any competitor, but there were fairly frequent deviations, especially in department stores and gift shops. Also, fairly frequently a retailer seasonally stocked Cleo wrap near a large permanent display of products made by Hallmark or American Greetings. Gibson and its major competitors provided credit to stores for seasonal merchandise for an average of six months and in a few instances for as long as eleven months. Consistent with industry practice, the company permitted retailers to return unsold seasonal cards, of which there were many.

Gibson employed a direct field sales force that regularly visited most of the company's customers. For retail accounts that had branches, such visits might be to central offices or district headquarters or both. A much larger merchandising service force called on the stores themselves.

Traditionally, there was a difference between the types of retailers the three leading card makers emphasized. Gibson Greetings, Inc., was a bit more varied and had had a multiple strategy For a long time the company had cultivated card shops, drugstores, and middle-of-the-road department stores with Gibson brand cards and the rest of the product types the company manufactured while cultivating variety stores, supermarkets, and discount department stores with the Buzza brand. Simultaneously, it tried to reach lower-end stores of several types (drugstores, supermarkets, and discount department stores) with Cleo brand products. Gibson brand was priced higher than Buzza; and the latter, higher than Cleo. However, the Cleo brand did not have a fully developed line of cards. American Greetings had used supermarkets, drugstores, variety stores, and discount department stores.

Hallmark had emphasized gift shops and conventional department stores and also developed a large network of franchised Hallmark shops that stressed cards but also carried other Hallmark products such as paper party goods, stationery, candles, albums, and coffee mugs. Objectively considered, Hallmark brand cards were of good quality, but the company had heavily emphasized quality for decades in its public relations work and corporate image advertising. Its crown symbol was extremely familiar to people. Its main promotional slogan, "When you care enough to send the very best," was one of the best known in the nation. Ironically, however, many customers associated that expression with all three of the leading card manufacturers. On the other hand, company identification and prestige had benefited handsomely from its longtime, intermittent television series, "Hallmark Hall of Fame." The name of the program and its content implied something of special quality.

In recent years, a few of the more upscale department stores and a small number that were trading up vigorously had dropped greeting cards even though space productivity and markup rates of cards were attractively high. Retailers normally sold cards at about twice what they paid for them. As one retailing executive put it, "Our store cannot do everything and be everything. Moreover, some merchandise, such as washing machines and greeting cards, does not seem to fit into the image of fashionable merchandise for people and their homes that we want. In addition, a card department makes us look too much like a drugstore or supermarket."

American Greetings had recently altered some of its strategy and was attempting to cultivate gift shops, conventional department stores, and national and regional chains of nondiscount department stores. This manufacturer signed up Sears, Roebuck to carry its cards exclusively whereas Hallmark, anticipating the American Greetings action, countered by signing up the 2,000-store J. C. Penney chain to carry the Hallmark brand exclusively. Hallmark additionally countered by vastly enlarging its Ambassador brand line of products (composed of cards, wrapping supplies, and stationery) and pushing hard for placement of Ambassador in the types of stores American Greetings emphasized. Hallmark worked out an arrangement with A & P, Giant Food, and some other supermarket chains. Ambassador brand carried the word "Ambassador" prominently, of course. Hallmark did not legally have to print the word "Hallmark" on Ambassador brand goods. However, it did so but in a size of print most consumers would not notice and many could not read and in a place where most consumers would not look. American Greetings began to reallocate its product line and called the part of it aimed at grocers and similar retailers "Forget-Me-Not." An arrangement was worked out with Safeway supermarkets. The name "American Greetings" also appeared prominently on the Forget-Me-Not products but in a different typeface.

Advise Gibson Greetings, Inc.

HEAD SPORTS WEAR, INC.

Alex Schuster, an executive of a leading sportswear manufacturer, made a proposal in 1966 to Howard Head, inventor and owner of Head Ski. Schuster proposed: Why not allow skiers to find their entire ski outfit under the Head name? Apply the same standards of quality, design, and engineering to a line of ski wear. The proposal was convincing. Head Ski and Sports Wear, as it was then known, was born, with Alex Schuster as president. Production of quality ski wear under the Head name began in Cockeysville, Maryland. Within four years the company advanced from a newcomer to a solid second place in annual ski wear sales.

Just a year after its ski wear debut, Head Ski and Sports Wear introduced its first line of tennis wear. One reason for the expansion was to achieve a seasonal production balance. Another reason was to apply the same principles of fashionable and functional appeal to sports other than skiing. And for these same reasons, swim and running wear were later added to the sportswear offerings.

The company's rapid growth warranted a new home, and in 1969 it moved to a new corporate headquarters in the newly created town of Columbia, Maryland. In 1970 Head also entered the tennis racquet field, and the hardware division of the company moved its headquarters to Boulder, Colorado. Head became a subsidiary of AMF in 1971. AMF was a conglomerate with annual sales of more than $1.5 billion.

Up to this point the Head Sports Wear collections had always represented top-of-the-line quality and had been priced accordingly.

This case was prepared by Dee Wewer. Ms. Wewer is vice-president of Head Sports Wear, Inc.

Schuster saw a void between the mid-priced range of ski wear and Head sportswear and he set out to produce a line of ski wear that would have Head's heritage of design and engineered construction, but which would be priced competitively within the mid-price range. The line became Number One Sun—to indicate its Head heritage and also because it would be produced in Hong Kong, although it would be designed by Head people in the United States, as were the other lines. The line grew from a collection of twenty pieces in 1970 to 116 pieces in 1980. In that year the possiblity of dropping the Sun line was considered because of the line's drop in sales from $6 million to $4 million in two years. This decision and its implementation are emphasized in the present case.

At the time of Alex Schuster's proposal to Howard Head in 1966, 75 per cent of all skis owned in the United States were Head skis, a remarkable market penetration. There was tremendous brand awareness of the name Head, and the decision to expand upon it was a wise one. Also, the personality and charisma of Howard Head, who had become an important figure in this close-knit industry, were complemented by the equally dynamic and charismatic personality of Alex Schuster. These factors were not taken lightly in the ski industry. Most ski shops were small, privately owned, and operated by people very close to the sport. It was definitely a "family" industry.

Howard Head and Alex Schuster, well aware of this fact, serviced their accounts accordingly. Howard Head sat with every account that wrote an order for Head skis. Alex Schuster became "the" personality in the ski wear industry, known for his parties and personal attention to all the elements of his business. Also, Schuster was considered a progressive merchandiser with innovative designs that ranged from elegant to provocative.

Until 1978, Alex Schuster had headed the merchandising department of the sportswear company. He had a superb image within the industry for his ability to know what was "right" in fashion, and he brought a sophistication to ski wear never before equaled. The Sun line had had his attention during its birth and early adolescence, but it began to wane as he lessened his responsibilities in the specific departments and took on more of a managerial role. This alteration of responsibilities was partly caused by the demands of the new owners, AMF.

Besides Head Ski, Head Sports Wear, and Head Tennis Racquets, AMF also owned Tyrolia, an Austrian-based ski binding manufacturer, and several other leisure-oriented businesses. The joint ownership of these companies had some impact on the marketing of their individual products, and this became an important part of many product decisions over the years.

It should also be noted that during the time of the AMF purchase, many ski retailers worried greatly that the personal attention they had received from their entrepreneurial friends, Howard and Alex, would change into a "corporate attitude." This fear received constant attention from Schuster, which won him an even firmer place in the ski family. His attention was forced away from this continuing problem, however, when in 1979 he was sent by AMF to the European division of Head Sports Wear in Munich, Germany, to manage its growth and design.

At this time the management of Head Sports Wear USA was turned over to the executive vice-president, who had never had the exposure and did not have the same image as his forerunner. The "personality" of Head was closely watched by the industry. Every person in management was aware of the "Schuster following," and efforts to be honest, open, friendly, and, above all, service-oriented were established and enforced in order not only to overcome the space created by Schuster's absence but also to take advantage of improving service and quality in any tangible way possible.

Until 1981, Head Sports Wear's revenues were primarily from ski wear sales. However, by the end of the second quarter of 1981, sales had reached a fifty-fifty balance between ski wear on the one hand and sportswear for tennis, swimming, and running on the other.

In the winter of 1980–1981, after reviewing the previous year's sales, production, and delivery of ski wear, both with the Head label and the 1 Sun label, the decision was reached that there was a problem with the demand for the 1 Sun label. Opinions as to the cause of the demand drop varied from lack of promotional funds, poor design, and too much competition to the reality of the poor snow season in the East during the winter of 1979–1980.

The revenue had to be forecasted for 1981, and it was questionable that the 1 Sun label could pull enough in sales for the company to carry the fixed costs previously budgeted to support it. One solution was suggested that became a focal point for creativity in the promotion, design, and budgeting areas: Because (1) AMF also owned the company which produced the Tyrolia binding, as well as Head Sports Wear; and (2) the Tyrolia name had benefitted from a $6 million expenditure in America over the past three years to make the public brand-aware; and (3) the Head Ski Wear line had found its success from the awareness of the Head ski, why not develop a ski wear line and give it the already brand-aware name of Tyrolia?

Most management personnel thought this was a good direction, as long as the continuity between the labels rang true. That is, it would have to be an authentic ski wear line, not a fashion line, in order for the Tyrolia name on both the bindings and the garments to have credibility.

Another major decision was what to do with 1 Sun Ski Wear. Should design continuation for product presentation be cancelled and all efforts be devoted to a new Tyrolia line? If the 1 Sun line were now (November 1980) dropped, would the dealers who heard of it cancel their remaining orders for delivery in December 1980 through March 1981? Would all closeout sales of 1 Sun be cut off if ski retailers knew too soon of the elimination of the line? Closeout goods were those which did not sell during the prime selling period and therefore had to be offered at reduced prices to eliminate inventory before a new line was produced. Would the competition be given too much time for creativity if the company let anyone know too early of the development of the Tyrolia line?

The ski industry had one large national trade show each year, organized by Ski Industries of America, in mid-March in Las Vegas, Nevada. All major manufacturers and dealers participated and did the majority of their buying and selling there. However, Head Sports Wear also maintained permanent showrooms in New York, Los Angeles, and Atlanta, and several sales representatives in the field.

In the past years, 1 Sun had always been introduced to the market a month and a half before the Las Vegas show, whereas the Head Ski line was never introduced until the opening of the show. If it was decided not to produce 1 Sun, yet not introduce Tyrolia too early, what would the ski dealers be told in early February when they asked about the new 1 Sun line?

It was a ski industry practice to advertise and editorialize heavily in the Las Vegas show issues of ski publications, specifically *Ski* and *Skiing* magazines. Both had vast editorial coverage of the new lines to be introduced, and almost all manufacturers advertised their surprises to the industry through these two vehicles. This year, to make matters more difficult, the advertising deadlines for both these magazines were backed up to mid-January. This date was far in advance of the ideal time for Head Sports Wear to introduce Tyrolia, or the news of "no 1 Sun." Could the editorial or advertising staffs of these magazines be trusted with the information of either of these pieces of news? Would keeping back the news regarding the elimination of 1 Sun have ethical overtones? Was it possible, it was considered, to tease the industry with a "Guess what's ahead with Head" campaign, referring to Tyrolia?

The Tyrolia line, if produced, would be dramatically different from the Head or 1 Sun lines. It would be a hardware-oriented line—all-black zippers, buckles, snaps, lining—to represent its birth from the ski binding of the same name. And the colors offered for the line would be those also offered in the bindings, ski-oriented primary colors of red, royal blue, white, black, and bright yellow. The Tyrolia line would have fewer colors and only 78 pieces instead of 1 Sun's 120 pieces. Moreover, it would be a medium-price line. A new brand of ski wear introduced to the industry after two bad snow years was also a major business news story.

After another bad ski winter (this time no snow in the West), should the key dealers across the country be forewarned about the coming of Tyrolia? If they were not and they did not see 1 Sun at the usual introduction time, would they commit their purchase dollars elsewhere? Was this another question of ethics? Considering the family nature of the industry and Schuster's previous image, this was perceived as having extreme importance to dealer-manufacturer relationships.

Head Sports Wear was also wondering what the proper steps of introduction should be for the Tyrolia line. One must remember that little if any research had gone into deciding what the true problems of 1 Sun had been. And the demand for a new ski wear line, even if different in concept, had not been researched. This was a highly argued subject within management, and the decision was made because of "a lack of time for further research or delay."

Advise Head Sports Wear, Inc.

PELKUS'S OAK GROVE MOTEL

Paul and Anna Pelkus owned and operated a motor hotel of seventy rental units in an Ohio community of about 75,000 population. This community had about a dozen other motels. The facility, named Pelkus's Oak Grove Motel,[1] was a few hundred feet away from a busy interstate highway that was completed only a few years before. The

---

[1] Among the many helpful references are the following: Shelby D. Hunt and John R. Nevin, "Full Disclosure Laws in Franchising: An Empirical Investigation," *Journal of Marketing,* **40** (April 1976), pp. 53–62, and the citations therein; Charles M. Lillis, Chem L. Narayana, and John L. Gilman, "Competitive Advantage Variation Over the Life Cycle of a Franchise," *Journal of Marketing,* **40** (October 1976), pp. 77–80, and the citations therein. Although the latter research focuses on fast-food franchises, it is useful background.

motel had a heated swimming pool, a wading pool, black-and-white television in every rental unit, and was fully air-conditioned. The Pelkus business had no restaurant, but there were eating places within one fourth of a mile.

Mr. and Mrs. Pelkus also owned eight acres of land, for which they paid $46,000, near another Ohio city of about 50,000 population some sixty miles away. The Pelkuses had just begun to consider establishing a second motel on that undeveloped tract when Henry Arliss, a field representative of Biarritz Inns, approached them and inquired if they would be interested in taking franchises for both their old and new locations. He told them that he was thinking of a four-year contract.

In recent years franchising had been adapted to many types of businesses. In addition to the low-priced restaurant, typified perhaps by McDonald's, there were franchising systems in such disparate activities as soft-drink bottling, art galleries, travel agencies, shoe-repair shops, nursing homes, and weight-reduction salons. Many franchisors had developed sophisticated systems of management and had reached great size. There had also been many fly-by-nighters. Perhaps the best known fact was that both the franchisor and the franchisee participated in a common public identity.

Biarritz Inns, Inc., owned motels and also maintained a system under which independent motel operators were franchised to use the Biarritz name. It also had a restaurant chain operating under the name Continental House.

The Biarritz operation was integrated to a considerable degree. There was market research on the geographical area and the particular acreage for each prospective motel. Then there was architectural planning, including building and room plans, planning for furnishings and decorations, brokerage for construction and mortgage financing (but no Biarritz guarantees on financing), central purchasing of operating supplies, operation of a reservation system, training and refresher training of motel personnel, and supervision and monitoring of advertising and public relations. There was considerable inspection, but this was usually announced in advance from headquarters. Considerable physical similarity existed among most of the motels in the chain and all were identified by a standardized sign and the name Biarritz Inn, a properly registered mark.

The motor hotels owned and franchised by Biarritz contained a total of 19,500 rental units and were spread over Ohio, Indiana, Illinois, Michigan, Wisconsin, Minnesota, North Dakota, South Dakota, Iowa, Nebraska, Missouri, Kansas, Oklahoma, Colorado, New Mexico, and Arizona. In the last year alone 1,101 rental units had been added to the chain's motels. This number included seventy-five units in a new motel in North Dakota, the company's first penetration into that state. Expansion plans for the current year were emphasizing Ohio, Indiana, and Arizona. Biarritz's motels ranged in size from sixty to 290 rental units, and the mean was 112 units. All motels in the chain had air-conditioning, a heated swimming pool, color television, twenty-four-hour switchboard service, room service, restaurant facilities, on-premises parking for all guests, and reservations by teletype.

Biarritz's current franchise agreement specified that the franchisee would pay to the franchisor (a) a one-time fee of $20,000, of which 40 per cent was payable on signing the contract and the remainder when construction began or in seven months, whichever was sooner; (b) a royalty of 3.1 per cent of gross receipts, payable the first and fifteenth of each month; and (c) a contribution of 8 cents per rental unit per day for advertising. The $20,000 fee was applicable to every location separately.

Motor hotels owned by the chain also paid the 8 cents charge into the advertising fund. National media, local media, and roadside billboards were utilized. Biarritz did not practice cooperative advertising with its franchisees. However, it did issue a highly detailed directory that listed all of the Biarritz franchisees and explained how to find them.

Biarritz Inns, Inc., operated food service facilities in all of its motels, but most of these food service facilities were in adjacent buildings. Approximately one fifth of the restaurants in the chain were on sites where no motel of the chain existed. Restaurants were operated in all the states in which motels were operated and California. The restaurants were a separate operating division of Biarritz and all accounting was kept separate from the lodging operation.

Biarritz Inns honored all major credit cards, a point that was extensively featured in its national advertising. In fact, slightly over two thirds of gross rental income in the chain's motels came through credit cards. Pelkus's advertising had been largely on the themes of cleanliness, convenient location, and restfulness. About 60 per cent of their rental income was through credit cards.

Expenses, income, and other data for Pelkus's Oak Grove Motel are presented in Exhibits 1 and 2 for 19XX, a representative year.

Arliss called the Pelkuses' attention to the fact that Biarritz motels had an occupancy rate of 73.0 per cent the past year and 72.6 per cent the year before, a net profit of 13.5 per cent of sales, and total operating expenses of 60.0 per cent.

The Pelkuses were aware that Biarritz owned around one tenth of

EXHIBIT 1 Accounting Data for the Oak Grove Motel 19XX

Income		
Room rentals	96	%
Merchandise sales	4	
	100	%

Operating Expenses		
Salaries and wages	24	%
Salaries for owners	4	
Repairs and maintenance	5	
Cleaning and other supplies	3	
Heat and electricity	5.5	
Laundry	4	
Linens and glassware	0.5	
Payroll taxes and insurance	6.5	
Telephone and telegraph	1.5	
Advertising	4.8	
Stationery	0.2	
Other	3	
Total operating expenses	62.0%	
Gross operating profit	38.0	
Sales	100.0%	

Nonoperating Expenses	
Real estate and property taxes	4.6%
Interest	5.5
Insurance	1.9
Depreciation and amortization	14.0
Total nonoperating expenses	26.0%
Net Profit	12.0%

the motels in its chain and that the franchisor had bought out two franchised Biarritz Inns in Chicago last year. Moreover, they knew that several franchises had as many as eight locations operating with Biarritz, which amounted to having chains within a chain.

The Pelkuses were also aware of potential deviations beyond their control. An old friend who managed a franchised sweet shop had told them that a day-old doughnut sold as fresh or a weak cup of coffee served in one shop could lose a customer for the other shops. If a customer was dissatisfied he could blame the entire chain instead of the offender.

Advise the Pelkuses.

EXHIBIT 2 Miscellaneous Data for Oak Grove Motel 19XX

Original investment in motel building	$355,000
Original investment in furniture	$205,000
Original investment in land	$50,000
Occupancy rate	67.0%
Mean daily rate per rental unit rented	$28.50

POWER TOOLS, INC. (B)

Harvey Beeson had just been named president of the United States Operations Group of Power Tools, Inc., the largest branch of this worldwide company. He was justifiably proud of his new appointment. It meant that he would now sit on the board of directors of this corporation, which was listed in the *Fortune* 500. He believed the promotion was merited because he had overseen the impressive growth of the Consumer Products Division over the last several years. Beeson had started out as a company salesman about twenty years earlier and later became the head of the Asian-Pacific Division of the organization. Although born in the United States, he was a Canadian citizen. His office was in one of the company's older establishments in the Middle Atlantic states.

Sales of the Consumer Products Division had risen at a compound annual rate that approached 15 per cent during the last several years. Beeson had been at the helm of the division while all this rapid growth had occurred. Although the profitability of this division was not as impressive as its sales, profitability too had grown rapidly over the last several years.

However, Beeson knew that all was not as well in the other units under his control. Principally, Beeson was concerned about the serious situation that prevailed in the Air Products Division. He knew that the Air Products Division was not performing profitably and for three years had not met its goals. It was the only unprofitable division in the company.

In order to clarify his understanding, Beeson asked the Air Products Division general manager, Arthur Molnar, to meet with him. Beeson requested that a summary of the current situation be presented to him.

This case was prepared by Richard Rosecky, Ph.D., who is on the staff of the company being considered.

In order to comply with Beeson's request, Molnar first met with two Air Products Division officers, comptroller Bob Roberts and marketing manager Tom Solow. At the conference with Solow and Roberts, Molnar saw a very displeasing picture. The following two viewpoints emerged at the conference.

Marketing's View

Molnar asked Solow to summarize marketing's picture of the situation. Solow portrayed the situation as being a problem thrust upon the Air Products Division from corporate headquarters, which in Solow's view clearly failed to understand the economic characteristics and problems of air-powered tools. A successful small maker of precision power tools located in Ohio, the General Precision Pneumatic Corporation, had been taken over by the much larger Power Tools, Inc., about three years ago. As the marketing manager saw it, the subsidiary had been asked to perform as if it were a rapid growth company. Solow related how the General Precision Pneumatic product line had been stripped of all the various specialty items that it had and how it had been forced to streamline its product offerings. Worse yet, in Solow's view, General Precision Pneumatic had been forced to drop its established direct-to-the-user method of selling in favor of selling through industrial distributiors. Solow stated that the traditional strength of General Precision Pneumatic had been its highly capable sales engineers, who could meet directly with users and potential users and design virtually custom-made products to suit their desires. These sales engineers had been redirected by management to cover the entire nation through a type of middleman, the industrial distributors serving the Electric Tool Division of Power Tools, Inc. In addition, the parent company was so confident that it approximately doubled the capacity of the Ohio plant. Solow stated that he had certainly been able to foresee the disaster that followed. He then explained somberly that division sales dropped rapidly. Solow related that the remaining employees at General Precision Pneumatic, now renamed the Air Products Division of Power Tools, Inc., were disappointed with the entire merger.

Finally, Solow remarked that in his view the marketing policies of a consumer-products-oriented organization would not work when applied to the industrial customers served by the Air Products Division. Solow advocated a return to the limited number of customers who had been served previously by General Precision Pneumatic and a return to the high profit products that were better suited to the customers' quasi-individual needs.

The Corporate View

Bob Roberts had grown up with the parent company and was clearly an unofficial emissary from its headquarters. When Molnar asked him to present his view, Roberts took the opportunity with apparent relish.

The Air Products comptroller related that he understood the problem quite differently from the view presented by Solow. Roberts stated that the major source of growth in the parent company had been the concept of positive price elasticity of demand for power tools. As Roberts put it, "This concept means that as prices drop, volume in units will increase rapidly, and subsequent dollar sales will increase even faster." Roberts explained that the Consumer Products Division was a clear example of this valuable principle at work.

Roberts related that in the Consumer Products Division, as prices were reduced, great economies of scale in production and marketing generated rapid growth in profits. In addition, there was a greatly expanded market for power tools. In fact, prices for power tools were about one-half the level they had been ten years ago whereas the dollar market was easily two to three times as large.

The Air Products comptroller then explained that the parent firm believed if the very expensive air products were reduced in price and marketed through a channel of distribution that would reach many new users, the same principle would operate. In his eyes, this would have occurred had there been cooperation on the part of General Precision Pneumatic employees. Instead, Roberts related, there had been a small strike, and this difficulty had been followed by considerable personnel turnover in the administrative levels.

A Telephone Conversation

While Roberts and Solow were presenting their points of view to Molnar, a very important telephone call came in for Molnar. It illustrated a problem that contributed further to his perplexing situation.

Paul Fitzgerald, the sales manager for the Automotive Products Division, called to confirm a last-minute plan to increase the production for the division's half-inch air impact wrench. In Fitzgerald's view, the success or failure of his division depended upon the Air Products Division's ability to supply that organization with a reliable and inexpensive air wrench with which he could offer the broader product line that wholesale distributors of automotive products demanded.

The Automotive Products Division sales manager envisaged a sales campaign that would reverse earlier failures on the part of Power

Tools, Inc., to consolidate its position in the automotive products market. Just as Power Tools, Inc., had been in the process of gaining an important market share in the automotive marketplace, the Japanese had invaded the air wrench market with very inexpensive products that Fitzgerald described as "inferior or perhaps even cheap." Undeniably, the Japanese had been able to price their products well below the current prices of domestic manufacturers. Worse, they had captured an important part of the market. Fitzgerald was telephoning to be sure that there would be no delay in the latest product redesigns, which would allow costs to be reduced to a level at which the Automotive Products Division would be able at least to meet the prices of the Japanese competition, even if it could not beat this formidable competition.

Molnar's Conference with Beeson

As Beeson had requested, Molnar put together a summary of what he thought of the current situation in the Air Products Division. It was not really a pretty picture to present to his new boss, Molnar thought.

Molnar agreed with Solow that marketing policies that worked with a consumer product would not always work with industrially oriented products. However, Molnar had to agree with Roberts that the considerably reduced prices instituted by Power Tools, Inc., had not been given a real chance to have an impact. There had been great friction between the employees of the General Precision Pneumatic Company and the employees of the new parent company. This had subsided, Molnar thought, as time had progressed. He thought that it really could not be considered a problem today.

In his conference with Beeson, Molnar outlined the situation in simple terms. He related that the concept of altering the General Precision Pneumatic manner of distributing the product from custom representatives to the idea of industrial distributors most likely would not work. He suggested a return to a sales engineer calling upon an industrial user. Molnar also suggested that the pricing strategy put forth by the parent company should be given a chance to work in the Automotive Products Division. He stated, however, that the prices for the Air Products Division output sold directly to industrial users should be increased to reflect the new costs of marketing directly.

Beeson listened intently to the presentation from Molnar, but he was not pleased. He knew that any substantial reduction in the sales of the Air Products Division would most likely mean that division's demise, and that would mean a large loss to the parent company. In his first year as president, Beeson did not want to incur a new loss. On the other hand, Beeson did not need to be told that the situation as it stood could not be sustained for any long period of time. Something simply had to be done. Beeson viewed Fitzgerald's idea of the Automotive Division's pursuit of the air wrench market as a good one. Perhaps it was the only action that would increase the demand on the Air Products Division's factory and thus reduce losses there while stimulating sales in the lagging Automotive Products Division.

Advise Power Tools, Inc.

CRINSHAW COMPANY

Kenneth McMindle was manager of store number 220 in the Crinshaw Company, a large chain of department stores. Although this organization was the principal owner of a thriving insurance company, its main business was its several hundred stores. McMindle had been with the company for twenty-four years and had been adjudged an outstanding manager. He was quite loyal to Crinshaw's and had never worked for any other retailer. He had become an assistant store manager within three years, an accomplishment made by very few people in less than six years unless one worked in an extremely small store. By the time McMindle was in his early forties he had become a district manager over seventeen stores. He did well in that position for three years, but he had been very fond of merchandising and wanted to return to store management. In addition, he did not enjoy traveling, although his district did not cover a particularly large geographic area. McMindle was given his choice of nine stores that were either about to be opened or in which the manager was about to retire. This freedom of choice was a major compliment paid him by top management.

McMindle had chosen store number 220, a new suburban store in a Midwestern metropolitan area of about 150,000 population. It was in the same district over which he had been manager. His replacement as district manager was Ralph Jungkind, an old friend who had operated a Crinshaw store in a city forty-five miles away but in the same district. Planners in company headquarters intended this new store to carry the usual department store merchandise lines except for the full furniture line. Only patio and camping furniture was to be carried, and that was restricted to the late spring and summer seasons. The store was not intended to be large by department store industry standards, but was to be above average size for the Crinshaw Company. The average store in that chain did an annual volume of about $2,200,000, but this store was expected to do about $3,600,000.

Crinshaw was conservative and not given to flashy promotion. Its merchandise was medium quality and seldom included fads. Crinshaw enjoyed a reputation for ethical and dependable if not fashionable and exciting merchandising. The company's financial condition was sound and the stock was widely held.

The Crinshaw organization operated one other store (number 131) in the metropolitan area. It was located about seven miles away in a shopping center on the opposite edge of town and was essentially stable at about $2,050,000 net sales a year. It handled no hard lines except small appliances, but had been under no pressure from the headquarters people to change. Its manager, who was due to retire in ten months, had spent thirty-three years with the company. No replacement had been selected. It was possible that McMindle would be consulted for advice on making the replacement choice in that he knew this metropolitan area and its characteristics well. The store facilities occupied by store number 131 were in need of refurbishment, but it was not an urgent matter. The store had occupied that building for seventeen years and the lease had another two and a half years to run.

Crinshaw emphasized soft goods, and until about fifteen years ago restricted itself to such lines. The chain's net sales were still nearly 84 per cent soft goods, but this percentage was declining every year. The hard lines earned satisfactory markups, and the company was eager to increase such sales. However, it required time to sharpen the company's buying expertise and to change the public's expectation that no hard lines would be found at Crinshaw's. In addition, the company had always shown extreme regard for the views of its local managers. On this factor they were often the envy of managers in competing companies. Some Crinshaw store managers had resisted the addition of hard lines and delayed their introduction by two or three years, and some stores devoted a disproportionately small amount of floor space to the new hard lines. Some store managers protested (many with justification) that the amount of space in the building leased by the company could not accommodate a greater variety of goods without hurting the established lines. Most of these leases would run several more years. Furthermore, moving to another building could be disruptive of established patronage. In addition, some fixtures might not fit a new facility. The problem was compounded in the 7 per cent of the stores that were located in structures the company owned.

The market researchers at the home office of Crinshaw in New York City had predicted $3,600,000 for store number 220, which was located in Wagonwheel Plaza, a shopping center developed by Hoadly Brothers of Chicago. Under McMindle's leadership the store did $3,803,000 its first year, $4,256,000 in the second year, and $5,003,000 in the third year, which had just ended. Net profits as a percentage of net sales were satisfactory. The sales per square foot were well above the average for the company and the department store industry. McMindle's personal sales forecasts, which he had not reported to New York, were $5,550,000 for the fourth year, $6,000,000 for the fifth year, and $6,175,000 for the sixth year.

Instead of a fixed lease payment annually, the owner of the store number 220 building had asked for 1.1 per cent of net sales. Crinshaw's headquarters organization had agreed to this arrangement for a six-year contract because they had tacitly assumed that a fixed monetary sum for six years would have cost them about 11 per cent more the first year. Executives of Hoadly Brothers had known McMindle for several years and had had great confidence in the Wagonwheel Plaza location and in him. Hoadly Brothers were willing to gamble on the percentage instead of a riskless fixed payment. According to the contract, the cost to cancel the lease early was a flat $18,000.

The average Crinshaw store did 7 per cent of its volume in major appliances (excluding stero equipment), whereas the Wagonwheel Plaza store did 5 per cent of its business in such appliances. For small appliances, the figures were 2 per cent and 4 per cent, respectively. The average figure for sporting goods was 2 per cent, whereas the Wagonwheel Plaza store figure was 3 per cent. The typical Crinshaw store did 3 per cent of its volume in stereo equipment, records, and tapes.

Hugh Bock, senior buyer for stereo equipment, records, and tapes at the home office of Crinshaw, was perturbed by the number of stores doing little volume in his line. One such store was Wagonwheel Plaza, which confined itself to two models of stereo sets on the floor. It would order a unit like one of those two demonstrators if the customer wanted to buy. The salespeople in major appliances and small appliances took turns answering the inquiries customers made about the stereo equipment. The store handled no records or tapes. In the first year Wagonwheel Plaza sold four units at an aggregate of $1,110, in the second year five units for $1,455, and in the third year six units for 1,895. Bock noted and commented widely that store number 220 did 83 per cent of its volume in soft goods this year and 84 per cent the year before, and that as a new and "progressive" store it probably should be doing no more than 74 per cent in soft goods. Stereo equipment, records, and tapes had been the largest movers in hard-lines sales in about one fifth of the Crinshaw stores.

Bock had the ear of all the top executives at headquarters. Two years before he had been hired away from a chain of hard-lines stores where he had been extremely successful as the stereo buying supervisor at headquarters. Although only thirty, Bock had already worked successfully for a stereo equipment manufacturer as well as for the chain mentioned previously.

McMindle had answered Bock without undue delay, and he advised the buyer that his opportunities with stereo equipment, records, and tapes were extremely limited because the shopping center had a store specializing in such merchandise and because another shopping center just one mile away also had such a specialty store. The second plaza, Lyndale Center, had the stereo store, plus a hardware store, a supermarket, a drugstore, a women's and girls' apparel store, a shoe store, a cafeteria, a jewelry shop, a gift shop, a gas station, a coffee shop, and parking for 695 cars. In addition to Crinshaw's and the stereo shop in Wagonwheel Plaza, there were two women's and girl's apparel stores, two shoe shops, a gift shop, a fabric shop, a men's and boys' apparel store, a sporting-goods store, a bake shop, a gourmet food shop, a table-service restaurant, a hairdresser, a barber shop, a drugstore, a supermarket, a travel agency, and a parking lot for 500 cars. McMindle estimated that the Wagonwheel Plaza stereo shop had a volume of about $340,000 and the Lyndale Center stereo shop just under $400,000. Both carried a limited line of records and tapes, but they did not push them hard. For the whole metropolitan area he estimated the demand for stereo equipment at around $1,650,000, but he could not make an estimate for tapes and records. His past estimates had proved rather accurate. McMindle also knew that in the metropolitan area three department stores, one music store, one home appliance store, two furniture stores, and one other stereo specialty shop offered stereo equipment for sale, and that another department store had withdrawn from stereo equipment about six months before.

Bock retorted to McMindle's letter of explanation, "You have avoided full-line furniture, which about 20 per cent of Crinshaw stores are handling. And you have virtually avoided stereo equipment. Two demonstrators are worth less than none at all. You make us look like Hicksville! Why don't you consider putting your management expertise to the making of a balanced variety of merchandise in your store? The two stereo shops should constitute a challenge for you, not an insuperable obstacle."

McMindle became provoked. In the letter to Bock, with a carbon copy to each vice-president and the district manager, McMindle challenged Bock to negotiate a contract with a stereo manufacturer such that McMindle could reduce the prevailing stereo set price in

Crinshaw stores by about 10 or 11 per cent and thus slightly under-price the two stereo shops nearby. "Then I will sell them as fast as you can have them shipped to me!" After a day of reflection Mc-Mindle was bothered by a fact that he knew very well. Expressed as a per cent of cost, Crinshaw's had a markup of about 40 per cent on stereo sets, but the two independent stereo shops nearby had a markup of about 50 per cent.

Two days later McMindle received a telegram from Hugh Bock stating that in about twelve days sixty-five stereo sets (seven dif-ferent models) would arrive at store number 220, and that the retail price would be 8 per cent below the ordinary retail price. The sets would carry a markup of 25 per cent of retail selling price, he said. More would follow when inventory levels were worked down. In-stead of the manufacturer's brand name appearing on the merchan-dise, as it ordinarily did on stereo equipment sold at Crinshaw's, a Crinshaw house brand would appear. (About 50 per cent of Crin-shaw Company sales came through their own house brands. About the same figure applied in store number 220.) In getting this price, Bock advised, he had not sacrificed any functional quality in the product. Rather he had economized on the quality and workman-ship of the wood, plastic, and chrome used in the composition of the cabinets and cabinet trim. McMindle realized that under existing company policy he could reject the shipment of stereo equipment when it arrived. In addition, he could cancel it immediately.

Advise Kenneth McMindle, the manager of Crinshaw's store num-ber 220.

8

PHYSICAL DISTRIBUTION

UNIVERSAL MOTORS PARTS DIVISION

Six months ago, William Frank, general manager of the parts division of Universal Motors Corporation began to feel uneasy about certain trends that had been developing in the automotive parts aftermarket. Products in this market fall into two major categories, service parts and accessories. Service parts are those used in repair and replacement, including mechanical, body/frame, and chassis components. Accessories, either appearance or functional items used to improve performance or dress up the car, include fog lights, outside rearview mirrors, or interior floor mats.

Over the past ten years, total aftermarket parts sales in the United States had stabilized in the $70 billion to $80 billion range after growing steadily along with new car sales since World War II. In the last two years, the total number of outlets selling aftermarket parts had declined dramatically, and it was predicted by industry analysts that in five years there would be 20 per cent fewer outlets than there are today. Last year the average U.S. car owner spent $405 per vehicle on tires, batteries, accessories, and service parts. In the last three years, service parts sales had increased from $19 billion to $23 billion nationwide.

Like many firms, Universal Motors had also seen its sales patterns shift to follow population trends. Sales in the South and West were expanding at a faster rate than in the North and East.

The major types of outlets for aftermarket parts are service stations,

---

This case was prepared by Robert Krapfel, Ph.D., who is on the staff of the company that is being considered.

garages, new vehicle dealers, specialized repair shops (for example, muffler shops), mass merchandisers, and jobbers. Exhibit 1 shows how market shares of these types of outlets have changed over the last five years.

Fifty-three years ago, the parts division of Universal Motors was established by consolidating the aftermarket service parts warehousing and distribution activities of three marketing divisions. Twelve years ago, the parts division of Universal Motors Corporation became a separate operating division with aftermarket parts responsibility for all six of the North American marketing divisions. This had been done to provide one centralized service parts organization which was devoted entirely to the nationwide distribution of replacement parts to UM dealers. Sales and marketing activities continued to be performed by the marketing divisions, whereas the parts division concentrated on improving service, warehousing, and distribution.

Then, six years ago, sales and marketing functions were also assigned to the parts division, thus giving it total responsibility for marketing and distribution of parts to UM dealers. This move was soon followed by incorporation of all truck division service parts into the parts division system, and finally, two years ago operations were expanded from North America to include all aftermarket parts marketing and distribution activities to UM dealers worldwide. This remains its current status today.

Universal Motors Parts Division (UMPD) and Allied Division are UM's marketing and distribution arms that service the automotive aftermarket. UMPD distributes only to UM dealers, whereas Allied serves independent distributors. Each division maintains its own sales force and network of distribution centers. Many of the parts inventoried are identical; yet, for sales and merchandising reasons, the two divisions operate independently of each other. Also, many of the accessory items sold by both UMPD and Allied are contract-manufactured for UM by independent manufacturers.

In an indirect way UMPD and Allied actually compete because independent jobbers are free to sell to UM dealers, as is shown in Figure 1.

William Frank realized that the sales trends he had observed, if continued, would call for adjustments in the distribution system. He called in his director of operations, Dave Hert.

"Dave, I want to re-evaluate our entire operational network. This division needs to operate even better and more efficiently than it has in the past. I know there is no fat to cut, but we have to trim someplace, and I'm depending on you to come up with some answers. Let's get together in thirty days and you show me what you've got."

Hert knew from past experience that such requests from the boss

EXHIBIT 1 Percentage Market Shares by Type of Retail Outlet

| Year | | | Type of Outlet | | | |
Number of years ago	Service Stations	Garages	New Car Dealers	Specialized Repair Shops	Mass Merchandisers	Jobbers	Total
5	25	12	30	18	10	5	100
4	24	11	31	17	11	6	100
3	23	10	30	20	14	5	100
2	18	11	29	24	13	5	100
1	21	9	27	22	17	4	100

FIGURE 1. UM's Aftermarket Parts Distribution Channels

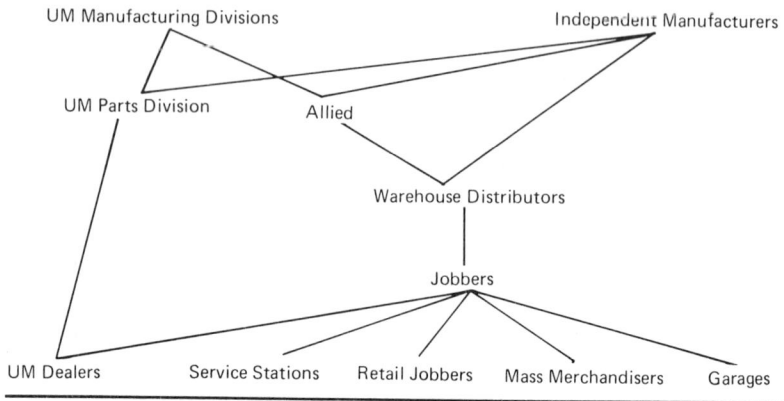

were not to be taken lightly and that completing an entire operational review in thirty days would be no easy task. He worked late that night and the next two deciding what information would be required. On the fourth day after his meeting with Frank, he drafted a memo to each of his twenty-three regional distribution center managers, requesting a selected audit of the previous twelve months' operations.

Specifically, he wanted monthly average figures in each of the following categories.

1. Inbound freight volume in tons, broken down by shipment size. That is, what amount was received in less-than-truckload (LTL) shipments and what amount was received in full truckload (TL) quantities. For both the LTL and TL inbound freight he wanted to know average distance travelled and total freight charges billed. All of this information could be obtained directly from trucking company invoices and internal records.
2. Inventory handled in tons, again in two categories, high versus low turnover items. High turnover items include routine service parts such as spark plugs, oil filters, and shock absorbers. Low turnover parts include sheetmetal and frame parts such as door panels and bumpers. Total inventory carrying costs for each category would also be needed.
3. Outbound freight volumes in tons, reported in the same manner as inbound freight.

Hert asked that the information be in his hands in two weeks. This was pressing things, but he wanted the remaining two weeks to absorb the information and do follow-up if needed.

After one week reports from the field began to come in. Soon twenty of the twenty-three distribution center managers' figures were in hand. Two had not been received because key people were on vacation, and in one location a newly installed minicomputer was experiencing start-up problems. Nevertheless, Hert was satisfied that he would be able to present an accurate picture of the current state of affairs when he met with Frank. Deciding to group the distribution center data by sales regions, he displayed the highest and lowest cost operation in each region. The data for two of these regions appear in Exhibit 2.

Looking at these figures, it was obvious to Hert which operations were most and least costly; yet he still was unsure that the figures

EXHIBIT 2 Distribution Center Operating Review
(For average 30-day period)

	Midwest		South	
	Toledo	Indianapolis	Atlanta	Memphis
	Inbound Freight			
LTL				
Volume (tons)	125	260	152	171
Distance (miles)	77	86	380	275
Cost (thousands)	157.85	366.70	901.05	733.59
TL				
Volume	195	196	228	114
Distance	91	88	410	320
Cost	230.68	224.22	1,112.41	434.11
	Inventory Carrying			
HIGH TURNOVER				
Amount (tons)	174	319	180	130
Cost (thousands)	22.45	37.64	19.44	11.96
LOW TURNOVER				
Amount	146	137	200	155
Cost	24.82	25.35	26.80	20.30
	Outbound Freight			
LTL				
Volume	170	237	304	200
Distance	55	68	40	75
Cost	153.34	264.30	189.70	234.00
TL				
Volume	150	219	76	85
Distance	31	42	62	90
Cost	20.15	119.57	56.07	91.04

EXHIBIT 3 Inventory Carrying Cost Factors

	Midwest		South	
	Toledo	Indianapolis	Atlanta	Memphis
COST FACTOR				
Number of Employees	20	26	17	14
Total Average Monthly Wage (thousands)	30.60	39.78	18.79	15.47
Cubic Feet of Storage Space (thousands)	200	275	220	140
Utilization (%)	78	84	87	88
Building Age (years)	12	19	14	6

clearly pointed to any particular course of action. To get a clearer picture, Hert went back to the original reports and zeroed in on the sources of the inventory carrying costs. He believed these were the most directly controllable and therefore deserved the greatest attention. For each distribution center, he reviewed the figures on number of employees, total monthly wages, number of cubic feet of storage space in the building, per cent of space utilized, and building age. These figures for the Toledo, Indianapolis, Atlanta, and Memphis distribution centers are shown in Exhibit 3.

In the meeting, Frank mentioned that the sales figures continued to be unencouraging and that something would have to be done to reduce operational costs fairly quickly. Hert had been in the industry many years and he knew that it was highly cyclical. Sales often expanded dramatically during the early stages of a business cycle upturn, and he did not want to jeopardize the overall ability of the distribution network to respond. The ability to serve customers reliably and on time was still most important in the long run.

After an hour and a half of going over the figures in some detail, Frank turned to Hert and said, "What do you think we should do?"

Advice Universal Motors parts division.

COLÓN FREE TRADE ZONE

The governments of several nations have authorized the establishment of free trade zones within their borders. This entity is an enclosed policed area in, adjacent to, or near a port of entry, into which foreign products not otherwise prohibited may be brought without formal customs entry or payment of customs duties. It has no resident population, and it is subject to the various other laws of the authorizing jurisdiction, such as those dealing with labor, carrier inspection, public health, and postal service. One international business magazine has referred to the free trade zone entity as a "combination transshipment center and industrial park where a company can enter into the intense competition of world marketing unencumbered by the usual restrictions of import-export business."[1] It is often simultaneously a design for attracting job-producing activities into underdeveloped regions. If products are reshipped out of the free trade zone to foreign destinations, whether or not they have incurred any processing, there is no customs interference or even supervision. Of course, if the goods are reshipped into the interior of the country operating the free trade zone, ordinary regulations and customs duties apply.

Free trade zones, often known as foreign trade zones, are found in a good many places. There are several small operations in the United States: for example New York City, Buffalo, San Francisco, San Jose, Seattle, Honolulu, Toledo, New Orleans, Little Rock, Kansas City, Charleston (South Carolina), and McAllen (Texas). In addition, such zones are planned for many cities, for example Chicago, Atlanta, Boston, Salt Lake City, Omaha, Louisville, Wilkes-Barre (Pennsylvania), New Bedford (Massachusetts), Portsmouth (Virginia), Port Everglades (Florida), and Bay City and Sault Ste. Marie (Michigan). Some examples of established zones abroad are Monrovia, Liberia; Hamburg, Germany; and Colón, Panama.

Panama

The Republic of Panama links South and Central America. Formerly part of Colombia, Panama achieved independence in 1903. With an area of 29,700 square miles (including the Panama Canal Zone), it is a narrow, curving isthmus extending generally in an east-west direction. It is about fifty miles wide in the vicinity of Colón and Panama City. Its tropical climate is divided into a rainy season extending from mid-May to mid-December and a dry season occupying the rest of the year. The Caribbean side of the country receives about 150 inches of rainfall a year, and the Pacific side receives about

---

[1] "New Life for Free Zones," *International Management,* 18 (March 1963). Other helpful material can be found in "Free Trade Zones Abroad Can Aid U.S. Exporters as Competition Mounts," *Commerce Today,* Feb. 5, 1973, pp. 13–16; " 'In' But 'Out' Foreign Trade Zones Merit Community Attention Today." *Commerce Today,* Dec. 9, 1974, p. 12.

EXHIBIT 1 Population of Major Communities,
Panama, 1986 (Estimated)

City	Population
Panama City	600,000
Colón	90,000
David	40,000
La Chorrera	30,000
Panama Canal Zone	44,000

seventy inches. Spanish is the official language, but a majority of the population in the two leading cities also speaks English. Many educated persons know a third language. Public sanitation and health conditions in Panama are among the best in the underdeveloped world.

The 1986 population of Panama was 2,000,000, of which about 50 per cent was urban. The main cities and their populations are given in Exhibit 1. As in most of Latin America, the rate of population growth in Panama is quite high, in recent years about 3 per cent.

There are no foreign exchange controls in Panama. The national unit of currency, the balboa, is at par with the United States dollar. The government issues its own coins but not paper currency. Panama utilizes United States paper currency, United States coins, and Panamanian coins. The banking services situation is very good. More than seventy foreign banks operate in Panama City, several with branches in Colón. Wages are higher than the average for Latin America but remain at a level only about one third as high as in the United States.

The Panamanian economy has always been internationally oriented, and trade and services have always been important.[2] Residence papers for foreigners are generally not difficult to obtain. Some United States citizens have felt a bit uneasy about living in Panama because of the former disagreements over the presence of United States government and military personnel in the Panama Canal Zone. However, Panamanian attitudes toward private United States citizens and companies are extremely cordial and supportive.

Transportation

Panama is unique in its transportation setting. The foremost feature is the fifty-one-mile long Panama Canal connecting the Pacific and

[2] See Thomas V. Greer, "The Mercantile Potpourri Called Panama," *Journal of Inter-American Studies and World Affairs*, 14 (August 1972), pp. 347–359; and David McCullough, *The Path Between the Seas* (New York: Simon & Schuster, Inc., 1977).

the Atlantic Oceans. An engineering triumph that opened in 1914, the Canal is incapable of handling some United States Navy ships today but is wide and deep enough for 96 per cent of all the world's ocean-going vessels to use. There are excellent port facilities on both coasts, including modern piers and equipment in Colón that are assigned to the Free Trade Zone. There is a very good international airport at Tocumen, a suburb of Panama City about fifty-one miles from Colón. The airport received a $45 million improvement and enlargement in 1977. Sixty-four steamship lines and twenty-eight scheduled airlines serve Panama City-Colón. Only the busiest North American, European, and Asian cities equal such numbers. No other Latin American location has access to as many ships, regular schedules, routes, steamship companies, and air carriers.

A good highway and a railroad connect Colón and Panama City, which are fifty miles apart, and an expressway is planned. Rail service to other Latin American nations is unavailable. Motor freight is possible only to the Central American nations by way of the Pan American Highway, which is excellent in some sections and very poor in others. Trucks need about eleven hours to reach San José, Costa Rica, the next large city and business center to the north. About forty hours of actual driving time is required for a truck to travel from Colón to Guatemala City, which lies at the northern end of Central America. The Pan American Highway connection south to Colombia is in various stages of surveying and construction and will probably open in about 1990. In Colombia the highway will link up with a fairly good existing network in that nation and the excellent highway system of Venezuela to the east. Poor but passable routes are available from Colombia south to the republics down the west coast of South America, Ecuador, Peru, and Chile. The nearest large industrial center, Medellin, Colombia, is on the Pan American Highway. Timing of the completion of the road is dependent mainly on the level of United States subsidies and possible money from international lending organizations.

Colón Free Trade Zone

The Colón Free Trade Zone, originally comprising about 120 acres, is located in the city of Colón, on the Atlantic coast of the isthmus [3] The Zone was created in 1948 and actually started opera-

[3] Helpful information can be found in the following: "Panama's Colón Free Trade Zone Can Facilitate Latin American Sales," *Commerce Today*, April 14, 1975, pp. 29-30; "Panama's Colón Free Zone: Another Record Year," *World Ports*, February, 1975; "Panama's Colón Free Trade Zone Profitable to International Firms," *Metropolitan Purchasor*, Septemper 1976.

tions in 1953. Although a government institution, it is administered by a board of experienced business people. Retail trade is forbidden in this enclave. Warehouse receipts for goods stored there can be used as collateral to borrow money.

The basic law of Panama covering the Free Trade Zone defines the allowable activities as follows:

> to bring in, store, exhibit, unpack, manufacture, put in containers, mount, assemble, refine, purify, blend, alter and, in general, perform operations with and handle all kinds of merchandise, products, raw materials, containers and other articles of commerce, with the sole exception of articles whose importation is prohibited by the law of the Republic.

Physical facilities for operations in the Free Trade Zone can be provided in several ways. First, space can be leased in buildings owned by the Colón Free Trade Zone. One can have a complete building or a portion of a building for a lease period of one to twenty years. Second, one can lease land and erect a building under a twenty-year agreement that has a customer option of renewal. Construction specifications must be approved by the Free Trade Zone. Third, public warehouse space is available in any amount for any time period. Charges for space must be paid at least once a month and are based on total usage. Fourth, in addition to storage, other services such as receiving and checking merchandise, repacking, reshipping, documentation, freight forwarding, and the maintenance of accounting and inventory records are available for reasonable fees.

Various payroll taxes are charged companies who operate in the Colón Free Trade Zone. However, there are several income tax advantages for companies who make sales to customers outside of Panama. The net combined effect of United States and Panamanian corporate income taxes is to save the company a sizable fraction of the taxes it would pay if it were conducting this business back in the United States. The saving is not uniform, for the Panamanian corporate income tax, unlike that of the United States, is divided into twenty-four ascending gradations.

The lowest cost physical distribution may be a sea-air combination. Normal oceangoing vessels may bring the goods in large quantities to the Colón Free Zone, after which small shipments of individual orders may be made by air cargo. In most years the aggregate value of air shipments from the Colón Free Zone exceeds that of ocean shipments. See Exhibit 2.

In an average year, about 600 European, Asian, and North American companies use the facilities of the Colón Free Trade Zone. Examples are presented in Exhibit 3 broken down by industry.

EXHIBIT 2 Value of Imports and Re-exports, Colón Free Trade Zone, By Mode of Transportation

	Value of Imports		Value of Re-exports	
	Latest Year	Two Years Ago	Latest Year	Two Years Ago
Air	27.6%	25.5%	60.7%	65.7%
Sea	72.1	74.1	35.7	32.1
Overland	0.3	0.4	3.6	2.2
	100.0%	100.0%	100.0%	100.0%

EXHIBIT 3 Examples of Companies Regularly Using Colón Free Trade Zone

Cosmetics	Beverages	Photographic Equipment
Givinchy	Heineken	Zeiss
Chanel	Ballantine & Sons	Yashica
Dior	Anheuser-Busch	Minolta
Jean Patou	Hiram Walker	Polaroid
Revlon	Courvoisier	Kodak
Colgate-Palmolive	Pedro Domecq	Nikon
Toni	Pepsi Cola	Canon
	Coca Cola	

Electrical and Electronic Equipment	Pharmaceuticals	Foods
Sony	Upjohn	Swift
Sylvania	Pfizer	Gerber
Hitachi	Parke-Davis	McCormick
Mitsubishi	Farbwerke Hoechst	Stokley-Van Camp
Panasonic	Zyma	Kraft
Norelco	Geigy	Heinz
Matsushita	Roche	Beechnut
Schick	Ciba	
	Schering	
	Riker	
	Wyeth	
	Warner-Lambert	

Tobacco	Automotive	Miscellaneous
Phillip Morris	Jeep	McGraw-Hill
American Tobacco	Chrysler	Singer
Brown & Williamson	General Motors	Gillette
P. Lorillard	Toyota	Xerox
Liggett & Myers	Goodyear	3-M
British Tobacco	General Tires	Paper Mate
	Mercedes Benz	

EXHIBIT 4 Distance from Port of Colón and Tocumen International Airport to Selected Cities

City and Region	Statute Miles	
	By Sea	By Air
Latin America and the Caribbean:		
La Guaira, Venezuela (Port of Caracas)	967	850
Maracaibo, Venezuela	797	531
Kingston, Jamaica	634	636
La Romana, Dominican Republic	965	916
Mayaguez, Puerto Rico	1,054	*
San Juan, Puerto Rico	1,142	1,103
Quito, Ecuador	—	633
Guayaquil, Ecuador	897	777
Puerto Limón, Costa Rica	218	253
Puntarenas, Costa Rica	587	362
San José, Costa Rica	—	334
Medellin, Colombia	—	326
Bogotá, Colombia	—	470
Buenaventura, Colombia	458	402
Cali, Colombia	—	435
Barranquilla, Colombia	386	336
Havana, Cuba	1,139	982
Veracruz, Mexico	1,634	1,321
Mexico City, Mexico	—	1,495
Willemstad, Curaçao	803	740
Oranjestad, Aruba	710	702
Managua, Nicaragua	—	507
San Salvador, El Salvador	—	731
Puerto Barrios, Guatemala	897	771
Callao, Peru (Port of Lima)	1,598	1,465
Valparaiso, Chile	3,060	2,943
Rio de Janeiro, Brazil	5,026	3,294
Buenos Aires, Argentina	6,311	3,381
Port of Spain, Trinidad	1,334	1,230
Georgetown, Guyana	1,743	1,484
Port-au-Prince, Haiti	985	817
La Paz, Bolivia	—	1,925
United States:		
Tampa	1,399	1,320
Miami	1,397	1,156
New Orleans	1,598	1,603
Mobile	1,603	1,599
Galveston	1,709	1,753

*Not available.

EXHIBIT 4 (Continued)

City and Region	Statute Miles	
	By Sea	By Air
Jacksonville	1,744	1,484
Charleston	1,800	1,657
Norfolk	2,047	2,020
Washington, D.C.	—	2,080
Baltimore	2,240	2,120
New York City	2,272	2,231
Los Angeles	3,402	3,001
San Francisco	3,779	3,322
Seattle	*	3,651
Chicago	*	2,325
Honolulu	5,395	5,245
Canada:		
Toronto	3,975	2,389
Halifax	2,641	2,693
Vancouver	4,678	3,740
St. John (New Brunswick)	2,640	*
Montreal	3,637	2,534
Europe:		
Le Havre, France	5,302	5,283
Antwerp, Belgium	5,516	5,477
Rotterdam, Netherlands	5,522	5,493
Liverpool, U.K.	5,341	5,167
Hamburg, West Germany	5,825	5,699
Zurich, Switzerland	—	5,657
Lisbon, Portugal	4,968	*
Gibraltar	5,038	4,926
Rome, Italy	—	5,903
Madrid, Spain	—	5,064
Barcelona, Spain	5,571	*
Other:		
Tokyo-Yokohama, Japan	8,898	8,419
Hong Kong	10,635	10,084
Manila, Philippines	10,764	10,283
Bombay, India	14,921	9,742
Singapore	12,097	11,687
Melbourne, Australia	9,130	9,022
Wellington, New Zealand	7,491	7,433
Haifa, Israel	7,296	7,303

*Not available.

About two thirds of the companies using the zone are based in the United States.

In recent years the Free Trade Zone reached the capacity of its 120 acres. Anxious to expand further, it brought about negotiations between the United States and Panamanian governments concerning extra space in the Canal Zone, since the town of Colón is an enclave within the Canal Zone. The result was that in 1975 the United States gave the Free Trade Zone an abandoned airport, Old France Field, for a period of ninety-nine years. This 540-acre airfield lies in marshy land on the other side of a saltwater inlet from the existing Free Trade Zone. It has few facilities, but the three hangars were immediately put to use. A causeway several hundred yards long is planned to connect the two tracts of land.

Other Free Trade Zones in the Region

The Colón Free Trade Zone is the largest in the region and one of the largest in the world in terms of monetary value of business conducted. Small zones have been proposed for the cities of Buenaventura and Cali, in southern Colombia a little over 400 miles south of Colón; in Puerto Limón, Costa Rica; and Puerto Cortes, Honduras. Small zones already exist in Managua, Nicaragua; Margarita, Vene-

EXHIBIT 5 Imports from and Re-exports to Leading Countries, Latest Years, Colón Free Trade Zone

Country in Rank Order	$ Amount (in thousands) Imported from	Country in Rank Order	$ Amount (in thousands) Re-exported to
1. Japan	$166,024.7	1. Aruba	$73,741.3
2. United States	93,439.0	2. Brazil	60,055.7
3. Taiwan	61,372.1	3. Venezuela	56,137.7
4. Hong Kong	40,146.4	4. Ecuador	53,793.2
5. Switzerland	29,141.4	5. Colombia*	49,616.4
6. United Kingdom	23,574.4	6. United States	35,567.9
7. West Germany	14,708.9	7. Mexico	25,401.7
8. Colombia	13,604.0	8. El Salvador	22,630.6
9. France	12,598.0	9. Chile	22,083.7
10. South Korea	12,012.8	10. Costa Rica	18,725.7
11. Puerto Rico	9,832.9	11. Guatemala	17,002.4
12. Italy	8,274.7	12. Bolivia	16,642.5
13. Spain	7,226.2	13. Nicaragua	15,481.4

*Of this amount, $14,905 thousand went to San Andres Island, a possession of Colombia about 120 miles off the Atlantic coast of Nicaragua and 250 miles northwest of Colón.

zuela; San Bartolo, El Salvador; Santa Marta, San Andres, Providencia islands, and Barranquilla, Colombia; La Romana, Dominican Republic; and Mayaguez, Puerto Rico; as well as in Oranjestad, Aruba, and Willemstad, Curaçao, in the Dutch West Indies. The Mayaguez Zone is fairly aggressive, but it has chosen to specialize. Its forty-four acres of space currently serve only eight firms. About six tenths of its business is processing Australian and New Zealand beef and reshipping it. The Mayaguez Zone also manufactures industrial uniforms, towels, and napkins; attaches buttons to ready-made apparel; and makes small amounts of pharmaceuticals. Total value of annual business is about $19 million, versus well over $1 billion in the Colón Free Trade Zone.

Advise the Colón Free Trade Zone, its users, and its potential users.

9

SALES
MANAGEMENT

LIBERTY STATESMAN CORPORATION

Liberty Statesman Corporation was a large life insurance company operating throughout the United States and Canada. The manager of the Louisiana-Mississippi district, Cyrus Baker, had just retired after eight years in that post. His replacement was thirty-six-year-old Lyman Danner, who had been with the company six years and with a competitor for about seven years before that. For the past two years Danner, a native of New Jersey, had been manager for his home state for Liberty Statesman. The results in that territory had pleased top management. Danner, his wife, and three young children immediately moved to New Orleans, where district headquarters was located.

The first thing Danner did on arrival was to order the district office refurbished at a cost of about $7,500. He conferred at length during a series of meetings with an interior decorator on how the project was to be done. After about ten days he started a task that he described to many persons as "the most important for any new district manager, learning the sales force." Simultaneously he investigated the paper handling and limited bookkeeping activities the district office engaged in, for his observations indicated that things were not smoothly or efficiently handled and that applicable services of Liberty Statesman's national office were not being fully utilized. Using the national office for any available service might increase the expertise with which it was done and might save the district office some money, he explained.

Danner was accustomed to being in charge of one of the seven leading districts in terms of sales volume. As he discovered when he began to study the records in his new office, the Louisiana-Mississippi dis-

215

trict had never finished in this elite group in any year. The best it had ever done was nineteeth among the thirty-eight districts and that was four years ago. The past year it had been twenty-fourth. It had been rumored in the company that Cyrus Baker was winding down toward his retirement the past two years. Therefore, Danner took the view that his new district had much more potential than the actual sales figures of the past implied. He wondered about trying to transfer in some of the highly able and motivated sales representatives he knew from his old district. He discussed the idea briefly with Sam Autier, his assistant district manager and right-hand man. Autier advised him not to waste valuable time and psychic energy even considering it, because insurance sales representatives do not transfer as readily as many other types of sales representatives. They are on their own most of the time and can benefit handsomely from a detailed knowledge of and "feel" for the area in which they work. They need networks of contacts and referrals from friends, acquaintances, and customers. Many sales require periodic visits for several years before the sale is consummated. Insurance on one member of the family may lead to insurance on another member.

Danner began to think. He knew all of this as well as Autier did and was embarrassed that he had even brought up such an idea. Perhaps, he reflected to himself, it was symptomatic of his anxiety. But he considered that Sam Autier was a good listener and he had to have someone with whom to "bat ideas around." After all, every manager had some ideas that could be improved on. And everyone in a position of responsibility needs people around him with whom he can talk without entering into commitments and promises.

What he actually said to Autier was: "Of course, you are so right. I was daydreaming. But if I had my druthers, that is about what I would do."

A few days later Danner and Autier set up a contest to furnish additional incentive for the twenty-eight sales representatives in the district. These salesmen did not represent any other company. There had been no contest in this district for about eighteen months. This one would last three months during the slow season and would be based on percentage increases over the same three months the previous year. There were to be three prizes. First prize was an all-expense-paid five-day vacation in Montego Bay, Jamaica. The second prize was a $100 U.S. savings bond, and the third prize was a bond of $50. All three winners would be presented handsome certificates on Danner's next field visit to their vicinity.

As soon as the three-month period was over, Danner eagerly began to examine the results, which are shown in Exhibit 1 for the ten persons with the highest percentage increases. He had never conducted a

EXHIBIT 1 Selected Results of Sales Contest: The Ten Sales Representatives with the Highest Percentage Increases

Salesman	Location	Sales During Contest	Sales, Same Period Last Year	Percentage Increase
Leary	Shreveport	$800,000	$705,000	13.4%
Caruthers	New Orleans	720,000	650,000	
Bymel	Baton Rouge	640,000	590,000	
Beatty	Jackson	635,000	590,000	
Verier	Lafayette	620,000	581,000	
Sutkin	Lake Charles	481,000	455,000	
Hemingway	Monroe	422,000	400,000	
Rymanson	Ruston	430,000	409,000	
Breaux	Hammond	430,500	410,000	
Belton	Natchitoches	435,750	415,000	

contest with such an outcome. Aggregate sales had gone up only about 4 per cent. He was surprised and keenly disappointed and said so, but he gave the three awards anyway. Moreover, he immediately announced to the sales force that there would be another contest, the details of which would be given out in a few weeks.

A few days later Danner made a field visit swing through Jackson, Oxford, Starkville, Hattiesburg, and Gulfport. At a party in his honor on this trip there was enough conversation, some of it oblique and some overheard, for him to realize that his remarks about wanting to transfer in some sales representatives from his former territory had gotten out and had apparently been repeated with some enlargement. There were no scenes at the party and Danner deftly avoided saying anything awkward or embarrassing, despite the strong temptation. Nevertheless, he returned to New Orleans perplexed.

Advise Lyman Danner of Liberty Statesman Corporation.

KRUGER-MONTINI MANUFACTURING COMPANY

The management of Kruger-Montini Manufacturing Company had just entered a new fiscal year and was rethinking its specific policies and general position on transfers of sales representatives. The decision was the responsbility of the sales manager.

Founded many years earlier, this well-established corporation was a medium-sized manufacturer of several related industrial products in rather wide use. The majority of customers were manufacturers. For quite a few years Kruger-Montini did not do its own personal selling. Starting about twenty years ago, it gradually phased out the various intermediaries and manufacturers' agents. After about five years of difficult transition, Kruger-Montini relied strictly on sales representatives who were on the company's payroll and who worked for no one else. Kruger-Montini was not truly national in coverage in its early years but became so nine years ago when it added five sales representatives in one year and relocated thirteen.

The size of the sales force had increased as the company grew and prospered and had now reached thirty-eight. The sales manager had found it necessary to divide his organization into four geographical regions because of span of control difficulties as Kruger-Montini grew. Because the product line was fairly narrow, it was decided that geography, not type of products, would be the best basis for the organization structure. Thus each sales representative sold all products. A contributing reason for deciding against product specialization as the basis for organizing selling efforts was that it would have resulted necessarily in a larger geographical territory for each employee to cover. That would have meant his being away from home overnight much more than under the policy adopted. The present sales manager, Henry Rosas, estimated that the average person on his sales force spent six nights a month away from home. This figure was a little lower, he knew, for people in the highly industrialized and densely populated areas of the Northeast, the Michigan, Ohio, Indiana, Illinois, Wisconsin region in the Middle West, and parts of California. The figure was a little higher for his people in all other areas. Rosas estimated that the difference was about five versus eight nights per month. During the past few years the company had noticed a sizable number of its customers relocate to the Sun Belt and many customers open branch factories in those milder climate areas of the nation. The demand for Kruger-Montini's products was slowly becoming more evenly spread across the country, and this trend was expected to continue.

Rosas had been with the organization about three years. He had been a successful salesman with one company and then assistant sales manager with another company before coming with Kruger-Montini. He had a good personality and was well liked by the sales representatives.

The company had always used a salary plus commission pay plan. For the average representative the commission provided 25 per cent of his compensation.

Kruger-Montini manufactured nine products, two of which had been introduced only in the past three years. Prior to that three-year period there had been no new product introductions for a great many years. It appeared highly probable that Kruger-Montini would introduce two more new products, closely related to the existing product line, and delete one during the next two years.

During the most recent fiscal year Kruger-Montini had transferred six sales representatives to different territories. In the four years previous to that, the company had transferred seven each year. Each was moved because of company need and/or the assigning of better territories to deserving sales representatives. See Exhibit 1 for earlier years and additional data on size of the sales force and average distances people were transferred. The mean distance of a relocation at Kruger-Montini had shown a downward trend for several years.

Every person on the sales force had moved at least once. The longest time in one place anyone on the present sales force had experienced with Kruger-Montini was seven years. Rosas was tentatively thinking about moving from five to seven members of the sales force later this year.

EXHIBIT 1 Data on Sales Force of Kruger-Montini Manufacturing Company

	Size of Sales Force	Number Transferred	Mean Distance Transferred (miles)
Latest year	38	6	798
Two years ago	37	7	872
Three years ago	37	7	682
Four years ago	36	7	1122
Five years ago	35	7	1254
Six years ago	34	9	1360
Seven years ago	32	9	597
Eight years ago	32	12	1070
Nine years ago	31	13	793
Ten years ago	26	10	1035
Eleven years ago	25	10	640
Twelve years ago	24	11	510

The management did not know much about the geographical preferences of its sales representatives or their family life. Rosas could not legally inquire systematically about whether the spouses were also employed and whether that work was professional and managerial, which might make one less willing to move. Dual careers made it difficult for couples to handle relocations well, and some probably would not consider it at all. However, Rosas and his four regional sales managers had been trying recently to make observations and record facts and inferences about these matters for all the sales representatives. Three of the sales representatives were young, unmarried men who seemed to be mobile and flexible. Three middle-aged men were divorced, and one was a widower. The remaining thirty-one were all married. It appeared that twenty of them had working spouses and that fifteen of these women had professional or managerial careers. Rosas also began to understand that most nonworking married women had developed community ties and that moving for them could also be difficult and unsettling.

The unwritten understanding of personnel at Kruger-Montini had been that turning down a transfer would be suicidal. At the minimum such a rejection would classify a person as unaggressive and unambitious. The United States culture for many years had perceived frequent transfers as evidence of fast-track career progress. Staying mobile was a "badge of honor," as business newspapers and magazines usually described it.

No one on the Kruger-Montini sales force had ever declined a transfer until two years ago, as far as Rosas could determine. The sales manager and other headquarters personnel had been surprised and perplexed when Charles Hopkins, a very satisfactory employee, had declined a move from a small, pleasant southeastern city to a much more lucrative territory in another part of the United States. Age thirty-seven and a native of the upper Middle West, Hopkins explained that he liked Kruger-Montini and wanted to continue working for the company but did not want to move. His wife was a business manager in another company, and they had a thirteen-year-old daughter in school.

The costs to relocate a sales representative had been rising quite rapidly. The most recently transferred person was Alex Kendall, a man with a wife and three children. It cost Kruger-Montini $30,880 to move them approximately 2,900 miles from one coast to the other, although the company was not any more generous than the typical American company. Of this amount, $11,475 was to ship household goods, $4,100 was for the pre-move housing search, and $3,680 was for one extra month of this man's average compensation in lieu of incidental expenses. Final travel and temporary living expenses accounted for another $4,550. The remaining costs had to do with company subsidies on the sale of the couple's house and purchase of a replacement house. The management of Kruger-Montini was beginning to note the financial impact of moving costs of the company.

Kruger-Montini also recognized that a transferred sales representative required several months to get his work productivity back to normal. The recovery of productivity was much more difficult for people who worked with the public and who needed to understand the characteristics of a market than for other types of workers. A sales representative also needed time to establish rapport with the regular clients.

One managerial colleague whom Rosas respected was outspoken about the issue of moving. Bert Crane, who managed another department at Kruger-Montini and had been with the company about twelve years, believed that if employees were permitted to put down roots in a community they would lose their sense of corporate identity. Loyalties to the geographical community would overcome loyalties to the corporation. He stated that perhaps this had been an unconscious motivation of Kruger-Montini in past years.

Another colleague, Robert Mason, mentioned that a nice compromise might be to confine transfers to the region in which the sales representative was already living. For example, the ten sales representatives in eleven Northeastern states would be transferred only within that region. Mason noted that each region had some lifestyle characteristics that set it apart from the others. He was an experienced manager and had been with the company for about nine years.

Advise Henry Rosas of the Kruger-Montini Manufacturing Company.

NORTHERN NEW JERSEY MANUFACTURING COMPANY

Northern New Jersey Manufacturing Company was a producer of several kinds of industrial equipment listed in Exhibit 1. It developed from the efforts in the late 1940s of a gifted engineer and inventor, Sidney Hovey, who patented several of his idea for variations on standard products. He founded and was active in the firm for more than twenty-six years until his death.

EXHIBIT 1 Northern New Jersey Manufacturing Company Sales by Product, Selected Months

Product	September	July	September Last Year	September Two Years Before
Dryers	$21,000	$34,500	$35,000	$32,200
Sprayers	7,700	7,500	8,000	7,800
Planers	4,100	4,300	4,000	3,900
Power saws	3,200	3,000	3,000	3,100
Drills	4,200	4.100	4,000	3,900
Sanders	9,500	7,300	7,200	7,000
Metal buffers	7,500	4,900	5,000	4,800

Hovey had been very interested in the selling activity of his company and had a strong sense of professionalism that he used in personally selecting people for his sales force. He managed the sales force until it grew to a size of three men, at which time he secured the services of Herbert Staley as sales manager.

Before Staley's arrival and for several years thereafter, Hovey told the salesmen expressly the names of firms he wanted them to call on. The founder was acutely interested in the reputation of his young company. His concern with reputation included product characteristics as promised, delivery on time (critical to customers for these goods), and ethical, highly reserved business conduct by the salesmen. However, this concern for reputation was not restricted to these factors. Hovey also wanted to have as his customers those who enjoyed the finest reputations. For example, he told his salesmen never to solicit the orders of a small firm then known by the name of Reihnan and Loykas, for he considered the owners to be social climbers without proper backgrounds. In addition, he did not like an advertisement of theirs he once saw in a weekly business newspaper. He also instructed his salesmen not to call on Heather Glow, Inc., because it had been turned down for a loan at the bank that Hovey used. This was despite the fact that Heather Glow found credit at another bank.

Not all the instructions were negative, however. Hovey had the salesmen, all of whom were engineers, visit Camden Mills, Stone & Kruger, and South Coast Metals time after time even though all three were committed to other sellers and other product designs. He wanted Northern New Jersey Manufacturing Company to be a name that such firms knew and respected. He also cultivated several large national companies, such as Combustion Engineering, American Machine and Foundry, Kaiser Industries, Westinghouse, and Melpar.

After Hovey's death, Staley continued these policies for the better part of a year. At that point James Watts, the new president hired from the outside, had a long talk with the sales manager and explained that he thought some changes were desirable. The firm should try to maximize sales and abandon all the "notions and pretentions," as he termed them. The salesmen should be put on a combination salary plus commission. The two other executives in the company, the finance man and the production man, spoke up with thorough endorsements of such changes. The existing policy was straight salary.

With some misgivings, Staley devised a new compensation structure for his four salesmen. Under this plan he estimated that a salesman would earn about 80 per cent of his compensation through salary and about 20 per cent through commissions. The plan was announced on August 1 and the men were told it would go into effect in thirty days. Sales in August slumped about 17 per cent from the same month one year earlier and 14 per cent from the same month two years earlier.

After one month of use, the sales manager conducted a preliminary inquiry into the results of the new compensation policy. The results appeared to be that the easier to sell items in the product line were moving well, those of average difficulty to sell were moving adequately, and the one item that was rather difficult to sell (the dryer) was moving very poorly. Exhibit 1 gives the comparisons of September to the last month under the old policy (July) and to September one year before. Staley presented his analysis to Watts but cautioned him about premature inferences from these data. The sales manager said that he would repeat his comparisons after another month. In the meanwhile, the president told the sales manager to urge the salesmen to solicit orders for dryers.

At the beginning of November, Staley anxiously studied the results for October, as presented in Exhibit 2. He had taken a preliminary look at some fragmentary data about October 16 but knew that those data were undependable. In addition, the company had usually experienced a mild upswing in the fall season.

EXHIBIT 2 Northern New Jersey Manufacturing Company
Sales by Product, Selected Months

Product	October	October Last Year	October Two Years Before
Dryers	$23,000	$36,000	$35,400
Sprayers	7,900	8,400	8,200
Planers	4,300	4,200	4,000
Power saws	3,300	3,200	3,000
Drills	4,200	4,300	4,100
Sanders	11,500	7,500	7,200
Metal buffers	9,700	5,300	5,100

Staley was in his office reflecting on the figures in Exhibits 1 and 2 when Douglas Guglielmi, the production manager, and Richard Acker, the finance and accounting manager, both walked in. After several minutes of friendly conversation about sports and the weather, Guglielmi said that he and Staley jointly had a problem. To be specific, the mix of sales was apparently changing radically, which was upsetting his production schedule, company general plans, and deliveries. Richard Acker then added what Staley already knew, that the dryers had been earning the highest unit margin, whereas the sanders and metal buffers had been earning the lowest unit margin. Total profits were beginning to go down.

Advise Herbert Staley, sales manager for the Northern New Jersey Manufacturing Company.

10

ADVERTISING
AND
PUBLIC RELATIONS

TONKA TOYS

Tonka was established in 1946 by L. E. Baker, Avery F. Crouse, and Alvin F. Tesch in the basement of an abandoned school building in Mound, Minnesota, a western suburb of Minneapolis. It was incorporated on September 18, 1946, as Mound Metalcraft, Inc. The name was changed to Tonka Toys, Inc., in 1956 and Tonka Corporation in 1965.

The three founders and a small number of employees began by producing only two toy designs, a steam shovel and a crane. These items rapidly proved to be quite popular, and very soon demand exceeded production. Other toys were added, and the corporation grew. Tonka was most widely known for its die-cast steel toy trucks. At one time Tonka had about 45 per cent of the U.S. market for this type of toy. Without really intending to aim so narrowly, the company appealed principally through the years to a market of boys in the age bracket of two to ten. Two generations of little boys dug up their back yards with Tonka-made trucks, Mighty Crane, Mighty Dozer, and other construction toys. The all-time favorite was the little yellow dump truck.

The high birthrates of the baby boom following World War II helped Tonka very much. This trend line turned down, however, in the early 1960s. There was a baby boomlet in the early 1980s, and it had helped throughout the 1980s, but it would not continue to help, of course. The number of children in the late 1980s and through the

225

1990s would probably not increase, according to the majority of forecasts from the government, private industry, and universities. A pattern of low birthrates was expected to continue indefinitely. On the other hand, slowly rising real incomes and the growth of two-earner households meant that there was potential to give children more or better toys or both. In addition, more children would be first children. On average, parents spent more on the first child than on later children except when the last child was born many years after its siblings.

Making toys was a relatively risky business. Although sales of the whole toy industry did not show large changes from year to year, the sales of individual toys were extremely volatile. Because a toy manufacturer necessarily had a limited selection of toys in its product line, the sales of a given company were apt to exhibit noteworthy changes from year to year. Until the early 1980s, Tonka tried to combat volatility by emphasizing staple products, that is, those less subject to trends and, especially, fads. Examples of staples were toy boats, airplanes, trucks, and construction equipment. Nevertheless, the average life cycle of a toy truck was only around three or four years. Several new variations of basic products were brought out each year. The tooling necessary to make several new products normally amounted to $1.5 to $3 million in total every year. Two other factors added to the riskiness of the toy manufacturing business. Substantial time was required between the design of a toy and its reaching the shelves of the retailer. Even if the manufacturer guessed right in January, tastes might have changed by the important November-December period. Most toys were exhibited at the industry's Toy Fair held in February every year for buying representatives. Moreover, the industry offered credit on rather generous terms for extended periods of time, and quite a few toy retailers and some wholesaler-distributors were questionable credit risks. For example, recently Tonka had found it necessary to write off as uncollectibles the $1.1 million account of a California wholesaler-distributor. The industry was seasonal. Tonka normally did about 64 per cent of its sales in the second half of the year. The third quarter was normally slightly better than the fourth quarter.

The toy industry in the United States was composed of about 25 U.S. companies and many importers. Several Oriental sources were becoming important. The main U.S. organizations were Mattel, Inc., Hasbro Bradley, and Coleco Industries, in that order, plus Tonka and Fisher-Price, a subsidiary of Quaker Oats Company. Tonka was the smallest of these major toy operations. Mattel was taken over in 1984 by F. M. Warburg Pincus as part of a financial restructuring, and it was considered plausible that in a few years time Mattel might be offered for sale. Two small but aggressive new toy manufacturers were Axlon, Inc., and Worlds of Wonder, Inc. Both emphasized talking suffed animals, and the former was beginning to make robotic stuffed animals and dolls. The moving force in Axlon was Nolan Bushnell, the founder and former owner of Atari Corporation and Pizza Time Theatre, Inc.

As Tonka matured, it made several acquisitions. In October 1963 it purchased Gresen Manufacturing Company of Minneapolis, a maker of pumps, filters, motors, directional control valves, and accessory valves used in hydraulic systems. Tonka sold this subsidiary to Dana Corporation in January 1981. In December 1964, Tonka acquired selected assets of Mell Manufacturing Company, a Chicago producer of outdoor barbecue grills, but sold this subsidiary in 1968. In 1973, Tonka acquired Vogue Dolls, Inc., a small maker of dolls, with the objective of quickly extending its toy line to have more appeal to little girls. However, this attempt did not work out, and the subsidiary was sold in 1976. In December 1973, Tonka acquired Ceramichrome, Inc., a small firm that made paints, stains, glazes, and molds used by ceramics hobbyists. In 1966, Tonka acquired a majority holding in Mercury Tool & Stamping, Rexdale, Ontario. Tonka now had a sizable manufacturing subsidiary in Toronto, Canada, and a small one in Rhodes, Australia.

The average age of boys who played with trucks and other constuction toys was going down. Boys of six or eight now tended to want toys that came with a story line. Truly imaginative play emanating from the boy himself was becoming confined to the very young who watched rather little television. In the past, the company's trucks and other construction toys had strong appeal to boys up to about age ten or eleven. Girls had never been significant consumers of Tonka's line of traditional toys.

The president of Tonka, Peter Wimsatt, was dismissed in 1979 following a disagreement with the board of directors. He opposed significant diversification of the product line, which was described by unhappy shareholders as sturdy, reliable, traditional, and dull. Business journalists, securities brokers, and many others continuously described Tonka as "sleepy." In the main, they believed Tonka was facing at best a no-growth future with its present product line and lack of concern for market factors. Instead, the organization had a strong production orientation. Wimsatt went to Ertl Toy Company, located in Dyersville, Iowa, as manufacturing vice president, and Stephen Shank, the company's 34-year-old chief legal counsel, was elevated to the presidency. The corporation was undergoing a major rethinking about itself and continued to do so for a lengthy time period. In 1982, Shank raided Mattel and hired two marketing executives, including that company's marketing vice president.

The performance of Tonka had been troubled and uneven in

recent years. Sales reached $81.1 million in 1982, but there was a net loss of $2.7 million. In 1983 sales rose to $87.8 million, but there was a net loss of $3.9 million. Losses in 1983 would have been greater if there had not been an extraordinary gain of $3.0 million that year from the reserves related to the termination of the old pension plan for workers and establishment of a new one. Sales reached $139 million in 1984, and there was a net profit of $5.0 million. Sales surged in 1985 to $244 million, and the net profit was $19.5 million. See Exhibit 1.

EXHIBIT 1 Consolidated Statements of Operations

Tonka Corporation and Subsidiaries
(In millions, except per share data)

	Fiscal Year		
	1984	1983	1982
Sales	$139.0	$87.8	$81.1
Cost of goods sold	93.9	66.5	54.9
Gross Profit	45.1	21.3	26.2
Selling, general, and administrative expenses	33.0	25.8	26.1
Other (income) expense	(1.7)	1.9	3.5
Interest expense—Net	5.5	3.7	1.8
Earnings (loss) before income taxes	8.3	(10.1)	(5.2)
Income taxes	3.3	(3.2)	(2.5)
Earnings (loss) before extraordinary gain	5.0	(6.9)	(2.7)
Extraordinary gain	—	3.0	—
Net earnings (loss)	$ 5.0	$ (3.9)	$ (2.7)
Earnings (loss) per share:			
Before extraordinary gain	$ 2.34	$ (3.22)	$ (1.24)
Extraordinary gain	—	1.43	—
Net earnings (loss)	$ 2.34	$ (1.79)	$ (1.24)
Average number of common shares	2.1	2.1	2.1

Consolidated Statements of Retained Earnings

(In millions)

	Fiscal Year		
	1984	1983	1982
Retained earnings at beginning of year	$22.7	$27.0	$47.4
Net earnings (loss)	5.0	(3.9)	(2.7)
Dividends	(.4)	(.4)	(.4)
Retirement of treasury stock	—	—	(17.3)
Retained earnings at end of year	$27.3	$22.7	$27.0

New Products and the Supporting Advertising and Sales Promotion

Coleco Industries scored the industry's largest hit in 1983 with its Cabbage Patch Kids dolls, and the product continued important for several years. However, in 1984 and 1985, Tonka enjoyed the distinction of having the industry's top-selling new toy, GoBots in 1984 and Pound Puppies in 1985.

The new marketing management people at Tonka did some thinking and conducted some research in trying to identify some breakthrough toys. As part of that process, they studied what was happening in Japan and, in doing so, discovered that GoBots were extremely popular with children in that country. Therefore, Tonka secured a license from Bandai Company, located in Tokyo, for the concept and started producing them. These were small, die-cast metal and plastic action-figure robots having movable arms and legs that could be folded and rearranged, thus converting these little space-age creatures into miniature trucks, sports cars, and other vehicles. Tonka also raised its advertising budget, nearly all the increase going for GoBots. See Exhibit 2. The product was a great success, in fact, beyond Tonka's expectations. Having little experience in forecasting sales of hot items and monitoring the actual movement off the retailers' shelves, Tonka decreased production after the pre-Christmas rush season. Demand continued strong, however, and soon demand far exceeded supply. Meanwhile, Hasbro Bradley had introduced Transformers, its version of this product type. More sophisticated at sales forecasting and having a better working relationship between marketing and production processes, Hasbro did not cut back on production and then forged ahead to be number one in the robotics toy market. Tonka had forfeited its lead of several months with this product type. Hasbro attained 40 per cent—and Tonka 26 per cent—of the market for this type of toy. Matchbox Toys, Ltd., a well-known British company, also entered this market aggressively with its Voltron.

**EXHIBIT 2 Tonka's Advertising Costs, Six Recent Years
(in millions)**

1985	1984	1983	1982	1981	1980
$40.2	$13.8	$7.6	$7.5	$6.8	$5.5

Hasbro launched an animated miniseries for television in 1984 made by Sunbow Productions, a subsidiary of Griffin Bacal Advertising. This series, featuring Transformers, in time became a weekly, then daily syndicated series. Considerably later, Tonka added its own television miniseries featuring GoBots. Shown on Saturday morning television, this five-part series was made by the successful cartoon producer Hanna-Barbera Productions of Hollywood. As part of the supportive promotion, there were coupons on packages of some snack foods that offered a chance for a free GoBot. Despite the popularity of the GoBots group of products, at the end of 1984 the traditional toys still accounted for almost 60 per cent of Tonka's sales.

For 1985, Tonka added 28 new GoBots, and it expanded the television show to a 65-part series. In 1986, Tonka offered its GoBots again but also offered a variation, a line of mechanized GoBots with motors. Seventy-eight new television episodes of GoBots were prepared for 1986 to promote this group of toys.

Pound Puppies from Tonka were the industry hit of 1985. They were modeled after the Cabbage Patch Kids dolls. They were individually designed, soft-sculptured dogs that, like Cabbage Patch products, came with optional adoption papers. The puppies were adoptable by means of a mail-in $2 certificate of ownership. Tonka sold more Pound Puppies in 1985 than Coleco sold Cabbage Patch dolls at their peak. As part of the promotion supporting the product, Tonka sponsored a "bark-off" in twelve cities. In this event, children competed for prizes by barking like their favorite dogs.

The line of Pound Puppies was then extended to include Newborns, one-fourth the size of Pound Puppies. Newborns were priced at retail at $8 compared to $20 for Pound Puppies. Tonka anticipated that children would want a litter of Newborns, especially if they had a Pound Puppy. Therefore, the company was counting on multiple-unit sales of the product. Also introduced were a Supreme Pound Puppy, much larger than any Pound Puppy, so as to head the whole group, plus doghouses, carriers, and dog clothing. Pound Purries, a cat version, were introduced as well. Also in 1986, Tonka brought out a set of products promoted solely to girls called Keypers. Soft, sculptured animals with hidden storage compartments, the assortment consisted of a ladybug, a snail, and a turtle, each attached to a carrying case. Another version was a plastic form of Keypers that doubled as a jewelry box and case with a key. An arrangement was reached with Current, Inc., a Colorado manufacturer, to picture soft and plastic versions of Keypers on greeting cards.

On the other hand, Tonka's Star Fairies series of dolls introduced for young girls in 1985 was a distinct disappointment. This product was a small girl doll, in six variations, with wings and wand, and there were accessories. Magical abilities were emphasized. The company supported this group of toys with a syndicated cartoon special, offered back-to-back with another that starred its Pound Puppies, but there was little effect. Tonka felt a little better, however, in that a similar product, Rainbow Brite, did not work out very well for Mattel. Cabbage Patch Kids were still rather popular, but the doll category throughout the industry was slowly declining in size. Nevertheless, Tonka decided to modify the Star Fairies group of products and give it another costly opportunity in 1986. The new version had longer hair and a larger wardrobe selection, but the company was not optimistic. Executives and designers considered girls a more difficult type of customer than boys.

In the spring of 1986 Tonka brought out several more GoBots but shifted its emphasis to a new generation of the basic product concept of transformable robots. This market entry, named the Rocklords line, consisted of boulder-shaped pieces of plastic that unfolded to reveal fantasy figures, many of them highly muscled. The behavioral principle of the product was people's interest in elemental things such as rocks. It was hoped that this principle would also widen the age appeal of the new product group. The introductory advertising campaign, largely on television, used the theme "Rocks that will rock the world." Tonka contracted with Hanna-Barbera to make a full-length movie that featured the Rocklords and seven new GoBot characters. This film was meant for theaters rather than television. Thus, if the movie were successful, people would be paying to watch an extremely long advertisement.

Tonka also launched Legions of Power in 1986. It was a space-age construction set that reminded one of Lego building blocks from Lego System, a Danish organization. It came with a futuristic group of transformable characters.

Corporate Image and Public Relations

Something of Tonka's corporate image was presented in the previous parts of the case. However, there were two problems of corporate image and public relations in a short time period. Each was of such major proportions that most companies of similar size would go for several decades without anything equaling them. The first problem was primarily with employees, the community around metropolitan Minneapolis-St. Paul, politicians, and the state government of Minnesota. Some consumers were concerned also in that they were becoming worried about preservation of jobs in the United States. One could see "Buy American" campaigns emerging. The second problem was primarily with lenders and stockholders, and it also captured the critical attention of many potential investors and some potential lenders.

Location of Production

Tonka Corporation had owned a small plant in Mississauga, Ontario for two decades. Tonka invested in a new plant of 74,256 square feet in Ciudad Juárez, Mexico, in 1982 and shifted some of its manufacturing from Minnesota. There were minor start-up problems. Simultaneously, there was a minirecession in the United States, and the interest in video games drained off some toy sales potential. Like some others, the company operated at a loss in 1982. Nevertheless, Tonka was basically pleased with the Mexican operation. Therefore, in 1983 the company moved the remainder of its domestic production, opening two new plants, each with 187,000 square feet, in El Paso, Texas, directly across the Rio Grande from Ciudad Juárez. The Mound, Minnesota, factory stayed open through 1983, at first as a precaution in case there were major start-up problems in El Paso and later for the sake of orderly wind-down operations. Headquarters remained in suburban Minneapolis. El Paso was a community of about 500,000 population at the western tip of Texas, and Ciudad Juárez was of similar size. Despite being in two nations, these facilities would be operated as one integrated production and physical distribution complex. About 1,200 were employed permanently, 350 of them in Ciudad Juárez and 850 in El Paso. In addition, there were 400 to 500 seasonal workers. By far the most important reason for moving was to achieve lower operating costs. The hourly rate of the production workers hired in El Paso was only 49 per cent as high as what Tonka was paying in Minnesota. The wages across the border in the Ciudad Juárez facility were much lower than those in El Paso.

Legislation was adopted in both the United States and Mexico in 1971, establishing an in-bond program, creating an opportunity for U.S. firms to use abundant, low-cost labor south of the border. The Mexican government allowed processing, assembling, packaging, or repair facilities or a combination of these in the in-bond area to import parts and processed materials without import taxes provided the finished goods were reexported to the United States or some other foreign country. In turn, the U.S. government allowed the reimportation of the processed, assembled, packaged, or repaired products with only a low tariff applied; and this tariff was applied only to the value that had been added in Mexico. This tariff cost was much lower than the savings in labor costs. Facilities in the program had to be within a specified distance of the U.S.-Mexican border. Over 400 U.S. manufacturers in various industries, such as electronics, apparel, furniture, and automotive parts, decided to participate. This whole idea was a variation on the long-established concept of a free trade zone (also known as a foreign trade zone) but put into a larger context.

Several key items in the Mighty Tonka construction toy group were redesigned in 1983 to reduce their materials costs. Because the materials costs for some products and the labor costs for all products went down, unit production costs declined markedly. When these facts were taken in conjunction with the fact that demand was slightly soft, Tonka decided to decrease the prices of its line of traditional toys substantially in late 1983. This pricing action was taken in order to become more competitive and gain a larger share of this market. The share for such toys rose from about 23 per cent to about 30 per cent.

In addition, Tonka's management was troubled by trying to match production capacity needs with prudent fixed investment. Like some other corporations from time to time, Tonka became financially vulnerable every time there was a significant decline in sales. This vulnerability was principally because of large fixed investment in manufacturing facilities. The facilities were there, whether needed in total, in the majority, or just a fraction, tying up and using scarce capital. This set of concepts was not appreciated or even understood by consumers. Tonka adopted a policy of moving toward reliance on a combination of its own manufacturing capacity and that of independent suppliers under contract to Tonka. Such a contract might be for any time period from a few months to a few years, or it might be for a definite number of units of product. The new policy was implemented immediately and vigorously. In 1984 and 1985 approximately 40 per cent of Tonka's sales came from goods manufactured for the company by others to Tonka's specifications, and this figure was slowly trending upward. Nearly all of the newer products were made in this manner and came from outside North America. The El Paso and Ciudad Juárez plants made the line of traditional toys.

Critics had a field day. Tonka was attacked by critics of all political persuasions for allegedly abandoning its heritage, loyal employees, and the community that helped it get started and grow up. Critics did not note that some employees had not been terribly loyal; that the company's marketing area was widespread, not local, from the beginning; and that some prices were coming down. As with all companies participating in the Mexican border program, Tonka was also taken to task by liberals for "exploiting" and "abusing" Mexican workers in that it was not paying them as high wages and fringe benefits as it paid American citizens. The same critical comparisons were made between the workers in the El Paso plants, many of whom were American citizens of Mexican ancestry, and the former workers. Critics said virtually nothing then or later about the new contracts for supply from abroad.

Political conservatives got into this situation also. A group called Independent Republicans of Minnesota designed and ran an advertising campaign on the relocation in March 1984. The advertisement, which ran on 27 radio stations spread throughout the state, began with the following highly emotional wording: "Were you there when Tonka left Minnesota for Texas? How many jobs were lost that day? How many tears?" Apparently, sponsors of this campaign were not militantly anti-Tonka but were trying to raise public support for the repeal of a 10 per cent surcharge on state income taxes in Minnesota, which was already a high-tax state anyway. The Democratic party in Minnesota opposed the repeal. The overall promotional strategy of the Republican group included the argument that Tonka moved its production because of excessive, unjustified levels of state income tax in Minnesota. The president of Tonka made a public statement that the high income tax "played no part" in the decision.

Financial Scandal

The second trouble spot in corporate image and public relations revolved around an alleged misappropriation of funds discovered by outside auditors. The corporation's financial vice-president was accused of investing about $2 million of Tonka's money in a closely held company with which, according to Tonka's president, Stephen Shank, the financial vice-president had "a close relationship." Also he allegedly received "substantial payments" from that company. Later Tonka described the company as "a personal business venture." That company failed. Shank stated that the financial officer had led Tonka to believe the money was invested in a cash management fund. Using prudent and conservative accounting practices, Tonka recorded the loss and took a $1.3 million charge against corporate earnings. Tonka's earnings were already negative, about $2.6 million, and this action drove the figure to a loss of $3.9 million for 1983. The financial vice president was fired in early 1984. Tonka also filed a claim with its insurance carrier, Federal Insurance Company, a subsidiary of Chubb Corporation. In late 1984 the insurer paid $1.7 million in settlement of its obligations on the loss, and Tonka recorded an extraordinary gain on its books. Some observers were concerned about inadequate internal controls at Tonka, and some potential buyers of the corporate stock were put off by the whole affair.

Advise Tonka.

EXHIBIT 3 Consolidated Balance Sheets

Tonka Corporation and Subsidiaries (In millions)	Fiscal Year-End	
	1984	1983
Assets		
Current Assets:		
Cash and short-term investments	$ .5	$ 2.0
Accounts receivable—Net	31.6	4.6
Inventories	12.1	14.2
Prepaid expenses and other current assets	3.0	6.5
Assets identified for sale	4.4	—
Total Current Assets	51.6	27.3
Land, Buildings and Equipment		
Land	1.8	3.3
Buildings	10.4	17.1
Equipment	39.9	42.9
Total land, buildings and equipment	52.1	63.3
Less accumulated depreciation	32.0	36.8
Net Land, Buildings and Equipment	20.1	26.5
Other Assets	.4	.8
Total Assets	$72.1	$54.6
Liabilities and Stockholders' Equity		
Current Liabilities:		
Notes payable	$ 9.8	$ —
Accounts payable	8.7	5.2
Accrued taxes	1.5	1.0
Accrued payroll	2.3	1.4
Accrued advertising	2.8	1.6
Other current liabilities	4.3	7.4
Total Current Liabilities	29.4	16.6
Long-Term Debt	8.2	8.0
Deferred Income Taxes	2.6	2.1
Total Liabilities	40.2	26.7
Stockholders' Equity:		
Common stock	1.4	1.4
Additional paid-in capital	5.0	4.9
Retained earnings	27.3	22.7
Cumulative translation adjustments	(1.8)	(1.1)
Total Stockholders' Equity	31.9	27.9
Total Liabilities and Stockholders' Equity	$72.1	$54.6

NEW YORK METS BASEBALL CLUB

The New York Mets baseball team, a member of the National League, was established in 1962 after New York City had been without a participant in that league for four years. Through 1957 both the old New York Giants and Brooklyn Dodgers represented New York in the National League. At the beginning of the 1958 season, the former became the San Francisco Giants; and the latter, the Los Angeles Dodgers, as professional baseball at last decided to serve the large and lucrative sports markets of California.

The Paysons, a prominent New York business family, founded the Mets and immediately did an unconventional thing. They persuaded Casey Stengel, the seventy-one-year-old baseball veteran, to come out of a one-year retirement to manage the new club. Many considered this action a great coup. Many wondered why the highly successful Stengel would try his hand at the difficult task of building a new team.

One of the most colorful characters in baseball history, Stengel had been a player for several teams, including Philadelphia, Pittsburgh, Brooklyn, Boston, and New York—all in the National League. Later he managed Brooklyn and Boston. Stengel managed the New York Yankees for twelve seasons, 1949 through 1960, in which period they won the pennant ten times and finished in second place once and third place once. He then retired.

Although the talkative Stengel was a man who got much notice from the fans, the media, and the general public and was an acknowledged baseball wizard, the Mets finished in the cellar each of the four years 1962–1965. Because of an injury, Stengel semiretired at that point but served as a vice president for several more years. He died in 1975.

The Mets' low standings continued. In 1966 under Manager Wes Westrum the Mets finished ninth in the ten-team National League. The 1967 team, managed first by Westrum and then by Salty Parker, finished in last place. The 1968 team, under Manager Gil Hodges, ended the season in ninth place.

The year 1969 brought two major events. First, two teams were added to the National League, Montreal and San Diego, and the league began to play in two divisions, the East and the West. Besides the Mets, the East Division was composed of Chicago, St. Louis, Philadelphia, Pittsburgh, and Montreal. Second, there was what many sportswriters called "the miracle of Flushing Meadows." Under Gil Hodges, the Mets won the National League pennant, beating the Atlanta Braves in the play-offs, and then beat the Baltimore Orioles, winners of the American League, in the World Series by four games to one. They were termed "the Cinderella team" and "the unlikeliest champions in baseball history." The "Amazin' Mets" were called a mystical experience.

In 1970 the Mets finished third in the six-team East Division; and in 1971, fourth, as Gil Hodges continued as manager. In 1972 the Mets finished third. Yogi Berra replaced Hodges during that season. In 1973, Berra's Mets surprised everyone by winning the National League pennant, but they lost to Oakland by four games to three in the World Series. The league championship was achieved with the lowest winning statistic (.509) any champion had ever turned in. After 1973 the Mets again fell into a long period of mediocre to poor performance. In the mid-1980s performance improved.

The founders sold the franchise in 1980 for $21.6 million. The principal purchaser was Doubleday & Co., Inc., a long-established, family-owned book publishing enterprise, based in New York City. Nelson Doubleday, president of the acquiring organization, became chairperson of the board of directors of the Metropolitan Baseball Club of New York, the legally proper name of the Mets. Doubleday bought about 80 per cent of the corporate stock, and City Investing Company bought the remaining 20 per cent. Although mainly a publisher, Nelson Doubleday had already shown a strong business interest in sports and was a minority stockholder in the New York Islanders hockey team. Doubleday's friend John O. Pickett, Jr., who headed the Islanders and was a major investor in them, had brought about massive improvements in the Islanders, both athletically and commercially.

Nelson Doubleday did not regard the Mets as just a hobby. He was keenly interested and an active administrator, but he left technical-professional baseball decisions to his baseball experts. He was well acquainted with baseball, of course, and attended many of the Mets games. As a teenager he had been an enthusiastic Dodgers fan. Doubleday was a quiet, reticent man who did not cultivate publicity about himself.

The great-grand-uncle of Nelson Doubleday, General Abner Doubleday, was generally credited with formalizing the sport into the game as it is known today. Although the origins of baseball are obscure, it started in the colonial era of America and had several variations In 1839, Abner Doubleday, while a college student at West Point, devised at Cooperstown, New York, several basic rules of play and designed the playing field as used today. Some called him the inventor of baseball.

The Mets' playing field was Shea Stadium, a publicly owned facility built specifically for this club and finished in 1964. The first two seasons the Mets played at the Polo Grounds. Shea was in the middle-class Flushing Meadows section of the borough of Queens in New York City. This facility was about seven miles east of midtown Manhattan and was close to two major expressways, the subway, bus lines, and La Guardia Airport. Shea Stadium had a seating capacity of 55,300. Like about half of the National League playing fields, the diamond was perfectly symmetrical at Shea Stadium. The center field line, 410 feet, was about average for National League parks. The left and right center field lines were 371 feet. The left and right field lines were 338 feet.

Attendance at the Mets' home games was highly erratic, but the long-term average was certainly very poor. It had been as high as 2.7 million and as low as 700,000. There had been some improvement in the mid-1980s compared to the late 1970s and early 1980s. See Exhibit 3. Low attendance resulted in not only low gate receipts but also low sales of foods, beverages, and souvenirs. From 1977 through 1983 the Mets drew much larger crowds on the road than at home. Undependable attendance remained a source of concern.

The competition was really all other forms of recreation, but the most relevant was other professional sports. The New York City metropolitan area had professional clubs in all major sports, including basketball, hockey, soccer, and football, as well as baseball. There was, naturally, special concern about the other New York baseball club, the Yankees. These crosstown rivals in the American League played in Yankee Stadium in the Bronx in the northwest part of the city, about six miles from Shea Stadium and also the same distance from midtown Manhattan. Built in the early 1920s specifically for baseball, Yankee Stadium had a capacity of 57,545. It was extensively rebuilt in the years 1975–1976, and during this time the Yankees played in Shea. Yankee Stadium had slightly less field depth than Shea Stadium. Both stadiums were lighted. The Mets played some of their home games at night, and the proportion had been slowly rising. The Yankees played about three-fourths of their home games at night. See Exhibits 1, 2, and 3.

Professional baseball was considering expansion to more than the present 26 cities, 14 of which were in the American League and 12 in the National League. Many cities wanted teams, but baseball was a risky business, and the majority of teams were losing money. It was not expected that any new team would be located in or near New York City.

The owner of the Yankee franchise was George Steinbrenner, an outspoken and controversial person who attracted enormous news media attention. This activist owner was the most-discussed person in professional baseball and was fond of proclaiming, "I do it my

EXHIBIT 1 Mets Home Attendance 1980

Time of Game	Number of Games		Total Attendance		RATIO	Average Attendance
Daytime Mon.-Thurs	11	14.5%	86,904	7.4%	.51	7,900
Night Mon.-Thurs.	27	35.5%	285,181	24.2%	.68	10,562
Daytime Fri.-Sun.	23	30.3%	450,956	38.3%	1.26	19,606
Night Fri.-Sun.	15	19.7%	355,618	30.2%	1.53	23,708
Totals	76		1,178,659			15,508

EXHIBIT 2 Mets' Home Game Schedule and Attendance, 1984

Date No.	Game No.	Date	Day	Vs.	Game	Series	Season
1	1	4-17	Tue (D)	Mon	46,637		46,637
2	2	4-18	Wed (D)	Mon	11,147		57,784
3	3	4-19	Thu (D)	Mon	10,705	68,489	68,489
4	4	4-27	Fri (N)	Pha	18,171		89,660
5	5	4-28	Sat (D)	Pha	14,292		100,952
6	6	4-29	Sun (D)	Pha	28,562	61,025	129,514
7	7	5-1	Tue (N)	Chi	13,906		143,420
8	8	5-2	Wed (N)	Chi	11,059	24,965	154,479
9	9	5-4	Fri (N)	Hou	9,717		164,196
10	10	5-5	Sat (N)	Hou	16,895		181,091
11	11	5-6	Sun (D)	Hou	39,294	65,906	220,385
12	12	5-7	Mon (N)	Cin	6,942	6,942	227,327
13	13	5-9	Wed (N)	Atl	8,141		235,468
14	14	5-10	Thu (D)	Atl	6,900	15,041	242,368
15	15	5-22	Tue (N)	SF	14,834		257,202
16	16	5-24	Thu (N)	SF	12.363	27,197	269,565
17	17	5-25	Fri (N)	LA	27,340		296,905
18	18	5-26	Sat (D)	LA	20,051		316,956
19	19	5-27	Sun (D)	LA	26,465	73,856	343,421
20	20	5-28	Mon (D)	SD	36,204	36,204	379,625
21	21	5-31	Thu (N)	StL	7,440		387,065
22	22	6-1	Fri (N)	StL	20,968		408,033
23	23	6-2	Sat (N)	StL	24,879		432,912
24	24	6-3	Sun (D)	StL	13,723	67,010	446,635
25	25	6-11	Mon (N)	Pit	19,596		466,231
26	26	6-12	Tue (N)	Pit	14,255		480,486
27	27	6-13	Wed (N)	Pit	12,124	45,975	492,610

EXHIBIT 2 Mets' Home Game Schedule and Attendance, 1984 (Continued)

Date No.	Game No.	Date	Day	Vs.	Game	Series	Season
28	28	6-19	Tue (N)	Pha	28,061		520,671
29	29	6-20	Wed (N)	Pha	28,082		548,753
30	30	6-21	Thu (D)	Pha	20,094	76,237	568,847
31	31	6-22	Fri (N)	Mon	39,586		608,433
32	32	6-23	Sat (D)	Mon	46,301		654,734
33	33	6-24	Sun (D)	Mon	22,633	108,520	677,367
34	34	6-28	Thu (N)	Atl	15,077		692,444
35	35	6-29	Fri (N)	Atl	21,458		713,902
36	36-37	7-1	Sun (D)	Atl	8,949	45,484	722,851
37	38	7-2	Mon (N)	Hou	21,923		744,774
38	39	7-3	Tue (N)	Hou	16,601		761,375
39	40	7-4	Wed (N)	Hou	51,010	89,534	812,385
40	41	7-5	Thu (N)	Cin	14,041		826,426
41	42-43	7-6	Fri (N)	Cin	19,908		846,334
42	44	7-7	Sat (N)	Cin	35,004		881,338
43	45	7-8	Sun (D)	Cin	48,916	117,869	930,254
44	46	7-23	Mon (N)	StL	27,350		957,604
45	47	7-24	Tue (N)	StL	36,749		994,353
46	48	7-25	Wed (D)	StL	37,697	101,796	1,032,050
47	49	7-27	Fri (N)	Chi	51,102		1,083,152
48	50	7-28	Sat (D)	Chi	37,518		1,120,670
49	51-52	7-29	Sun (D)	Chi	50,443	139,063	1,171,113
50	53	8-9	Thu (N)	Pit	27,604		1,198,717
51	54	8-10	Fri (N)	Pit	28,355		1,227,072
52	55	8-11	Sat (N)	Pit	28,326		1,255,398
53	56	8-12	Sun (D)	Pit	36,135	120,420	1,291,533
54	57-58	8-24	Fri (N)	SF	31,834		1,323,367
55	59	8-25	Sat (N)	SF	23,823		1,347,190
56	60	8-26	Sun (D)	SF	22,046	77,703	1,369,236
57	61	8-27	Mon (N)	LA	33,765		1,403,001
58	62	8-28	Tue (N)	LA	25,854		1,428,855
59	63	8-29	Wed (N)	LA	26,290	85,909	1,455,145
60	64-65	8-31	Fri (N)	SD	38,323		1,493,468
61	66-67	9-1	Sat (N)	SD	35,688		1,529,156
62	68	9-2	Sun (D)	SD	36,915	110,926	1,566,071
63	69	9-7	Fri (N)	Chi	46,301		1,612,372
64	70	9-8	Sat (N)	Chi	42,810		1,655,182
65	71	9-9	Sun (D)	Chi	34,956	124,067	1,690,138
66	72	9-10	Mon (N)	StL	9,995		1,700,133
67	73	9-11	Tue (N)	StL	14,968	24,963	1,715,101
68	74	9-12	Wed (N)	Pit	12,876		1,727,977
69	75	9-13	Thu (D)	Pit	6,076	18,952	1,734,053
70	76	9-21	Fri (N)	Mon	15,458		1,749,511

EXHIBIT 2 Mets' Home Game Schedule and Attendance, 1984 (Continued)

Date No.	Game No.	Date	Day	Vs.	Game	Series	Season
71	77	9-22	Sat (D)	Mon	27,666		1,777,177
72	78	9-23	Sun (D)	Mon	22,171	65,295	1,799,348
73	79	9-24	Mon (N)	Pha	11,071		1,810,419
74	80	9-25	Tue (N)	Pha	13,812		1,824,231
75	81	9-26	Wed (D)	Pha	5,251	30,134	1,829,482

EXHIBIT 3 Mets' Home Game Schedule and Attendance, 1985

Date No.	Game No.	Date	Day	Vs.	Game	Series	Season
1	1	4-9	Tue (D)	StL	46,781*		46,781
2	2	4-11	Thu (D)	StL	18,864	65,645	65,645
3	3	4-12	Fri (N)	Cin	31,120		96,765
4	4	4-13	Sat (D)	Cin	26,212		122,977
5	5	4-14	Sun (D)	Cin	30,456	87,788	153,433
6	6	4-26	Fri (N)	Pit	31,846		185,279
7	7	4-27	Sat (D)	Pit	24,786		210,065
8	8	4-28	Sun (D)	Pit	36,423	93,055	246,488
9	9	4-30	Tue (N)	Hou	31,558		278,046
10	10	5-1	Wed (N)	Hou	17,973	49,531	296,019
11	11	5-7	Tue (N)	Atl	21,342		317,361
12	12	5-8	Wed (N)	Atl	20,905	42,247	338,266
13	13	5-10	Fri (N)	Pha	46,143		384,409
14	14	5-11	Sat (D)	Pha	29,635		414,044
15	15	5-12	Sun (D)	Pha	32,597	108,375	446,641
16	16	5-17	Fri (N)	SF	23,428		470,069
17	17	5-18	Sat (N)	SF	32,646		502,715
18	18	5-19	Sun (D)	SF	50,369*	106,443	553,084
19	19	5-20	Mon (N)	SD	36,672		589,756
20	20	5-22	Wed (N)	SD	23,468	60,140	613,224
21	21	5-24	Fri (N)	LA	37,124		650,348
22	22	5-25	Sat (D)	LA	40,052		690,400
23	23	5-26	Sun (D)	LA	36,234		726,634
24	24	5-27	Mon (N)	LA	24,458	137,868	751,092
25	25	6-7	Fri (N)	StL	34,490		785,582
2C	26	6-8	Sat (D)	StL	36,424		822,006
27	27-28	6-9	Sun (D)√	StL	41,431	112,345	863,437
28	29	6-17	Mon (N)	Chi	41,986		905,423
29	30	6-18	Tue (N)	Chi	41,325		946,748
30	31	6-19	Wed (N)	Chi	51,778*		998,526
31	32	6-20	Thu (D)	Chi	37,203	172,292	1,035,729

EXHIBIT 3 Mets' Home Game Schedule and Attendance, 1985 (Continued)

Date No.	Game No.	Date	Day	Vs.	Game	Series	Season
32	33	6-21	Fri (N)	Mon	38,554		1,074,283
33	34	6-22	Sat (N)	Mon	51,513*		1,125,796
34	35	6-23	Sun (D)	Mon	44,506	134,573	1,170,302
35	36	7-1	Mon (N)	Pit	21,610		1,191,912
36	37	7-2	Tue (N)	Pit	22,651		1,214,563
37	38	7-3	Wed.(N)	Pit	46,220*	90,481	1,260,783
38	39	7-18	Thu (N)	Atl	30,496		1,291,279
39	40	7-19	Fri (N)	Atl	36,572		1,327,851
40	41	7-20	Sat (D)	Atl	35,650		1,363,501
41	42	7-21	Sun (D)	Atl	50,876*	153,594	1,414,377
42	43	7-22	Mon (N)	Cin	27,471		1,441,848
43	44	7-23	Tue (N)	Cin	34,720		1,476,568
44	45	7-24	Wed (D)	Cin	30,154	92,345	1,506,722
45	46	7-25	Thu (N)	Hou	28,421		1,535,143
46	47-48	7-27	Sat (N) ✓	Hou	51,284*		1,586,427
47	49	7-28	Sun (D)	Hou	34,298	114,003	1,620,725
48	50	7-29	Mon (N)	Mon	30,693		1,651,418
49	51	7-30	Tue (N)	Mon	45,118		1,696,536
50	52	7-31	Wed (D)	Mon	26,055	101,866	1,722,591
51	53	8-9	Fri (N)	Chi	44,309		1,766,900
52	54	8-10	Sat (D)	Chi	48,306		1,815,206
53	55	8-11	Sun (D)	Chi	40,311	132,926	1,855,517
54	56	8-12	Mon (N)	Pha	26,577		1,882,094
55	57	8-13	Tue (N)	Pha	31,186		1,913,280
56	58	8-14	Wed (N)	Pha	31,549		1,944,829
57	59	8-15	Thu (D)	Pha	36,663	125,975	1,981,492
58	60	8-20	Tue (N)	SF	31,758		2,013,250
59	61	8-21	Wed (N)	SF	22,450		2,035,700
60	62	8-22	Thu (N)	SF	24,536	78,744	2,060,236
61	63-64	8-23	Fri (N) ✓	SD	45,156		2,105,392
62	65	8-24	Sat (N)	SD	40,863		2,146,255
63	66	8-25	Sun (D)	SD	37,350	123,369	2,183,605
64	67	8-26	Mon (N)	LA	43,063		2,226,668
65	68	8-27	Tue (N)	LA	42,764	85,827	2,269,432
66	69	9-10	Tue (N)	StL	50,195*		2,319,627
67	70	9-11	Wed (N)	StL	52,616*		2,372,243
68	71	9-12	Thu (D)	StL	46,295	149,106	2,418,538
69	72	9-16	Mon (N)	Pha	30,606		2,449,144
70	73	9-17	Tue (N)	Pha	22,440	53,046	2,471,584
71	74	9-18	Wed (N)	Chi	25,424		2,497,008
72	75	9-19	Thu (N)	Chi	26,812	52,236	2,523,820
73	76	9-20	Fri (N)	Pit	33,803		2,557,623
74	77	9-21	Sat (D)	Pit	49,931		2,607,554
75	78	9-22	Sun (D)	Pit	35,679	119,413	2,643,233

M-Th	D	7 (9%) 34574	242015	8.8%	.98
m-Th	N	33 (42%) 32147	1,060,841	38.6%	.91
F-S	D	22 (28.2) 38,128	838,820	30.5%	1.08
F-S	N	16 (20.5) 38110	609,761	22.2%	1.08
		78 dates			

EXHIBIT 3 Mets' Home Game Schedule and Attendance, 1985 (Continued)

Date No.	Game No.	Date	Day	Vs.	Game	Series	Season
76	79	10-4	Fri (N)	Mon	30,910		2,674,143
77	80	10-5	Sat (D)	Mon	45,404		2,719,547
78	81	10-6	Sun (D)	Mon	31,890	108,204	2,751,437

*denotes sellout

way." He believed strongly that one cannot just call it "the grand old game" and expect people to walk through the turnstiles. Steinbrenner took the long-held mystique of the Yankees and added to it.

A fundamental strategy of the Mets' management and coaching had been joint effort, with emphasis on the team instead of on individual stars. Some cynics believed that this was more of a money-saving device than a strategy. At any rate, the Mets had hired or developed (or both) few widely known performers. The National League's Most Valuable Player Award had never gone to a Met. The same was true for the Home Run Leader Award and the Batting Championship. The most notable exception to the nonstar theme was Tom Seaver, who was voted the National League's Rookie of the Year in 1967 and won the Cy Young Award for pitching in 1969, 1973, and 1975. Three Mets players had won the award of National League Rookie of the Year. These were pitcher Jon Matlack in 1972, outfielder Darryl Strawberry in 1983, and pitcher Dwight Gooden in 1984. Gooden won the Cy Young award in 1985. Both Seaver and Matlack moved on to other clubs at much higher salaries. Management mishandled Seaver's request for contract negotiations in 1977, and tempers flared. Seaver was articulate and witty and enjoyed good relations with the news media. For a short while, he held the extra job of player representative, doing some negotiation and acting in a liaison capacity. This fact plus his stardom hastened his rupture with the Mets management. Seaver was reaquired from the Cincinnati Reds in 1983, but on January 20, 1984, he was claimed by the Chicago White Sox in a free agent compensation pool.

One of the behavioral principles of sports business management that had emerged in the last decade or so was that good batting is more satisfying to most fans than is good pitching. According to this line of reasoning, finely controlled pitching is appreciated and admired by people who like baseball, but, if given a choice, they would prefer to watch a good display of hitting. Although an active task, pitching was not as active as batting and perhaps not as active as fielding. Contemporary sports fans and journalists seemed to admire action more than those of a generation past. Some purists among baseball fans insist that perfect balance among pitching, batting, and fielding is the goal for which a team should strive.

The conventional wisdom in sports management had always been that a winning team brought out large crowds; and a losing team, small crowds. Commercial success came from a high rate of winning according to tradition. However, recently some people of a more analytical frame of mind had started questioning this idea and called it nothing more than a naive assumption. There was only limited evidence to support the assumption if one gathered the economic data and analyzed them objectively. Many poor teams drew large crowds, and many good teams drew small crowds. This was true even after adjustments for size of the population in the territory around the team and the income levels of that population. A specific example sometimes cited was that of the Yankees in 1977, 1978, and 1979. In the first two of those three years, the Yankees were the world champions. In 1979 the Yankees finished fourth in the American League, but home attendance rose more than 200,000 (9 per cent) over 1978. See Exhibit 4.

High-quality management of factors other than the team's on-the-field performance could and should overcome most, if not all, of the effect of poor team performance and thus permit the club to earn a satisfactory level of profit. None of this meant that winning games was unimportant. It meant that winning games was not the only factor in the economic success of a team. The conventional wisdom that guided most professional sports businesses was simplistic and out of touch with reality.

One of the most respected voices in athletics, *Sports Illustrated* magazine, recently noted that the Mets did not understand who their fans were and where these fans came from. The Mets management assumed a preponderance of affluent suburbanites from north of the city but finally found, after hiring marketing research consultants, that the fans were mostly working-class people who lived close by in the Brooklyn and Queens portions of the city and from some close working-class suburbs on Long Island. Matthew Levine, president of Pacific Select Corporation, a marketing research and consulting firm retained by the Mets, concluded that the owners prior to Doubleday were among the most disliked owners in sports.[1]

Many observers believed that the Mets had become rather well known, both at home and on the road. Yet that image was not very good. Among the prevailing perceptions of the Mets team were the following recurring descriptions: laughable, juvenile, and inept but

[1] "More Victories Equals More Fans Equals More Profits, Right? Wrong, Wrong, Wrong," *Sports Illustrated,* April 28, 1980, pp. 34–45.

EXHIBIT 4 Home Attendance by Year,
Yankees and Mets

Year	Yankees	Mets		
1956	1,491,784			
1957	1,497,134			
1958	1,428,438			
1959	1,552,030			
1960	1,627,349			
1961	1,747,736			
1962	1,493,574	922,530		
1963	1,308,920	1,080,108		
1964	1,305,638	1,732,597		
1965	1,213,552	1,768,389		
1966	1,124,648	1,932,693		
1967	1,141,714	1,565,492		
1968	1,125,124	1,781,657		
1969	1,067,996	2,175,373		
1970	1,136,879	2,697,479		
1971	1,070,771	2,266,680		
1972	966,328	2,134,185		
1973	1,262,077	1,912,390		
1974	1,273,075	1,722,209		
1975	1,288,048	1,730,566	3.02m	57.3%
1976	2,012,434	1,468,754	3.48m	42.2%
1977	2,103,092	1,066,825	3.17m	33.6%
1978	2,335,871	1,007,328	3.34m	30.2%
1979	2,537,765	788,905	3.33m	23.7%
1980	2,627,417	1,178,659	3.81m	30.9%
1981*	1,614,353	704,244	2.32m — strike 30.3%
1982	2,041,219	1,320,055	3.36m	39.3%
1983	2,257,976	1,103,808	3.36m	32.9%
1984	1,821,815	1,829,482	3.65m	50.1%
1985	2,214,587	2,751,437	4.97m	55.4%

Doubleday bought → (handwritten, at 1980)

*A strike shortened the 1981 season for all
teams. The Mets played only 52 home dates
and the Yankees 50.

occasionally lovable. A large part of the time they were referred to
by a diminutive form of their name, the Metsies. Use of the diminutive was sometimes an approval and sometimes a put-down. Nearly
all the sports news media consistently expressed the viewpoint,
"What's the latest thing the Mets have done to blow the ball game?"
Public relations was certainly not used to its potential to assist the
organization.

Advise the management of the New York Mets.

DR. PEPPER COMPANY

Dr. Pepper, formerly a large but only regional producer of a brand holding fifth place in the United States in the soft-drink industry, expanded to national coverage in 1969. By 1981 it had captured third place in the industry after the first place Coca-Cola brand and the second place Pepsi-Cola brand. From 1982 to 1984, 7–Up regained the third place, but Dr. Pepper and 7–Up were of almost identical size and virtually tied for third place among brands. However, Dr. Pepper was consistently profitable, and 7-Up was not. Dr. Pepper regained third place in 1985.

About 800 brands of soft drinks were produced in the United States, but the top ten commanded about three-fourths of the market. Besides the brands just mentioned, important ones included Sprite, Tab, Mello Yello, and Fanta from Coca-Cola Co.; Mountain Dew from Pepsico, Inc.; Royal Crown Cola and Nehi from Royal Crown Company; Sunkist, Canada Dry ginger ale, and Schweppes from Cadbury-Schweppes; Orange Crush and Hires root beer from Procter and Gamble; Shasta; Squirt; Faygo; Nu-Grape; Dad's root beer; and the diet and caffeine-free versions of several of these brands. Pepsi-Cola became the leading brand in the United States in 1985 after Coca-Cola's patronage was split into Classic Coke and New Coke. Coca-Cola Co. remained the largest soft drink organization, but Pepsico was growing faster. The industry's unit volume was expected to increase about 5 to 6 per cent per year during the late 1980s and early 1990s.

In 1984, Dr. Pepper Company was bought by Forstmann Little & Co., a New York City investment firm backed by several financiers and large pension funds in a leveraged transaction for $623 million. The other aggressive suitor was Castle & Cooke, Inc., producers of Dole brand products. In such a transaction the buyers work largely with borrowed money, pledging assets about to be acquired to secure the new debt. Dr. Pepper Company officials were hoping that this maneuver was a way to high growth. In an earlier leveraged buyout, Forstman Little had purchased Topps Chewing Gum, Inc., and several small firms. Forstmann Little saw in Dr. Pepper Company the crucial factors for a profitable buyout: good and fairly predictable cash flow; a loyal base of customers; and, most important, undervaluation of the assets as perceived by the financial publics. This last factor meant that the individual assets of the company were worth more than their combined worth in one company. In other words, it was the *reverse* of the old expression, "The whole is worth more than the sum of its parts." Following the buyout, Dr. Pepper's chairperson of the board, W. W. Clements, stayed on, but the president, Richard Armstrong, resigned.

In 1986 Forstmann agreed to sell Dr. Pepper to Coca-Cola. The Federal Trade Commission and RC Cola filed suit to block this sale, alleging that there would be too much concentration in the industry and too little competition. The parties cancelled the arrangement. A few weeks later Dr. Pepper was sold for $416 million to a group of investors, including Shearson-Lehman Brothers, Inc., several Dr. Pepper executives, Cadbury-Schweppes PLC, and Hicks & Haas. Cadbury-Schweppes, a large British maker of candy and beverages, bought about 30 per cent of the shares. Hicks & Haas already owned one-third of A & W Beverages, makers of root beer.

The archrival 7-Up Company became a wholly owned subsidiary of Philip Morris, Inc., in 1981 at a purchase price of $520 million cash. With access to new talent and additional capital, 7-Up was expected to become quite aggressive after a year or two of reevaluation and planning under the new ownership. This brand was widely promoted as "the Uncola" by both the old and the new owners. However, 7-Up lost money four out of the five years 1981–1985, and Philip Morris sold it to Pepsico, Inc., in January 1986 at a small loss. The FTC and RC Cola filed suit to block this sale, on the same grounds as their complaint against Dr. Pepper. The parties cancelled the sale. Schweppes was considering trying to buy 7-Up.

Dr. Pepper brand enjoyed 5.1 per cent of the U.S. market whereas Sugar Free Dr. Pepper had 1.0 per cent; Sugar Free Pepper Free, 0.1 per cent; and Pepper Free, another 0.1 per cent. Dr. Pepper Company's Welch brand line of fruit-flavored drinks had 0.5 per cent. Thus, the company had a total market share of approximately 6.8 per cent, selling about 470 million cases annually.

Based in Dallas, Dr. Pepper Company had sales of about $550 million and net profits of about $60 million in the latest year. Sales and profits were on a strong trend of improvement. The company employed about 400 persons at its Dallas headquarters. Sales of Dr. Pepper Company's products at the retail level were several times the $550 million, of course. Dr. Pepper made soft drink concentrates and fountain syrups and sold them to about 500 bottlers that were unaffiliated with Dr. Pepper Company. These franchised firms converted the concentrates to bottled and canned beverages by adding sweeteners and carbonated water. Some bottlers also held franchises for one or more competitive brands, using the same physical facilities. Dr. Pepper Company sold fountain syrups to franchised bottlers and wholesale distributors and directly to some fountain accounts, such as fast-food restaurant chains. Until the purchase by Forstmann Little, Dr. Pepper was partially integrated vertically, conducting its own bottling operations in ten locations: Dallas-Fort Worth, Los Angeles, Houston, San Antonio, Waco, Corpus Christi, Albuquerque, Mobile, Pensacola, and Washington, North Carolina. These plants provided about 50 per cent of company sales dollars and served well over 10 per cent of the national demand for Dr. Pepper products. All these facilities were in areas where Dr. Pepper enjoyed large sales and high brand loyalty. As an independent, Dr. Pepper had been expanding its investments in bottling. It had purchased the Los Angeles, Houston, Albuquerque, Mobile, Pensacola, and Washington, North Carolina, plants between 1977 and 1983. Forstmann Little divested all these bottling facilities one at a time during its two years of ownership. In a leveraged buyout, the new owners normally pay off part of the debt incurred in buying the organization by selling off selected assets whose loss would not destroy the company but would bring good prices. The dismemberment of the Dr. Pepper Company came as a surprise to some of the veteran managers and former shareholders.

Although national in scope, Dr. Pepper's deepest market penetration was in Texas and California. However, it was also strong throughout the Sun Belt. Because population and incomes were rising faster there than in the nation as a whole, Dr. Pepper considered itself to be in a fairly promising situation. In addition, in the regions where Dr. Pepper was strong, teenagers and young adults comprised a larger share of the population than in the country as a whole. Such age groups consumed more sodas per capita than did middle-aged and elderly people.

Dr. Pepper Company bought the exclusive marketing rights to the Welch's line of carbonated soft drinks in late 1981. Started in 1974 by Welch Foods, Inc., this line consisted of several fruit flavors but emphasized grape and strawberry. Welch's was targeted to the traditional users of these sodas, black and Hispanic teenagers, especially for consumption away from home. Dr. Pepper Company set up a subsidiary, Premier Beverages, Inc., to handle this group of products.

In early 1982, Dr. Pepper Company purchased Canada Dry Corp. from Norton Simon, Inc., a conglomerate. Canada Dry made and marketed a successful bitter lemon soda and ginger ale, both successful but not in the top ten sellers. It also had a popular line of mixers, including tonic water and club soda (a sparkling water). Tonic water was occasionally drunk by itself but was usually mixed with vodka or gin. American liquor consumption was slowly shifting toward more "white goods" and less whiskey. Forstmann Little sold Canada Dry to R. J. Reynolds Industries, the tobacco-based conglomerate, a few months after purchasing Dr. Pepper Company. Cadbury

Schweppes PLC bought Canada Dry and Sunkist from R. J. Reynolds in 1986.

For several years before the purchase of Canada Dry, Dr. Pepper Company had been interested in buying Crush International, Ltd., of Vancouver, Canada, whose major products were Orange Crush and Hires root beer. However, giant detergent, toiletries, and food manufacturer Procter and Gamble, looking for further diversification, beat out Dr. Pepper Company and bought that organization in 1980. Dr. Pepper maintained that its offer was about $2 million higher than Procter and Gamble's but that Crush sold to the other company because of the prospect of lengthy litigation by Procter and Gamble if Crush selected Dr. Pepper. It was expected that Procter and Gamble would develop a cola drink soon to add to the acquired line of beverages. Procter and Gamble soon bought an established bottler so as to gain experience with the whole spectrum of soft-drink operations.

Like all soft-drink enterprises, Dr. Pepper was vitally concerned about the high and often volatile costs of sugar. The company was expanding its use of high-fructose corn sweetener, which cost much less than traditional sugars. Most other soft-drink organizations were making similar adaptations.

At the head of the Dr. Pepper organization was seventy-one-year-old W. W. "Foots" Clements, who worked his way through college by driving a Dr. Pepper truck and serving the accounts on a route. After college he worked in sales and later on the corporate marketing staff. He became general sales manager, then president, and finally chief executive and chairperson of the board of directors. In that capacity, he worked mainly on long-range planning. There had been a high turnover in the position of president and chief operating officer. From 1980 to 1982, Charles L. Jarvie, formerly corporate vice president for Procter and Gamble's Food Products Division filled this position. However, when the national share of the market stopped growing and the product line continued to languish in the northeast (where the share of the market was only 2 per cent), he resigned. Jarvie had pushed television network advertising and held a million-dollar lottery, which Clements called "ill-conceived." Richard Q. Armstrong, who had been president of Canada Dry at the time Dr. Pepper purchased that organization, replaced Jarvie. Armstrong left immediately when the sale to Forstmann Little was decided on. The president and chief operating officer then became fifty-nine-year-old Joe K. Hughes, formerly the Dr. Pepper Company's executive vice president. He had been with the company almost twenty years. That did not work out. By the end of 1984, Hughes was named vice chairperson of the board without line authority over the president. The new president was John Albers, who had served briefly as executive vice-president. In 1985, Robert Hamlin was appointed vice president for marketing. He had been Young & Rubicam's account executive for Dr. Pepper advertising for many years.

The Dr. Pepper beverage was invented in 1885 by a pharmacist working for Wade Morrison, a young druggist, in Waco. Morrison was quite interested in the daughter of Dr. Charles Pepper, a physician. However, Pepper had not allowed Morrison to court his daughter. Morrison thought that surely the father would relent if he named his great new beverage for him. The tactic did not work, but the brand name continued.

Morrison's design objective was to combine a great many of the attractive aromas of the sodas of his day. Therefore, the highly secret formula for this brand had twenty-three ingredients, many of them old-fashioned fruit extracts. There was also a sizeable amount of caffeine. Many people who tried Dr. Pepper concluded that cherry was the single most important flavor, but the company indicated several years ago that cherry was not in the formula. Even Clements assumed that there was cherry until he had been with the organization for twenty years. Many people thought they detected prunes. Some people thought the beverage had laxative characteristics, whether or not prunes were included.

Unfortunately, both the name and the taste of Dr. Pepper suggested to most people something medicinal or, at least, partly medicinal. Clements readily admitted, "People never knew whether to drink it or rub it on." Besides the simplistic implication of medication, the words "Dr. Pepper" did not seem to convey any particular meaning to people, unlike the names of several competitive soft drinks. In addition, the taste was not easily described. The producer had always had difficulty describing the taste to people in its consumer advertising and in its face-to-face selling to accounts.

Because the Dr. Pepper drink was difficult to classify by taste and, in all fairness, could be said to be unique, competitors had worked on the development of items of a similar taste to compete with it. This task became more important as the sales of Dr. Pepper grew. Coca-Cola introduced Mr. Pibb in 1972, but it was not very successful. It had only 0.3 per cent of the market, but it remained in the product line. Then Coca-Cola introduced Cherry Coke in early 1985, and Royal Crown introduced Cherry R. C. in the spring of 1985. Pepsico launched Cherry Pepsi in Canada in late 1985 and, without test marketing, launched it in Great Britain in January 1986. Pepsico planned to introduce the product in the United States quickly. All three organizations publicly stated that these cherry flavored drinks were not aimed at Dr. Pepper, but most industry observers, market analysts, and journalists believed otherwise. The cherry emphasis was stronger than in the Dr. Pepper products, but there were definite similarities. Coca-Cola had done tests on Cherry Coke for several years. Its research indicated that potential Cherry Coke consumers would be close to the mainstream but willing to be a little different.

Advertising and Sales Promotion

Some of the advertising in the early years of the product was curious. One theme used for many years was a cartoon trademark called "The Old Doc," a character who resembled "Reddy Kilowatt." This theme probably reinforced the suspicion that Dr. Pepper was an effective laxative. Later, in 1927, Dallas advertising specialist Earle Racy created the theme "Drink a Bite to Eat at 10, 2, and 4 O'Clock." This was based on a book, *The Liquid Bite,* by a Columbia University professor, Walter H. Eddy, whose research into the human diet revealed in-between-meal times when blood sugar reached its low points. The rationale for the theme was that because Dr. Pepper metabolized quickly, it restored energy during the valley hours of 10:30 A.M. and 2:30 and 4:30 P.M. This theme was used for more than a quarter of a century. Racy received a $25 bonus for creating this advertising theme. The theme and rationale were so persuasive that J. B. O'Hara, then president of Dr. Pepper Company, took the lead for the industry and, in conjunction with the chief executives of several other soft-drink companies, convinced the War Rationing Board to rescind a ruling that would have severely rationed the sugar allowed to the soft-drink industry during World War II.

The advertising and sales promotion of Dr. Pepper since it went national had been extremely interesting. In 1969 Dr. Pepper placed its account with Young & Rubicam, Inc., a large New York advertising agency. This agency attempted to remove the fuzzy and sometimes medicinal image of Dr. Pepper and build for it a distinctive image. In the first phase of the long-range plan, the agency introduced this beverage in an audacious manner that was very unconventional: "America's most misunderstood soft drink." Manufacturers and advertising agencies almost never consider any admission of public confusion about a product, preferring to be constantly positive. This musical jingle theme stated, "Dr. Pepper, so misunderstood . . . It's not a cola, it's not a root beer, it's something much, much more . . . ." Young & Rubicam wanted to establish that Dr. Pepper was different from other soft drinks, and it and the manufacturer were willing to take the risk of approaching the misunderstanding directly. Several television special shows with big-name stars were sponsored by Dr. Pepper. This phase ran for more than two years.

The second phase was the "Most Original" theme campaign. This phase sought to position Dr. Pepper as a soda in a class by itself. While most major competitors were using variations of the "kids on the beach" sorts of themes, Young & Rubicam developed a series of large-scale, highly theatrical production numbers complete with elaborate singing and dancing routines in the old tradition of producer-director Busby Berkeley. Dr. Pepper was promoted as the change-of-pace drink for special people. The social self-confidence of users and those first trying the drink needed to be built up. Phase two also later included the theme, "You've got to try it to love it," followed by the theme "Once you try it you'll love the difference." It was vital to keep talking about trying it, not only because so many people had not done so, but also because the first try did not usually make a convert. The consumer regarded the first few trials as just that. Four to six servings were usually necessary before a person adopted this beverage, if at all. Phase two, which won many awards in the advertising profession, lasted about five years.

By 1977 the manufacturer and Young & Rubicam were ready to go into phase three, which was supposed to position Dr. Pepper in the mainstream of the American life-style. They wanted to picture it as the popular beverage for every occasion. They developed "The Pepper," a Pied Piperlike character who danced from town to town and coast to coast leading a joyous crowd in a groundswell of support for this universally enjoyed, admired beverage. A "Pepper" was portrayed as a self-confident, bold, and popular person. David Naughton, an unknown 23-year-old actor, was hired as the Pepper. Emphasis was targeted towards the 13- to 30-year-old segment of consumers. Advertisements in phase three were less sophisticated and used simpler story lines and songs than in phase two. Naughton's amateur voice was used for the songs. As the Pepper character became more recognizable to viewers, the age target was broadened a little, and celebrities and cartoon characters were built in, for example, Ron Guidry, Charlie Rich, Fred Flintstone, Tweetie Bird, Sylvester, and Popeye.

With the success of company sales, phase three was altered somewhat in 1981 to try to convert nonusers, including specifically those who still had never heard of Dr. Pepper and those who knew of it but had not tried it. Naughton was continued, and each new advertisement explored a fanciful facet of his persona. For example, in a thirty-second spot entitled "Sign," he magically produced a rainbow that swirled across the scene to become a glittering Dr. Pepper sign. In a sixty-second spot entitled "Whistling," the Pepper was paired with Mickey Rooney in a production number containing only music and a whistle in the sound track. The idea was to encourage viewers to become participants in the commercial. The jingle had become much more familiar to viewers than the jingles of most other advertisers.

With hindsight, both Dr. Pepper Company and Young & Rubicam were unhappy with the series of advertising campaigns built around "The Pepper." Awareness of the product rose but share of the market did not. According to the advertising agency, this drink tried to become a soda for the masses. That mass appeal made Dr. Pepper's advertising too much like that of Coca-Cola and Pepsi. Psychographic studies showed that consumers who tended to like Dr. Pepper's taste were apt to be "inner-directed" rather than "outer-directed" or "other-directed." They did not place a great deal of weight on doing what other people expected them to do, instead emphasizing their own personal values. What is more, Coke and Pepsi already had better-accepted flavors and several times as much money to spend on advertising. Therefore, in 1984, Dr. Pepper returned to the advertising strategy that had helped it grow in the 1970s. In 1975 the company had been extremely pleased with the slogan "the most original soft drink ever in the whole wide world." In 1984 and 1985 the company went with a slogan "Hold out for the out-of-the-ordinary." The intended image was that Dr. Pepper was the choice of the independent thinker who was looking for an alternative to colas.

Exhibit 1 presents selected advertisements from the planned 1986 and 1987 television campaigns. The overall theme line was "Out of the ordinary. Like you." On radio the Dr. Pepper commercials were to be in the style of hit songs of 30 seconds, 60 seconds, and two minutes in length and rendered in the singing styles of several star performers. Each song had a story to tell with Dr. Pepper cleverly worked in. Both television and radio were aimed primarily at the youth audiences and stressed two psychological moods, fun and irreverence for the traditional.

For Sugar Free Dr. Pepper, now renamed Diet Dr. Pepper, there were multiple series of advertisements built around "Stargazers," "Godzilla Too," and "Droids." The theme line was "Diet Dr. Pepper. The taste for out of the ordinary bodies." The wording suggested the health benefit of this brand but still tied in with the advertising for the flagship brand. The company had always been cautious about the word "diet" but now felt that the word carried more positive than negative connotations for the consumer.

Robert Hamlin, the company marketing vice president, tried to sum up the advertising strategy: "Dr. Pepper commercials tell a story, often with a twist at the end, and they involve the consumer.

This is captivating entertainment value that pays off in long-lasting awareness." Hamlin had been involved in Dr. Pepper's advertising since 1977.

Dr. Pepper became more agressive in 1986 with its sales promotions. In-store sweepstakes were organized, one for each quarter of the year with seasonally appropriate premiums and colorful point-of-sale material. Cooperative advertising on radio, on television, and in newspapers was offered to bottlers.

Advise Dr. Pepper Company.

UNITED WAY

The United Way[1] was probably the best known name in the business of charity. It traced its roots back under a series of former names to 1887 in Denver when the first United Community Campaign was organized. From the 1920s through the 1940s the prevailing name was the Community Chest. After that time it was widely known as the United Fund and, in places, United Givers. In the 1970s the designation of United Way became prevalent.

Along the route of development several innovations occurred at the local level. In 1908, in Pittsburgh, the first organized fact-finding group in charity was created. In 1913, Cleveland introduced the concept of budgeting for charity fund raising. And, in 1919, Rochester, seeing the need for a permanent name for the movement that had some promotional qualities, coined the name Community Chest.

The underlying concept of the United Way was a federation for seeking contributions. It raised money simultaneously for many good causes, thus cutting down on duplication of fund-raising drives and saving time and frustration for donors. Individual charities within local United Ways received about one fourth of their funding from the annual United Way campaign on the average. The remainder of funding came from grants and bequests, from government agencies in fees

[1] Helpful material can be found in the following: William A. Mindak and H. Malcolm Bybee, "Marketing's Application to Fund Raising," *Journal of Marketing*, 35 (July 1971), pp. 13–18; Ben M. Enis, "Deepening the Concept of Marketing," *Journal of Marketing*, 37 (October 1973), pp. 57–62; Philip Kotler, "Defining the Limits of Marketing," in Boris Becker and Helmet Becker, Eds., *Combined Proceedings of the 1972 Conferences* (Chicago: American Marketing Association, 1972), pp. 48–56; Sidney J. Levy and Philip Kotler, "Beyond Marketing: The Furthering Concept," *California Management Review*, 12 (Winter 1969), pp. 67–73; Philip Kotler and Sidney J. Levy, "Broadening the Concept of Marketing," *Journal of Marketing*, 33 (January 1969), pp. 10–15; David J. Luck, "Broadening the Concept of Marketing–Too Far," *Journal of Marketing*, 33 (July 1969), pp. 53–55; Philip Kotler and Sidney J. Levy, "A New Form of Marketing Myopia: Rejoinder to Professor Luck," *Journal of Marketing*, 33 (July 1969), pp. 55–57; and Philip Kotler, "A Generic Concept of Marketing," *Journal of Marketing*, 36 (April 1972), pp. 46–54.

for contracted services, and from supplemental fund-raising drives. These supplemental drives were approved or condoned by the United Way.

By any standard of measurement, charity in the United States was large, totaling about $47 billion in the most recent year. Sources of donations in most years tended to break down in approximately the following shares: individuals, 80 per cent; wills of recently deceased individuals, 8 per cent; foundations, 7 per cent; corporations, 5 per cent. Most of the foundations received their original endowments from major entrepreneurs in the business world. Most of the bequests in wills were in the form of securities, real estate, and objects of art rather than cash. Approximately 43 per cent of giving went to religious bodies and the rest went to a large variety of civic, welfare, humanitarian, educational, artistic, and health-related organizations. Of the money for nonreligious use, approximately 6 per cent, or more than $1.5 billion, was collected and allocated by the United Way. Sources of funds and their shares of contributions to the United Way in the three most recent years are shown in Exhibit 1. This table indicates that this organization received relatively much more from corporations and relatively much less from individuals than did charity at large.

Although large in amounts of money, charity had a difficult time keeping up with inflation throughout the 1970s and early 1980s, and in several years the contributions actually declined when adjusted for inflation. United Way had the same difficulty. In ten of the twelve latest years the percentage increase in collections was less than the inflation rate. In addition, the growth rate in federal spending on the needy was decreased, but absolute amounts continued to rise slightly.

United Way of America was the name for the national movement

EXHIBIT 1 United Way Support By Source, in Percentages, Four Most Recent Years

Source	Latest Year	Two Years Ago	Three Years Ago	Four Years Ago
Corporations	26.5%	27.5%	27.7%	28.4%
Employees and executives	47.6	47.3	46.0	46.1
Education	3.4	3.2	3.1	3.1
Government	7.2	7.2	7.2	7.1
Other nonprofit	1.3	2.0	2.0	1.6
Professions	3.9	3.2	3.1	3.2
Foundations	2.0	1.6	1.5	1.5
Residential	3.1	3.8	3.7	3.9
Other (includes small business)	5.0	4.2	5.7	5.1
	100.0%	100.0%	100.0%	100.0%

and for the umbrella organization that maintained national headquarters. Local United Ways were autonomous. Of late the headquarters budget had tended to run a little over $13 million per year. The national level received annual support on the basis of an allocation from the collections of most local United Ways. The national level also received small amounts of money directly from a few people who wanted to support the headquarters. It received small amounts of program service fees and an extremely small amount of income from rentals and various investments.

The national level was necessary for coordination, long-range planning, and some services to the approximately 2,100 local United Ways in the United States and Canada. Headquarters furnished the local organizations technical support for local campaigns and tried to build and maintain good relations with large corporations. More specific activities had to do with the development and production of films and other materials for use by voluntary solicitors and the media, development and production of planning and budgeting manuals, review of national agency programs, publication of various newsletter series, training of locals in management techniques and fund raising, maintenance of a lending library of pertinent reports, and the execution of public opinion and market research. An example of recent market research was the test marketing in Seattle and Richmond of a telethon format to recruit volunteer labor for local charities.

United Way of America recently decided that it needed truly year-round communication with the public instead of just at the time when most local campaigns were held, late fall and early winter. This communication should educate and inform people about the United Way, according to C. P. McColough, vice-chairman of the board of directors. He indicated that they had found a direct correlation between contributor knowledge of United Way and support. The Advertising Council, a social marketing organization formed for the purpose of supporting selected nonprofit causes with the creation and placement of donated professional advertising, became supportive of the United Way. An advertising agency, Bozell & Jacobs, International, volunteered to create the advertising and the National Football League agreed to support the United Way on its televised games. A short while later the National Hockey League and the National Basketball Association agreed to similar arrangements. United Way had to pay for the production costs of the advertisements, but the electronic and print media contributed the time and space. For example, an elaborate series on television with the National Football League cost United Way only $200,000, the cost of producing the advertisements.

In 1972, United Way officials took the lead in establishing the Alexis de Tocqueville Society Award, named for the famous French scholar, author, and admirer of voluntarism. Taking this action meant that some deserving voluntarism leaders would be rewarded, but it also meant that some publicity and positive feelings for voluntarism in general and the United Way in particular would probably result. Recent recipients included the Adams family descendants of President John Adams and Vernon E. Jordan, Jr., executive director of the Urban League and civil rights leader. In a speech accepting this award, Jordan stated that because the voluntary sector provided the opportunity for personal involvement, it constituted the cement binding our society together.

After several scandals in recent years in organizations unaffiliated with the United Way, the United States and some state governments had become concerned about the percentage of funds contributed for charity that were used for charity administration. The United States national average for charitable organizations appears to be just over 20 per cent. For the United Way the figure was about 10.5 per cent. About 4.6 per cent was attributable directly to fund raising and the remaining 5.9 per cent was for planning and general management. It was sometimes difficult to classify expenditures perfectly. There was noteworthy hostility and misinformation about the amounts of money that went into administration in any charitable organization, especially in geographic areas that had experienced well-publicized scandals. In a few charities unaffiliated with United Way more than 80 per cent of funds collected went to administrative costs.

Criticisms of the United Way

Criticisms were always offered against all charitable organizations. Because of its sheer size the United Way seemed to receive a considerable amount of criticism. Some of the criticism was not based on fact, whereas on some other points intelligent, well-informed persons of goodwill could differ.

The fundamental and perhaps unsolvable criticism was that the role United Way assigned itself was inherently arrogant; that is, it ran one campaign on behalf of many worthy causes and then allocated the proceeds among them as it saw fit. Professional envy by administrators in channels undoubtedly played some part in this criticism. This envy was enhanced by the fact that United Way was virtually the only organization with which an employer would cooperate with employee-authorized payroll deductions.

Among the several other criticisms of United Way was that many recipients of United Way money, such as the American Red Cross, Salvation Army, and Boy Scouts, conducted additional fund raising, thus violating the concept of federated fund raising. This was true, but defenders pointed out that these organizations could not carry out their work on the amounts allocated to them from United Way and that they did not want to lose their individual public identities.

Another criticism was that the money a person contributed and designated for a particular charity did not go specifically to that charity, because the bookkeeping involved would be burdensome and the United Way had already reached a tentative agreement in advance with recipients as to the amounts that would be given them. Despite tentative allocations and costly paper work caused by donors specifying recipient charities, the United Way did honor those directions. Because so many people specified nothing and there were offsets, the draft amount and the final amount for each recipient tended to be the same.

Some people believed that United Way was the indirect cause of pressure on employees, because much of the United Way campaign

EXHIBIT 2 Organization Chart for Headquarters, United Way of America

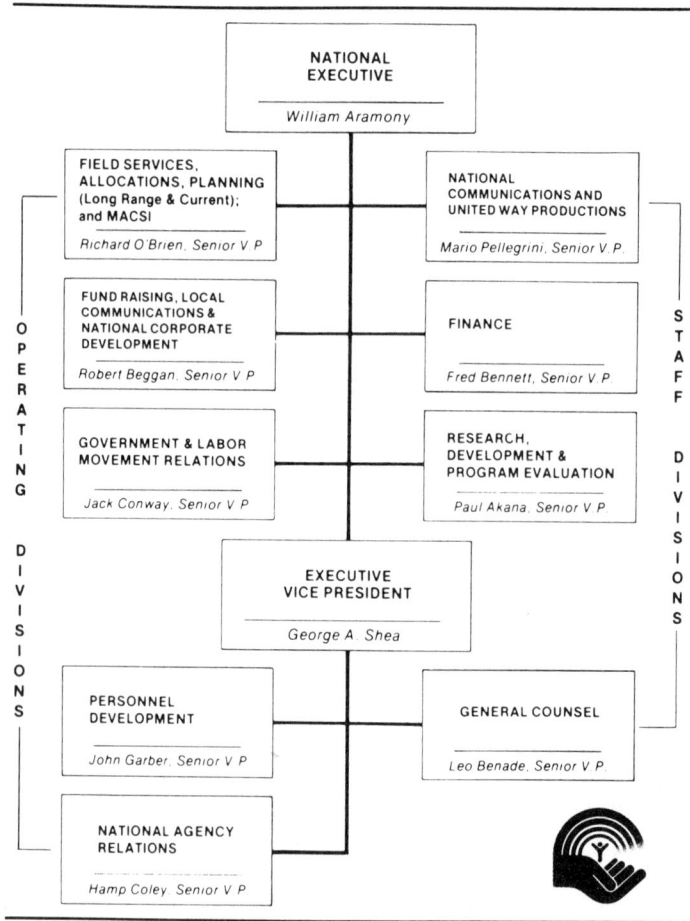

was carried out at places of employment and the payroll deduction was encouraged. Moreover, a certain percentage of one's pay was suggested as the contribution. Although there might have been pressure from some employers, there was infrequent evidence of such pressure, and 100 per cent participation by employees in any firm was extremely rare. The United Way investigated all such charges.

EXHIBIT 3 A Partial List of Agencies and Services Receiving United Way Allocations

American Diabetes Association	National Cystic Fibrosis Research
American National Red Cross	Foundation
American Social Health Association	National Easter Seal Society for
Arthritis Foundation	Crippled Children and Adults
Big Brothers	National Hemophilia Foundation
Big Sisters	National Kidney Foundation
Boys Clubs	National Multiple Sclerosis Society
Boy Scouts	National Recreation and Park
Camp Fire Girls	Association
Catholic Charities	Neighborhood Centers and
Child Adoption Services	Settlements
Child Guidance Clinics	Planned Parenthood Services
Day Care Centers	Residential Treatment Centers for
Epilepsy Foundation of America	Children
Family Counseling Services	Salvation Army
Foster Care of Children	Services for the Aging
Girls Clubs	Services for the Handicapped
Girl Scouts	Services for Unwed Mothers
Homemaker—Home Health Aide Service	Summer Camps
Homes for Dependent and Neglected	Temporary Shelters for Children
Children	Travelers Aid
Hospitals	United Cancer Council, Inc.
Information and Referral Services	United Cerebral Palsy Association
Inner City Projects	United Seamen's Service
Legal Aid Services	United Service Organizations (USO)
Leukemia Society of America	United Way Planning Organizations
Mental Health Services	Urban League
Medical Clinics	Visiting Nurse Services
National Association for Mental Health	Volunteer Bureaus and Voluntary
National Association for Retarded	Action Centers
Citizens	Volunteers of America
National Association of Hearing and	YMCA
Speech Action	YWCA
National Council on Alcoholism	YMHA
National Council on Crime and	YWHA
Delinquency	

Another criticism was that the types of services subsidized by the United Way were not the services that were needed the most. According to this line of thought, many needed services were not supported and the United Way was slow to alter its list of recipients. This kind of criticism particularly came from many blacks, and, as a result, in 1975 the National Black United Fund, Inc., was formed. With affiliated groups in about fifteen cities, the national organization set up headquarters of the Black United Way in Los Angeles. The crux of the criticism from blacks was that the set of services supported by United Way did not stress the subjects that mattered the most to blacks: employment, job training, legal assistance, housing, health services, and crime. In a few places whites got into serious dispute about the mix of recipients of United Way funds. For example, in Prince George's County, Maryland, a suburban area near Washington, D.C., the United Way organization split into two groups in the mid-1970s.

An additional criticism was that the United Way employed too many people and compensated them too well. At local and national levels combined there were about 3,500 professionals on the payroll.

Income Tax Developments and Problems

Among the United Way officials and advisors there had long been concern that the structure of personal income tax regulations in the United States was affecting contributions adversely. Instead of itemizing deductions, about 78 per cent of taxpayers took the standard deduction (also known as the zero bracket amount), a proportion that had grown of late. People who used the standard deduction had had no financial incentive to donate to any charitable organization, in that their income taxes were unaffected by donations. The federal government had built into the standard deduction an assumed amount of contributions for the typical person. If the person selecting the standard deduction made few or no donations, he was automatically ahead financially. In 1981 as part of the overhaul of federal income tax policies this characteristic was changed, effective in 1982, the result largely of intense lobbying by charitable organizations, including the United Way. For tax filings for the years 1981 through 1986, taxpayers who used the standard deduction instead of itemizing their deductions were able to reduce their income tax obligation by a percentage of qualifying donations made during the year. For 1982 and 1983, 25 per cent of contributions up to a $100 maximum could be claimed for a top deduction of $25. For 1984 the ceiling rose to $300 and the rate stayed at 25 per cent for a maximum deduction

EXHIBIT 4 Themes in Past United Way Campaigns

I gave	Fair Share
I care	Do your share
Keep on caring	Be a good neighbor
Suppose nobody cared	Help the unfortunate
Give more	Brighten a life
I give the United Way	It's working
I did not forget	Thanks to you it's working
Open your heart	Thanks to you it works. For all of us
	Now more than ever

of $75. In 1985 the rate went to 50 per cent and in 1986 to 100 per cent, with no dollar ceilings in either year (except for the traditional limitation to 50 per cent of adjusted gross income. This section of the tax code was meant to expire at the end of 1986. The purpose of this provision was financially to motivate people of average income to contribute to charity.

In addition, 1981 reforms in income tax regulations reduced tax rates for all people at all income levels and for corporations. The net impact of the 1981 change was to decrease dollars of tax obligations significantly and the top personal rate to 50 per cent. The impact of a planned overhaul in late 1986 was to redistribute tax obligations, eliminate many deductions, and cut the top rate to about 33 per cent. Thus, in just five years the whole structure of rates went down dramatically, and the incentive to donate for people who itemized their deductions decreased. For example, a person might find his effective marginal rate dropping from 53 to about 33 per cent. Thus his cost to make each $100 contribution to charity would become $67 rather than the old $47. Corporate rates were also cut but not as much.

Advise United Way.

ROBERTSHAW CONTROLS COMPANY

Robertshaw Controls Company could be traced back to a thermostat device invented by Frederick W. Robertshaw in Pittsburgh in 1899. A prolific inventor who obtained forty-one patents, Robertshaw guided the early growth of the organization. Soon after World War II the Grayson Company, based upon the inventions of John H. Grayson in California, and the Fulton Company, based upon the inventions of Weston M. Fulton in Tennessee, merged with Robertshaw to form the present corporation.

A major participant in the industrial controls industry, Robertshaw manufactured automatic controls and control systems for industry, commercial buildings, and the home. The product line included controls for regulating and measuring temperatures and pressure, for heating and cooling, for appliances, for transportation, and for industrial processes and systems, and instrumentation for other precise control requirements. The company specialized in the applications of the physical sciences, that is, electronics, pneumatics, hydraulics, mechanics, and electromagnetics, to control energy and to enable products to work automatically. It also made a line of clocks and timers for household use, but this represented a very small part of the company's sales. In total, the company manufactured more than 10,000 different products.

The company distributed its industrial products to original equipment manufacturers, contractors, replacement parts wholesalers, governmental agencies, the military, automotive and aircraft manufacturers, shipbuilding yards, public utility service departments, and various other industrial users. The clocks and timers for household use were sold to wholesalers, retailers, and trading stamp companies.

The demand for industrial goods is, of course, derived; the demand depends completely on the demand for the consumer goods produced by the particular industry. For example, there is little need for a new temperature and pressure control system on the production line of a fruit canning factory unless a viable demand exists for the canned fruit.

Manufacturing plants owned and operated by the company included three in Pennsylvania, two in Ohio, four in California, two in Connecticut, one in Tennessee, and one in New Hampshire. In addition, Robertshaw leased and operated two plants in Tennessee and one each in Michigan, Pennsylvania, Georgia, and Virginia. Foreign subsidiary plants were located in Toronto and Oakville, Ontario, Canada; Sydney, Australia; Skelmersdale, England; Reims, France; Amsterdam, The Netherlands; Tokyo, Japan; and Caxias do Sul, Brazil. An affiliate plant was located in Mexico City, Mexico. There were 9,900 employees. Plant size varied from fifty to 1,500 employees. Selling efforts extended to fifty-one nations.

Justifiably proud of its technological expertise and its long tradition of inventions, Robertshaw continued to have a strong commitment to technological advancement. In the latest year inventors in the company were issued eighty-eight patents, compared with sixty-four the previous year and ninety-nine the year before that. The company was consistently among the most prolific firms in the number of patents obtained. Although each manufacturing division conducted some product research and development and was expected to do so, the company operated three facilities devoted exclusively to research and development, one in California and two in Pennsylvania. To permit a more coordinated approach and a cross-fertilization of ideas, the Advanced Technology Forecast Committee was formed in 1974 to monitor advanced technological developments that might be utilized in the controls industry and suggest potential new products. This committee consisted of representatives from the research and development, marketing, manufacturing, and patent departments.

In the most recent year the company's sales were $247,145,000, up 27.9 per cent from the previous year's $193,280,000. Sales for each of the five most recent years broken down by type of market are presented in Exhibit 1. A five-year summary operating statement of the company is presented as Exhibit 2.

In earlier years Robertshaw Controls Company was organized strictly by product type. There was a manufacturing division for a cluster of related products, and a sales department and an advertising department for the same cluster of products. Manufacturing was still organized by type of product into twelve divisions, but marketing was now organized by type of customer into eight groups. For example, the Industrial Instrument Marketing Group was in Richmond, Virginia, but the products that the customers of this group needed might come from the Grayson Manufacturing Division in Long Beach, California, the Simicon Manufacturing Division in Holland, Michigan, the Milford Manufacturing Division in Milford, Connecticut, or the Sylphon Manufacturing Division in Knoxville, Tennessee. Without this organizational structure a particular customer or potential customer might be called on by four different Robertshaw sales representatives.

Robertshaw spent $500,000 annually for space purchases for its advertising. Like most other industrial goods firms, the company exhibited a preference for personal selling efforts over advertising. The corporation had used the same advertising agency for ten years and was satisfied with it. Robert W. Pendergast, Robertshaw's corporate director of public relations and advertising, noted that an agency's cooperative attitude was as important as its professional competence.

Perhaps the central difficulty in meeting Robertshaw's advertising needs was that most of the company's products were not highly visible. Most of the time the products were completely hidden and thus unseen by nearly everyone. The company had not engaged in consumer advertising until late in the past year, when it launched a small, limited campaign in selected newspapers and do-it-yourself-type magazines to support its automatic setback thermostat. This was a home control device that had the ability to adjust the temperature at times programmed by the residents.

EXHIBIT 1 Robertshaw Controls Company Five-Year Sales by Markets

(To nearest million)	Temperature Controls for Homes and Commercial Buildings	Controls for Home Appliances	Industrial Controls and Instrumentation	Transportation, Consumer, and Other	Total
Latest year: Volume	$92	$82	$37	$36	$247
Per cent of total	37%	33%	15%	15%	100%
Two years ago: Volume	$73	$55	$34	$31	$193
Per cent of total	38%	28%	18%	16%	100%
Three years ago: Volume	$64	$60	$34	$32	$190
Per cent of total	34%	31%	18%	17%	100%
Four years ago: Volume	$65	$65	$31	$32	$193
Per cent of total	34%	34%	16%	16%	100%
Five years ago: Volume	$62	$59	$27	$24	$172
Per cent of total	36%	34%	16%	14%	100%

EXHIBIT 2 Robertshaw Controls Company Five-Year Summary of Operations (Amounts in thousands, except per share data) Year ended December 31

	Latest Year	Two Years Ago	Three Years Ago	Four Years Ago	Five Years Ago
Net sales	$247,145	$193,280	$189,899	$193,335	$172,459
Cost of products sold	194,443	156,701	155,292	150,007	129,217
Equity income (loss)	352	(85)	1,511	2,253	1,245
Other revenue	1,481	871	1,184	1,077	909
Interest expense	1,834	1,963	2,337	1,690	910
Taxes on income	7,607	2,157	1,399	6,780	7,940
Net income	9,382	2,943	5,020	10,438	9,798
Earnings per share of common stock based on average shares outstanding	2.42	.76	1.30	2.70	2.55
Cash dividends per share	.90	.75	.90	.83	.72
Average shares outstanding	3,876,591	3,871,726	3,871,709	3,871,525	3,838,504

Some of the advertising effort was decentralized to the eight marketing groups. In addition, each marketing group could retain its own advertising agency. The groups had been using their present agencies for periods of time varying from one to several years. The director of public relations and advertising explained as follows:

As an arm of marketing, advertising of products and systems now follows the same group approach. Advertising strategies are keyed to portraying Robertshaw as a single source for a variety of controls and systems. Advertising to the chemical process industry, for example, is programmed to present Robertshaw's total instrumentation capability. In the appliance field, advertising backs up the marketing approach wherein an appliance maker looks to a single Robertshaw representative to supply all his control needs.

Decisions on marketing group advertising objectives, plans, media, and budgets generally are made by the groups themselves. In most cases, however, these plans are formulated only after discussion and consultation with the corporate director of advertising. Budgets are prepared by the groups and submitted to the corporate advertising director for approval. Written permission must be obtained for all additional programs not previously budgeted.

Each marketing group had additional promotional responsibilities, such as participation in appropriate trade shows and exhibitions. The total for all marketing groups combined was usually ten shows-exhibitions per year. Moreover, each marketing group prepared its own product catalog, which required approval from Pendergast.

A sizable amount of the advertising effort was centralized at corporate headquarters. The director of public relations and advertising summarized corporate advertising, media selection, and copy themes in the following manner:

Corporate Advertising

For several years now, Robertshaw's prime corporate objectives have continued to be building a favorable awareness in the financial and investment community. Advertising strategy has centered on creating an understanding among target audiences of our involvement in many and diverse markets. Corporate messages are directed to the decision makers who influence investment decisions, and they also reach individual investors.

Media Choices

To make the most efficient use of our corporate budget, advertising has been concentrated in *The Wall Street Journal*, acknowledged leader in financial circles. Its readership also includes a broad reach among business executives. This provides a "bonus" in awareness among this audience because they are also decision makers in purchasing Robertshaw products as well as potential personal investors. Smaller campaigns are used in *Business Week* to re-

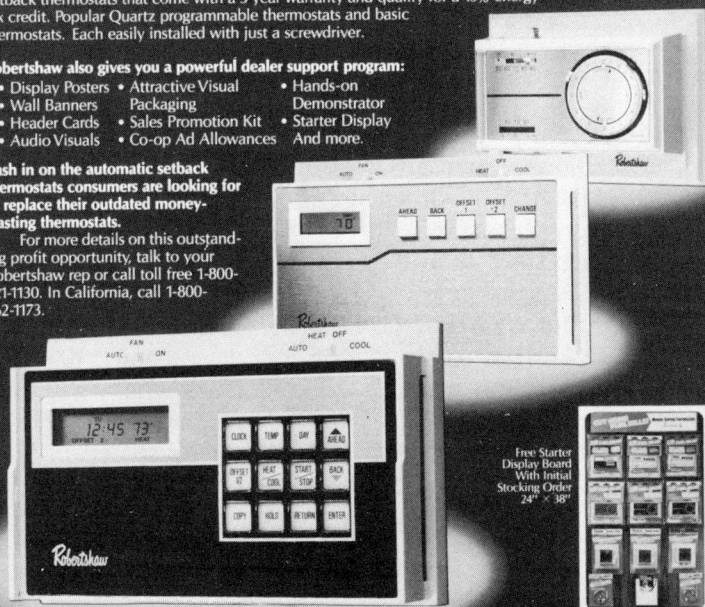

inforce the message to the general business community, and in *Institutional Investor* to reach their audience of major investors.

Copy Themes

Each ad in the campaign spotlights a Robertshaw product and its benefits to the user. Generally the headlines name one or more well-known customers for this Robertshaw control or control system. A closing paragraph points out Robertshaw's diversity, including its international involvement . . . and asks for action by offering more information. Separately and together, these messages convey a picture of leadership in a basic field—controls . . . diversity of markets for a broad base of sales . . . R & D capability . . . proven performance record for blue chip companies. For several years, the ads have also pointed up our ability to perform as the Energy Control Company.

Results

This campaign has fulfilled its objective of contributing to a wider awareness of Robertshaw's total corporate capability. Because the ads talk about specific products, they produce inquiries—particularly on new products and controls that function to provide energy savings.

However, recently the company reexamined its media mix, and it reached a decision to try a different combination of print media. The periodicals chosen had audiences of quite specialized people who were identified with particular types of businesses. The mix consisted of business magazines such as *InTech, Appliance, Appliance Manufacturer, LP Gas, Building Supply Home Centers, National Home Center News,* and *Hardware Age.* Robertshaw's Consumer Products Marketing Group planned to use the last three named in an attempt to interest retailers and buyers for retail chains who were considered highly relevant to that product line. The Appliance Controls Marketing Group planned to run the advertisement presented in Exhibit 3 in *Appliance* and *Appliance Manufacturer.* The Consumer Products Control Group planned to run the advertisement presented in Exhibit 4 in *Building Supply Home Centers, National Home Center News,* and *Hardware Age.*

Advise Robertshaw Controls Company.

11

PRICING

CROFTON-WAGLEY, INC.

Charles McDowell was worrying about a sales contract that he had counted on signing in a few days but that was now in danger of falling through. He thought, "If only those people in the accounting department and in navigation instrumentation would cooperate sometimes and get a team effort going."

McDowell was a sales representative and contract negotiator in the sales department of Crofton-Wagley, Inc., a large company engaged in the manufacture of electronics, aerospace products, and sophisticated marine equipment. About 80 per cent of its sales volume was to the military. Most of the military sales were to the U.S. armed forces, but there was significant business with the military procurement offices of Canada, Australia, and West Germany. Crofton-Wagley's plants were located in California, Texas, and the Middle West, and the company had just opened a small experimental facility in Appalachia following federal government pressure to "spread the jobs around."

Sales volume fluctuated somewhat more from year to year than in most other firms in this type of industry. Sales last year were $499 million, but the year before were $538 million. The ratio of net profit after taxes to sales was a disappointing 2.0 per cent in the latest year. Long-term trends are given in Exhibit 1.

Experienced and age thirty-five, Charles McDowell had been with Crofton-Wagley, Inc. about six years and was with an aerospace company for about seven years before that. He graduated from a well-known university with a BS in a combination engineering-business administration curriculum. In industry he had had experience in product design, product laboratory testing, liaison between various engineering departments and the marketing department, and

EXHIBIT 1 Sales and Profit Trends
of Crofton-Wagley, Inc.

Number of Years Ago	Sales	Net Profit After Taxes	
1	$499 million	$10,023,000	2.00%
2	538	12,975,000	2.41%
3	485	10,045,000	2.07%
4	456	9,902,000	2.17%
5	491	10,450,000	2.13%
6	461	10,076,000	2.19%
7	485	13,240,000	2.73%
8	440	13,210,000	3.00%
9	441	13,230,000	3.00%

was currently in sales. He was on a straight salary. McDowell was considered a competent, personable, and loyal employee.

Recently McDowell had been negotiating a sale with Ronninger Corporation for $4 million worth of navigation equipment. He and some others deemed it highly important not just for the large amount of money involved but for the possibility of follow-on orders from Ronninger and also because it would get Crofton-Wagley deeper into civilian markets. The president of the company wanted Crofton-Wagley to be less dependent on military orders.

Crofton-Wagley's pricing had been systematized. This meant that certain procedures adopted a little over a year before had to be followed in determining the asking price. The Crofton-Wagley approach was essentially cost-based pricing. Company practice was to figure the costs involved, then add a small contingency charge (sometimes hidden in slight overestimates of detailed items but sometimes spelled out separately) of about 2 per cent of the costs, and then add a markup that averaged 14 per cent. Special facilities needed for a specific contract, such as specialized testing equipment or new construction of testing rooms tailor-made for the contract, were charged to the contract and thus became part of the price quoted to the potential customer. The navigation equipment on which McDowell and Ronninger were negotiating required a special testing room that had to be constructed from the ground up. Estimates of cost to construct this room were $135,000, and the special testing equipment would add another $25,000. There seemed to be no significant error in these two estimates that anyone could discover. These two figures were part of the exactly $4 million total figure McDowell was asking the potential customer.

Ronninger had bought similar but technologically less advanced navigation equipment in the past from one of Crofton-Wagley's major competitors, Kingston, Inc. McDowell was able to learn that there had been only one such purchase, but Ronninger Corporation had been happy with the product. This competitor was about the same size as Crofton-Wagley and enjoyed a similar reputation in the industry. However, McDowell and many of his colleagues in the sales areas considered Kingston more aggressive than Crofton-Wagley.

To his great chagrin, McDowell had just learned that Kingston was now trying to obtain the same contract on which he was working. Furthermore, Kingston was quoting a total price of $3,930,000 or $70,000 less than Crofton Wagley. McDowell had no doubt that this information about the competitor was correct. Said McDowell, "It not only is cheaper than our quotation by one and three-quarters per cent but sounds a lot cheaper because it stays below $4 million."

At this point, Charles McDowell approached the senior cost accountant, Louise Bascomb. The cost accounting group had been directed to participate in the paperwork for price quotations in transactions expected to total $2 milllion or more since the new price setting system had been installed. He attempted to get a special exception to the company's new costing procedure so as to delete from the estimate the $135,000 cost of the construction. Bascomb appeared to want to cooperate but replied in the negative. She called to McDowell's attention that this costing policy was the result of the work of a pricing committee that included the marketing vice president, the sales manager, two other vice presidents, and the company president. In vain, McDowell argued that the testing room would still be in place and have some value and usefulness after the sales order had been filled. An immediate appeal to Bascomb's superior, the head of finance and accounting, did not change matters.

Undaunted, McDowell next sought the exclusion of the $25,000 worth of special testing equipment, arguing that this equipment would have a lengthy life and some other potential uses. This line of attack was not successful, however. Next, McDowell began questioning the 2 per cent contingency factor, but the reply to that from everyone was a resounding no. It was even added that the company's cost estimating was so imprecise that perhaps the figure of 2 per cent should be raised in the future. Finally, McDowell questioned the 14 per cent markup but again without positive results.

At this point, these thoughts went through Charles McDowell's mind: "Perhaps Ronninger would pay this price differential just to get what amounts to 'second sourcing' because we all realize that Kingston can give Ronninger just as sophisticated technology as we can. On the other hand, they already know Kingston and Kingston's people quite well. And $70,000 is a lot of money." The term "second sourcing" referred to an idea in which many industrial buyers believed strongly: that is, a company was likely to get into a poor position if over the long run it relied on only one vendor for an important product or category of products. For a very few products that were patentable, there might be only one lawful supplier, of course. For some technical products, however, even when no patent was possible, there might still be only one maker because the demand was so small. Some buyers liked to divide their company's purchases of such an item between two suppliers in an attempt to keep both available. This tactic would insure the buying organization against interruptions resulting from such matters as strikes, fires, and floods.

McDowell then determined again the exact date that the price quotation had to be in the hands of Ronninger Corporation's buyers. He had one week.

Advise Charles McDowell of Crofton-Wagley, Inc.

DENVER ART MUSEUM

The Denver Art Museum, the major visual arts institution for the Rocky Mountain region, was founded as an artists' club in 1893. It had no collection and no permanent building. By 1932 it had become the official art institution for Denver, but until 1971 the collection was divided among various locations, including an old mansion and a remodeled automobile showroom.

In 1971 the Denver Art Museum's spectacular six-story building was opened. The striking silver-gray structure, designed by Gio Ponti of Milan and James Sudler of Denver, was located near downtown in the city's Civic Center. The opening of that new building marked a significant boost to the visual arts of the area. According to Thomas Maytham, director of the museum from 1974 to 1983, "In the new building we had a doubled budget, a new board of trustees, quadrupled attendance, and a challenging question: How can we best use this building?"

The answer continued to change, but by most measures the museum had been very successful. The permanent collection numbered 50,000 objects in 1985. The major areas in the collection were European art, American art, New World art (including Pre-Columbian art), Asian art, native arts (including American Indian art), and Contemporary art. The largest single area in the museum's collection was American Indian art, which numbered more than 20,000 objects and was among the finest assemblages of its type in the world. It had

This case was prepared by Professor Patricia Stocker of the University of Maryland based on information provided by Helen Masterson, director of public relations for the Denver Art Museum.

been described as the finest collection of American Indian works in any art museum.

About eight major special circulating exhibitions were also shown at the museum each year. These were usually borrowed from other museums or from private collections. The collections ranged in scope from the well-known Armand Hammer collection of European and American masterpieces and the Thyssen-Bornemiza Collection to "Art of the Muppets" and "Secret Splendors of the Chinese Court," a costume collection. (See Exhibit 1.) The museum had not been on the tour for such "blockbuster" exhibitions as King Tut or Picasso.

The museum also had a number of educational programs, including lectures, tours, films, seminars, and other performing arts. These programs were generally planned around the circulating exhibitions or the museum's permanent collection and were designed to increase the visitors' appreciation of the visual arts they were seeing. A "Top of the Week" program featuring jazz groups playing in the museum's restaurant area was instituted in 1984, and, for 11 consecutive Wednesday nights in 1985, this event attracted a total of 12,648 visitors.

EXHIBIT 1 Attendance at Selected Temporary Exhibitions (six-week showings)

Armand Hammer Collection	152,106
Masterpieces of French Art	56,836
The Art of the Muppets	115,531
Heritage of American Art	22,583
Frederick Remington: The Late Years	35,000
Silver in American Life	30,000
American Photographers and National Parks	31,045
Museum of Modern Art Collection	40,924
Thyssen-Bornemiza Collection	54,644

Background Information

Although the Denver Art Museum was not strictly a government agency, its assets were held by a Colorado nonprofit educational corporation for the benefit of the public. It served as the official arts agency of the city and county of Denver. (The city and the county were one entity.) The museum was managed by an elected, unpaid board of trustees including civic leaders in the community, lawyers, advertising agency executives, professional artists, business managers, and others.

Prior to the imposition of a front-door admission fee to the museum in 1982, attendance at the museum averaged between

500,000 and 600,000 a year (See Exhibit 2), which put it ahead of the Boston, Houston, and Philadelphia art museums. Perhaps more significantly, prior to the admission fee, the museum boasted the highest attendance on a per capita basis of any major art museum in the country. Following the imposition of the front-door fee, attendance dropped dramatically. Of the visitors to the Denver Art Museum, about 25 per cent came from out of state, another 45 per cent came from Colorado but outside of Denver, and the remaining 30 per cent from the city and county of Denver. Of those who are from Colorado but not from Denver, the vast majority are from suburban communities. About 70 per cent of museum visitors can be identified as from either Denver or nearby suburban areas. Included in these attendance figures were visits from students as part of the gallery tours led by museum guides. The largest community in the Rocky Mountains region, Denver had a population of 500,000, but the population of the metropolitan area was 1,650,000.

The museum was open 48 hours a week, including one evening. It was closed on Mondays, and, as a cost-cutting measure, some galleries would be closed a half-day a week on a rotating basis. There were 100 full-time and part-time employees, about half on the security force and the other half in curatorial and administrative positions.

EXHIBIT 2 Total Yearly Denver Art Museum Attendance

1972	674,299
1973	527,311
1974	555,058
1975	524,193
1976	527,859
1977	530,000
1978	608,178[a]
1979	466,361
1980	598,648
1981	467,917
1982	291,619
1983	284,034
1984	293,698

[a]The popular Armand Hammer Collection was included this year.

The Denver Art Museum had been free to the public until January 1, 1982. However, admission fees had been charged for major circulating exhibitions. At that time, the museum had collected an average of $160,000 per year in fees for these special exhibitions.

In 1985 there were about 18,500 museum members, the majority of these being family memberships at $35 per family per year. The greatest impetus to membership was the free admission granted to members. Among other membership benefits were 10 per cent discounts at the museum gift shop, a monthly newsletter about museum activities, and previews of the major traveling exhibitions. At each preview showing, light refreshments were served free of charge, and there was a cash bar. At a few previews, an arts celebrity, patron, or collector appeared. A recent example was Baron Thyssen von Bornemiza when a portion of his collection was exhibited.

The museum had been more marketing-oriented than most other art museums, with marketing considerations in terms of exhibitions, educational programs, fund raising, and acquisitions of art objects for the permanent collection. The museum's trustees had commissioned a marketing plan in 1983 that focused on the promotional needs of the museum. The museum had traditionally been supported financially by local, state, and federal allocations; gifts from private foundations; and museum memberships. The trend had been toward having a greater percentage of the budget each year raised from private sources. To succeed in this change, the museum had instituted a number of innovative funding ideas, such as the successful museum associates program, for which membership was limited to those individuals who contributed at least $1,500 each year in unrestricted funds for museum support. This was in contrast to restricted funds contributed by individuals and others for specific purposes, such as the support of special exhibitions or the purchase of a specific piece of art for the museum's permanent collection. The museum had also instituted creative benefit events to raise extra dollars. Among the most creative of these events was the annual "Collectors' Choice" benefit at which those attending an expensive benefit party would vote on the particular acquisition to be purchased by the proceeds of that event. The alternative selections were made by the museum's curators.

In its solicitation of funds from private foundations, companies, and individuals for restricted uses, the museum had been successful by demonstrating its relationship to the quality of life in Denver and by including recognition of the donors, such as associating a special exhibition with the sponsoring organization in the publicity about that exhibition.

The museum also had received substantial support from the federal government. In 1984 the museum received about $221,000 from federal sources, including the National Endowment for the Arts, the National Endowment for the Humanities, the Institute for Museum Services, and the National Museum Act of the Smithsonian Institution. Much of this support had come as matching grants. Matching grants generally required the museum to raise $1 for each $1 of the grant. Walter Rosenberry, former chairperson of the museum's board of trustees, explained that these challenge grants had had a "tremendously stimulating effect" on private contributions.

The museum budget for 1981 was $3.8 million. The city provided about 24 per cent of that amount, with state appropriations making up another 10 per cent of the total. The museum budget for 1984 was $4.3 million. The city provided about 29 per cent of that amount, with direct state appropriations eliminated completely and only $12,000 in an indirect appropriation from the State Legislature via the Colorado Council on the Arts and Humanities.

The Funding Crunch

A combination of government cuts, inflation, and potential changes in tax deductions for private contributions was forcing changes in the museum's funding picture. The museum generated over $1.92 million of its operating budget of $4.3 million in 1984 from grants, gifts, and memberships. The city provided $1.25 million in support. In total, these sources accounted for nearly 75 per cent of the museum's budget. The remaining income was generated by front-door admission fees ($234,634), interest income, educational programs, gift-shop income, and volunteer benefits. Unfortunately, these sources were not sufficient to match expenditures even when the expenditures were cut dramatically, and $50,000 was taken from the museum's endowment in 1984 to meet expenses. It was clear that the gap between revenue and expenses was a continuing problem for the museum.

Bridging the Gap

Over the past several years, museum employees had responded to the cuts from funding sources by increasing their solicitation of individual, corporate, and foundation gifts. They also cut back on the number of traveling exhibitions, with more emphasis on the museum's own permanent collection. Galleries were closed on a rotating basis to reduce security expenses.

The museum's retail gift shop was expanded to increase sales, and a small gallery was closed to accommodate this expansion. The museum's management also worked toward establishing a substantial endowment through foundation and individual gifts. Because of the pressure of generating operating expenses and the depletion of the endowment to meet current operating expenses, this effort was large-

ly unsuccessful. Many trustees and staff felt that the lack of a substantial endowment limited the museum's flexibility in meeting
unpredictable contingencies.

However, the most noticeable action taken by the museum over
the past few years was the institution of an admission fee in January
1982. For about a decade prior to that, the museum had vigorously
opposed such a fee although the city administration and others
had proposed the charge as a way to avoid increasing city and state
aid to the museum.

Museum officials had debated not only the imposition of a fee
but also what form of admission charge would be most effective in
terms of generating the greatest revenue with the smallest drop in
attendance. Thomas Maytham, then the director of the museum, suggested as an alternative to a mandatory entrance fee, a "recommended contribution" along with a sign saying, "Pay what you wish but
you must pay something." This flexible type of admission fee was
pioneered by New York's Metropolitan Museum of Art, where it had
been used with success since 1971. The Metropolitan had signs
suggesting certain donations. Several months after the flexible fee
was introduced by the Metropolitan Museum, the Art Institute of
Chicago adopted the system, which it continues to use.

The Denver Art Museum trustees decided to adopt this "recommended" admission fee. They felt that such a fee would have the
smallest impact on attendance. Maytham explained that "while we
regret that we must institute the fee, we hope the flexible system
will encourage people to come to the museum regardless of their
financial means."

"Our two major goals connected with the inauguration of the
fee are an increase in critically needed revenue and retention of our
healthy attendance goals," he continued. Recommended contributions at the Denver Art Museum started at $2 for adults and $1 for
senior citizens and students. Museum members and children under
12 were admitted free. There were no separate charges for special
traveling exhibitions, which had previously brought in about
$160,000 each year. On Labor Day 1983, the recommended fees
increased to $2.50 for adults, and in mid-1985 the museum dropped
the optional nature of the fee, instituting a standard, required
admission fee.

Costs of implementing the fee collection were $60,000, which
included such items as cash registers and turnstiles. The museum
had expected to generate a large increase in memberships following
the institution of the fee, and such an increase did occur. When the
admission fee was instituted in 1982, membership was at 15,000.
By mid-1985 membership was 18,500, and museum officials expect-

ed to have 20,000 memberships by the end of 1985.

The Denver Art Museum admission fee decision relied heavily on the experience at the Metropolitan Museum and Chicago's Art Institute, yet the differences in the Denver museum and its audience apparently made the flexible fee less successful. Attendance dropped dramatically, by about 40 per cent, in the first year after the admission fee was begun. This was alarming to museum officials who had gone with the flexible fee to have less impact on attendance. "With a fixed fee, we'd expected a drop in attendance of 20 to 30 per cent at first," a museum official explained, "with rebuilding after that." Unfortunately, even the flexible fee produced a much greater drop in attendance. The drop was of particular concern in terms of the museum's efforts to attract lower-income visitors. It saw its mission as education, and museum officials worried that attendance might become restricted to middle and upper economic classes.

The museum had tried discounting the fixed admission fee heavily through the use of coupons and free days. In addition, it had used more aggressive promotion of the museum's collections and other activities. However the fee failed to meet its objectives, which were to enhance income significantly for the museum and maintain high attendance figures.

Advise the Denver Art Museum.

WOMEN'S EXERCISE AND FITNESS CENTERS, INC.

Women's Exercise and Fitness Centers was a local chain with nine locations in a large northeastern metropolitan area. Eight of the locations were spaced around the circular Interstate by-pass highway that ran through the suburbs, and the original location was in the heart of downtown. The downtown location was oversubscribed by working women and had a waiting list. The four southside suburban locations were all in relatively affluent communities and had a profitable volume of memberships. The four locations in the northern suburbs were all relatively new and not yet heavily utilized. The company was owned and operated by Anne Martin, a former dancer in her late fifties.

Clients could visit the facilities at any hour between 10 A.M. and 9 P.M. Monday through Friday, and from 10A.M. to 5 P.M. on Saturday. All locations were open Saturday and closed Sunday, despite the fact that two locations were in suburbs with 15 to 20 per cent Jewish population and had some Jewish members. Visits from 10 to 11:30 A.M. were almost entirely from retirees and stay-at-home mothers of

This case was prepared by Joanne G. Greer, Ph.D.

nursery school children. School teachers most often came between 3:30 and 5:00 and nurses between 1:30 and 4. Other working women clogged the facilities from 5:30 to 9:00 P.M., the period of greatest use. A minimum of three visits a week, of at least thirty minutes each, was recommended to clients. Dance classes lasted fifteen minutes and were held on the hour. Each woman also had a custom-designed program of weight lifting for at least fifteen minutes.

When founded in 1955, Martin's centers had originally been called "Women's Figure Salons," and until 1979 the emphasis had been on increasing the client's physical attractiveness. "Counselors," usually college students who were dance or physical education majors, were employed at the minimum wage. They also received free unlimited use of the facilities and every effort was made to adapt to their school schedules in assigning shifts. The counselors weighed and measured the clients on every fifth visit, exhorted, scolded, and praised them, and adjusted their exercise programs individually. On slow days a counselor would work out with each client.

Many members seemed to enjoy the attention of the counselors, and Martin was careful to select for these jobs only personable young women who related well to others. She also expected the counselors to set an example for clients in maintaining proper weight and a fit appearance. Counselors were required to dress in black leotards and tights and to wear name tags so that they could be readily identified by clients needing assistance on the exercise floor. A ratio of one counselor to five clients was maintained. Counselors were rotated from facility to facility every three months, and branch managers were rotated once a year, to prevent any one location from developing an esoteric style of dealing with clients. Martin also made unannounced visits to the nine facilities.

The salons, or centers, were located in shopping plazas with ample free parking, on or near major traffic arteries. To economize on rent, the suburban locations were in smaller shopping plazas, and often in the least convenient parts of those plazas. Only the downtown location, which catered exclusively to employed women, had showers and lockers. Each of the locations had a changing room with curtained booths and several rest rooms, open hanging space for street clothing, and a secure place for purses. Each facility had several tiny sales offices, an attractive lobby, a private area for counselors, and a large, carpeted and mirrored exercise room. Various kinds of exercise equipment lined the four walls, and the center of the room was kept clear for group activities and for exercise that did not employ equipment. Decor was "feminine," using lots of the color pink and flowers.

For many years Martin's business had grown steadily. This appeared to be the result of a number of factors: (1) Her prices were thought to be more reasonable and her ambience less intimidating when compared with her chief downtown competitor, high-fashion Elizabeth Arden, Inc.; (2) she offered considerable locational convenience, by plowing much of her profit back into additional locations; (3) she trained and encouraged counselors to be friendly and supportive, especially to women who seemed lonely or were very overweight; (4) she used a complicated structure of special rates, discounts, and coupons, combined with effective personal selling, to recruit new members. For example, every November she offered a "Get Ready for the Holidays" promotion, allowing those who signed up for a membership beginning January 1 to start using the facility the day they signed the contract at no extra charge. Counselors were required to learn her personal selling techniques, and those who could not bring in new business were terminated. Counselors who were especially successful were promoted through a series of increasingly impressive managerial titles, and received bonuses and modest pay increases.

Martin utilized only two kinds of advertising, television spots and mail coupons. Except for a telephone number, the television spots were noninformative, utilizing vague statements, such as "Become the woman you've always wanted to be," set to music and featuring shapely young women. They were, however, of professional quality, done by a good local advertising agency. Martin supplied the wording for these advertisements. The coupons offered two free "get acquainted" visits. Martin never gave price information in her advertising or over the telephone.

When a prospective client telephoned to inquire or to arrange for the free visits, counselors made every effort to be both charming and supportive. A specific appointment was made, as soon as possible, and the prospect's telephone number and address were noted for follow-up if she did not come. Prospects were scheduled to visit at slow times, so that the counselors could devote at least 45 minutes to each one. The prospect was weighed, measured, and escorted to the changing room, to the accompaniment of bright, friendly chatter and much genuinely sound and useful information on diet and exercise. About half an hour was spent in one-on-one exercise instruction, with the counselor taking care to select routines hard enough to be challenging but easy enough for the prospect to complete without aching the next day. Martin devoted considerable effort to teaching counselors how to visually assess a woman's current fitness level and put together a suitable routine from memory, while continuing to entertain the prospect with friendly conversation.

Some time was also spent in explaining the equipment and in commenting on the exercise being performed by advanced clients. Finally, the prospect was taken to one of the small private offices to discuss enrollment.

A variety of plans were offered, for three months, six months, one year, two years, and six years. The prospect was told primarily that these plans all permitted unlimited use at any time of day, unlike those of competitors. Martin had never actually checked this out, but she had the impression that her competitors offered time-limited plans with scheduled "classes." Martin preferred that the prospect buy the six-year plan, priced at $60 a month for the first year plus $50 a year renewal thereafter, because it was almost all paid during the first year and few clients used it more than two years. For those who did use it six years, the per month rate figured out to only about $13.00. The per month rates for the three-month and six-month plans were set much higher, at $35 and $30 a month, respectively. Most clients on these two plans used all the time for which they contracted.

If the prospect signed the contract on the first visit, she received a flat 10 percent discount. Twice when Martin needed working capital, she offered by mail an additional 20 per cent discount to clients who paid their entire enrollment obligation within ten days. The installment contracts were held by Martin Associates, a small finance company she also owned. Every effort was made to obtain a signed contract on the first visit without applying pressure or deviating from a friendly, concerned stance. Few women who signed a contract later took advantage of the three-day cancellation feature which was required by law. Aware that the decision to enroll was difficult for many reasons, the counselors encouraged prospects to revisit the next day. For the first five visits following enrollment, a counselor stayed with the woman constantly, instructing and encouraging her. For each enrollment they sold, counselors received a commission of 5 per cent of the sale.

In the early 1980s Martin suddenly realized that the competition had become much stiffer. Within two years, three additional competitors, Spa Lady, Swim and Exercise, Inc., and Club Nautilus, had staged grand openings. Of these only Spa Lady advertised prices in dollar figures per month or year. Spa Lady's advertised price for a three-month contract was approximately half of Martin's. Spa Lady also offered diet advice. Martin was aware of the value of this service but was concerned about legal liability issues. She always advised clients to obtain reducing diets from their physicians. Swim and Exercise, Inc. was offering whirlpool, sauna, and swimming pool facilities, none of which was feasible in the spaces currently under long-term lease by Martin. Club Nautilus was coed and emphasized muscle building with the use of complicated machinery. Martin wondered if her clients would have any interest in joining Club Nautilus. She suspected they would not and that they enjoyed the feminine "women only" privacy of her centers and the companion-ableness of her all-female staff. Many of her clients were over age thirty, and she had attracted many retirees at one of her locations that was close to a suburban retirement community. Some who were exercising under doctor's orders deducted their membership fees on their income tax returns as a medical expense.

To increase volume without overloading facilities, Martin was con-sidering offering a special rate to women over fifty, for long-term enrollments of two to five years good only on weekdays from 11:30 A.M. to 2:30 P.M., the slowest time of the day. Recently she had also expanded the poorly attended noon dance class to a one-hour aerobics class. Two month's attendance at the aerobics class was offered to nonmembers for a flat $39. The only promotion was on 8-½ by 11-inch offset-printed flyers posted on location doors. Response was low, and persons buying the package were in poor shape physically and could not handle a full hour of such strenuous exercise as aerobics. The program was quickly redesigned to include a lot of stretching and bending to slow ballet music. The women enjoyed it and several inquired about full membership. The most enthusiasm, however, came from women who were already members and who enjoyed the challenge of the hour-long class in place of the usual fifteen minutes.

Until now, all Anne Martin's clients had to select one branch and use it only. However, she had just decided that she would offer for an additional $20 fee on anyone's contract the right to use all the nine locations. However, Martin did not feel completely at ease with her decision and wondered what use would be made of this offer and what its effects would be on operations.

Swim and Exercise, Inc., had just recently received some unfavor-able publicity. Seventy members at one of the three locations had signed a letter to Maria Panos, the consumer advocate reporter on a local evening television news show. This letter stated that the whirl-pool and swimming pool had fungus and mold in and around them and that often no staff person showed up to lead the scheduled exercise classes. The owners refused to be interviewed, but Panos succeeded in interviewing a staff member. He remarked spontane-ously that he certainly would not pay $800 per year for such ser-vices. Panos asked, "But isn't it true that some of the memberships are as much as $1,200 a year?"

Around the nation there had been several bankruptcies of spas and some fraudulent operators of such businesses. To combat fly-by-night operators of spas and exercise salons, local government jurisdictions in Martin's trade area had just put in a requirement that each branch of such a business had to post a small bond. Because she had nine branches, the total bond would be quite substantial. Martin and all her competitors would now have a higher cost of doing business.

Advise Anne Martin.

THOMPSON FUNERAL HOME[1]

Lawrence and Joseph Thompson owned and operated a funeral home that they had inherited from Horace Thompson, their late father. The business had been successful under Horace Thompson, who established it many years ago when he was a young man. Horace Thompson was always very promotion-minded about the firm but had to be discreet to stay in the good graces of his suppliers, other funeral directors, and the public. In that era a mortician, another term for funeral director, was expected to be extremely dignified and somber in all that he did and said personally and on behalf of his firm. This expectation extended even to the immediate family of the funeral director.

The Thompson brothers ran a successful operation in a metropolitan area. Considerably larger than the average funeral home in

[1]For economic, behavioral, and philosophical background the following are useful references: Elisabeth Kübler-Ross, *Death: The Final Stage of Growth* (Englewood Cliffs, N.J.: Prentice-Hall, Inc., 1975), especially Roy and Jane Nichols, "Funerals: A Time for Grief and Growth," pp. 87–96; Elisabeth Kübler-Ross, *On Death and Dying* (London: Collier Macmillan Publishers, 1969); Howard C. Raether, *Successful Funeral Service Practice* (Englewood Cliffs, N.J.: Prentice-Hall, Inc., 1971); Arnold van Gennys, *The Rites of Passage* (Chicago: University of Chicago Press, 1960); Vanderlyn Pine, *Caretaker of the Dead: The American Funeral Director* (New York: Irvington Publishers, 1975); William M. Kephart, "Status After Death," *American Sociological Review*, 15 (Oct. 1950), pp. 635–643; Paul E. Irion, *The Funeral and the Mourners* (New York: Abingdon Press, 1954); Edgar N. Jackson, *Understanding Grief* (New York: Abingdon Press, 1957); LeRoy Bowman, *The American Funeral* (Washington, D.C.: Public Affairs Press, 1959); Geoffrey Gorer, *Death, Grief, and Mourning* (New York: Doubelday & Company, 1965); Robert W. Haberstein and William M. Lamers, *The History of American Funeral Directing* (Milwaukee: Bulfin Printers, 1955); Jacques Choron, *Death and Western Thought* (New York: Collier Books, 1963); Maurice Lamm, *The Jewish Way in Death and Mourning* (New York: Jonathan David Publishers, 1969); Robert Fulton, *The Sacred and the Secular: Attitudes of the American Public Toward Death* (Milwaukee: Bulfin Printers, 1963); Roger D. Blackwell, "Price Levels in the Funeral Industry," *Quarterly Review of Economics and Business*, 7 (Winter 1976), p. 80; Wilbur M. Krieger, *A Complete Guide to Funeral Service Management* (Englewood Cliffs, N.J.: Prentice-Hall, Inc., 1962); Philippe Aries, *Western Attitudes Toward Death: From the Middle Ages to the Present* (Baltimore: Johns Hopkins University Press, 1974).

the United States, their establishment conducted approximately 200 funerals in an average year. The brothers were conscientious about promises, cognizant of detail, and practiced good cost control. They were in particularly good financial condition in that most physical facilities had already been paid for and there was little debt. In addition, the two brothers did a sizable amount of the work themselves. All in all, the firm was incurring fairly low costs of doing business.

After considerable thought the Thompsons were leaning toward the opinion that their volume of business would increase if they reduced their prices. They could still make a profit that they regarded as satisfactory if they cut their prices significantly. They reasoned that they would make only a modest amount of profit per funeral, but with many more funerals their total profit should increase considerably. They realized that if their analysis proved to be correct there would be much more work to do. Of course, they also realized that the total industry could not take such pricing action, for total units of demand were fixed by the number of deaths. Despite the fact that they leaned toward significant price cuts, the Thompsons were hesitant and unsure. As did nearly all mortuaries, Thompson's required payment within sixty days after the funeral.

A coffin, usually the largest item in a funeral bill, ranged in wholesale price from about $50 to $700. If Thompson's sold the coffin separately, the retail price ranged from about $125 to about $2,000. Such figures for costs, prices, and markups were also true of the entire industry. Most people in the industry preferred the word *casket* to coffin.

The cheapest model of casket, called a *flattop*, was made of plain pine and covered and lined in cloth, whereas the most popular model was made of walnut, mahogany, or steel and sold separately for around $800 to $900. At the high end of the scale was a copper-coated coffin, usually termed the *halfcouch*, which featured a velvet interior, a mattress and springs that could be raised with a crank for the viewing of the body, and a hermetic seal. Most people, however, did not purchase a coffin separately, or confine their purchase to a coffin. Instead, they purchased a package of goods and services whose price was all-inclusive.

Similar to most other funeral homes, Thompson's had a casket merchandising area referred to as the "selection room," where the medium- and higher-priced models were displayed. The higher-priced models were displayed to the right as one entered, because it was known that the majority of people turn to the right on entering a room in a commercial building. Low-priced models were available in a smaller adjoining area separated from the main part of the room by a partition about six feet high. Separation in such an area or in another room or a basement was the practice in at least half of all mortuaries. Customers were always shown the low-priced caskets if they inquired.

Lawrence and Joseph Thompson were seriously thinking of charging as low as $499 for a packaged funeral and $379 for a cremation. Moreover, they were inclined to advertise these prices in a clear manner but with dignity. They thought that placement of advertisements in the newspapers and the Yellow Pages would be appropriate, since that was where the rather small amount of institutional advertising for funeral homes appeared. Only one other funeral home in the metropolitan area, Kirby's, advertised its prices. The largest in the metropolitan area, Kirby's offered the same packages at $499 and $369 that the Thompson brothers were considering. Kirby's had advertised these package deals in newspapers and the Yellow Pages in a dignified manner for several years. The Kirby firm was old and well established and was the largest in the metropolitan area even before it started advertising the low-priced packaged services. There was little reference to economic matters in the advertising of the many other competitors. One firm advertised "Superior funerals at moderate prices"; another stated "Low-cost funeral plan. Terms arranged if necessary"; and a third stated "The expense depends on your desire." A firm owned and operated by blacks, self-identified as black, and actively seeking black customers stated in its advertising that "Expense is a matter of your own selection." Although it was seldom advertised, the majority of funeral homes in the United States had a package funeral available but not as low-priced as what the Thompsons were considering. Thompson's had had some medium and high-medium price packages for several years but had never promoted them. One alternative for Thompson's was, of course, to adopt lower prices but not to advertise them. In packaged arrangements the customer still chose the casket, but the casket had to be from a designated assortment.

The Thompsons were thinking of including simple, clear statements that the majority of people were entitled to certain funeral subsidies, for which their firm was willing to file the necessary paper work and subtract from the bill. Everyone covered by Social Security had a right to a funeral subsidy of $255, whereas military veterans with honorable discharges had a right to $250 and an additional $150 if they needed a plot in a private cemetary. Three other mortuaries in the metropolitan area mentioned that "Veterans' benefits are assured" and one other substituted the word "allowances" for benefits. Two others mentioned "Full Social Security Benefits if allowed." Kirby's, the large mortuary that advertised its package prices, mentioned both Social Security and Veterans Administration allowances in its advertisements.

The proposed $499 package price for a funeral included the cost of a simple casket; picking up the body from the home, hospital, or other institution; obtaining the death certificate and filing it with the public authorities (the public recording fee was from $2 to $4 in most states); placing funeral notices in the local newspapers (about $15 to $40 per newspaper depending on the length of the notice and the circulation of the newspaper); writing an obituary and sending it to the newspapers (if desired); providing a guest registry, acknowledgment cards and envelopes, and space in the mortuary for a funeral service; transporting the deceased in a hearse and the family in a limousine to the cemetery; furnishing and setting up a seating area under a canopy at the cemetary; and filing for government death benefits on behalf of the estate of the deceased. If embalming and public viewing of the body in the mortuary were desired, the price was $999 because this tied up large amounts of valuable space for long periods of time and required an employee near the front door to receive guests.

This $999 package figure did not include burial, for there was a wide variation in the price of digging and filling in the grave. This price was usually set by the cemeteries rather than the morticians and ranged from about $60 to about $250. A package price that included burial had to be high enough to cover the highest grave-handling fee in the trade territory. If burial was desired and the family did not buy the package, the Thompson's firm would charge $65 for a hearse and $45 for a limousine for the family. In either case, if friends of the deceased were not to be used as pallbearers, there was an additional charge of $12 for each of six pallbearers to carry the coffin, and if there were so many flowers that a van was required to carry them from the mortuary or church to the cemetery, there was another $30 charge.

The price of a burial plot ranged from about $100 to several thousand dollars, depending on the location of the cemetery, the physical characteristics of the specific plot and the cemetery, the size of the plot, and whether maintenance of the grounds and the grave surface was included. "Perpetual care" referred to maintenance of the grounds and grave into the long-run future. Many people bought double-size or family-size plots at the time a family member died, which had the effect of shifting part of the cost of other deaths to the present one. Grave markers ranged from a simple flat granite slab flush to the ground at about $80 (or $125 if in bronze) to up-right stones with angular surfaces and elaborate carving at $500 or even more. Many cemeteries of recent design prohibited headstones that protruded more than one or two inches above the ground, because they interferred with lawn mowing machinery. A decision to bury above ground, always a high-status phenomenon, added thousands of dollars to the cost. An individual tomb building might cost $10,000 to $20,000, but even a crypt ranged from about $2,000 to $10,000.

Most cemeteries required the use of a vault or a grave liner, both of which were durable containers for a casket. The purpose was to prevent the grave from caving in after a few years when the coffin and its contents disintegrated. The caving in presented a hazard to visitors and cemetery employees and caused expensive refilling of the hole. A vault, which was a large metal box, varied in price from several hundred dollars to about $1,000, the higher priced ones being guaranteed waterproof for ten years. A grave liner, which was composed of six slabs of some material, usually concrete or fiberglass, was priced at about $135 and was not waterproof. All mortuaries and most cemeteries had these products for sale.

In addition, the family of the deceased usually had two other types of funeral costs. In the United States about $1 billion a year was spent on funeral flowers, or almost $500 per funeral. The family's share of this figure was usually from $75 to $150. The other cost was an honorarium for the clergyman. Although some Protestant ministers expected nothing, the practice was usually to give them something and always to give rabbis and priests an honorarium. The figure ranged from $25 to $100. Some families encountered a third type of charge. If they asked for live music at the funeral the price might be from $20 to $50.

The legal requirements on embalming were diverse, but no state required it. However, a good many states required embalming after a designated period, usually twenty-four or thirty-six hours, unless the body was properly refrigerated. The United States culture fully expected embalming and had put a high value on it since the 1860s. This process gained acceptance at that time because of the families' wishes to return the bodies of Civil War deceased to their home communities. Body preparation also usually included the use of cosmetics. Morticians also were willing to call in hairdressers for a fee, usually $25, and supply clothing, if necessary, at $35 to $75. Embalming consisted of replacing the blood with a formalin solution, which made the deceased appear more lifelike for a brief period but was not a long term preservative. Embalming was necessary to make the remains presentable if public viewing was to occur some twelve to thirty-six hours after death, as was the majority practice, because decomposition started immediately. The Thompsons made an itemized charge of $225 for embalming when it was not included in a package, a fee that was in line with the average in the community. Most scientific evidence indicated that there was no sanitation hazard from the underground decomposition of embalmed corpses of people who had an infection when they died, but a small amount of research suggested the contrary.

The cremation for $379 included wrapping the body in a plain sheet and no use of a container. Containers for cremation came in various qualities, including some for several hundred dollars, but a pressed wood or cardboard container at $20 was functionally adequate. Two states, Michigan and Massachusetts, prohibited cremation unless the body was in a casket, Cremation was growing in popularity in the United States except among blacks, who almost never used it, and accounted for about 6 per cent of all dispositions. The ashes were usually put in a bronze urn, which cost from $100 to $250. The ashes were sometimes buried, which required the purchase of a small plot, but sometimes the urn was placed in a niche in an above-ground facility designed for such purposes. A niche cost from about $75 to about $800. However, along the East and West coasts it had become popular to scatter the ashes at sea from an airplane, with or without an impressive container. Such a flying service, called Ecologic Service Company, had been established recently in the Thompsons' trade territory and charged low prices.

A possible but seldom used alternative for the consumer was speedy cremation or burial, without embalming, followed by a memorial service rather than being preceded by a funeral. A memorial service was usually held in a church. Churches did not charge for the use of their space for a funeral service or a memorial service, but a considerable number of people were not affiliated with a church. In addition, almost no church would permit its facilities to be tied up for public viewing of the remains except for a few minutes preceding a funeral.

The Industry and Its Image

The Thompson Funeral Home was part of a large industry which, according to the latest United States Census of Business, included 18,966 firms operating 20,854 establishments. This industry was dominated by small, single-location businesses owned and operated by families. There were slightly under two million deaths per year and the figure was slowly rising. Thus, the average funeral home handled about 105 dispositions per year, or about two per week. Most physical facilities were underutilized. The average total cost of a disposition to a family in the United States was between $2,000 and $2,100. About one fourth (5,111) of all funeral establishments were so small that they had no employees, whereas another 3,482 had only one employee and 2,488 had two paid employees. Only 295 had twenty or more employees. Even most of the mortuaries located in large metropolitan areas were small.

Despite the absence of big business in this type of economic activity, the funeral industry was controversial. The Federal Trade Commission conducted extensive investigations from the early 1970s through 1977 and held wide-scale public hearings in six communities in the later years.[2] The industry had been controversial since at least the early 1960s. In 1963, two provocative books that were critical of funeral directors were published, Ruth Harmer's *The High Cost of Dying*,[3] and Jessica Mitford's *The American Way of Death.*[4] The latter, written by a journalist rather than a scholar, proved to be a best-seller and is even now highly influential. Although it looked at many facts, this book rested fundamentally on the author's personal values and those she wished others to adopt. The gist of her belief was that funerals were extravagant and excessively sentimental. This book was particularly galling to the industry not just because of its content but because Mitford formerly was a self-avowed Communist party member for fifteen years. Her survey considered but largely rejected the work of cultural anthropologists, psychiatrists, psychologists, sociologists, and other behavioral scientists that collectively pointed to the necessity and value of funeral practices and expenditures. Mitford believed that funeral practices in the United States were an exploitation by funeral directors of consumers at a time when their bereavement was having a disorienting effect on them, when they might have feelings of guilt, and when there was too little time for them to make rational arrangements.

Most of what the social critics said was at odds with the research literature. For example, one of the pillars of modern behavioral research and thought, Bronislaw Malinowski, concluded the following:

[Death] threatens the very cohesion and solidarity of the group . . . [and the funeral] counteracts the centrifugal forces of fear, dismay, demoralization, and provides the most powerful means of reintegration of the group's shaken solidarity and of re-establishment.[5]

[2] See Report of the Presiding Officer on Proposed Trade Regulation Rule Concerning Funeral Industry Practices (16 C.F.R. Part 453, Public Record 215-46), which is a 165-page summary of the matter. This document contains citations to many FTC supporting documents.

[3] Ruth Harmer, *The High Cost of Dying* (New York: Macmillan Publishing Co., Inc., 1963).

[4] Jessica Metford, *The American Way of Death* (New York: Simon & Schuster, Inc., 1963).

[5] Bronislaw Malinowski, *Magic, Science and Religion* (New York: Doubleday & Company, 1948), p. 53.

Behavioral science accepts the principle that people should express their grief and come to terms with death. The funeral achieves closure. Raymond Firth summed up a considerable amount of the literature with these words:

> A funeral rite is a social rite par excellence. Its ostensible object is the dead person, but it benefits not the dead, but the living.[6]

The characteristics of the rite are determined partly by the individual but mainly by the culture and the subculture in which the individual lives.

V. R. Pine, probably the only behavioral scientist who was also a funeral director, and D. L. Phillips stated that "[People's] funeral expenditures serve as evidence of their concern for both the dead and the conventional standards of decency in their community of residence."[7] They added the following concerning one sizable portion of the population:

> It may be that for those who have, to a great extent, abandoned a religious outlook in favor of a secular one, the act of buying, receiving, and paying for funerals represents a secular and economic ritual of payment formerly performed by more religious customs and ceremonies. If expenditures are viewed as a secular ritual, then money spent for funerals is serving a far different need than one of mere exchange of cash between two agents: the funeral purchaser and the funeral producer.[8]

Behavioral science finds it noteworthy that formal funerals and private expenditures for them and for memorialization survive in the Soviet Union, despite the clear opposition of the state. From 1917 until the mid-1930s government regulations required unceremonial and immediate disposal of the remains, but after that time regulations were relaxed and a system of grants was established. A grant was made to the bereaved family to be used to purchase the family's selections from state stores and state services. Although the funeral arrangements provided after the mid-1930s were fully adequate for the disposition of the remains, many Soviet families chose to add to and embellish the arrangements.[9]

---

[6] Raymond Firth, *Elements of Social Organization* (Boston: Beacon Press, 1964), p. 63.

[7] Vanderlyn R. Pine and Derek L. Phillips, "The Cost of Dying: A Sociological Analysis of Funeral Expenditures," *Social Forces*, **17** (Winter 1970), pp. 405–417 at p. 416. This article resulted from a research grant from the National Institute of Mental Health, a federal agency.

[8] Ibid.

[9] See Robert W. Haberstein and William M. Lamers, *Funeral Customs the World Over* (Milwaukee: Bulfin Printers, 1960); John Manning, "Soviet Funeral Service." *The American Funeral Director*, **89**, No. 1 (1966), p. 30; V. R. Pine, "Comparative Funeral Practices,' *Practical Anthropology*, 16 (March–April 1969), pp. 49–62.

Although the FTC hearing examiner recommended that the commissioners adopt some modest trade regulations for the funeral industry, he concluded that

> The "traditional" funeral has the merit of achieving closure in the sense a gestalt psychologist would approve. As a widely known and recognizable societal ritual, it would signify to many that a life had ended and do it in a way no other form of disposition could. In a society with few rituals, this one is of great value to those who are accustomed to it. Many people derive comfort from its familiarity.
> There is also a therapeutic benefit to be gained from being "forced" to go through certain motions. The various motions expected of the bereaved in the "traditional" funeral may bring structure to a temporarily disorganized family, perhaps helping all through a difficult time.
> Throughout this proceeding funeral directors and their representatives focused on the trust relationship which exists between funeral directors and their clientele. That it exists is not rebutted despite many witnesses to the contrary.[10]

Advertising of prices had always been extremely uncommon in the United States funeral industry and had been prohibited in many states. Massachusetts and Nebraska still had laws forbidding the advertising of funeral prices, but there was some likelihood that these two state laws would be declared unconstitutional. Price advertising had also been prohibited by the code of ethics of the National Funeral Directors Association, the most powerful professional association in the industry. However, in 1968 the Justice Department brought suit against the NFDA for violation of the antitrust laws in prohibiting its members from advertising prices. The defendant signed a consent decree. However, the presiding officer at the Federal Trade Commission (FTC) hearings concluded in the late 1970s:

> The result of the attitude of funeral directors is considerable peer pressure directed toward those who advertise prices. It appears that such advertisers are the outsiders in this industry and are generally scorned by their peers.[11]

After long controversy the FTC decided that some regulations were in the public interest and put them into effect on April 30, 1984. Like many adopted over the past decade, this set of rules contained a "sunset" provision requiring the agency to decide in four years whether they should continue. Political scientists and experts on government administration had been urging greater use of the sunset feature in regulations so as to combat inertia and obsolescence of rules. A potential penalty of up to $10,000 per violation was

[10]Report of the Presiding Officer, op. cit., pp. 126–127
[11]Ibid., p. 116.

written into the regulation. Such penalty would be imposed only if the Justice Department agreed with the FTC that there was a pattern of abuse by a given mortuary. Under the FTC rules, funeral directors had to do the following:

1. Give customers an itemized list of prices at the beginning of any discussion of funeral goods and services.
2. Disclose prices over the telephone when asked.
3. Disclose in writing the existence of any markups imposed on "cash advance items," such as flowers or death notices.
4. Tell customers that embalming is not legally required in most cases.

Furthermore, funeral directors were forbidden to do the following:

1. Tell customers that they need to buy a casket if they want a "direct" cremation.
2. Tell customers that there is a legal requirement to buy an outside burial container for a casket, unless state, local law, or a cemetery requires it.
3. Tell customers that any law, cemetery, or crematory rules require them to buy a certain item or service if it is not true.
4. Claim that any funeral goods (such as sealed caskets) or services (such as embalming) will delay a body's decomposition for a long, or indefinite, time after burial. Customers cannot be told that a casket or vault will protect a body from water, insects, and so on, if that is not true.

Advise Thompson Funeral Home.

12

INTERNATIONAL MARKETING

DENTSU ADVERTISING

The Japanese advertising agency Dentsu was one of the most admired of Japanese companies among North American and European businesspeople. However, its background and manner of operation were not understood well. Even more important, it was not appreciated that Dentsu had some problems and underexploited opportunities.

Dentsu was the largest advertising agency in the world in 1985 if measured in billings to clients, the prevailing way in which businesspeople and journalists judged the size of an advertising agency. In some people's minds, this corresponded to sales. However, it was really the costs of space and time in the media that the agency bought on behalf of clients whose advertising messages it prepared. In the latest fiscal year, that figure at Dentsu was the equivalent of U.S. $3.5 billion.

An alternative, preferable, and growing way of judging size of advertising agencies was to look at their gross income, that is, revenue. See Exhibit 1. The Japanese firm's gross income in 1985 placed it just behind Young & Rubicam and Ogilvy Group. Ted Bates & Company, a U.S. agency, was only slightly behind Dentsu and had risen from fifth place in 1980. For the period 1973–1983 the Japanese agency had been first in both billings and gross income, but its share in the billings of the world's ten largest agencies had fallen for six consecutive years. Dentsu was eager to regain first place, lock it

297

EXHIBIT 1 World's Largest Advertising Agencies in 1985

Rank	Agency	Home Country	Gross Income (in millions)	Billings (in billions
1.	Young & Rubicam	U.S.	$536.0	$3.58
2.	Ogilvy Group	U.S.	481.1	3.32
3.	Dentsu Inc.	Japan	473.1	3.62
4.	Ted Bates Worldwide	U.S.	466.0	3.11
5.	J. Walter Thompson Co.	U.S.	450.9	3.01
6.	Saatchi & Saatchi Compton Worldwide	Great Britain	440.9	3.03
7.	BBDO International	U.S.	377.0	2.52
8.	McCann-Erickson Worldwide	U.S.	345.1	2.30
9.	D'Arcy Masius Benton & Bowles	U.S.	319.5	2.18
10.	Foote, Cone & Belding	U.S.	284.5	1.90
11.	Leo Burnett Company	U.S.	269.4	1.87
12.	Grey Advertising	U.S.	259.3	1.73
13.	Doyle Dane Bernbach Group	U.S.	231.8	1.67
14.	Hakuhodo International	Japan	198.9	1.53
15.	SSC&B; Lintas Worldwide	U.S.	190.9	1.30
16.	Bozell, Jacobs, Kenyon & Eckhardt	U.S.	173.7	1.22
17.	Marschalk Campbell-Ewald	U.S.	150.1	1.00
18.	Eurocom Group	Several West European nations	129.1	.87
19.	Needham Harper Worldwide	U.S.	127.1	.85
20.	Dancer Fitzgerald Sample	U.S.	121.5	.88

in permanently, and improve its financial showing. Dentsu enjoyed its high rank because of domestic dominance. It had rather little foreign business.

There was, however, something of an anomaly in the economic statistics. McCann-Erickson, founded in 1912 and eighth in both gross income and billings, was the largest of three large advertising agencies jointly owned by The Interpublic Group of Companies, Inc., a U.S. holding company. The other two were SSC&B:Lintas, which was fifteenth in both gross income and billings, and Marschalk Campbell-Ewald, which was seventeenth in both gross income and billings. McCann-Erickson alone operated 113 agencies in 60 countries and received 65 per cent of its gross income abroad. For several reasons, including tradition, the preservation of corporate cultures, wariness about bigness, and a respect for internal competition, each of the three operated in a quasi-independent manner. If their data had been added together, Interpublic Group would have been the largest in the world in 1985, with $686 million in gross income and $4.60 billion in billings.

Before the 11-year period of Dentsu supremacy, the largest agency in the world was J. Walter Thompson Co. Young & Rubicam, J. Walter Thompson, and Ted Bates were old, respected U.S. organizations established in 1923, 1864, and 1940 respectively. Typically, Young & Rubicam made about 40 per cent of its gross income abroad; and J. Walter Thompson, about 57 per cent. The latter was something of a pioneer and in many nations had been the first American advertising agency to go into business.

The advertising industry was going through a pronounced merger trend, but two 1986 transactions in particular were of great significance. First, BBDO, Doyle Dane Bernbach Group, and Needham Harper Worldwide agreed to merge. Their combined 1985 gross income would have been $735.9 million and their billings $5.037 billion. The agreement provided that the new holding company would run two separate and independent international networks of offices and a third subsidiary composed of all the specialty and regional firms of the three. Name of the holding company had not been decided. Second, Saatchi & Saatchi Compton, established in 1970, purchased Ted Bates Worldwide. Their combined 1985 gross income would have been $906.9 million and their billings $6.14 billion. Saatchi's rise had been meteoric. It agreed to let Bates operate quasi-independently and with its present managers.

Several expansion strategies had been followed by U.S.-based advertising agencies. D'Arcy favored joining forces with agencies owned in other countries to establish third companies, which they then owned together. Ted Bates Advertising and BBDO (Batton, Barton, Durstine, & Osborne) mainly purchased existing overseas organizations whereas both J. Walter Thompson and McCann-Erickson expanded abroad mainly by setting up wholly owned subsidiaries. McCann-Erickson also acquired a few foreign agencies. Its acquisition policy was 100 per cent or majority ownership wherever local law permitted. The company owned 80 of its 113 agencies around the world. In three Asian countries, Indonesia, South Korea, and Taiwan, the law prohibited foreign ownership interests in an agency, but McCann-Erickson had established "association arrangements" with locally owned and operated agencies. Taken together, the Interpublic Group was the most important advertising business in Asia outside of the Japanese market. All three Interpublic companies shared a joint venture with Matheson-Jardine of Hong Kong and Bermuda in the People's Republic of China. Called Interpublic-Jardine (China) Ltd., it maintained offices in Beijing (Peking), Shanghai, and Guangzhou. This joint venture and Dentsu were the first foreign advertising agencies receiving permits to do business in the People's Republic of China.

Dentsu was founded in 1901, and its name literally translates as "telegraphic communication." The corporate stock was not publicly traded. The two largest shareholders were the two Japanese news services, Kyodo News and Jiji Press. The former was owned, like Associated Press in the United States, by a sizable number of news papers, and the latter was owned principally by an employees' trust.

The Japanese agency was, of course, the largest advertising firm in Japan and was two and one-third times as large as its nearest domestic rival, Hakuhodo, Inc., and over seven times as large as the number three Daiko Advertising. Dai-Ichi Kikaku, based in Tokyo, was fourth. Dentsu was pervasive in the Japanese economy, but Hakuhodo and Dai-Ichi Kikaku were growing much faster than Dentsu. Daiko was rather stable. Founded in 1944 and employing 1.420, Daiko was based in Osaka and had branches in Tokyo, Nagoya, Kobe, Kyoto, and Fukuoka but no overseas branches. Established in 1895 and employing 2,950, Hakuhodo was based in Tokyo and had branches in all large Japanese cities. It had partial ownership in agencies in Hamburg, Düsseldorf, New York, Los Angeles, Singapore, Bangkok, and Kuala Lumpur. Dentsu maintained branches in all large Japanese cities and maintained small offices in London, Paris, Los Angeles, New York, Taipei, Beijing, and Shanghai.

Hakuhodo entered into a joint venture in 1960 with McCann-Erickson. This venture was a pioneering initiative that provided both organizations with great assistance in bridging the gulf separating the U.S. and Japanese cultures. McCann-Erickson Hakuhodo was by far the largest agency there that had majority ownership held by non-Japanese. Other Japanese and U.S. agencies set up several similar arrangements later on in the 1960s and 1970s.

Asahi Advertising, the ninth largest agency in Japan, signed an agreement in 1985 to cooperate with Saatchi & Saatchi Compton. A British organization, Saatchi was the largest agency in Europe, one of the fastest-growing in the world, and one of the most imaginative in its work. Asahi Advertising had annual billings of $194 million and gross income of $30 million.

The majority of Dentsu's Japanese clients did not use it for advertising supporting their exports. Such work constituted no more than 5 per cent of Dentsu's billings. The Japanese manufacturers tended to use local, U.S.-based, or European-based agencies for their foreign advertising. In 1966, Dentsu attempted to follow some of its major Japanese clients into the United States and established Dentsu Corporation of America. It did not work out well. Executives later attributed the disappointment to lack of the right personnel for the subsidiary. By 1986 there were 48 large Japanese corporations spending about $1.5 billion abroad on advertising every year. About 85 per cent of that amount was spent in Western Europe and North America.

It was not until 1981 that Dentsu got together with someone for a joint venture abroad. After years of sporadic dialogue, Dentsu-Young & Rubicam was established. Hakuhodo executives hypothesized that Dentsu's holding back for so long could be explained by corporate personality, managerial style, orientation, and ownership pattern. By personality Dentsu was cautious and conservative. It practiced decision making by consensus, which took a great deal of time but was a revered goal in that culture. As an example of togetherness, observers noticed that as many Dentsu employees as possible climbed Mt. Fuji together annually. Dentsu was domestically rather than internationally oriented in thinking and tradition. Also, there were numerous spokespersons for the owners. On the other hand, Hakuhodo was not conservative, had a cosmopolitan world view, and was closely held by just a few individuals who had similar philosophies and objectives.

The purpose of Dentsu-Young & Rubicam (DYR) was to provide an organization that would let each partner capitalize on reciprocal strengths in markets where they were weak. Dentsu would take Young & Rubicam intensively into Japan and other parts of Asia; and Young & Rubicam would let Dentsu put roots down in Western Europe, the United States, and Latin America. After establishment, it took an abnormally long time for this joint venture to organize itself and begin seriously to conduct business. The president of Dentsu was appointed chairperson of the board and an American was appointed president and chief executive officer of DYR. The firm opened branches in New York, Tokyo, Los Angeles, Kuala Lumpur, Singapore, Hong Kong, and Melbourne. Among the first clients signed up were Pacific Southwest Airlines and Hawaiian Punch. By 1985 the venture was doing over $330 million in billings in the United States, Japan, Malaysia, Singapore, Hong Kong, and Australia; and among foreign agencies it ranked seventh in Malaysia, fourth in Singapore, third in Hong Kong, and twenty-ninth in Australia.

If an advertising agency could attract a client from its own country abroad, there was interesting potential at home as well as abroad. An important example was that of McCann-Erickson, which years earlier got its foot in the door providing service to Coca-Cola in some foreign countries before D'Arcy, which held the Coca-Cola account at home, expanded into other nations. Coca-Cola subsequently shifted to McCann-Erickson.

The corporate culture of Dentsu was quite noteworthy in ways other than what has already been mentioned. At its core was an interlocking set of connections throughout the Japanese economy. The company constantly tried to improve this set. The agency recruited many of its employees from the families of top executives in many client companies and from the families of Diet (Congress) members. There was in essence an "old boy" network. This network was so intricate that some people had termed it the "Tsukiji CIA" after the section of Tokyo in which the organization was located.

There were sometimes complaints in Japanese business circles that Dentsu was favored by the media. To be specific, it was alleged that on occasion when time and space were scarce, Dentsu could always get whatever its clients needed. Moreover, in all periods Dentsu could obtain the most desirable time and space. This set of feelings, whether always true or not, assisted Dentsu in holding clients. In addition, many corporate advertising managers reasoned that if Dentsu conducted a campaign for them and it did not succeed, then they would not be blamed, for others would feel that if Dentsu could not do it, nobody could. If they hired another agency and the campaign failed, the company superiors would ask why they had not hired Dentsu.

Japanese industry traditionally put much more emphasis on personal selling and healthy, harmonious relationships with the other member firms in the channel of distribution than on advertising. In that country, the fraction of the gross national product (GNP) spent on advertising in a typical year was about 1 per cent, compared to about 2.1 per cent in the United States. See Exhibit 2.

The Japanese economy, although quite healthy, was showing some signs of maturation. The economy was growing, but the long-term rate of growth was slowing. As part of this trend, the growth in national spending on advertising was slowing. In recent years that growth rate was only about one-half as much as in the 1970s. In addition, the mix of promotion showed a small but noteworthy change. See Exhibit 3. There was an increase in clients' requests for Dentsu to help with sales promotion. This term, of course, referred to a miscellany of promotional activities such as contests, sweepstakes, cents-off coupon offers, and short- and long-term exhibitions. Sales promotion work had risen to about 15 per cent of Dentsu's billings. Instead of the traditional 15 per cent commission on media time and space, sales promotion by an advertising agency was paid for by negotiated fees. The clients negotiated aggressively. Such fees

EXHIBIT 2 Advertising Expenditures as a Percent of
GNP in Selected Countries

Argentina	1.3	Pakistan	.1
Australia	1.8	Peru	.6
Austria	1.0	Philippines	.4
Belgium	.6	Portugal	.2
Brazil	.7	Puerto Rico	1.8
Canada	1.3	Saudi Arabia	.1
Chile	.8	Singapore	1.0
Colombia	1.0	South Africa	1.7
Denmark	1.3	South Korea	.7
Finland	1.8	Spain	.8
France	.8	Sri Lanka	.2
Greece	.3	Sudan	.1
Hong Kong	.7	Surinam	.3
India	.3	Sweden	1.1
Indonesia	.2	Switzerland	1.4
Ireland	.8	Syria	.3
Israel	.7	Taiwan	1.3
Italy	1.3	Thailand	.3
Japan	1.0	Trinidad and Tobago	.6
Kenya	.4	Turkey	.3
Luxembourg	.6	United Kingdom	1.8
Malaysia	.5	Uruguay	.5
Mexico	.6	United States	2.1
Netherlands	1.8	Venezuela	1.0
New Zealand	1.8	West Germany	.8
Norway	1.5		

were running only 5 to 8 per cent of the cost of the services rendered. Sales promotion work was labor-intensive and thus costly to furnish a client. The sales promotion services rendered to some clients were loss leaders, offered mainly to keep their high commission billings on the books. Overall, Dentsu was netting only about 5.6 per cent on gross income and about 10 per cent on shareholders' equity. Interpublic Group was making over 18 per cent on sharholders' equity.

There were at least two extremely important differences in professional practices, from an ethical viewpoint, between Japanese advertising agencies on the one hand and all American and most European agencies on the other hand. First, it was considered perfectly all right in Japan for an agency to serve two or more clients who were in direct competition with each other. In the United States and most other developed economies, an advertising agency avoided this practice, regarding it as a conflict of interest although local laws did not

EXHIBIT 3 Breakdown of Billings by Agency by Media Type[a]

	Dentsu	Hakuhodo	Daiko	DYR
Newspapers	23%	18.3%	32%	5.6%
Magazines	5	6.2	4	22.8
Business publications	Included in other	Included in other	Included in other	4.8
Farm publications	Included in other	Included in other	Included in other	0.3
Outdoor	14	Included in other	Included in other	0.7
Transit	Included in other	Included in other	Included in other	0.2
Television	42	43.6	34	43.8
Radio	4	3.6	4	5.2
Direct mail	Included in other	Included in other	Included in other	13.3
Yellow Pages	Included in other	Included in other	Included in other	0.5
Point of purchase	Included in other	Included in other	17	Included in other
Sales promotion	Included in other	12.7	Included in other	Included in other
Other	12	15.6	9	2.8

[a]Dai-Ichi Kikaku is not available.

prohibit it. Even if a Western advertising agency were to assign most personnel to work exclusively on just one client account, rather inefficient and a rarity, the organization would still suspect that some commercially valuable information would leak between these groups of staff members, and also simple observation would provide significant insights into the rival's plans and accomplishments. Even the sharing of equipment could offer opportunities for leakage. Also, of course, the agency's top managers would inevitably have some degree of conflict in overseeing the work of their employees even if there were substantial delegation of authority.

Second, Japanese agencies could have ownership interests in media. Although this was not totally unknown in Europe, it was uncommon there and did not exist in the United States. Dentsu owned 3 per cent of the stock of Tokyo Broadcasting System, the largest privately owned telecaster in Japan. It also owned small fractions of the Yomiuri Group's television operations, Mainichi Shimbun, a major newspaper, and eleven other newspapers.

Employees of Dentsu numbered 5,700, about 17 per cent of

whom were female. Salaries and wages were average for the advertising industry in Japan, but bonuses, paid twice a year, were quite generous even by Japanese standards. The Japanese culture and some other cultures, especially in Asia, were characterized by modest salaries but also by the expectation of significant bonuses once or twice a year and quite a few recreational benefits paid for by the employer as well as the normal vacation, retirement, and health insurance benefits. The employer saw bonuses as a way of building and keeping morale high and rewarding some people for particularly fine work performance. The bonus could be linked directly to the work, instead of building it into the base salary. In twice-a-year bonus systems like that of Dentsu, the reward could come without a long passage of time intervening, thus putting a good psychological principle into practice. In most situations the bonuses were optional with the management, not required. Of course, the reputation of a company could be damaged easily if it wandered too far from cultural expectations unless some other employers began to do the same. All forms of compensation together amounted to about 60 per cent of all Dentsu revenue, well above the corresponding figure in North American and European agencies. In Japan there was also the expectation of lifetime employment with the same firm. This expectation was strong, and it was part of the thinking of both employer and employee. Only a tiny percentage of employees violated this idea.

The Japanese government was interested in expanding Japanese-based service businesses abroad. In part, this was because of a desire to move toward balance, but there was another reason. If tariffs should rise against foreign products or strict quotas be imposed on many foreign products that Japan exported in large quantities or both, then the provision of services, such as advertising, could help take up the slack.

Advise Dentsu.

UNILEVER

Unilever, the giant London-Rotterdam-based manufacturer of consumer household goods, ranked as the world's fourteenth largest multinational corporation, with some 500 subsidiaries in seventy-five nations around the world, more than 300,000 employees, and sales volume of more than U.S. $24.1 billion in 1980. Unilever's products

This case was prepared by Sheryl Ferrucci, who is on the staff of Leo Burnett and Company, Milan, Italy.

were grouped into nine major categories in that year: edible fats and oils and dairy products; other foods; detergents; personal products; chemicals; paper, plastics, and packaging; animal feeds; The United Africa Corporation (a trading company); and plantations, transport, and other concerns.

Most of Unilever's products had some links among them. Many of them used similar raw materials (for example, margarines and soaps), or similar research and development expertise. The history of Unilever's expansion showed a gradual diversification from soaps into related industries.

The company developed a rather unusual joint management technique. Dual officers were established in both London and Rotterdam; each one's actions mirrored those of his counterpart. A special committee of three officers from both London and Rotterdam directed the company, backed up by an international board of twenty-three directors, each of whom had jurisdiction over some functional area, geographical region, or coordinating role.

Unilever offered unique insights into the problems encountered in the management and integration of such a large and diversified concern. The organization had to allow for maximum flexibility to respond to problems faced by individual subsidiaries, divisions, or countries. At the same time, it had to provide a framework by which information and resources could be transmitted between the parent and subsidiaries and among the subsidiaries.

Unilever's Corporate Structure

The company that most people knew as Unilever was, in fact, two legal entities. Unilever Ltd., with offices in London, was given nominal (for legal purposes) charge of most subsidiaries in Africa, the United Kingdom, and Commonwealth nations. Unilever N.V., the Dutch arm of the firm, with home offices in Rotterdam, had control over most of the U.S. and European companies. Each of these had its own chairman and top management staff. However, the two operated as one firm, and all earnings, resources, and responsibilities were pooled.

A special committee of three was established to preside over all major decisions and was given ultimate responsibility and decision-making power. Directly under the special committee, the board of directors, made up of the executive directors of the two branches, was assigned responsibility for deciding on the appointment, promotion, and salaries of Unilever's top management, for giving final approval of all one-and five-year plans for each product division, for making the final decision on large capital projects, and for approving overall financial policy.

Lever Brothers

Lever Brothers, the original British branch of what was later to become Unilever, was founded in 1885 by William Lever with the opening of a soap factory in Port Sunlight, England. Lever Brothers grew quickly. By 1890, agencies had been established on the Continent to market Sunlight brand soap. By the turn of the century, these agencies had been replaced by Lever Brothers factories in Germany, Switzerland, Australia, Canada, and the United States. At about this time, Lever began to seriously consider vertical integration to ensure a steady supply of vegetable oil for his factories. The company acquired plantations in the Pacific, Africa, and the Middle East for this purpose.

During World War I, Lever Brothers diversified into margarines and other edible fats. This was in part the result of necessity imposed by war and the halting of trade and in part the realization of an expansion plan that Lever management had long been considering. This was a logical expansion, given the similarity of raw materials utilized in soap and margarine manufacture. The better-quality oils from the plantations were used to manufacture margarine and the residue was used in soap making.

Jurgens Ltd. and Van den Burgh Ltd.

Jurgens Ltd. and Van den Burgh Ltd., both Dutch companies, began manufacturing the first margarine-type butter substitutes during the 1870s. The new product caught on quickly and, by 1890, both firms had established a network of factories and marketing organizations across Europe. As long as the market offered opportunity for growth, the two companies could afford to compete, but by 1908, competition from abroad and the maturation of the market led them to form a pool. This became a full-scale merger in 1927, when the two companies combined to form the Margarine Union.

The Formation of Unilever

By 1929, the Margarine Union and Lever Brothers were engaged in open battle for markets and for raw material supplies. The merger of these two organizations and the acquisition of several smaller companies was undertaken to gain greater control over both the market and raw material supplies. In 1930, the two companies were combined into one, Unilever, with home offices in London and Rotterdam. A board of twenty-three directors was appointed to oversee the new company, and a special committee, appointed by the board, was designed to coordinate the firm's vast interests. Certain points of

Unilever's overall policy guidelines were noteworthy. These were broad policies which Unilever followed in delineating company strategies and tactics, and they made up part of the framework within which subsidiaries operated. These points were decentralization of structure, use of local managers, sharing equity with host-country nationals, and advertising practices.

Decentralization

Unilever long had a decentralized organizational structure. Individual subsidiaries were virtually autonomous within the broad guidelines set by the parent company. One- and five-year plans were drawn up by product line and by geographic area. These plans, approved by the special committee, covered such areas as sales, capital budgeting, and management availability. Individual firms were expected to meet the goals set in these plans, but just how these goals were achieved was up to the firm's management. Product line coordinators and regional directors were developed to monitor the progress of firms within their jurisdiction and to bring problems to the attention of the parent organization.

This organizational approach underwent drastic changes starting in the early 1970s, and the trend was toward greater integration and control over operations. Before these changes, managerial decisions were made strictly on a country by country basis, with little communication with the home offices. By the late 1970s, as a result of recognition that consumers in different countries had become more similar in their tastes, this nation by nation approach was streamlined. It was replaced by an emphasis on product line specialists who designed overall policies for an entire product category.

Use of Local Managers

Unilever attempted, whenever possible, to employ host country nationals in management positions. Local managerial talent was actively recruited and trained. In 1979, 94 per cent of all managers were employed in their home country.[1] In addition, the training of most seniors managers included temporary assignments in at least one country other than their own, in order to instill an understanding of the international scope of Unilever's operations.

---

[1] H. van den Hoven, "Business in a Changing International Society," speech to the Food Marketing Institute's Mid-Winter Conference held at the Americana Hotel, Bal Harbor, Florida, on January 24–26, 1979, p. 2.

Practice of Sharing Equity with Locals

Although Unilever always preferred 100 per cent ownership of subsidiaries because of the greater control and flexibility it gives, management recognized the growing wish of developing nations to share in the commercial and industrial growth of their countries. Unilever had been faced with forced divestment in several cases (for example, Nigeria, where it was forced to sell 60 per cent of its stock at very low prices), but in other cases it anticipated compulsory divestment. For example, Unilever voluntarily offered local participation in India as early as 1956 and in parts of Africa in 1959.

Advertising

Unilever was primarily in the highly competitive consumer products market, in which mass advertising was vitally important. In 1978, Unilever spent $570 million worldwide on mass media advertising for consumer products. About $300 million, more than 50 per cent of that total, was spent in Western Europe.[2] Expenditures varied among product groups. For example, they tended to be highest for toiletries but relatively low for food products. All in all, however, they tended to be less than 3 per cent of the product's final consumer price.[3] Again, the decentralized nature of Unilever's organization showed through here. The subsidiary was given full freedom to select the optimal level of advertising expenditure per brand, the media to be used, the advertising copy, and even the advertising agency.

Since 1964, Unilever had attempted to streamline its advertising by making use of international brand strategies wherever possible. Management believed the increasing similarity in consumer tastes and perceptions in the developed world would allow greater use of internationalized promotion approaches in the future, giving economies of scale in the creation of advertising strategies.

Unilever's Experience With Frozen Foods In Europe

Unilever could be credited with having created a market for quick frozen foods in Europe by use of aggressive marketing campaigns to educate the European consumer. The newest medium, television, was particularly useful in this education effort. In the United Kingdom,

[2] Elspeth Durie, "Unilever Eyes Changes in 'Sacred' Agency Policy," *Advertising Age,* July 9, 1979, p. 38.

[3] "Advertising–The Unilever View," Unilever Briefing Sheet, Information Division, Unilever, London/Rotterdam, July 1978.

a two-stage television ad campaign was carried out. First, introductory ads were used to acquaint consumers with the concept of frozen foods. After this, ads specifically for the Unilever brand (Birds Eye) were featured.

Unilever first entered the frozen food market in 1943 with the formal establishment of Birds Eye Foods in Great Britain.[4] Processing and sales began in 1946. Growth was slow during the first few years. Adequate transportation and storage facilities for these new products were often lacking. Retailers and wholesalers often did not have freezer containers. Also, and more difficult to resolve, frozen foods were relatively expensive and it was often difficult to convince consumers that they were worth the high price. By the early 1960s, however, frozen foods were firmly established in the United Kingdom, and Birds Eye Foods was the top seller. Sales of Unilever frozen foods in the U.K. grew from £2.5 million in 1953 to £45 million in 1965.[5]

Sales on the Continent were much less successful. Unilever first introduced frozen foods there at the same time they were introduced in Great Britain, but losses were so high that Unilever was forced to withdraw from the Continental frozen food market altogether by 1949. Consumers saw frozen foods as more expensive than fresh foods and of lower quality, and no amount of advertising could convince them otherwise.

Unilever stayed out of the Continental market for eight years, but by 1957, conditions were judged to be ripe for reentry. Vita, a small Dutch firm with expertise in the field but limited capital resources for demand expansion, was acquired. The brand name was changed to Iglo, a name easily pronounced in all European languages.

The Market Today

Much had changed since Unilever's first attempt (and failure) to build a market for frozen foods in Continental Europe. Unilever's share of the Western European frozen food market was recently between 60 per cent and 70 per cent.[6] Sales increased each year from 1975 to 1980, with the exception of 1977 when poor performance of the economy and relatively plentiful and inexpensive fresh foods combined to produce a drop in sales volume.

[4] Birds Eye Foods in Great Britain was related to Birds Eye Foods in the United States only by name. The British firm was a wholly owned subsidiary of Unilever, with rights to use the name and the process invented in the United States by Clarence Birdseye. The American firm was a subsidiary of General Foods.

[5] Charles Wilson, *The History of Unilever—A Study in Economic Growth and Social Change,* 3 volumes. (New York: Praeger Publishers, Inc., 1968), p. 165.

[6] "Unilever: A Multinational's New Route to Profits," *Business Week,* April 13, 1974, p. 57.

The consumption of frozen foods was dependent upon several factors. One, the availability and cost of fresh foods, could be expected to fluctuate from year to year. Other factors included:

- The amount of disposable income and expectations about the economy. These determined whether or not people were willing and able to pay the extra cost for added convenience.
- The number and percentage of households within a given market area that owned freezers and the average size of a freezer unit.
- The percentage of women who worked in a given nation. This affected not only the need for quick, convenient processed foods but also per capita disposable income of the household.
- The number of retail food outlets and their locations. The more convenient it was for consumers to shop, the more often they would do so, and the less need there would be for foods that kept for a long time.
- Finally, the character of the region or nation and the unique personality of the individual consumer were important, if virtually impossible to measure or quantify.

Nowhere in Europe did the consumption of frozen foods approach the level reached in the Unted States (approximately 43.6 kilograms per person in 1979).[7] However, Western Europe represented a large and growing market. More working women, increased incomes, a rise in the number of households owning freezers, and the trend toward concentration in the retail food industry were likely to lead to continued growth in the future.

Problems and Opportunities for the Future

Frozen convenience foods offered a vivid example of the problems encountered by an organization as large and complex as Unilever. Frozen foods were a relatively new type of product. Although they were widely accepted in the United States, in many countries consumers were still skeptical about their benefits. Advertising campaigns often needed to teach the consumer about frozen foods in general (how to prepare and use them) before they could get the consumer to prefer a given brand. Next, success in this market required the existence of certain factors:

1. A relatively high level of home freezer ownership.

---

[7]This figure is an estimate by the American Frozen Food Institute, McLean, Virginia. It is based on total frozen food production in the United States in 1979.

EXHIBIT 1

Country	Major Languages	Literacy Rates	Member of Trade Blocks	Frozen Food Consumption[8]	Per Capita Income[9]
Belgium	French, Flemish, German	99%	Belgo-Luxembourg Economic Union; European Community; Benelux Economic Union	6.4 Kg. per person	US$ 9,025
West Germany	German	99%	European Community	6.0 Kg. per person	$ 9,278
Denmark	Danish	99%	European Community	13.7 Kg. per person	$ 9,869
France	French	99%	European Community	5.4 Kg. per person	$ 7,908
Ireland	English, Gaelic	99%	European Community	3.9 Kg. per person	$ 2,711*
Great Britain	English	99%	European Community	13.1 Kg. per person	$ 4,955
Italy	Italian	94%	European Community	2.2 Kg. per person	$ 3,076*
Netherlands	Dutch	99%	European Community; Benelux Economic Union	9.6 Kg. per person	$ 8,509
Austria	German	99%	European Free Trade Association	6.1 Kg. per person	$ 6,739
Portugal	Portuguese	72%	European Free Trade Assocation; Associate member of the European Community	1.8 Kg. per person	$ 1,577*

Spain	Spanish	Associate Member of the European Community	2.2 Kg. per person	$ 3,625
Switzerland	German, French, Italian	European Free Trade Association	8.4 Kg. per person	$ 12,408
Norway	Bokmal (80%) Nyndrysk (20%)	European Free Trade Association	11.2 Kg. per person	$ 7,949
Greece	Greek	European Community	3.1 Kg. per person	$ 3,209
Sweden	Swedish	European Free Trade Association	18.8 Kg. per person	$ 9,274

*Per capita income in 1977. All other income figures are for 1978.

Country	Distribution Systems and Trends	Ownership of Freezers [10]	Women as a % of the Labor Force [11]
Belgium	Relatively inefficient. Sixty % of all retail food outlets are unaffiliated independents. A trend toward concentration has been slowed but not halted by lobbying on the part of small retailers.	42% of households	35.6%
West Germany	Marked trend toward larger, more efficient operations. Retail chains are very important in food distribution. Only 24% of all food retailers are classified as unaffiliated independents.	45% of households	37.7%
Denmark	Marked trend toward concentration aided by rising labor costs and the concentration of population in the urban areas. Only 7% of food retailers are unaffiliated independents.	69% of households	42.8%

EXHIBIT 1 (Continued)

Country	Distribution Systems and Trends	Ownership of Freezers[10]	Women as a % of the Labor Force[11]
France	A conscious effort on the part of distributors to increase efficiency through greater concentration in food distribution. Independent retailers are 61% of the total, but this situation is changing because of the formation of buying groups, cooperatives, and chains.	22% of households	36.1%
Ireland	The system is dominated by small, family-owned firms. Although there is a trend toward concentration, 20% of food retailers are still unaffiliated independents.	41% of households	26.5%
Great Britain	Distribution is relatively concentrated. Only 22% of food retailers are unaffiliated independents. Vertical integration (manufacturers that sell through their own retail outlets) has been particularly popular here, sparking the formation of voluntary chains as small firms have sought to protect themselves from the giants.	35% of households	38.2%
Italy	Both wholesalers and retailers tend to be small firms, with one or two employees. Wholesalers are usually limited in scope and serve only small retailers. Larger retailers buy directly from manufacturers. Unaffiliated independents are 74% of all food retailers. Legislation has tended to discourage the establishment of larger, more efficient firms.	29% of households	32.2%

Country			
Netherlands	Distribution is rapidly becoming more and more concentrated. The total number of grocery stores has been declining, and the number of supermarkets has increased sharply. Thirty per cent of all food retailers are unaffiliated independents.	44% of households	28.4%
Austria	The trend toward concentration is relatively advanced in Austria. Unaffiliated independent retailers make up only 25% of the total. Voluntary chains are particularly important, making up 46% of the total.	44% of households	38.9%
Portugal	Distribution is composed almost entirely of small, independent shops (90% of all food retailers). Although some concentration is taking place, change will be slow.	9% of households	39.5%
Spain	Eighty-four per cent of food stores are small, independent retailers. Only 10% of all food retailers can be classified as supermarkets, and these are located almost exclusively in urban areas.	21% of households	29.3%
Switzerland	One of the most concentrated systems in Western Europe. Fewer than 1% of all food retail outlets are unaffiliated independents. Cooperatives are particularly important, making up 69% of the total.	39% of households	34.1%
Norway	There is a strong trend toward concentration (35% of food retailers are unaffiliated independents). Voluntary chains and cooperatives are particularly important.	77% of households	39.2%
Greece	The system is dominated by small, family-run shops that sell a limited range of goods (97% of food retailers are unaffiliated independents). Some supermarkets have begun to appear, but only in large urban areas.	11% of households	28%

EXHIBIT 1 (Continued)

Country	Distribution Systems and Trends	Ownership of Freezers[10]	Women as a % of the Labor Force[11]
Sweden	There is a strong trend toward concentration, paralleling similar trends in the U.S. Shopping centers have become particularly popular in recent years. The number of super-markets has grown rapidly and consumer cooperatives are very strong. Only 19% of food retailers are unaf-filiated independents.	90% of households	43%

Country	Media		
	Newspapers[12]	Radio[13]	Television[14]
Belgium	Circulation per 1,000 inhabitants, 241; total circulation, 2,369,000. There are 45 major dailies, 14 of which have regional editions.	Government-owned, no advertising allowed. Radio Luxembourg broadcasts both programming and advertising in five languages into most Western European nations, including Belgium. Radio ownership, 428 per 1,000 persons.	Government-owned, no advertising allowed. TV programs and advertising from Luxembourg can be received in Belgium through the Cable TV network. TV ownership, 291 per 1,000 persons.

	Newspapers	Radio	Television
West Germany	Circulation per 1,000 inhabitants, 423; total circulation, 25,968,000. Newspapers are primarily regional and local, but about 50% are regional editions of large city dailies. Many of the papers published in Munich, Frankfurt, and Hamburg have national readership.	Owned and operated by federal or regional authorities. Advertising is allowed, but the number of available time spots is limited. Radio ownership, 338 per 1,000 persons.	Owned and operated by federal or regional authorities. Advertising is allowed, but the number of available time spots is limited. TV ownership, 310 per 1,000 persons.
Denmark	Circulation per 1000 inhabitants, 362; total circulation, 1,840,000. Denmark has a large number of daily papers and a higher than average readership rate. There are over 50 daily papers, approximately 10 of which are published in Copenhagen. The largest paper has a weekday circulation of less than 200,000.	State-owned, no advertising permitted. Radio ownership, 340 per 1,000 persons.	State-owned, no advertising permitted. TV ownership, 356 per 1,000 persons.
France	Circulation per 1,000 inhabitants, 205; total circulation, 10,863,000. There are over 100 daily papers in France, most of which are either regional or local in scope.	Government-owned and controlled. No advertising is allowed. Radio programs and ads broadcast from nearby countries can be received in all of France. Radio ownership, 358 per 1,000.	Government-owned and operated. Advertising is permitted, but time is limited to seven 15-minute periods per day. The government decides which products and firms will have access to scarce advertising time. TV ownership, 288 per 1,000.

EXHIBIT 1 (Continued)

Country	Media		
	Newspapers [12]	Radio [13]	Television [14]
Ireland	Circulation per 1,000 inhabitants 220; total circulation, 702,000. Of the approximately 60 newspapers in Ireland, only 7 have national distribution. Weeklies, published in all county seats and Dublin, are very influential but tend to have very small circulation.	State monopoly. There is only one channel, and it broadcasts from 7:30 A.M. to 11:30 P.M. every day. Advertising time is limited to 10% of broadcasting time. Programs can also be received from Great Britain. Radio ownership, 311 per 1,000 persons.	State monopoly. The one channel broadcasts from 4 P.M. to 11:30 P.M. every day. Advertising is limited to 10% of broadcasting time. Programming is in both English and Gaelic. Cable broadcasts form Great Britain can be received. TV ownership, 204 per 1,000 persons.
Great Britain	Circulation per 1,000 inhabitants, 409; total circulation, 22,900,000. Newspapers account for the largest share of ad expenditures. Nine nationally distributed dailies account for 60% of newspaper readership. Sunday papers have the highest circulation. Most dailies have clearly indentifiable political outlooks.	No advertising is allowed on the BBC radio stations. Ads can be placed with Radio Luxembourg's English language network. Radio ownership, 786 per 1,000 persons.	TV advertising is allowed through the 91 stations affiliated with the Independent Television Authority (ITA). Ads can be placed on either a regional or a local level through ITA. No advertising is allowed on the British Broadcasting Corporation networks. TV ownership, 329 per 1,000 persons.

Italy

Circulation per 1,000 inhabitants, 97; total circulation, 5,941,000. Newspapers are the most popular ad medium. Most daily papers are either regional or local in scope, but many of those published in large cities have national circulation. Many papers have strong political or Church affiliations.

The three national stations are state-owned and controlled. The amount of advertising time is limited. Recently, many private stations have sprung up. These are generally local in character, and virtually all accept advertising. Radio ownership, 236 per 1,000 persons.

The three national channels are state-run. Little ad time is available, and all ads are grouped in scheduled blocks of 15 minutes. A number of private local stations have appeared recently. These accept advertising and show ads both during and between scheduled programs. TV ownership, 227 per 1,000 persons.

Netherlands

Circulation per 1,000 inhabitants, 314; total circulation, 4,371,000. Most newspapers are small and regional in scope, but there are newspaper chains that will place ads in all affiliated papers, thus giving national coverage.

Radio broadcasting is by private firms licensed and monitored by the government. Total broadcasting time is 300 hours per week. Advertising immediately precedes and follows regular news programs and is limited to 15 minutes per day for each station. Radio ownership, 305 per 1,000 persons.

TV broadcasting is run in the same manner as radio broadcasting. Total broadcasting time is 63 hours per week. Advertising precedes and follows regular news programs and is limited to 15 minutes per day. TV ownership, 289 per 1,000 persons.

Austria

Circulation per 1,000 inhabitants, 336; total circulation, 2,529,000. There are about twenty-four major national newspapers. The major press center is Vienna, with nine dailies that have a combined circulation of 1,759,000.

State-owned, advertising is allowed only at certain designated times. There are three radio channels. Radio ownership, 299 per 1,000 persons.

State-owned. The two channels reach 85% of Austria's land area. Advertising is limited to 2½ hours per week of a total broadcasting time of 87½ hours per week. TV ownership, 272 per 1,000 persons.

EXHIBIT 1 (Continued)

Country	Media		
	Newspapers[12]	Radio[13]	Television[14]
Portugal	Circulation per 1,000 inhabitants, 54; total circulation: 527,-000. Newspapers tend to be local in orientation, but the Lisbon and Oporto newpapers have national circulation.	Radio broadcasting is both state- and privately owned. The state-owned station has no advertising. The privately owned stations often are small and local in character. Radio ownership, 181 per 1,000 persons.	The RTP, a private corporation of which the government owns 60%, serves about 90% of Portugal and accepts advertising. Ad time is limited to 5% of broadcasting time. TV ownership, 120 per 1,000 persons.
Spain	Circulation per 1,000 inhabitants, 123; total circulation, 4,710,000. The strongest ad medium. There are about 150 dailies, most of which are local or regional in scope. In addition, many have strong connections with political, religious, or commercial organizations.	A fast-growing ad medium. All broadcasting, public and private, is government-controlled. Advertising is limited to 5 minutes per hour. Radio ownership, 235 per 1,000 persons.	The second largest ad medium. All 32 stations are government-owned and operated and all carry advertising. TV spots are generally 20 to 30 seconds in length. TV ownership, 222 per 1,000 persons.
Switzerland	Circulation per 1,000 inhabitants, 414; total circulation, 2,622,000. Switzerland has a large number of local newspapers. Space brokers and ad agencies that specialize in ad placement are available to aid in nationally run newspaper ad campaigns.	No radio advertising is allowed, but programs broadcast on foreign stations can be received in Switzerland. Radio ownership, 343 per 1,000 persons.	TV broadcasting is operated solely by the Société Suisse de Radio-diffussion et Télévision, a public corporation. Advertising is permitted but is limited to a maximum of 15 minutes per day, in three time blocks each evening. TV ownership 299 per 1,000 persons.
Norway	Circulation per 1,000 inhabitants, 430; total circulation,	No radio advertising is allowed. Radio ownership, 330 per	No TV advertising is allowed. TV ownership, 283 per 1,000

	Press	Radio	TV
	1,740,000. Norway's daily newspaper network is highly decentralized. There is a large number of papers, each of which has a very small circulation. Most papers have unofficial political party connections.	1,000 persons.	persons.
Greece	Circulation per 1,000 inhabitants, 107; total circulation, 962,000. Newspapers are the second most popular ad medium, with about 30% of ad expenditures. Papers are published in 30 towns, and most have circulations under 100,000. The language used by the press is an official revival of classical Greek (Katharevousa), not the popular vernacular (Demotiki).	The state-run network (EIRT) has three stations, only one of which carries advertising. Private stations also carry a combined total of 120 hours per week of advertising time. Radio ownership, 290 per 1,000 persons.	TV broadcasting is run by EIRT. Total broadcasting time is 58 hours per week, two of which are devoted to advertising. TV ownership, 160 per 1,000 persons.
Sweden	Circulation per 1,000 inhabitants, 528; total circulation, 4,358,000. Sweden has one of the world's highest rates of newspaper readership. Major metropolitan newspapers have rather wide circulation throughout Sweden, and advertising in these can be supplemented by ads placed in smaller local dailies to provide complete national coverage.	No radio advertising is allowed. Radio ownership, 378 per 1,000 persons.	No TV advertising is allowed. TV ownership, 372 per 1,000 persons.

EXHIBIT 1 (Continued)

Country	Media		Other Important Media
	Cinema [15]	Magazines [16]	
Belgium	Attendance: 23.2 million. Average number of times attend per year: 2.4.	Circulation: Not available. A wide variety of magazines exists in each of the three major languages. Women's magazines boast the highest circulation rates.	Direct mail, point of sale promotions, posters, billboards.
West Germany	Attendance: 124.2 million. Average number of times attended per year: 2.0	Circulation: 1.378 per 1,000 persons. Magazines are available to appeal to a broad range of general and specialized tastes. There is a large number of nationally distributed titles, many of which have relatively large circulations.	Posters.
Denmark	Attendance: 16.7 million. Average number of times attend per year: 3.3.	Circulation: Not available. Publication of illustrated periodicals is concentrated; most belong to four large publishing houses. Family, women's, and TV/Radio journals have the highest circulation rates.	Direct mail, point of sale displays.

France	Attendance: 177 million. Average number of times attend per year: 3.3.	Circulation: 3.439 per 1,000 persons. A wide variety of general and special interest magazines is distributed throughout France. Most important titles have large circulations.	Direct mail, billboards.
Ireland	Attendance: Not available. Average number of times attend per year: Not available.	Circulation 5.210 per 1,000 persons. There are relatively few Irish periodicals, but many English magazines also circulate here. The number of titles and readership rates have shown rapid growth in recent years.	Direct mail.
Great Britain	Attendance: 103.9 million. Average number of times attend per year: 1.9.	Circulation: Not available. Among large number of general and special interest magazines, many also have extensive circulation abroad. Several magazines in the women's and general interest categories have circulations in excess of 1 million copies each week.	
Italy	Attendance: 372.3 million. Average number of times attend per year: 6.5.	Circulation: Not available. Although there is a wide variety of general and specific interest magazines, most of these have small circulations.	Posters.

EXHIBIT 1 (Continued)

Country	Media		Other Important Media
	Cinema [15]	Magazines [16]	
Netherlands	Attendance: 23.8 million. Average number of times attend per year: 1.7.	Circulation: 1.104 per 1,000 persons. There is a wide variety of general and special interest periodicals. Radio/TV and women's magazines boast the highest circulation figures.	Posters, direct mail.
Austria	Attendance: 17.8 million. Average number of times attend per year: 2.4.	Circulation: Not available. There are about 300 major Austrian magazines. In addition, many German magazines are also sold here.	Posters, point of sale.
Portugal	Attendance: 39.1 million. Average number of times attend per year: 4.0.	Circulation: Not available. There is a wide variety of both general and special interest titles from which to choose. The highest circulations are boasted by women's and sports magazines.	Posters.
Spain	Attendance: 211.9 million. Average number of times attend per year: 5.2.	Circulation: 1.512 per 1,000 persons. Over 5,500 periodicals are published in Spain, but most have	Posters.

Country			
Switzerland	very small circulations. About 20 magazines are published in regional Spanish dialects. Circulation: 0.503 per 1,000 persons. In addition to the Swiss magazines, many German, French, and Italian periodicals are also sold here.	Attendance: 23 million. Average number of times attend per year: 3.7.	Posters, direct mail, point of sale, trade fairs.
Norway	Circulation: Not available. Many magazines, particularly those that are family-oriented, have relatively wide circulation. These are considered particularly important for advertising consumer goods.	Attendance: 16.4 million. Average number of times attend per year: 4.0.	Posters, point of sale, transit ads.
Greece	Circulation: Not available. The periodical press is relatively decentralized, with some 850 titles. In 1972, the 40 largest titles had a combined annual circulation of 116.4 million copies.	Attendance: Not available. Average number of times attend per year: not available.	Direct mail.
Sweden	Circulation: Not available. The readership of magazines approaches 90% of the adult population. A wide variety of periodicals is available, ranging from professional journals to general interest titles.	Attendance: 23 million. Average number of times attend per year: 2.7.	Posters, direct mail, point of sale, transit ads.

EXHIBIT 1 (Continued)

Country	Legal Restrictions on Advertising[17]
Belgium	False information regarding the origin, nature, composition, or quality of the product is forbidden. Also forbidden are denigrating comparisons with competitors, as well as slogans that may create confusion between one merchant (or manufacturer) and another. Any person or group that suspects an infraction may bring suit against the advertiser in the Commercial Court.
West Germany	Advertising that misleads the consumer about the quality, origin, production, or price is illegal. Any associations that may confuse the buyers are also forbidden (for example, the use of a French name for a non-French product). "Puffery," such as the use of such phrases as "the most beautiful," or "the best," are likewise considered misleading. Any person or group may bring suit against a manufacturer or merchant who engages in misleading advertising.
Denmark	The International Advertising Codex of the International Chamber of Commerce is considered the standard for advertising practice.[18] Any advertising that is deemed false or misleading is forbidden. All statements made by an advertiser must be absolutely correct and the advertiser should be prepared to prove any statements made. A consumer ombudsman has the authority to deal with any complaints made against an advertiser, as well as to instigate an investigation into any marketing practice, and to issue guidelines for commercial practice. The judgments of the consumer ombudsman are subject to judicial review.
France	The International Codex of Advertising Practice of the International Chamber of Commerce is the standard used to judge advertising.[18] In addition, the Civil Code prohibits any actions that may unnecessarily harm others, such as comparative advertising. Legal enforcement of these Codes is extremely rigorous.
Ireland	All advertising must be decent, legal, honest, and truthful. Ads must not be false or misleading. All advertisements must be identified as such, if not readily recognizable. They must not appeal to fear or superstition, and they must not unfairly attack any competitor. Any testimonial must be genuine, no more than three years old, and related to experience or expertise of the person giving it. In broadcast advertising, Radio-Telefis Eireann has

the power to reject any ad, or part of an ad, that does not conform to these requirements. In addition, complaints against an advertiser may be made to a government established commission, authorized to review and judge the complaint.

Great Britain

Unfair or misleading advertising is prohibited. "Puffery" and comparison advertising is allowed, if truthful, but in general, British advertising tends to be more restrained than that in other nations. Any statements made must be absolutely true and verifiable upon request, including such claims as "Product X gives more satisfaction. . . ." Any false or malicious statements may subject the advertiser to civil as well as criminal legal action. The authorized use of test results from independent laboratories is allowed. Self-regulation is provided by the Advertising Standards Authority (ASA), which includes representatives from advertisers, agencies, and media. The ASA gives general guidance to advertisers through bulletins, investigates complaints from competitors and the public, and randomly monitors advertising to ensure compliance with the British Code of Advertising Practice.

Italy

All advertising in Italy must follow norms of decency, good taste, honesty, and truthfulness. Any denigration of a competitor's product (such as comparative advertising) is illegal. In particular, existing laws for the advertising of food products forbid any names, phrases, or designs that may mislead the public as to the quality, ingredients, or nutritional value of the product. All claims must be substantiated beforehand, and all advertisements must be approved before publication by "SACIS," the government commission that oversees advertising.

Netherlands

All advertising must be truthful, in good taste, and lawful. Advertising must not mislead the public; it must not appeal to fear or superstition; and it must be clearly recognizable (or identified) as advertising. Any statistical data must be the most recent available and must be used with great care. All references to authority must be genuine and provable. The use of models posing as experts is forbidden. All advertising must be completely original and differentiatable, in order to avoid creating confusion between products and brands. All TV advertisements for candy or other sweets must show a toothbrush in the corner of the screen. Any claims made by an advertiser must be substantiatable upon request. Complaints may be brought by any person or group to the Advertising Commission, which has the authority to investigate and judge these complaints. The results of such an investigation may be presented in trade and general interest publications.

EXHIBIT 1 (Continued)

Country	Legal Restrictions on Advertising[17]
Austria	The "Law Against Unfair Competition" forbides any activities not in accordance with principles of fairness and equity. Advertising that is deceptive or misleading as to the value, price, or quality of the product is forbidden. If the "average consumer" can be misled by an ad, that ad is illegal. Direct comparisons are forbidden if derogatory. Parasitical use of a competitor's name or reputation ("as good as...") is forbidden. "Puffery" is not allowed, but the use of superlatives ("the best") is. No TV advertising can begin with phrases such as "official message" that might mislead the public as to the origin of the ad. No phrases such as "clinical" or "recommended by doctors" are permitted. No advertising with religious content is allowed. The Consumer Forum of the Austrian Trade Ministry has the authority to examine all ad campaigns for truthfulness, information value, and ethics. The Forum can initiate court proceedings against offenders.
Portugal	All advertising must be clearly identifiable as such. Ads may not play on the fears of superstitions of the audience. They may not use slang or foreign expressions, or terms such as "latest" or "latest news." They may not mislead the consumer about the nature, composition, origin, or qualities of the product. Any testimonials must be genuine and related to the experience of the person giving them. The use of models wearing the uniform of a given profession must be done in such a way as not to mislead the public. Advertising must not make use of a woman's figure as an object to promote the product, nor must it portray women as home-based in exclusion of other occupations. All advertising is screened by a regulatory body, which has the authority to ban or fine any advertiser that infringes the Code.
Spain	Commercial Law forbids all activities that are considered to be against good commercial practice, and particularly those that tend to discredit competitors and their products. Advertisements which deprecate a competitive product, whether the statement made is true or false, are strictly forbidden. Self-regulation is provided by the Advertising Jury of the National Advertising Board, which reports directly to the General Directorate for Advertising and Public Relations of the Ministry of Culture.

Switzerland

The International Code of Advertising Practice is the norm used to judge advertising in Switzerland.[18] In addition, according to the Swiss Unfair Competition Act, comparison advertising is allowed as long as it is rigorously objective, not misleading, and not unnecessarily injurious to competitors. Adherence to these norms is assured by the Swiss Committee for the Supervision of Advertising Fairness.

Norway

All advertising must conform to "good business practice." No advertisement may downgrade either men or women, or use men or women as a means of attracting attention to the ad or product. No misleading advertising is allowed, nor is any ad that does not provide sufficient information of importance to the consumer. Ads that may exploit the insufficient knowledge or experience of the consumer are considered unfair. All advertising must be strictly original, so as to avoid creating confusion between products or brands. A consumer ombudsman and a Market Council are authorized to enforce these standards. The consumer ombudsman is empowered to ban any advertising or marketing practice deemed illegal. The advertiser may appeal the ban to the Market Council, which will review the case and make a final decision. In addition, any person or group may submit a case directly to the Market Council in the event of inaction by the consumer ombudsman.

Greece

Advertising must be in accordance with good moral standards. The International Advertising Codex of the International Chamber of Commerce is used as the reference for good advertising practice by the industry.[18] Self-regulation is carried out by the executive committee of the Greek Advertising Agencies Association. Comparative advertising is generally considered to be offensive and is therefore illegal; however, self-laudatory and superlative advertising is allowed.

Sweden

All advertising must be in accordance with "good commercial standards." Specifically, misleading representations (other than rebates) are expressly forbidden. All information needed by the consumer must be included in the advertisement. The burden of proof for any claims made lies with the advertiser in the event of an investigation. A consumer ombudsman is charged with supervising the marketing practice of firms to ensure that they comply with these standards. The ombudsman is authorized to instigate investigations and to act on complaints made by any person, firm, or organization, and to issue bans against any practices judged to be unfair.

EXHIBIT 1 (Continued)

[8] Based in part on *European Marketing Data and Statistics 1981* (London: Euromonitor Publications, Ltd., 1980).

[9] *1979/80 Statistical Yearbook* (New York: United Nations Department of International Economic and Social Affairs, 1981).

[10] Op. cit.

[11] Op. cit.

[12] Circulation figures are in part based on *European Marketing Data and Statistics 1981* (London: Euromonitor Publications, Ltd., 1980).

[13] Radio ownership figures are in part based on *European Marketing Data and Statistics 1981*.

[14] Television ownership figures are in part based on *European Marketing Data and Statistics 1981*.

[15] Ibid.

[16] Ibid.

[17] The European Community has been attempting for several years to formulate a Standardized Advertising Code to be adopted by all member nations. The code is still being debated, and it is not certain when, if ever, it will be adopted. However, the Code in its present draft form states criteria for determining whether an advertisement is misleading or unfair and permits comparative advertising if it deals with important aspects of the product, is based on verifiable and objective facts, and does not discredit the competitor or his product. The burden of proof as to whether an advertisement is unfair or not lies with the person who makes the complaint, except where a factual chain is disputed. In this case, the advertiser must be able to substantiate the statement made. In addition, the Code specifies that national laws should be passed that allow persons and/or organizations to have quick, effective, and inexpensive legal recourse against advertising that does not conform to these standards.

[18] The International Chamber of Commerce International Code of Advertising Standards states the following basic principles:

Advertising should not offend against prevailing standards of decency.

Advertisements should not abuse the consumer's trust or exploit his lack of knowledge or experience.

Advertising should not, without reason, play on fear or superstition.

Advertising should not, directly or indirectly, mislead the consumer with regard to the characteristics or value of the product.

Any comparison must not mislead the consumer and must be based on fact.

Testimonials and endorsements are allowed only if genuine and related to the experience of the person giving it.

Advertising should not, directly or indirectly, denigrate a competitor's product.

Advertisements should not imitate the layout or slogan of other advertisements in any way that is likely to confuse the consumer.

Advertisements should be clearly distinguishable as such.

2. The acceptance of preprepared foods.
3. The willingness of women to surrender a part of their historic role as family cook.
4. A relatively high proportion of working women.
5. A relatively high disposable income.

The overwhelming bulk of Unilever frozen food products were sold in Europe. This region offered a wide variety of cultural and social factors that affect the success of frozen food products. The history of the introduction of frozen foods into Western Europe illustrated the importance of the unique social and cultural factors in each nation that determine whether an enterprise will be a success or a failure. One of Unilever's most important brands, Iglo, was sold in the following countries: Belgium, France, Denmark, Portugal, Spain, Austria, Switzerland, West Germany, and The Netherlands. The types of frozen foods sold in these countries included vegetables, fish and meat entrees, soups, snack items, and desserts. Other Western European nations of potential interest to Iglo were Ireland, Great Britain, Italy, Norway, Greece, and Sweden.

Exhibit 1 presents selected data pertinent to marketing and advertising strategies in each of the fifteeen nations of Western Europe.

Advise Unilever.

Note
  As this book went to press there were several relevant developments: (1) France had just permitted the establishment of a limited amount of privately owned television, which carried advertising, and had offered for sale one of the state owned television channels; (2) the Portuguese government was considering selling all or most of its television and radio investments to the private sector; (3) Spain was considering the establishment of private television; (4) a government study task force tentatively had recommended acceptance of advertising on BBC radio; and (5) small scale cable and satellite television broadcasting, which carried advertising, had begun in several countries and was crossing some international boundaries.

13

LEGAL
ENVIRONMENT
OF
MARKETING

A NOTE ON STUDYING THE LEGAL CASES

Three recent Court cases are included in this section on the legal environment of marketing. All are decisions of the United States Supreme Court.

It is extremely helpful to the student of marketing to become familiar with legal thinking, to pinpoint the issues, and to understand how the comparison of points of law is carried out. Look for the points of law being rejected, those being accepted, those given priority, and those raised on which the Court takes no position. Determine the important precedents set by the cases. Try to reconstruct the reasoning that led to the overturning of a lower court or regulatory agency decision or a Supreme Court decision from past years.

Note the ambiguity of statutes that the Court is trying to interpret and enforce. Attempt to determine the role of economic, political, psychological, and sociological beliefs in the decision. Laws operate in a behavioral milieu. Law is not a science in the conventional sense of that term.

Many courts and individual judges have been accused of being social and economic engineers, whereas many others regard their roles more narrowly as interpreters and clarifiers of law. Many judges seek to establish the executive or legislative intent and motivation. Do these cases reflect engineering or strict constructionism? Closely related to this question is what and how much respect is demonstrated in each of these cases for the executive and legislative branches of the government? This deals with the classic dilemma of the *separation of powers* doctrine, that is, separation of authority among the executive, legislative, and judicial branches of government.

What and how much respect is shown for the *division of powers* doctrine, which is sometimes called the *federalism* doctrine? This deals with the split of authority between the national government and the state governments. Does the case perhaps treat rights delegated to the states by the federal government, as opposed to state rights specified in the United States Constitution? What rights are irrevocable?

Dissents by judges are common. Note if they occur and their extent. Do they apply to peripheral areas or go to the heart of the case? Dissents often give rise to reversals, partial reversals, or reinterpretations by judges sitting on the same court later. Do you think there is a good basis for overturning the decisions in these cases? If so, explain your reasoning. Suppose that you were asked to challenge the decision. Organize your arguments from the case and add other ideas and facts of your own. Present them persuasively and anticipate the counterarguments.

Often a decision in a legal case is accompanied by one or more concurring opinions by judges who voted with the majority. Even a unanimous opinion may be accompanied by one or more concurring opinions. These concurring opinions may deal with a secondary issue in the case or the central issue, but the holder of the concurring opinion believes it is necessary to distinguish his line of reasoning, the stream of precedents, and/or the level of his doubt or conclusiveness on the issue from those of his colleagues. The concurring rationale of the judge(s) may imply the difference in degree to which he (they) may be willing to carry an idea or an interpretation. A judge who concurs on one case will not always concur on a similar case later, but the concurring opinion provides clues to that judge's future decision making.

Suppose that you were called by the United States government or a concerned company as an expert on marketing to support the legal decision. Organize the thoughts of the case into a presentation. Add ramifications and implications, using your present background and expertise in marketing.

Consider the practical effects of each case on the marketing policies and practices of the companies involved. What changes in the organizations will be necessary if the decision stands and is implemented? If an overturning or reversal is expected in the long term, what changes must be made for the short term? What new broad marketing strategies will be necessary, as opposed to narrow specific changes? What will be the effects on the day-to-day operating policies?

JEFFERSON COUNTY PHARMACEUTICAL ASSN., INC. *v.* ABBOTT LABORATORIES ET AL.

460 U.S. 150

Certiorari to the United States Court of Appeals for
the Fifth Circuit

No. 81-827. Argued November 8, 1982—Decided February 23, 1983
656 F. 2d 92, reversed and remanded.

POWELL, J., delivered the opinion of the Court, in which
BURGER, C. J., and WHITE, MARSHALL, and BLACKMUN, JJ.,
joined. STEVENS, J., filed a dissenting opinion, *post* p. 171.

O'CONNOR, J., filed a dissenting opinion, in which
BRENNAN, REHNQUIST, and STEVENS, JJ., joined, *post,* p. 174.

Joe L. Tucker, Jr., argued the cause and filed briefs for petitoner.

David Klingsberg argued the cause for respondents. With him on the brief for respondents Abbott Laboratories et al. was *Michael Malina. John J. Coleman, Jr., E. Mabry Rogers*, and *Ina B. Leonard* filed a brief for respondent Board of Trustees of the University of Alabama.*

JUSTICE POWELL delivered the opinion of the Court.

The issue presented is whether the sale of pharmaceutical products of state and local government hospitals for resale in competition with private retail pharmacies is exempt from the proscriptions of the Robinson-Patman Act.

I

Petitioner, a trade association of retail pharmacists and pharmacies doing business in Jefferson County, Alabama, commenced this action in 1978 in the District Court for the Northern District of Alabama as the assignee of its members' claims. Respondents are 15 pharmaceutical manufacturers, the Board of Trustees of the University of Alabama, and the Cooper Green Hospital Pharmacy. The University operates a medical center, including hospitals, and a medical school. Located in the University's medical center are two

---

*Briefs of *amici curiae* urging reversal were filed by *Paul L. O'Brien* and *Frank M. Northam* for the American Pharmaceutical Association; and by *John S. Hoff* and *Fred W. Geldon* for the National Association of Retail Druggists.

George H. Cross filed a brief for the National Association of Counties as *amicus curiae.*

pharmacies. Cooper Green Hospital is a county hospital, existing as a public corporation under Alabama law.

The complaint seeks treble damages and injunctive relief under §§ 4 and 16 of the Clayton Act, 38 Stat. 731, 737, 15 U. S. C. §§ 15 and 26, for alleged violations of §§ 2(a) and (f) of the Clayton Act, 38 Stat. 730, as amended by the Robinson-Patman Act (Act), 49 Stat. 1526, 15 U. S. C. §§ 13(a) and (f). Petitioner contends that the respondent manufacturers violated § 2(a)[1] by selling their products to the University's two pharmacies and to Cooper Green Hospital Pharmacy at prices lower than those charged petitioner's members for like products. Petitioner alleges that the respondent hospital pharmacies knowingly induced such lower prices in violation of § 2(f)[2] and sold the drugs to the general public in direct competition with privately owned pharmacies. Petitioner also alleges that the price discrimination is not exempted from the proscriptions of the Act by 15 U. S. C. § 13c.[3]

Respondents moved to dismiss the complaint on the ground that state purchases[4] are exempt as a matter of law from the sanctions of § 2. In granting respondents' motions, the District Court expressly accepted as true the allegations that local retail pharmacies had been injured by the challenged price discrimination and that at least some of the state purchases were not exempt under § 13c. 656 F. 2d 92, 98 (CA5 1981) (reprinting District Court's opinion as Appendix). The District Court held that "governmental purchases are, without regard to 15 U. S. C. § 13c, beyond the intended reach of the Robinson-Patman Price Discrimination Act, at least with respect to purchases for hospitals and other traditional governmental purposes."

---

[1] Section 2(a), 15 U. S. C. § 13(a), provides in relevant part:

"It shall be unlawful for any person engaged in commerce, in the course of such commerce, either directly or indirectly, to discriminate in price between different purchasers of commodities of like grade and quality, where either or any of the purchases involved in such discrimination are in commerce, where such commodities are sold for use, consumption, or resale within the United States . . . , and where the effect of such discrimination may be substantially to lessen competition or tend to create a monopoly in any line of commerce, or to injure, destroy, or prevent competition with any person who either grants or knowingly receives the benefit of such discrimination, or with customers of either of them . . . . "

[2] Section 2(f), 15 U. S. C. § 13(f), provides:

"It shall be unlawful for any person engaged in commerce, in the course of such commerce, knowingly to induce or receive a discrimination in price which is prohibited by this section."

[3] Section 13c provides:

"Nothing in [the Robinson-Patman Act] shall apply to purchases of their supplies for their own use by schools, colleges, universities, public libraries, churches, hospitals, and charitable institutions not operated for profit."

[4] "State purchases" are defined as sales to and purchases by a State and its agencies.

Id., at 102. The Court of Appeals for the Fifth Circuit, in a divided *per curiam* decision, affirmed "on the basis of the district court's Memorandum of Opinion." *Id.,* at 93.[5]

We granted certiorari to resolve this important question of federal law. 455 U. S. 999 (1982). We now reverse.

II

The issue here is narrow. We are not concerned with sales to the Federal Government, nor with state purchases for *use* in traditional governmental functions.[6] Rather, the issue before us is limited to state purchases for the purpose of competing against private enterprise—with the advantage of discriminatory prices—in the retail market.[7]

The courts below held, and respondents contend, that the Act exempts all state purchases. Assuming, without deciding, that Congress did not intend the Act to apply to state purchases for consumption in traditional governmental functions, and that such purchases are therefore exempt, we conclude that the exemption does not apply where a State has chosen to compete in the private retail market.

---

[5] The District Court, and thus the Court of Appeals, agreed that "[t]he claims against the Board must . . . be treated as equivalent to claims against the State itself." 656 F .2d, at 99. Accordingly, both courts held that the Eleventh Amendment bars petitioner's claim for damages against the University. Petitioner did not challenge this holding in its appeal from the District Court's decision.

[6] Respondents argue that application of the Act to purchases by the State of Alabama would present a significant risk of conflict with the Tenth Amendment and that we therefore should avoid any construction of the Act that includes such purchases. See *NLRB* v. *Catholic Bishop of Chicago,* 440 U. S. 490, 501 (1979). There is no risk, however, of a constitutional issue arising from the application of the Act in this case: The retail sale of pharmaceutical drugs is not "indisputably" an attribute of state sovereignty. See *Hodel* v. *Virginia Surface Mining & Reclamation Assn., Inc.,* 452 U. S. 264, 288 (1981). It is too late in the day to suggest that Congress cannot regulate States under its Commerce Clause powers when they are engaged in proprietary activities. See, *e.g., Parden* v. *Terminal Railway of Alabama State Docks Dept.,* 377 U. S. 184, 187–193 (1964). If the Tenth Amendment protects certain state purchases from the Act's limitations, such as for consumption in traditional governmental functions, those purchases must be protected on a case-by-case basis. Cf. *City of Lafayette* v. *Louisiana Power & Light Co.,* 435 U. S. 389, 413, and n. 42 (1978) (plurality opinion).

[7] Special solicitude for the plight of indigents is a traditional concern of state and local governments. If, in special circumstances, sales were made by a State to a class of indigents, the question presented, that we need not decide, would be whether such sales are "in competition" with private enterprise. The District Court correctly assumed that the private and state pharmacies in this case are "competing pharmacies." 656 F. 2d, at 98. See also n. 8, *infra.*

III

The Robinson-Patman Act by its terms does not exempt state purchases. The only express exemption is that for nonprofit institutions contained in 15 U. S. C. § 13c.[8] Moreover, as the courts below conceded, "[t] he statutory language—'persons' and 'purchasers'— is sufficiently broad to cover governmental bodies. 15 U. S. C. § § 12, 13(a, f)." 656 F. 2d, at 99.[9] This concession was compelled by several of this Court's decisions.[10] In *City of Lafayette* v. *Louisiana Power and Light Co.,* 435 U. S. 389, 395 (1978), for example we stated without qualifications that "the definition of 'person' or 'persons' embraces both cities and States."[11]

Respondents would distinguish *City of Lafayette* from the case before us because it involved the Sherman Act rather than the Robinson-Patman Act.[12] Such a distinction ignores the specific reference to the Robinson-Patman Act in our discussion of the all-inclusive nature of the term "person." *Id.,* at 397, n. 14. We do not perceive any reason to construe the word "person" in that Act any differently than we have in the Clayton Act, which it amends,[13] and it is undis-

[8] The District Court properly assumed, for purposes of making its summary judgment, that at least some of the hospital purchases would not be covered by the § 13c exemption. See n. 3, *supra,* and accompanying text. Therefore, we need not consider whether this express exemption would support summary judgment in cases against state hospitals purchasing for their own use. See n. 20, *infra.*

[9] The words "person" and "persons" are used repeatedly in the antitrust statutes. See 15 U. S. C. § § 7, 12, 15.

[10] See, *e. g., Georgia* v. *Evans,* 316 U. S. 159, 162 (1942) (State is a "person" under § 7 of the Sherman Act); *Chattanooga Foundry & Pipe Works* v. *City of Atlanta,* 203 U. S. 390, 396 (1906) (municipality is a "person" within the meaning of § 8 of the Sherman Act). See also *Pfizer Inc.* v. *Goverment of India,* 434 U. S. 308, 318 (1978) (foreign nation is a "person" under § 4 of the Clayton Act).

The Court has not considered it at all "anomalous to require compliance by municipalities with the substantive standards of other federal laws which impose . . . sanctions upon persons.' " *City of Lafayette* v. *Louisiana Power & Light Co., supra,* at 400. See *California* v. *United States,* 320 U. S. 577, 585–586 (1944); *Ohio* v. *Helvering,* 292 U. S. 360, 370 (1934). One case is of particular relevance. In *Union Pacific R. Co.* v. *United States,* 313 U. S. 450 (1941), the Court considered the applicability to a city of § 1 of the Elkins Act, 32 Stat. 847, as amended, 34 Stat. 587, 49 U. S. C. § 41(1)(repealed 1978), "a statute which essentially is an antitrust provision serving the same purposes as the anti-price-discrimination provisions of the Robinson-Patman Act." *City of Lafayette, supra,* at 402, n. 19. The *Union Pacific* Court expressly found that a municipality was a "person" within the meaning of the statute. 313 U. S., at 462–463. See also *City of Lafayette, supra,* at 401, n. 19.

[11] The word "purchasers" has a meaning as inclusive as the word "person." See 80 Cong. Rec. 6430 (1936)(remarks of Sen. Robinson) ("The Clayton Antitrust Act contains terms general to all purchasers. The pending bill does not segregate any particular class of purchasers, or exempt any special class of purchasers").

[12] The only apparent difference between the scope of the relevant laws is the extent to which the activities complained of must affect interstate commerce. Congress' decision in

puted that the Clayton Act applies to States. See *Hawaii* v. *Standard Oil Co.,* 405 U. S. 251, 260–261 (1972).[14] In sum, the plain language of the Act strongly suggests that there is no exemption for state purchases to compete with private enterprise.

IV

The plain language of the Act is controlling unless a different legislative intent is apparent from the purpose and history of the Act. An examination of the legistlative purpose and history here reveals no such contrary intention.

A

Our cases have been explicit in stating the purposes of the antitrust laws, including the Robinson-Patman Act. On numerous occasions, this Court has affirmed the comprehensive coverage of the antitrust laws and has recognized that these laws represent "a care-

---

the Robinson-Patman Act not to cover all transactions within its reach under the Commerce Clause, see *Gulf Oil Corp.* v. *Copp Paving Co.*, 419 U. S. 186, 199–201 (1974), does not mean that Congress chose not to cover the same range of "persons" whose conduct "in commerce" is otherwise subject to the Act.

[13] Indeed, the House and Senate Committee Reports specifically state that "[t]he special definitions of section 1 of the Clayton Act will apply without repetition to the terms concerned where they appear in this bill, since it is designed to become by amendment a part of that act." H. R. Rep. No. 2287, 74th Cong., 2d Sess., pt. 1, p. 7 (1936); S. Rep. No. 1502, 74th Cong., 2d Sess., 3(1936). See 80 Cong. Rec. 3116 (1936) (remarks of Sen. Logan) ("[M]any have complained because the provisions of the bill apply to 'any person engaged in commerce.' . . . The original Clayton Act contains the exact language, and it is carried into the bill under consideration. The language of the Clayton Act was used because it has been construed by the courts"). Given their common purposes, it should not be surprising that the common terms of the Clayton and Robinson-Patman Acts should be construed consistently with each other. See *id.*, at 8137 (remarks of Rep. Michener) ("The Patman-Robinson bill does not suggest a new policy or a new theory. The Clayton Act was enacted in 1914, and it was the purpose of that act to do just what this law sets out to do"); *id.*, at 3119 (remarks of Sen. Logan) (purpose of Robinson-Patman bill is to strengthen Clayton Act); *id.*, at 6151 (address by Sen. Logan) (same).

[14] JUSTICE O'CONNOR, in her dissenting opinion, questions our use of antitrust cases to define a word common to the antitrust laws. She would distinguish all of these cases uniformly holding States to be included in the word "persons," because none has held "that States or local governments are persons for purposes of exposure to *liability* as purchasers under the provisions of the Clayton Act." *Post,* at 177 (emphasis in original). The dissent takes no notice, however, of our decision last Term in *Community Communications Co.* v. *City of Boulder,* 455 U. S. 40, 56 (1982), in which the Court stated that the antitrust laws, "like other federal laws imposing civil or criminal sanctions upon 'persons,' of course apply to municipalities as well as to other corporate entities." No authority is cited for the dissent's distinction between "persons" entitled to sue under the antitrust laws and "persons" subject to suit under those laws.

fully studied attempt to bring within [them] every person engaged in business whose activities might restrain or monopolize commercial intercourse among the states." *United States* v. *South-Eastern Underwriters Assn.*, 322 U. S. 533, 553 (1944).[15] In *Goldfarb* v. *Virginia State Bar*, 421 U. S. 773 (1975), the Court observed that "our cases have repeatedly established that there is a heavy presumption against implicit exemptions" from the antitrust laws. *Id.*, at 787 (citing *United States* v. *Philadelphia National Bank*, 374 U. S. 321, 350–351 (1963); *California* v. *FPC*, 369 U. S. 482, 485 (1962)).[16] In *City of Lafayette, supra*, applying antitrust laws to a city in competition with a private utility, we held that no exemption for local governments would be implied. The Court emphasized the purposes and scope of the antitrust laws: "[T]he economic choices made by public corporations . . . , designed as they are to assure maximum benefits for the community constituency, are not inherently more likely to comport with the broader interests of national economic well-being than are those of private corporations acting in furtherance of the interests of the organization and its shareholders." 435 U. S., at 403. See also *id.*, at 408.[17]

These principles, and the purposes they further, have been helpful in interpreting the language of the Robinson-Patman Act. As JUSTICE BLACKMUN stated for the Court in *Abbott Laboratories* v. *Portland Retail Druggists Assn., Inc.*, 425 U. S. 1, 11–12 (1976):

> It has been said, of course, that the antitrust laws, and Robinson-Patman in particular, are to be construed liberally, and that the exceptions from their

[15] See, *e. g.*, *Pfizer Inc.* v. *Government of India, supra*, at 312–313 (noting "broad scope of the remedies provided by the antitrust laws") (applying Sherman Act cases to construe Clayton Act); *Mandeville Island Farms, Inc.* v. *American Crystal Sugar Co.*, 334 U. S. 219, 236 (1948) ("[Sherman] Act is comprehensive in its terms and coverage, protecting all who are made victims of the forbidden practices by *whomever* they may be perpetrated") (emphasis added).

[16] See, *e. g.*, *National Gerimedical Hospital & Gerontology Center* v. *Blue Cross of Kansas City*, 452 U. S. 378, 388 (1981); *City of Lafayette*, 435 U. S. at 398, 399; *Abbott Laboratories* v. *Portland Retail Druggists Assn., Inc.*, 425 U. S. 1, 11–12 (1976); *United States* v. *National Assn. of Securities Dealers, Inc.*, 422 U. S. 694, 719–720 (1975).

[17] In one important sense, retail competition from state agencies can be more invidious than that from chainstores, the particular targets of the Robinson–Patman Act. Volume purchasing permits any large, relatively efficient, retail organization to pass on cost savings to consumers, and, to that extent, consumers benefit merely from economy of scale. But to the extent that lower prices are attributable to lower overhead, resulting from federal grants, state subsidies, free public services, and freedom from taxation, state agencies merely redistribute the burden of costs from the actual consumers to the citizens at large. An exemption from the Robinson-Patman Act could give state agencies significant *additional* advantage in certain commercial markets, perhaps enough to eliminate marginal or small private competitors. Consumers, as citizens, ultimately will pay for the full costs of the drugs sold by the state agencies involved in this case. Because there is no reason to assume that such agencies will provide retail distribution more efficiently than private retail pharma-

application are to be construed strictly. *United States* v. *McKesson & Robbins,* 351 U. S. 305, 316 (1956); *FMC* v. *Seatrain Lines, Inc.,* 411 U. S. 726, 733 (1973); *Perkins* v. *Standard Oil Co.,* 395 U. S. 642, 646-647 (1969). The Court has recognized, also, that Robinson-Patman "was enacted in 1936 to curb and prohibit all devices by which large buyers gained discriminatory preferences over smaller ones by virtue of their greater purchasing power." *FTC* v. *Broch & Co.,* 363 U. S. 166, 168 (1960); *FTC* v. *Fred Meyer, Inc.,* 390 U. S. 341, 349 (1968). Because the Act is remedial, it is to be construed broadly to effectuate its purposes. See *Tcherepnin* v. *Knight,* 389 U. S. 332, 336 (1967); *Peyton* v. *Rowe,* 391 U. S. 54, 65 (1968).

B

The legislative history falls far short of supporting respondents' contention that there is an exemption for state purchases of "commodities" for "resale." There is nothing whatever in the Senate or House Committee Reports, or in the floor debates, focusing on the issue.[18] Some Members of Congress were aware of the possibility that the Act would apply to governmental purchases. Most Members, however, were concerned not with state puchases, but with possible limitations on the Federal Government. The most relevant legislative history is the testimony of the Act's principal draftsman, H. B. Teegarden, before the House Judiciary Committee.[19] Although the testimony is ambiguous on the application of the Act to state purchases for consumption, one conclusion is certain: Teegarden expressly stated that the Act would apply to the purchases of munici-

---

cists, consumers will suffer to the extent that state retail activities eliminate more efficient private retail distribution systems.

[18] JUSTICE O'CONNOR's dissenting opinion repeatedly emphasizes that Congress in 1936 did not focus specfically on the issue presented here. See *post,* at 180, 182, 187, and n. 10. This may well be true, as the likelihood of state entities competing in the private sector was remote in 1936. It cannot be contended, however, that Congress specifically intended to *allow* the competition at issue here. In any event, the absence of congressional focus is immaterial where the plain language applies. See, *e. g., United States* v. *South-Eastern Underwriters Assn.,* 322 U. S. 533, 556–558 (1944); *Browder* v. *United States,* 312 U. S. 335, 339 (1941); *De Lima* v. *Bidwell,* 182 U. S. 1, 197 (1901).

[19] "[Rep.] LLOYD: Would this bill, in your judgment, prevent the granting of discounts to the United States Government?

"Mr. TEEGARDEN: Not unless the present Clayton Act does so. . . .

"[Rep.] LLOYD: For instance, the Government gets huge discounts. . . . Now, would that discount be barred by this bill?

"Mr. TEEGARDEN: I do not see why it should, unless a discount contrary to the present bill would be barred—that is, the present law—would be barred by that bill.

"Aside from that, my answer would be this: *The Federal Government is not in competition* with other buyers from these concerns. . . .

"The Federal Government is saved by the same distinction . . . . They are not in competition with anyone else who would buy."

pal hospitals in at least some circumstances.[20] Thus, his comments directly contradict the exemption found by the courts below for all such purchasing.[21] In the absence of any other relevant evidence, we find no legislative intention to enable a State, by an unexpressed exemption, to enter private competitive markets with congressionally approved price advantages.[22]

"[Rep.] HANCOCK: It would eliminate competitive bidding all along the line, would it not, in classes of goods that would be covered by this bill?

"Mr. TEEGARDEN: You mean competitive bidding on Government orders?

"[Rep.] HANCOCK: Government, State, city, municipality.

"Mr. TEEGARDEN: No; I think not.

"[Rep.] MICHENER: If it did do it, you would not want it, would you?

"Mr. TEEGARDEN: No; I would not want it. It certainly does not eliminate competitive bidding anywhere else, and I do not see how it would with the Government.

"[Rep.] HANCOCK: You would have to bid to the city, county, exactly the same as anybody else; same quantity, same price, same quality?

"Mr. TEEGARDEN: No.

"[Rep.] HANCOCK: *Would they or could they sell to a city hospital any cheaper than they would to a privately-owned hospital, under this bill?*

"Mr. TEEGARDEN: I would have to answer it in this way. In the final analysis, it would depend upon numerous questions of fact in a particular case. *If the two hospitals are in competition with each other, I should say then that the fact that one is operated by the city does not save it from the bill.* If they are not in competition with each other, then they are in a different sphere.

"The facts of the situation are not present upon which to predicate a discrimination, in the nature of the case. I do not see that that question becomes any different under this bill from what it is under the present section 2 of the Clayton Act, for that bill also prohibits discrimination generally in the same terms that this does. But it differs in the breadth of the exceptions. That is the only difference between the two bills." Hearings on H. R. 8442 et al. before the House Committee on the Judiciary, 74th Cong., 1st Sess., 208–209 (1935) (emphasis added) (hereinafter 1935 Hearings).

[20] JUSTICE STEVENS agrees that state and local governments may be "purchasers" within the meaning of the Robinson-Patman Act. See *post*, at 171. He joins in JUSTICE O'CONNOR's dissent, however, on the basis of a novel theory: that state and local agencies may never be in "competition" with private parties within the meaning of the Act. See *ibid.* This is an economic fiction: If in fact a State participates in the private retail pharmaceutical market, it competes with the private participants. JUSTICE STEVENS relies on one statement by witness Teegarden in the 1935 House Hearings, but attaches no significance to a further statement by the same witness: "In the final analysis, it would depend upon *numerous questions of fact in a particular case.* If the two hospitals are *in competition* with each other, I should say then that the fact that one is operated by the city does not save it from the bill." See 1935 Hearings, at 209 (emphasis added).

[21] Teegarden subsequently submitted a written brief to the House Committee. He first rejected outright the desirability of *any* exemptions. See *id.*, at 249. He then posed the question whether "the bill [would] prevent competitive bidding on Governmental purchases below trade price levels." He stated that "[t]he answer is found in the principle of statutory construction that a statute will not be construed to limit or restrict in any way the rights, prerogatives, or privileges of the sovereign unless it so expressly provides—a principle inherited by American jurisprudence from the common law . . . ." But he also noted that "requiring a showing of effect upon competition . . . will further preclude any possibility of the bill affecting the Government." *Id.*, at 250.

V

Despite the plain language of the Act and its legislative history, respondents nevertheless argue that subsequent legislative events and decisions of District Courts confirm that state purchases are outside the scope of the Act. We turn therefore to these subsequent events.

All the cases Teegarden cited suggest that this sovereign-exception rule of statutory construction simply means that a government, when *it* passes a law, gives up only what it expressly surrenders. While the Robinson-Patman Act was pending before Congress, the Court stated that it could "perceive no reason for extending [the presumption against binding the sovereign by its own statute] so as to exempt a business carried on by a state from the otherwise applicable provisions of an act of Congress, all-embracing in scope and national in its purpose, which is as capable of being obstructed by state as by individual action." *United States* v. *California*, 297 U. S. 175, 186 (1936). See *California* v. *Taylor*, 353 U. S. 553, 562–563 (1957). In the context of the Robinson-Patman Act, the rule of statutory construction on which Teegarden relied supports, at the most, an exemption for the *Federal* Government's purchases. The existence of such an exemption is not before us. Cf. *United States* v. *Cooper Corp.*, 312 U. S. 600, 604–605 (1941) (United States not a "person" under the Sherman Act for purposes of suing for treble damages). Moreover, Teegarden clearly assumed that governmental purchasing would not compete with private purchasing. That assumption, however, is inapplicable here.

[22] Six months after the Act was passed, the Attorney General of the United States responded to an inquiry from the Secretary of War regarding the Act's application "to government contracts for supplies." 38 Op. Atty. Gen. 539 (1936). In ruling that such contracts are outside the Act, the Attorney General explained:

"[S]tatutes regulating rates, charges, etc., in matters affecting commerce do not ordinarily apply to the Government unless it is expressly so provided; and it does not seem to have been the policy of the Congress to make such statutes applicable to the Government. . . .

"The [Robinson-Patman Act] merely amended the [Clayton Act] and, in so far as I am aware, the latter Act has not been regarded heretofore as applicable to Government contracts." *Id.,* at 540.

Later in the letter, the Attorney General clarified that his reference was to "the Federal Government," *ibid.,* and gave other reasons "for avoiding a construction that would make the statute applicable to the Government in violation of the apparent policy of the Congress in such matters," *id.,* at 541. The Attorney General expressly relied upon *Emergency Fleet Corp.* v. *Western Union Telegraph Co.*, 275 U. S. 415, 425 (1928), in which the Court upheld the granting of favorable telegraph rates to a *federal* corporation that competed with private enterprise.

The Attorney General's opinion says nothing about the Act's applicability to state agencies. Indeed, in the following year, the Attorney General of California expressly concluded that state purchases were within the Act's proscriptions. See 1932–1939 Trade Cases ¶ 55,156, pp. 415–416 (1937). Two other early State Attorney General opinions simply do not consider whether the Act applies to state purchases for *retail* sales. See Opinion of Attorney General of Minnesota, 1932–1939 Trade Cases ¶ 55,157, p. 416 (1937); 26 Wis. Op. Atty. Gen. 142 (1937).

Representative Patman "presumed that the [United States] Attorney General's reasons may be also applied to municipal and public institutions." W. Patman, The Robinson-Patman Act 168 (1938). See also W. Patman, Complete Guide to the Robinson-Patman Act 30 (1963) (interpreting Attorney General's opinion as exempting all governmental purchases). His interpretation is entitled to some weight, but he appears only to be interpreting—or

A

Respondents cite the hearings on the Robinson-Patman held in the late 1960's.[23] Testimony before the House Subcommittee investigating practices in the pharmaceutical industry indicated that the Act did not cover price discrimination in favor of state hospitals,[24] and Federal Trade Commission Chairman Paul Dixon disclaimed any authority over transactions involving state health care programs.[25] It is not at all clear, however, whether Chairman Dixon contemplated cases in which the state agency competed with private retailers, although he was aware of such practices by institutional purchasers.[26] Other statements expressed little more than informed, interested opinions on the issue presented, and are not entitled to the consideration appropriate for the constructions given contemporaneously with the Act's passage.[27] See *supra*, at 159–162, and n. 22.

It is clear from the House Subcommittee's conclusions that it did not focus on the question presented by this case. The Subcommittee

---

erroneously extending—the Attorney General's opinion and reasoning. Representative Patman's personal intentions probably are better reflected in his introduction in 1951 and 1953 of bills to amend the Act to define "purchaser" to include "the United States, any State or any political subdivision thereof." H. R. 4452, 82d Cong., 1st Sess. (1951); H. R. 3377, 83d Cong., 1st Sess. (1953). There is no legislative history on these bills, but it is arguable that he believed that the original intent needed to be stated expressly to negate his reading of the Attorney General's contrary construction of the Act. In any case, Congress' failure to pass these bills may be attributable to a reluctance to subject *federal* purchases to the Act. For example, in 1955, 1957, 1959, and 1961, Representative Keogh also unsuccessfully introduced bills to extend the Act to federal purchases only *for resale*. See H. R. 430, 87th Cong., 1st Sess. (1961); H. R. 155, 86th Cong., 1st Sess. (1959); H. R. 722, 85th Cong., 1st Sess. (1957); H. R. 5213, 84th Cong., 1st Sess. (1955).

It bears repeating, moreover, that none of these views—including Representative Patman's—focuses on the state purchases alleged here: purchases to gain competitive advantage in the private market rather than purchases for use in traditional governmental functions. For the Department of Justice's most recent statements regarding an exemption or immunity for state enterprises, see n. 37, *infra*.

[23] The most important relevant event in the Robinson-Patman Act's postenactment history is the amendment in 1938 excluding eleemosynary institutions, 52 Stat. 446, 15 U. S. C. § 13c. Whether the existence of an exemption in § 13c supports an exemption for certain state purchases depends upon whether § 13c is interpreted to apply to state agencies that perform the functions listed. That is a substantial issue in its own right. Compare H. R. Rep. No. 1983, 90th Cong., 2d Sess., 7–8, 78 (1968) (suggesting that § 13c does not include government agencies), with 81 Cong. Rec. 8706 (1937) (remarks of Rep. Walter) (§ 13c would apply to institutions financed by cities, counties, and States). See also *City of Lafayette,* 435 U. S., at 397, n. 14 (§ 13c includes "public libraries," which "are, by definition, operated by local government"); *Abbott Laboratories,* 425 U. S., at 18, n. 10; 81 Cong. Rec. 8705 (1937) (remarks by Rep. Walter) (exemption codifies the intention of the drafters of the Robinson-Patman Act). We need not address that issue here.

[24] See, *e. g.,* Small Business and the Robinson-Patman Act: Hearings before the Special Subcommittee on Small Business and the Robinson-Patman Act of the House Select Committee on Small Business, 91st Cong., 73–77 (1969–1970) (William McCamant,

found that the difference between drug prices for retailers and government customers "is extremely substantial" and "not always fully explainable by either cost justifiable quantity discounts, economies of scale, or other factors inherent in bulk distribution." H. R. Rep. No. 1983, 90th Cong., 2d Sess., 77 (1968). In the next conclusion, it stated that "[n]umerous acts and policies of individual manufacturers seem . . . violative of the Robinson-Patman Act . . . ." *Ibid.* Thus, it is quite possible that the Subcommittee considered some state purchasing at discriminatory prices—about which it had heard testimony—to be unlawful. The Subcommittee Report did include the awkwardly worded statement: "There is no basis apparent . . . why the mandate of the Robinson-Patman Act should not be applied to discriminatory drug sales favoring nongovernmental institutional purchasers, profit or nonprofit, to the extent there is prescription drug competition at the retail level with disfavored retail druggists." *Id.,* at 79. This unexceptional opinion, however, simply says that *private* institutional purchases may not facilitate unfair retail

---

Director of Public Affairs, National Association of Wholesalers); *id.,* at 623 (Harold Halfpenny, counsel for the Automative Service Industry Association); Small Business Problems in the Drug Industry: Hearings before the Subcommittee on Activities of Regulatory Agencies of the House Select Committee on Small Business, 90th Cong., 15–16 (1967–1968) (hereinafter 1967–1968 Hearings) (Earl Kintner, former FTC Commissioner, counsel for the National Association of Retail Druggists) (state purchases "probably" exempt). But see *id.,* at 80 (remarks of Charles Fort, President, Food Town Ethical Pharmacies, Inc.) ("Robinson-Patman Act may prohibit this practice"); *id.,* at 86 (same). There also was testimony that institutional purchasers frequently obtain drugs at lower prices than do retail pharmacies, see *id.,* at 14, 258, 318, 1093-1904, and many witnesses complained that this discrimination adversely affected competition, see *id.,* at A-140 to A-141, 253-262, 273, 292.

[25] See H. R. Rep. No. 1983, *supra* n. 23, at 74.

[26] After hearing his testimony, the Subcommittee posed further questions for Chairman Dixon about the eroding influence on the retail druggists' market presented by: (i) expanding federal, state, and private group health care programs; (ii) the Federal Government's ability to purchase from drug manufacturers at prices substantially below wholesale cost; and (iii) instances of hospitals, "both nonprofit and proprietary, selling to outpatients or even nonpatients." *Id.,* at 73. In his response to the Subcommittee, Chairman Dixon declined to discuss further the last category, which involved §13c issues. *Id.,* at 74. His disclaimer of FTC authority envisioned state purchases for welfare programs, not for resale in competition with private enterprise. Thus, the issue presented here is most similar to the issue *not* discussed by Chairman Dixon.

[27] Assuming that this postenactment commentary before the Subcommittee can be imputed to Congress—quite a leap given the failure of the Subcommittee Report to rely on it for its conclusions—"the views of a subsequent Congress form a hazardous basis for interring the intent of an earlier one." *United States* v. *Price,* 361 U. S. 304, 313 (1960). See, *e. g., Consumer Product Safety Comm'n* v. *GTE Sylvania, Inc.,* 447 U. S. 102, 117–118, and n. 13 (1980); *Oscar Mayer & Co.* v. *Evans,* 441 U. S. 750, 758 (1979); *United Air Lines, Inc.,* v. *McMann,* 434 U. S. 192, 200, n. 7 (1977) ("Legislative observations 10 years after passage of the Act are in no sense part of the legislative history").

competition through sales at discriminatory prices. The Subcommittee said nothing expressly about the unfair competition at issue in this case.[28]

B

Respondents also argue that, without exception, courts considering the Act's coverage have concluded that it does not apply to government purchasers. They insist that no court has imposed liability upon a seller or buyer, under either § 2(a) or § 2(f), when the discriminatory price involved a sale to a State, city, or county. See Brief for Respondent University 31-32. There are serious infirmities in these broad assertions: (i) this Court has never held nor suggested that there is an exemption for state purchases;[29] (ii) the number of judicial decisions even *considering* the Act's application to purchases by state agencies is relatively small;[30] (iii) respondents cite no Court of Appeals decision that has expressly adopted their interpretation of

---

[28] The Subcommittee also concluded that the 1938 amendment was "designed to afford immunity to private nonprofit institutions . . . to the extent the sales are for the nonprofit institution's 'own use,'" H. R. Rep. No. 1983, *supra* n. 23, at 78, but that would indicate more the construction of § 13c than it would the intent of the 1936 Congress.

[29] Indeed, our opinions suggest precisely the opposite. See *City of Lafayette, supra,* at 397, n. 14; *Abbott Laboratories, supra,* at 18-19, no. 10; *California Motor Transport Co.* v. *Trucking Unlimited,* 404 U. S. 508, 513 (1972).

[30] The parties cite fewer than a dozen cases, many with unpublished opinions, that involve the application of the Robinson-Patman Act to state purchases. See nn. 31-33, *infra.* Cf. *Blue Chip Stamps* v. *Manor Drug Stores,* 421 U. S. 723, 731 (1975) (affirming rule adopted by "virtually all lower federal courts facing the issue in the *hundreds* of *reported* cases presenting this question over the past quarter century") (emphasis added); *Gulf Oil Corp.* v. *Copp Paving Co.,* 419 U. S., at 200-201 (adopting consistent, "longstanding" construction of Robinson-Patman Act after "nearly four decades of litigation").

[31] See *Pacific Engineering & Production Co.* v. *Kerr-McGee Corp.,* 1974-1 Trade Cases ¶ 75,054, p. 96,742 (Utah 1974) (dicta) (involving Federal Government as ultimate purchaser) (relying on Attorney General's opinion as sole support), aff'd in part and rev'd in part, 551 F. 2d 790, 798-799 (CA10) (finding legitimate competition despite different prices), cert. denied, 434 U. S. 879 (1977); *Sachs* v. *Brown-Forman Distillers Corp.,* 134 F. Supp. 9, 16 (SDNY 1955) (Act inapplicable because there was no proof that sales affected plaintiff adversely), aff'd on opinion below, 234 F. 2d 959 (CA2) (*per curiam*), cert. denied, 352 U. S. 925 (1956); *General Shale Products Corp.* v. *Struck Constr. Co.,* 37 F. Supp. 598, 602-603 (WD Ky. 1941) (finding no "sale" under the Act and alternatively holding the Act inapplicable because "[n]either the government nor a city in its purchase of property considered necessary for the purposes of *carrying out its governmental functions* is in competition with another buyer who may be engaged in *buying and reselling* that article") (emphasis supplied), aff'd, 132 F. 2d 425, 428 (CA6 1942) (expressly reserving issue whether Act applies to sales to state agency), cert. denied, 318 U. S. 780 (1943). The *Sachs* court also indicated, in dicta, that it was unclear whether the Act applied to state purchases. 134 F. Supp., at 16.

[32] Cf. *Mountain View Pharmacy* v. *Abbott Laboratories,* No. C-77-0094 (Utah, Sept. 6, 1977) (unpublished opinion) (consent by plaintiffs to dismiss with prejudice Act claims

§2 before the decision below; (iv) some of the District Court cases upon which respondents rely are simply inapposite;[31] (v) it is not clear that *any* published District Court opinion has relied solely on a state purchase exemption to dismiss a Robinson-Patman Act claim alleging injury as a result of government competition in the private market;[32] and (vi) there are several cases that suggest that the Robinson-Patman Act *is* applicable to state purchases for resale purposes.[33] This judicial track record is in no sense comparable to the unbroken chain of judical decisions upon which this Court previously has relied for ascertaining a construction of the antitrust laws that Congress over a long period of time has chosen to preserve. See cases cited, n. 27, *supra.*

Respondents also seek support in the interpretations of various commentators and executive officials. But the most authoritative of these sources indicate that the question presented is unsettled;[34]

---

based on sales to state agencies), aff'd in part and rev'd in part, 630 F. 2d 1383 (CA10 1980) (complaint insufficient because it failed to identify products or purchasers subject to discriminatory treatment); *Portland Retail Druggists Assn.* v. *Abbott Laboratories,* No. 71-543 (Ore., Sept. 11, 1972) (unpublished, oral opinion), vacated and remanded, 510 F. 2d 486 (CA9 1974) (§13c applied), vacated and remanded, 425 U. S. 1 (1976). One District Court has suggested in an alternative holding that there is an exemption for state purchases for nonconsumption use. *Logan Lanes, Inc.* v. *Brunswick Corp.,* No. 4-66-5, (Idaho, May 26, 1966) pp. 4–5 (unpublished opinion), aff'd, 378 F. 2d 212, 215–216 (CA9) (purchases by Utah State University within scope of §13c; expressly declined to address "so-called governmental exemption"), cert. denied, 389 U. S. 898 (1967). All of these cases predate our decision in *City of Lafayette.*

[33] See *Burge* v. *Bryant Public School District,* 520 F. Supp. 328, 330–332 (ED Ark. 1980), aff'd, 658 F. 2d 611 (CA8 1981) (*per curiam*); *Champaign-Urbana News Agency, Inc.* v. *J. L. Cummins News Co.,* 479 F. Supp. 281, 286–287 (CD Ill. 1979) (although Act inapplicable to federal purchases, state agencies might face an opposite result), aff'd, 632 F. 2d 680 (CA7 1980); *A. J. Goodman & Son* v. *United Lacquer Manufacturing Corp.,* 81 F. Supp. 890, 893 (Mass. 1949). Other cases cut against *any* exemption for state purchases. See *Municipality of Anchorage* v. *Hitachi Cable, Ltd.,* 547 F. Supp. 633, 637–641 (Alaska 1982); *Sterling Nelson & Sons* v. *Rangen, Inc.,* 235 F. Supp. 393, 399 (Idaho 1964), aff'd, 351 F. 2d 851, 858–859 (CA9 1965), cert. denied, 383 U. S. 936 (1966); *Sperry Rand Corp.* v. *Nassau Research & Development Associates,* 152 F. Supp. 91, 95 (EDNY 1957). Cf. *Reid* v. *University of Minnesota,* 107 F. Supp. 439, 443 (ND Ohio 1952) (expressly not addressing whether state agency exempt from Act when engaged in a business in the same manner as other business corporations).

[34] See 5A Z. Cavitch, Business Organizations §105D.01[8][c] (1973 and Supp. 1982) (opinions "divided" whether Act is applicable); 4 J. von Kalinowski, Antitrust Laws and Trade Regulation §24.06, p. 24–70 (1982) ("there is some conflict among the authorities as to whether sales to states and municipalities are covered by the Act"); *id.,* §24.06[2]; E. Kintner, A Robinson-Patman Primer 203 (1970) ("Although [the Attorney General's] opinion appears to have settled the matter where the federal government is concerned, some controversy has arisen over the applicability of the act to purchases by state and local governments"); F. Rowe, Price Discrimination Under the Robinson-Patman Act §4.12, p. 84 (1962).

others are not necessarily inconsistent with our holding;[35] and in some cases they support it.[36] Thus, Congress cannot be said to have left untouched a universally held interpretation of the Act.[37]

In sum, it is clear that postenactment developments—whether legislative, judicial, or in commentary—rarely have considered the specific issue before us. There is simply no unambiguous evidence of congressional intent to exempt purchases by a State for the purpose of competing in the private retail market with a price advantage.[38]

VI

The Robinson-Patman Act has been widely criticized, both for its effects and for the policies that it seeks to promote. Although Congress is well aware of these criticisms, the Act has remained in effect for almost half a century. And it certainly is "not for [this Court] to indulge in the business of policy-making in the field of antitrust legislation. . . . Our function ends with the endeavor to ascertain from the words used, construed in the light of the relevant material, what was in fact the intent of Congress." *United States* v. *Cooper Corp.*, 312 U. S. 600, 606 (1941).

"A general application of the [Robinson-Patman] Act to all combinations of business and capital organized to suppress commercial competition is in harmony with the spirit and impulses of the times which gave it birth." *South-Eastern Underwriters*, 322 U. S., at 553. The legislative history is replete with references to the economic evil of large organizations purchasing from other large organizations

[35] Some deal only with sales to the Federal Government. See Letter from Comptroller General to Robert F. Sarlo, Veterans Administration (July 17, 1973), reprinted in 1973-2 Trade Cases ¶ 74,642. Almost all fail to mention, much less decide, whether the Act applies to state purchases for *retail* sales. See Report of the Attorney General Under Executive Order 10936, Identical Bidding in Public Procurement 11 (1962).

[36] See 62 Cal. Op. Atty. Gen. 741 (1979); 47 N. C. Atty. Gen. 112, 115 (1977); [1948–1949] Ga. Op. Atty. Gen. 723, 727 (1949) (if state agency competes with private enterprise, it is subject to Act).

[37] In its 1977 Report of the Task Group on Antitrust Immunities, at 25, the Department of Justice stated:

"The mere fact that a state has authorized a state-owned enterprise to engage in commercial activity should not be sufficient to immunize all activities of the enterprise from the antitrust laws. That test removes the clearly sovereign activities of a state from the antitrust scrutiny of the federal government while holding the commercial activities of a state-owned enterprise to the same standards requir[ed] of all who engage in commercial transactions in the market." Reprinted in Antitrust Exemptions and Immunities: Hearings before the Subcommittee on Monopolies and Commercial Law of the House Committee on the Judiciary, 95th Cong., 1st Sess., 1890 (1977).

Cf. *Victory Transport Inc.* v. *Comisaria General de Abastecimientos y Transportes*, 336

for resale in competition with the small, local retailers. There is no reason, in the absence of an explicit exemption, to think that Congressmen who feared these evils intended to deny small businesses, such as the pharmacies of Jefferson County, Alabama, protection from the competition of the strongest competitor of them all.[39] To create an exemption here clearly would be contrary to the intent of Congress.

VII

We hold that the sale of pharmaceutical products to state and local government hospitals for resale in competition with private pharmacies is not exempt from the proscriptions of the Robinson-Patman Act. The judgment of the Court of Appeals accordingly is reversed, and the case is remanded for further proceedings consistent with this opinion.

It is so ordered.

JUSTICE STEVENS, dissenting.

While I join JUSTICE O'CONNOR's dissenting opinion, I believe an additional comment on the text of the Robinson-Patman Act may help to explain my vote. For purposes of interpreting that statute, I think that federal, state, and local agencies are "purchasers," but that such governmental agencies are not engaged in "competition" with private parties even when they resell purchased goods to consumers who might otherwise have patronized a private retailer. Both before and after the 1936 statute amended § 2 of the Clayton Act, the requirement of proving an adverse effect on "com-

---

F. 2d 354, 360–362 (CA2 1964) (the charter of a ship to haul grain by a state instrumentality not a sovereign activity that would justify applying the sovereign immunity doctrine).

[38] The dissent of JUSTICE O'CONNOR relies in large part, not on the words of the statute, or its legislative history, but on assertions that a "general consensus [existed] in the legal and business communities that sales to governmental entities are not covered by the Robinson-Patman Act." *Post*, at 182. See also *post*, at 174 (STEVENS, J., dissenting). JUSTICE O'CONNOR is correct that some in the business and legal community did think that an exemption existed for all state purchases. See *post*, at 185–187, and nn. 19 and 20. But to say there is a "consensus" is to disregard the opinion of commentators, see n. 34, *supra*; the views expressed that the Act is applicable to state purchases, see *supra*, at 161, 162–163, n. 22, and 169, and n. 37; and the most recent, relevant opinion of the Department of Justice, see *supra*, at 169, and n. 37. It is more accurate to say that this was an unsettled question of federal law that demanded this Court's attention.

[39] Under our interpretation, the Act's benefits would accrue, precisely as intended, to the benefit of small, private retailers. See 1935 Hearings, at 261 (Teegarden recommending passage "for the protection of private rights").

petition" played an important part in limiting the coverage of the statute.

It is universally agreed that federal purchases are not covered by the Act. Even though it has always been obvious that primary line competition might be injured by discriminatory prices on sales to the Federal Government, and also that goods sold to military post exchanges would normally be resold at a substantial discount, no one in the 1936 legislative deliberations questioned the inapplicability of the Act to these sales. The explanation, in my opinion, does not rest on the sovereign status of the Federal Government,* but rather on the assumption embodied in the Act that federal agencies do not compete with nongovernmental entities.

Mr. Teegarden, the lobbyist, made this assumption clear in his statement at the 1935 House hearings, quoted in part by the opinion of the Court. *Ante,* at 160–161, n. 19:

> Mr. LLOYD: Would this bill, in your judgment, prevent the granting of discounts to the United States Government?
>
> .   .   .   .   .
>
> For instance, the Government gets huge discounts. Take that electric fan, for instance. You go to the ordinary store and the list price is $35. The Procurement Division procures them delivered, one at a time, for $13.18. Now, would that discount be barred by this bill?
>
> Mr. TEEGARDEN: I do not see why it should . . . .
>
> Aside from that, my answer would be this: The Federal Government is not in competition with other buyers from these concerns. Therefore a discrimination—it is so applied universally in interstate commerce law, in the railroad law—to have a discrimination, there must be a relative position between the parties to the discrimination which constitutes an injury to one as against the other. I think the answer is to be found in that.
>
> In other words, if seller A makes a price to a retailer in New York and a different price to a retailer in San Francisco, all other

---

*When Mr. Teegarden responded to specific written questions about the Act, he gave two reasons why the bill would not prevent competitive bidding on government purchases below trade price levels. First, he stated that a statute would not be construed to restrict the rights, prerogatives, or privileges of the sovereign unless it expressly so provided. This reason would apply only to the Federal Government, as the Court's opinion points out. *Ante,* at 159–161, nn. 18, 19. In addition, however, Mr. Teegarden gave a reason that applies to governmental entities at state and local levels as well. "The further insertion of the clause proposed under topic 4 below, requiring a showing of effect upon competition, will further preclude any possibility of the bill affecting the Government." Hearings on H. R. 8442 et al. before the House Committee on the Judiciary, 74th Cong., 1st Sess., 250 (1935).

things aside, no case of discrimination could be predicated there, because the two are not in the same sphere at all.

The Federal Government is saved by the same distinction, not of location but of function. They are not in competition with any one else who would buy. Hearings on H. R. 8442 et al. before the House Committee on the Judiciary, 74th Cong., 1st Sess., 208–209 (1935).

I would interpret the "distinction, not of location but of function" somewhat more broadly than does the majority. It is not merely a question of whether government agencies do or do not resell the goods they have purchased. Even when they resell items to the public, governmental entities do not engage in competition with private retailers in the same sense that chainstores compete with independent retailers. Most importantly, their activities are seldom affected by a profitmaking motivation; rather they are undertaken in connection with the provision of services to the public. Further, their merchandising and price-setting decisions take a different set of factors into accout. As the Court notes, *ante*, at 158, n. 17, they need not include a profit component, their overhead may be subsidized, and they may be exempt from state or federal taxation. In short, governmental agencies are in an entirely different category of market participants.

I am convinced that the same analysis applies to purchases and resales by state and local agencies. I do not believe that a municipal hospital that operates a pharmacy is any more engaged in competition with a retail druggist than a military post exchange is engaged in competition with a retail grocer or a retail clothing store. To be sure, this analysis is not entirely consistent with the conclusion implied by Mr. Teegarden's somewhat equivocal answer to Congressman Hancock. Although he did not say that purchases by a city hospital would be covered by the bill, he did state that, *"[i]f the two hospitals are in competition with each other,"* the fact that one was operated by the city would not save it from the bill. But he went on to stress: *"If they are not in competition with each other, then they are in a different sphere."* Hearings on H. R. 8442, *supra*, at 209 (emphasis added). In my view, if not in Mr. Teegarden's, the differences between a city hospital and a private hospital justify the conclusion that, for purposes of construing this statute, they should not be considered in competition with each other.

I therefore would hold as a matter of law that neither purchases nor sales by governmental agencies—federal, state, or local—constitute "competition" with private persons to which the statute has any application. The Act has no impact on any governmental agency's ability to provide hospital and related services to its constituents. For the reasons JUSTICE O'CONNOR has set forth in greater detail, I believe such a holding more accurately reflects the understanding of the Congress that enacted the statute and the lawyers and businessmen who have lived with the statute on a day-to-day basis for almost half a century.

JUSTICE O'CONNOR, with whom JUSTICE BRENNAN, JUSTICE REHNQUIST and JUSTICE STEVENS join, dissenting.

The issue that confronts the Court is one of statutory construction: whether the Robinson–Patman Act covers purchases of commodities by state and local governments for resale in competition with private retailers.[1] The Court's task, therefore, is to discern the intent of the 1936 Congress which enacted the Robinson-Patman Act. I do not agree with the majority that this issue can be resolved by reference to cases under the Sherman Act or other statutes, or by reliance on the broad remedial purposes of the antitrust laws generally. The 1936 Congress simply did not focus on this issue. The business and legal communities have assumed for the past four decades that such purchases are not covered. For these reasons, as explained more fully below, I respectfully dissent.

I

A

The majority relies extensively on the interpretation this Court has given to the term "person" under the Sherman Act and other statutes as a guide to whether the terms "person" and "purchasers," as used in § 2 of the Clayton Act, 38 Stat. 730, as amended by the Robinson-Patman Act (Act), 49 Stat. 1526, 15 U. S. C. § 13, include state and local governmental entities. See *ante*, at 155–156. In my view, such reliance is misplaced. The question of the Robinson-Patman Act's treatment of governmental purchases requires an independent examination of the legislative history of *that* Act to ascertain congressional intent.[2] Indeed, the cases cited by the majority emphasize that the key question regarding coverage or non-

---

[1] This case does not require us to consider, as the cases cited by the majority suggest, *ante*, at 157–158, whether compliance with other federal statutes necessitates an implied exemption from the provisions of the Act. The question is simply one of congressional intent—*i. e.*, what Congress intended when it enacted the Robinson-Patman Act with respect to coverage of governmental purchases for resale.

[2] The majority cites *Pfizer Inc.* v. *Government of India*, 434 U. S. 308 (1978), as a case in which the Court applied Sherman Act cases to construe the Clayton Act, which the Robinson-Patman Act amends. *Ante*, at 157, n. 15. In *Pfizer* the Court held that a

coverage of governmental entities is the intent of Congress *in enacting the statute in question.*[3] Resolution of the statutory construction question cannot be made to depend upon the abstract assertion that the term "person" is broad enough to embrace States and municipalities.[4] For these reasons, the mere fact that in *City of Lafayette* v. *Louisiana Power & Light Co.,* 435 U. S. 389, 397, n. 14 (1978), a Sherman Act case, the Court referred to the Robinson-Patman Act in its discussion of the breadth of the term "person" cannot resolve the question now before us.

Further, the majority opinion propounds a misleading syllogism when it (1) suggests that the term "person" in the Clayton and Robinson-Patman Acts should be construed similarly, (2) cites *Hawaii* v. *Standard Oil Co.,* 405 U. S. 251 (1972), for the proposition that the Clayton Act applies to States, and (3) then opines that the terms "person" and "purchasers" under §2 therefore should be

---

foreign nation is a "person" entitled to bring a treble damages action under §4 of the Clayton Act, 15 U. S. C. §15. As the Court acknowledged, 434 U. S., at 311, §4 is a reenactment of the virtually identical language of §7 of the Sherman Act. In fact, §7 was eventually repealed as redundant. §3, 69 Stat. 283; see S. Rep. No. 619, 84th Cong., 1st Sess., 2 (1955). Reliance on prior interpretation of §7 of the Sherman Act was therefore uniquely appropriate.

[3] See *Pfizer Inc.* v. *Government of India, supra,* at 315 (§4 of the Clayton Act) ("The word 'person' . . . is not a term of art with a fixed meaning wherever it is used, nor was it in 1890 when the Sherman Act was passed"); *Georgia* v. *Evans,* 316 U. S. 159, 161 (1942) (§7 of the Sherman Act) ("Whether the word 'person' . . . includes a State or the United States depends upon its legislative environment"); *Ohio* v. *Helvering,* 292 U. S. 360, 370 (1934) (Rev. Stat. §§3140, 3244) ("Whether the word 'person' or 'corporation' includes a state . . . depends upon the connection in which the word is found"). See also *United States* v. *Cooper Corp.,* 312 U. S. 600, 604–605 (1941) ("[T]here is no hard and fast rule of exclusion. The purpose, the subject matter, the context, the legislative history, and the executive interpretation of the statute are aids to construction which may indicate intent, by the use of the term, to bring state or nation within the scope of the law").

It is also worth noting that many of the cases upon which the majority relies involved construction of the term "person" for the purpose of determining whether a particular governmental entity is a "person" entitled *to sue. Pfizer Inc.* v. *Government of India, supra; United States* v. *Cooper Corp., supra* (United States is not "person" entitled to sue under §7 of the Sherman Act); *Georgia* v. *Evans, supra* (State is "person" entitled to sue under §7 of the Sherman Act); *Chattanooga Foundry & Pipe Works* v. *City of Atlanta,* 203 U. S. 390 (1906) (municipality is "person" entitled to sue under §7 of the Sherman Act).

[4] I would also note that the majority overstates the significance of Senator Robinson's remarks in connection with its observation that "[t]he word 'purchasers' has a meaning as inclusive as the word 'person.'" *Ante,* at 155, n. 11. The remarks of Senator Robinson should not be read to suggest that the word "purchasers," as used in the Robinson-Patman Act, embraces States or municipalities. The Senator's observation reflects an affirmative response to Senator Vandenberg's concern that, although the bill was drafted with a view toward the problems of large chain-store buying power in the retail merchandising field, the Act would apply to *private* enterprise in the field of industrial production as well. See 80 Cong. Rec. 6429–6430 (1936).

construed to include state purchases. *Ante*, at 155–156. Because, as the majority observes, *ante*, at 156, n. 13, the definitional section of the Clayton Act, 15 U. S. C. § 12, was intended to apply to the Robinson–Patman Act, I do not dispute the first proposition. However, *Hawaii* v. *Standard Oil Co.* stated only that a State is a "person" for purposes of *bringing* a treble damages action under § 4 of the Clayton Act. 405 U. S., at 261.[5] Conspicuously absent from the majority's discussion is any authority holding that States or local governments are persons for purposes of exposure to *liability* as purchasers under the provisions of the Clayton Act.[6] Although Congress might now decide that the purchasing activities of States and local governments *should* be subject to the limitations imposed by § 2, that is a policy judgment appropriately left to legislative determination.

B

Nor do I find persuasive the majority's invocation of presumptions regarding the liberal construction and broad remedial purposes of the antitrust laws generally. Without derogating the usefulness of those principles or suggesting that they should never play a role in the Robinson-Patman context, one may nevertheless candidly acknowledge that the Court also has identified a certain tension between the Robinson-Patman Act, on the one hand, and the Sherman Act and other antitrust statutes, on the other. The Court frequently has recognized that strict enforcement of the anti-price-discrimination

[5] Were Congress to consider the specific question of *liability* of governmental entities as purchasers under the Robinson-Patman Act, it seems reasonable to assume that it would approach that question with a different set of policy concerns than those bearing on the decision whether to extend the benefit of the Act's protections to those entities. Cf. *Parker* v. *Brown*, 317 U. S. 341, 351 (1943) ("In a dual system of government in which, under the Constitution, the states are sovereign, save only as Congress may constitutionally subtract from their authority, an unexpressed purpose to nullify a state's control over its officers and agents is not lightly to be attributed to Congress").

[6] Indeed, one basis for the United States Attorney General's conclusion in 1938 that the Robinson-Patman Act is inapplicable to purchases of supplies by the Federal Government was the absence of any judicial decision construing the Clayton Act, prior to its amendment by the Robinson-Patman Act, to apply to governmental contracts. 38 Op. Atty. Gen. 539, 540 (1936).

Prior to 1929, courts interpreted the original § 2 as addressed only to the problem of primary line competition—*i.e.*, injury to competition among sellers. See, *e. g.*, *National Biscuit Co.* v. *FTC*, 299 F. 733 (CA2), cert. denied, 266 U. S. 613 (1924). Not until 1929 did this Court hold that § 2 also protected against the type of injury alleged in the present case—*i. e.*, secondary line injury, or injury to competition among buyers. See *George Van Camp & Sons Co.* v. *American Can Co.*, 278 U. S. 245, 253 (1929). The Robinson-Patman amendment to § 2 clarified that the Act was designed to redress the latter type of injury.

provisions of the former may lead to price rigidity and uniformity in direct conflict with the goals of the latter. See, *e. g., Great Atlantic & Pacific Tea Co. v. FTC*, 440 U. S. 69, 80, 83, n. 16 (1979); *Automatic Canteen Co. v. FTC*, 346 U. S. 61, 63, 74 (1953); *Standard Oil Co. v. FTC*, 340 U. S. 231, 249, and n. 15 (1951).[7]

At the very least, this recognition raises doubts that the Court should liberally construe the Robinson-Patman Act in favor of broader coverage. Those doubts are enhanced by the fact that Congress' principal aim in enacting the Robinson-Patman Act was to protect small retailers from the competitive injury suffered at the hands of large chain stores.[8] It is consistent with that intent for Congress also to have displayed special solicitude for the well-established, below-trade price-buying practices of governmental institutions.

II

As the majority documents, *ante*, at 160, n. 19, the legislative history of the Robinson-Patman Act clearly indicates that Congress envisioned *some* sort of immunity for governmental bodies.[9] The

---

[7] Indeed, the tension between the Robinson-Patman policy of protection of competitors and the Sherman Act goal of protection of the competitive process has prompted the Court to achieve a partial reconciliation of the two by liberal interpretation of the "meeting competition" defense under § 2(b) of the Clayton Act, as amended by the Robinson-Patman Act, 15 U. S. C. § 13(b). See *Standard Oil Co. v. FTC*, 340 U. S., at 251.

[8] H. R. Rep. No. 2287, 74th Cong., 2d Sess., pt. 1, pp. 3–4 (1936); S. Rep. No. 1502, 74th Cong., 2d Sess., 4 (1936); see FTC, Final Report on the Chain Store Investigation, S. Doc. No. 4, 74th Cong., 1st Sess. (1935).

[9] Members of the House expressed concern with the effect of the bill on the established below-market buying practices of federal, *state, county, and municipal governments.* Hearings on H. R. 8442 et al. before the House Committee on the Judiciary, 74th Cong., 1st Sess., 209 (1935). In response H. B. Teegarden, a principal draftsman of the Act, assured members of the House Judiciary Committee that he "would not want" the Act if it prohibited, all along the line, the competitive bidding practices of those governments. *Ibid.*

Moreover, with respect to subsequent legislative history, I find significant the fact that later attempts in Congress to expressly include governmental entities within the coverage of the Act failed. See H. R. 4452, 82d Cong., 1st Sess. (1951); H. R. 3377, 83d Cong., 1st Sess. (1953); H. R. 5213, 84th Cong., 1st Sess. (1955); H. R. 722, 85th Cong., 1st Sess. (1957); H. R. 155, 86th Cong., 1st Sess. (1959); H. R. 430, 87th Cong., 1st Sess. (1961). In particular, I would not dismiss as readily as does the majority, *ante*, at 163, n. 22, the bills introduced by Representative Patman in 1951 and 1953 to amend the Act to define "purchaser" to include "the United States, any State or any political subdivision thereof." The majority speculates that Representative Patman introduced these bills to reaffirm his original intent that these entities would be covered. In light of Representative Patman's agreement in his book, W. Patman, The Robinson-Patman Act 168 (1938), with the United States Attorney General's construction of the Act to exclude purchases by the Federal Government and his extension of the Attorney General's rationale to "municipal and public institutions," *ibid.*, it is more plausible to infer that he viewed the bills as *extending* the Act's coverage.

question before the Court is the extent of that immunity—in particular, whether the purchase of goods by state and local governments for resale in competition with private retailers is within the intended scope of the Robinson-Patman Act. As the majority acknowledges, *ante*, at 159, the 1936 Congress that enacted the Robinson-Patman Act did not focus on the precise issue before the Court. Notwithstanding this admission, the majority announces the surprising conclusion that "[t]o create an exemption here *clearly* would be contrary to the intent of Congress." *Ante,* at 171 (emphasis added).

The majority is correct in stating that it is not the business of this Court to engage in "policy-making in the field of antitrust legislation'" in order to fill gaps where Congress has not clearly expressed its intent. *Ante,* at 170 (quoting *United States* v. *Cooper Corp.,* 312 U. S. 600, 606 (1941)). It is precisely because I concur in that admonition that I would refrain from attributing to Congress an intent to cover the state and local governmental purchases in question here.[10]

A

In attempting to supply the unexpressed intent of Congress, the majority fails to offer satisfactory guidelines for determining the scope of the Act's coverage of governmental agencies.[11] The majority assumes, "without deciding, that Congress did not intend the Act to apply to state purchases for consumption in traditional governmental functions" and suggests that state purchases of pharmaceuticals for the purpose of resale to indigent citizens may not expose the State to antitrust liability. *Ante*, at 154, and n. 7.

---

[10] My resolution of the statutory issue here should not be construed to reflect a policy judgment that the Robinson-Patman Act *should* protect "a State's entrepreneurial personality." *City of Lafayette* v. *Louisiana Power & Light Co.,* 435 U. S. 389, 422 (1978) (BURGER, C. J., concurring in part). We are not concerned here with whether the kind of activity in which these governmental entities are engaged *appropriately* exposes them to antitrust liability under the Act. Cf. *id.,* at 418. That question raises policy concerns lying peculiarly within the institutional province of Congress. "A court, without the benefit of legislative hearings that would illuminate the policy considerations if the question were left to Congress, is not competent in my opinion to resolve this question . . . . It is regrettable that the Court today finds it necessary to rush to this essentially legislative judgment." *Pfizer Inc.* v. *Government of India,* 434 U. S., at 331 (POWELL, J., dissenting) (footnote omitted). Because the question before us is one of congressional intent and it is far from clear that Congress has supplied an answer to that question, I would refrain from substituting the policy judgments of the judiciary for those Congress might embrace. Cf. *id.,* at 320 (BURGER, C. J. dissenting); *id.,* at 330–331 (POWELL, J., dissenting).

[11] To the extent the majority purports to "divine" the will of Congress, it comes as no surprise, given Congress' inattention to this precise question, that no "bright lines" for coverage and noncoverage emerge from its opinion.

The majority's assumption, however, is inconsistent with the principles of statutory construction upon which it purports to rely. If, absent a clear expression of legislative intent to the contrary, the plain language of the statute controls, then by the majority's own assertions one would have to conclude that even purchases for the State's own use or for resale to indigents would fall within the Act's proscriptions. For, as the majority remarks, *ante*, at 155, the terms "person" and "purchasers" are broad enough to include governmental entities, and the legislative history is "ambiguous on the application of the Act to state purchases for consumption. . . . " *Ante*, at 160–161.

Moreover, to the extent the majority implies that a State's coverage or noncoverage under the Act turns on the distinction between purchases for resale and purchases for consumption,[12] that distinction is inconsistent with the competition rationale elsewhere suggested, *ante*, at 170, to underlie the prohibitions of § 2(a). For example, a state university hospital might limit the use of its pharmacy to its own faculty and staff, thereby falling within the "for their own use" exception.[13] Nevertheless, the university pharmacy may be inflicting competitive injury on private pharmacies that the university's faculty and staff might otherwise patronize.[14] Thus, the majority's conflicting suggestions leave in doubt what principle— the presence of functional competition or the consumption/resale dichotomy—guides the determination whether a state or local government's purchases fall within the Act's proscriptions.

B

Against the backdrop of a legislative history that even the majority concedes does not focus on the issue before us stands the general consensus in the legal and business communities that sales to governmental entities are not covered by the Robinson-Patman Act. The majority devotes considerable effort to distinguishing or under-

---

[12] The majority thus suggests, though it refrains from holding, that the scope of coverage under § 2(a) is coextensive with the "for their own use" line drawn by the Nonprofit Institutions Act of 1938, 15 U. S. C. § 13c, and interpreted by the Court in *Abbott Laboratories* v. *Portland Retail Druggists Assn., Inc.*, 425 U. S. 1 (1976). This proposed resale/consumption distinction has no foundation in the language of § 2(a), which prohibits discrimination "in price between different purchasers of commodities . . . , where such commodities are sold *for use, consumption or resale* . . . . " 15 U. S. C. § 13(a) (emphasis added).

[13] See *Abbott Laboratories* v. *Portland Retail Druggists Assn., Inc.*, *supra*, at 16–17.

[14] Or, to take another example, a cafeteria operated by a governmental agency for the benefit of its employees also might inflict some competitive injury on restaurants in the same area that otherwise might enjoy the employees' patronage.

cutting the authorities cited by the respondents. In so doing, and in observing that these authorities cannot reveal Congress' intent in 1936, *ante*, at 165, n. 27, the majority misunderstands the significance of this evidence. These authorities simply illustrate the virtually unanimous assumption over the past 47 years of noncoverage of governmental entities—an assumption that has served as the basis of well-established governmental purchasing practices and marketing relationships. In the past the Court has relied upon the widespread understanding of the provisions of the Robinson-Patman Act in limiting the scope of the Act's prohibitions.[15] To do so here is no less appropriate.

Despite its attempt to discount the significance of the judicial authorities cited by the respondents, the majority cannot dispute that no court has imposed liability upon a seller or buyer, under either § 2(a) or § 2(f), 15 U. S. C. § § 13(a) and (f), in a case involving an alleged price discrimination in favor of a federal, state, or municipal governmental purchaser.[16] Commentators confirm the general judicial consensus that sales to States and municipalities are

---

[15] See *Standard Oil Co.* v. *FTC*, 340 U. S., at 246–247 (reliance on widespread understanding that the meeting-competition proviso of § 2(b) of the Clayton Act, as amended by the Robinson-Patman Act, provides a complete defense to a charge of price discrimination).

[16] See *Champaign-Urbana News Agency, Inc.* v. *J. L. Cummins News Co.,* 632 F. 2d 680, 688–689 (CA7 1980) (Robinson-Patman Act inapplicable to purchases by instrumentality of Federal Government for resale); *Mountain View Pharmacy* v. *Abbott Laboratories Pharmaceutical Products Division,* No. C-77-0094 (Utah, Sept. 6, 1977) (unpublished opinion) (order of consent dismissing with prejudice Robinson-Patman claims based on sales to any governmental entity), aff'd in part and rev'd in part on other grounds, 630 F. 2d 1383 (CA10 1980); *Logan Lanes, Inc.* v. *Brunswick Corp.,* No. 4-66-5 (Idaho, May 26, 1966) (unpublished opinion) (sale of bowling equipment to State not within provisions of Act; alternative holding that sales exempt under 15 U. S. C. § 13c), aff'd, 378 F. 2d 212, 217 (CA9) (sales to state university within § 13c exemption), cert. denied, 389 U. S. 898 (1967); *Sperry Rand Corp.* v. *Nassau Research & Development Associates,* 152 F. Supp. 91, 96 (EDNY 1957) (disclaiming, on motion for reargument, any intention that original opinion could be "construed to suggest that sales to the Government can be thought to be subject to the provisions of the Robinson-Patman Act"); *Sachs* v. *Brown-Forman Distillers Corp.,* 134 F. Supp. 9, 16 (SDNY 1955) ("It is doubtful at best whether the Robinson-Patman Act applies at all to sales to Government agencies, state or federal") (holding Act inapplicable to sales by liquor distiller to state liquor commissions; alternative holding that no competitive injury suffered by plaintiff liquor wholesaler), aff'd on opinion below, 234 F. 2d 949 (CA2), cert. denied, 352 U. S. 925 (1956); *General Shale Products Corp.* v. *Struck Constr. Corp.,* 37 F. Supp. 598, 602–603 (WD Ky. 1941) (alternatively holding Robinson-Patman Act inapplicable to sales to municipal housing commission and suggesting that "the Act does not apply to sales to the government, state or municipalities"), aff'd, 132 F. 2d 425 (CA6 1942), cert. denied, 318 U. S. 780 (1943).

While one may concede that most of these cases do not focus on the precise situation of purchases by state or local governments for resale, they nonetheless reflect the consensus of judicial opinion that governmental bodies are not subject to liability under § 2 of the

not covered by the Act.[17] Moreover, Congress' failure to enact bills extending Robinson-Patman coverage to these entities buttresses this interpretation of the Act. See n. 9, *supra.*

This same understanding has been expressed in testimony before Congress. In 1967 and 1968 a congressional Subcommittee conducted public hearings on the problems of small businesses in the pharmaceutical industry. The Subcommittee heard testimony from both representatives of pharmaceutical manufacturers and retail pharmacists regarding the industrywide practice of price discrimination in sales of pharmaceuticals to governmental purchasers—federal, state, county, and municipal.[18] Several witnesses also directly expressed

---

Clayton Act, as amended by the Robinson-Patman Act. The majority would dismiss many of these cases with the simple observation that they predate the Court's decision in *City of Lafayette* v. *Louisiana Power & Light Co.,* 435 U. S. 389 (1978). *Ante,* at 167–168, n. 32. For reasons already noted, however, in my view *City of Lafayette* does not resolve the issue before us in this case.

Moreover, cases that the majority suggests are supportive of its position, *ante,* at 168, n. 33, are similarly distinguishable. For example, both *Municipality of Anchorage* v. *Hitachi Cable, Ltd,* 547 F. Supp. 633 (Alaska 1982), and *Sterling Nelson & Sons, Inc.* v. *Rangen Inc.,* 235 F. Supp. 393 (Idaho 1964), aff'd, 351 F. 2d 851, 858–859 (CA9 1965), cert. denied, 383 U. S. 936 (1966), indicate only that the Robinson-Patman Act may apply where the State, as in *Sterling,* or the municipality, as in *Hitachi,* is the *victim* of commercial bribery under § 2(c), 15 U. S. C. § 13(c), rather than the favored customer.

[17] E. Kintner, A. Robinson-Patman Primer 224 (2d ed. 1979) ("In spite of [any] contrary indications [among state attorneys general], it is generally believed that the exemption applies to governmental purchases at any level"); W. Patman, Complete Guide to the Robinson-Patman Act 30 (1963) (indicating the Act is inapplicable to sales to government, municipal, or public institutions); F. Rowe, Price Discrimination Under the Robinson-Patman Act 84 (1962) ("The preponderance of reasoned opinion treats State or municipal bodies on a par with the Federal Government's exemption"); 4 J. von Kalinowski, Antitrust Laws and Trade Regulation § 24.06, p. 24–70 (1982) ("[T]he prevailing view is that such sales [to States and municipalities] are excluded from Robinson-Patman liability"). See also 5A Z. Cavitch, Business Organizations § 105D.01[8][c] (1973) (indicating that lower federal courts have generally held the Act inapplicable to sales to States and municipalities, that one lower federal court has held the Act may be applicable if the State is the disfavored customer, and that opinions among state attorneys general are divided).

Although not specifically addressing any consumption/resale distinction, a past Attorney General of the United States also has opined that purchases by state and local governments are not within the Act's prohibition against price discrimination. Report of the Attorney General Under Executive Order 10936, Identical Bidding in Public Procurement 11 (1962) (identical bidders on contracts with state and local governments cannot contend that the Act prohibits bidding below the schedule price, because the Act is not applicable to government contracts).

[18] Small Business Problems in the Drug Industry: Hearings before the Subcommittee on Acitivies of Regulatory Agencies of the House Select Committee on Small Business, 90th Cong., 1st Sess., 48 (1967–1968) (hereinafter 1967–1968 Hearings) (Merritt Skinner, community pharmacist); *id.,* at 258 (William Apple, executive director of the American Pharmaceutical Association); *id.,* at 296, 318–319 (Hyman Moore, H. L. Moore Drug Exchange,

their assumption that the Robinson-Patman Act does not apply to such sales.[19]

In 1969 and 1970, the same House Subcommittee investigated the problems of small businessmen under the Robinson-Patman Act. In these hearings witnesses again expressed the view that governmental purchases at any level are not covered, highlighting the problem of favorable prices on governmental purchases *for resale* and making a plea for a change in the law.[20]

Inc.); *id.*, at 500 (Henry DeBoest, vice president of Eli Lilly & Co.); *id.*, at 705 (Donald van Roden, vice president and general manager of pharmaceutical operations for Smith Kline & French Laboratories); *id.*, at 792 (Joseph Ingolia, vice president and general manager of Schering Laboratories); *id.*, at 817 (Lyman Duncan, vice president of American Cyanamid Co.

id., at 705 (Donald van Roden, vice president and general manager of pharmaceutical operations for Smith Kline & French Laboratories); *id.*, at 792 (Joseph Ingolia, vice president and general manager of Schering Laboratories); *id.*, at 817 (Lyman Duncan, vice president of American Cyanamid Co.).

Based upon this overwhelming evidence, the Select Committee on Small Business concluded in its Report to the House: "The difference between drug prices charged retailers and wholesalers as compared to those charged . . . governmental customers is extremely substantial, often being over 50 percent." H. R. Rep. No. 1983, 90th Cong., 2d Sess., 77 (1968).

[19] See 1967–1968 Hearings, at 15–16 (Earl Kintner, former FTC Commissioner, counsel for the National Association of Retail Druggists) ("When a drug supplier sells drugs to Federal, State, or municipal government institutions, the price charged by the supplier may be without regard to the Robinson-Patman Act, because such sales are probably exempt from the Robinson-Patman Act"); *id.*, at 731 (W. Abrahamson, president of Ortho Pharmaceutical Corp.) ("[T]he only special pricing we have ever engaged in are [sic] in bidding situations to [federal, state, or local government] agencies excluded from the Robinson-Patman Act"); *id.*, at 1069 (C. Stetler, president of the Pharmaceutical Manufacturers Association) ("There is nothing immoral or unlawful about incremental cost pricing in cases—such as sales to the Government . . . —where the Robinson-Patman Act does not apply").

Even one Congressman on the Subcommittee expressed his understanding that the Act does not apply to governmental purchasers. See *id.*, at 1092 (Rep. Corman) ("[I]f there were no exemption under Robinson-Patman for the Government . . . , what would be the situation as to their purchases?"). The colloquy that followed Representative Corman's question further evidences the assumption that governmental purchases are outside the scope of the Act, *even in the case of resales.*

"Mr. STETLER. If there was no exemption under Robinson-Patman, I presume some of these practices would be illegal under Robinson-Patman.

"Mr. CUTLER. If I could try to answer that, [Representative] Corman. . . .

"[A]bsent the one case of these resales . . . , I suppose the lack of exemption would make no difference, because the Robinson-Patman Act would not apply for other reasons, because you are not discriminating between two people engaged in commerce and competing with one another.

"Further, there is a real question as to whether the Robinson-Patman Act applies *under any circumstances* where you are bidding under a competitive bid. So for both of these reasons, the answer to your question would be that the same pricing practices might still lawfully prevail under Robinson-Patman without *the exemption for the government . . . .* "
Ibid., (emphasis added).

[20] William McCamant, Director of Public Affairs for the National Association of Wholesalers, testified:

III

The legislative history of the Robinson-Patman Act clearly reveals that Congress intended to exclude governmental entities from the Act's proscriptions to some extent. However, Congress did not focus on the issue before us and therefore did not provide a clear rationale governing coverage and noncoverage. In an area in which bright lines are needed to guide state and local governments in their purchasing practices, the majority fails to identify any principle triggering inclusion or exclusion.

Moreover, one cannot doubt that state, county, and municipal governments and manufacturers of commodities have structured their marketing relationships with each other on the longstanding assumption that the Robinson-Patman Act does not apply to those transactions. That understanding finds substantial support among the courts and commentators. State and local governments have developed programs for providing services to the public, including medical care to the indigent and the medically needy,[21] based on the

---

"Over the years, the Robinson-Patman Act has not been extended to cover sales to the Government. In the days when Government purchases constituted a relatively small volume in the marketplace, this exemption posed few problems. But today, with the vast growth in Government purchases, Federal, State, and local, . . . the continued exemption creates many unfair competitive situations.

"We believe that Congress must turn its attention to this problem." Small Business and the Robinson-Patman Act, Hearings before the Special Subcommittee on Small Business and the Robinson-Patman Act of the House Select Committee on Small Business, 91st Cong., 1st Sess., 73–74 (1969–1970).

See *id.,* at 76–77 (Everette MacIntyre, Acting Chairman of the Federal Trade Commission) (affirming that sales to the Federal Government, even in the resale context, are not subject to the Robinson-Patman Act).

Harold Halfpenny, legal counsel for the Automotive Service Industry Association, focused most precisely on the problem of which petitioners complain–*i.e.,* competitive injury to private industry when governmental entities receive more favorable prices on purchases of commodities for resale.

"[W]hile the Act is silent on the subject, its legislative history and subsequent interpretation support the proposition that sales made to Federal or *State governmental bodies* are not subject to the provisions of the Act.

"This may be injurious to competition in several ways. . . .

"[T]here are *'second line' situations where competition exists between the Government and private industry in the resale of commodities.*

"The Federal Trade Commission has not recommended legislation to make the Robinson-Patman Act applicable to sales to governmental purchases. However, in our opinion, Congress should consider acting on its own volition." *Id.*, at 623 (emphasis added).

[21] See, *e. g.,* Cal. Welf. & Inst. Code Ann. §§ 14100–14126 (West 1980 and Supp. 1982); Ill. Ann. Stat., ch. 23, ¶¶ 5–1 to 5–14 (Supp. 1982–1983); Mont. Code Ann. § § 53–6–103 to 53–6–144 (1981); N. Y. Soc. Serv. Law §§ 365, 365–a (McKinney 1976 and Supp. 1982–1983); Tex. Human Res. Code Ann. §§ 32.001–32.037 (1980); Va. Code §§ 63.1–134 to 63.1–140 (1980).

same assumption. The majority's holding that sales of commodities to state and local governments for resale in competition with private enterprise are covered by the Act will engender significant disruption—not only through government and industry reexamination and restructuring of marketing relationships, but also, unfortunately, through possible termination of services and supplies to needy citizens[22] and through litigation associated with the process of reexamination.[23] The Court rests its decision primarily on one statement in the legislative history,[24] taken in isolation from other remarks designed to assure concerned House Members that the Act would *not* force the abandonment of governmental below-market buying practices which the majority's holding now calls into question. Given Congress' failure to delineate the extent of the Robinson-Patman Act's coverage or noncoverage of state and local governments, I would allow Congress to speak on this issue rather than disrupt long-standing practices and programs and judicially arm private litigants with a powerful treble-damages action against these governments. Therefore, I would affirm the judgment below.

IN RE R. M. J.

455 U. S. 191
Appeal from the Supreme Court of Missouri
No 80-1431. Argued November 9, 1981—Decided January 25, 1982
609 S. W 2d 411, reversed.
POWELL, J., delivered the opinion for a unanimous Court.

Charles B. Blackmar argued the cause for appellant. With him on the briefs were *Charles A. Blackmar, Bruce J. Ennis,* and *Charles S. Sims.*

John W. Inglish argued the cause and filed a brief for appellee.*
JUSTICE POWELL delivered the opinion of the Court.

[22] The administrative burden of developing internal accounting and recordkeeping procedures to segregate commodities purchased for resale, plus the additional financial strain of paying higher prices for these purchases, may induce state and local governments to terminate programs and services already in place. More significantly, however, the uncertainty generated by the majority's failure to establish clear lines of demarcation for coverage and noncoverage and the fear of exposure to treble-damages liability might well cause cautious legislators facing budgetary dilemmas to eliminate these programs.

[23] I note that the Court has not indicated that today's holding will have only prospective effect.

[24] See *ante,* at 161.

Thomas Lumbard and *Harry M. Philo* filed a brief for the Association of Trial Lawyers of America as *amicus curiae* urging reversal.
Jerry L. Zunker filed a brief for the State Bar of Texas as *amicus curiae.*

The Court's decision in *Bates* v. *State Bar of Arizona,* 433 U. S. 350 (1977), required a reexamination of long-held perceptions as to "advertising" by lawyers. This appeal presents the question whether certain aspects of the revised ethical rules of the Supreme Court of Missouri regulating lawyer advertising conform to the requirements of *Bates.*

I

As with many of the States, until the decision in *Bates,* Missouri placed an absolute prohibition on advertising by lawyers.[1] After the Court's invalidation of just such a prohibition in *Bates,* the Committee on Professional Ethics and Responsibility of the Supreme Court of Missouri revised that court's Rule 4 regulating lawyer advertising. The Committee sought to "strike a midpoint between prohibition and unlimited advertising,"[2] and the revised regulation of advertising, adopted with slight modification by the State Supreme Court, represents a compromise. Lawyer advertising is permitted, but it is restricted to certain categories of information, and in some instances, to certain specified language.

Thus, part B of DR 2-101 of the Rule states that a lawyer may "publish . . . in newspapers, periodicals and the yellow pages of telephone directories" 10 categories of information: name, address and telephone number; areas of practice; date and place of birth; schools attended; foreign language ability; office hours; fee for an initial consultation; availability of a schedule of fees; credit arrangements; and the fixed fee to be charged for certain specified "routine" legal services.[3] Although the Rule does not state explicitly that these 10

[1] Prior to the 1977 revision, Rule 4 provided in pertinent part:

"(A) A lawyer shall not prepare, cause to be prepared, use, or participate in the use of, any form of public communication that contains professionally self-laudatory statements calculated to attract lay clients; as used herein, 'public communication' includes, but is not limited to, communication by means of television, radio, motion picture, newspaper, magazine, or book.

"(B) A lawyer shall not publicize himself, his partner, or associates as a lawyer through newspaper or magazine advertisements, radio or television announcements, display advertisements in city or telephone directories, or other means of commercial publicity, nor shall he authorize or permit others to do so in his behalf . . . ." Mo. Sup. Ct. Rules Ann. Rule 4, DR 2-101, p. 63 (Vernon 1981) (historical note).

[2] Report of Committee to Chief Justice of Supreme Court of Missouri (Sept. 9, 1977), reprinted in App. A-30.

[3] The 10 listed "routine" services are: an uncontested dissolution of marriage; an uncontested adoption; an uncontested personal bankruptcy; an uncomplicated change of name; a simple warranty or quitclaim deed; a simple deed of trust; a simple promissory note; an individual Missouri or federal income tax return; a simple power of attorney; and a simple will. Mo. Rev. Stat., Sup. Ct. Rule 4, DR 2-101(B) (1978) (Index Vol.). The Rule authorizes the Advisory Committee to approve additions to this list of routine services. *Ibid.*

categories of information or the 3 indicated forms of printed advertisement are the only information and the only means of advertising that will be permitted,[4] that is the interpretation given the Rule by the State Supreme Court and the Advisory Committee[5] charged with its enforcement.

In addition to these guidelines, and under authority of the Rule, the Advisory Committee has issued an addendum to the Rule providing that if the lawyer chooses to list areas of practice in his advertisement, he must do so in one of two prescribed ways. He may list one of three general descriptive terms specified in the Rule—"General Civil Practice," "General Criminal Practice," or "General Civil and Criminal Practice." Alternatively, he may use one or more of a list of 23 areas of practice, including, for example, "Tort Law," "Family Law," and "Probate and Trust Law." He may not list both a general term and specific subheadings, nor may he deviate from the precise wording stated in the Rule. He may not indicate that his practice is "limited" to the listed areas and he must include a particular disclaimer of certification of expertise following any listing of specific areas of practice.[6]

---

[4] Indeed, on its face, the Rule would appear to suggest that its specific provisions are intended only to provide a safe harbor, and not to prohibit all other forms of advertising or categories of information. This impression is conveyed by the Rule's inclusion of a general prohibition on misleading advertising in DR 2-101(A):

"A lawyer shall not, on behalf of himself, his partner, associate or any other lawyer affiliated with him or his firm, use or participate in the use of any form of public communication respecting the quality of legal services or containing a false, fraudulent, misleading deceptive, self-laudatory or unfair statement or claim." Rule 4, DR 2-101(A).

[5] The Advisory Committee is a standing committee of the Supreme Court of Missouri and is responsible for prosecuting disciplinary proceedings and for giving formal and informal opinions on the Canons of Professional Responsibility. See Rule 5.

[6] The addendum to the rule promulgated by the Advisory Committee provided in relevant part as follows:

"[T]he following areas for fields of law may be advertised by use of the specific language hereinafter set out:

1. 'General Civil Practice'
2. 'General Criminal Practice'
3. 'General Civil and Criminal Practice.'

"If a lawyer or law firm uses one of the above, no other area can be used . . . . If one of the above is *not* used, then a lawyer or law firm can use one or more of the following:

1. 'Administrative Law'
2. 'Antitrust Law'
3. 'Appellate Practice'
4. 'Bankruptcy'
5. 'Commercial Law'
6. 'Corporation Law and Business Organizations'
7. 'Criminal Law'
8. 'Eminent Domain Law'
9. 'Environmental Law'

Finally, one further aspect of the Rule is relevant in this case. DR 2-102 of Rule 4 regulates the use of professional announcement cards. It permits a lawyer or firm to mail a dignified "brief professional announcement card stating new or changed associates or addresses, change of firm name, or similar matters." The Rule, however, does not permit a general mailing; the announcement cards may be sent only to "lawyers, clients, former clients, personal friends, and relatives." [7] Mo. Rev. Stats., Sup. Ct. Rule 4, DR 2-102 (A)(2) (1978) (Index Vol.).

II

Appellant graduated from law school in 1973 and was admitted to the Missouri and Illinois Bars in the same year. After a short stint with the Securities and Exchange Commission in Washington, D. C., appellant moved to St. Louis, Mo., in April 1977, and began practice as a sole practitioner. As a means of announcing the opening of his office, he mailed professional announcement cards to a selected list of addressees. In order to reach a wider audience, he placed several advertisements in local newspapers and in the yellow pages of the local telephone directory.

The advertisements at issue in this litigation appeared in January, February, and August 1978, and included information that was not expressly permitted by Rule 4. They included the information that appellant was licensed in Missouri and Illinois. They contained, in

---

10. 'Family Law'
11. 'Financial Institution Law'
12. 'Insurance Law'
13. 'International Law'
14. 'Labor Law'
15. 'Local Government Law'
16. 'Military Law'
17. 'Probate and Trust Law'
18. 'Property Law'
19. 'Public Utility Law'
20. 'Taxation Law'
21. 'Tort Law'
22. 'Trial Practice'
23. 'Workers Compensation Law.'
No deviation from the above phraseology will be permitted and no statement of limitation of practice can be stated.
    "If one or more of these specific areas of practice are used in any advertisement, the following statement must be included . . . :
'Listing of the above areas of practice does not indicate any certification of expertise therein.'" Rule 4, Addendum III (Adv. Comm. Nov. 13, 1977).
    [7] This provision of Rule 4 was not altered by the 1977 amendments.

large capital letters, a statement that appellant was "Admitted to Practice Before THE UNITED STATES SUPREME COURT." And they included a listing of areas of practice that deviated from the language prescribed by the Advisory Committee—e. g., "personal injury" and "real estate" instead of "tort law" and "property law"—and that included several areas of law without analogue in the list of areas prepared by the Advisory Committee—e. g., "contract," "zoning & land use," "communication," "pension & profit sharing plans."[8] See n. 6, *supra.* In addition, and with the exception of the advertisement appearing in August 1978, appellant failed to include the required disclaimer of certification of expertise after the listing of areas of practice.

On November 19, 1979, the Advisory Committee filed an information in the Supreme Court of Missouri charging appellant with unprofessional conduct. The information charged appellant with publishing three advertisements that listed areas of law not approved by the Advisory Committee, that listed the courts in which appellant was admitted to practice, and, in the case of two of the advertisements, that failed to include the required disclaimer of certification. The information also charged appellant with sending announcement cards to "persons other than lawyers, clients, former clients, personal friends, and relatives" in violation of DR 2–102(A)(2). In response, appellant argued that, with the exception of the disclaimer requirement, each of these restrictions upon advertising was unconstitutional under the First and Fourteenth Amendments.

In a disbarment proceeding, the Supreme Court of Missouri upheld the constitutionality of DR 2–101 of Rule 4 and issued a private reprimand. 609 S. W. 2d 411 (1981). But the court did not

---

[8] In an advertisement published in the August 1978 yellow pages for St. Louis, and typical of appellant's other advertisements, appellant included a listing of 23 areas of practice. Four of the areas conformed to the language prescribed in the Rule—"bankruptcy," "anti-trust," "labor," and "criminal." Eleven of the areas deviated from the precise language of the Rule—"tax," "corporate," "partnership," "real estate," "probate," "wills, estate planning," "personal injury," "trials & appeals," "workmen's compensation," "divorce-separation," and "custody-adoption," instead of, respectively, and as required by the Rule, "taxation law," "corporation law and business organizations," "property law," "probate & trust law," "tort law," "trial practice," "appellate practice," "workers compensation law," and "family law." Eight other areas listed in the advertisement are not listed in any manner by the Advisory Committee's addendum: "contract," "aviation," "securities-bonds," "pension & profit sharing plans," "zoning & land use," "entertainment/sports," "food, drug & cosmetic," and "communication."

A photograph of the advertisements as they appeared in the St. Louis, Suburban West, Telephone Directory for February 1978, and in the January/February 1978 issue of the West End Word is reproduced as an Appendix to this opinion. In all of appellant's advertisements the statement as to his membership in the Bar of the United States Supreme Court was printed conspicuously in large capital letters.

explain the reasons for its decision, nor did it state whether it found appellant to have violated each of the charges lodged against him or only some of them. Indeed, the court only purported to uphold the constitutionality of DR 2-101; it did not mention the propriety of DR 2-102, which governs the use of announcement cards.

Writing in separate dissenting opinions, Chief Justice Bardgett and Judge Seiler argued that the information should be dismissed. The dissenters suggested that the State did not have a significant interest either in requiring the use of certain, specified words to describe areas of practice or in prohibiting a lawyer from informing the public as to the States and courts in which he was licensed to practice. Nor would the dissenters have found the mailing of this sort of information to be unethical.[9]

III

In *Bates* v. *State Bar of Arizona*, 433 U. S. 350 (1977), the Court considered whether the extension of First Amendment protection to commercial speech announced in *Virginia Pharmacy Board* v. *Virginia Citizens Consumer Council*, 425 U. S. 748 (1976), applied to the regulation of advertising by lawyers.[10] The *Bates* Court held that indeed lawyer advertising was a form of commercial speech, protected by the First Amendment, and that "advertising by attorneys may not be subjected to blanket suppression." 433 U. S., at 383.

---

[9] The dissenting judges differed in several respects. Chief Justice Bardgett considered that appellant's listing of the fact that he was admitted to practice before the United States Supreme Court was not improper; Judge Seiler argued that this information was more misleading than helpful. Moreover, Judge Seiler argued that appellant should not be penalized for having omitted a disclaimer of certification when the addendum requiring the disclaimer was not available until after appellant had placed the advertisements and after it was too late to add the disclaimer. Chief Justice Bardgett's dissent omits any mention of appellant's failure to include a disclaimer. See n. 18, *infra*. Finally, Chief Justice Bardgett expressed his belief that our decision in *Central Hudson Gas & Electric Corp.* v. *Public Service Comm'n,* 447 U. S. 557 (1980), concerning the regulation of commercial speech, does not apply in its entirety to the regulation of lawyer advertising. Judge Seiler appeared to take the opposite position. Both of the dissenting opinions reflect a thoughtful examination of the charges made against appellant.

[10] The Court in *Virginia Pharmacy,* expressly reserved this question:

"We stress that we have considered in this case the regulation of commercial advertising by pharmacists. Although we express no opinion as to other professions, the distinctions, historical and functional, between professions, may require consideration of quite different factors. Physicians and lawyers, for example, do not dispense standardized products; they render professional *services* of almost infinite variety and nature, with the consequent enhanced possibility for confusion and deception if they were to undertake certain kinds of advertising." 425 U. S., at 773, n. 25.

More specifically, the *Bates* Court held that lawyers must be permitted to advertise the fees they charge for certain "routine" legal services. The Court concluded that this sort of price advertising was not "inherently" misleading, and therefore could not be prohibited on that basis. The Court also rejected a number of other justifications for broad restrictions upon advertising including the potential adverse effect of advertising on professionalism, on the administration of justice, and on the cost and quality of legal services, as well as the difficulties of enforcing standards short of an outright prohibition. None of these interests was found to be sufficiently strong or sufficiently affected by lawyer advertising to justify a prohibition.

But the decision in *Bates* nevertheless was a narrow one. The Court emphasized that advertising by lawyers still could be regulated.[11] False, deceptive, or misleading advertising remains subject to restraint,[12] and the Court recognized that advertising by the professions poses special risks of deception—"because the public lacks sophistication concerning legal services, misstatements that might be overlooked or deemed unimportant in other advertising may be found quite inappropriate in legal advertising." *Ibid.* (footnote omitted). The Court suggested that claims as to quality or in-person

[11] Even as to price advertising, the Court suggested that some regulation would be permissible. For example, the bar may "define the services that must be included in an advertised package . . . ." 433 U. S., at 373, n. 28, and the bar could require disclaimers or explanations to avoid false hopes, *id.*, at 384 ("[S]ome limited supplementation, by way of warning or disclaimer or the like, might be required of even an advertisement of the kind ruled upon today so as to assure that the consumer is not misled").

Presumably, too, the bar may designate the services that may be considered "routine." Moreover, the Court might reach a different decision as to price advertising on a different record. If experience with particular price advertising indicates that the public is in fact misled or that disclaimers are insufficient to prevent deception, then the matter would come to the Court in an entirely different posture. The commercial speech doctrine is itself based in part on certain empirical assumptions as to the benefits of advertising. If experience proves that certain forms of advertising are in fact misleading, although they did not appear at first to be "inherently" misleading, the Court must take such experience into account. Cf. *Bates* v. *State Bar of Arizona*, 433 U. S., at 372 ("We are not persuaded that restrained professional advertising . . . will be misleading").

[12] See *Friedman* v. *Rogers,* 440 U. S. 1, 11, n. 9 (1979) ("When dealing with restrictions on commercial speech we frame our decisions narrowly, 'allowing modes of regulation [of commercial speech] that might be impermissible in the realm of noncommercial expression'" (quoting *Ohralik* v. *Ohio State Bar Assn.*, 436 U. S. 447, 456 (1978)); *Virginia Pharmacy Board* v. *Virginia Citizens Consumer Council*, 425 U. S., at 771–772, and n. 24 ("Untruthful speech, commercial or otherwise, has never been protected for its own sake. . . . Obviously, much commercial speech is not provably false, or even wholly false, but only deceptive or misleading. We foresee no obstacle to a State's dealing effectively with this problem. The First Amendment, as we construe it today, does not prohibit the State from insuring that the stream of commercial information flow cleanly as well as freely") (citations and footnote omitted).

solicitation might be so likely to mislead as to warrant restriction. And the Court noted that a warning or disclaimer might be appropriately required, even in the context of advertising as to price, in order to dissipate the possibility of consumer confusion or deception.[13] "[T]he bar retains the power to correct omissions that have the effect of presenting an inaccurate picture, [although] ·the preferred remedy is more disclosure, rather than less." *Id.*, at 375.[14]

In short, although the Court in *Bates* was not persuaded that price advertising for "routine" services was necessarily or inherently misleading, and although the Court was not receptive to other justifications for restricting such advertising, it did not by any means foreclose restrictions on potentially or demonstrably misleading advertising. Indeed, the Court recognized the special possibilities for deception presented by advertising for professional services. The public's comparative lack of knowledge, the limited ability of the professions to police themselves, and the absence of any standardization in the "product" renders advertising for professional services especially susceptible to abuses that the States have a legitimate interest in controlling.

Thus, the Court has made clear in *Bates* and subsequent cases that regulation—and imposition of discipline—are permissible where

[13] In addition, the *Bates* Court noted that reasonable restrictions on the time, place, and manner of advertising would still be permissible, while "the special problems of advertising on the electronic broadcast media will warrant special consideration." 433 U.S., at 384.

[14] The Model Rules of Professional Conduct proposed by the American Bar Association Commission on Evaluation of Professional Standards provide that "a lawyer may advertise services through public media, such as a telephone directory, legal directory, newspaper or other periodical, radio or television, or through written communication not involving personal contact." Rule 7.2(a). Rule 7.1 prohibits misleading advertising in the following terms:

"A lawyer shall not make any false or misleading communication about the lawyer or the lawyer's services. A communication is false or misleading if it:

"(a) contains a material misrepresentation of fact or law, or omits a fact necessary to make the statement considered as a whole not materially misleading;

"(b) is likely to create an unjustified expectation about results the lawyer can achieve, or states or implies that the lawyer can achieve results by means that violate the Rules of Professional Conduct or other law; or

"(c) compares the lawyer's services with other lawyers' services, unless the comparison can be factually substantiated."

Commentary following the Rule suggests that the Rule would prohibit "advertisements about results obtained on behalf of a client, such as the amount of damage award or the lawyer's record in obtaining favorable verdicts, and advertisements containing client endorsements."

It is understood that the format of the proposed new Rules will be considered by the House of Delegates of the American Bar Association at its 1982 midyear meeting and that the substance of the Rules will be considered at the 1982 annual meeting. We, of course, imply no view as to these proposals.

the particular advertising is inherently likely to deceive or where the record indicates that a particular form or method of advertising has in fact been deceptive. In *Ohralik* v. *Ohio State Bar Assn.*, 436 U. S. 447, 462 (1978), the Court held that the possibility of "fraud, undue influence, intimidation, overreaching, and other forms of 'vexatious conduct'" was so likely in the context of in-person solicitation, that such solicitation could be prohibited. And in *Friedman* v. *Rogers*, 440 U. S. 1 (1979), we held that Texas could prohibit the use of trade names by optometrists, particularly in view of the considerable history in Texas of deception and abuse worked upon the consuming public through the use of trade names.

Commercial speech doctrine, in the context of advertising for professional services, may be summarized generally as follows: Truthful advertising related to lawful activities is entitled to the protections of the First Amendment. But when the particular content or method of the advertising suggests that it is inherently misleading or when experience has proved that in fact such advertising is subject to abuse, the States may impose appropriate restrictions. Misleading advertising may be prohibited entirely. But the States may not place an absolute prohibition on certain types of potentially misleading information, *e. g.,* a listing of areas of practice, if the information also may be presented in a way that is not deceptive. Thus, the Court in *Bates* suggested that the remedy in the first instance is not necessarily a prohibition but preferably a requirement of disclaimers or explanation. 433 U. S., at 375. Although the potential for deception and confusion is particularly strong in the context of advertising professional services, restrictions upon such advertising may be no broader than reasonably necessary to prevent the deception.

Even when a communication is not misleading, the State retains some authority to regulate. But the State must assert a substantial interest and the interference with speech must be in proportion to the interest served. *Central Hudson Gas & Electric Corp.* v. *Public Service Comm'n*, 447 U. S. 557, 563–564 (1980).[15] Restrictions

---

[15] See *Central Hudson Gas & Electric Corp.* v. *Public Service Comm'n*, 447 U. S., at 566:

"In commercial speech cases, then, a four-part analysis has developed. At the outset, we must determine whether the expression is protected by the First Amendment. For commercial speech to come within that provision, it at least must concern lawful activity and not be misleading. Next, we ask whether the asserted governmental interest is substantial. If both inquiries yield positive answers, we must determine whether the regulation directly advances the governmental interest asserted, and whether it is not more extensive than is necessary to serve that interest."

As the discussion in the text above indicates, the *Central Hudson* formulation must be applied to advertising for professional services with the understanding that the special characteristics of such services afford opportunities to mislead and confuse that are not present when standardized products or services are offered to the public. See n. 10, *supra.*

must be narrowly drawn, and the State lawfully may regulate only to the extent regulation furthers the State's substantial interest. Thus, in *Bates*, the Court found that the potentially adverse effect of advertising on professionalism and the quality of legal services was not sufficiently related to a substantial state interest to justify so great an interference with speech.[16] 433 U. S., at 368–372, 375–377.

IV

We now turn to apply these generalizations to the circumstances of this case.[17]

The information lodged against appellant charged him with four separate kinds of violation of Rule 4: listing the areas of his practice in language or in terms other than that provided by the Rule, failing to include a disclaimer, listing the courts and States in which he had been admitted to practice, and mailing announcement cards to persons other than "lawyers, clients, former clients, personal friends, and relatives." Appellant makes no challenge to the constitutionality of the disclaimer requirement,[18] and we pass on to the remaining three infractions.

Appellant was reprimanded for deviating from the precise listing of areas of practice included in the Advisory Committee addendum to Rule 4. The Advisory Committee does not argue that appellant's listing was misleading. The use of the words "real estate" instead of "property" could scarcely mislead the public. Similarly, the listing of areas such as "contracts" or "securities," that are not found on the Advisory Committee's list in any form, presents no apparent danger of deception. Indeed, as Chief Justice Bardgett explained in dissent, in certain respects appellant's listing is more informative than that provided in the addendum. Because the listing published by the

[16] We recognize, of course, that the generalizations summarized above do not afford precise guidance to the bar and the courts. They do represent the general principles that may be distilled from our decisions in this developing area of the law. As they are applied on a case-by-case basis—as in Part IV of this opinion—more specific guidance will be available.

[17] We note that the restrictions placed upon appellant's speech by Rule 4 imposed a restriction only upon commercial speech—"expression related solely to the economic interests of the speaker and its audience." *Central Hudson Gas & Electric Corp.* v. *Public Service Comm'n, supra*, at 561. By describing his services and qualifications, appellant's sole purpose was to encourage members of the public to engage him for personal profit.

[18] At oral argument counsel for appellant stated that the constitutionality of the disclaimer requirement was not before the Court, and that "[t]he disciplinary action was not based on a failure to include the disclaimer." Tr. of Oral Arg. 16.

Although, the Supreme Court of Missouri did not explicitly indicate whether appellant was in violation of each and every one of the charges made against him, that is the implication of the opinion particularly when read in light of the more detailed dissenting opinions.

appellant has not been shown to be misleading, and because the Advisory Committee suggests no substantial interest promoted by the restriction, we conclude that this portion of Rule 4 is an invalid restriction upon speech as applied to appellant's advertisements.

Nor has the Advisory Committee identified any substantial interest in a rule that prohibits a lawyer from identifying the jurisdictions in which he is licensed to practice. Such information is not misleading on its face. Appellant was licensed to practice in both Illinois and Missouri. This is factual and highly relevant information particularly in light of the geography of the region in which appellant practiced.

Somewhat more troubling is appellant's listing, in large capital letters, that he was a member of the Bar of the Supreme Court of the United States. See Appendix to this opinion. The emphasis of this relatively uninformative fact is at least bad taste. Indeed, such a statement could be misleading to the general public unfamiliar with the requirements of admission to the Bar of this Court. Yet there is no finding to this effect by the Missouri Supreme Court. There is nothing in the record to indicate that the inclusion of this information was misleading. Nor does the Rule specifically identify this information as potentially misleading or, for example, place a limitation on type size or require a statement explaining the nature of the Supreme Court Bar.

Finally, appellant was charged with mailing cards announcing the opening of his office to persons other than "lawyers, clients, former clients, personal friends and relatives." Mailings and handbills may be more difficult to supervise than newspapers. But again we deal with a silent record. There is no indication that an inability to supervise is the reason the State restricts the potential audience of announcement cards. Nor is it clear that an absolute prohibition is the only solution. For example, by requiring a filing with the Advisory Committee of a copy of all general mailings, the State may be able to exercise reasonable supervision over such mailings.[19] There is no indication in the record of a failed effort to proceed along such a less restrictive path.[20] See *Central Hudson Gas & Electric Corp.* v. *Public Service Comm'n,* 447 U. S., at 566 ("we must determine

---

[19] Rule 7.2(b) of the proposed Model Rules of Professional Conduct of the American Bar Association requires that "[a] copy or recording of an advertisement or written communication shall be kept for one year after its dissemination."

[20] The Advisory Committee argues that a general mailing from a lawyer would be "frightening" to the public unaccustomed to receiving letters from law offices. If indeed this is likely, the lawyer could be required to stamp "This is an Advertisement" on the envelope. See *Consolidated Edison Co.* v. *Public Service Comm'n*, 447 U. S. 530, 541–542 (1980) (billing insert is not a significant intrusion upon privacy, and privacy interest can be protected through means other than a general prohibition).

whether the regulation . . . is not more extensive than is necessary to serve" the governmental interest asserted).

In sum, none of the three restrictions in the Rule upon appellant's First Amendment rights can be sustained in the circumstances of this case. There is no finding that appellant's speech was misleading. Nor can we say that it was inherently misleading, or that restrictions short of an absolute prohibition would not have sufficed to cure any possible deception. We emphasize, as we have throughout the opinion, that the States retain the authority to regulate advertising that is inherently misleading or that has proved to be misleading in practice. There may be other substantial state interests as well that will support carefully drawn restrictions. But although the States may regulate commercial speech, the First and Fourteenth Amendments require that they do so with care and in a manner no more extensive than reasonably necessary to further substantial interests. The absolute prohibition on appellant's speech, in the absence of a finding that his speech was misleading, does not meet these requirements.

Accordingly, the judgment of the Supreme Court of Missouri is

Reversed.

Appendix to Opinion of the Court

```
                          LAW OFFICES
                    R     M. J
                 CHROMALLOY PLAZA—SUITE 1404
                   120 SOUTH CENTRAL AVENUE
                 ST. LOUIS (CLAYTON), MISSOURI 63106
                           721-5321

                 Admitted to Practice before
              THE UNITED STATES SUPREME COURT
                 Licensed in: MISSOURI and ILLINOIS

  • Corporate        • Trials & Appeals      • Personal Injury
  • Partnership      • Criminal              • Divorce, Separation,
    • Tax            • Real Estate             Custody, Adoption
    • Securities-Bonds  • Wills, estate        • Workman's
      • Pension          planning, probate      Compensation
        Profit Sharing   • Bankruptcy           • Contracts
```

The advertisement above appeared in the January/February 1978 issue of the West End Word and was the basis for Count I of the Information.

The advertisement above appeared in the yellow pages of the Southwestern Bell Telephone Co. telephone directory for St. Louis Suburban West issued in February 1978, and was the basis for Count II of the Information.

FALLS CITY INDUSTRIES, INC. v. VANCO BEVERAGE, INC.

460 U. S. 428
Certiorari to the United States Court of Appeals for
the Seventh Circuit
No. 81-1271. Argued October 13, 1982–Decided March 22, 1983
654 F. 2d 1224, vacated and remanded.
BLACKMUN, J., delivered the opinion for a unanimous Court.

Howard Adler, Jr., argued the cause for petitioner. With him on the briefs was *Lionel Kestenbaum.*

John T. Cusack argued the cause for respondent. With him on the briefs was *Gordon B. Nash.*

Deputy Solicitor General Shapiro argued the cause for the United States as *amicus curiae* urging reversal. With him on the brief were *Solicitor General Lee, Assistant Attorney General Baxter, John H. Garvey, Barry Grossman,* and *Nancy C. Garrison.*

JUSTICE BLACKMUN delivered the opinion of the Court.

Section 2(b) of the Clayton Act, 38 Stat. 730, as amended by the Robinson-Patman Act, 49 Stat. 1526, 15 U. S. C. § 13(b), provides that a defendant may rebut a prima facie showing of illegal price discrimination by establishing that its lower price to any purchaser or purchasers "was made in good faith to meet an equally low price of a competitor."[1] The United States Court of Appeals for the Seventh Circuit has concluded that the "meeting-competition" defense of § 2(b) is available only if the defendant sets its lower price on a customer-by-customer basis and creates the price discrimination by lowering rather than by raising prices. We conclude that § 2(b) is not so inflexible.

I

From July 1, 1972, through November 30, 1978, petitioner Falls City Industries, Inc., sold beer f.o.b. its Louisville, Ky., brewery to wholesalers throughout Indiana, Kentucky, and 11 other States. Respondent Vanco Beverage, Inc., was the sole wholesale distributor of Falls City beer in Vanderburgh County, Ind. That county includes the city of Evansville. Directly across the state line from Vanderburgh County is Henderson County, Ky., where Falls City's only wholesale distributor was Dawson Springs, Inc. The city of Henderson, Ky., located in Henderson County, is less than 10 miles from Evansville. The two cities are connected by a four-lane interstate highway. The two counties generally are considered to be a single metropolitan area. App. 124.

Vanco and Dawson Springs each purchased beer from Falls City and other brewers and resold it to retailers in Vanderburgh County and Henderson County, respectively. The two distributors did not compete for sales to the same retailers. This was because Indiana wholesalers were prohibited by state law from selling to out-of-state retailers, Ind. Code § 7.1-3-3-5 (1982), and Indiana retailers were not permitted to purchase beer from out-of-state wholesalers. See § 7.1-3-4-6. Indiana law also affected beer sales in two other ways relevant to this case. First, Indiana required brewers to sell to all Indiana wholesalers at a single price. § 7.1-5-5-7. Second, although it was ignored and virtually unenforced, see Tr. 122-123, 135-136, state law prohibited consumers from importing alcoholic beverages without a permit. § 7.1-5-11-1.

In December 1976, Vanco sued Falls City in the United States District Court for the Southern District of Indiana, alleging, among other things, that Falls City had discriminated in price against Vanco, in violation of § 2(a) of the Clayton Act, 38 Stat. 730, as amended

---

[1] Section 2(b)'s "meeting-competition" proviso reads:

"[N]othing herein contained shall prevent a seller rebutting the prima-facie case thus made by showing that his lower price or the furnishing of services or facilities to any purchaser or purchasers was made in good faith to meet an equally low price of a competitor, or the services or facilities furnished by a competitor."

by the Robinson-Patman Act, 49 Stat. 1526, 15 U. S. C. § 13(a),[2] by charging Vanco a higher price than it charged Dawson Springs. Vanco also claimed that Falls City had violated § § 1 and 2 of the Sherman Act, 15 U. S. C. § § 1 and 2, by conspiring with other brewers and unnamed wholesalers to maintain higher prices in Indiana than in Kentucky.

After trial, the District Court dismissed Vanco's Sherman Act claims, finding no evidence to support the allegations of conspiracy or monopolization. 1980-2 Trade Cases ¶ 63,357, pp. 75,809, 75,820. The court held, however, that Vanco had made out a prima facie case of price discrimination under the Robinson-Patman Act. The District Court found that Vanco competed in a geographic market that spanned the state border and included Vanderburgh and Henderson Counties. *Id.*, at 75,813-75,814. Although Vanco and Dawson Springs did not sell to the same retailers, they "competed for sale of [Falls City's] beer to . . . consumers of beer from retailers situated in [that] market area." *Id.*, at 75,814. Falls City charged a higher price for beer sold to Indiana distributors than it charged for the same beer sold to distributors in other States, including Kentucky. *Ibid.*[3] This pricing policy resulted in lower retail prices for Falls City beer in Kentucky than in Indiana, because Kentucky distributors passed on their savings to retailers who in turn passed them on to consumers. Finding that many customers living in the Indiana portion of the geographic market ignored state law to purchase cheaper Falls City beer from Henderson County retailers, the court concluded that Falls City's pricing policies prevented Vanco from competing effectively with Dawson Springs, *id.*, at 75,815-75,816, and caused it to sell less beer to Indiana retailers. *Id.*, at 75,814-75,817, 75,818.[4]

The District Court rejected Falls City's § 2(b) meeting-competition defense. The court reasoned that, instead of reducing its prices

[2] That section provides in relevant part:

"It shall be unlawful for any person engaged in commerce, in the course of such commerce, either directly or indirectly, to discriminate in price between different purchasers of commodities of like grade and quality, where either or any of the purchases involved in such discrimination are in commerce . . . and where the effect of such discrimination may be substantially to lessen competition or tend to create a monopoly in any line of commerce, or to injure, destroy, or prevent competition with any person who either grants or knowingly receives the benefit of such discrimination, or with customers of either of them . . . ."

[3] Falls City charged Vanco and other Indiana distributors 10-30% more than it charged Dawson Springs and other Kentucky distributors. The District Court concluded that this price differential was not explained by differing costs. Falls City's distributors—wherever located—picked up the beer at Falls City's Louisville brewery. 1980-2 Trade Cases, at 75,814.

[4] The District Court acknowledged that during the period at issue, sales of Falls City beer dropped precipitously throughout Indiana and Kentucky. *Id.*, at 75,815. This decline

to meet those of a competitor, Falls City had created the price disparity by raising its prices to Indiana wholesalers more than it had raised its Kentucky prices. Instead of "adjusting prices on a customer to customer basis to meet competition from other brewers," id, at 75,822, Falls City charged a single price throughout each State in which it sold beer. The court concluded that Falls City's higher Indiana price was not set in good faith, instead, it was "raised" for the sole reason that it followed the other brewers . . . for its profit." *Ibid.*.

The United States Court of Appeals for the Seventh Circuit, by a divided vote, affirmed the finding of liability. 654 F. 2d 1224 (1981).[5] The court held that Vanco had established a prima facie case of illegal price discrimination and that Falls City had not demonstrated that the discrimination "was a good faith effort to defend against competitors." *Id.,* at 1230. We granted certiorari to review the Court of Appeals' holdings respecting injury to competition and the "meeting-competition" defense. 455 U. S. 988 (1982).

II

To establish a prima facie violation of § 2(a), one of the elements a plaintiff must show is a reasonable possibility that a price difference may harm competition. *Corn Products Refining Co.* v. *FTC*, 324 U. S. 726, 742 (1945). In keeping with the Robinson-Patman Act's prophylactic purpose, § 2(a) "does not 'require that the discriminations must in fact have harmed competition.'" *J. Truett Payne Co.* v. *Chrysler Motors Corp.*, 451 U. S. 557, 562 (1981), quoting *Corn Products*, 324 U. S., at 742. This reasonable possibility of harm is often referred to as competitive injury. Unless rebutted by one of the Robinson-Patman Act's affirmative defenses, a showing of competitive injury as part of a prima facie case is sufficient to support.

---

paralleled a significant nationwide trend that favored national brands of beer and harmed or eliminated many regional brewers like Falls City. See generally, FTC, Staff Report of Bureau of Economics, The Brewing Industry 13–28 (1978). But Vanco's sales of Falls City beer declined more rapidly than did Falls City's sales in Indiana as a whole, or in Henderson County. Moreover, Falls City's rate of decline in Henderson County was less than that in Kentucky as a whole. The District Court found that the difference between Vanco's rate of decline and the rate of decline elsewhere was caused by Falls City's price discrimination. 1980–2 Trade Cases, at 75,815.

[5] The Court of Appeals remanded the case to the District Court for a redetermination of damages because, contrary to our decision in *J. Truett Payne Co.* v. *Chrysler Motors Corp.*, 451 U. S. 557 (1981), the District Court had found, 1980–2 Trade Cases, at 75,823, that the aggregate overcharges to Vanco—$575,293.79—were "automatic damage[s]," and had entered judgment for treble that amount. 654 F. 2d, at 1231. The damages issue is not before this Court.

injunctive relief, and to authorize further inquiry by the courts into whether the plaintiff is entitled to treble damages under §4 of the Clayton Act, 38 Stat. 731, as amended, 15 U. S. C. §15 (1976 ed., Supp. V). *J. Truett Payne Co.* v. *Chrysler Motors Corp.*, 451 U. S., at 562.[6]

Falls City contends that the Court of Appeals erred in relying on *FTC* v. *Morton Salt Co.*, 334 U. S. 37 (1948), to uphold the District Court's finding of competitive injury. In *Morton Salt* this Court held that, for the purposes of §2(a), injury to competition is established prima facie by proof of a substantial price discrimination between competing purchasers over time. 334 U. S., at 46, 50–51; see *id.*, at 60 (Jackson, J., dissenting in part). In the absence of direct evidence of displaced sales, this inference may be overcome by evidence breaking the causal connection between a price differential and lost sales or profits. F. Rowe, Price Discrimination Under the Robinson-Patman Act 182 (1962) (Rowe); see *Chrysler Credit Corp.* v. *J. Truett Payne Co.*, 670 F. 2d 575, 581 (CA5 1982).

According to Falls City, the *Morton Salt* rule should be applied only in cases involving "large buyer preference or seller predation." Brief for Petitioner 31. Falls City does not, however, suggest any economic reason why *Morton Salt's* "self-evident" inference, 334 U. S., at 50, should not apply when the favored competitor is not extraordinarily large. Although concerns about the excessive market power of large purchasers were primarily responsible for passage of the Robinson-Patman Act, see generally Rowe, at 3–23; U. S. Dept. of Justice, Report on the Robinson-Patman Act 101–139 (1977) (1977 Report), the Act "is of general applicability and prohibits discriminations generally," *FTC* v. *Sun Oil Co.*, 371 U. S. 505, 522 (1963). The determination whether to alter the scope of the Act must be made by Congress, not this Court, as is recognized by the commentators on which Falls City relies. See 1977 Report, at 221–228 and 290–291; ABA Antitrust Section, Monograph No. 4, The Robinson-Patman Act: Policy and Law, Vol. I, 102–103 (1980).

The *Morton Salt* rule was not misapplied in this case. In a strictly literal sense, this case differs from *Morton Salt* because Vanco and Dawson Springs did not compete with each other at the wholesale level; Vanco sold only to Indiana retailers and Dawson Springs sold only to Kentucky retailers. But the competitive injury component of a Robinson-Patman Act violation is not limited to the injury to competition between the favored and the disfavored purchaser; it also encompasses the injury to competition between their custom-

---

[6] Section 4 of the Clayton Act requires "some showing of actual injury attributable to something the antitrust laws were designed to prevent." *J. Truett Payne Co.* v. *Chrysler Motors Corp.*, 451 U. S., at 562. In this case, the Court of Appeals affirmed the District Court's finding of antitrust injury, 654 F. 2d, at 1230, and that issue is not before us.

ers—in this case the competition between Kentucky retailers and Indiana retailers who, under a District Court finding not challenged in this Court, were selling in a single, interstate retail market.[7]

After observing that Falls City had maintained a substantial price difference between Vanco and Dawson Springs over a significant period of time, the Court of Appeals, like the District Court, considered the evidence that Vanco's loss of Falls City beer sales was attributable to factors other than the price difference, particularly the marketwide decline of Falls City beer. Both courts found it likely that this overall decline accounted for some—or even most—of Vanco's lost sales. Nevertheless, if some of Vanco's injury was attributable to price discrimination, Falls City is responsible to that extent. See *Perma Life Mufflers, Inc.* v. *International Parts Corp.*, 392 U.S. 134, 144 (1968) (White, J., concurring).

The Court of Appeals agreed with the District Court's findings that "the major reason for the higher Indiana retail beer prices was the higher prices charged Indiana distributors," and "the lower retail prices in Henderson County attracted Indiana customers away from Indiana retailers, thereby causing the retailers to curtail purchases from Vanco." 654 F. 2d, at 1229. These findings were supported by direct evidence of diverted sales,[8] and more than established the competitive injury required for a prima facie case under § 2(a). See *J. Truett Payne Co.* v. *Chrysler Motors Corp.*, 451 U. S., at 561–562; *Morton Salt*, 334 U. S., at 50–51. We therefore turn to Falls

[7] The Court of Appeals upheld the District Court's findings that the sale of Falls City beer to Vanco was in interstate commerce and that Henderson County and Vanderburgh County constituted a unified retail market for beer. *Id.*, at 1227–1229. These holdings are not before us. Falls City does not argue, and never has argued, "that Indiana's consumer-level non-importation law *compels* a finding that Evansville and Henderson are separate retail beer markets." Reply Brief for Petitioner to Supplemental Brief after Oral Argument 3. Indeed, Falls City's counsel affirmatively waived this argument in a letter written to the District Court before trial, App. to Supplemental Brief for Respondent after Oral Argument. Nor is the broader question whether Indiana and Kentucky constitute separate markets fairly included within the scope of the questions presented in Falls City's petition for certiorari. Counsel for Falls City made this very clear at oral argument, stating that "I'm not asking this Court to delve into the record to second guess that determination by the lower courts." Tr. of Oral Arg. 5–6.

[8] Falls City's own sales agent reported that the different prices charged in the two States accounted—at least in part—for the substantial difference in Vanco's and Dawson Spring's sales performances. App. 97–98, 157, 166. The local press reported substantial purchases of beer in Kentucky by Indiana residents. Tr. 114–122, 128. Kentucky retailers located just south of the Indiana state line on the four-lane highway between Evansville and Henderson advertised their low prices extensively in the Evansville media and utilized "drive-in windows" at which customers could purchase beer without leaving their cars. E. g., *id.*, at 336. Witnesses testified that they observed cars with Indiana license plates parked at Henderson County carryout retailers, to which drivers would return carrying cases of beer. *Id.*, at 86–112, 629–632. One Indiana resident testified that he purchased beer in Kentucky because of lower prices there. *Id.*, at 121–122, 218–222, 229. The District Court also relied on the differing rates of decline. See n. 4, *supra*.

City's "meeting-competition" defense.

III

When proved, the meeting-competition defense of § 2(b) exonerates a seller from Robinson-Patman Act liability. *Standard Oil Co.* v. *FTC*, 340 U. S. 231, 246–247 (1951). This Court consistently has held that the meeting-competition defense "'at least requires the seller, who has knowingly discriminated in price, to show the existence of facts which would lead a reasonable and prudent person to believe that the granting of a lower price would in fact meet the equally low price of a competitor.'" *United States* v. *United States Gypsum Co.*, 438 U. S. 422, 451 (1978), quoting *FTC* v. *A. E. Staley Mfg. Co.*, 324 U. S. 746, 759–760 (1945); see *Great A&P Tea Co.* v. *FTC*, 440 U. S. 69, 82 (1979). The seller must show that under the circumstances it was reasonable to believe that the quoted price or a lower one was available to the favored purchaser or purchasers from the seller's competitors. See *United States Gypsum Co.*, 438 U. S., at 451. Neither the District Court nor the Court of Appeals addressed the question whether Falls City had shown information that would have led a reasonable and prudent person to believe that its lower Kentucky price would meet competitors' equally low prices there; indeed, no findings whatever were made regarding competitors' Kentucky prices, or the information available to Falls City about its competitors' Kentucky prices.

Instead, the Court of Appeals reasoned that Falls City had otherwise failed to show that its pricing "was a good faith effort" to meet competition. 654 F. 2d, at 1230. The Court of Appeals considered it sufficient to defeat the defense that the price difference "resulted from price increases in Indiana, not price decreases in Kentucky," *ibid.*, and that the higher Indiana price was the result of Falls City's policy of following the Indiana prices of its larger competitors in order to enhance its profits. The Court of Appeals also suggested that Falls City's defense failed because it adopted a "general system of competition," rather than responding to "individual situations." *Ibid.* The court believed that *FTC* v. *A. E. Staley Mfg. Co., supra,* supported this holding. 654 F. 2d, at 1230.

A

On its face, § 2(b) requires more than a showing of facts that would have led a reasonable person to believe that a lower price was available to the favored purchaser from a competitor. The showing required is that the "lower price . . . *was made* in good faith to *meet*" the competitor's low price. 15 U. S. C. § 13(b) (emphasis added). Thus, the defense requires that the seller offer the lower price in good faith *for the purpose* of meeting the competitor's price, that is, the lower price must actually have been a good-faith response to that competing low price. See Rowe, at 234–235. See generally Kuenzel & Schiffres, Making Sense of Robinson-Patman: The Need to Revitalize Its Affirmative Defenses, 62 Va. L. Rev. 1211, 1237–1255 (1976). In most situations, a showing of facts giving rise to a reasonable belief that equally low prices were available to the favored purchaser from a competitor will be sufficient to establish that the seller's lower price was offered in good faith to meet that price. In others, however, despite the availability from other sellers of a low price, it may be apparent that the defendant's low offer was not a good-faith response.

In *Staley,* this Court applied that principle. The Federal Trade Commission (FTC) had proceeded against Staley and six competing manufacturers of glucose, all of whom adhered to the same Chicago basing-point pricing system. See C. Edwards, Price Discrimination Law 372–379 (1959). See generally FTC Policy Toward Geographic Pricing Practices, 1 CCH Trade Reg. Rep. ¶¶ 3601.27, 3601.40–3601.42, pp. 5346, 5351–5352 (10th ed. 1959). Like its competitors, Staley, whose plant was located in Decatur, Ill., sold glucose to candy and syrup manufacturers at a delivered price that included the freight rate from Chicago to the point of delivery. Purchasers nearer Decatur thus were charged an element of "phantom" freight, while Staley "absorbed" an element of freight in sales to buyers nearer Chicago. 324 U. S., at 749. Customers located near Staley's Decatur plant were harmed because, despite being located closer to the plant, they were forced to pay more for glucose than did their Chicago area competitors. *Id.,* at 756.

The FTC eventually charged all seven manufacturers individually for price discrimination and jointly under the Federal Trade Commission Act for price fixing. See *Corn Products Refining Co.,* 47 F. T. C. 587 (1950). At the time of the *Staley* decision, both the FTC and this Court had determined that use of the pricing system by Staley's competitors was illegal under § 2(a). See *Corn Products Refining Co.* v. *FTC,* 324 U. S., at 732, 737–739. And, although neither the FTC nor this Court directly relied on the fact in finding price discrimination, Staley itself had been found to be a party to an interseller conspiracy aimed at maintaining "oppressive and uniform net delivered prices" throughout the country. See *A. E. Staley Mfg. Co.* v. *FTC,* 4 F. T. C. Stat. & Dec. 795, 805 (1943).

The Court observed that § 2(b) could exonerate Staley only if that section permitted a seller to establish "an otherwise unlawful system of discriminatory prices" in order to benefit from "a like unlawful system maintained by his competitors." 324 U. S., at 753. Staley could not claim that its low Chicago prices were set for the purpose of meeting the equally low prices of competitors there; the Chicago prices could be seen only as part of a collusive pricing system designed to exact artificially high prices throughout the country. Since the low prices were set "in order to establish elsewhere the artificially high prices whose discriminatory effect permeates respondents' entire pricing system," *id.*, at 756, the Court sustained the FTC's finding "that respondents' price discriminations were not made to meet a 'lower' price and consequently were not in good faith," *id.*, at 758.

Thus, even had Staley been able to show that its prices throughout the country did not undercut those of its competitors, its lower price in the Chicago area was not a good-faith response to the lower prices there. Staley had not priced in response to competitors' discrete pricing decisions, but from the outset had followed an industrywide practice of setting its prices according to a single, arbitrary scheme that by its nature *precluded* independent pricing in response to normal competitive forces.

B

Almost 20 years ago, the FTC set forth the standard that governs the requirement of a "good-faith response":

> "At the heart of Section 2(b) is the concept of 'good faith.' This is a flexible and pragmatic, not a technical or doctrinaire, concept. The standard of good faith is simply the standard of the prudent businessman responding fairly to what he reasonably believes is a situation of competitive necessity." *Continental Baking Co.*, 63 F. T. C. 2071, 2163 (1963).

Whether this standard is met depends on "'the facts and circumstances of the particular case, not abstract theories or remote conjectures.'" *United States* v. *United States Gypsum Co.*, 438 U. S., at 454, quoting Continental Baking Co., 63 F. T. C., at 2163.

The "facts and circumstances" present in *Staley* differ markedly from those present here. Although the District Court characterized the Indiana prices charged by Falls City and its competitors as "artificially high," there is no evidence that Falls City's lower prices in Kentucky were set as part of a plan to obtain artifically high profits in Indiana rather than in response to competitive conditions in Kentucky. Falls City did not adopt an illegal system of prices maintained by its competitors.[9] The District Court found that Falls City's prices rose in Indiana in response to competitors' price increases there; it did not address the crucial question whether Falls City's Kentucky prices remained lower in response to competitors' prices in that State.

Vanco attempts to liken this case to *Staley* by arguing that the existence of industrywide price discrimination within the single geographic retail market itself indicates "tacit or explicit collusion, or . . . market power" inconsistent with a good-faith response. Brief for Respondent 39. By its terms, however, the meeting-competition defense requires a seller to justify only its *lower* price. See *Staley*, 324 U. S. at 753. Thus, although the Sherman Act would provide a remedy if Falls City's higher Indiana price were set collusively, collusion is relevant to Vanco's Robinson-Patman Act claim only if it affected Falls City's lower Kentucky price. If Falls City set its lower price in good faith to meet an equally low price of a competitor, it did not violate the Robinson-Patman Act.

Moreover, the collusion argument founders on a complete lack of proof. Persistent, industrywide price discrimination within a geographic market should certainly alert a court to a substantial possibility of collusion.[10] See Posner, Oligopoly and the Antitrust Laws: A Suggested Approach, 21 Stan. L. Rev. 1562, 1578–1579 (1969). Here, however, the persistent interstate price difference could well have been attributable, not to Falls City, but to extensive state regulation of the sale of beer. Indiana required each brewer to charge a single price for its beer throughout the State, and barred direct

[9] Except through its rejected Sherman Act claim, Vanco has never attempted to prove that the competing prices Falls City claims to have met were themselves illegal, or that Falls City met those prices knowing them to be unlawful. The plaintiff bears the burden of proving that the prices met were actually illegal. *Cadigan* v. *Texaco, Inc.*, 492 F. 2d 383, 387 (CA9 1974); *National Dairy Products Corp.* v. *FTC*, 395 F. 2d 517, 524 (CA7), cert. denied, 393 U. S. 977 (1968); see *Standard Oil Co.* v. *Brown*, 238 F. 2d 54, 58, and n. 7 (CA5 1956).

[10] Indeed, in some circumstances there may be no other plausible explanation for persistent "economic" price discrimination. Cf. *FTC* v. *Cement Institute*, 333 U. S. 683, 715 (1948) ("the multiple basing point system of delivered prices as employed by respondents contravened accepted economic principles and could only have been maintained through collusion"); *Staley*, 324 U. S., at 756 (it "seems inescapable" that basing point system was adopted not to meet equally low prices of competitors, but to establish artificially high prices elsewhere).

"Economic" price discrimination consists in selling a product to different customers at prices that bear different ratios to the marginal costs of sales to those customers, for example, charging the same price to two customers despite the fact that the seller incurs higher costs to serve one than the other, or charging different prices to two customers despite the fact that the seller's costs of service are the same. Price discrimination under the Robinson-Patman Act, however, "is merely a price difference." *FTC* v. *Anheuser-Busch, Inc.*, 363 U. S. 536, 549 (1960).

competition between Indiana and Kentucky distributors for sales to retailers. In these unusual circumstances, the prices charged to Vanco and other wholesalers in Vanderburgh County may have been influenced more by market conditions in distant Gary and Fort Wayne than by conditions in nearby Henderson County, Ky. Moreover, wholesalers in Henderson County competed directly, and attempted to price competitively, with wholesalers in neighboring Kentucky counties. App. 52–53. A separate pricing structure might well have evolved in the two States without collusion, notwithstanding the existence of a common retail market along the border. Thus, the sustained price discrimination does not itself demonstrate that Falls City's Kentucky prices were not a good-faith response to competitors' prices there.

C

The Court of Appeals explicitly relied on two other factors in rejecting Falls City's meeting-competition defense: the price discrimination was created by raising rather than lowering prices, and Falls City raised its prices in order to increase its profits. Neither of these factors is controlling. Nothing in § 2(b) requires a seller to *lower* its price in order to meet competition. On the contrary, § 2(b) requires the defendant to show only that its "lower price . . . was made in good faith to meet an equally low price of a competitor." A seller is required to justify a price difference by showing that it reasonably believed that an equally low price was available to the purchaser and that it offered the lower price for that reason; the seller is not required to show that the difference resulted from subtraction rather than addition.

A different rule would not only be contrary to the language of the statute, but also might stifle the only kind of legitimate price competition reasonably available in particular industries. In a period of generally rising prices, vigorous price competition for a particular customer or customers may take the form of smaller price increases rather than price cuts. Thus, a price discrimination created by selective price increases can result from a good-faith effort to meet a competitor's low price.

Nor is the good faith with which the lower price is offered impugned if the prices raised, like those kept lower, respond to competitor's prices and are set with the goal of increasing the seller's profits. A seller need not choose between "ruinously cutting its prices to all its customers to match the price offered to one, [and] refusing to meet the competition and then ruinously raising its prices to its remaining customers to cover increased unit costs." *Standard Oil Co.*

v. *FTC*, 340 U. S., at 250. Nor need a seller choose between keeping all its prices ruinously low to meet the price offered to one, and ruinously raising its prices to all customers to a level significantly above that charged by its competitors. A seller is permitted "to retain a customer by realistically meeting in good faith the price offered to that customer, without necessarily changing the seller's price to its other customers." *Ibid.* The plain language of § 2(b) also permits a seller to retain a customer by realistically meeting in good faith the price offered to that customer, without necessarily freezing his price to his other customers.

Section 2(b) does not require a seller, meeting in good faith a competitor's lower price to certain customers, to forgo the profits that otherwise would be available in sales to its remaining customers. The very purpose of the defense is to permit a seller to treat different competitive situations differently. The prudent businessman responding fairly to what he believes in good faith is a situation of competitive necessity might well raise his prices to some customers to increase his profits, while meeting competitors' prices by keeping his prices to other customers low.

The Court in *Staley* said that the meeting-competition defense "presupposes that the person charged with violating the Act would, by his normal, non-discriminatory pricing methods, have reached a price so high that he could reduce it in order to meet the competitor's equally low price." 324 U. S., at 754. In that case, however, the Court was not dealing with a seller whose "normal, non-discriminatory pricing methods" called for a price increase but who wished to exempt certain customers from the increase in order to meet prices, lower than the increased price, available to those customers from competitors. Of course, a seller could accomplish the same result within the guidelines the Court of Appeals would impose by instituting across-the-board price increases followed by selective reductions. But far from being flexible and pragmatic, a rule requiring such costly behavior would be nonsensical.[11]

D

Vanco also contends that Falls City did not satisfy § 2(b) because its price discrimination "was not a *defensive* response to competition." Brief for Respondent 47 (emphasis supplied). According to Vanco, the Robinson-Patman Act permits price discrimination only

---

[11] "Section 2 (b) should not require proof that the seller departed from a previously uniform price schedule. Such *previous* pricing is not relevant to evaluation of genuine responses to a *current* competitive situation." Report of the Attorney General's National Committee to Study the Anti-trust Laws 182 (1955) (1955 Report) (emphasis in original).

if its purpose is to retain a customer. *Id.*, at 32–33. We agree that a seller's response must be defensive, in the sense that the lower price must be calculated and offered in good faith to "meet not beat" the competitor's low price. See *United States Gypsum Co.*, 438 U. S., at 454. Section 2(b), however, does not distinguish between one who meets a competitor's lower price to retain an old customer and one who meets a competitor's lower price in an attempt to gain new customers.[12] See Stevens, Defense of Meeting the Lower Price of a Competitor, in Summer Institute on International and Comparative Law, University of Michigan Law School, Lectures on Federal Antitrust Laws 129, 135–136 (1953). Such a distinction would be inconsistent with that section's language and logic, see *Sunshine Biscuits, Inc.* v. *FTC*, 306 F. 2d 48, 51–52 (CA7 1962), "would not be in keeping with elementary principles of competition, and would in fact foster tight and rigid commercial relationships by insulating them from market forces." 1955 Report, at 184; see 1977 Report, at 26, 265.[13]

IV

The Court of Appeals also relied on *Staley* for the proposition that the meeting-competition defense "places emphasis on individual [competitive] situations, rather than upon a general system of competition,'" 654 F. 2d, at 1230 (quoting *Staley*, 324 U. S., at 753), and "does not justify the maintenance of discriminatory pricing among classes of customers that results merely from the adoption of a competitor's discriminatory pricing structure," 654 F. 2d, at 1230. The Court of Appeals was apparently invoking the District Court's findings that Falls City set prices statewide rather than on a "customer to customer basis," and the District Court's conclusion that this practice disqualified Falls City from asserting the meeting-competition defense. 1980–2 Trade Cases, at 75,817. At least two

---

[12] At least three Courts of Appeals have held that the defense is not limited to attempts to retain customers. *Cadigan* v. *Texaco, Inc.*, 492 F. 2d, at 387, and n. 3; *Hanson* v. *Pittsburgh Plate Glass Industries, Inc.*, 482 F. 2d 220, 226–227 (CA 5 1973), cert. denied, 414 U.S. 1136 (1974); *Sunshine Biscuits, Inc.* v. *FTC*, 306 F. 2d 48, 51–52 (CA7 1962). But see *Standard Motor Products, Inc.* v. *FTC*, 265 F. 2d 674, 677 (CA2), cert. denied, 361 U. S. 826 (1959) (defense available only if lower price responds to individual competitive demand).

[13] *Standard Oil Co.* v. *FTC*, 340 U. S. 231 (1951), is not to the contrary. The Court there referred to the defense's being available to a seller seeking to "retain" customers, *id.*, at 242, 249, 250, simply because the petitioner had so framed its defense in that particular case. *Id.*, at 234, 236; see 1955 Report, at 184; Kuenzel & Schiffres, Making Sense of Robinson-Patman: The Need to Revitalize its Affirmative Defenses, 62 Va. L. Rev. 1211, 1253–1254 (1976).

other Courts of Appeals have read *Staley* to hold that the defense is unavailable to sellers pricing on other than a customer-by-customer basis, while two Courts of Appeals have held that a customer-by-customer response is not required.[14]

There is no evidence that Congress intended to limit the availability of § 2(b) to customer-specific responses. Section 2(b)'s predecessor, § 2 of the original Clayton Act, stated that "nothing herein contained shall prevent . . . discrimination in price in the same or different communities made in good faith to meet competition." 38 Stat. 730. The Judiciary Committee of the House of Representatives, which drafted the clause that became the current § 2(b), see *Standard Oil Co.* v. *FTC,* 340 U. S., at 247–248, n. 14, explained the new section's anticipated function: "It should be noted that while the seller is permitted to meet *local* competition [§ 2(b)] does not permit him to cut *local* prices until his competitor has first offered lower prices, and then he can go no further than to meet those prices." H. R. Rep. No. 2287, 74th Cong., 2d Sess., 16 (1936) (emphasis supplied). Congress intended to allow reasonable pricing responses on an area-specific basis where competitive circumstances warrant them. The purpose of the amendment was to "restric[t] the proviso to price differentials occurring in actual competition." *Standard Oil Co.* v. *FTC*, 340 U. S., at 242. We conclude that Congress did not intend to bar territorial price differences that are in fact responses to competitive conditions.

Section 2(b) specifically allows a "lower price . . . to any purchaser or purchasers" made in good faith to meet a competitor's equally low price. A single low price surely may be extended to numerous purchasers if the seller has a reasonable basis for believing that the competitor's lower price is available to them.[15] Beyond the requirement that the lower price be reasonably calculated to "meet not beat" the competition, Congress intended to leave it a "question of fact . . . whether the way in which the competition was met lies

---

[14] Compare *Exquisite Form Brassiere, Inc.* v. *FTC*, 123 U. S. App. D. C. 358, 359, 360 F. 2d 492, 493 (1965), cert. denied, 384 U. S. 959 (1966) (customer-by-customer response required), and *Standard Motor Products, Inc.* v. *FTC*, 265 F. 2d, at 677 (same), with *William Inglis & Sons Baking Co.* v. *ITT Continental Baking Co.,* 668 F. 2d 1014, 1046 (CA9 1981), cert. denied, 459 U. S. 825 (1982) (customer-by-customer response not necessarily required), *Callaway Mills Co.* v. *FTC*, 362 F. 2d 435, 442 (CA5 1966) (same), and *Balian Ice Cream Co.* v. *Arden Farms Co.,* 231 F. 2d 356, 366 (CA9 1955), cert. denied, 350 U. S. 991 (1956) (same).

[15] See also *Standard Oil Co.* v. *FTC*, 340 U. S., at 247, n. 13, quoting statement of Herbert A. Bergson, Assistant Attorney General, at Hearings on S. 236 before a Subcommittee of the Senate Committee on Interstate and Foreign Commerce, 81st Cong., 1st Sess., 77 (1949) ("'The section presently permits sellers to justify otherwise forbidden price discriminations on the ground that the lower prices to one set of buyers were made in good faith to meet the equally low prices of a competitor'").

within the latitude allowed." 80 Cong. Rec. 9418 (1936) (remarks of Rep. Utterback). Once again, this inquiry is guided by the standard of the prudent businessman responding fairly to what he reasonably believes are the competitive necessities.

A seller may have good reason to believe that a competitor or competitors are charging lower prices throughout a particular region. See *William Inglis & Sons Baking Co.* v. *ITT Continental Baking Co.,* 668 F. 2d 1014, 1046 (CA9 1981), cert. denied, 459 U. S. 825 (1982); *Balian Ice Cream Co.* v. *Arden Farms Co.,* 231 F. 2d 356, 366 (CA9 1955), cert. denied, 350 U. S. 991 (1956); Rowe, at 235–236. In such circumstances, customer-by-customer negotiations would be unlikely to result in prices different from those set according to information relating to competitors' territorial prices. A customer-by-customer pricing "would be burdensome, unreasonable, and competition unrealistically expensive for smaller firms such as Falls City, which was attempting to compete with larger national breweries in 13 separate States. Cf. *Callaway Mills Co.* v. *FTC,* 362 F. 2d 435, 442 (CA5 1966) (in some circumstances, requirement of customer-by-customer pricing "would be burdensome, unreasonable, and practically unfeasible").

In *Staley,* 324 U. S., at 753, as in each of the later cases in which this Court has contrasted a "general system of competition" with "individual competitive situations," see, *e. g., FTC* v. *National Lead Co.,* 352 U. S. 419, 431 (1957); *FTC* v. *Cement Institute,* 333 U. S. 683, 708 (1948), the seller's lower price was quoted not "*because* of lower prices by a competitor," but "*because* of a preconceived pricing scale which [was] operative regardless of variations in competitor's prices." Rowe, at 234 (emphasis in original). In those cases, the contested lower prices were not·truly "*responsive* to rivals' competitive prices," *ibid.* (emphasis in original), and therefore were not genuinely made to meet competitors' lower prices. Territorial pricing, however, can be a perfectly reasonable method—sometimes the most reasonable method—of responding to rivals' low prices.[16] We choose not to read into § 2(b) a restriction that would deny the meeting-competition defense to one whose areawide price is a well-tailored response to competitors' low prices.

---

[16] See Rowe, at 240 ("a seller's area-wide and blanket lower price, if made in good faith to meet competitors' lower prices, may be justified . . . as responsive to an "individual competitive situation'"). Cf. *Maryland Banking Co.* v. *FTC,* 243 F. 2d 716, 719 (CA4 1957) (FTC permits competitive area price variations to avert placing "prices in a straight-jacket throughout the country"); *Anheuser-Busch, Inc.,* 54 F. T. C. 277, 301 (1957) (suggesting that offer of lower price throughout particular area might be responsive to "individual competitive situation"); *C. E. Niehoff & Co.,* 51 F. T. C. 1114, 1130, 1146 (1955) (rejecting position that "showing that the seller's discriminations were temporary and localized in area is an indispensable prerequisite" to defense).

Of course, a seller must limit its lower price to that group of customers reasonably believed to have the lower price available to it from competitors. A response that is not reasonably tailored to the competitive situation as known to the seller, or one that is based on inadequate verification, would not meet the standard of good faith. Similarly, the response may continue only as long as the competitive circumstances justifying it, as reasonably known by the seller, persist.[17] One choosing to price on a territorial basis, rather than on a customer-by-customer basis, must show that this decision was a genuine, reasonable response to prevailing competitive circumstances. See *International Air Industries, Inc.* v. *American Excelsior Co.*, 517 F. 2d 714, 725–726 (CA5 1975), cert. denied, 424 U. S. 943 (1976); *Callaway Mills Co.* v. *FTC*, 362 F. 2d, at 441–442. See generally 1977 Report, at 265. Unless the circumstances call into question the seller's good faith, this burden will be discharged by showing that a reasonable and prudent businessman would believe that the lower price he charged was generally available from his competitors throughout the territory and throughout the period in which he made the lower price available. See *William Inglis & Sons Baking Co.* v. *ITT Continental Baking Co.*, 668 F. 2d, at 1045–1046.

V

In summary, the meeting-competition defense requires the seller at least to show the existence of facts that would lead a reasonable and prudent person to believe that the seller's lower price would meet the equally low price of a competitor; it also requires the seller to demonstrate that its lower price was a good-faith response to a competitor's lower price.

Falls City contends that it has established its meeting-competition defense as a matter of law. In the absence of further findings, we do not agree. The District Court and the Court of Appeals did not decide whether Falls City had shown facts that would have led a reasonable and prudent person to conclude that its lower price would meet the equally low price of its competitors in Kentucky throughout the period at issue in this suit. Nor did they apply the proper standards to the question whether Falls City's decision to set a single statewide price in Kentucky was a good-faith, well-tailored response to the competitive circumstances prevailing there. The absence of allegations to the contrary is not controlling; the statute places the burden of establishing the defense on Falls City, not Vanco. There

[17] See Klein, Meeting Competition by Price Systems Under § 2(b) of the Robinson-Patman Act: Problems and Prospects, 16 Antitrust Bull. 213, 233–234, 238 (1971); Kuenzel & Schiffres, 62 Va. L. Rev., at 1244–1249.

is evidence in the record that might support an inference that these requirements were met,[18] but whether to draw that inference is a question for the trier of fact, not this Court.

Accordingly, the judgment of the Court of Appeals is vacated, and the case is remanded for further proceedings consistent with this opinion.

It is so ordered.

---

[18] Were the courts below to find that Falls City reasonably believed that low prices were available to Dawson Springs and other Kentucky wholesalers from Falls City's competitors, a factfinding that we decline to address on this record, Falls City could not easily have eliminated price discrimination between Dawson Springs and Vanco. In such circumstances, had Falls City raised prices in Kentucky in lockstep with price increases in Indiana, it would have lost sales in Kentucky because its competitors would have been offering far lower prices. Raising its Kentucky prices only in Henderson County would not only have cost Falls City sales there, but also might have exposed Falls City to new Robinson-Patman Act claims, since Dawson Springs competed for sales with wholesalers in neighboring Kentucky Counties. Nor, in such circumstances, could Falls City reasonably be required to charge Vanco the lower Kentucky price. Indiana law prohibited Falls City from doing so without simultaneously offering the same price to all other Indiana wholesalers. This approach might well have harmed Falls City's economic interests, since most of Falls City's Indiana sales were in areas far removed from lower Kentucky prices and competition.

14

SOCIAL
RESPONSIBILITY

NATIONAL PEACH COUNCIL

Among the several pesticides used on agricultural crops was dibromo-chloropropane, usually termed DBCP. This chemical was widely used on fruit trees, cotton, and soybeans to combat wormlike nematodes and some other pests that imperil these crops. A total of about thirty million pounds of this pesticide was produced and marketed annually by several companies. The three main suppliers were Dow Chemical Company, Shell Oil Company, and Occidental Chemical Company. Dow sold this product under the trade name Fumazone, Shell under the trade name Nemagon Soil Fumigant, and Occidental under the trade names Green Light, Garden Fume, and CHA-KEM-CO.

Evidence of the effect of DBCP on people working closely with it came to light in at least three locations in August. In Dow Chemical Company's DBCP plant at Magnolia, Arkansas, there was evidence of sterility in twelve male workers, whereas in Shell's installations in Denver and Mobile, sixteen of twenty-one male workers tested after exposure to the chemical showed abnormally low sperm counts. The Oil, Chemical, and Atomic Workers Union filed complaints with the government, especially the Occupational Safety and Health Administration (OSHA), a unit of the Department of Labor, and the Environmental Protection Agency. These agencies imposed emergency restrictions on the handling of the substance and began studying the imposition of permanent restrictions or a banning of the product. The manufacturers of the product voluntarily halted its production.

Following the reaction of OSHA to the DBCP health threat, the executive secretary of the National Peach Council, Robert K. Phillips, sent the letter reproduced as Exhibit 1 and dated September 12

EXHIBIT 1 Letter from National Peach Council to OSHA

National Peach Council

Dr. Eula Bingham
Assistant Secretary for Occupational
   Safety and Health
U.S. Department of Labor
Washington, D.C. 20210

Recently we received the interesting DOL news release concerning worker exposure to DBCP.

It appears to us that you and Secretary Marshall may have overreacted, or at least that is your public posture.

While involuntary sterility caused by a manufactured chemical may be bad, it is not necessarily so. After all, there are many people who are now paying to have themselves sterilized to assure they will no longer be able to become parents.

How many of the workers who have become sterile were of an age that they would have been likely to have children anyway? How many were past the age when they would want to have children? These, too, are important questions.

If possible sterility is the main problem, couldn't workers who were old enough that they no longer wanted to have children accept such positions voluntarily? They would know the situation, and it wouldn't matter. Or could workers be advised of the situation, and some might volunteer for such work posts as an alternative to planned surgery for a vasectomy or tubal ligation, or as a means of getting around religious bans on birth control when they want no more children.

We do believe in safety in the work place, Dr. Bingham, but there can be good as well as bad sides to a situation.

Above all, please don't try to get a ban on the manufacture and sale of the chemical DBCP, because that would cause some losses of agricultural production which would be serious.

Sincerely,

Robert K. Phillips
Executive Secretary

---

to Dr. Eula Bingham, assistant secretary of labor for Occupational Safety and Health. A few days later the National Cancer Institute, a federal agency, released the results of a research project in which it was shown that large doses of DBCP caused cancer in laboratory rats and mice. Phillips did not have advance knowledge of these research results. According to Phillips, someone employed by OSHA gave a copy of his September 12 letter to a *New York Times* reporter on September 26. That newspaper and the news wire services carried portions of the letter on September 27.

There followed considerable news coverage about the product, the manufacturers, the workers, and the proposal from the National Peach Council. Phillips stated that the suggestion was made in good faith and with sincerity. He noted further that people might think he was speaking tongue in cheek but he definitely was not. Phillips stated to the press "All these government agencies overdo everything. I know they carry things to extremes. They should at least consider alternatives to banning this material." He added that "After all, people take some kind of chance every day."

In mid-November Phillips made the following statement:

> It is . . . only in the last few years that peach producers, and many others in agriculture have come to the somewhat belated realization that Congress can and will pass laws which allow Federal *bureaucrats* powers which would have been undreamed of only a few years ago.
>
> The situation which has developed in Washington requires more checking and more direct contact than ever before, and it seems the situation will build more in that direction.
>
> That is just one of the reasons that National Peach Council, as an organization which speaks only for the nation's peach industry, is so important to each and every peach grower.

Eula Bingham replied to Phillips on November 21, ten weeks after Phillips had written her. Her letter arrived on November 25 and is reproduced as Exhibit 2.

On December 13 Phillips added the following:

> It [Bingham's letter] is a nice enough letter, but does not in my opinion serve as an answer to the letter I wrote to her on September 12.
>
> Dr. Bingham certainly deserves praise for the recent moves to wipe out a large number of trivial job-safety standards and loosen enforcement standards. At least there is progress in that direction.

The National Peach Council

The National Peach Council was an agricultural federation representing the interests of growers of fresh market peaches throughout the United States. Established in 1942, it was the only peach farmers trade association of national scope in the United States, and had 6,300 members and associate members. The latter were manufacturers of equipment and supplies needed by this industry, sales agencies, and other interested firms. Production and per capita consumption of fresh peaches had exhibited small decreases for several years.

EXHIBIT 2 Letter from OSHA to National Peach Council

Office of the Assistant Secretary

Mr. Robert K. Phillips
Executive Secretary
National Peach Council
Post Office Box 1085
Martinsburg, West Virginia 25401

Dear Mr. Phillips:

In response to your letter of September 12 regarding the sterilization of workers, I can think of no situation where the material impairment of an employee's health or reproductive capacity as a result of exposure to a toxic substance could be regarded as beneficial. The right to have children is a fundamental human right entitled to serious protection under the Occupational Safety and Health Act of 1970. There is no comparison between involuntary sterilization resulting from exposure to a chemical in the workplace and voluntary sterilization achieved by a medical procedure. Voluntary sterilization involves a conscious, deliberate choice by a man or woman to end one's reproductive capability. It also involves medical supervision in order to control any other adverse health consequences. Moreover, the reproductive period varies between men and women and between individuals. Therefore, it would be inappropriate for an employer or the government to make any general assumptions regarding the end of an individual employee's reproductive capability. Instead, the Occupational Safety and Health Administration (OSHA) must set standards which assure that no employee will suffer material impairment of health or functional capacity during the entire lifetime.

Sterility is only one hazard of exposure of 1,2-Dibromo-3-Chloropropane ("DBCP"). Degenerative changes occur in several organs of the body, and there is also a cancer hazard. OSHA intends to treat DBCP as a carcinogen because well-designed studies have demonstrated the carcinogenicity of DBCP in both sexes of two mammalian species at multiple dose levels. Therefore, the Agency's decision to issue an emergency temporary standard is based not only on the sterilant effects of DBCP but also on other serious health effects, including the carcinogenicity of DBCP.

In light of the serious health effects from worker exposure to DBCP, I believe that the issuance of an emergency temporary standard was necessary and appropriate to protect employees from this grave danger.

Please be assured that your letter has been included in the official record of the permanent standard for DBCP.

Sincerely,

Eula Bingham
Assistant Secretary
Occupational Safety and Health

The council had various activities. For example, it published a monthly newspaper and employed a professional home economist to assist in its educational public relations efforts to increase the use of fresh peaches. The Council also held a large national convention lasting four days once a year at which there were speeches, panels, and technical papers on horticulture and the economics of the industry. The latest convention, held in San Antonio, included sessions on peach tree disease control, nursery certification, use of computers and aerial photography in orchard management, chemical and mechanical thinning of fruit, evaporative cooling to delay blooming, herbicides in orchard floor management, peach varieties by production area, peaches and competitive fruits around the world, and wholesale and retail marketing. Another activity of the Council was the preparation and dissemination of news releases and direct contact with the United States Department of Agriculture. For example, many growers found that their peaches were not selling one mid-August. When these growers notified the National Peach Council, that organization Mailgrammed factual but promotional information to the major networks. The organization also contacted the Plentiful Foods section at the Department of Agriculture, which prepared a radio news release and got it out immediately rather than using the regular release system, which would have required seven to ten days.

One recent interesting activity of the National Peach Council was participation in the planning of proposed enabling legislation known as the Freestone Peach Research and Education Act. This proposed statute called for a plan of action and a nongovernmental board to oversee the resulting program of research and promotional education. Research would be on all phases of the production and marketing of freestone peaches. The promotional education would consist of preparation and dissemination of materials to households, institutional food buyers, restaurant chains, teachers, and others. Costs would be met by assessments on fresh peaches marketed. Rates of half a cent per bushel to several cents per bushel were being considered. Under the proposed enabling legislation the plan of action would have to go to a referendum among freestone peach farmers. The federal government would only monitor that the resulting work adhered to the statutes and the guidelines established by the plan of action that had been approved by a vote of the growers.

Occupational Safety and Health Administration

The Occupational Safety and Health Administration was a relatively new agency, but had quickly established itself as an activist group. It was considered unreasonable, arbitrary, capricious, and indifferent to cost by much of the business community. A survey of

Congressmen's opinions of OSHA conducted by the White House revealed several criticisms, including harassment of business organizations, too many forms, and unnecessary paper work. Even liberal Senator George McGovern (Democrat, South Dakota) attacked OSHA for "overregulation of small business [and] nitpicking enforcement."

Advise the National Peach Council.

FIRENZE GROCERY STORES[1]

Anthony Firenze opened a grocery store near Rhode Island Avenue in northeast Washington, D.C., in the late 1940s. The neighborhood could be characterized as middle-middle class. Firenze prospered and in the late 1950s opened a second store in northwest Washington in an affluent area west of Rock Creek Park.

Both stores were in areas of high-density population. Although the areas were zoned for land use, there were within easy walking distance single-family homes, duplexes, small apartment buildings, and large apartment buildings. Each store was located on a bus route and each was to be within walking distance of new subway stations then under construction. About 45 per cent of the households in the trade territory of the northeast store owned an automobile.

Firenze had paid off the mortgage on the northeast building and had only one more year of mortgage payments on the northwest building. Both buildings were well constructed and in good condi-

[1] Some publications that would assist in dealing with the problems of this case include the following: Donald E. Sexton, Jr., "Comparing the Cost of Food to Blacks and to Whites," *Journal of Marketing*, 35 (July 1971), pp. 40–46; Lola M. Ireland, Ed., *Low Income Life Styles* (Washington, D.C.: Department of Health, Education, and Welfare, 1966); Joseph B. Mason and Charles S. Madden, "Food Purchases in a Low-Income Negro Neighborhood: The Development of a Socio-Economic Behavorial Profile as Related to Movement and Patronage Patterns," in Fred C. Allvine, Ed., *Combined Proceedings of 1971 Conferences* (Chicago: American Marketing Association, 1971), pp. 634–639; Leonard Berry and Paul Solomon, "Generalizing About Low-Income Food Shoppers: A Word of Caution," *Journal of Retailing*, 47 (Summer 1971), pp. 41–51, 92; Leonard Berry, "The Low-Income Marketing System: An Overview," *Journal of Retailing*, 48 (Summer 1972), pp. 44–63, 90; Lawrence Feldman and Alvin Star, "Racial Factors in Shopping Behavior," in Keith Cox and Ben Enis, Eds., *A New Measure of Responsibility for Marketing* (Chicago: American Marketing Association, 1968); Arieh Goldman, "Do Lower Income Consumers Have a More Restricted Shopping Scope?" *Journal of Marketing*, 40 (Jan. 1976), pp.46–54; Gerald Hills, Donald Granbois, and James M. Patterson "Black Consumer Perceptions of Food Store Attributes," *Journal of Marketing*, 37 (April 1973), pp. 47–57; Hiram Barksdale and Warren French, "Response to Consumerism: How Change is Perceived by Both Sides," *MSU Business Topics*, 23 (Spring 1975), pp. 55–67.

tion. Each had been set up on a twenty-year life basis for purposes of depreciation accounting. Most of the northeast store's patronage came from a radius of about six blocks, whereas that of the northwest store was a little more spread out.

The census tract in which the northeast store was opened had been 100 per cent white in 1940 and 98 per cent white in 1950. During the 1950s it was obvious to Firenze that many blacks were moving into the neighborhood. This trend was a cause for temporary anxiety on the part of Firenze and other businessmen in the area, but they immediately discerned that the blacks moving in were almost all middle-class federal government employees. The transition for residents, both black and white, was not easy but was accomplished with no violence and little overt rancor. The 1960 census showed that the tract was 52 per cent white, but by 1970 this figure had declined to about 10 per cent. A similar trend had occurred in adjoining areas of the city. One adjoining tract was only 5 per cent white. Anthony Firenze observed that most of the whites in the vicinity appeared to be in their late fifties or older, and that many of them were retired.

An additional trend had taken place. Some of the middle-class blacks had moved out and had been replaced by lower-middle-class and lower-class blacks. This trend was beyond Firenze's ability to measure, but he suspected that about 60 to 70 per cent of the original blacks had moved on to more expensive neighborhoods in the city or into the suburbs. In addition, the physical condition of most rental housing units in the vicinity showed considerable deterioration. Apparently the landlords were not performing maintenance adequately or at least not up to the level of past years. Several commercial buildings were not being maintained well, but the commercial structures were not deteriorating as rapidly as were the residential buildings. Two small businessmen had relocated out of the neighborhood because of vandalism.

The number of grocery stores in the city belonging to corporate chains had declined from 91 to 42 over the past ten years. For example, A&P, the nation's sixth largest chain, had six stores then but had only one now. Grand Union, which operated throughout most of the northeastern United States, closed all of its District of Columbia locations. In the city's northeast quadrant the number of chain supermarkets declined from 23 to 9 over the ten-year period. The corresponding figures in the other quadrants were as follows: northwest, 54 to 22; southwest, one to two; southeast, 13 to 8.

Firenze was perplexed by the disappointing net profits of his northeast store for the past two years. This was rather galling to him for several reasons. First, it was his first store and he was sentimentally attached to it. Second, he gave this store just as much attention as he

EXHIBIT 1 Operating Statements for Firenze Stores, Most Recent Year

	Northeast Store	Northwest Store
Net sales	$700,000	$730,000
Cost of goods sold	595,000	606,630
Gross profit on sales	$105,000	$123,370
Expenses		
Property taxes	5,300	5,600
Advertising	7,300	7,600
Wages	49,900	48,900
Inventory shrinkage	8,770	7,010
Electricity, heat, water, trash		
removal, telephone, etc.	4,200	4,220
Salary to Anthony Firenze	10,000	10,000
Insurance	1,200	800
Depreciation on building	0	3,600
Depreciation on fixtures	950	975
Mortgage interest expense	0	2,705
Office expenses	1,950	1,650
	$ 89,570	$ 93,060
Net profit before income taxes	$ 15,430	$ 30,310

gave the northwest location. Third, with a sales volume of $700,000, the northeast store did about as much business as the $730,000 of the northwest store. The operating statements for the fiscal year just completed are presented as Exhibit 1.

From time to time Firenze did some comparison shopping, principally to gain perspective on prices but also to gain other merchandising ideas. In his most recent comparisons he found a long-standing situation to be continuing. His prices were slightly higher than the four chain stores located within a one-mile radius. On the average

EXHIBIT 2 Population and Age in District of Columbia

	1980	1970	1960	1950
White	171,768	209,272	345,263	517,865
Negro and all other races	466,565	547,238	418,693	284,313
	638,333	756,510	763,956	802,178
Median age for whites	N/A	41.0	40.0	34.4
Median age for Negro				
and all other races	N/A	25.1	27.1	29.6

Source: 1980 Census of Population.

EXHIBIT 3 Population in District of Columbia, 1980, by Quadrant

Quadrant	Total	White	Negro	Other	Median Age
Northeast	150,738	14,573	134,635	1,530	31.2
Northwest	301,032	132,462	154,768	13,802	33.7
Southeast	159,923	14,972	143,610	1,341	26.9
Southwest	26,640	9,761	15,833	986	28.8
Total	638,333	171,768	448,906	17,659	31.1

Source: 1980 Census of Population.

his prices were 3½ per cent higher than in those stores. For his price comparison he utilized a "shopping basket" of thirty specified items, a measurement popularized by some officials in the federal government and several consumer groups. Using the same technique Firenze had determined that his prices were about 4 per cent below other owner-managed grocery stores within a one-mile radius in the northeast. None of these chain or independent stores, including Firenze, offered home delivery or charge accounts. The prices in Firenze's northeast store were identical to those in his northwest store. Because his profits in the northeast were lower than in the northwest, Firenze was seriously considering charging more in his northeast store than in the northwest store for identical items.

Advise Anthony Firenze.

15

PLANNING
AND
FORECASTING

IMPERIAL LAWNS, INC.

Imperial Lawns, Inc., was established slightly over nine years ago in the northern suburbs of a large city. The founders and present owners were Stephen Nolan and George Pleshette, both age 23 at the time and just out of college. The first two years were extremely difficult for the owners as they got the firm going and looked for customers. Sales figures are given in Exhibit 1. Both men graduated from the agricultural college of the state university, Nolan majoring in agronomy, and Pleshette in horticulture, with strong supporting study in chemistry and biology. Agronomy is the agricultural science that studies relationships between soils and plant life and seeks improved methods of soils management and crop production.

The lawn care industry in the United States was a rather recent phenomenon but was estimated now to be a $1.5 billion per year business. This type of service, often called turf management, typically was provided by small firms. Approximately 5,000 companies averaged about $300,000 in sales per year. There was one large firm in the industry, Chem-Lawn, based in Ohio, which was estimated to do about $98 million in sales annually. Nationally, about 6.1 per cent of households in single-family, detached houses used a lawn care service. A typical company always fertilized the lawn and treated it for weeds and, if necessary, debugged it and reseeded it. Imperial Lawns, Inc., like most other companies, did not provide mowing.

The chemicals applied were either in pellet or liquid form in this

EXHIBIT 1 Price, Customer, and Sales Data, Imperial Lawns, Inc.

	Nine-Month Service				Winter Service				Total	
Year	Price	No. of Customers	Sales	% Change	Price	No. of Customers	Sales	% Change	Sales	% Change
Latest Year	$240	2,067	$496,080	11.9	$80	201	$16,080	94.9	$512,160	13.4
Two years ago	220	2,015	443,300	11.2	73	113	8,249	92.3	451,549	12.1
Three years ago	198	2,013	398,574	11.3	66	65	4,290	110.3	402,864	11.8
Four years ago	180	1,990	358,200	16.5	60	34	2,040	—	360,240	18.4
Five years ago	160	1,921	307,360	34.8	—	—	—	—	307,360	34.8
Six years ago	152	1,500	228,000	39.8	—	—	—	—	228,000	39.8
Seven years ago	145	1,125	163,125	69.1	—	—	—	—	163,125	69.1
Eight years ago	137	704	96,448	24.6	—	—	—	—	96,448	24.6
Nine years ago	131	591	77,421	—	—	—	—	—	77,421	—

industry. Imperial used the liquid form, which the company considered safer for the customer and his pets. In addition, the liquid form worked faster in helping the lawn.

In some ways lawn care was a luxury service. Some people considered it extravagant. Any homeowner who would order and read government-issued pamphlets and/or contact his local Agricultural Extension Service advisor and would read and follow the instructions on lawn care products available in countless stores could provide the service for himself. However, some customers disliked yard work, some had allergies, and some had too little time to learn about or look after their own lawns. An advertising theme that Imperial used often was "Imperial works while you play." Interestingly enough, some people who enjoyed gardening and had a knowledge of lawns nevertheless used a lawn service. The reason many gave was that lawn care was not as creative and satisfying as the care of flowers, shrubbery, and trees. Most real estate people believed that an attractive lawn added to the market value of a house, and the figure usually given by such persons was 2 to 3 per cent.

The most persuasive argument for a lawn service and the one used the most in primary promotion was that in the pricing of lawn fertilizers, herbicides, fungicides, and insecticides, there was a large quantity discount. Small sales were priced much higher per pound than were bulk sales. In addition, of course, lawn care organizations bought at wholesale rather than retail prices. The net effect was that the chemical supplies alone for an individual consumer for a nine-month period would probably cost him approximately $120 for an average-size lawn. The incremental cost to buy the lawn service from Imperial was thus about $120.

For this $120 increment the homeowner's lawn received the right things in the right quantities at the right times and the homeowner was relieved of the shopping, labor, scheduling, and the necessity of owning a spreader, which came in varying weights and qualities but averaged about $50 at retail. Virtually no homeowners applied these chemicals in liquid form, because they were wet, messy, usually malodorous, and best applied with a sprayer under pressure. Imperial used a large pressurized sprayer with a long hose attached to the truck.

Fertilizers needed to be selected to suit the types of grass and soils. Herbicides, which were chemicals designed to kill or discourage weeds and undesirable types of grasses, had to be measured properly or harm might come to the lawn. In addition, they had to be applied at just the right time or they would have little effect, and allowances had to be made for how sunny or shady the various parts of the yard were.

About half of the northern, northwestern, northeastern, and eastern suburban population was in Cabot County, which Nolan and Pleshette considered their trade territory. Both lived in Cabot County, which had a population of 497,200, according to the professional planners and statisticians in the county government. Their annual estimates of economic and demographic data for the county tended to be of high quality. For example, virtually all these planners' relevant estimates for December 31, 1979 were proved true in the April 1980 national census of population and housing.

Cabot County's population and that of the entire metropolitan area were rising but more slowly than the national average. The annual population growth rates for the nation, the metropolitan area, and the county were approximately 0.9, 0.7, and 0.8 per cent, respectively. Such rates were expected to continue until the late 1980s, after which the national rate would probably decline. It appeared likely that the rates for the metropolitan area and the Cabot County portion of the metropolitan area would stay almost constant. Average household income was about 20 per cent higher in Cabot County than for the city and the remainder of the suburbs. The county had about 167,000 dwelling units, of which about 110,300 were detached single-family houses and about 7,000 were townhouses. Nolan and Pleshette aimed at the people in the detached single-family houses. They had noticed in the last two or three years that most of the newly constructed houses were on slightly smaller lots. The typical Cabot County lot contained 11,000 square feet.

Nolan and Pleshette estimated that about 5,750 households in the county subscribed to a lawn care service at an average nine-month price of about $240. They also estimated that about 580 households in the county subscribed to winter service at an average of $80. These were also the prices charged by Imperial.

Nolan and Pleshette's organization was the oldest and largest in the lawn care business in Cabot County and enjoyed a good reputation. Two companies preceded Imperial but failed many years ago. Sales of Imperial Lawns, Inc., in the most recent year were $512,160, of which $16,080 came from sales of winter service to 201 families. Of these 201, all but three also took the nine-month service. Imperial's winter lawn care service was begun four years ago and was furnished during the annual downtime for this industry, December through February.

Five other such companies operating in Cabot County each did a smaller sales volume in the county than did Imperial. However, two of these five were larger than Imperial in that they operated also in the city and/or the other suburban counties. One was Chem-Lawn. All five competitors started providing winter service in Cabot County the same year as Imperial. The national figure for use of winter lawn service was estimated to be about 1.5 per cent.

The scientific rationale for the winter service was that the root system of the lawn could grow and gain strength when the top was dormant. When mild weather returned, the lawn would be healthier and more beautiful. The following message was used by Imperial in its advertising of the winter service:

> Heavy nitrogen fertilization of grasses during the winter months will promote a stronger root system. The root system is vital to turfgrass development because it is responsible for nutrient and water uptake and also anchors plants in the soil. Development of the root system depends on cooler soil temperatures. Therefore it is important to have a readily available supply of nitrogen in the soil during periods of cool soil temperatures to enhance this growth.

Mainly because of the climate and the natural soil conditions, fine lawns were harder to develop and maintain in this metropolitan area than in most others. Moreover, many people unknowingly abused their lawns by poor watering practices. They watered too lightly, too often, erratically, or at night, all of which were bad. Also some people mowed their grass too short or let it grow tall and then cut it short, sending the grass into shock.

The nine-month service consisted of five lawn treatments, not spaced quite evenly for unavoidable scientific reasons. The winter service consisted of one treatment, but it required about one-fourth longer to perform than did the treatments during the nine-month period. After each treatment the Imperial representative left a short prepared note explaining what he had done on that visit. He added a comment if he thought the height of the grass was inappropriate to its health, or if the chemical just applied needed water or the avoidance of water for a certain time period.

The average time required for a treatment during the nine-month period was twenty-six minutes. When one took into account the driving time between the houses, one person and his truck could cover fifteen accounts in a typical eight-hour workday during the nine-month period. Imperial owned four route trucks, all modern and in excellent condition. For customers who had outdoor dogs and/or fences with gates that were kept locked, it was necessary for the driver to telephone ahead and make arrangements.

Advise Imperial Lawns, Inc.

WALKER FURNITURE

Wayne and Lorna Walker owned and operated a store dealing in furniture and small appliances in the inner city of a large metropolitan area. They were black, as was the great majority of the population within a radius of several miles of their store. There was a sizable Hispanic neighborhood fairly near.

This establishment did not look large, but it was about the average size for furniture stores in the United States. It provided an income that the owners found satisfactory and met their drive for independence. However, they wanted to build their business and were looking to the future. They had in mind two routes for growth. One was to keep offering the present range of merchandise with no shift in relative emphasis within the line. Better personal selling and friendly service would be stressed. The other route for growth was to give additional emphasis to a product category that was already handled but that was uncommon for this type of store, wood-burning stoves. This type of merchandise appeared to have an interesting future.

Stoves had originally been stocked because some customers and potential customers who moved to this metropolitan area had rural Southern backgrounds, were quite familiar with the product, and liked it. Others saw this product as a necessity to supplement the heating systems that were too small in capacity, inefficient, or undependable in older city homes. Sometimes the purpose was to heat an extra room that was added or a newly finished basement or attic. A few customers were interested in an authentic-looking wood-burning stove to complement Early American family room or den furniture.

The stoves stocked by Walker's came in plain utilitarian models, historical reproductions, and Scandinavian-style decorator models. Stove manufacturers in recent years had made utilitarian stoves more compact. Some were as small as twelve inches wide by nineteen inches long and twenty inches tall, exclusive of legs. Many utilitarian stoves were made in the United States but some came from Scandinavia. In recent years, four Scandinavian stove producers, Jotul, Lange, Trolla, and Morsa, had substantially increased their exports to the United States. Their products included utilitarian and decorator models. Stoves were extremely popular for heating homes in the Scandinavian countries, as well as in several other European countries. In the United States, reproductions were made of several period stoves, including Victorian and Early American, such as the famous Franklin stove.

Scandinavian-style decorator stoves were available either with or without a frontal opening for viewing the fire. Those stoves with the view thus constituted combination fireplace-stoves and offered an aesthetic advantage, for fireplaces seemed to create an intimate focal point in a room. The image of flames and flickering light was emotionally as well as physically warm. However, stoves with the view of the fire cost more. These decorator stoves came in a range of colors, usually orange, red, yellow, gold, or black, and were finished in enamel or enameled porcelain. Such stoves were conical, barrel shaped, and trapezoidal in shape. The stoves were particularly favored by customers who enjoyed modernistic decor. Many of the Scandinavian-style decorator stoves were now made in other countries as well, including the United States. Of late, several large chains, including J. C. Penney, Montgomery Ward, and Sears, Roebuck had added these stoves to their lines but at much lower prices than what had been prevalent previously.

Because their working capital and floor space were both limited, in a store whose merchandise was bulky, the Walkers carried only nine to twelves stoves at a time. In addition, they had to be conscious of inventory turnover in all departments, and they tried to keep inventory turnover high. This frequently meant that they did not have in stock the model of stove that a customer wanted. Thus, some of the stove sales consisted of orders that were delivered to customers several weeks later. The Walkers observed with great interest that in January and February of the three most recent years they sold out of stoves, despite raising the planned stock level appreciably each year. Sales of stoves had reached the point that they were bringing in about 7 per cent of overall sales. Store sales are presented in Exhibit 1 and sales of stoves, in units and dollars, are presented in Exhibit 2. All stoves in stock were displayed.

The Walkers estimated that during the period when they were out of stoves in the most recent year about forty-eight to fifty shopping parties inquired about stoves. One sale was made to these shoppers for later delivery. The firm's experience had been that about one third of the people who discussed stoves with the store personnel purchased a stove from Walker's. The store owners estimated that out-of-stock conditions had caused no significant amount of lost stove sales except in the most recent year. Stoves occupied a selling area measuring fifteen by twenty and a half feet.

One store in the metropolitan area, Rosansky's, sold nothing but stoves. It was widely known in the mercantile community that this firm sold more than 1,500 stoves per year. Another company with

EXHIBIT 1 Walker Furniture Store Sales

Most recent year	$300,004
Two years ago	272,950
Three years ago	250,215
Four years ago	230,203
Five years ago	209,501
Six years ago	196,968

EXHIBIT 2 Sales of Stoves, Walker Furniture Company

	Utilitarian Models		Reproduction Models		Scandinavian Style Decorator Stoves	
	Units	$ Sales	Units	$ Sales	Units	$ Sales
Latest year	10	2,507	20	4,905	17	14,260
Two years ago	6	1,498	13	3,121	13	10,901
Three years ago	5	1,124	7	1,575	8	6,322
Four years ago	5	1,050	6	1,264	5	3,704
Five years ago	4	798	5	1,020	5	3,518
Six years ago	3	567	4	781	1	695

two locations specialized in stoves and fireplace equipment and appeared to be doing extremely well.

The Walkers had given some thought to expanding the space that was devoted to the display of stoves. Of course, it was possible to rearrange floor space and give the stoves a more prominent location without giving them more space. They also considered converting a small adjacent storage area measuring about twelve by eighteen feet to expansion of the stove department. It would be inconvenient to sacrifice this storage area but the firm had enough storage space in a warehouse building not far away. The total selling area of the store was currently about 4,500 square feet.

Financial institutions were more willing than ever to make loans in the inner city for people to buy houses and to improve the houses they already owned. Several large churches in the inner city had become involved in housing in recent years through loans from the federal government. Operating on a nonprofit basis, the churches built a number of houses, but primarily they rehabilitated old houses. Architects had determined that 60 to 75 per cent of the housing stock of the inner city was structurally quite good. Expenditures for new plumbing, new electrical wiring, new or improved heating, and insulation and storm windows, plus decorating touches, would put them in very good condition. The former practice of indiscriminately tearing down large numbers of buildings seemed to be ending. Lately there was a strong feeling that urban renewal probably should preserve communities to the extent possible. In the Walkers' area, a federally sponsored program was making twenty to thirty abandoned houses a year available to inner city homesteaders for the nominal price of $1. Local families were chosen by lot and had to commit themselves to renovate the house and live in it a minimum of five years. Both white and black families were participating enthusiastically in this program.

EXHIBIT 3 Cost of Fuels per Million BTUs

Fuel Type	Cost per Million BTUs
Natural gas	$ 3.05
Fuel oil	4.80
Electricity	
Without heat pump	8.00
With heat pump	5.60
Wood	
Stove	3.90
Fireplace	22.00

Source: Energy Research and Development Administration.

Exhibit 3 presents the approximate cost per million BTUs[1] for natural gas, fuel oil, electricity, and wood in the Walkers' metropolitan area; these figures were very near the national average. A heat pump made electric heating much cheaper, but it was still more costly than gas or fuel oil. The data indicated that a fireplace was quite inefficient. Coal is not included in the exhibit because almost everyone objected to the labor, dust, and odor involved in using this fuel. Many wood-burning stoves would, however, also burn coal if desired. The prices of natural gas, fuel oil, and electricity were expected to rise more rapidly than the overall Consumer Price Index, but the price of wood was expected to rise in line with the CPI. The CPI had been rising from 5 to 8 per cent each year and was expected to rise at a rate of 4 to 6 per cent in the next one or two years.

Experts in forestry management indicated that a sizable fraction of United States homes could be shifted to the use of wood for heat without interfering with other current uses of wood and without harvesting more than the annual forest growth, thus assuring no net resource depletion. Proven reserves of natural gas were quite low. It was difficult to get a new building connected to a natural gas distribution system in some parts of the United States, including the area where the Walkers lived.

Advise Walker Furniture.

[1] BTU = British Thermal Unit, a standard measure of heat generated.

16

MARKETING
PROGRAMS
(OVERVIEW)

MACK TRUCKS, INC.

Mack Trucks, Inc., one of the world's most respected names in truck manufacturing, was facing several problems of varying severity. The picture of the Mack bulldog, wearing the collar with the word "Mack" on it and carrying the promotional themes of toughness and "bulldog protection," was one of the best-known trade symbols in the commercial art field. A statue of the dog, over twenty feet tall, stood in front of headquarters. Moreover, the expression "built like a Mack truck" had taken its place in American colloquial English.

The truck-building industry was not generally considered a growth industry. In fact, Mack executives characterized it as "mature" and felt that the long-run growth of any company in this industry had to come at the expense of the competitors.

This organization, employing 12,193 people, maintained headquarters in Allentown, Pennsylvania; truck assembly plants in Allentown, nearby Macungie, Pennsylvania, Oakville, Ontario, and Brisbane, Australia; and a power-train plant in Hagerstown, Maryland. A plant in Hayward, California was eliminated in 1983. The company operated an engineering development and test laboratory at Hagerstown, Maryland, on a site that included a three-quarter mile, banked, oval test track on 62 acres, leading to a 1,100 feet long skid path with 13 lanes and three different road surfaces. This site included space for off-road testing also. Mack operated parts distribution centers in Baltimore, Atlanta, Dallas, Chicago, Hayward (California),

411

Toronto, Vancouver, and Antwerp (Belgium). In New Bern, North Carolina, the company operated the Mack Remanufacturing Center, where worn Mack diesel engines, transmissions, water pumps, injection pumps, cylinder heads, and other items were remanufactured to "like new" standards. For example, an engine was completely disassembled; and high wear items, replaced with new parts. In earlier years Mack did this work in Middletown, Pennsylvania.

Mack owned and operated 23 sales and service branches, 1 parts store, and 5 used truck centers in the United States. Mack acquired many trucks as trade-ins at its company-owned sales branches. The historical average was about 50 trade-ins for every 100 new trucks sold at these branches. There were 242 independently owned sales and service outlets and 503 independently owned service centers. Mack also supplied parts to 55 independently owned parts and service outlets in the United States for Brockway trucks, a vehicle line formerly produced by a discontinued division of the company. Mack's Canadian subsidiary operated a network of sales, parts, and service facilities scattered through that country. Mack considered that it had greater distributor strength in the East and the South than elsewhere in the United States. In recent years, Mack had converted several of its own sales and service branches to independent ownership. Its long-range plans were to retain only 20 of these branches, all located in major market cities of the United States. Mack maintained inventory on 83,000 different parts. Adequate parts stocks were important to its customers, all of whom were business users of trucks. Company sales and operating results are presented in Exhibit 1; and a recent balance sheet, in Exhibit 2.

Most Mack truck sales were to customer order rather than from stock. Extremely large customers who were probably going to need many hundreds of units sometimes observed or even participated in Mack's product development. For example, one of the manufacturer's largest customers was United Parcel Service (UPS), and they had had a good relationship for 27 years. Equipment specialists from UPS evaluated Mack's Ultra-Liner model in the prototype stages and suggested modifications and specifications. Subsequently UPS bought 830 of these units.

A new manufacturing plant, costing about $80 million and extremely modern and efficient in design, was planned for the late 1980s; and the old Allentown plant, built in 1926 and excessively costly to operate, was to be closed down. There had been very little modernization of plant and equipment since the mid 1960s. The planned new plant, it was figured, would cut production costs for a new truck line by 20 to 25 per cent. Location of the manufacturing facility was in doubt, a fact that was contributing considerably to the employee relations problems of the firm as well as to the community and general public relations problems. There was great pressure from the state and local governments to place Mack's new investment in the Allentown vicinity.

The old plant suffered not only from obsolete equipment and too little mechanization but from high hourly labor rates as well. The top management referred to the labor arrangement in this plant as "high button shoes." United Auto Workers labor costs there were about $23 per hour, including cost of fringe benefits, and the union contract called for a maze of over 90 separate job classifications and very limited ability to move between classifications to perform work. The company asked the union for concession of $3.85 per hour and said that, without such a concession, it would construct the new plant outside of Pennsylvania. Both the Middle West and the South, expecially the Carolinas, had been under consideration.

The reduction requested was the amount that Mack calculated it overpaid compared to its most direct U.S. competitors, Paccar, Freightliner, and Volvo-White Truck Corporation. The other noteworthy competitors were General Motors, Ford, and International Harvester, which was in process of establishing Navistar as a new name for itself. Because the United States represented one-third of the world's total truck market, new competitors had come in. Daimler-Benz of West Germany bought Freightliner, based in Portland, Oregon, in 1981; and AB Volvo, of Sweden, bought bankrupt White Motor, based in Greensboro, North Carolina, the same year. The Japanese truck makers, Nissan, Isuzu, Hino, and Mitsubishi, were now entering the market, too.

After about a year of negotiation, Mack set a deadline in early 1986 for the union to accept the reduction in the pay package. Straw votes and polls in the union's local branches in Pennsylvania and Maryland implied strongly that a majority of the workers were willing to accept the cut. The leadership, especially at the national level, was opposed, fearing a domino effect across the country. The Maryland plant workers were involved in the dispute not only through wages and fringe benefits but also in two other ways. First, if the Maryland workers did not accept compensation reductions, Mack would definitely start "outsourcing" (this practice is explained and developed later in the case) some items now made in Hagerstown, and the number of jobs in the facility would be decreased correspondingly. Regardless of union action on the proposed pay cut, some outsourcing would be considered. Second, a relocation of the Allentown plant to any point at great distance from Hagerstown would make it tempting to Mack to move Hagerstown activities closer to the proposed plant gradually. Hagerstown and Allentown were only

EXHIBIT 1 Mack Trucks, Inc. Operating Statements in Recent Years

SUMMARY OF OPERATIONS	in thousands, except per share amounts		
	1985	1984	1983
Net sales			
United States	$1,714,483	$1,801,603	$ 999,335
International	348,829	303,855	217,495
	2,063,312	2,105,458	1,216,830
Cost of sales	1,934,649	1,885,065	1,134,121
Depreciation and amortization	29,663	27,981	26,199
Gross profit	99,000	192,412	56,510
Selling, general and administrative expenses	101,102	107,025	97,027
Income (loss) from operations	(2,102)	85,387	(40,517)
Interest income	8,465	12,978	15,233
Interest expense	(20,534)	(19,727)	(25,983)
Other income (deductions)—net	(89,599)	(35,887)	(14,544)
Earnings (loss) before taxes, net income of unconsolidated financial subsidiaries and extraordinary item	(103,770)	42,751	(65,811)
Taxes on earnings	(22,738)	4,546	(26,435)
Net income—unconsolidated financial subsidiaries	21,249	26,377	13,201
Earnings (loss) before extraordinary item	(59,783)	64,582	(26,175)
Extraordinary item (tax benefits)	567	10,371	—
Net earnings (loss)	$ (59,216)	$ 74,953	$ (26,175)
Net earnings (loss) per common and common equivalent share:*			
Primary	$ (2.07)	$ 2.29	$ (.97)
Assuming full dilution	(2.07)	2.24	(.97)
Average common and common equivalent shares outstanding	30,056	30,993	28,388
Average common shares outstanding—assuming full dilution	30,056	33,049	28,388
Cash dividends per common share*	$ —	$ —	$ —
% to net sales:			
Earnings (loss) before taxes and net income of unconsolidated subsidiaries and extraordinary item	(5.0)%	2.0%	(5.4)%
Net earnings (loss)	(2.9)	3.6	(2.2)
Selected Financial Data			
Working capital	$ 358,509	$ 372,462	$ 371,991
Current ratio	2.22	1.90	2.58
Property—net	189,021	185,464	191,056
Capital expenditures	42,459	24,107	21,374
Total assets	1,061,822	1,174,275	972,995
Long-term debt (including redeemable preference shares)	120,616	95,415	149,171
Shareholders' equity	535,811	614,100	545,208
Per share	18.17	20.22	17.97
Capitalization ratio*	18.37	13.45	21.48
Number of employees	12,193	15,268	12,574

*After giving effect to the 21,600 for 1 stock split on July 21, 1983.
**The capitalization ratio is the sum of the company's redeemable preference shares and long-term debt divided by the sum of the redeemable preference shares, long-term debt and shareholders' equity.

1982	1981	1980	1979	1978	1977	1976
$ 988,230	$1,130,419	$1,131,599	$1,441,416	$1,306,017	$1,055,597	$ 706,771
303,322	395,654	405,061	392,421	333,993	275,468	319,033
1,291,552	1,526,073	1,536,660	1,833,837	1,640,010	1,331,065	1,025,804
1,189,464	1,368,010	1,404,158	1,571,964	1,388,956	1,141,720	883,406
24,306	22,322	22,579	21,057	19,770	19,686	21,375
77,782	135,741	109,923	240,816	231,284	169,659	121,023
99,887	98,779	97,987	92,492	77,750	69,118	67,405
(22,105)	36,962	11,936	148,324	153,534	100,541	53,618
6,323	7,062	3,177	3,317	2,568	3,512	4,181
(45,665)	(44,403)	(47,639)	(38,162)	(23,881)	(24,074)	(24,062)
(25,343)	(23,410)	(38,631)	(20,047)	(15,749)	(23,948)	(4,839)
(86,790)	(23,789)	(71,157)	93,432	116,472	56,031	28,898
(38,151)	(13,154)	(35,479)	42,585	59,407	29,097	14,234
16,345	19,272	17,480	16,451	11,732	10,105	9,096
(32,294)	8,637	(18,198)	67,298	68,797	37,039	23,760
—	—	—	—	—	—	—
$ (32,294)	$ 8,637	$ (18,198)	$ 67,298	$ 68,797	$ 37,039	$ 23,760
$ (1.26)	$ .36	$ (.76)	$ 2.91	$ 3.19	$ 1.71	$ 1.10
(1.26)	.36	(.76)	2.79	3.19	1.71	1.10
25,530	24,019	24,019	23,138	21,600	21,600	21,600
25,530	24,019	24,019	25,032	21,600	21,600	21,600
$ —	$ —	$ .27	$ .92	$ 4.28	$ .88	$ .56
(6.7)%	(1.6)% $	(4.6)%	5.1% $	7.1% $	4.2% $	2.8%
(2.5)	.6	(1.2)	3.7	4.2	2.8	2.3
$ 294,021	$ 358,811	$ 386,305	$ 396,118	$ 365,544	$ 348,053	$ 318,952
2.31	2.36	2.72	2.25	2.45	2.53	2.73
197,336	203,366	187,757	185,515	164,923	153,850	167,236
26,688	40,570	29,103	43,137	33,682	8,855	16,901
886,929	984,362	943,738	1,024,664	895,203	831,199	763,416
219,645	308,407	318,839	280,828	271,502	214,178	198,444
399,645	369,562	360,925	385,629	334,730	358,313	340,182
14.80	15.39	15.03	16.06	15.50	16.59	15.75
35.47	45.49	46.90	42.14	44.79	37.41	36.84
10,525	13,011	14,083	17,027	17,100	15,685	14,711

EXHIBIT 2 Recent Balance Sheets of Mack Trucks, Inc.*

Assets	December 31	
	1984	1983
	in thousands	
CURRENT ASSETS		
Cash and short-term investments (including $20,000,000 invested with an affiliate at December 31, 1984 and 1983)	$ 100,601	$145,038
Refundable taxes	1,129	6,985
Trade receivables:		
Accounts	76,703	77,614
Affiliated companies	3,525	1,041
Installment notes and contracts	717	766
Total	80,945	79,421
Less allowance for uncollectable accounts	10,197	12,923
Trade receivables–net	70,748	66,498
Accounts receivable from financial subsidiaries	41,328	17,799
Inventories:		
Finished units (new and used)	201,162	111,354
Service parts	146,529	112,541
Raw materials and work in process	182,317	117,102
Total inventories	530,008	340,997
Deferred income taxes	42,907	27,619
Prepaid expenses	1,870	2,190
Total current assets	788,591	607,126
INVESTMENT IN FINANCIAL SUBSIDIARIES	173,418	167,597
LONG-TERM RECEIVABLE FROM MACK FINANCIAL CORPORATION	18,950	
SUNDRY INVESTMENTS, ETC.	7,443	6,539
PROPERTY—AT COST		
Land and improvements	22,254	21,583
Buildings and improvements	121,067	120,731
Machinery and equipment	247,989	238,883
Motor vehicles leased to customers	419	504
Leased property under capital leases	8,928	9,038
Production model tools, etc.	34,425	30,209
Total	435,082	420,948
Less accumulated depreciation and amortization	249,618	229,892
Property–net	185,464	191,056
OTHER ASSETS	409	677
Total	$1,174,275	$972,995

*1985 not available *Statements continued on following page*

Liabilities	December 31	
	1984	1983
	in thousands	
CURRENT LIABILITIES		
Notes payable—banks	$ 25,517	$ 22,142
Current portion of long-term debt	63,398	22,600
Accounts payable		
Trade	112,978	61,611
Affiliated companies	33,812	28,183
Total accounts payable	146,790	89,794
Accrued U.S. and foreign income taxes	20,099	
Excise and other taxes payable	10,654	7,680
Accrued warranty	37,726	24,143
Accrued wages and commissions	40,610	22,625
Accrued liabilities to distributors	32,294	17,572
Other accrued liabilities	39,041	28,579
Total current liabilities	416,129	235,135
LONG-TERM DEBT		
Notes and loans	78,402	142,100
Obligations under capital leases	6,799	7,071
Total long-term debt	85,201	149,171
OTHER LIABILITIES AND DEFERRED CREDITS		
Deferred income taxes	35,784	33,346
Payable to an affiliate	7,170	5,696
Other	5,679	4,439
Total other liabilities and deferred credits	48,633	43,481
CONTINGENT LIABILITIES AND COMMITMENTS		
REDEEMABLE PREFERENCE SHARES	10,212	
SHAREHOLDERS' EQUITY		
Series A Cumulative Convertible Preferred stock, par value $1 per share—authorized, 25,000,000 shares; outstanding, 2,020,202 shares at December 31, 1984 and 1983 (redemption and liquidation value $33,333,333)	2,020	2,020
Common stock, par value $1 per share—authorized, 100,000,000 shares; outstanding, 30,373,930 and 30,333,334 shares at December 31, 1984 and 1983, repectively	30,374	30,333
Additional paid-in capital	345,833	345,274
Retained earnings	243,435	172,243
Equity adjustment from foreign currency translation	(7,562)	(4,662)
Shareholders' equity	614,100	545,208
Total	$1,174,275	$972,995

170 miles apart. In addition, a reduction of the size of the Hagerstown plant might bring it down to the point where it could not enjoy any economies of scale, and then it might be tempting to eliminate it.

The union offered only to make some of the work rules more rational and economical and to decrease compensation temporarily in Pennsylvania and Maryland, the savings going directly into an account to pay the cost to construct the new Allentown plant. Mack waited for 5 days after the deadline, and then it decided to relocate the Allentown facility to Winnsboro, South Carolina, a town of about 3,000 population about 30 miles north of Columbia. It also announced that it would start purchasing several items it was making at Hagerstown. The 3,100 jobs at the Maryland factory would probably decline by 40 to 60 per cent.

Founded in 1900 as Mack Brothers, the company later offered its stock to the general public. Then, in 1967, it became a subsidiary of the Signal Companies, which were based in La Jolla, California. In 1979, while Mack was still a Signal subsidiary, Regie Nationale des Usines Renault, a French organization, bought into Mack, investing $50 million for a 10 per cent common stock interest. Renault at that time also acquired convertible subordinated debentures for $65 million, which in 1982 it converted into an additional 10 per cent of Mack's common stock. Then, in 1983, through complex transactions pursuant to a stock and warrant purchase agreement, Renault purchased more shares from Signal and a fifteen-year warrant to purchase still more shares. Thus, Renault had paid $228 million beyond the first $50 million and now owned 41.9 per cent of the stock. Of the amounts Renault paid, $94 million went directly to Mack. The current chairperson of the board at Mack, John Curcio, was head of Mack's international operations in 1979 and helped persuade Renault to invest in Mack. In 1983, Signal sold all but 10.6 per cent of its Mack holdings to the general public, for which it received an aggregate of $144 million.

If it exercised all its rights under existing agreements, Renault could buy enough stock to take majority control if it so chose. Signal owned 10.6 per cent of Mack's common stock; and the general public, the remainder. In practical terms, however, it was difficult to get enough stockholders to agree on any policy position to swing a majority vote against someone who owned over four-tenths of the stock. The Renault and Signal blocks together accounted for 52 per cent of the common stock.

The Signal Companies were later absorbed by Allied. The resulting company, named Allied-Signal, Inc., was mainly in the chemical business.

In 1983, Mack issued 2,020,202 shares of its Series A Cumulative Preferred Stock for a purchase price of $33,333,333. This stock was redeemable at the option of Mack at any time at the price of $16.50 per share plus accrued dividends; and it was convertible into common stock at a rate of $16.21 per share, subject to antidilution adjustments. Signal had the right to require Renault to purchase this preferred stock if it had not been previously redeemed by Mack or if Mack had not given notice of its intention to redeem the shares. Renault had the right to purchase these shares from Signal at any time. In either case, the purchase price would be $33,333,322 plus accrued dividends.

Founded as a private enterprise, Renault had been a French government-owned corporation since 1946. The usual but not totally proved explanation for the nationalization was punishment for Renault's alleged cooperation with the German authorities who had occupied France during World War II and the extremely large amounts of war goods Renault supplied the German military forces during the occupation. With its private enterprise heritage, Renault performed well after nationalization for a time and intermittently well thereafter for many years. By the mid-1980s it was incurring heavy losses, in fact, the equivalent of over U.S. $1 billion per year. Under conservative, moderate, liberal, and, ironically, socialist government regimes, Renault had experienced severe labor relations problems. The reasons for the losses revolved around inadequate management, questionable decisions on the composition of the product line, and, in particular, the French government policy of keeping many thousands of workers for whom the company had no need. Moreover, in addition to its investment in Mack, Renault owned 46 per cent of American Motors and had an option to buy more.

Mack made fifteen lines of domestic "on" and "on-off" highway trucks and tractors, including a line of fire truck chassis units. The company's lines of trucks and tractors were distinguished by features such as cab style (conventional or cab-over-engine), size (engine compartment, frame, and axle size), and use-related design characteristics (highway or in-city tractor, dumper-mixer, all-wheel-drive snowplow, all-wheel-drive block hauler and mixer, refuse hauler). Models within each line were distinguished by such feature options as engines, transmissions, axles, frames, front-axle placement, and gross vehicle or gross combination weight.

Vehicles generally consisted of a chassis and cab without a body. Cab and chassis units were designed to accommodate many different types of bodies and trailers, including dry and refrigerated vans; dumps; concrete mixers; block haulers; liquid tanks; powder hopper tanks; stake, flatbed, front-side, and rear-loading refuse bodies; well-servicing equipment platforms; and beverage vans. Mack also made cab and chassis units designed especially for extraheavy-duty hauling, such as oil field, logging, and coal hauling. Truck tractors were used primarily on highway by long-distance freight carriers of dry and liquid cargoes. Mack engineered and built its trucks to meet the requirements of the industries in which they were to be used. Annual models were not produced. However, improvements, refinements, and modifications were made whenever deemed advantageous.

The U.S. truck-building industry suffered from overcapacity in class eight trucks, that is, equipment with gross vehicle weight of over 33,000 pounds. The classification system was created by the Motor Vehicle Manufacturers Association. Often called "heavy-duty trucks," class eight carried about three-fourths of the freight in the United States. Mack itself, the second largest of 12 producers of such trucks in the United States, suffered from overcapacity, and such trucks were its principal business. Total U.S. demand for class eight trucks dropped from a peak of 164,000 units in 1979 to 70,000 in 1982 and partially recovered to a projected 127,000 in 1986 whereas total industry capacity was 230,000 units. U.S. deregulation of the trucking (i.e., freight carrying by truck) industry had led to more efficient hauling, and aggressive competition from railroads plus the lack of growth in U.S. manufacturing kept demand for large trucks down. The average selling price of a class eight truck declined for five consecutive years. In 1985 that average price was $54,000.

The general strength of the U.S. economy pulled demand up for heavy trucks in 1984. Class eight units sold by the entire industry rose 79 per cent over 1983, and classes six and seven combined rose 45 per cent. The industry's exports of heavy-duty trucks declined slightly from 1983 to 1984. In 1984, Mack sold worldwide 29,003 class eight units, an increase of 103 per cent over 1983, and 5,778 medium-duty (classes six and seven) units, an increase of 63 per cent over 1983, thus outperforming the industry. Mack's share of the U.S. class eight truck market rose from 15 per cent in 1983 to 17.5 per cent in 1984 and 18.5 per cent in 1985. The industry sold 128,674 such units in the U.S. in 1985. The percentage breakdown between sales of new trucks and sales of parts is given in Exhibit 3.

EXHIBIT 3 Sales of Mack Trucks, Inc. by Major Type by Year in Percentages

	1985	1984	1983	1982	1981	1980	1979
Trucks	77	77	69	72	75	77	80
Parts and service	23	23	31	28	25	23	20

The company's share of the U.S. market for truck classes six and seven combined was 7.3 per cent in 1983, 8.2 per cent in 1984, and 6.4 per cent in 1985. The company's unit sales were 5,146 in the U.S. Mack's product offering was termed the Mid-Liner series, the best-selling import in the United States in this size range. It was built in France by Renault Vehicles Industriels, a wholly owned subsidiary of Renault. Mack was the exclusive distributor of the Mid-Liner in the United States, Canada, and several Central American and Caribbean countries. Mack did not make or sell trucks lighter than class six.

With a product named the FR-1 coach, Mack reentered the intercity bus market in 1984. Introduced in Europe by Renault in 1983, this rather advanced product had an aluminum and stainless steel structure and electronic technology. It was assembled with a Mack diesel engine and transmission. In 1986, Volvo-White closed down its U.S. bus manufacturing operation, which was located in Chesapeake, Virginia.

The new Japanese competitors in truck manufacturing had entered the market with small and midsize trucks and were not expected to launch class eight trucks before 1989 or 1990, in Mack's estimation. Mack officials noted that makers of class eight trucks in the United States had kept quality up better than Detroit had done in the late 1970s and early 1980s with passenger cars. Furthermore, the Japanese had had very little experience using or making heavy-duty trucks, a product type little used outside of the United States, Canada, and Australia. The Japanese were doing fairly well making earthmoving equipment and farm tractors. Mack and other U.S. and European firms building large trucks in the United States were reasonably optimistic about competing well against the Japanese companies.

Mack had a wholly owned subsidiary in the United States, Mack Financial Corporation (MFC), engaged in financing the sale of trucks to customers. MFC, in turn, had a wholly owned subsidiary in Canada. Varying by year, from 13 to 17 per cent of Mack's new truck sales in the United States and Canada were so financed. The service was available on trucks sold by both company-owned branches and independent dealers.

The company had long been a highly integrated manufacturer. It had made nearly all its own parts, such as front and rear axles, axle housings, axle shafts, support frames, engines, and transmissions, and did not offer such components to any other manufacturer This high degree of manufacturing integration gave rise to the expression "all-Mack," "the all-Mack truck," and occasionally "Mack-Mack." The first two of these expressions had been widely used, and the third was occasionally used in company advertising, personal salesmanship, and public relations. According to company officials, "Mack's greatest strength has always been the design and production of the total vehicle . . . the concept of balanced design." This strongly implied supplying from within the company. Nearly all competitors used outsourcing, that is, buying some key components from outside suppliers. All U.S. competitors for class eight vehicles used outsourcing for engines, transmissions, and rear axle carriers. Contrary to laypeoples expectations, outsourcing was often cheaper than making one's own parts because the outside supplier was a specialist and also gained large economies of scale by making a larger number of units than the customer organization needed to make for itself. Such parts makers served multiple-manufacturing customers. The mass component manufacturers, which produced for both truck and carmakers, included at least five U.S. firms: Eaton Corporation of Cleveland; Dana Corporation of Toledo; Cummins Engine Company of Columbus, Indiana; and two conglomerates, Rockwell International of Pittsburgh and TRW Inc. of Cleveland. All of them had foreign as well as domestic plants.

Mack was in the process of reducing its manufacturing integration and had already set up contracts with several parts-manufacturing specialists. It cost about $3,500,000 to close down selected parts-making operations in Allentown, but savings from outsourcing were estimated at $30 million per year. This included the termination of several hundred workers. Some of these new arrangements called for just one supplier of certain components, and others called for two suppliers. The new corporate policy was to "review its component manufacturing program periodically to determine which components it will continue to manufacture and which it will purchase from vendors."

Most Mack trucks contained Mack-built major components, such as engine and transmission, front axles, and single and tandem rear axles (including the gear-drive carriers). However, if specified by a customer, Mack was willing to substitute major components made by other firms. The company had a long-range objective of developing "a high degree of interchangeability of basic components among its truck models," which would permit flexibility in adapting models to a wide range of uses and reduce the size and complexity of parts inventories.

In recent years, the research and development effort on the powertrain, that is, the engine, transmission, and rear axle carriers, was on two fronts. First and more emphasized, there was work that management described as "evolutionary," taking products and product concepts to higher levels. This was perfecting what was already done well. Examples were the new engines in the company's six-cylinder, eleven-liter series and a six-cylinder, twelve-liter engine. Evolutionary work was very much influenced by scheduled and forecast future rises in government standards for emissions controls. Second, there was research and development that management described as "revolutionary," the increased application of electronic controls. Such electronics had to do mainly with engine fuel controls, vehicle instrumentation, a road-speed governor, and a transmission shifting system.

Mack's products were regularly exported to 80 countries although Canada and Australia were the principal foreign markets. Sales of Mack products abroad were made through 121 franchised distributors and branches in 80 countries and occasionally through independent agents not under franchise. These representatives abroad received a commission, the rate of which varied based on the amount of the representative's involvement in transactions or local custom on rates or both. On the whole, Mack's exports made a higher rate of profit than did domestic sales, mainly because of higher prices the company could usually command abroad.

Much of the organization's export volume was in the form of CKD (completely knocked down) chassis shipped for assembly in the country of destination, with varying degrees of local content added. CKD assembly operations were conducted in seven foreign nations by local firms, but Mack had an ownership interest in three of them.

From 1983 to 1985, Mack Trucks Australia Pty., Ltd., the wholly owned Australian subsidiary, delivered 1,000 eight-ton trucks to the Australian army, beating 24 other builders for the contract. The major criterion for winning was projected life-cycle cost. Using one standard chassis and both Australian and U. S. content, several vehicle variations were made for this contract. The company received the Defence Industry Quality and Achievement Award from the Australian government. With the encouragement of the host government, the Australian subsidiary had plans to develop exports of its own, but probably they would not be military vehicles.

Advise Mack Trucks, Inc.

POLAROID CORPORATION

Polaroid Corporation, based in Cambridge, Massachusetts, designed, manufactured, and marketed worldwide a line of products stemming from its inventions. This line was almost entirely in the photographic field. The products included instant cameras and film, light-polarizing filters and lenses, and diversified chemical and optical products. Polaroid produced more than forty types of film in eight different formats and in a variety of emulsion characteristics. The main products of the company were used in amateur and professional photography, industry, science, medicine, and education.

There was considerable concern about the well-being of the company and its future although it was still profitable. Sales were weak; profits, low; and the trends, not encouraging. See Exhibits 1 through 4 for data. About one-third of the company's workers had been dismissed. Nevertheless, Polaroid had almost two-thirds of the world's sales of instant cameras and instant film and had a hoard of cash of several hundred million dollars. Moreover, it held about 150 patents and continued to win some new patents from time to time.

Development of Polaroid and Its Corporate Culture

Edwin H. Land established Polaroid in 1937, when he was 28 years old. He was universally acknowledged to be an inventor of impressive talent and skill, one of the best physicists of his generation. He was also well prepared in chemistry and could make creative and useful ties between physics and chemistry. Land founded and built up the company around his own inventive work. He began by inventing new solutions to very old problems in the field of light polarization. Land invented additional optical devices for the U.S. military effort in World War II, and in 1948 he introduced his famous Land camera for instant photographs. A prolific professional, Land was second only to the legendary Thomas A. Edison in the number of U.S. patents issued to him. Over his career Land received dozens of awards from scientific socieities and honorary degrees from twelve universities. He still found time to teach a course occasionally at M.I.T. in Cambridge.

In 1980 the founder retired as chief executive officer and director of research and in 1982 as chairperson of the board of directors. He chose not to keep a seat on the board although, with 8.3 per cent of the company stock, he was the largest individual shareholder. However, Land continued to express opinions from time to time and was known to hold some views rather strongly.

Land built a technological empire and yet a supportive, warm, almost family-style corporate culture. It was his policy (Polaroid Corporate Personnel Policy #251) that anyone who had been employed for ten years with Polaroid had a job for life. There was rapid growth at Polaroid, inventions came quickly and frequently, and there was an extremely high esprit de corps. Land envisioned the company as a gathering place for talented scientists and engineers to exchange ideas and invent products "that bring science and technology to bear on filling . . . a deep human need." He spoke of making Polaroid "a noble prototype of industry." Land added, in one of

EXHIBIT 1 Polaroid Corporation's Operating Statements in Recent Years (dollar amounts in millions except per share data)

	1985	1984	1983	1982	1981	1980	1979	1978
CONSOLIDATED STATEMENT OF EARNINGS								
Net sales								
United States	$ 779.3	$ 743.5	$ 730.1	$ 752.5	$ 817.8	$ 791.8	$ 757.2	$ 817.4
International	515.9	528.0	524.4	541.4	601.8	659.0	604.3	559.2
Total net sales	1295.2	1271.5	1254.5	1293.9	1419.6	1450.8	1361.5	1376.6
Cost of goods sold	756.0	735.2	698.3	769.6	855.4	831.1	876.8	778.3
Marketing, research, engineering, and administrative expenses	505.6	492.6	462.1	472.6	520.8	483.9	449.4	418.2
Total costs	1261.6	1227.8	1160.4	1242.2	1376.2	1315.0	1326.2	1196.5
Profit from operations	33.6	43.7	94.1	51.7	43.4	135.8	35.3	180.1
Other income	28.9	39.5	32.5	45.5	49.2	25.4	13.3	20.3
Interest expense	22.3	20.9	26.5	35.5	29.9	17.0	12.8	5.9
Earnings before income taxes	40.2	62.3	100.1	61.7	62.7	144.2	35.8	194.5
Federal, state and foreign income taxes (credit)	3.3	36.6	50.4	38.2	31.6	58.8	(.3)	76.1
Net earnings	36.9	25.7	49.7	23.5	31.1	85.4	36.1	118.4
Earnings per share	$ 1.19	$ .83	$ 1.61	$ .73	$ .95	$ 2.60	$ 1.10	$ 3.60
Cash dividends per share	$ 1.00	$ 1.00	$ 1.00	$ 1.00	$ 1.00	$ 1.00	$ 1.00	$ .90
Average shares outstanding (in thousands)	30,959	30,959	30,959	32,144	32,855	32,855	32,855	32,855

EXHIBIT 2 **Polaroid Corporation and Subsidiary Companies Consolidated Balance Sheet December 31, 1984 and 1983 (in millions)***

Assets	1984	1983
Current assets		
Cash and short-term investments	$ 350.2	$ 366.5
Receivables, less allowances of $9.4 ($8.6 in 1983)	269.7	241.0
Inventories	344.9	372.4
Prepaid expenses	74.6	62.2
Total current assets	1,039.4	1,042.1
Property, plant and equipment		
Land	11.9	11.9
Buildings	200.6	197.3
Machinery and equipment	645.9	617.0
Construction in process	47.7	31.3
Gross property, plant and equipment	906.1	857.5
Less accumulated depreciation	599.5	580.5
Net property, plant and equipment	306.6	277.0
Total assets	$1,346.0	$1,319.1
LIABILITIES AND STOCKHOLDERS' EQUITY		
Current liabilities		
Short-term debt	$ 82.6	$ 66.9
Payables and accruals	126.6	116.4
Compensation and benefits	71.1	68.2
Federal, state and foreign income taxes	24.9	21.6
Total current liabilities	305.2	273.1
Long-term debt	124.5	124.4
Stockholders' equity		
Common stock, $1 par value, authorized 36,000,000 shares, issued 32,855,475 shares	32.9	32.9
Additional paid-in capital	122.0	122.0
Retained earnings	808.3	813.6
Less treasury stock, at cost, 1,896,300 shares	963.2	968.5
Total stockholders' equity	916.3	921.6
Total liabilities and stockholders' equity	$1,346.0	$1,319.1

*1985 not available

EXHIBIT 3 Number of Consumer Cameras Sold
by Polaroid Corporation by Year

Year	Number (in millions)
1985	3.5
1984	3.6
1983	3.8
1982	4.0
1981	5.6
1980	6.6
1979	7.3

his most famous pronouncements, "We're not here to make profits.
. . . We're here to make innovation." Yet many former employees
alleged that over the years a country club, minimum-work attitude
began and finally took over the organization.

The founder disapproved of the acquisition of products invented
or developed by people outside the Polaroid family and of companies
that would have made logical—and often needed—additions to Polaroid's lines of goods and services. He disdained joint ventures. Land
even disapproved of Polaroid's conducting basic research or product
development work anywhere but in the headquarters laboratories in
Cambridge although the organization had become multinational. He
thought poorly of present and potential industrial and commercial
applications of Polaroid goods and ideas and did not encourage them.
Somewhat incongruously for a man of such sophisticated scientific
expertise, Land was extremely enthusiastic about amateur photography and managed the corporation so as to try to be preeminent in
that field. Land saw photography as "the most elegant of arts." He
made it clear that he did not think of photography as a toy or mere
hobby and did not want others to do so. He wanted people to be
seriously interested in photography and make it part of their lives.

Although Polaroid Corporation had been willing, or course, to
talk to industrial, commercial, medical, and educational organizations about its products and adaptations of them for nonconsumers,
the corporate culture did not encourage promotional initiative. The
sales force was not aggressive by normal business standards. Sales
representatives normally waited for prospects to contact them. The
advertising was unusually educational in tone although creative and
typically interesting.

Polaroid's International Involvement

Polaroid Corporation owned manufacturing subsidiaries in Enschede, Holland, where it employed about 900 people, and Vale of Leven, Scotland, where it employed slightly over 1,000 people. In Holland, Polaroid made pack film, integral film, and film backs for industrial cameras; and in Scotland, cameras, pack film, and sunglasses. In conjunction with the manufacturing plant in Holland, Polaroid operated its International Distribution Center to supply products to most of its foreign marketing subsidiaries. The majority of Polaroid products for non-U.S. markets came from these two factories and flowed through this physical distribution center. The company closed a film-manufacturing facility in Ireland in 1982 and wrote off a loss of $20 million on the plant and equipment in so doing. The overseas manufacturing facilities received batteries, all light-sensitive materials and receiving sheet, some chemicals, and some components from the U.S. manufacturing plants of the company and selected components from the Far East made specifically for Polaroid, and they purchased some materials locally.

By the mid-1970s, shortly after major international currencies went off fixed rates of exchange, Polaroid found it advisable to create its Monetary Control Center in Holland to manage its exposure to changes in values of the many currencies in which it did business. Nevertheless, it lost money on foreign currency exposure during the period 1979–1984. The net after-tax effect of foreign currency exchange amounted to losses of $5.4 million in 1984, $4.8 million in 1983, $1.7 million in 1982, $1.3 million in 1981, $0.6 million in 1980, and $1.0 million in 1979.

The company first entered foreign markets with exports of its sunglasses. Then in 1959 it established its first subsidiaries outside the United States, Polaroid Canada, Inc., and Polaroid G.m.b.H. in West Germany. Approximately 42 per cent of Polaroid's sales came from abroad each year from 1981 through the mid-1980s compared to 44 per cent in 1979 and 45 per cent in 1980. See Exhibit 4. The extremely high foreign exchange rate of the U.S. dollar in the early and mid-1980s hurt Polaroid's exports of products, components, and supplies; but, of course, it was impossible to determine exactly how much.

Polaroid had an extensive marketing effort abroad through its wholly owned subsidiaries in 21 countries: Canada, West Germany, Italy, France, Holland, United Kingdom, Switzerland, Belgium, Holland, Sweden, Norway, Denmark, Austria, Spain, Singapore, Japan, Hong Kong, Australia, New Zealand, Panama, and Brazil. Polaroid also had such an organization in Puerto Rico. Most of the wholly owned marketing subsidiaries did business only within the territorial

EXHIBIT 4 **Polaroid Corporation and Subsidiary Companies Consolidated Statement of Changes in Financial Position**
Years ended December 31, 1984, 1983, and 1982 (in millions)*

Source and use of funds	1984	1983	1982
Source of funds			
Net earnings	$ 25.7	$ 49.7	$ 23.5
Items not requiring current outlay of funds			
Depreciation of property, plant, and equipment	50.8	51.8	62.2
Write-downs of property, plant, and equipment	—	—	18.6
Other	.7	.1	.1
Funds derived from operations	77.2	101.6	104.4
Disposals of property, plant, and equipment	1.7	3.1	1.8
Total source of funds	78.9	104.7	106.2
Use of funds			
Additions to property, plant and equipment	82.7	50.1	31.5
Cash dividends	31.0	31.0	31.9
Purchase of common stock for treasury	—	—	46.9
Total use of funds	113.7	81.1	110.3
Increase (decrease) in working capital	$ (34.8)	$ 23.6	$ (4.1)
CHANGES IN COMPONENTS OF WORKING CAPITAL			
Current assets—increase (decrease)			
Cash and short-term investments	$ (16.3)	$ 33.0	$ 1.7
Receivables	28.7	(20.8)	(27.7)
Inventories	(27.5)	(14.2)	(26.1)
Prepaid expenses	12.4	2.3	(7.9)
Total change in current assets	(2.7)	.3	(60.0)
Current liabilities—(increase) decrease			
Short-term debt	(15.7)	19.2	21.6
Payables and accruals	(10.2)	7.9	11.0
Compensation and benefits	(2.9)	(9.6)	12.7
Federal, state and foreign income taxes	(3.3)	5.8	10.6
Total change in current liabilities	(32.1)	23.3	55.9
Increase (decrease) in working capital	$ (34.8)	$ 23.6	$ (4.1)

*1985 not available

limits of the country where located and attempted to be part of the local business community. The company also marketed abroad through unrelated selected distributors in more than 100 other nations.

Polaroid created the European Marketing Council at the end of

1982 to address common concerns among the Polaroid marketing subsidiaries located in the European Economic Community. The council was designed to deal with policies and issues in marketing, and "marketing" was envisioned to include public affairs. In nearly all years since the 1960s Europe accounted for about 60 per cent of Polaroid's foreign sales, and most of that figure was in countries having membership in the European Economic Community, sometimes known as the European Common Market.

With over $100 million sales per year, Japan was the most important country for Polaroid's foreign sales. Polaroid set up Nippon Polaroid Kabushiki Kaisha (NPKK), its wholly owned marketing subsidiary, in 1960. It maintained headquarters and a central distribution center in Tokyo and branch offices in Osaka, Nagoya, Sendai, Sapporo, Hiroshima, and Fukuoka. NPKK marketed Polaroid products through an exclusive distributor, Konishiroku Photo Ind. Co. Ltd., maker of Konica brand cameras, to more than 12,000 retail stores. However, the Japanese market was different in that nonconsumer sales accounted for almost one-half of Polaroid sales in that nation. Staffed almost entirely by Japanese nationals, NPKK used traditional Japanese operating practices, such as measurement of performance of the group rather than the individual, considerations of age and seniority in advancement, and lifetime employment. Japan was doubly important to Polaroid in that in 1983 the company established in Tokyo a special subsidiary, Polaroid Asia/Pacific Ltd., to monitor and oversee all Polaroid activities in Asia and the South Pacific.

The Current Situation

In the early and middle 1980s, sales of instant cameras and instant film, the life blood of Polaroid Corporation, declined for six consecutive years. Sales of such cameras declined both in the United States and abroad but declined by a slightly lower percentage abroad than in the United States.

Some people spoke of Polaroid as having a mid-life crisis. In all fairness, the majority of high-tech firms seemed to have gone through a mid-life crisis in which they had to find themselves, and it was perhaps inevitable that all high-tech organizations would do so. Many, of course, had not survived such an experience.

As Land departed in 1982, the company was reorganized, and there were many changes in the ranks of management. Two vice presidents left as Land left. They were the executive vice president and director of worldwide marketing and the vice president and director of the Patent Department. William J. McCune, Jr., an engineer who had joined the company in 1939 at the age of twenty-four, became chairperson of the board, president, and chief executive officer. McCune had become vice president for engineering while still in his thirties, then executive vice president in 1969, president and chief operating officer in 1975, and president and chief executive officer in 1980. He relinquished the position of president (only) in 1983 in favor of I. M. Booth, who became president and chief operating officer. An engineer, Booth had joined the company in 1958 at the age of twenty-seven and in 1975 had been named assistant vice president and assistant to the president, in 1976 vice president and assistant to the president, in 1977 senior vice president, in 1980 executive vice president, and in 1982 executive vice president and chief operating officer. Sheldon Buckler, a scientist, who had joined Polaroid in 1964 at the age of thirty-three, remained as executive vice president. Buckler had been appointed assistant vice president in 1969, vice president of the research division in 1972, group vice president in 1975, senior vice president in 1977, and executive vice president in 1980.

Sales of nonconsumer products were given high priority by the new or newly elevated executives. By 1985 such markets constituted about 40 per cent of Polaroid sales. The new top management also decided that not all research had to be centralized in Cambridge. Land, now conducting basic research in his own private laboratory, the Rowland Institute for Science in Cambridge, let it be known that he did not like the diversification of products and market segments at Polaroid. The new top management also raised the percentage of sales devoted to research and development. This figure became 10.6 in 1984 compared to 9.8 in 1983, 9.1 in 1982, and 8.5 in 1981. However, the proportion of R & D devoted to basic research declined while the proportion devoted to direct product development and improvement increased.

The new top management made several acquisitions. In 1982, Polaroid bought a 25 per cent interest in Image Resource Corporation, whose product line made print images from video cassette recorders and from computer screens. However, in its long tradition of not trusting anyone else to develop a new product, Polaroid decided to develop such products itself and in 1985 sold its interest in Image Resource Corporation for about one-third of what it had paid. In 1983, Polaroid bought 1984 Inc., a research and development firm specializing in single-mode fiber optics but without any goods in actual production, in order to gain its expertise and patents. In 1984, Polaroid acquired a 20 per cent interest in Sage Technology, Inc., a California-based maker of plateroom chemistry and imaging products used in printing processes. Also in 1984, Polaroid bought a 30 per cent interest in Advanced Color Technology, Inc., a Chelmsford, Massachusetts, maker of ink-jet printers for color graphics, and bought an additional 8 per cent in 1985. Founded in 1980, Advanced Color Technology made products priced around $6,000 used principally with computers.

In another management innovation at Polaroid, the company began in 1985 to market an 8 mm video camera-recorder for Toshiba. The latter was a very large Japanese corporation engaged mainly in electronics.

Although the new top management was aiming at a partial reorientation of Polaroid's marketing efforts so as not to be so dependent on the ultimate consumer and was doing reasonably well in moving toward that objective, the corporation was still extremely dependent on instant photography. By 1986 almost 90 per cent of company sales were still in instant photography. Several new markets and potential adaptations of the company's products were being developed, but they did not diversify the company out of instant photography significantly. The diversification sought was to go in two directions, more nonconsumer sales and less dependence on instant photography, but there was sizable progress on only the former.

The entire amateur portion of the photographic industry, not just instant photography, slumped in the early and middle 1980s. In part, this was because of recession in nearly all the world. The United States recovered far faster than the rest of the world. The slump was also because consumers were becoming rather blasé about instant photography. Many simple 35 mm cameras were brought to the market by competitors at a variety of prices In addition, film-developing service for consumers became widely and conveniently available and cheaper than in former times. Most U.S. consumers had access to storefront developing service in a fraction of a day. This new fact of life discouraged interest in instant photography. In addition, some outspoken consumers disparaged instant photography as suitable for only the unsophisticated dabbler.

Over 90 per cent of U.S. households already owned at least one camera, and a sizable fraction had multiple units. A few business analysts had described cameras as a "sunset industry." This was rather exaggerated, but the industry certainly had problems. Although the recession of the early 1980s and all recessions had hurt the industry because cameras are basically a luxury item and purchase is infinitely postponable, the more powerful, long-term factor was probably the near saturation in several affluent countries, including the United States, West Germany, and Japan. Cameras were a type of product with a very long functional life. Thirty years' use was not uncommon. If consumers were going to judge it worthwhile to replace their old cameras or upgrade or add another unit, a stream of genuine innovations seemed necessary. Moreover, several Japanese companies were aggressively cultivating the U.S. market for the first time and were entering the European markets. U.S.-based organizations had long been faced with competition from many European and several other Japanese camera makers.

Ernst Leitz Wetzlar G.m.b.H., the West German manufacturer of Leica brand equipment, and Hasselblad of Sweden were probably the most prestigious camera companies in the world. The German firm was primarily engaged in making binoculars and scientific instruments, such as microscopes. Leica cameras were important in World War II, and the Allies spent a great deal of scientific and espionage effort to obtain and copy the most advanced versions of Leica cameras and other Leica optical goods. Other prominent European companies were Rollei and Zeiss-Ikon, both West German.

Several camera makers had recently brought out a new generation of equipment often referred to as "smart cameras." They were 35 mm models that automatically set aperture openings and shutter speed, adjusted the focus, rewound the film, and even activated a flash attachment. Most models were priced under $100. Minolta, a large Japanese organization, introduced a "talking" camera. With an electronically synthesized voice, this camera, priced about $200, told the user, for example, when film required reloading. In addition, many improvements had been introduced throughout the camera industry in the inexpensive lines, even those lines under $40.

Eastman Kodak made an extremely important product introduction in May 1982 and called it the Disc. Sandwich-thin and small enough to go in a shirt pocket, the product was described in promotion as "decision-free." This fully automatic camera, which virtually allowed the user simply to point and shoot, replaced several heavier, cumbersome Kodak models. Because of its thinner body, it was easier to handle for most people and less likely to be jiggled while the shutter was pressed. The product took its name from the film format, a disc with fifteen exposures that rotated automatically after each exposure. Because of the generic nature of the word, it appeared that it was going to be difficult for Eastman Kodak to assert and keep legal rights to the term "Disc." By 1983, Konica, Minolta, Continental, Ansco, Keystone, and several other makers introduced similar products, most at lower prices; and Eastman brought out three additional models of the basic product. The various brands of disc-type cameras, ranging from about $30 to $150 in price, accounted for an impressive 21 per cent of the U.S. camera market by 1984.

Sony of Japan began marketing a totally electronic photographic system at a premium price, approximately $800 for the Mavica camera and almost $1,000 for the optional printer, in 1983. The

Mavica was similar to the thin disc cameras and contained a magnetic disc that could hold up to fifty exposures. Sony's early introduction of this product to the market surprised other camera companies although the technology was not terribly surprising. Several companies, such as Polaroid, had been researching these concepts. Electronic photography, also known as "video imaging," converts light into electronic impulses that can be viewed on a television screen instead of photographic paper. Such impulses can be easily stored on magnetic tapes and are potentially more versatile for consumer than chemical photography because the images can be modified and put back into storage. Sony brought out its prototype in 1981 but did not ship it to commercial outlets until late 1983. Sony then offered a color version in 1985. Both Eastman Kodak and Polaroid had developed experimental models but were waiting to see the public reaction to the Sony product. Polaroid's top executives saw that photography and electronics would increasingly be used together. This would be of extreme importance in industrial, technical, and medical photography and of some yet-to-be-determined use in amateur photography. Unlike the Sony model, Eastman's experimental model was not completely electronic but still used film.

The overall market for electronic photography would probably grow more quickly if an electronics company joined with a camera company to develop much lower-price models. Such work would merge electronic and chemical technologies. No company really had adequate expertise in both at this time.

Some interesting changes occurred in advertising and sales promotion. Polaroid terminated Doyle Dane Bernbach as its domestic advertising agency for consumer photography in 1982 after a thirty-year relationship. The company said, "It's easier to get fresh ideas from a new agency." Polaroid hired the much smaller Ally & Gargano, Inc., to handle this work, which constituted nearly half of its advertising budget. This budget, which had been at $97 million, was cut by the new top management to $88 million per year. Polaroid left the industrial and professional photography account with Doyle Dane Bernbach. The company then hired the Ogilvy & Mather advertising agency to handle its new video cassette and computer diskette products. It was one of Doyle Dane Bernbach's smaller client accounts, but the dismissal was intriguing to the advertising industry because that agency had won innumerable awards from the advertising industry for creative excellence in advertising, including a sizable number of advertisements done for Polaroid products. Polaroid was one of Ally & Gargano's large client accounts.

Promotional tie-ins with air carriers were tried with some success. This work was with Delta in late 1982 and TWA in late 1984 and early 1985. Each purchaser of selected Polaroid cameras got a coupon entitling him or her to one-fourth off any TWA coach flight, domestic or foreign, except the London route, through April 30, 1985, or between October 15, 1985, and March 15, 1986, including fares that might be already discounted. For many people this meant that a $20 Polaroid 600-series camera produced a $200 to $250 saving on a foreign flight. The promotion was a success for Polaroid but not for TWA. With hindsight, TWA regretted that the offer had not been limited one to a customer and to the least popular routes.

Another type of promotion, simultaneously a public service, was the Polaroid Education Project. Started in 1979, this ongoing endeavor explored the relation of visual experience to children's learning. Project staff developed "curricula which apply the immediacy and simplicity of instant photography to the basic skills that determine how children perceive themselves and understand their relationship to the world and to those in their lives." School teachers were offered numerous exercises in natural science, mathematics, social studies, and language arts—all utilizing instant pictures. The instant photographic records of the children's gently guided inquiry served as visible, sharable evidence of their expanding interest and accomplishment. This built on the principles that rapid feedback and tangible evidence are more important when students are young. Using Polaroid cameras and film, well over one million U.S. and Canadian children had participated in the Polaroid Education Project, and large amounts of goodwill had been created, as well as widened familiarity with parts of Polaroid's product line.

The Patent Dispute with Eastman Kodak Company

Eastman Kodak introduced a camera and film for instant photography in April 1976, thus ending Polaroid's monopoly position. Polaroid filed a lawsuit against Eastman six days later in a U.S. district court, charging that Eastman was thus infringing several Polaroid patents. The action asked for an injunction against Eastman to halt all sales and that Polaroid be awarded treble damages and reimbursement of all legal costs of the action. Eastman countersued and counterclaimed, seeking a declaratory judgment that the Polaroid patents identified in Polaroid's complaint and several other Polaroid patents were invalid and not infringed. Eastman alleged that Polaroid's own designs were nothing more than new patents on Eastman's own patented processes. The complex trial of the issues was not completed until February 26, 1982, and no judgment was rendered at that time.

From 1957 to 1969, Polaroid had shared some of its instant color secrets with Eastman. Apparently, Polaroid, then much smaller, needed the technical know-how of the industry leader to make negatives for its pull-apart instant prints. In the trial, Polaroid charged that Eastman stole some of the proprietary technology that it learned during those years. Moreover, it alleged that Eastman "reverse-engineered" certain features of the Polaroid SX-70 after that camera was introduced in 1972. This term referred to the practice of taking a competitor's product, tearing it apart, and determining how to get the same result differently. An innovation, the SX-70 produced a color print without requiring the user to strip "garbage," as it was called in the photographic industry, or apply chemicals.

The complex five-month trial was completed in September 1985 after more than nine years of litigation and over $10 million in legal costs for Polaroid. The judge ruled in favor of Polaroid. She issued an injunction October 11, 1985, ordering Eastman to withdraw its instant cameras and film from the market by January 9, 1986. Eastman appealed at once.

Under a new arrangement of the U.S. judicial system, the Eastman appeal went to the Court of Appeals for the Federal Circuit, a new institution established in 1982 in Washington, D.C. This new tribunal was needed to bring logic and consistency to patent disputes. Many federal courts and individual judges were friendly to patent protection, many were unfriendly, and many were totally unqualified for the complex technical disputes about which they were rendering decisions. The lack of understanding by judges contributed to the inexcusable length of such disputes. Despite inconsistencies, in the United States only about 30 per cent of patents survived competitors' challenges.

Out of this untenable judicial situation came a solution. All appeals of patent cases from federal district courts had to come to this specialized court composed of fifteen specialized judges. This court was to handle patent disputes, customs disputes, and claims against the U.S government. The creation of the specialized court meant not only future consistency and predictability but probably also that patents would be upheld more often and thus become of more economic worth.

Another reason for the prediction that patents would hold up more often under challenge in the future had to do with the perennial U.S. government policy rivalry between antitrust forces and pro-patent forces. Antitrust enthusiasts wanted more and keener domestic competition and perceived patents as essentially damaging to the process of competition. Historically, no other country had pursued as vigorous an antitrust policy as the United States. The highly aggressive and successful competition from firms in Japan, Europe, and the newly industrializing countries such as South Korea, Taiwan, and Singapore, however, was forcing the U.S. government to give more attention to the international competitive process and less to the domestic competitive process. Thus there was need and empathy for better protection of patents of U.S. firms in order to make the U.S. economy stronger in the world business arena.

At the appeals hearing, Polaroid stated, "They saw the SX-70, and they copied it." Eastman's attorney, Francis T. Carr, placed the different-looking Eastman and Polaroid products side by side in the courtroom and stated, "If Kodak is a clone of the SX-70, I hope Kodak never gets into biotechnology." Polaroid noted that it was referring to the working internal principles, not the looks.

Eastman's attorneys noted the phenomenon of "inventing around existing patents," also known as "designing around existing patents." This expression describes the situation in which one firm is able to accomplish essentially the same product objective as another firm in a somewhat similar manner without exact copying and thus without infringing the patent. When a patent is granted, the ideas, techniques, and drawings go on public record for all to see if they wish. Eastman maintained that the U.S. Patent Office encouraged "innovating and designing around."

One day before it was to take effect, the appeals court declined to overturn the injunction. So on January 9, 1986, there were 16.5 million Eastman instant cameras with no further source of film. Moreover, Eastman and retailers had millions of dollars tied up in unsalable inventory, and the manufacturer had a $230 million investment in plant and equipment for instant cameras and instant film to close down. Several hundred Eastman workers were without jobs. Polaroid declined to manufacture film for the obsolete Eastman cameras, a dubious public relations posture. Fuji Photo, a Japanese company, made film compatible with Eastman's instant camera but did not offer that film in the United States. The question of how much the damages would be and whether they would be trebled remained to be settled in more litigation. What is more, the appeals court had not ruled on the merits of the case. If the appeal on merits failed, as was extremely likely, Eastman could ask the U.S. Supreme Court to hear an appeal, but, of course, had no right to be heard. In fact, it seemed likely, based on earlier public statements from Eastman, that that company would not even attempt to appeal the appeals court decision. A Supreme Court reversal of the appeals court was considered extemely unlikly. And once the ill will of the consumers and retailers had been incurred at the time of the market withdrawal, it would be quite difficult to get back into this product market.

Faced with 16.5 million irate consumers, Eastman within twenty-four hours offered three options. First, each consumer could exchange his or her camera, most purchased for $30 of less, for $50 worth of company coupons, or, second, for a telephoto disc camera currently selling for $50. Third, the consumer could exchange the camera for one share of Eastman Kodak corporate stock, which closed that day on the New York Stock Exchange at $47.50. Eastman offered to reimburse retailers for inventory and encouraged them to send it back immediately. Many consumers tried to speculate, but within a day Eastman Kodak had imposed a limit of three per household.

The several types of costs involved in this lost dispute were quite substantial for Eastman, as was the future loss of sales of instant cameras and film, about $300 million per year. Eastman had about one-fourth of the instant camera market in the United States, versus 40 per cent in 1977. However, this annual loss of sales amounted to only about 3 per cent of Eastman's total sales. On the other hand, over $1 billion of Polaroid's sales per year, about 90 per cent of that company's annual sales, were involved in the dispute. Eastman Kodak, with $10.6 billion per year in sales, was many times more product-diversified than smaller Polaroid. Despite the long, heated controversy, it was not clear if Eastman had ever turned a profit on the instant camera in ten years and, indeed, if it had recovered its research and development costs on this product. The fragmentary evidence that leaked out suggested that Eastman had sustained a loss on instant photography.

A few days after the court decision in January 1986, Eastman Kodak announced that it was reentering the 35 mm market, a quality segment from which it withdrew in the United States in 1970. It unveiled two cameras of that type, priced at $200 and $130 at retail. These two battery-powered, fixed-lens cameras offered automatic loading, focus, exposure, and flash functions. Eastman Kodak decided not to make these new products itself although it did not say so publicly for some time. Instead, it would use manufacturers in the Orient that already supplied Eastman Kodak with the 35 mm cameras it sold under its own name in Southeast Asia. Moreover, Eastman Kodak acknowledged that it was suffering from many serious internal problems, sluggish sales, and low profits and that it would need to dismiss permanently about 10 per cent of all its employees.

Advise Polaroid Corporation.

ADOLPH COORS BREWING COMPANY

One of the largest, oldest, and most interesting brewers in the United States was the Adolph Coors Brewing Company. It faced a perplexing set of circumstances, opportunities, and problems as an organization and was part of an industry that showed great structural change, extensive modifications of traditional consumer behavior, and public relations problems.

The U. S. Beer Industry

After the prohibition era, about 750 brewing companies went into business in the United States. Of course, many failed quickly, and the number of firms kept going down. However, the industry underwent a massive shakeout and restructuring between the late 1960s and the mid-1980s. About 60 brewing companies disappeared, some by closing down and some by merging with stronger organizations. Among the approximately 43 remaining, a few were in difficulty, a few faced significant problems, and some others faced problem-laden opportunities. Two thirds of the 43 were extremely small and insignificant in the industry. The top 5 firms sold about 87 per cent of the beer made in the United States.

For a long time fourth in size behind Anheuser-Busch, Inc., Joseph Schlitz Brewing Company, and Pabst Brewing Company, Coors fell to number 5 as the seventh-ranked Miller Brewing Company of Milwaukee surged into second place in the late 1970s. Formerly independent, Miller had been acquired by Philip Morris, Inc., the tobacco-based firm, in 1970 and had been given needed fixed investment, working capital, and marketing expertise for growth. Coors fell to sixth in 1981 as G. Heileman Brewing Company expanded.

In late 1981 the number 4 producer, G. Heileman Brewing Company, attempted to take over number 3 Schlitz, which was in difficulty with declining sales and profits. The Schlitz brand was in severe difficulty for several reasons, perhaps the most important of which was an ill-considered change in the recipe or brewing formula. A second reason was the greater sophistication of marketing at archrival Miller. Schlitz agreed to the proposed takeover. However, the Antitrust Division of the U.S. Justice Department was displeased with the additional ownership concentration that the deal would bring to the brewing industry and with the potential for significantly reduced competition. When the Justice Department announced that it would file suit to block the acquisition, it was canceled. This government action surprised many people because, in a much larger and more important merger about two months earlier, Du Pont had acquired Conoco. The reason for the different government posture was that, without the Du Pont action, Conoco, an important oil, natural gas, and coal producer, would have been taken over by Seagram, a Canadian corporation. In mid-1982 seventh-ranked Stroh Brewing Company took over the ailing Schlitz. Thus, the rank order became the following for the next few years: Anheuser-Busch, Miller,

Stroh-Schlitz, Heileman, Pabst, Coors.

Heileman, of La Crosse, Wisconsin, was one of the fastest-growing companies in the country, but Schlitz would have been Heileman's first nationally distributed brand. In an unusual strategy, Heileman operated a network of regional brewers offering over thirty brands. Among its better-known brands were Carling Black Label and National Bohemian along the East Coast, Rainier in the Northwest, and Blatz and Old Style in the Middle West and parts of the East. Colt 45, Blitz, Mickey's Malt Liquor, and Weinhard were also popular brands belonging to Heileman. Heileman's fundamental strategy was to revitalize the acquired regional brands, gradually bring in some of its other regional brews, and then promote heavily.

There were only a few other important brewing organizations. An independent regional firm that was growing was Pittsburgh Brewing Company, which made Iron City brand. Genessee Brewing Company, Christian Schmidt Brewing Company, Hudepohl Brewing Company, and Joseph Huber Brewing Company were other noteworthy regional corporations. With a capacity of 500,000 barrels per year in its Monroe, Wisconsin, plant, Huber made Augsburger brand beer, a Bavarian-style favorite in the Middle West.

A number of tiny local breweries had started up and were referred to in the trade as "boutique breweries" or microbrewers or both. By common consent, the term was confined to those making only 10,000 barrels or less per year. Interestingly, Coors had spillage of almost 70,000 barrels per year. The number of small brewers was variable, but it averaged about 28. Prominent examples were Sierra Nevada of Chico, California, Anchor Brewery of San Francisco; and Independent Ale of Seattle, the three that got the movement going in the 1970s. Other examples were Kessler of Helena, Montana; Samuel Adams (Boston Beer) of Boston; Reinheitsgebot (approximate translation: legal code of purity) of Plano, Texas; New Amsterdam of New York City; William S. Newman Brewing Company of Albany, New York; White Tail of Fordyce, Arkansas; Chesapeake Bay of Virginia Beach, Virginia; Hibernia Dunkel Weizen Fest of Eau Claire, Wisconsin; Snake River of Caldwell, Idaho; Boulder Brewing of Longmont, Colorado; and Grant's Imperial Stout of Yakima, Washington. White Tail added 10 per cent rice to give crispness, and Imperial was the strongest beer offered in North America. Chesapeake Bay called its Munich-style lager Chesbay Amber and distributed it in the eastern parts of Pennsylvania, Maryland, Virginia, and North Carolina. All boutique beers were high-priced, usually above prestige imports, and all taken together held less than half of 1 per cent of the U.S. market. A few, such as Anchor, were outgrowing their placement in this category. Anchor Brewing, owned by Fritz

Maytag, heir to the Maytag home appliance fortune, made about 30,000 barrels of Anchor Steam annually and distributed it in 30 states. Whether this operation was just fun and a hobby or a serious enterprise remained to be seen.

Many beer drinkers preferred to consume regional beers for various reasons, such as perceived unique taste, desire to enjoy local color, a wish to support local business and thus local jobs, or avoidance of beers that were thought to be mass-appeal, mass-produced goods. In the case of the boutique beers there was also a strong prestige factor for most brands. However, it was well understood in the industry and had been demonstrated experimentally countless times that most beer consumers could not recognize their favorite brands in blindfold tests that compared several brands. The majority of taste differences among popular U.S. brands were imaginary or too slight for the average beer consumer to detect.

The demand for beer in the United States rose rather rapidly in the 1950s, 1960s, and 1970s, but the growth rate slowed down markedly in the early 1980s. Despite an increasing population, in 1984 there was a small decrease, the first in over three decades. This was followed by another small decrease in 1985. The 1985 demand was almost exactly the same as the 1981 demand. The demand for light beer was still growing but not enough to offset the decrease in demand for regular beer. See Exhibit 1. Most of the industry was pessimistic and believed that there would be very little growth in the future.

EXHIBIT 1 U.S. Beer Sales by Segment and Year in Percentages

Segment	1981	1982	1983	1984	1985
Domestic					
Superpremium-priced	7.0%	7.0%	6.3%	5.0%	4.1%
Premium-priced	51.5	48.5	47.0	45.0	43.8
Popular-priced	21.4	20.1	21.3	23.0	24.3
Light	13.8	17.7	18.5	19.9	20.5
Malt Liquor	3.4	3.5	3.5	3.2	3.0
Imports	2.9	3.2	3.4	3.9	4.3

There was significant production overcapacity in the industry. Most large and medium-size firms built in the late 1960s and 1970s as though the high-growth trend line of the industry would go on indefinitely. This was despite the clear demographic evidence that the age distribution of the U.S. population would no longer be as encouraging for this industry after the early 1980s. In late 1984, Miller Brewing decided to write down part of the value of a new

$450 million brewery in Trenton, Ohio, because some of it was not needed then and would not be needed in the future. The amount was $140 million after income tax effects. In 1985, Stroh abandoned its Detroit headquarters brewery, the oldest and least efficient facility in that company, because of lack of need. Although there was clearly overcapacity in the industry, there might still be some construction of new breweries. This was primarily because some of the unused capacity was poorly located in relation to the geographical demand patterns. Beer was bulky, heavy, and costly to transport long distances. A secondary reason was that a few plants were underautomated and required too much expensive labor.

There were several reasons for the lack of growth in the brewing industry, among them the decrease in the number of people in the traditionally heaviest per capita beer-consumption stage of the life cycle. This stage was from the drinking age to age thirty-four, especially from the drinking age to age twenty-four. The U.S. population was much older on average than a generation earlier. The older that people became, the less beer they consumed. Second, the minimum drinking age was being raised in almost every state to twenty-one under extreme pressure from the federal government and the threat of cancellation of federally provided subsidies and matching funds for many programs if the states did not do so. There certainly were violations of the age requirement, but retailers, restaurateurs, and bar owners were anxious not to lose valuable licenses and had become rather careful. Third, there was greater concern about physical fitness and being "in shape." Fourth, there was a ground swell of public concern about misuse of alcoholic beverages, including the weak products such as beer. The Mothers Against Drunk Driving organization was influential and effective. A broad coalition of groups ranging from the Consumer Federation of America to the National Parents and Teachers Association was pushing hard for a legal ban on television and radio advertising of all alcoholic beverages similar to that imposed on cigarettes in 1969. According to William K. Coors, chairperson of the board of Coors Brewing, "The image of the alcohol beverage industry is the greatest challenge facing brewers today." He went on to argue that sanctions against advertising have little influence on the alcohol abuser. "This is an individual behavior problem, the solution to which is to teach people how to accommodate the pressure and stress of everyday life without the crutch of alcohol." He added that sanctions would reduce the consumption of alcohol by responsible users. Coors was a leader in "Drink safely" messages placed on point-of-purchase displays and packages. The large U.S. and Canadian brewers established and funded the Alcohol Beverage Medical Research Foundation at Johns Hopkins University School of Medicine in Baltimore.

Anheuser-Busch launched an interesting product in May 1984 in response to criticism of the industry. Called L.A., for low alcohol, it was the first such beer from a major company. This product was difficult to place with accounts. Sports facilities looked promising, for managers of stadiums and arenas were anxious to prevent and control rowdyism. Tiger Stadium in Detroit decided to offer only low-alcohol beers. Following that breakthrough, several other sports complexes added L.A. to their assortment. Michael Roarty, marketing vice president of Anheuser-Busch, noted that there was a problem getting people to try L.A. However, when Anheuser-Busch could get people to try it, the repeat sale rate was almost twice what this company normally experienced with a new product.

The brewing industry's promotion targeted to college-age people proved to be especially upsetting to critics and some executives in the industry itself. This part of the industry's promotional efforts was criticized for poor taste as well as possibly raising the risk of abuse. Included were advertising, personal selling, and sales promotion practices such as chug-a-lug contests and wet T-shirt competitions. These practices raised the ire of William Coors. He said that he personally thought they were "outrageous" and that everyone else in the company agreed with him. He doubted that the members of the industry would cooperate to change them.

Peter Coors delivered a major speech to the National Beer Wholesalers Association annual convention, in which he talked about both the abuse and tastefulness issues. Coors dared wholesalers

> to be even more responsive to societal concerns about the proper use of alcoholic beverages. . . . It is our challenge for all three tiers of the industry to promote beer properly and with good taste and common design to enhance the credibility of the product and its quality. . . . Ideally, we need to be so good at what we do that we are never placed in the position of having to run around putting out fires. If we are sensitive to our many publics and listen to what they are telling us, we can take action that will never let the fires get started in the first place. We're fully aware of the intense competitive environment in which we operate, but the industry can unite in common purposes.[1]

Pabst Brewing was an old, established company with headquarters in Milwaukee, but it had been suffering from sluggish sales and profits and high managerial turnover for a decade. An offer by Pabst to buy Schlitz for a larger sum of money than Heileman proposed was rejected by the Schlitz board of directors. Much of the business public and the brewing industry saw this rejection as a slap in the face for Pabst and a commentary on how Pabst's future was perceived. Pabst itself was clearly vulnerable to a takeover, dissolution, or split-

[1] *Beverage World,* (December 1985), p. 53.

ting up. Its marginal performance grew worse, but in 1983 it acquired Olympia Brewing Company in Tumwater, Washington, which held about 3 per cent of the U. S. market. Olympia had viable subsidiaries, Hamm's in Minneapolis and Lone Star in San Antonio.

In 1983, G. Heileman Brewing Company was poised to make a friendly takeover of Pabst to save it from two aggressive, unfriendly bidders, Paul Kalmanovitz and Irwin Jacobs. Kalmanovitz owned Falstaff Brewing Company, Pearl Brewing Company, and General Brewing Company. The Antitrust Division of the U.S. Justice Department agreed at the end of 1984 to a complex arrangement by which Heileman was to acquire within a reasonable time period about two-thirds of Pabst. However, Heileman was required to give up the Tumwater brewery and the Olympia, Hamm's, and Olde English 800 Malt Liquor brands to S & P of Vancouver, Washington, the Kalmanovitz holding company.

Thus, by 1986 the rank order of the largest U.S. brewing companies was the following: Anheuser-Busch, Miller, Heileman, Stroh-Schlitz, and Coors. See Exhibit 2. A secure hold on sixth place for the next few years had not been established. It could be Pabst, or it could be the several companies controlled by the Kalmanovitz family if one added their sales together.

EXHIBIT 2 Largest Brewing Companies in U.S. and Their Share of U.S. Market

Company	1980	1982	1984	1985
Anheuser-Busch	28.2%	32.4%	35.0%	37.0%
Miller	20.9	21.5	20.5	20.5
Stroh	13.9	12.6	13.1	12.9
G. Heileman	7.5	7.9	9.2	8.9
Coors	7.8	6.5	7.2	8.0

Coors was eager to improve its sales and profits and move up in the industry rankings. For the company to climb to fourth or third place and lock in that rank without marketing nationwide would be a noteworthy accomplishment, but, of course, it planned to be in all states fairly soon. Nevertheless, its coverage of many markets was quite thin, and it had little more than a token presence in a number of states. Some concerned people thought it was more realistic to approach this objective another way, that is, seek an extraordinary penetration of selected geographical markets and high brand loyalty among a hard core of consumers.

Beer Imports

Imported beers amounted to 7.8 million barrels, or 4.3 per cent of the American market, in 1985. The dollar amount was $1.54 billion. This category did not include beers made in the United States under license from foreign brewing concerns, such as Lowenbrau. Imported beer competed with domestic premium and superpremium beers. Imports' share of the market was rising. In 1971 the figure was only 0.6 per cent, but it rose to 2.9 per cent in 1981, 3.2 per cent in 1982, 3.4 per cent in 1983, and 3.9 per cent in 1984 The bulk of market analysts believed that the import segment would total about 10 per cent by 1991.

Heineken from Holland was the leading foreign-made beer. Imported since 1933 by Van Munching & Company of New York, it held about 34 per cent of the import market in 1985, compared to about 40 per cent in 1981. Molson from Canada with 13 per cent was second. Other highly important ones were Beck's from West Germany with 10 per cent, Moosehead from Canada with 7 per cent, Labatt from Canada with 4 per cent, and St. Pauli Girl from West Germany with 4 per cent. An Irish import, Guinness-Harp; a Dutch import, Amstel Light; and five Mexican imports, Corona Extra, Dos Equis, Carta Blanca, Tecate, and Bohemia all did well but much less than the brands mentioned earlier. Moosehead had had a meteoric rise in the United States that was doubly impressive in view of the fact that the other Canadian brands suffered a small decrease in the United States. Moosehead was a small company and did not even have nationwide distribution in Canada. It was imported by All Brands Importers, Inc., of New York City, a subsidiary of Heublein, Inc., the large distiller, which was itself a subsidiary of R. J. Reynolds Industries, Inc., the tobacco-based conglomerate. The importer had taken the initiative and done all the planning. Grizzly was a new import from Canada but was made by Heineken in Canada. Exotic brews were now being imported from such places as Ivory Coast, Congo, Thailand, Venezuela, and the People's Republic of China. In total, there were about 250 foreign brands imported. G. Heileman Brewing Company became the U.S. distributor of Hacker-Pschorr beers from Munich, West Germany, in 1985, and Anheuser-Busch became the U.S. importer-distributor of highly regarded Carlsberg and Carlsberg Elephant beers from Denmark in 1986.

Americans bought imported beer for three major reasons: prestige, variety, and flavor. Beer was often perceived as a blue-collar beverage. Accordingly, many people, certainly not the majority, in the middle and upper classes found it psychologically necessary to separate themselves from the blue-collar consumers by choice of brands. The same thinking or emotional process sometimes applied to domestic higher-priced beers. Nearly all imports have a heavier, stronger, and more distinctive flavor than American beers. Most foreign tourists in the United States and a small percentage of Americans were contemptuous of U.S. beers, regarding them as caramel-colored carbonated water. American commentators and writers on food and beverages almost all agreed that American beers were bland by prevailing world standards and were rather similar to each other. In addition, there was some speculation but no evidence that some ethnic groups in the United States might begin to look favorably on beers from foreign cultures with which they partially identified.

Curiously enough, the physical characteristics of the vast majority of beers produced in the United States and Canada made them harder, not easier, to produce than the beers from other countries. This refers to knowledge of chemistry, extreme precision in the blending, perfect consistency, and meticulous quality control. Finn Knudsen, director of brewing research and development for Coors Brewing, stated that it took greater skill to make North American lighter-flavored beers consistently than to make European beers. He had twenty-four years of brewing experience, including ten in Europe. As a general principle, the lighter a beer is in flavor, color, and calories, the more difficult is the manufacturing process. Carelessness and inconsistency could not be masked. Yet almost no North American consumers had any inkling of this principle.

The Coors Company

For many years, Coors was the only large brewer in the United States that was not national in scope. Based in Golden, Colorado, a suburb of Denver, this organization distributed its output in only sixteen states, all of them in the West or the western edge of the Middle West, at the beginning of the 1980s. At that time it covered all the West except Oregon and Alaska. In the early 1980s it gradually added one to three states each year. Then in 1983, Coors added Florida, Georgia, North Carolina, South Carolina, Alabama, Virginia, eastern Tennessee, the District of Columbia, Hawaii, and Alaska. In 1984 the company added Kentucky, West Virginia, Ohio, Maryland, and Oregon. Although it was a logical part of Coors's early market territory, Oregon was not available until it repealed its law barring the sale of packaged unpasteurized beer. Illinois and the six New England states were added in 1985 and Michigan in 1986. As of that time, Coors did not distribute in Pennsylvania, New Jersey, New York, Delaware, and Indiana but had plans to add those states in the future. Despite this rather orderly spread, the distribution was quite thin in many of the states added in the 1980s. The Coors company had always had a distinctly western image among both business people and consumers.

The company had beer sales of $1,077,880 in 1985, compared to $937,876,000 in 1984, $947,445,000 in 1983, and $765,909,000 in 1982. See Exhibit 3. The company's share of the U.S. market for beer was 8.0 per cent in 1985, 7.2 per cent in 1984, 6.5 per cent in 1982, 7.4 per cent in 1981, 7.8 per cent in 1980, and 8.0 per cent in 1977. In 1985 the company sold 14,738,000 barrels of beer.

EXHIBIT 3 Adolph Coors Company Statements of Income and Retained Earnings

	For the years ended		
	December 29, 1985	December 30, 1984	December 25, 1983
	(In thousands)		
Sales	$1,424,533	$1,262,903	$1,242,182
Less — federal and state beer excise taxes	143,411	130,260	131,776
	1,281,122	1,132,643	1,110,406
Costs and expenses:			
Cost of goods sold	864,193	804,793	720,152
Marketing, general and administrative	307,320	258,557	221,402
Research and project development	19,401	18,420	14,532
	1,190,914	1,081,770	956,086
Operating income	90,208	50,873	154,320
Other (income) expense:			
Interest income	(12,081)	(12,033)	(11,320)
Interest expense	1,714	1,407	1,796
Miscellaneous — net	4,159	4,068	7,983
	(6,208)	(6,558)	(1,541)
Income before income taxes	96,416	57,431	155,861
Income taxes	43,000	12,700	66,600
Net income	$ 53,416	$ 44,731	$ 89,261
Net income per share of common stock	$1.52	$1.28	$2.55

Canada had looked attractive to Coors for several years for its first international expansion. Consumer awareness of Coors was already high in western Canada. Yet it was perplexing to think seriously about distributing in that country when there were still a few states in the United States without Coors products and many states in the United States with only scattered availability of Coors products. Distribution in Quebec would require French-speaking salespersons and French language advertising. Montreal-based Molson Companies, Ltd., and Coors held extensive talks in 1985 about three possibilities: distribution of imported Coors products in Canada by Molson, licensing Molson to make Coors products, and a joint venture in Canada. The Coors executives commented, "We have a product that is difficult to replicate and we want to protect the Coors mystique." Nevertheless, an agreement was reached with Molson for that company to make Coors products in Canada. They became available in Canada, except for the Maritime Provinces, by the end of 1985. For the first time not all Coors products were being made in the same plant and using the fabled "Pure Rocky Mountain Spring Water." A few independent financial analysts suggested a merger between the Coors and Molson corporations.

Coors Company operated only one brewery, but this facility in Golden was the largest brewing plant in the United States. For several years the company had had tentative plans to enlarge the facility, but there had not been a need so far. See Exhibit 8. No finished product was stored at the plant. Golden was reasonably centrally located for the company's geographical distribution area until the middle 1970s. Yet even by the early 1970s, in terms of the population density of the markets served, the plant could not be considered logistically well located. This was primarily because of the importance of the Calfornia demand for the product. Among the secondary reasons for marketing area geographical expansion, mainly eastward and southeastward, was making logistics more rational. In particular, the cultivation of Texas, the nation's second most important beer market, was desirable for logistical balance. Another interesting point was that the average shipping distance for a unit of beer had been rising rapidly for several years, going up 20 per cent between 1982 and 1984 alone, as the company pushed farther afield. Intensive cultivation of the upper East Coast would push this figure up drastically. Three-fourths of Coors output was sent by rail; and one-fourth, by truck.

EXHIBIT 8 Production in 1985 As Percentage of Production Capacity

Company	Percentage
Anheuser-Busch	91%
Miller	85
Stroh	99
G. Heileman	62
Coors	96
Total U.S. Beer Industry	81

This organization took an option in 1979 to buy a large parcel of rural land in the Shenandoah Valley near Elkton, Rockingham County, Virginia, in case it should actually expand nationwide and might need additional production capacity, storage space, or packaging operations on the East Coast or a combination of these. The tract consisted of 2,245 acres. At first there were aggressive, noisy demonstrations by temperance groups, but they stopped. In 1985 the company announced that it would build a $70 million plant on this tract to package Coors beers in cans, bottles, and kegs. Considering the number of brands of beers, the types of container, sizes of containers, and variations by state on legal requirements for labeling, the plant would need to work with 238 different containers. Beer would arrive by refrigerated rail tank car from Golden. Employing 250 and involving no borrowing, this facility was to open in 1987. Annual packaging capacity was 2.4 million barrels.

Whether a brewery would be built on the tract remained undecided, but the economic evidence was favorable on balance. Moreover, Peter Coors stated that the company had found an exceptional source of pure spring water there that matched the quality of Golden's pure Rocky Mountain spring water. If built, the brewery would be put up in phases as eastern demand warranted. If built in the early and middle 1990s, the cost of such a brewery would probably be about $550 to $600 million for an annual capacity of ten million barrels.

The Coors company was partially integrated up-channel in that it produced its own bottles and cans. In fact, it owned and operated the nation's largest aluminum can factory. Moreover, the company supplied itself with natural gas and coal from its own fields and mines and grew all its own barley. The company was slightly integrated down-channel in that it owned its own beer wholesale distribution firms in Tustin (California), Spokane, Omaha, Denver, and Boise. These distribution investments furnished profit as well as what management termed "better insight in working with the company's independent distributor network."

The Coors company was in excellent financial health. See Exhibit 4. It did not have any significant debt, short- or long-term. In fact, the management was philosophically opposed to borrowing money and financed its expansion and other needs through its stream of profits.

The U.S. beer industry exhibited a seasonal pattern in demand. Sales rose in the warm weather and fell in the cool weather. Coors Brewing experienced the same pattern as the industry. The third quarter, July–September, at Coors typically accounted for about 34 per cent of sales, whereas the first quarter, January–March,

EXHIBIT 4 Recent Balance Sheets of Adolph Coors Company

Assets	December 29, 1985	December 30, 1984
	(In thousands)	
Current assets:		
Cash, including short-term interest bearing investments of $125,927,000 in 1985 and $70,562,000 in 1984	$ 166,131	$ 87,603
Accounts and notes receivable	90,698	75,050
Refundable income taxes		14,400
Inventories:		
Finished	14,927	12,009
In process	26,738	22,387
Raw materials	70,296	67,000
Packaging materials	30,989	28,226
	142,950	129,622
Prepaid expenses and other assets	51,567	52,332
Accumulated income tax prepayments	3,238	6,322
Total current assets	454,584	365,329
Properties, at cost, less accumulated depreciation, depletion and amortization of $621,968,000 in 1985 and $549,026,000 in 1984	827,928	835,254
Excess of cost over net assets of businesses acquired, less accumulated amortization	3,513	3,754
Other assets	10,682	10,806
	$1,296,707	$1,215,143

accounted for only about 19 per cent. The second quarter and fourth quarter accounted for about 25 per cent and 22 per cent, respectively.

Established in 1873, Adolph Coors Company was now managed by the founder's grandsons, William K. and Joseph Coors, and Joseph's sons, Jeffrey and Peter Coors. William Coors was chairperson of the board of directors. Joseph Coors had been vice chairperson of the board and president until June 1985, when he yielded the presidency to Jeffrey Coors. The latter had been serving as divisional president of operations and technical affairs. At the same time, Peter Coors, who had been serving as divisional president for marketing, sales, and administration, was appointed president of the newly carved-out brewing division. The company's attempt at diversification of the business and the ages of William and Joseph Coors, both in their late sixties, made it advisable to make some changes. Jeffrey Coors was age forty and Peter Coors age thirty-nine. Early in their careers, both sons had been what were essentially unspecialized

EXHIBIT 4 Recent Balance Sheets of Adolph Coors Company (Continued)

Liabilities and Shareholders' Equity	December 29, 1985	December 30, 1984
	(In thousands)	
Current liabilities:		
Accounts payable	$ 69,953	$ 66,463
Accrued salaries and vacations	38,725	31,155
Taxes, other than income taxes	26,105	24,650
Federal and state income taxes	5,127	4,846
Accrued expenses and other liabilities	43,392	45,309
Total current liabilities	183,302	172,423
Accumulated deferred income taxes	165,462	136,409
Other long-term liabilities	11,482	15,366
Shareholders' equity		
Capital stock:		
Class A common stock, voting, $1 par value, authorized and issued 1,260,000 shares	1,260	1,260
Class B common stock, non-voting, no par value, authorized and issued 46,200,000 shares	11,000	11,000
	12,260	12,260
Paid-in capital	7,330	2,011
Retained earnings	942,506	903,129
	962,096	917,400
Less — treasury stock, at cost, Class B shares, 12,062,276 in 1985 and 12,448,376 in 1984	25,635	26,455
Total shareholders' equity	936,461	890,945
Commitments and contingencies		
	$1,296,707	$1,215,143

vice presidents. There were several other vice presidents. Peter Coors, who held a master's degree in business administration, was the only member of the family who had done graduate study in management. The family owned 86 per cent of the corporate stock, and the remaining 14 per cent of the shares of stock carried no voting rights. The Coors family was close-knit, inward-looking, and conservative. This philosophical stance and personality characteristic had been reinforced by a family tragedy in 1960, when Joseph Coors's other son, Adolph III, was kidnapped and murdered.

The company was rethinking its philosophies of marketing and general management. Some officials, including Peter Coors, described the corporation as arrogant about itself and its output. Ideas that did not originate within the family were not even considered. The firm was frequently referred to by outsiders, investment counselors, and workers as "baronial" and "feudal" and a "nineteenth-century industrial dynasty." Yet more potential changes were coming in the form of the younger Coors men and a new marketing officer. A new senior vice president for marketing, Robert A. Rechholtz, then age forty-two, arrived in 1982 from Schlitz, where he had held the same title.

However, allegations of rigid inflexibility were a little exaggerated. It was worth noting that Coors was the first brewer to adopt aluminum cans, now widely used in the industry. Management admitted, on the other hand, that its improved Press-Tab II, a can that was environmentally appealing to the company's largely western market because it had no pop-top, was a mistake because the average consumer found it impossible to open.

Top management's old-fashioned views, provincialism, and egotism had been temporarily reinforced by a fad occurrence on college campuses during the mid-1970s. Coors beer was the "in" beer among millions of educated young adults, people who were likely to enjoy good incomes and community positions in the future. This voguish product was carried long distances outside the normal trade territory by students. An informal distribution network arose among enthusiasts, and few college parties were complete without Coors. The bubble burst by 1977.

Labor relations in recent years had been stormy and harmful to Coors. In 1977, Local 366 of the Brewery Workers Union struck the company's plant, and it was quickly joined in a boycott by several other groups that were strongly opposed to the Coors family's conservative political stands. The effect of the boycott was particularly noteworthy in California, the company's largest market. Greatly increased advertising by Miller and Anheuser-Busch simultaneously affected Coors in California, so it was not known how much effect the unions and their political sympathizers had had on the sales. Coors's share of the important California market dropped from 40 per cent to 20 per cent. By the early 1980s, this figure had risen to only a little over 20 per cent and essentially stabilized thereafter. Opponents of Coors claimed all the credit. To the consternation of the labor movement, about two-thirds of Coors employees returned to work soon after the strike began. Not only did the strike fail, but the workers even petitioned the U.S. Department of Labor to hold an election on the fate of the local union. In accordance with normal legal machinery, such an election was held under government supervision, and the workers overwhelmingly rejected Local 366 as their bargaining agent. Thus, the Carter administration decertified the local union. However, embarrassed and infuriated national union leaders, some local union leaders in other states, plus some radical left political groups kept the boycott alive. The Coors company became the object of great pressure and vilification, which still existed. The Coors fad on college campuses might have lasted longer if it had not been for the boycott call. Many students in particular embraced the boycott even though the Coors workers had over-whelmingly voted out their union. Many students were also extreme-ly angry that the members of the Coors family made generous dona-tions to conservative political groups.

Relations between Coors and minorities received much adverse publicity in the early and mid-1980s. A tiny number of people alleged ethnic discrimination. However, two large, respected national civil rights groups, one predominantly black and one predominantly His-panic, conducted their own inquiries and concluded the allegations were without merit. A national television news program of investiga-tive journalists made an inquiry and concluded the same. The televi-sion program questioned the true motivations of the complainants in this matter. Clearly, Coors was no community leader in ethnic rela-tions, but it was not engaged in discrimination.

On the other hand, the company clearly made a major public rela-tions blunder in 1984. William Coors, not known as an articulate, smooth public speaker who could build goodwill for the organiza-tion, nevertheless addressed a meeting of minority business owners in Denver. He aggressively criticized the political and economic leader-ship of the new black African republics, including their educational and technical preparation. He organized and phrased the speech so poorly that it was misinterpreted as a criticism of the black race and received international publicity. Despite Coors's explanations, clari-fications, and apologies for the lack of clarity, significant public rela-tions harm had been done and would linger.

The Coors organization had always been production-oriented rather than marketing-oriented. It had concentrated on perfect uni-formity and turned out only one beer until 1978. It was a medium-to premium-priced product made in an unusual process that avoided pasteurization because the family was convinced that heat caused deterioration. The lack of pasteurization meant that extra care was used in handling and storing Coors goods. The company used refrig-erated rail cars and trucks and had a corporate policy in effect in the channel of distribution to avoid offering Coors products to the public if they were more than sixty days old. In 1978 the company belatedly introduced a second product, Coors Light. Some family members, especially Jeffrey Coors, admitted to being furious that chemists in the organization had been secretly conducting some experimental work leading to the development of a light beer for the company. Management had previously told them not to do so.

The primary competitor in the reduced calorie category was Miller Lite, a successful brand that came out in 1975 and started the entire category of products. Miller Lite came out in response to consumer consciousness about feelings of fullness and the high calorie count in beers. However, the new Coors Light had 105 calories per 12-ounce serving versus 96 for Miller Lite. Coors's regular beer had 145 calories versus 150 for Miller High Life. See Exhibit 5.

EXHIBIT 5 Calories per 12-ounce Serving, Selected Brands of Beer

Brand	Number of Calories
Michelob	168
Budweiser	156
Miller High Life	150
Schlitz	148
Stroh	148
Coors	145
Pabst	140
Budweiser (low alcohol)	137
Pearl	136
Michelob Light	134
Heidelberg	133
Stroh Light	115
Budweiser Light	108
Coors Light	105
Miller Lite	96
Schlitz Light	96
Heidelberg Light	96
Pabst Extra Light	70
Pearl Light	68

Whether Coors Light was going to succeed was extremely questionable for several years. Michelob Light and Natural Light, both made by Anheuser-Busch, were number 2 and number 3 in the reduced-calorie category. At least fifteen other brands of light beer were launched in the industry. Yet Miller Lite, the innovator, was still hanging on to 57 per cent of the light market in 1981 and, in fact, had surpassed its owner's flagship brand, Miller High Life. In 1982, Anheuser-Busch introduced Budweiser Light nationally after an eleven-month period of meticulous test marketing and supported it with heavy advertising. Regular Budweiser was the number 1 selling brand in the country, and its name carried great commercial value for the light version. Bud Light outperformed Natural Light quickly, and it became questionable whether the latter should be retained. By 1982, Coors Light was judged a modest success. By 1984 it was a major success, second in the reduced-calorie category and tenth in the industry. It moved to eighth place in the industry in 1985 with 3.1 per cent of the industry's sales. However, Bud Light was only an insignificant distance behind, with 3.0 per cent of the industry's sales, third place in the light category, and ninth in the industry. Bud Light was growing much faster than Coors Light.

Coors, the flagship brand of the Coors Company, suffered a declining share of the market for several consecutive years. Even temporary rises in Coors sales did not obscure the long-run trend line downward. Production of Coors brand dropped from 12.1 million barrels in 1977 to 8.7 million barrels in 1985. The company was finding it difficult to position this brand in the industry. See Exhibit 7.

EXHIBIT 7 Largest-Selling Beer Brands in the U.S. in 1985
By Percent of Market

Brand	Company	Percent of U.S. Market
Budweiser	Anheuser-Busch	24.8%
Miller Lite	Miller	10.1
Miller High Life	Miller	7.0
Coors	Coors	4.8
Old Milwaukee	Stroh	4.1
Michelob	Anheuser-Busch	3.3
Busch and Busch Bavarian	Anheuser-Busch	3.3
Coors Light	Coors	3.1
Bud Light	Anheuser-Busch	3.0
Pabst	Pabst	2.7
Stroh	Stroh	2.7
Old Style	G. Heileman	2.7
Schaefer	Stroh	2.2

After appropriate test marketing in the early 1980s, Coors Brewing added a premium Irish beer called George Killian's. It was under license from a French brewer, Société Brasserie Pelforth. However, Coors Brewing decided later to call it Killian's Irish Red. Offered in only twenty-four states, it was growing in sales and popularity. Geographical expansion for it had not been decided.

A test market was conducted in early 1984 for a proposed new product called Golden Lager. It was to appeal to consumers who wanted a little heavier taste and was aimed directly at Budweiser. Taste tests with blindfolded consumers showed that Coors brand was as full-bodied as Budweiser, but consumers had a strong nonrational perception that the Coors brand was lighter than Budweiser. Golden Lager was provided in the advertising with the theme "a rich, full-bodied beer that could remind you of Budweiser." It failed badly. The constant comparisons to Budweiser were later considered a mistake. Moreover, the executives suspected that many people falsely perceived Golden Lager as a superpremium-priced beer.

Therefore, a test market for a new premium beer, Coors Extra Gold, was begun in early 1985 in selected regions of California, Florida, Texas, Idaho, and Nevada. This product was positioned to appeal to consumers who desired a more full-bodied beer. It had a distinctly darker color. The advertising was placed in the hands of Tatham-Laird & Kudner of Chicago. This brand was presented as "the beer with a taste you can see." It was characterized as "bolder, golder, broad shouldered beer, the way beer oughta be." Advertisements featured power, muscles, sports prowess, and whimsical violence. There was a little humor, but the appeal was strongly to those who longed to be seen as extremely masculine.

The company began a test market of Colorado Chiller in late 1985. It was to compete in the wine cooler segment of the beverage industry, but it was not wine-based. Instead, like White Mountain Cooler from Stroh, it was based on malt and citrus. Anheuser-Busch had failed with a similar type of product quite a few years earlier.

The Coors organization had had in test market for five years a superpremium beer named Herman Joseph's 1868 to honor the founder of the company and the year he arrived in the United States as a young stowaway. If the tests were successful, it was planned to roll out the new product, introducing it in several cycles of a few states each until it was distributed everywhere the company offered Coors and Coors Light. The test area was expanded to include parts of Florida, Georgia, and Virginia, but the data were distinctly mixed. The length of the test market was one of the longest ever recorded on any type of product in the United States. The emotional involvement with the name of the founder made it difficult to perform an evaluation in a completely rational manner.

A joint venture was formed in August 1985 by Coors Brewing, Molson Companies, Ltd., of Montreal, and Kaltenberg Castle Brewery of Neuschwanstein, West Germany. They created Masters Brewing Company "to investigate new products that might be marketable here in the U.S." A new beer that had been under development since mid-1984 was on the market by the end of 1985 in four selected metropolitan areas, Miami, Boston, Columbus, and Washington, D.C. The product, made in the Coors plant, was named Masters Beer, and the launch was not considered a test market. Geographical expansion was to follow. Advertising for the new beer heavily emphasized the ages and experience of the three members of the joint venture. One of Canada's big three brewing firms, Molson was founded in 1786, and the venerable Kaltenberg Castle company was founded in 1260. There was some consideration of constructing brewery capacity for this product on the tract of land Coors owned near Elkton, in Rockingham County, Virginia.

Molson and Coors began their joint planning for Masters Beer in early 1982. The Bavarian firm was brought into the venture in September 1984 because the fundamental concept for the product and the joint company required a German presence. A German participant could provide technical knowledge and advice. Just as important, if not more so, was the consumer perception that Germany was the home of beer and the place where the finest beer in the world was made. As part of the $2.5 million spent on research and development by Molson and Coors for the joint venture, there was research on American consumer behavior. It showed clearly that the Americans who were studied perceived European-made beers as of finer quality than American beers and perceived Germany as the finest source of beer in Europe.

The Masters Brewing Company was a prominent part of an emerging industry reaction to imports and the additional segmentation of consumers. This reaction dealt with "specialty beers," that is, those outside the United States and Canadian tradition but not foreign-made. It was especially important in view of a nongrowing demand for beer. There was the feeling or suspicion among some industry executives that, if some consumers were going to drink less beer at any given time, then those people might want the product to be "more advancing" or have "more bite" or both. Jeffrey Coors stated that if there were a trend toward specialty beers, Coors Brewing wanted to lead that trend. This posture was unlike the corporate tradition of Coors. G. Heileman countered quickly, opening a Milwaukee facility costing $6 million in 1986 to make European-style beer. Russell Cleary, president of G. Heileman, stated that his new product was "goof-proof to make."

Until recent years, Coors Brewing spent little on advertising. At the beginning of the 1970s, it budgeted $3 million to $4 million annually, but this figure grew rapidly. By the early 1980s, despite dramatic increases in its advertising expenditures, Coors Brewing was still underspending its major national competitors if advertising were expressed as a ratio to barrels of beer produced. The discrepancy ranged from about 10 per cent to 50 percent depending on which firm one compared against. The company continued to push the advertising budget upward.

By 1984, Coors Brewing's advertising reached $138,750,000, which was 14.8 per cent of its beer sales, and in 1985 the corresponding figures were $165,050,000 and 15.3 per cent. See Exhibit 6. If advertising were expressed as spending per barrel, Coors Brewing apparently had become the largest spender in the industry whereas it had been one of the smallest spenders fifteen years earlier. It was ordinarily to be expected that advertising per unit of product would have to rise in a period when extensive new geographical territories were being entered. Whether this percentage leadership in the industry would continue was very much a topic for internal discussion. The Coors brand beer, the company's flagship product, was the fifth-largest dollar spender for advertising in the industry, behind the number 1 spender, Budweiser; number 2, Miller High Life; number 3, Michelob; and number 4, Stroh's. The second five spenders were in order, L.A., Meister Brau, Lowenbrau, Old Milwaukee, and Heineken. Both Budweiser and Miller High Life outspent Coors brand by about three to one. Coors augmented print and electronic media with sponsorship of concerts and some sporting events, such as rodeos, motor sports, and the Coors International Bicycle Classic.

EXHIBIT 6 **Advertising Expenditures of Coors Brewing by Year, 1980–1985**

1985	$165,050,000
1984	138,750,000
1983	118,742,000
1982	88,103,000
1981	85,817,000
1980	66,752,000

In the last few years, Coors brand advertising had been using a theme, "Coors is the One." The expression "the difference worth tasting" was repetitively used. Actor Mark Harmon was featured in many of the messages built around this theme. The objectives were two fold: to gain consumer awareness of Coors and to position the brand as "a distinctive superlative product—the desired choice among premium beers." Killian's Irish Red employed the tag line "Killian's Red, Instead" quite effectively, and Coors Light used the "Silver Bullet" theme.

Until recent years, Coors Brewing relied on a conservative, in-house advertising department to a greater extent than most other brewers. The company retained a large national advertising agency under contract for at least media relations but would not delegate much decision-making authority to the agency. For the light beer, Peter Coors was able in 1978 to switch the advertising to a large international agency based in New York. By the mid-1980s, each Coors product was in the hands of a large advertising agency.

The Coors company was making some effort to diversify. The largest attempt was Roberts Rice Mill in Weiner, Arkansas. Others included Coors Energy Company, which owned or had interests in 355 oil or gas wells or both and held oil and gas leases on 466,000 acres of land, and Coors BioTech Products Company in Johnstown, Colorado. Using the Coors knowledge of fermentation chemistry, this plant produced refined starch, fructose syrup, and animal nutrition supplements. Coors owned grain elevators in seven western and southern cities and paper converting plants in Boulder, Colorado, and Lawrenceburg, Tennessee. Suncoa Foods, Inc., of Greeley, Colorado. manufactured snack foods. In 1984, Suncoa test marketed the CocoMo candy bar made with brewer's yeast by a patented process. The product provided chocolate flavor without caffeine or other potentially objectionable ingredients. Coors owned an aluminim recycling plant that produced aluminum coil. It was not yet profitable. Coors Porcelain Company was another subsidiary, and it itself had some related subsidiaries, including Royal Worcester Industrial Cermaics, Ltd., in Wales, which was bought in 1984. Other ceramics locations were in Norman, Oklahoma; Hillsboro, Oregon; Lakewood, Grand Junction, and Denver, Colorado; El Cajon, California; Benton, Arkansas; Glenrothes, Scotland; and Rio Claro, Brazil. The nonbeer subsidiaries provided $197,767,000 of the company's $1,132,643 sales revenue in 1984, compared to $203,242,000 in 1985. Taken as a whole. the subsidiaries were marginally profitable in most years but lost money in 1984. However, the procelain subsidiaries earned acceptable profits in most years.

Advise the Coors organization.

MACY'S

There was considerable concern about the New York Division of R. H. Macy and Company[1] and about the main New York store in particular. The corporation, which operated seventy-six department stores, seven furniture clearance centers, and twenty-seven automotive centers in ten states, had sales of $1,660,684,000 in the latest year. Men's, women's, and children's apparel and accessories accounted for 64 per cent of sales, whereas home furnishings, appliances, and housewares accounted for 31 per cent. Two years earlier, apparel and accessories were responsible for 62 per cent of sales, and home furnishings, appliances, and housewares were responsible for 31 per cent. Besides the stores, the corporation owned five large shopping centers and a 50 per cent interest in three others. Thus, Macy's was the landlord of several other department stores and hundreds of specialty shops. These rental properties produced a net profit of $2,616,000, before federal income taxes, in the latest year. Total net corporate profits before federal income taxes were $99,051,000. After federal income taxes were subtracted, total net corporate profits were $52,794,000. Fifty-eight per cent of sales were on credit, up from 56 per cent two years earlier.

Retailing operations were organized into six geographical divisions: Macy's New York; Lasalle's (Ohio); Davison's (Georgia); Bamberger's (New Jersey); Macy's Missouri-Kansas; and Macy's California. It had been decided that it was commercially advantageous to retain the local family names of former owners in Ohio, Georgia, and New Jersey. The seventy-six department stores had a square footage of 18,758,000, of which 5,998,000 or 32.0 per cent was in the New York division. The main New York store accounted for 2,151.000 square feet, which represented 35.9 per cent of the New York division total and 11.5 per cent of the corporate total.

Bamberger's, predominantly a medium-priced operation and the most profitable of the six company divisions in most years, had grown rapidly in square footage and sales. In the latest year it operated nineteen stores, more than any other division, totaling 5,305,000 square feet. The corresponding figures ten years earlier were eight stores and 2,746,000 square feet. Bamberger's operated a large downtown store measuring 1,245,000 square feet in Newark, New Jersey, a location approximately ten miles west of Macy's main New York store. Starting in 1949 with the Morristown, New Jersey, store, Bam-

[1] For helpful background see the following: Ralph M. Howes, *History of Macy's of New York: 1858-1919* (Cambridge: Harvard University Press, 1946); Tom Mahoney, *The Great Merchants*, rev. ed. (New York: Harper & Row, Publishers, 1974).

EXHIBIT 1 F. H. Macy & Co., Inc. Consolidated Five-Year Summary of Operations

(All amounts in thousands, except per share)	Latest Year	Two Years Ago	Three Years Ago	Four Years Ago	Five Years Ago
Net retail sales	$1,660,684	$1,469,363	$1,297,672	$1,241,501	$1,133,483
Less:					
Cost of goods, sold, including occupancy and buying costs	1,173,280	1,049,404	933,387	905,838	822,507
Selling, publicity, general and administrative expenses	335,738	289,144	263,126	243,994	220,690
Provision for doubtful accounts	20,806	20,331	22,755	17,291	14,521
Interest expense—net	34,425	30,874	28,030	24,930	18,479
Add:					
Income from non-merchandising sources—net	2,616	1,813	759	2,736	1,632
Earnings before federal income taxes	99,051	81,423	51,133	52,184	58,918
Federal income taxes	46,257	38,450	23,998	23,642	26,987
Net earnings	52,794	42,973	27,135	28,542	31,931
Dividends on preferred shares	652	679	758	838	918
Net earnings applicable to common shares	52,142	42,294	26,377	27,704	31,013
Per common share:					
Earnings	$5.33	$4.37	$2.72	$2.80	$3.13
Cash dividends	1.32½	1.15	1.10	1.10	1.00
Average number of common shares outstanding used to compute:					
Earnings per share	9,787	9,686	9,687	9,905	9,915

EXHIBIT 2 R. H. Macy & Co., Inc., Consolidated Statement of Financial Condition

ASSETS
Dollars in thousands
Current Assets

Cash (includes certificates of deposit of $17,000)	$ 43,227
Short-term investments, at amortized cost (approximate market)	60,467
Customers' accounts receivable	40,275
Due from Macy Credit Corp.	2,333
Other receivables	11,445
Merchandise inventories	233,722
Prepaid expenses and supplies	13,120
Total current assets	404,589

Other Assets	
Investment in Macy Credit Corp., at equity	70,816
Investment in, at equity, and advances to 50% owned shopping centers and affiliated companies	8,618
Deferred pension charges	10,192
Miscellaneous	10,204
	99,830

Property and Equipment, at cost	
Land	53,829
Buildings and improvements on owned properties	219,913
Buildings and improvements on leased properties and leaseholds	110,546
Fixtures and equipment	220,432
Construction in progress	20,791
	625,511
Accumulated depreciation and amortization	190,936
	434,575
	$938,994

berger's added branches to the west, south, and southwest. Thus, both Macy's New York division and Macy's Bamberger division spatially resembled complementary half circles. However, in the 1960s the Bamberger division began expanding into the suburbs of Philadelphia, the nation's fourth largest metropolitan area, the center of which is just about seventy-five miles southwest of Newark. In the latest year Bamberger's operated four suburban stores there and had approximately a 5 per cent share of the Philadelphia SMSA (Standard Metropolitan Statistical Area) department store trade. Bamberger's also had under construction a large suburban store there and one in Wilmington, Delaware, approximately thirty miles south of Philadelphia.

EXHIBIT 2 R. H. Macy & Co., Inc., Consolidated Statement of Financial Condition (Continued)

LIABILITIES AND INVESTMENT OF SHAREHOLDERS
Dollars in thousands, except per share
Current Liabilities

Accounts payable and accrued liabilities	$176,579
Income taxes	
Current	9,735
Deferred	77,245
Long-term debt due within one year	7,322
Total current liabilities	270,881
Deferred Credits and Other Liabilities	
Deferred income taxes	46,500
Deferred gains on shopping center joint ventures	10,517
Deferred investment credit	11,978
Deferred compensation	7,915
Other deferred credits	8,396
	85,306
Long-Term Debt, due after one year	
R. H. Macy & Co., Inc.	31,724
Real estate subsidiaries	158,230
	189,954
Investment of Shareholders	
Cumulative preferred shares, 400,000 authorized; par value $100 per share—	
4¼% Series A—153,360 shares outstanding, callable at $107.50 per share	15,336
Preference shares, par value $5.00 per share—1,000,000 authorized and unissued	—
Common shares, par value $0.25, assigned value $3.75 per share—	
20,000,000 authorized, 10,776,933 and 10,154,505 issued	38,079
Additional paid-in capital	48,111
Retained earnings	295,068
Less 302,596 and 262,650 common shares held in treasury, at cost	(3,741)
Total investment of shareholders	392,853
	$938,994

In the latest year, Bamberger's had a sales volume of about $350 million in the southern, western, and southwestern suburbs of New York.

Macy's California division operated eleven stores in the San Francisco-Oakland SMSA, San Jose, Monterey, and Sacramento totaling

3,126,000 square feet of space. The corresponding figures ten years earlier were nine stores and 1,939,000 square feet. This division had under construction three stores near San Francisco and one in Reno, Nevada. In addition, Macy's Missouri-Kansas division and Davison's division (Georgia), each of which operated eleven stores, were building one new store each. The Lasalle division (Ohio), which operated seven stores, had no new branches under construction.

The oldest division of the company was New York. This division had fifteen department stores, four furniture clearance centers, and eight automotive centers. Exhibit 3 lists the New York division department stores, their square footage, and the year opened. The Parkchester branch, which opened in 1941 next to a large housing development in the eastern part of The Bronx, a borough in New York City, was one of the first branch department stores in the United States. Expert observers had considered that expansion innovative for its era.

EXHIBIT 3 Macy's New York Stores*

Stores	Current Size (square feet)	Year Opened
Herald Square	2,151,000	1902
Parkchester	200,000	1941
Flatbush	145,000	1948
White Plains	352,000	1949
Roosevelt Field	452,000	1956
Huntington	230,000	1962
Bay Shore	321,000	1963
New Haven, Conn.	310,000	1964
Queens	334,000	1965
Colonie	257,000	1966
New Rochelle	225,000	1967
Smith Haven	232,000	1969
Kings Plaza	340,000	1970
Staten Island	236,000	1972
Massapequa	213,000	1973
Total (15 stores)	5,998,000	

*Plus four Furniture Clearance Centers and eight Auto Centers.

The Jamaica store in a section of the borough of Queens, the Flatbush store in a section of the borough of Brooklyn, and the White Plains store in a suburban location about eight miles north of the city limits and about twenty-one miles north of the main store, were added in 1947, 1948, and 1949, respectively, long before most other department store companies had given any serious thought to the addition of branches.

Macy's New York division grew greatly through the years. In 1973 it added its sixteenth store, Massapequa, at a Nassau County location about thirteen miles east of the city limits and about twenty-six miles east of the main store. In late 1977, however, the company chose not to renew its lease on the 166,000 square feet facility in Jamaica, a section of town undergoing physical decline and decreases in average household real income. The New York division accounted for a little over one third of the company's sales.

During the latest year, R. H. Macy & Company's six downtown stores (one in each of the six geographic divisions) produced $351 million of the company's sales volume, versus $291 million ten years earlier. These six downtown stores accounted for 21 per cent of corporate sales in the latest year versus 38 per cent ten years earlier. In the latest ten years, the sales of these six had risen 20 per cent, whereas sales of the nondowntown stores had risen 180 per cent and the whole corporation had risen 119 per cent. Among major department store firms in the United States the downtown stores produced from 18 to 36 per cent of company sales volume. Thus, Macy's was near the bottom of the range in the importance of its downtown stores to company sales volume. The main New York store had sales of approximately $190 million in the latest year, or about one third of the New York division total. The main store was showing some year-to-year sales increases and was marginally profitable. The troubled New York division had had several chief executives in recent years but remained the largest sales volume department store operation in the New York-Northeastern New Jersey Standard Consolidated Area.

History and Development of the Company

In 1858, Rowland H. Macy founded an eleven-foot-wide store on Sixth Avenue near 14th Street in New York City. His first retailing venture, in 1844 in Boston, had been a failure, as had his second, also in Boston. He went west in the California Gold Rush and was successful with a store in Marysville, California. With the resulting funds Macy opened the Haverhill Cheap Store in the 1850s in Haverhill, Massachusetts, but it too failed. Macy's 1858 investment in New York City specialized in what was then known as "fancy dry goods," laces, ribbons, embroideries, feathers, handkerchiefs, cambric flouncings, hosiery, gloves, and artificial flowers. The store succeeded, largely because of a fine location at the heart of the shopping district and the large amount of well-planned and designed advertising utilized.

Rowland Macy died in 1877 in Paris while on a buying trip for the store. Ownership and management of the store were in the hands of relatives until 1896, when Nathan and Isidor Straus, who had contractually operated china, glassware, and crockery departments in several stores, including Macy's, bought control. Many lines were added and sales grew, reaching $10,800,000 in 1902. In that year the company made a bold and risky move north to Thirty-Fourth Street, its present location. Extensive commercial development of the Thirty-Fourth Street corridor followed, consisting of hotels, shops, other department stores, and office buildings, including the 1930 construction of the Empire State Building at Thirty-Fourth Street and Fifth Avenue. The Thirty-Fourth Street corridor became one of the world's most intensively developed commercial areas.

Macy's New York division stressed medium-priced merchandise, but it had some of lower medium and upper medium prices. The company attempted successfully to build a reputation for selling a little below going market prices for many well-known brands and never above the market on anything. Macy's was in litigation several times for alleged unlawful price cutting. It utilized a large crew of comparison shoppers who reported to management valuable information about the competition, such as the displays, features, and most important of all, the prices of the competition.

Advertising and sales promotion were always aggressive and often showed great creativity. For example, Macy's famous Thanksgiving Day parade, usually one or two miles of bands, floats, celebrities, sixty-foot-tall balloons, and other attractions, was started in 1924 and often drew more than one million onlookers. The parade had been nationally televised for the past quarter century and had drawn more than 65 million viewers annually. This parade inspired a popular movie, *Miracle on 34th Street*, which was later adapted into a television program and a Broadway musical. This movie is still shown on television.

The company incorporated in 1919 and made its first public offering of corporate stock in 1922. An ambitious acquisition drive began. During the speculative years of the 1920s Macy's bought Lasalle's in Toledo, Davison's in Atlanta, and L. Bamberger in Newark. In 1945, Macy's bought O'Connor Moffatt & Co. in San Francisco and followed this up in 1947 with the purchase of the John Taylor Company in Kansas City. After 1947 Macy's turned its attention from acquisitions to the creation of new stores.

Present Situation

Macy's flagship store and the main store of Marshall Field and Company on Chicago's State Street vied for rank as the largest store in the world, as measured in physical size. The two were really about the same size. Occupying a large city block bounded by Broadway, Seventh Avenue, Thirty-fourth Street, and Thirty-fifth Street. Macy's had 2,151,000 square feet of floor space in two adjoining buildings. The building on Broadway, constructed in 1902, was ten stories high, whereas the one on Seventh Avenue, constructed in 1924, was twenty stories high. Some upper floors were used for Macy company offices. A little over one million square feet were devoted to public sales areas. The two buildings were in good structural condition, but some parts were rather unattractive. For example, there were exposed pipes in places. Several elevators and escalators were safe but strikingly old. The air inside the store was often stuffy. The store employed more than 4,000 people and added many others seasonally. On an average day there were more than 100,000 customers, but this approximately tripled in the peak shopping season between Thanksgiving and Christmas.

Sales per square foot of store space were a source of concern. Although within reason by industry standards, this figure was lower than several other New York City department stores, such as Bloomingdale's and Abraham & Straus. Those two competitors did almost the same sales volume as Macy's main store but in much smaller buildings.

Several trends helped explain the difficulties of the main store. A pioneer in the branch store movement, Macy's saw huge amounts of its sales potential shift to the suburbs. Many middle-class shoppers completely abandoned the main store. Several other conventional city department stores became aggressive. Discount-type stores drained off considerable trade in many lines of goods, despite Macy's relatively aggressive pricing policies.

In addition, portions of the district in which the main store was located were undergoing change. Most observers and business executives saw significant decay in these changes. The media gave considerable attention to these changes and exaggerated the literal truth. Although the immediate neighborhood was still in good condition, the area starting about three blocks north and extending to Times Square, and the area one block to the west had shown a great decline. Adult book shops, adult cinemas, massage parlors, bars, inexpensive shops, fast-food places, and other services predominated there. There were many prostitutes on the streets just to the west of the store. During the previous ten years the number of paying passengers using the Herald Square subway station fell by almost one half.

For several decades, long predating the decay in and near Times Square, the retailing district had been slowly shifting in a northeast direction. Such major fashionable stores as Lord and Taylor, Saks

Fifth Avenue, Bergdorf Goodman, Arnold Constable, and Blooming-dale's, plus several hundred fashionable small specialty shops were a considerable distance away to the northeast. These establishments were scattered in an area that was from a half mile to two miles from Macy's. Moreover, in that same area two other large merchants emphasizing lower medium prices had put in department stores. Alexander's established a large store at Fifty-eighth Street and Lexington Avenue, just one block from trendy Bloomingdale's, whereas Korvette's in 1962 put in a seven-floor store at Fifth Avenue and Forty-seventh Street in a building vacated by a highly regarded furniture dealer. Korvette's closed in 1981. In the early 1970s Gimbel's expanded well outside this area by opening a branch called Gimbel's East on East Eighty-sixth Street about three miles northeast of the main Gimbel's and Macy's stores.

On the other hand, retailing in Manhattan had been experiencing some difficulties for several years. Best and Company, S. Klein & Company, and Stern's had closed their department stores, and Abercrombie & Fitch, a famous specialty store, had been dissolved in bankruptcy and also closed its store. Along fashionable Fifth Avenue, and to a lesser extent Madison Avenue, there was concern as new office buildings displaced many dozens of shops. Many shoppers did not feel the need to come to the central city, even though it contained the nation's largest complex of stores. The population of Manhattan was reasonably stable at about 1,500,000.

The Thirty-fourth Street commercial corridor, about one third of a mile long, remained reasonably popular with shoppers and contained several dozen specialty shops and several large department stores, such as Ohrbach's. Across the street from Macy's, E. J. Korvette's had moved in 1967 into the building vacated by Saks 34th Street, a medium-price defunct affiliate of Saks Fifth Avenue, but had now closed. Gimbel's, at Broadway and Thirty-third Street one block south of Macy's, was a highly aggressive competitior. Macy's and Gimbel's had had an almost legendary rivalry since the 1910 opening of the latter. B. Altman's department store, at the corner of Thirty-fourth Street and Fifth Avenue, anchored the corridor near its east end, just as Macy's did at its west end. At Thirty-second Street and Seventh Avenue, two blocks south of Macy's, Pennsylvania Railroad Station was remodeled in the late 1960s and the new Madison Square Garden was constructed directly above it.

For almost four years there had been a program of major renovation in Macy's main store costing almost $10 million. Many upstairs departments were relocated and redecorated. There were also changes on the important main floor. A notions department was moved off this floor to permit setting up a jeans shop that included piped-in rock music. The use of large tables holding vast quantities of socks, scarves, other accessories, and health aids was halted. A plush green carpet was laid down a twelve-feet wide center aisle on the main floor. Many of the other aisles were widened through the store, and lighting was improved either functionally or aesthetically or both. In many departments airier, less heavy fixtures and partitions were installed. Partitions were necessary to separate dissimilar types of products and to try to overcome the cavernous size of the sales floors. The bargain basement, one of the first in the world, was abolished, and replaced by The Cellar, which consisted of a quasi-street of large shops, including stationery, cookware, cutlery, gourmet foods, an art gallery, a pottery shop with demonstrations by a working potter, and an 1890s style Irish pub. Management began to stock larger quantities of medium-priced fashionable merchandise, but medium-priced staple merchandise was still in the majority.

One noteworthy change that many department stores around the United States had made in recent years was to narrow the range of goods and prices within each type of merchandise. Some basement-type departments were closed. A few large establishments, such as Woodward and Lothrop in downtown Washington, D. C., abandoned their bargain basements completely. As some observers described such stores, "They stopped trying to be all things to all people." Another change found in many department stores was a reduced emphasis on low markup items, especially those that were bulky. For example, major home appliances, mattresses, and box springs usually carried a markup of 22 to 25 per cent, but most apparel and accessories carried a markup of 30 to 44 per cent. Moreover, apparel and accessories gave the merchant a better opportunity to build continuing customer identification with the store. A more sharply focused image, if desired, was then possible. With the rate of population growth down and several department store chains, such as J. C. Penney, increasingly trying to cultivate a share of the market for fashionable merchandise, department store companies were locked in a vigorous competitive battle all over the United States.

In the New York-Northeastern New Jersey Standard Consolidated Area department stores operated by Abraham & Straus, the SCA's second largest retailer with ten locations, Alexander's, the SCA's third largest with thirteen locations, and Mays were successfully catering to the budget-minded shopper and had taken many such customers away from Macy's. Abraham & Straus was a semiautonomous operating division of Federated Department Stores, as was Bloomingdale's. The highly aggressive Federated owned several other operations, such

EXHIBIT 4 Number of Stores of Selected Types

	Borough of Manhattan	New York City	New York SMSA[1]	New York SCA[2]
Department stores	21	58	105	264
Sporting goods and bicycles	81	286	487	967
Hobby, toy, and games	80	333	465	750
Jewelry	919	1,805	2,076	2,828
Camera and photographic supplies	166	290	364	550
Luggage and leather goods	56	115	140	198
Sewing, needlework, and piece goods	253	890	1,118	1,685
Radio, television, music and records	337	865	1,116	1,740
Books	255	405	483	645
Variety stores	170	592	741	1,142
Household appliances	121	421	591	1,078
Furniture	483	1,336	1,684	2,705
House furnishings	425	1,366	1,768	2,749
Men's and boys' clothing and furnishings	822	1,673	1,957	2,768
Women's clothing, specialty stores, and furriers	1,562	3,734	4,506	6,477
Family clothing stores	146	490	617	1,015
Shoe stores	560	1,560	1,895	2,857
Other apparel and accessory stores	340	887	1,044	1,486

[1] Standard Metropolitan Statistical Area.
[2] Standard Consolidated Area of New York, N.Y.—Northeastern New Jersey.
Source: U.S. Bureau of the Census, Census of Retail Trade, 1972. Vol. 11 Area Statistics, Part 2 Iowa—North Carolina, pp. 33-6–33-7, 33-18–33-19, 33-61–33-62, 33-102–33-103, Washington, D.C.: U.S. Government Printing Office, 1976.

EXHIBIT 5 Population, Income, and Relative Income, Past and Forecasted for Selected Years, Seven SMSAs

	1950	1969	1971	1980 Forecast	1990 Forecast
New York SMSA					
Population, midyear	9,578,371	11,440,827	11,620,292	12,258,200	13,326,200
Per capita income (Constant 1967 $)	2,886	4,693	4,803	6,360	7,964
Per capita income relative (U.S. = 1.00)	1.40	1.37	1.36	1.33	1.29
Newark SMSA					
Population, midyear	1,479,594	1,840,112	1,879,600	2,067,200	2,306,200
Per capita income (Constant 1967 $)	2,606	4,267	4,391	5,856	7,383
Per capita income relative (U.S. = 1.00)	1.26	1.24	1.24	1.23	1.20
Atlanta SMSA					
Population, midyear	729,821	1,377,348	1,413,709	1,690,800	2,107,600
Per capita income (Constant 1967 $)	2,185	3,701	3,953	5,157	6,543
Per capita income relative (U.S. = 1.00)	1.06	1.08	1.12	1.08	1.06
San Francisco-Oakland SMSA					
Population, midyear	2,154,251	3,088,491	3,122,121	3,445,600	3,839,200
Per capita income (Constant 1967 $)	2,891	4,658	4,802	6,271	7,899
Per capita income relative (U.S. = 1.00)	1.40	1.36	1.35	1.31	1.28
Toledo SMSA					
Population, midyear	533,151	685,180	699,204	764,700	840,900
Per capita income (Constant 1967 $)	2,509	3,611	3,723	5,025	6,482
Per capita income relative (U.S. = 1.00)	1.22	1.05	1.05	1.05	1.05

EXHIBIT 5 Continued

	1950	1969	1971	1980 Forecast	1990 Forecast
Kansas City SMSA					
Population, midyear	851,402	1,236,380	1,266,571	1,449,500	1,634,800
Per capita income (Constant 1967 $)	2,295	3,829	3,999	5,192	6,647
Per capita income relative (U.S. = 1.00)	1.11	1.11	1.13	1.09	1.08
Philadelphia SMSA					
Population, midyear	3,677,748	4,769,714	4,905,144	5,277,800	5,678,500
Per capita income (Constant 1967 $)	2,417	3,781	3,843	5,156	6,598
Per capita income relative (U.S. = 1.00)	1.17	1.10	1.08	1.08	1.07

NOTE: This set of forecasts utilizes the Series E national population projections of the Bureau of the Census. Series E assumes a fertility rate in 1990 roughly the same as the current rate.

Source: U.S. Department of Commerce, Social and Economic Statistics Administration, Area Economic Projections 1990, pp. 80, 110, 126, 131, 142, 151.

as Bullock's in California, Sanger-Harris in Dallas-Fort Worth, The Boston Store in Milwaukee, Shillito's in Cincinnati, and Filene's in Boston.

Experienced managers and observers believed that Macy's main store had three major advantages. First, it had a large sales volume. Second, it provided a place to test market new merchandise before buying it for branches. Third, the store's location adjoining the garment production and wholesaling district permitted company buyers to respond quickly to new fashions. In addition, the company apparently had some emotional attachment to the store.

The main store was in competition with many other department stores belonging to other companies. Within the borough of Manhattan there were twenty-one department stores, according to the most recent Census of Retail Trade conducted by the Bureau of the Census. In all of New York City there were fifty-eight department stores, whereas in the New York Standard Metropolitan Statistical Area there were 105 department stores, and in the New York City-Northeastern New Jersey SCA (Standard Consolidated Area) there were 264.

In addition to other department stores, Macy's main store was in competition with several thousand specialty stores. Many of the main store's departments had the wide assortment and depth of stock of specialty stores, contrary to the practices of some department store companies. According to this line of thinking, the Macy's book department, for example, was in competition with 255 book shops in Manhattan, 405 in New York City, 483 in the New York SMSA, and 645 in the SCA. Exhibit 4 gives additional data for selected types of stores from the most recent Census of Retail Trade. Exhibit 5 presents Bureau of the Census forecasts for population and per capita income in New York and the six other metropolitan areas in which Macy's operated. The income is expressed in constant 1967 dollars. This exhibit also shows the ratio of SMSA per capita income to United States per capita income.

Advise Macy's.